Explorations in CORE MATH

Algebra 1

HOUGHTON MIFFLIN HARCOURT

Printed in the U.S.A.

ISBN 978-0-547-88200-0

11 0982 22 21 20 19 18 17 16 15 14 13

4500452979 C D E F G

Contents

Chapter 1 Equations

Chapter 2 Inequalities

Chapter 3 Functions

Chapter 4 Linear Functions

Chapter 5 Systems of Equations and Inequalities

Chapter 6 Exponents and Polynomials

Chapter 7 Factoring Polynomials

Chapter 8 Quadratic Functions and Equations

Chapter 9 Exponential Functions

Chapter 10 Data Analysis

Learning the Standards for Mathematical Practice

The Common Core State Standards include eight Standards for Mathematical Practice. Here's how *Explorations in Core Math Algebra 1* helps you learn those standards as you master the Standards for Mathematical Content.

1 Make sense of problems and persevere in solving them.

In *Explorations in Core Math Algebra 1*, you will work through Explores and Examples that present a solution pathway for you to follow. You will be asked questions along the way so that you gain an understanding of the solution process, and then you will apply what you've learned in the Practice for the lesson.

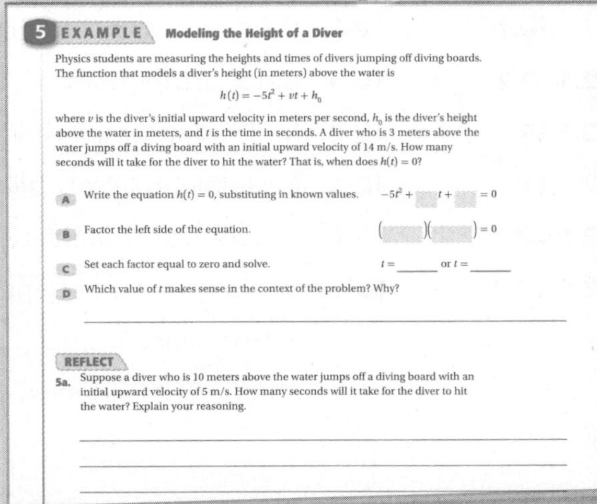

5 EXAMPLE **Modeling the Height of a Diver**

Physics students are measuring the heights and times of divers jumping off diving boards. The function that models a diver's height (in meters) above the water is

$$h(t) = -5t^2 + vt + h_0$$

where v is the diver's initial upward velocity in meters per second, h_0 is the diver's height above the water in meters, and t is the time in seconds. A diver who is 3 meters above the water jumps off a diving board with an initial upward velocity of 14 m/s. How many seconds will it take for the diver to hit the water? That is, when does $h(t) = 0$?

A Write the equation $h(t) = 0$, substituting in known values. $-5t^2 + \_\_\_\_ t + \_\_\_\_ = 0$

B Factor the left side of the equation. $(\_\_\_\_)(\_\_\_\_) = 0$

C Set each factor equal to zero and solve. $t =$ ____ or $t =$ ____

D Which value of t makes sense in the context of the problem? Why?

____

REFLECT

5a. Suppose a diver who is 10 meters above the water jumps off a diving board with an initial upward velocity of 5 m/s. How many seconds will it take for the diver to hit the water? Explain your reasoning.

____

2 Reason abstractly and quantitatively.

When you solve a real-world problem in *Explorations in Core Math Algebra 1*, you will learn to represent the situation symbolically by translating the problem into a mathematical expression or equation. You will use these mathematical models to solve the problem and then state your answer in terms of the problem context. You will reflect on the solution process in order to check your answer for reasonableness and to draw conclusions.

2 EXAMPLE **Writing and Solving Inequalities**

Kristin can afford to spend at most $50 for a birthday dinner at a restaurant, including a 15% tip. Describe some costs that are within her budget.

A Which inequality symbol can be used to represent "at most"? ____

B Complete the verbal model for the situation.

Cost before tip (dollars)		15%		Cost before tip (dollars)		Budget limit (dollars)

C Write and simplify an inequality for the model. ____

REFLECT

2a. Can Kristin spend $40 on the meal before the tip? Explain.

____

2b. What whole dollar amount is the most Kristin can spend before the tip? Explain.

____

③ Construct viable arguments and critique the reasoning of others.

Throughout *Explorations in Core Math Algebra 1*, you will be asked to make conjectures, construct a mathematical argument, explain your reasoning, and justify your conclusions. Reflect questions offer opportunities for cooperative learning and class discussion. You will have additional opportunities to critique reasoning in Error Analysis problems.

REFLECT

1a. Why should the parts of the domain of a piecewise function $f(x)$ have no common x-values?

REFLECT

2a. Describe how the graph of $f(x) = ab^x$ compares with the graph of $f(x) = b^x$ for a given value of b when $a > 1$ and when $0 < a < 1$.

23. **Error Analysis** A student says that the graph of $g(x) = |x + 3| - 1$ is the graph of the parent function, $f(x) = |x|$, translated 3 units to the right and 1 unit down. Explain what is incorrect about this statement.

④ Model with mathematics.

Explorations in Core Math Algebra 1 presents problems in a variety of contexts such as science, business, and everyday life. You will use mathematical models such as expressions, equations, tables, and graphs to represent the information in the problem and to solve the problem. Then you will interpret your results in context.

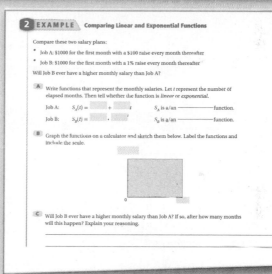

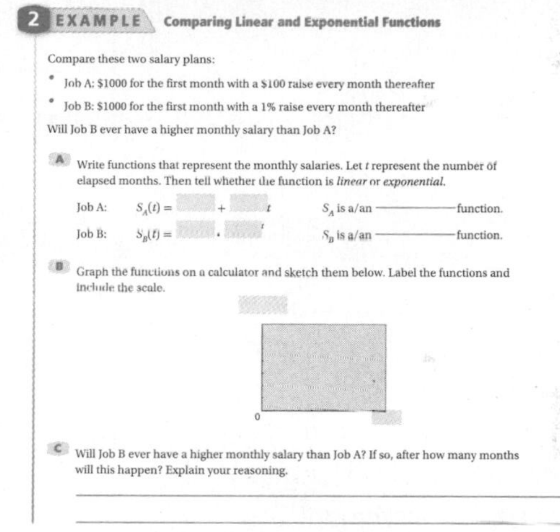
2 EXAMPLE **Comparing Linear and Exponential Functions**

Compare these two salary plans:

- Job A: $1000 for the first month with a $100 raise every month thereafter
- Job B: $1000 for the first month with a 1% raise every month thereafter

Will Job B ever have a higher monthly salary than Job A?

A Write functions that represent the monthly salaries. Let t represent the number of elapsed months. Then tell whether the function is *linear* or *exponential*.

Job A: $S_A(t) =$ ___ + ___ t S_A is a/an ______ function.

Job B: $S_B(t) =$ ___ · ___^{t} S_B is a/an ______ function.

B Graph the functions on a calculator and sketch them below. Label the functions and include the scale.

0

C Will Job B ever have a higher monthly salary than Job A? If so, after how many months will this happen? Explain your reasoning.

REFLECT

2a. Revise $S_B(t)$ and use the Table feature on your graphing calculator to find the interval in which the monthly salary for Job B finally exceeds that for Job A if the growth rate is 0.1%. Use intervals of 1,000. Repeat for a growth rate of 0.01%, using intervals of 10,000.

2b. Why does a quantity increasing exponentially eventually exceed a quantity increasing linearly?

Getty Images/Image Source

5 Use appropriate tools strategically.

You will use a variety of tools in *Explorations in Core Math Algebra 1,* including manipulatives, paper and pencil, and technology. You might use manipulatives to develop concepts, paper and pencil to practice skills, and technology (such as graphing calculators, spreadsheets, or geometry software) to investigate more complicated mathematical ideas.

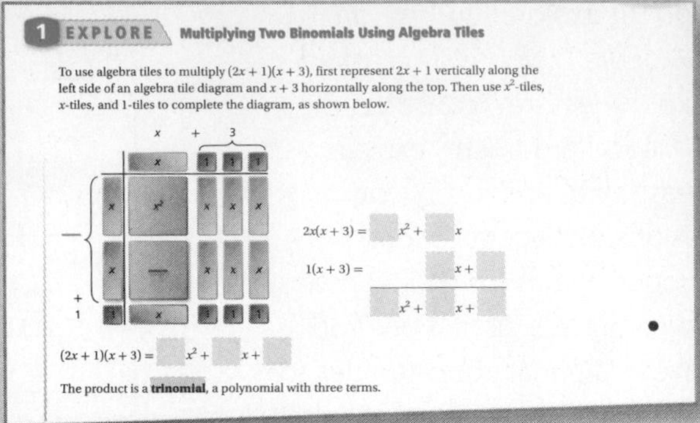

1 EXPLORE **Multiplying Two Binomials Using Algebra Tiles**

To use algebra tiles to multiply $(2x + 1)(x + 3)$, first represent $2x + 1$ vertically along the left side of an algebra tile diagram and $x + 3$ horizontally along the top. Then use x^2-tiles, x-tiles, and 1-tiles to complete the diagram, as shown below.

$2x(x + 3) =$ ___ $x^2 +$ ___ x

$1(x + 3) =$ ___ $x +$ ___

___ $x^2 +$ ___ $x +$ ___

$(2x + 1)(x + 3) =$ ___ $x^2 +$ ___ $x +$ ___

The product is a **trinomial**, a polynomial with three terms.

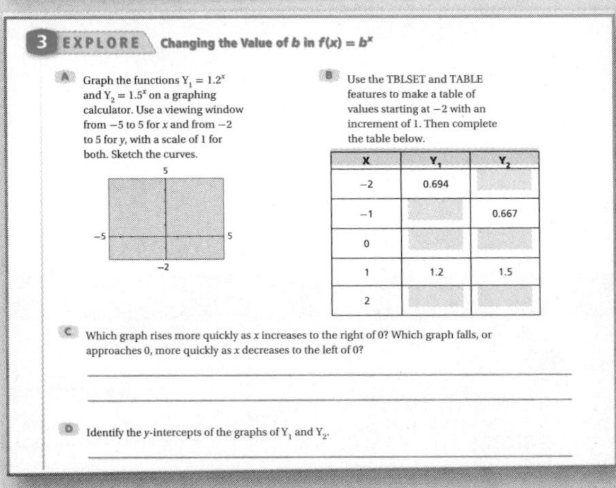

3 EXPLORE **Changing the Value of b in $f(x) = b^x$**

A Graph the functions $Y_1 = 1.2^x$ and $Y_2 = 1.5^x$ on a graphing calculator. Use a viewing window from −5 to 5 for x and from −2 to 5 for y, with a scale of 1 for both. Sketch the curves.

B Use the TBLSET and TABLE features to make a table of values starting at −2 with an increment of 1. Then complete the table below.

X	Y_1	Y_2
−2	0.694	
−1		0.667
0		
1	1.2	1.5
2		

C Which graph rises more quickly as x increases to the right of 0? Which graph falls, or approaches 0, more quickly as x decreases to the left of 0?

D Identify the y-intercepts of the graphs of Y_1 and Y_2.

6 Attend to precision.

Precision refers not only to the correctness of arithmetic calculations, algebraic manipulations, and geometric reasoning but also to the proper use of mathematical language, symbols, and units to communicate mathematical ideas. Throughout *Explorations in Core Math Algebra 1* you will demonstrate your skills in these areas when you are asked to calculate, describe, show, explain, prove, and predict.

REFLECT

1a. Identify the property being illustrated.

- $2x + 7x = (2 + 7)x$, which equals $9x$
- $(x + 1) + 9 = x + (1 + 9)$, which equals $x + 10$
- $5 + x + 3 = x + 5 + 3$, which equals $x + 8$

1b. *Like terms* contain the same variables raised to the same power. In part a, how was the Distributive Property used to combine like terms?

1c. Constant terms are also considered like terms. In part a, how were properties used to combine constant terms?

3c. If you write only the units for the expression $100 + 12.5t$, you get $\text{mi} + \frac{\text{mi}}{\text{h}} \cdot \text{h}$ where "mi" is the abbreviation for miles and "h" is the abbreviation for hours. Explain what the following *unit analysis* shows:

$$\text{mi} + \frac{\text{mi}}{\cancel{\text{h}}} \cdot \cancel{\text{h}} = \text{mi} + \text{mi} = \text{mi}$$

7 Look for and make use of structure.

In *Explorations in Core Math Algebra 1*, you will look for patterns or regularity in mathematical structures such as expressions, equations, geometric figures, and graphs. Becoming familiar with underlying structures will help you build your understanding of more complicated mathematical ideas.

This method of using the distributive property to multiply two binomials is referred to as the FOIL method. The letters of the word FOIL stand for First, Outer, Inner, and Last and will help you remember how to use the distributive property to multiply binomials.

You apply the FOIL method by multiplying each of the four pairs of terms described below and then simplifying the resulting polynomial.

- **First** refers to the first terms of each binomial.
- **Outer** refers to the two terms on the outside of the expression.
- **Inner** refers to the two terms on the inside of the expression.
- **Last** refers to the last terms of each binomial.

Now multiply $(7x - 1)(3x - 5)$ using FOIL. Again, think of $7x - 1$ as $7x + (-1)$ and $3x - 5$ as $3x + (-5)$. This results in a positive constant term of 5 because $(-1)(-5) = 5$.

Outer, Inner, First, Last

$$(7x - 1)(3x - 5) = 21x^2 - 35x - 3x + 5$$

First, Inner, Outer, Last

$$(7x - 1)(3x - 5) = 21x^2 - 38x + 5$$

Notice that the trinomials are written with variable terms in descending order of exponents and with the constant term last. This is a standard form for writing polynomials: Starting with the variable term with the greatest exponent, write the other variable terms in descending order of their exponents, and put the constant term last.

8 Look for and express regularity in repeated reasoning.

In *Explorations in Core Math Algebra 1*, you will have the opportunity to explore and reflect on mathematical processes in order to come up with general methods for performing calculations and solving problems.

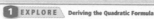

1 EXPLORE Deriving the Quadratic Formula

Solve the general form of the quadratic equation, $ax^2 + bx + c = 0$, by completing the square to find the values of x in terms of a, b, and c.

A Subtract c from both sides of the equation.

$$ax^2 + bx = \underline{\quad}$$

B Multiply both sides of the equation by $4a$ to make the coefficient of x^2 a perfect square.

$$4a^2x^2 + \underline{\quad}\, x = -4ac$$

C Add b^2 to both sides of the equation to complete the square. Then write the trinomial as the square of a binomial.

$$4a^2x^2 + 4abx + b^2 = -4ac + \underline{\quad}$$

$$\left(\underline{\quad}\right)^2 = b^2 - 4ac$$

D Apply the definition of a square root and solve for x.

$$\underline{\quad} = \pm\sqrt{\underline{\quad}}$$

$$2ax = -\underline{\quad} \pm \sqrt{\underline{\quad}}$$

$$x = \underline{\qquad}$$

The formula $x = \frac{-b \pm \sqrt{b^2 - 4ac}}{2a}$ is called the **quadratic formula**. For any quadratic equation written in standard form, $ax^2 + bx + c = 0$, the quadratic formula gives the solutions of the equation.

PhotoDisc/Getty Images

CHAPTER 1

Equations

Chapter Focus

This chapter helps you transition from performing operations with numbers to working with variables, expressions, and equations, which are the building blocks of algebra. You will apply the order of operations and properties of real numbers and equations to simplify algebraic expressions and solve equations. You will also apply unit analysis as you write proportions to solve measurement problems and learn how to express answers to the desired degree of accuracy.

Chapter at a Glance

COMMON CORE

Lesson		Standards for Mathematical Content
1-1	Variables and Expressions	CC.9-12.A.SSE.1, CC.9-12.A.SSE.1a, CC.9-12.A.SSE.1b
1-2	Solving Equations by Adding or Subtracting	CC.9-12.A.REI.1, CC.9-12.A.REI.3
1-3	Solving Equations by Multiplying or Dividing	CC.9-12.A.REI.1
1-4	Solving Two-Step and Multi-Step Equations	CC.9-12.A.REI.1
1-5	Solving Equations with Variables on Both Sides	CC.9-12.A.REI.1
1-6	Solving for a Variable	CC.9-12.A.CED.4, CC.9-12.A.REI.3
1-7	Solving Absolute-Value Equations	CC.9-12.A.CED.2, CC.9-12.A.REI.1, CC.9-12.A.REI.11
1-8	Rates, Ratios, and Proportions	CC.9-12.N.Q.1, CC.9-12.A.SSE.1
1-9	Applications of Proportions	CC.9-12.N.Q.1, CC.9-12.A.CED.1
1-10	Precision and Accuracy	CC.9-12.N.Q.3
	Performance Tasks	
	Assessment Readiness	

CHAPTER 1

Unpacking the Standards

Understanding the standards and the vocabulary terms in the standards will help you know exactly what you are expected to learn in this chapter.

COMMON CORE **CC.9-12.A.SSE.1**

Interpret expressions that represent a quantity in terms of its context.

Key Vocabulary

expression *(expresión)*
A mathematical phrase that contains operations, numbers, and/or variables.

What It Means For You Lessons 1-1, 1-6, 1-8

Variables in formulas and other math expressions are used to represent specific quantities.

EXAMPLE

$A = \frac{1}{2}bh$

A = area of the triangle

b = length of the base

h = height

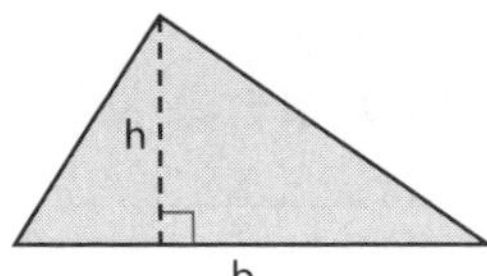

COMMON CORE **CC.9-12.A.CED.1**

Create equations ... in one variable and use them to solve problems.

Key Vocabulary

equation *(ecuación)* A mathematical statement that two expressions are equivalent.
variable *(variable)* A symbol used to represent a quantity that can change.

What It Means For You Lessons 1-1, 1-9

You can write an equation to represent a real-world problem and then use algebra to solve the equation and find the answer.

EXAMPLE

Michael is saving money to buy a trumpet. The trumpet costs \$670. He has \$350 saved, and each week he adds \$20 to his savings. How long will it take him to save enough money to buy the trumpet?

Let w represent the number of weeks.

cost of trumpet	=	current savings	+	additional savings
670	=	350	+	$20w$
320	=	$20w$		
16	=	w		

It will take Michael 16 weeks to save enough money.

CC.9-12.A.REI.3

Solve linear equations … in one variable, including equations with coefficients represented by letters.

Key Vocabulary

linear equation in one variable *(ecuación lineal en una variable)* An equation that can be written in the form $ax = b$ where a and b are constants and $a \neq 0$.

coefficient *(coeficiente)* A number that is multiplied by a variable.

solution of an equation in one variable *(solución de una ecuación en una variable)* A value or values that make the equation true.

What It Means For You — Lessons 1-2, 1-3, 1-4, 1-5, 1-6, 1-7, 1-9

You solve equations by finding the value of the variable that makes both sides equal.

EXAMPLE

The Fahrenheit temperature that corresponds to 35°C is the solution of the equation $35 = \frac{5}{9}(F - 32)$.

F	70	75	80	85	90	95
$\frac{5}{9}(F - 32)$	21.1	23.9	26.7	29.4	32.2	35

When it is 35°C, it is 95°F.

Equation is true.

CC.9-12.A.CED.4

Rearrange formulas to highlight a quantity of interest, using the same reasoning as in solving equations.

Key Vocabulary

formula *(fórmula)* A literal equation that states a rule for a relationship among quantities.

What It Means For You — Lesson 1-6

By rearranging a formula, you may be able to form a new formula for a different quantity.

EXAMPLE

You can rewrite a temperature conversion formula as follows.

$C = \frac{5}{9}(F - 32)$ *C = °Celsius, F = °Fahrenheit*

$\frac{9}{5}C = F - 32$ *Multiply both sides by* $\frac{9}{5}$.

$\frac{9}{5}C + 32 = F$ *Add 32 to both sides.*

CHAPTER 1

CC.9-12.N.Q.1

Use units as a way to understand problems and to guide the solution of multi-step problems; …

Key Vocabulary

unit analysis/dimensional analysis *(análisis dimensional)* A process that uses rates to convert measurements from one unit to another.

What It Means For You — Lessons 1-8, 1-9

Keeping track of units in problem solving will help you identify a solution method and interpret the results.

EXAMPLE

Li's car gets 40 miles per gallon of gas. At this rate, she can go 620 miles on a full tank. She has driven 245 miles on the current tank. How many gallons of gas g are left in the tank?

$$\underbrace{620 \text{ mi}}_{\textit{Distance}} = \underbrace{245 \text{ mi}}_{\textit{Distance}} + \underbrace{\frac{40 \text{ mi}}{1 \cancel{\text{gal}}} \cdot g \cancel{\text{gal}}}_{\textit{Distance}}$$

Key Vocabulary

coefficient *(coeficiente)* A number that is multiplied by a variable.

constant *(constante)* A value that does not change.

corresponding angles *(ángulos correspondientes)* Angles in the same relative position in polygons with an equal number of angles.

corresponding sides of polygons *(lados correspondientes de los polígonos)* Sides in the same relative position in polygons with an equal number of sides.

equation *(ecuación)* A mathematical statement that two expressions are equivalent.

evaluate *(evaluar)* To find the value of an algebraic expression by substituting a number for each variable and simplifying by using the order of operations.

expression *(expresión)* A mathematical phrase that contains operations, numbers, and/or variables.

formula *(fórmula)* A literal equation that states a rule for a relationship among quantities.

linear equation in one variable *(ecuación lineal en una variable)* An equation that can be written in the form $ax = b$ where a and b are constants and $a \neq 0$.

literal equation *(ecuación literal)* An equation that contains two or more variables.

order of operations *(orden de las operaciones)* A process for evaluating expressions:
First, perform operations in parentheses or other grouping symbols.
Second, simplify powers and roots.
Third, perform all multiplication and division from left to right.
Fourth, perform all addition and subtraction from left to right.

precision *(precisión)* The level of detail of a measurement, determined by the unit of measure.

similar *(semejantes)* Two figures are similar if they have the same shape but not necessarily the same size.

solution of an equation in one variable *(solución de una ecuación en una variable)* A value or values that make the equation true.

term of an expression *(término de una expresión)* The parts of the expression that are added or subtracted.

unit analysis/dimensional analysis *(análisis dimensional)* A process that uses rates to convert measurements from one unit to another

variable *(variable)* A symbol used to represent a quantity that can change.

CHAPTER 1

Name ______________________ Class ____________ Date ____________

1-1

Video Tutor

Variables and Expressions

Going Deeper

Essential question: *How do you interpret, evaluate and write algebraic expressions that model real-world situations?*

CC.9-12.A.SSE.1a

1 ENGAGE Interpreting Expressions

An **expression** is a mathematical phrase that contains operations, numbers, and/or variables. A **numerical expression** contains only numbers and operations, while an **algebraic expression** contains at least one variable.

A **term** is a part of an expression that is added. The **coefficient** of a term is the numerical factor of the term. A numerical term in an algebraic expression is referred to as a *constant term.*

Algebraic Expression	Terms	Coefficients
$2x^2 - 16x + 32$	$2x^2$, $-16x$, constant term 32	2 is the coefficient of $2x$. -16 is the coefficient of $-16x$.

Recall that the **order of operations** is a rule for simplifying a numerical expression:

1. **P**arentheses (simplify inside parentheses) $1 - 6 \cdot (7 - 4) + 5^2 = 1 - 6 \cdot \mathbf{3} + 5^2$
2. **E**xponents (simplify powers) $= 1 - 6 \cdot 3 + \mathbf{25}$
3. **M**ultiplication and **D**ivision (from left to right) $= 1 - \mathbf{18} + 25$
4. **A**ddition and **S**ubtraction (from left to right) $= \mathbf{8}$

REFLECT

1a. Write the expression $3m - 4n - 8$ as a sum. How does this help you identify the terms of the expression? Identify the terms.

____

____

1b. Explain and illustrate the difference between a term and a coefficient.

____

____

1c. What is the coefficient of x in the expression $x - 2$? Explain your reasoning.

____

1d. What is the value of $1 - 18 + 25$ if you subtract then add? If you add then subtract? Why is the order of operations necessary?

____

To **evaluate** an algebraic expression, substitute the value(s) of the variable(s) into the expression and simplify using the order of operations.

CC.9–12.A.SSE.1b

2 EXAMPLE Evaluating Algebraic Expressions

Evaluate the algebraic expression $x(4x - 10)^3$ for $x = 2$.

A Substitute 2 for x in the expression. $\square \cdot \left(4 \cdot \square - 10\right)^3$

B Simplify the expression according to the order of operations.

- Multiply within parentheses. ____________
- Subtract within parentheses. ____________
- Simplify powers. ____________
- Multiply. ____________

REFLECT

2a. Explain why x and $4x - 10$ are factors of the expression $x(4x - 10)^3$ rather than terms of the expression. What are the terms of the factor $4x - 10$?

____

____

2b. Evaluate $5a + 3b$ and $(5 + a)(3 + b)$ for $a = 2$ and $b = 4$. How is the order of the steps different for the two expressions?

____

____

2c. In what order would you perform the operations to correctly evaluate the expression $2 + (3 - 4) \cdot 9$? What is the result?

____

2d. Show how to move the parentheses in the expression $2 + (3 - 4) \cdot 9$ so that the value of the expression is 9.

____

CC.9–12.A.SSE.1

3 ENGAGE Writing Algebraic Expressions

The table shows some words associated with the four arithmetic operations. They can help you translate verbal phrases into algebraic expressions.

Operation	Words	Examples
addition	plus, the sum of, added to, more than, increased by, how many altogether	• the sum of a number and 3 • a number increased by 3 $n + 3$
subtraction	minus, less, less than, the difference of, subtracted from, reduced by, how many more, how many less	• the difference of a number and 3 • 3 less than a number $n - 3$
multiplication	times, multiply, the product of, twice, double, triple, percent of	• the product of 0.4 and a number • 40% of a number $0.4n$
division	divide, divided by, divide into, the quotient of, half of, one-third of, the ratio of	• the quotient of a number and 3 • one-third of a number $n \div 3$, or $\frac{n}{3}$

REFLECT

The verbal phrase "the quotient of 3 more than a number and 5" can be modeled as follows:

Quantity 1 ÷ Quantity 2

3a. What words in the phrase represent Quantity 1? Translate these words into an algebraic expression using n for the variable.

____

3b. Write an algebraic expression to represent the overall phrase. Explain why you have to use some sort of grouping symbol.

____

3c. Show two ways to rewrite the verbal phrase so that it could be represented by the algebraic expression $5 \div (n + 3)$.

____

____

You can create a verbal model to help you translate a verbal expression into an algebraic expression.

CC.9–12.A.SSE.1

4 EXAMPLE Modeling with Algebraic Expressions

Write an algebraic expression to model the following phrase: the price of a meal plus a 15% tip for the meal.

A Complete the verbal model.

Price of meal (dollars)	▭	15%	▭	Price of meal (dollars)

B Choose a variable for the unknown quantity. Include units.

Let ________ represent the ________________________________.

C Write an algebraic expression for the situation. Simplify, if possible.

____

REFLECT

4a. A 15% tip represents the ratio 15 cents to 100 cents. Why does this make 15% a *unit-less* factor?

____

____

4b. What units are associated with the total cost? Explain.

____

____

4c. What could the expression $\frac{p + 0.15p}{2}$ represent, including units?

____

____

____

4d. What if the tip is 20% instead of 15%? How can you represent the total cost with a simplified algebraic expression? Identify the units for the expression.

____

4e. What if the tip is 20% instead of 15% and 3 people are sharing the cost evenly? How can you represent the amount that each person pays with a simplified algebraic expression? Identify the units for the expression.

____

PRACTICE

Identify the terms of each expression and the coefficient of each term.

1. $7x + 8y$

2. $a - b$

3. $3m^2 - 6n$

Evaluate each expression for $a = 2$, $b = 3$, and $c = -6$.

4. $7a - 5b + 4$

5. $b^2(c + 4)$

6. $8 - 2ab$

7. $a^2 + b^2 - c^2$

8. $(a - c)(c + 5)$

9. $12 - 2(a - b)^2$

10. $a + (b - c)^2$

11. $(a + b) - ab$

12. $5a^2 + bc^2$

13. Alex purchased a 6-hour calling card. He has used t minutes of access time. Write an algebraic expression to represent how many minutes he has remaining and identify the units for the expression.

14. A store is having a sale on used video games. Each game costs $12. Write an algebraic expression to represent the cost of buying v video games. Identify the units for the expression.

15. Sara is driving home from college for the weekend. The average speed of her car for the trip is 45 miles per hour. Write a verbal model and algebraic expression to represent the distance Sara's car travels in h hours. Identify the units for the expression.

16. It costs $20 per hour to bowl and $3 for shoe rental. Write a verbal model and an algebraic expression to represent the cost for n hours and identify the units for the expression.

17. Jared earns 0.25 vacation days for every week that he works in a calendar year. He also gets 10 paid company holidays per year. Write a verbal model and an algebraic expression to represent the amount of time he gets off from work in a year after working for w weeks and identify the units for the expression.

18. Sam collects baseball cards. He currently has 112 cards in his collection. He plans to buy 5 new cards every month. Write a verbal model and algebraic expression to represent the total number of cards Sam has after m months. Identify the units for the expression.

____

____

19. There are 575 fireworks to be shot off in a fireworks display. Every minute 12 new fireworks are shot off for the display. Write a verbal model and algebraic expression to represent the number of fireworks left to be shot off after t minutes. Identify the units for the expression.

____

____

20. Lindsay gets paid a base salary of $400 per week plus a 0.15 commission on each sale she makes. Write a verbal model and algebraic expression to represent Lindsay's total salary for the week if she makes d dollars worth of sales during the week. Identify the units for the expression.

____

____

Name________________ Class__________ Date__________

1-1

Additional Practice

Give two ways to write each algebraic expression in words.

1. $15 - b$

2. $\frac{x}{16}$

3. $x + 9$

4. $(2)(t)$

5. $z - 7$

6. $4y$

7. Sophie's math class has 6 fewer boys than girls, and there are *g* girls. Write an expression for the number of boys.

8. A computer printer can print 10 pages per minute. Write an expression for the number of pages the printer can print in *m* minutes.

Evaluate each expression for $r = 8$, $s = 2$, and $t = 5$.

9. st

10. $r \div s$

11. $s + t$

12. $r - t$

13. $r \cdot s$

14. $t - s$

15. Paula always withdraws 20 dollars more than she needs from the bank.
   a. Write an expression for the amount of money Paula withdraws if she needs *d* dollars.
   b. Find the amount of money Paula withdraws if she needs 20, 60, and 75 dollars.

Problem Solving

Write the correct answer.

1. For her book club, Sharon reads for 45 minutes each day. Write an expression for the number of hours she reads in *d* days.

______

2. The minimum wage in 2003 was $5.15. This was *w* more than the minimum wage in 1996. Write an expression for the minimum wage in 1996.

______

3. According to the 2000 census, the number of people per square mile in Florida was about 216 more than the number of people per square mile in Texas. Write an expression for the number of people per square mile in Florida if there were *t* people per square mile in Texas.

______

4. The cost of a party is $550. The price per person depends on how many people attend the party. Write an expression for the price per person if *p* people attend the party. Then find the price per person if 25, 50, and 55 people attend the party.

______

______

Use the table below to answer questions 5–6, which shows the years five states entered the Union. Select the best answer.

State	Year Entered into Union
Florida	1845
Indiana	1816
Pennsylvania	1787
Texas	1845
West Virginia	1863

5. North Carolina entered the Union *x* years after Pennsylvania. Which expression shows the year North Carolina entered the Union?

   A $1845 + x$ C $1787 + x$

   B $1845 - x$ D $1787 - x$

6. The expression $f - 26$ represents the year Alabama entered the Union, where *f* is the year Florida entered. In which year did Alabama enter the Union?

   F 1819 H 1837

   G 1826 J 1871

7. The number of states that entered the Union in 1889 was half the number of states *s* that entered in 1788. Which expression shows the number of states that entered the Union in 1889?

   A $2s$ C $s + 2$

   B $s \div 2$ D $2 - s$

Name________________________ Class______________ Date__________

1-2

Video Tutor

Solving Equations by Adding or Subtracting

Going Deeper

Essential question: *What are some different methods for solving linear equations?*

The solution of an equation can be given as an equation of the form $x = a$ where a is a solution, as in $x = 6$, or listed in set notation, as {6}.

CC.9–12.A.REI.3

1 EXPLORE Solving Equations Using Different Methods

Find the solution set for the linear equation.

A Use guess and check to find the solution set of the equation $x - 5 = 4$.

Guess $x = 10$. $10 - 5 =$ ____ $5 > 4$, so 10 is too great.

Guess $x = 8$. $8 - 5 =$ ____ $3 < 4$, so 8 is too little.

Guess $x = 9$. $9 - 5 =$ ____ $4 = 4$, so 9 is correct.

The solution set is { ____ }.

B Use a table to find the solution set of the equation $y + 7 = 10$.

y	1	2	3	4
y + 7	1 + 7	2 + 7	3 + 7	4 + 7
Sum				

The solution set is { ____ }.

C Work backward to find the solution set of the equation $z - 2 = 8$.

Start with the number being subtracted, _______.

Working backward, add _______ since it is the inverse of subtracting _______.

You get $z - 2 + 2 = 8 + 2 =$ _______ or $z = 10$. The solution set is {_______}.

REFLECT

1a. Could you solve each of the three equations above by all three methods? Explain.

____

____

____

Two equations are **equivalent equations** if they have the same solution set. The two equations below are equivalent because they have the same solution set, {6}.

$$x + 3 = 9 \qquad x - 3 = 3$$
$$\mathbf{6} + 3 = 9 \qquad \mathbf{6} - 3 = 3$$

To solve an equation algebraically, you perform a series of inverse operations to isolate the variable on one side. When these inverse operations are completed, the other side of the equation is the solution. The Addition and Subtraction Properties of Equality can be used to justify the steps taken to solve an equation. These properties, as well as other useful properties, are listed below.

Addition Property of Equality	If $a = b$, then $a + c = b + c$.
Subtraction Property of Equality	If $a = b$, then $a - b = b - c$.
Inverse Property of Addition	$a + (-a) = -a + a = 0$
Identity Property of Addition	$a + 0 = 0 + a = a$
Associative Property of Addition	$(a + b) + c = a + (b + c)$

CC.9–12.A.REI.1

2 EXAMPLE Adding or Subtracting to Find the Solution Set

Add or subtract to find the solution set.

A $x + 5 = 13$

$x + 5 -$ ______ $= 13 -$ ______   ______________ Property of Equality

$x +$ ______ $= 13 -$ ______   ______________ Property of Addition

$x = 13 -$ ______   ______________ Property of Addition

$x =$ ______   Simplify.

The solution set is { ______ }.

B $y - 11 = 2$

$y - 11 +$ ______ $= 2 +$ ______   ______________ Property of Equality

$y +$ ______ $= 2 +$ ______   ______________ Property of Addition

$y = 2 +$ ______   ______________ Property of Addition

$y =$ ______   Simplify.

The solution set is { ______ }.

REFLECT

2a. Which property of equality would you use to solve $x - 47 = 100$? Explain.

____

____

CC.9–12.A.REI.1

3 EXAMPLE Using the Associative Property

Use properties to find the solution set of $(x + 5) + 4 = 16$.

$(x + 5) + 4 = 16$	Original equation
$x + (5 + \boxed{}) = 16$	Associative Property
$x + \boxed{} = 16$	Simplify.
$x + 9 - 9 = 16 - \boxed{}$	______________ Property of Equality
$x + \boxed{} = 16 - 9$	Inverse Property of Addition
$\boxed{} = 16 - \boxed{}$	______________ Property of Addition
$x = \boxed{}$	Simplify.

The solution set is $\{\boxed{}\}$.

REFLECT

3a. Solve $(x + 5) + 4 = 16$ by first subtracting 4 and then subtracting 5. Show your work and justify each step.

____

____

____

____

____

____

____

____

____

____

3b. Does performing the steps in a different order affect the solution of the equation? Compare the steps in the example with the steps for the question above. How do the two methods differ? Explain.

____

____

____

____

PRACTICE

Find the solution set for each equation. State the property you used.

1. $m - 7 = 13$

2. $r + 12 = 21$

3. $17 + p = 22$

4. $7 = q + 4$

5. $81 = 8 + z$

6. $42 = b - 21$

Solve using the Associative Property first. Justify your steps.

7. $(y + 8) - 3 = 16$

Solve using the Properties of Equality first. Justify your steps.

8. $(m - 3) + 5 = 12$

Name ________________ Class ________ Date ________

1-2

Additional Practice

Solve each equation. Check your answers.

1. $g - 7 = 15$ ________
2. $t + 4 = 6$ ________
3. $13 = m - 7$ ________
4. $x + 3.4 = 9.1$ ________
5. $n - \frac{3}{8} = \frac{1}{8}$ ________
6. $p - \frac{1}{3} = \frac{2}{3}$ ________
7. $-6 + k = 32$ ________
8. $7 = w + 9.3$ ________
9. $8 = r + 12$ ________
10. $y - 57 = -40$ ________
11. $-5.1 + b = -7.1$ ________
12. $a + 15 = 15$ ________

13. Marietta was given a raise of $0.75 an hour, which brought her hourly wage to $12.25. Write and solve an equation to determine Marietta's hourly wage before her raise. Show that your answer is reasonable.

____

____

14. Brad grew $4\frac{1}{4}$ inches this year and is now $56\frac{7}{8}$ inches tall. Write and solve an equation to find Brad's height at the start of the year. Show that your answer is reasonable.

____

____

15. Heather finished a race in 58.4 seconds, which was 2.6 seconds less than her practice time. Write and solve an equation to find Heather's practice time. Show that your answer is reasonable.

____

____

16. The radius of Earth is 6378.1 km, which is 2981.1 km longer than the radius of Mars. Write and solve an equation to determine the radius of Mars. Show that your answer is reasonable.

____

____

Problem Solving

Write the correct answer.

1. Michelle withdrew $120 from her bank account. She now has $3345 in her account. Write and solve an equation to find how much money *m* was in her account before she made the withdrawal.

____

____

2. Max lost 23 pounds while on a diet. He now weighs 184 pounds. Write and solve an equation to find his initial weight *w*.

____

____

3. Earth takes 365 days to orbit the Sun. Mars takes 687 days. Write and solve an equation to find how many more days *d* Mars takes than Earth to orbit the Sun.

____

____

4. In 1990, 53.4% of commuters took public transportation in New York City, which was 19.9% greater than the percentage in San Francisco. Write and solve an equation to find what percentage of commuters *p* took public transportation in San Francisco.

____

____

Use the circle graph below to answer questions 5–7. Select the best answer. The circle graph shows the colors for SUVs as percents of the total number of SUVs manufactured in 2000 in North America.

5. The percent of silver SUVs increased by 7.9% between 1998 and 2000. If x% of SUVs were silver in 1998, which equation represents this relationship?

   A $x + 7.9 = 14.1$ C $7.9x = 14.1$

   B $x - 7.9 = 14.1$ D $7.9 - x = 14.1$

6. Solve the equation from problem 5. What is the value of x?

   F 1.8 H 7.1

   G 6.2 J 22

7. The sum of the percents of dark red SUVs and white SUVs was 26.3%. What was the percent of dark red SUVs?

   A 2.3% C 12.2%

   B 3.2% D 18%

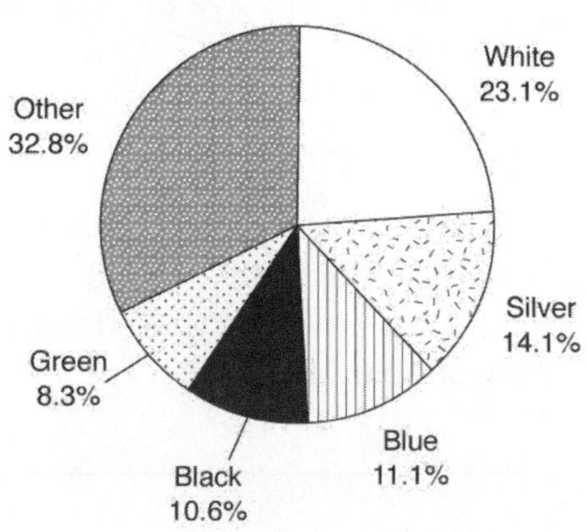

Name________________________ Class______________ Date______________

1-3

Video Tutor

Solving Equations by Multiplying or Dividing

Going Deeper

Essential question: *How can you use properties to justify solutions to equations that involve multiplication and division?*

You have solved addition and subtraction equations by performing a series of inverse operations that isolate the variable on one side of the equation. Multiplication and division equations can be solved in a similar way. The Multiplication and Division Properties of Equality, as well as the other properties below, can be used to justify the steps taken to solve a multiplication or division equation.

Multiplication Property of Equality	If $a = b$, then $ac = bc$.
Division Property of Equality	If $a = b$, and $c \neq 0$, then $\frac{a}{c} = \frac{b}{c}$.
Inverse Property of Multiplication	If $a \neq 0$, then $a\left(\frac{1}{a}\right) = \left(\frac{1}{a}\right)a = 1$.
Identity Property of Multiplication	$a \cdot 1 = 1 \cdot a = a$
Associative Property of Multiplication	$a(bc) = (ab)c$

CC.9–12.A.REI.1

1 EXAMPLE Multiplying or Dividing to Find the Solution Set

Find the solution set.

$\frac{5y}{3} = 20$

$\square\left(\frac{5y}{3}\right) = \square(20)$ ______________ Property of Equality

$\frac{\square}{3}(5y) = \square(20)$ Associative Property of Multiplication

$\square(5y) = \square(20)$ ______________ Property of Multiplication

$(5y) = \square(20)$ ______________ Property of Addition

$5y = \square$ Simplify.

$\frac{5y}{\square} = \frac{60}{\square}$ ______________ Property of Equality

$y = \square$ Simplify.

The solution set is { }.

REFLECT

1a. Solve $\frac{5y}{3} = 20$ using only the Multiplication Property of Equality. Show your work and justify each step.

1b. Which method of solving $\frac{5y}{3} = 20$ is more efficient? Explain.

PRACTICE

Find the solution set for each equation. State the property you used.

1. $\frac{4}{5}b = 16$

2. $7w = 105$

3. Solve $\frac{3}{4}\left(\frac{2}{3}m\right) = 24$. Use the Properties of Equality first. Justify each step.

Name________________________ Class________________ Date____________

1-3

Additional Practice

Solve each equation. Check your answers.

1. $\frac{d}{8} = 6$ ________
2. $-5 = \frac{n}{2}$ ________
3. $2p = 54$ ________
4. $\frac{-t}{2} = 12$ ________
5. $-40 = -4x$ ________
6. $\frac{2r}{3} = 16$ ________
7. $-49 = 7y$ ________
8. $-15 = -\frac{3n}{5}$ ________
9. $9m = 6$ ________
10. $\frac{v}{-3} = -6$ ________
11. $2.8 = \frac{b}{4}$ ________
12. $\frac{3r}{4} = \frac{1}{8}$ ________

Answer each of the following.

13. The perimeter of a regular pentagon is 41.5 cm. Write and solve an equation to determine the length of each side of the pentagon. ________
14. In June 2005, Peter mailed a package from his local post office in Fayetteville, North Carolina to a friend in Radford, Virginia for \$2.07. The first-class rate at the time was \$0.23 per ounce. Write and solve an equation to determine the weight of the package. ________
15. Lola spends one-third of her allowance on movies. She spends \$8 per week at the movies. Write and solve an equation to determine Lola's weekly allowance. ________

Problem Solving

Write the correct answer.

1. John threw a surprise birthday party for his friend. Food, drinks, and a DJ cost \$480 for a group of 32 people. Write and solve an equation to find the cost *c* per person.

____

____

2. One serving of soybeans contains 10 grams of protein, which is 4 times the amount in one serving of kale. Write and solve an equation to find the amount of protein *x* in one serving of kale.

____

____

3. Maria earned \$10.50 per hour working at an ice cream shop. She earned \$147 each week before taxes. Write and solve an equation to find the number of hours *h* she worked each week.

____

____

4. Ben is saving $\frac{1}{5}$ of his weekly pay to buy a car. Write and solve an equation to find what weekly pay *w* results in savings of \$61.50.

____

____

Use the table below to answer questions 5–7. Select the best answer. The table shows the maximum speed in miles per hour for various animals.

Animal	mi/h
Falcon	200
Zebra	40
Cat (domestic)	30
Black Mamba Snake	20
Snail	0.03

5. The speed of a snail is how many times that of a cat?

A $\frac{1}{1000}$

B $\frac{1}{100}$

C 100

D 1000

6. A cheetah's maximum speed of 70 mi/h is *x* times faster than a black mamba snake's maximum speed. Which equation shows this relationship?

F $20 + x = 70$

G $20 = 70x$

H $70 = \frac{20}{x}$

J $70 = 20x$

7. Use your equation in problem 6 to find how many times faster a cheetah is than a black mamba snake if they are both traveling at their maximum speed.

A 0.3 times

B 3.5 times

C 10 times

D 50 times

Name________________________ Class______________ Date__________

1-4

Video Tutor

Solving Two-Step and Multi-Step Equations

Going Deeper

Essential question: *How can you justify solutions to multi-step equations?*

The Properties of Equality, as well as the Commutative Properties, can be used to solve multi-step equations.

Addition Property of Equality	If $a = b$, then $a + c = b + c$.
Subtraction Property of Equality	If $a = b$, then $a - c = b - c$.
Multiplication Property of Equality	If $a = b$, then $ac = bc$.
Division Property of Equality	If $a = b$ and $c \neq 0$, then $\frac{a}{c} = \frac{b}{c}$.
Commutative Property of Addition	$a + b = b + a$
Commutative Property of Multiplication	$ab = ba$

CC.9-12.A.REI.1

1 EXAMPLE Solving Multi-Step Equations

Find the solution. Justify each step.

$x + 3 + 3x = 7 + 4$

$(x + 3x) + \_\_\_ = 7 + 4$ Commutative Property of Addition

$\_\_\_ = \_\_\_$ Combine like terms.

$4x + 3 - 3 = \_\_\_ - \_\_\_$ Subtraction Property of Equality

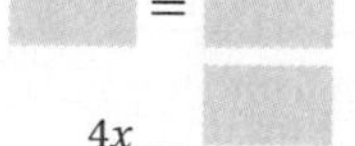

$\_\_\_ = \_\_\_$ Inverse Property of Addition; Simplify.

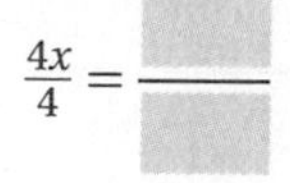

$\frac{4x}{4} = \frac{\_\_\_}{\_\_\_}$ Division Property of Equality

$x = \_\_\_$ Simplify.

REFLECT

1a. In the equation $4x - 8 + x = 18 - 7$, would you use the Addition Property of Equality to add 7 to each side? Why or why not?

You may need to use the Distributive Property to solve an equation.

Distributive Property	If a, b, and c are real numbers, then $a(b + c) = ab + ac$.

CC.9–12.A.REI.1

2 EXAMPLE Using the Distributive Property

Find the solution. Justify each step.

$2(x - 6) = -18$

$2x - 12 = -18$ ____________________

$2x - 12 + 12 =$ ______ ____________________

____ $=$ ____ Inverse Property of Addition; Simplify.

$\frac{2x}{2} = \frac{-6}{2}$ ____________________

____ $=$ ____ Simplify.

REFLECT

2a. Could you have solved $2(x - 6) = -18$ by dividing first? If so, how? When does it make sense to do this and when does it not?

PRACTICE

1. Solve $4(5x + 3) = 92$. Justify each step.

Without solving, explain which properties you would use to solve these equations. List the properties in order of use.

2. $\frac{x}{3} + 5 = 11$

3. $4(x + 6) = 30$

Name ________________________ Class ________________ Date ____________

1-4

Additional Practice

Solve each equation. Check your answers.

1. $-4x + 7 = 11$ ____________
2. $17 = 5y - 3$ ____________
3. $-4 = 2p + 10$ ____________
4. $3m + 4 = 1$ ____________
5. $12.5 = 2g - 3.5$ ____________
6. $-13 = -h - 7$ ____________
7. $-6 = \frac{y}{5} + 4$ ____________
8. $\frac{7}{9} = 2n + \frac{1}{9}$ ____________
9. $-\frac{4}{5}t + \frac{2}{5} = \frac{2}{3}$ ____________
10. $-(x - 10) = 7$ ____________
11. $-2(b + 5) = -6$ ____________
12. $8 = 4(q - 2) + 4$ ____________

13. If $3x - 8 = -2$, find the value of $x - 6$. ____________

14. If $-2(3y + 5) = -4$, find the value of $5y$. ____________

Answer each of the following.

15. The two angles shown form a right angle. Write and solve an equation to find the value of x.

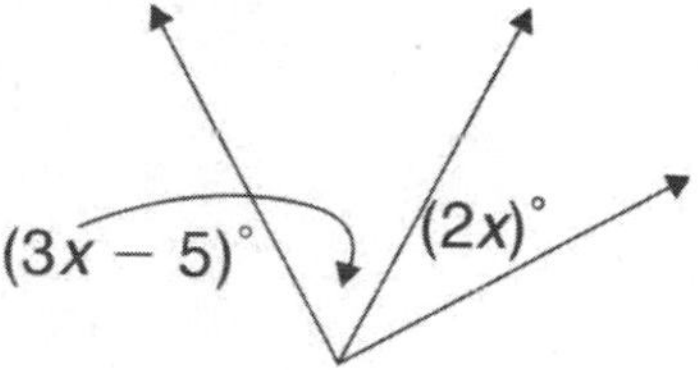

____

16. For her cellular phone service, Vera pays \$32 a month, plus \$0.75 for each minute over the allowed minutes in her plan. Vera received a bill for \$47 last month. For how many minutes did she use her phone beyond the allowed minutes? ____________

Problem Solving

Write the correct answer.

1. Stephen belongs to a movie club in which he pays an annual fee of $39.95 and then rents DVDs for $0.99 each. In one year, Stephen spent $55.79. Write and solve an equation to find how many DVDs *d* he rented.

____

____

2. In 2003, the population of Zimbabwe was about 12.6 million, which was 1 million more than 4 times the population in 1950. Write and solve an equation to find the population *p* of Zimbabwe in 1950.

____

____

3. Maggie's brother is three years younger than twice her age. The sum of their ages is 24. How old is Maggie?

____

4. Kate is saving to take an SAT prep course that costs $350. So far, she has saved $180, and she adds $17 to her savings each week. How many more weeks must she save to be able to afford the course?

____

Use the graph below to answer questions 5–7. Select the best answer. The graph shows the population density (number of people per square mile) of various states given in the 2000 census.

5. One seventeenth of Rhode Island's population density minus 17 equals the population density of Colorado. What is Rhode Island's population density?

A 425 C 714

B 697 D 1003

6. One more than sixteen times the population density of New Mexico equals the population density of Texas. To the nearest whole number, what is New Mexico's population density?

F 5 H 13

G 8 J 63

7. Three times the population density of Missouri minus 26 equals the population density of California. What is Missouri's population density?

A 64 C 98

B 81 D 729

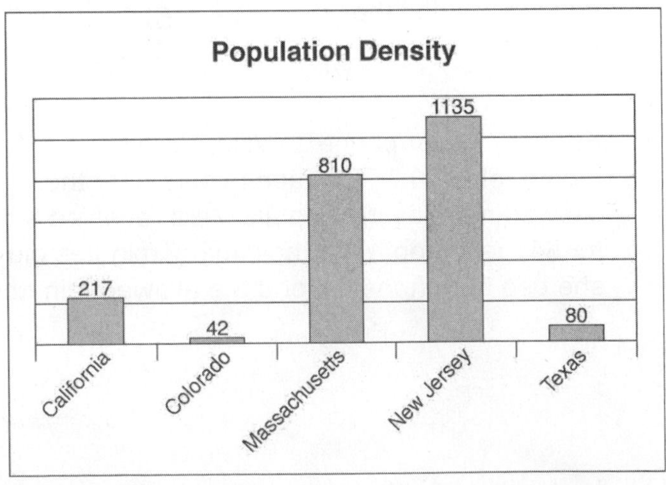

Name ______________________ Class ____________ Date ____________

1-5

Video Tutor

Solving Equations with Variables on Both Sides

Going Deeper

Essential question: *How can you use properties to justify solutions to equations that have variables on both sides?*

You can use the Properties of Equality and the Distributive Property to justify the steps to solutions of equations that have variables on both sides.

CC.9–12.A.REI.1

1 EXAMPLE Solving with Variables on Both Sides

Justify the steps in solving $3x + 2 = -x + 10$ by using the properties of equality.

$3x + 2 = -x + 10$	Original equation
$3x + 2 + x = -x + 10 + x$	____________________
______ = ______	Simplify.
$4x + 2 - 2 = 10 - 2$	____________________
$4x =$ ______	Simplify.
$\frac{4x}{\_\_\_} = \frac{8}{\_\_\_}$ 	____________________
$x =$ ______	Simplify.

The solution set is { ______ }.

REFLECT

1a. In the first step, suppose that you subtracted $3x$ from both sides. How would the rest of the steps change? Would the solution set be different?

____

____

____

____

1b. What is the solution set of $x = x$? Why?

____

____

1c. What statement do you get if you try to solve the equation $x + 2 = x$? Is this statement true or false? What does this mean in terms of the solution set?

____

____

CC.9–12.A.REI.1

2 EXAMPLE Solving a Multi-Step Linear Equation

Justify the steps in solving $\frac{3x}{2} + 7x - 7 = 3(2x + 1)$ by using the properties of equality and other properties.

$\frac{3x}{2} + 7x - 7 = 3(2x + 1)$ Original equation

$\frac{3x}{2} + 7x - 7 = 6x + 3$ ______________

$2 \cdot \left(\frac{3x}{2} + 7x - 7\right) = 2 \cdot (6x + 3)$ ______________

$3x + 14x - 14 = 12x + 6$ ______________

$(3 + 14)x - 14 = 12x + 6$ ______________

$17x - 14 = 12x + 6$ Simplify.

$17x - 14 - 12x = 12x + 6 - 12x$ ______________

$5x - 14 = 6$ Simplify.

$5x - 14 + 14 = 6 + 14$ ______________

$5x = 20$ Simplify.

$\frac{5x}{5} = \frac{20}{5}$ ______________

$x = 4$

The solution set is { }.

REFLECT

2a. In the example, could the steps have been performed in a different order? Explain.

____

____

____

2b. Would performing the steps in a different order affect the solution to the equation? Why or why not?

____

____

PRACTICE

Find the solution set for the equation. Use the properties of equality and other properties to justify your solution.

1. $2x - 3 = 9 - x$

2. $4x - 7 = x + 5$

3. $25 + 10(12 - x) = 5(2x - 7)$

4. $\frac{1}{2}(6x + 4) = x + 2(x + 1)$

5. Find the set of values of x such that $5x - 9 = 6$. Justify your solution by using the properties of equality.

6. Find the set of values of x such that $-12x + 7 = 4x - 9$. Justify your solution by using the properties of equality.

Name________________________ Class______________ Date__________

1-5

Additional Practice

Solve each equation. Check your answers.

1. $3d + 8 = 2d - 17$
2. $2n - 7 = 5n - 10$
3. $p - 15 = 13 - 6p$

_______________ _______________ _______________

4. $-t + 5 = t - 19$
5. $15x - 10 = -9x + 2$
6. $1.8r + 9 = -5.7r - 6$

_______________ _______________ _______________

7. $2y + 3 = 3(y + 7)$
8. $4n + 6 - 2n = 2(n + 3)$
9. $6m - 8 = 2 + 9m - 1$

_______________ _______________ _______________

10. $-v + 5 + 6v = 1 + 5v + 3$
11. $2(3b - 4) = 8b - 11$
12. $5(r - 1) = 2(r - 4) - 6$

_______________ _______________ _______________

Answer each of the following.

13. Janine has job offers at two companies. One company offers a starting salary of \$28,000 with a raise of \$3000 each year. The other company offers a starting salary of \$36,000 with a raise of \$2000 each year.

    a. After how many years would Janine's salary be the same with both companies? _______________

    b. What would that salary be? _______________

14. Xian and his cousin both collect stamps. Xian has 56 stamps, and his cousin has 80 stamps. Both have recently joined different stamp-collecting clubs. Xian's club will send him 12 new stamps per month, and his cousin's club will send him 8 new stamps per month.

    a. After how many months will Xian and his cousin have the same number of stamps? _______________

    b. How many stamps will that be? _______________

Problem Solving

Write the correct answer.

1. Claire purchased just enough fencing to border either a rectangular or triangular garden, as shown, whose perimeters are the same.

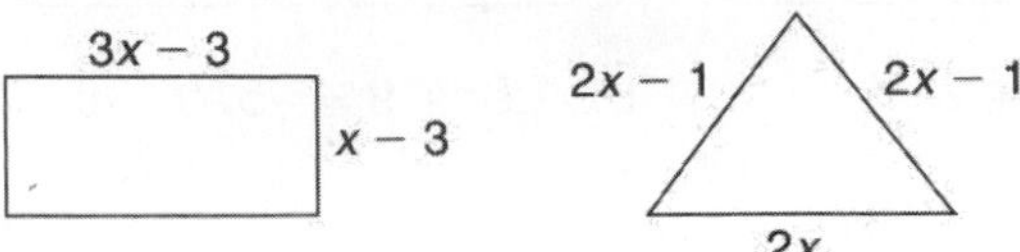

How many feet of fencing did she buy?

____

2. Celia and Ryan are starting a nutrition program. Celia currently consumes 1200 calories a day and will increase that number by 100 calories each day. Ryan currently consumes 3230 calories a day and will decrease that number by 190 each day. They will continue this pattern until they are both consuming the same number of calories per day. In how many days will that be?

____

3. A moving company charges $800 plus $16 per hour. Another moving company charges $720 plus $21 per hour. How long is a job that costs the same no matter which company is used?

____

4. Aaron needs to take out a loan to purchase a motorcycle. At one bank, he would pay $2500 initially and $150 each month for the loan. At another bank, he would pay $3000 initially and $125 each month. After how many months will the two loan payments be the same?

____

Use the table below to answer questions 5–7. Select the best answer. The table shows the membership fees of three different gyms.

Gym	Fees
Workout Now	$200 plus $45 per month
Community Gym	$50 plus $55 per month
Ultra Sports Club	$20 plus $60 per month

5. After how many months will the fees for Workout Now and Community Gym be the same?

   A 2.5   C 25

   B 15   D 30

6. Sal joined Workout Now for the number of months found in problem 5. How much did he pay?

   F $695   H $1325

   G $875   J $1550

7. After how many months will the fees for Workout Now and Ultra Sports Club be the same?

   A 7   C 12

   B 10   D 15

Name________________________ Class________________ Date________

1-6

Solving for a Variable

Going Deeper

Essential question: *How do you solve literal equations and rewrite formulas?*

Video Tutor

A **literal equation** is an equation in which the coefficients and constants have been replaced by letters. In the following Explore, you will see how a literal equation can be used to represent specific equations having the same form.

CC.9–12.A.REI.3

1 EXPLORE Understanding Literal Equations

A For each equation given below, solve the equation by writing two equivalent equations: one where the x-term is isolated and then one where x is isolated.

$3x + 1 = 7$ $-2x + 5 = 11$ $4x + 3 = -1$

________ ________ ________

________ ________ ________

B Identify the two properties of equality that you used in part A. List them in the order that you used them.

____

C Each equation in part A has the general form $ax + b = c$ where $a \neq 0$. Solve this literal equation for x using the properties of equality that you identified in part B.

$ax + b = c$	Write the literal equation.
$ax = \square - \square$	Subtract b from both sides.
$x = \frac{\square - \square}{\square}$	Divide both sides by a.

D Show that the solution of the literal equation gives the same solution of $3x + 1 = 7$ as you found in part A. Recognize that when $a = 3$, $b = 1$, and $c = 7$, the literal equation $ax + b = c$ gives the specific equation $3x + 1 = 7$.

$x = \frac{\square - \square}{\square}$	Write the literal equation's solution.
$x = \frac{\square - \square}{\square}$	Substitute 3 for a, 1 for b, and 7 for c.
$x = \square$	Simplify.

REFLECT

1a. Why must the restriction $a \neq 0$ be placed on the literal equation $ax + b = c$?

____

1b. Choose one of the other specific equations from part A. Show that the solution of the literal equation gives the solution of the specific equation.

____

____

When you solve a literal equation, you use properties of equality and other properties to isolate the variable. The result is not a number, but rather an expression involving the letters that represent the coefficients and constants.

CC.9–12.A.REI.3

2 EXAMPLE Solving a Literal Equation and Evaluating Its Solution

Solve the literal equation $a(x + b) = c$ where $a \neq 0$. Then use the literal equation's solution to obtain the solution of the specific equation $2(x + 7) = -6$.

A Solve $a(x + b) = c$ for x. Use the properties of equality to justify your solution steps.

$a(x + b) = c$ Original equation

$x + b = \frac{\square}{\square}$ ____________ Property of Equality

$x = \frac{\square}{\square} - \square$ ____________ Property of Equality

B Obtain the solution of $2(x + 7) = -6$ from the literal equation's solution by letting $a = 2$, $b = 7$, and $c = -6$.

$x = \frac{\square}{\square} - \square$ Write the literal equation's solution.

$x = \frac{\square}{\square} - \square$ Substitute 2 for *a*, 7 for *b*, and −6 for *c*.

$x = \square$ Simplify.

REFLECT

2a. When solving $a(x + b) = c$, why do you divide by a before you subtract b?

____

____

____

2b. Write an equation that has the form $a(x + b) = c$. Find the solution of your equation using the literal equation's solution.

____

2c. Another way to solve $a(x + b) = c$ is to start by using the Distributive Property. Show and justify the solution steps using this method.

____

____

____

____

2d. When you start solving $a(x + b) = c$ by dividing by a, you get $x = \frac{c}{a} - b$. When you start solving $a(x + b) = c$ by distributing a, you get $x = \frac{c - ab}{a}$. Use the fact that you can rewrite $\frac{c - ab}{a}$ as the difference of two fractions to show that the two solutions are equivalent.

____

CC.9–12.A.CED.4

3 EXAMPLE Solving a Formula for a Variable

Solve the formula for the given variable. Justify each step in your solution.

A The formula $V = lwh$ gives the volume of a rectangular prism with length l, width w, and height h. Solve the formula for h to find the height of a rectangular prism with a given volume, length, and width.

$V = lwh$ Original equation

$\frac{V}{\square} = \frac{lwh}{\square}$ ______________________________

$h = \frac{\square}{\square}$ Simplify.

B The formula $E = \frac{1}{2}kx^2$ gives the potential energy E of a spring with spring constant k that has been stretched by length x. Solve the formula for k to find the constant of a spring with a given potential energy and stretch.

$E = \frac{1}{2}kx^2$ Original equation

$\square \cdot E = \square \cdot \frac{1}{2}kx^2$ ______________________________

$2E = kx^2$ ______________________________

$\frac{2E}{\square} = \frac{kx^2}{\square}$ ______________________________

$k = \frac{\square}{\square}$ Simplify.

REFLECT

3a. The formula $T = p + sp$ gives the total cost of an item with price p and sales tax s, expressed as a decimal. Describe a situation in which you would want to solve the formula for s.

____

3b. What is true about the restrictions on the value of a variable in a formula that might not be true of other literal equations?

____

____

CC.9–12.A.CED.4

4 EXAMPLE Writing and Rearranging a Formula

The flower garden at the right is made up of a square and an isosceles triangle. Write a formula for the perimeter *P* in terms of *x*, and then solve for *x* to find a formula for the side length of the square in terms of *P*.

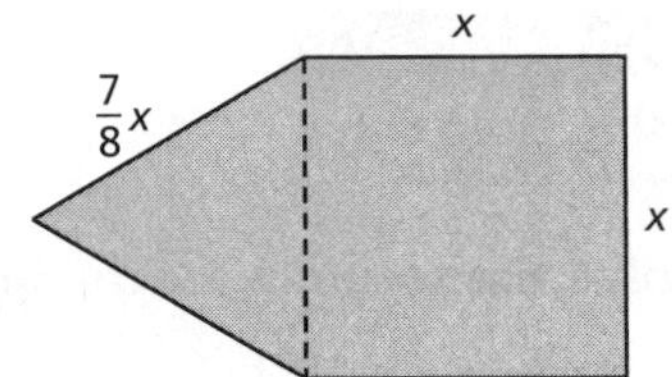

A Write a formula for the perimeter of each shape. Use only the sides of the square and the triangle that form the outer edges of the figure.

Perimeter of square = ____________

Perimeter of triangle = ____________

B Combine the formulas. $P = \square$

C Solve the formula for x.

$P = \square$ Write the combined formula.

$P = x(\square + \square)$ Distributive Property

$P = x\left(\frac{\square}{\square}\right)$ Find the sum. Write the result as an improper fraction.

$P\left(\frac{\square}{\square}\right) = x\left(\frac{\square}{\square}\right)\left(\frac{\square}{\square}\right)$ Multiplication Property of Equality

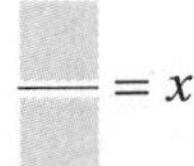

$\frac{\square}{\square} = x$ Simplify.

REFLECT

4a. What are the restrictions on the values of P and x? Explain.

4b. How could you write a formula for the area of the square in terms of P?

PRACTICE

1. Show and justify the steps for solving $x + a = b$. Then use the literal equation's solution to obtain the solution of $x + 2 = -4$.

2. Show and justify the steps for solving $ax = b$ where $a \neq 0$. Then use the literal equation's solution to obtain the solution of $3x = -15$.

3. Show and justify the steps for solving $ax = bx + c$ where $a \neq b$. Then use the literal equation's solution to obtain the solution of $2x = x + 7$.

Solve each formula for the indicated variable.

4. Formula for the surface area of a rectangular prism: $SA = 2(lw + hw + hl)$, for w

5. Formula for the area of a trapezoid: $A = \frac{1}{2}(a + b)h$, for b

6. An electrician sent Bonnie an invoice in the amount of a dollars for 6 hours of work that was done on Saturday. The electrician charges a weekend fee f in addition to an hourly rate r. Bonnie knows what the weekend fee is. Write a formula Bonnie can use to find r, the rate the electrician charges per hour.

7. The swimming pool below is made up of a square and two semicircles. Write a formula for the perimeter P in terms of x, and then solve for x to find a formula for the side length of the square in terms of P.

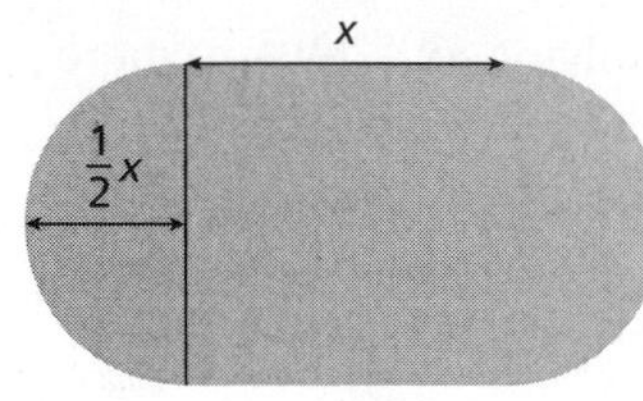

Name__________ Class__________ Date__________ 1-6

Additional Practice

Answer each of the following.

1. The formula $C = 2\pi r$ relates the radius r of a circle to its circumference C. Solve the formula for r.

2. The formula $y = mx + b$ is called the slope-intercept form of a line. Solve this formula for m.

Solve for the indicated variable.

3. $4c = d$ for c

4. $n - 6m = 8$ for n

5. $2p + 5r = q$ for p

6. $-10 = xy + z$ for x

7. $\frac{a}{b} = c$ for b

8. $\frac{h-4}{j} = k$ for j

Answer each of the following.

9. The formula $c = 5p + 215$ relates c, the total cost in dollars of hosting a birthday party at a skating rink, to p, the number of people attending.

   a. Solve the formula $c = 5p + 215$ for p.

   b. If Allie's parents are willing to spend $300 for a party, how many people can attend?

10. The formula for the area of a triangle is $A = \frac{1}{2}bh$, where b represents the length of the base and h represents the height.

   a. Solve the formula $A = \frac{1}{2}bh$ for b.

   b. If a triangle has an area of 192 mm^2, and the height measures 12 mm, what is the measure of the base?

Problem Solving

Use the table below, which shows some track and field gold medal winners, to answer questions 1–4. Round all answers to the nearest tenth.

1. Solve the formula $d = rt$ for r.

____

2. Find Johnson's average speed in meters per second.

____

3. Find Garcia's average speed in meters per second.

____

4. The world record of 19.32 seconds in the 200-meter race was set by Michael Johnson in 1996. Find the difference between Johnson's average speed and Kenteris' average speed.

____

2000 Summer Olympics		
Gold Medal Winner	**Race**	**Time (s)**
M. Greene, USA	100 m	9.87
K. Kenteris, Greece	200 m	20.09
M. Johnson, USA	400 m	43.84
A. Garcia, Cuba	110 m hurdles	13.00

Select the best answer.

5. The cost to mail a letter in the United States in 2008 was $0.41 for the first ounce and $0.26 for each additional ounce. Solve $C = 0.41 + 0.26(z - 1)$ for z.

A $z = \dfrac{C - 0.41}{0.26}$

B $z = \dfrac{C - 0.41}{0.26} + 1$

C $z = \dfrac{C + 0.15}{0.26}$

D $z = C - 0.67$

6. The formula $V = \dfrac{Bh}{3}$ shows how to find the volume of a pyramid. Solve for B.

F $B = \dfrac{3V}{h}$ H $B = 3Vh$

G $B = 3V - h$ J $B = 3V + h$

7. Degrees Celsius and degrees Fahrenheit are related by the equation $C = \dfrac{5}{9}(F - 32)$. Solve for F.

A $F = 9C + 27$ C $F = \dfrac{5}{9}C + 32$

B $F = \dfrac{9}{5}C$ D $F = \dfrac{9}{5}C + 32$

8. The cost of operating an electrical device is given by the formula $C = \dfrac{Wtc}{1000}$ where W is the power in watts, t is the time in hours, and c is the cost in cents per kilowatt-hour. Solve for W.

F $W = 1000C - tc$

G $W = \dfrac{Ctc}{1000}$

H $W = 1000C + tc$

J $W = \dfrac{1000C}{tc}$

Name________________________ Class________________ Date__________

1-7

Video Tutor

Solving Absolute Value Equations

Going Deeper

Essential question: *How can you use graphing to solve equations involving absolute value?*

The equation $2|x - 3| + 1 = 5$ is an example of an *absolute value equation.*

CC.9-12.A.REI.11

1 EXAMPLE Solving an Absolute Value Equation by Graphing

Use a graphing calculator to solve the equation $2|x - 3| + 1 = 5$.

A Treat the left side of the equation as the absolute value equation $y = 2|x - 3| + 1$. Treat the right side as the equation $y = 5$.

B Press Y=. Enter the first equation, $y = 2|x - 3| + 1$, as Y_1 and the second equation $y = 5$ as Y_2.

C Press GRAPH. Copy the graph from your calculator on the grid at the right. Use the intersect feature under the CALC menu to find the points of intersection of Y_1 and Y_2.

D Identify the x-coordinate of each point where the graphs of Y_1 and Y_2 intersect. Show that each x-coordinate is a solution of $2|x - 3| + 1 = 5$.

____

REFLECT

1a. Why is the y-coordinate of both points of intersection equal to 5?

____

____

1b. The vertex of an absolute value graph is the lowest point if the graph opens upward or the highest point if the graph opens downward. The vertex of the graph of $y = 2|x - 3| + 1$ is (1, 3). How are the coordinates of the vertex related to its equation?

____

____

____

CC.9–12.A.REI.1

2 EXAMPLE Solving an Absolute Value Equation Using Algebra

Solve the equation $2|x - 3| + 1 = 5$ using algebra.

A Isolate the expression $|x - 3|$.

$2\|x - 3\| + 1 = 5$	Write the equation.
$\underline{\qquad\ \square\quad \square}$	Subtract 1 from both sides.
$2\|x - 3\| = \square$	Simplify.
$\dfrac{2\|x - 3\|}{\square} = \dfrac{\square}{\square}$	Divide both sides by 2.
$\|x - 3\| = \square$	Simplify.

B Interpret the equation $|x - 3| = 2$: What numbers have an absolute value equal to 2?

____

C Set the expression inside the absolute value bars equal to each of the numbers from Part B and solve for x.

$x - 3 = \square$	or	$x - 3 = \square$	Write an equation for each value of $x - 3$.
		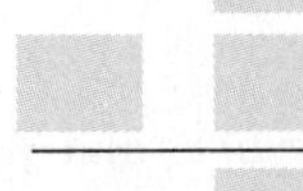 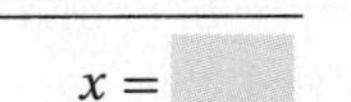	Add 3 to both sides of each equation.
$x = \square$	or	$x = \square$	Simplify.

REFLECT

2a. The left side of the equation is $2|x - 3| + 1$. Evaluate this expression for each solution of the equation. How does this help you check the solutions?

____

____

____

____

2b. Suppose the number on the right side of the equation was -5 instead of 5. What solutions would the equation have? Why? When answering these questions, you may want to refer to the graph of $y = 2|x - 3| + 1$.

____

____

CC.9-12.A.CED.2

3 EXAMPLE Solving a Real-World Problem

Sal exercises by running east 3 miles along a road in front of his home and then reversing his direction to return home. He runs at a constant speed of 0.1 mile per minute. Write and graph an absolute value equation that gives his distance d (in miles) from home in terms of the elapsed time t (in minutes). Use the graph to find the time(s) at which Sal is 1 mile from home.

A Determine the three key values of the distance equation:

- When Sal begins his run ($t = 0$ minutes), he is ________ miles from home, so $d =$ ________.
- When Sal reverses direction, he is ________ miles from home.

  He reaches this point in $t = \dfrac{\square \text{ miles}}{0.1 \text{ mile per minute}} =$ ________ minutes, so when $t =$ ________, $d =$ ________.
- When Sal returns home, he is ________ miles from home. Because he has run a total of 6 miles, he reaches this point in $t = \dfrac{\square \text{ miles}}{0.1 \text{ mile per minute}} =$ ________ minutes, so when $t =$ ________, $d =$ ________.

B Add axis labels and scales to the coordinate plane shown, then plot the points (t, d) using the time and distance values from part A. The equation is an absolute value equation, and the vertex of the equation's graph is the point that represents when Sal reverses direction. Draw the complete graph and then write the absolute value equation.

$d = -0.1\left|t - \square\right| + \square$

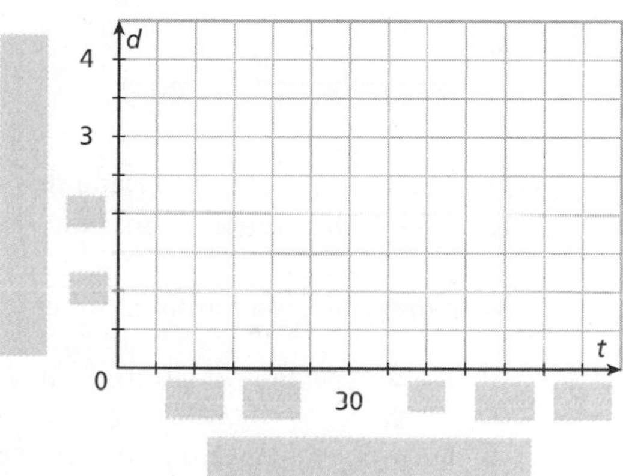

C To find the time(s) when Sal is 1 mile from home, draw the graph of $y = 1$. Find the t-coordinate of each point where the two graphs intersect.

____

REFLECT

3a. Show how to use algebra to find the time(s) when Sal is 1 mile from home.

____

____

PRACTICE

Use a graphing calculator to solve each absolute value equation. Sketch your graphs on the grids provided.

1. $-2|x + 1| + 4 = -4$

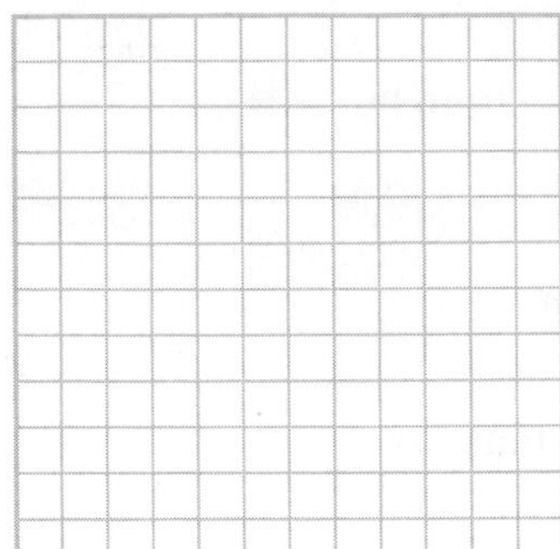

____

2. $0.5|x - 3| + 2 = 4$

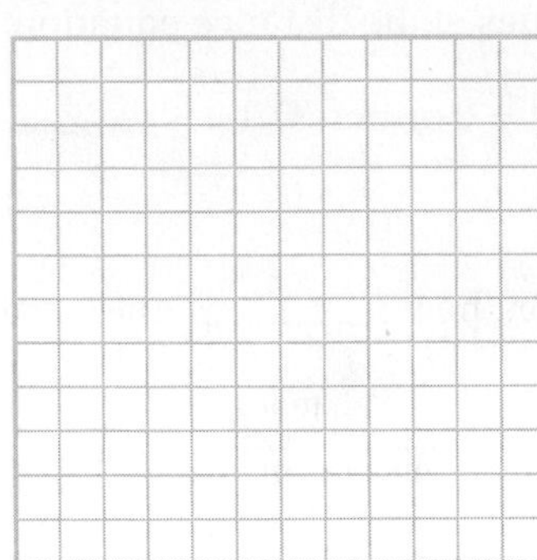

____

3. $|x + 2| - 2 = -2$

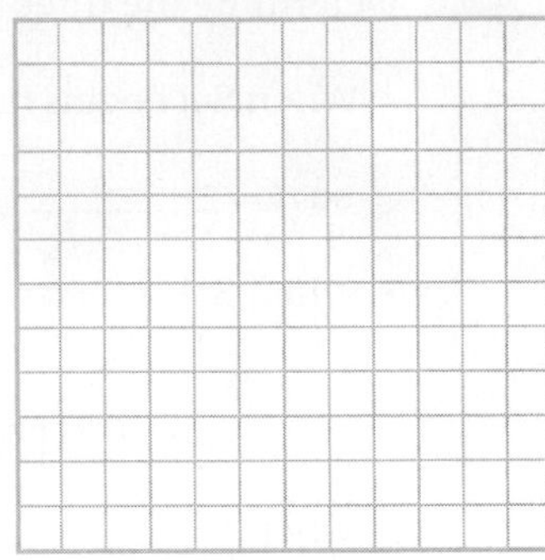

____

Solve each absolute value equation using algebra.

4. $4|x + 3| - 7 = 5$ ______________

5. $0.8|x + 4| - 3 = 1$ ______________

6. $-3|x - 1| + 5 = 8$ ______________

7. The number of gallons of water in a storage tank is given by $y = -40|h - 20| + 800$ where h is the time in hours since the tank was last empty.

a. What is the maximum number of gallons the tank can hold? ______________

b. For what values of h is the tank half empty? ______________

c. For what values of h is the tank empty? ______________

d. if the tank is empty, how long does it take to refill it? ______________

8. The number of shoppers in a store is modeled by $y = -0.5|t - 288| + 144$ where t is the time (in minutes) since the store opened at 10:00 A.M.

a. For what values of t are there 100 shoppers in the store? ______________

b. At what times are there 100 shoppers in the store? ______________

c. What is the greatest number of shoppers in the store? ______________

d. At what time does the greatest number of shoppers occur? ______________

Name________________ Class__________ Date__________

Additional Practice

Solve each equation.

1. $|x| = 12$ ________

2. $|x| = \frac{1}{2}$ ________

3. $|x| - 6 = 4$ ________

4. $5 + |x| = 14$ ________

5. $3|x| = 24$ ________

6. $|x + 3| = 10$ ________

7. $|x - 1| = 2$ ________

8. $4|x - 5| = 12$ ________

9. $|x + 2| - 3 = 9$ ________

10. $|6x| = 18$ ________

11. $|x - 1| = 0$ ________

12. $|x - 3| + 2 = 2$ ________

13. How many solutions does the equation $|x + 7| = 1$ have? ________

14. How many solutions does the equation $|x + 7| = 0$ have? ________

15. How many solutions does the equation $|x + 7| = -1$ have? ________

Leticia sets the thermostat in her apartment to 68 degrees. The actual temperature in her apartment can vary from this by as much as 3.5 degrees.

16. Write an absolute-value equation that you can use to find the minimum and maximum temperature. ________

17. Solve the equation to find the minimum and maximum temperature. ________

Problem Solving

Write the correct answer.

1. A machine manufactures wheels with a diameter of 70 cm. It is acceptable for the diameter of a wheel to be within 0.02 cm of this value. Write and solve an absolute-value equation to find the minimum and maximum acceptable diameters.

____

____

2. A pedestrian bridge is 53 meters long. Due to changes in temperature, the bridge may expand or contract by as much as 21 millimeters. Write and solve an absolute-value equation to find the minimum and maximum lengths of the bridge.

____

____

3. Two numbers on a number line are represented by the absolute-value equation $|n - 5| = 6$. What are the two numbers?

____

____

4. A jewelry maker cuts pieces of wire to shape into earrings. The equation $|x - 12.2| = 0.3$ gives the minimum and maximum acceptable lengths of the wires in centimeters. What is the minimum acceptable length of a wire?

____

____

The table shows the recommended daily intake of several minerals for adult women. Use the table for questions 5–7. Select the best answer.

5. Which absolute-value equation gives the minimum and maximum recommended intakes for zinc?

   A $|x - 8| = 32$ C $|x - 16| = 24$

   B $|x - 24| = 16$ D $|x - 40| = 32$

6. For which mineral are the minimum and maximum recommended intakes given by the absolute-value equation $|x - 31.5| = 13.5$?

   F Fluoride H Zinc

   G Iron J None of these

7. Jason writes an equation for the minimum and maximum intakes of fluoride. He writes it in the form $|x - b| = c$. What is the value of b?

   A 3 C 6.5

   B 3.5 D 7

Mineral	Daily Minimum (mg)	Daily Maximum (mg)
Fluoride	3	10
Iron	18	45
Zinc	8	40

Source:
http://www.supplementquality.com/news/multi_mineral_chart.html

Name_______________ Class_______________ Date_______________

1-8

Rates, Ratios, and Proportions

Extension: Dimensional Analysis

Essential question: *How can you use units to help solve real-world problems?*

Video Tutor

Unit Analysis When evaluating expressions that represent real-world situations, you should pay attention to the units of measurement attached to the parts of the expression. For instance, if p people go to a restaurant and agree to split the $50 cost of the meal equally, then the units in the numerator of the expression $\frac{50}{p}$ are *dollars*, the units in the denominator are *people*, and the units for the value of the expression are *dollars per person.*

CC.9–12.A.SSE.1

1 EXAMPLE Evaluating Real-World Expressions

A Sheila is participating in a multi-day bike trip. On the first day, she rode 100 miles in 8 hours. Use the expression $\frac{d}{t}$ where d is the distance traveled and t is the travel time to find her average rate of travel. Include units when evaluating the expression.

$\frac{d}{t} = \frac{\quad}{\quad} = \underline{\qquad}$

B If Sheila continues riding at her average rate for the first day, then the expression $100 + 12.5t$ gives the total distance that she has traveled after riding for t hours on the second day. Evaluate this expression when $t = 7$, and include units.

$100 + 12.5t = 100 \underline{\qquad} + 12.5 \underline{\qquad} \cdot \underline{\qquad}$

$= \underline{\qquad}$

REFLECT

1a. What are the terms in the expression $100 + 12.5t$? What does each term represent in the context of Sheila's bike trip?

____

____

1b. What is the coefficient of the term $12.5t$? What does it represent in the context of Sheila's bike trip?

____

____

1c. If you write only the units for the expression $100 + 12.5t$, you get $\text{mi} + \frac{\text{mi}}{\text{h}} \cdot \text{h}$ where "mi" is the abbreviation for miles and "h" is the abbreviation for hours. Explain what the following *unit analysis* shows:

$$\text{mi} + \frac{\text{mi}}{\cancel{\text{h}}} \cdot \cancel{\text{h}} = \text{mi} + \text{mi} = \text{mi}$$

____

____

1d. How can you modify the expression $100 + 12.5t$ so that the units are feet when the expression is evaluated?

____

CC.9–12.N.Q.1

2 EXAMPLE Using Unit Analysis to Guide Modeling

Lizzie has volunteered 20 hours at her town library. From now on, she plans to volunteer 5 hours per week at the library. Write an algebraic expression to represent the total number of hours she will volunteer.

A Use unit analysis to help you get the correct units for the expression.

$$\boxed{\text{hours}} + \frac{\boxed{\text{hours}}}{\boxed{\cancel{\text{week}}}} \cdot \boxed{\phantom{\text{weeks}}} = \boxed{\text{hours}}$$

B Write a verbal model.

____

C Choose a variable for the unknown quantity.

Let __________ represent the ______________________________.

D Write an algebraic expression to represent the situation.

____

REFLECT

2a. Explain why you chose the units you chose in Part A.

____

____

____

____

2b. How many hours will Lizzie have volunteered at the library by the end of 10 weeks?

2c. Lizzie has also volunteered 10 hours at an animal shelter and she plans to volunteer there for 3 hours a week beginning in 1 week. Rewrite the algebraic expression you wrote in Part D above based on this new information. (Assume that the number of weeks is at least 1.) Simplify, if possible.

2d. How many hours will Lizzie have volunteered at the library and the animal shelter combined by the end of 20 weeks?

PRACTICE

1. Henry drives in town at a rate of 25 miles per hour. It takes him 15 minutes to go to the library from his house. The algebraic expression rt represents distance traveled, where r is the average rate (in miles per hour) and t is the travel time (in hours).

a. Can you multiply 25 and 15 to find the distance Henry traveled to the library? Explain.

b. Show how to find the distance from Henry's house to the library. Include units in your calculation.

2. Sarah works 4 hours her first week of a part-time job and earns \$60. Her total pay after the second week can be represented by the expression $60 + \frac{p}{t} \cdot s$ where p represents her pay for t hours of work and s represents the hours she works in the second week.

a. What are the units of the fraction?

b. Rewrite the expression substituting the given values for p and t. What are the units of each term of your new expression? Explain.

c. Evaluate your expression for $s = 5$. Include units.

3. To convert dog years to human years, you count 10.5 dog years per human year for the first two human years and then 4 dog years per human year for each human year thereafter.

a. Show how to use unit analysis to get the correct units when you convert dog years to human years.

____

b. Write and simplify an algebraic expression for converting dog years to human years when the number of human years is 2 or more. Define what the variable represents.

____

4. Tracie buys tickets to a concert for herself and two friends. There is an 8% tax on the cost of the tickets and an additional $10 booking fee. Write an algebraic expression to represent the cost per person. Simplify the expression, if possible. Define what the variable represents and identify the units for the expression.

____

____

5. Write two different algebraic expressions that could represent the phrase "a number plus 2 times the number." Then rewrite the phrase so that only one of the algebraic expressions could be correct.

____

____

Additional Practice

1. Julia drove 135 miles in 4.5 hours. Find her average rate in miles per hour. ________

Find the average rate.

2. Four pounds of apples cost $1.96. ________

3. Sal washed 5 cars in 50 minutes. ________

4. A giraffe can run 32 miles per hour. What is this speed in feet per second? Round your answer to the nearest tenth. ________

Use unit analysis to write an algebraic expression to represent the situation.

5. Billie and Toni are driving from Chicago to Phoenix. The first day they drove 420 miles. They want to drive at 65 miles per hour for the rest of their trip.
   a. Write an algebraic expression to represent the situation. ________
   b. If they drive 8 hours a day for the next two days, how far have they traveled by the end of the third day? ________

6. Frank ordered playoff tickets for himself and three friends. There is a $7 service fee per ticket and an additional shipping cost of $12 for the entire ticket order.
   a. Write an algebraic expression to represent the situation. ________
   b. Write an algebraic expression to represent the ticket cost per person. ________

7. Sam is building a model of an antique car. The scale of his model to the actual car is 1:10. His model is $18\frac{1}{2}$ inches long. How long is the actual car in feet? Round your answer to the nearest tenth of a foot. ________

8. The scale on a map of Virginia shows that 1 centimeter represents 30 miles. The actual distance from Richmond, VA to Washington, DC is 110 miles. On the map, how many centimeters are between the two cities? Round your answer to the nearest tenth. ________

Problem Solving

Write the correct answer.

1. A donut shop bakes 4 dozen donuts every 18 minutes. Find the average rate to the nearest hundredth.

2. Sally volunteers at the youth center 14 hours per week. If Sally volunteers 4 days a week, what is her average rate in hours per day?

3. The birth rate in Namibia is 35 babies to every 1000 people. In 2001, the country had a population of about 1,800,000 people. How many babies were there?

4. A boat travels 160 miles in 5 hours. What is its speed in miles per minute to the nearest hundredth?

The Hendersons are driving cross country from Boston to Los Angeles. The first day they drove 300 miles. They plan to drive at an average speed of 60 miles per hour for the rest of the trip so that the trip will be completed in less than one week.

5. Write an algebraic expression to represent the length of the total trip.

   A $300t + 60$
   B $300 - 60t$
   C $60t + 300$
   D $60t - 300$

6. What are the units in the expression from Problem 5?

   F hours
   G miles
   H days
   J weeks

7. If the Hendersons drive for 9 hours per day, how many miles will they travel in a day?

   A 300 miles
   B $9t$ miles
   C 60 miles
   D 540 miles

8. The distance from Boston to Los Angeles is approximately 3000 miles. How many days should the Henderson's trip take if they drive 9 hours per day after the first day?

   F 4 days
   G 5 days
   H 6 days
   J 7 days

Name ______________________ Class ______________ Date ______________

1-9

Applications of Proportions

Connection: Dimensional analysis

Essential question: *How can you use units to write and solve proportions?*

Video Tutor

CC.9–12.N.Q.1

1 ENGAGE Writing Valid Proportions

Similar figures are figures that have the same shape, but not necessarily the same size. **Corresponding sides** of two similar figures are in the same relative position in the figures. Two figures are similar if and only if the lengths of the corresponding sides are proportional.

$\triangle ABC$ is similar to $\triangle DEF$. This can be written as $\triangle ABC \sim \triangle DEF$, with the corresponding vertices written in the same order. It is not correct to write $\triangle ABC \sim \triangle FED$.

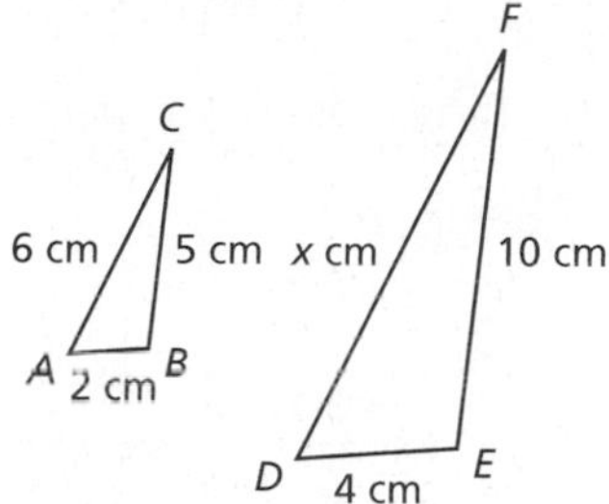

Side $\overline{AC}$ corresponds to side $\overline{DF}$.
Side $\overline{AB}$ corresponds to side $\overline{DE}$.
Side $\overline{BC}$ corresponds to side $\overline{EF}$.

In similar figures, the lengths of corresponding sides are proportional. To correctly set up a proportion, the corresponding side lengths must be in the same position in both ratios.

Correct: $\frac{AC}{DF} = \frac{AB}{DE}$ (corresponding sides; same position)

Incorrect: $\frac{AC}{DF} = \frac{DE}{AB}$ (second ratio reversed)

Incorrect: $\frac{AC}{DF} = \frac{AB}{EF}$ (non-corresponding sides)

Also, in a valid proportion the units must be the same for all entries.

Incorrect: $\frac{3 \text{ cm}}{8 \text{ m}} = \frac{9 \text{ cm}}{x}$ Correct: $\frac{3 \text{ cm}}{800 \text{ cm}} = \frac{9 \text{ cm}}{x}$

REFLECT

1a. What change was made to make $\frac{3 \text{ cm}}{8 \text{ m}} = \frac{9 \text{ cm}}{x}$ into a valid proportion? Why and how was this change made?

____

____

____

1b. Two figures are similar. One is measured in inches and the other is measured in feet. How could you write a valid proportion for these figures?

____

____

1c. Is it possible to write the proportion $\frac{6 \text{ m}}{x} = \frac{2 \text{ m}}{4 \text{ m}}$ in another way? If so, rewrite the proportion and then explain how you know that the new proportion is valid.

____

____

CC.9–12.A.CED.1

2 EXAMPLE Solving Real-World Proportions

A flagpole casts a shadow that is 12 feet long. At the same time, a 6-foot-tall man casts a shadow that is 2 feet long. Write and solve a proportion to find the height of the flagpole.

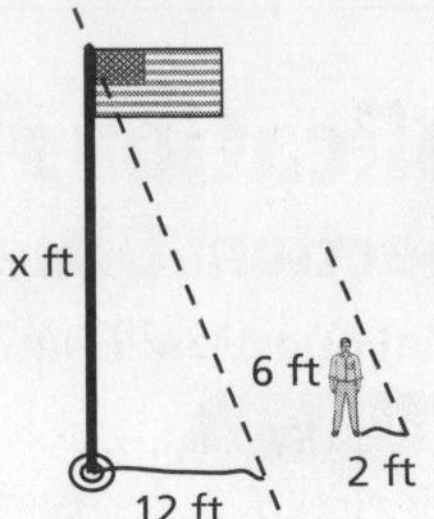

The man and the flagpole are both perpendicular to the ground, so they form right angles with the ground. The sun shines at the same angle on both, so similar triangles are formed.

A Write a proportion.

$\frac{\text{man's height}}{\text{pole's height}} = \frac{\text{man's shadow}}{\text{pole's shadow}}$ $\quad\quad \frac{6}{x} = \frac{2}{12}$

B Solve using cross products.

$\frac{6}{x} = \frac{2}{12}$

$6 \times 12 =$ ________________

____

____

____

REFLECT

2a. Write and solve a different proportion to find the height of the flagpole.

____

____

____

____

____

2b. Explain why your new proportion and solution are valid.

____

____

____

CC.9–12.N.Q.1

3 EXAMPLE Using Dimensional Analysis

A can of tuna has a shape similar to the shape of a large holding tank. The can of tuna has a diameter of 3 inches and a height of 2 inches. The holding tank has a diameter of 6 yards. What is the height of the holding tank?

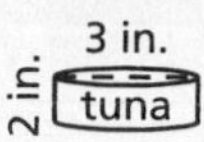

You can change the units by using dimensional analysis. In order to avoid using fractions or decimals, change yards to inches.

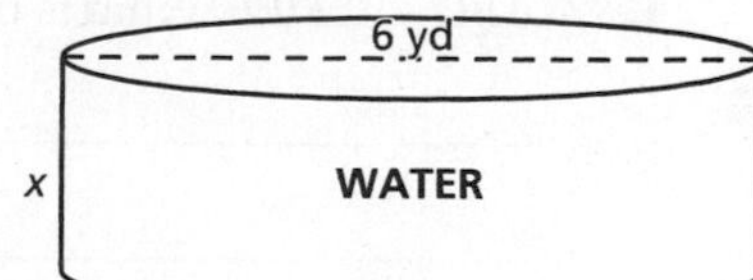

A Use dimensional analysis.

$$6 \text{ yd} \times \frac{\square \text{ ft}}{1 \text{ yd}} \times \frac{\square}{1 \text{ ft}} = \square \times \square \times \square = \square$$

B Write and solve a proportion.

$\frac{2 \text{ in.}}{3 \text{ in.}} =$ ______________________________

____

____

____

____

The holding tank is ______________ tall.

REFLECT

3a. Use dimensional analysis to write the height in feet and in yards.

____

____

3b. What other proportions could be used to find the height of the holding tank? Explain why these proportions could be used.

____

____

____

PRACTICE

Solve each problem using a proportion.

1. $\triangle ABC \sim \triangle DEF$. What is the length of $\overline{DF}$?

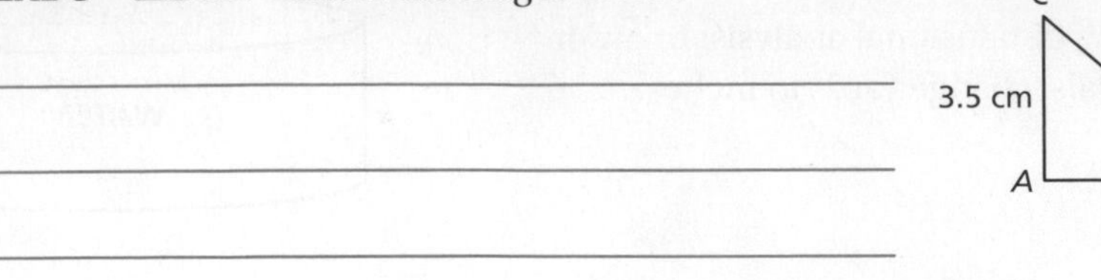

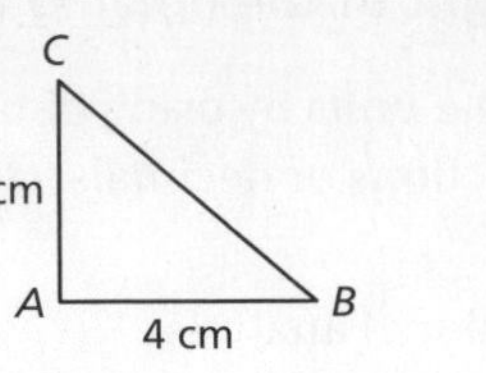

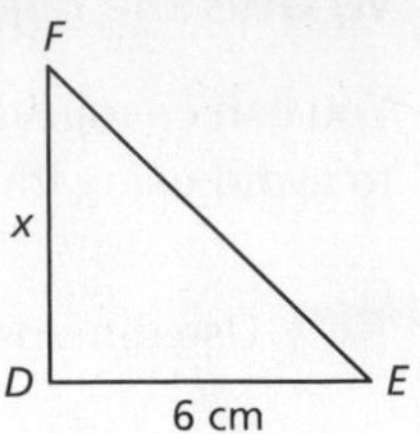

2. A building casts a shadow 48 feet long. At the same time, a 40-foot tall flagpole casts a shadow 9.6 feet long. What is the height of the building?

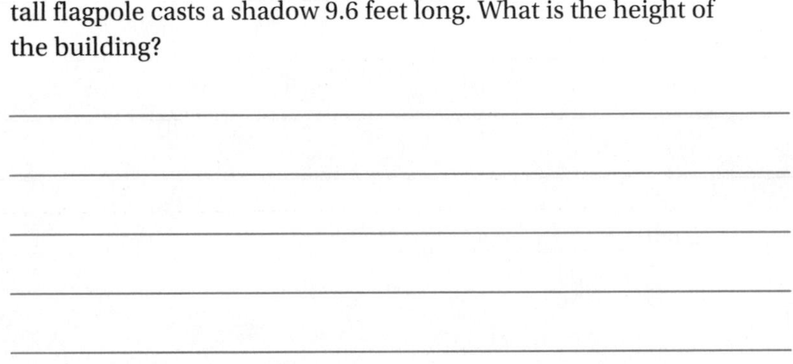

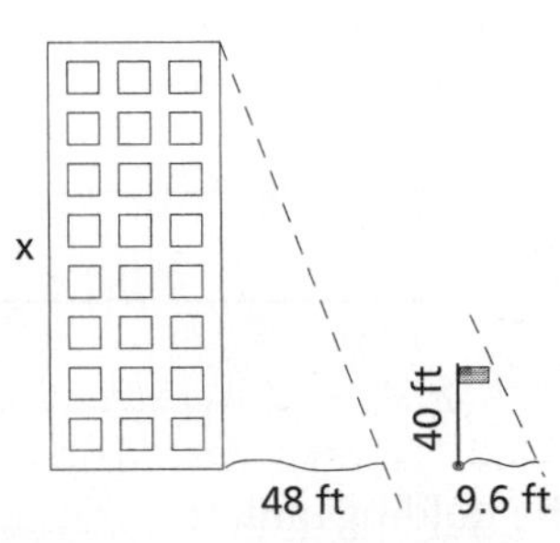

3. Rectangle *ABCD* is similar to rectangle *WXYZ*. Rectangle *ABCD* has a length of 8 inches and a height of 5 inches. Rectangle *WXYZ* has a height of 3 feet. What is the length of rectangle *WXYZ* in inches?

Name________________________ Class______________ Date__________

Additional Practice

Find the value of *x* in each diagram.

1. $\Delta ABC \sim \Delta DEF$

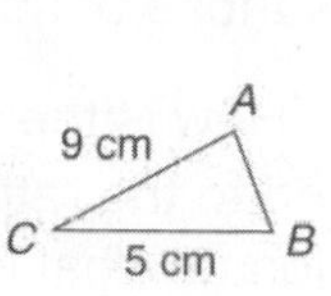

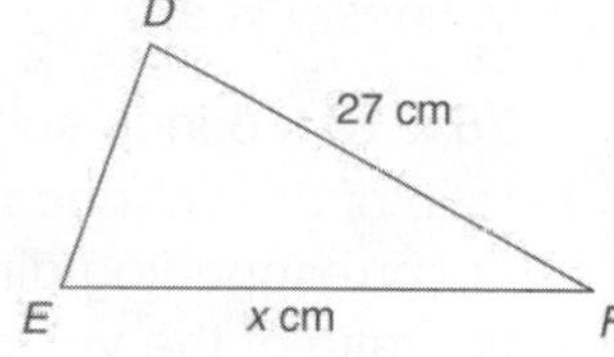

2. $FGHJK \sim MNPQR$

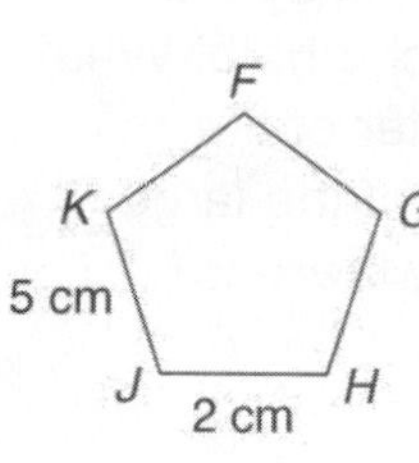

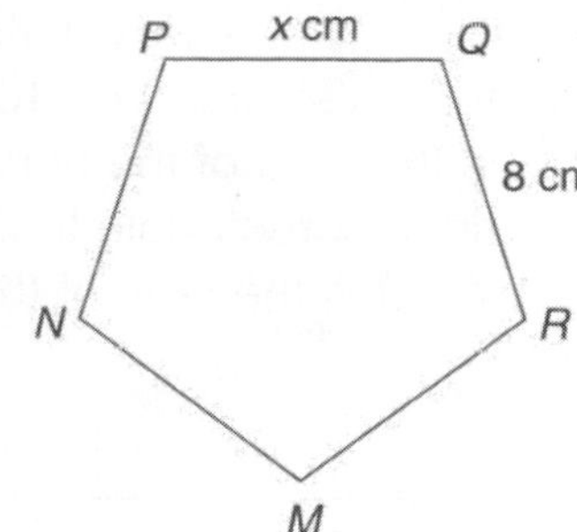

________________________ ________________________

3. A utility worker is 5.5 feet tall and is casting a shadow 4 feet long. At the same time, a nearby utility pole casts a shadow 20 feet long. Write and solve a proportion to find the height of the utility pole. ________________________

4. A cylinder has a radius of 3 cm and a length of 10 cm. Every dimension of the cylinder is multiplied by 3 to form a new cylinder. How is the ratio of the volumes related to the ratio of corresponding dimensions?

____

5. A rectangle has an area of 48 in^2. Every dimension of the rectangle is multiplied by a scale factor, and the new rectangle has an area of 12 in^2. What was the scale factor? ________________________

Problem Solving

Write the correct answer.

1. A 4 by 5 inch photo is enlarged by multiplying every dimension by 2 to form a similar 8 by 10 inch photo. What is the ratio of the perimeter of the smaller rectangle to that of the larger? What is the ratio of the two areas?

____

____

2. Pamela wants to buy a suitcase whose dimensions are $1\frac{1}{2}$ times those of her $28 \times 16 \times 8$ inch suitcase. How is the ratio of the volumes related to the ratio of corresponding dimensions? What is the ratio of the volumes?

____

____

____

____

3. The Taylors plan to expand their 80 square foot garage by tripling the dimensions. What will be the area of the new garage?

____

4. A tent has a volume of 26.25 in^3. Every dimension is multiplied by a scale factor so that the new tent has a volume of 1680 in^3. What was the scale factor?

____

Complete the table below and use it to answer questions 5–8. Select the best answer. Assume the shadow lengths were measured at the same time of day.

Object	Length of Shadow (ft)	Height (ft)
Flagpole	8	20
Oak tree	12	
Goal post	18	
Telephone pole		17.5
Fence		6.5

5. The flagpole casts an 8 foot shadow, as shown in the table. At the same time, the oak tree casts a 12 foot shadow. How tall is the oak tree?

   A 4.8 ft C 30 ft

   B 24 ft D 32 ft

6. How tall is the goal post?

   F 7.2 ft H 38 ft

   G 30 ft J 45 ft

7. What is the length of the telephone pole's shadow?

   A 5.5 ft C 25.5 ft

   B 7 ft D 43.8 ft

8. What is the length of the fence's shadow?

   F 1.5 ft H 16.25 ft

   G 2.6 ft J 21.5 ft

Name________________________ Class______________ Date________

1-10

Video Tutor

Precision and Accuracy

Extension: Significant Digits

Essential question: *How do you use significant digits to report the results of calculations based on measurements?*

Precision is the level of detail an instrument can measure. For example, a ruler marked in millimeters is more precise than a ruler that is marked only in centimeters.

You can use precision to compare measurements. For example, a measurement of 25 inches is more precise than a measurement of 2 feet because an inch is a smaller unit than a foot. Similarly, 9.2 kg is more precise than 9 kg because a tenth of a kilogram is a smaller unit than a kilogram.

In the following activity, you will investigate how precision affects calculated measurements, such as area.

CC.9–12.N.Q.3

1 EXPLORE Making Measurements to Calculate an Area

A Work with a partner. One of you should measure the width of a book cover to the nearest centimeter. Record the width below.

Width of book cover: ____________

The other person should measure the length of the book cover to the nearest tenth of a centimeter. Record the length below.

Length of book cover: ____________

B Determine the minimum and maximum possible values for the actual width and length of the book cover.

0cm 1 2 3 4 5

When measuring to the nearest centimeter, lengths in this range are rounded to 3 cm.

Example: When you measure an object to the nearest centimeter and get a measurement of 3 cm, the actual measurement is between 2.5 cm and 3.5 cm.

Minimum width: ____________ Maximum width: ____________

Minimum length: ____________ Maximum length: ____________

C Use the minimum width and minimum length to calculate the minimum possible area of the book cover. Then use the maximum width and maximum length to calculate the maximum possible area of the book cover.

Minimum area: ____________ Maximum area: ____________

REFLECT

1a. How does the precision of the linear measurements (width and length) affect the calculated measurement (area)?

____

____

In the preceding Explore, you may have discovered that there was a wide range of possible values for the actual area of the book cover. This raises the question of how a calculated measurement, like an area, should be reported. Significant digits offer one way to resolve this dilemma.

Significant digits are the digits in a measurement that carry meaning contributing to the precision of the measurement. The table gives rules for determining the number of significant digits in a measurement.

Rules for Determining Significant Digits			
Rule	**Example**	**Significant Digits (Bold)**	**Number of Significant Digits**
All nonzero digits	37.85	**37.85**	4
Zeros after the last nonzero digit and to the right of the decimal point	0.0070	0.00**70**	2
Zeros between significant digits	6500.0	**6500.0**	5

Note that zeros at the end of a whole number are usually not considered to be significant digits. For example, 4550 ft has 3 significant digits.

CC.9–12.N.Q.3

2 EXAMPLE Determining the Number of Significant Digits

Determine the number of significant digits in each measurement.

A 840.09 m **B** 36,000 mi **C** 0.010 kg

A The digits 8, 4, and 9 are significant digits because ______________________.

The zeros are significant digits because ______________________.

So, 840.09 m has __________ significant digits.

B The digits 3 and 6 are significant digits because ______________________.

The zeros are not significant because ______________________.

So, 36,000 mi has __________ significant digits.

C The digit 1 is a significant digit because ______________________________.

The zero after the 1 is a significant digit because ______________________________

____

So, 0.010 kg has ____________ significant digits.

REFLECT

2a. A student claimed that 0.045 m and 0.0045 m have the same number of significant digits. Do you agree or disagree? Why?

____

____

When you perform operations on measurements, use these rules for determining the number of significant digits you should report.

Rules for Significant Digits in Calculations	
Operations	**Rule**
Addition Subtraction	Round the sum or difference to the same place as the last significant digit of the least precise measurement.
Multiplication Division	The product or quotient must have the same number of significant digits as the measurement with the fewest significant digits.

CC.9-12.N.Q.3

3 EXAMPLE Calculating with Significant Digits

A student measures the width of a book cover to the nearest centimeter and finds that the width is 16 cm. Another student measures the length of the cover to the nearest tenth of a centimeter and finds that the length is 23.6 cm. Use the correct number of significant digits to write the perimeter and area of the cover.

A Find the perimeter: 16 cm + 23.6 cm + 16 cm + 23.6 cm = 79.2 cm

The least precise measurement is 16 cm. Its last significant digit is in the units place. Round the sum to the nearest whole number.

So, the perimeter is ____________.

B Find the area: 16 cm × 23.6 cm = 377.6 cm^2

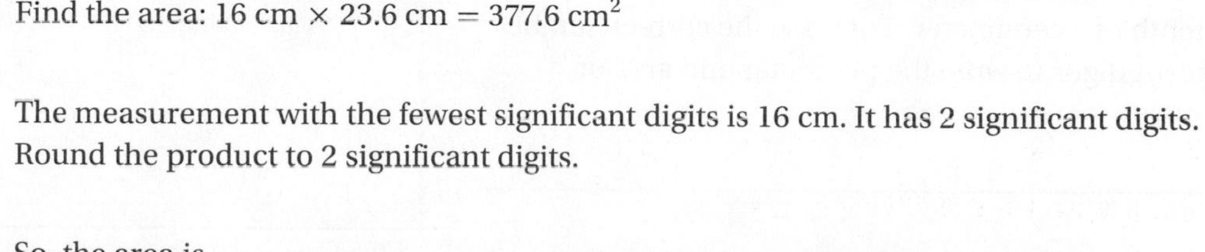

The measurement with the fewest significant digits is 16 cm. It has 2 significant digits. Round the product to 2 significant digits.

So, the area is ____________.

REFLECT

3a. Suppose the first student had measured the book cover to the nearest tenth of a centimeter and found that the width was 16.0 cm. Does this change how you would you report the perimeter and area? Explain.

PRACTICE

Choose the more precise measurement in each pair.

1. 18 cm; 177 mm

2. 3 yd; 10 ft

3. 40.23 kg; 40.3 kg

4. One student measures the length of a rectangular wall to the nearest meter and finds that the length is 5 m. Another student measures the height of the wall to the nearest tenth of a meter and finds that the height is 3.2 m. What are the minimum and maximum possible values for the area of the wall?

Determine the number of significant digits in each measurement.

5. 12,080 ft

6. 0.8 mL

7. 1.0065 km

8. You measure a rectangular window to the nearest tenth of a centimeter and find that the length is 81.4 cm. A friend measures the width to the nearest centimeter and finds that the width is 38 cm. Use the correct number of significant digits to write the perimeter and area of the window.

9. **Error Analysis** A student measured the length and width of a square rug to the nearest hundredth of a meter. He found that the length and width were 1.30 m. The student was asked to report the area using the correct number of significant digits and he wrote the area as 1.7 m^2. Explain the student's error.

10. Measure the length and width of the rectangle to the nearest tenth of a centimeter. Then use the correct number of significant digits to write the perimeter and area of the rectangle.

Name ______________________ Class ____________ Date ____________ 1-10

Additional Practice

Choose the more precise measurement in each pair.

1. 2.78 L; 2782 mL
2. 6 ft; 72.3 in.
3. 2 c; 15 oz
4. 52 mm; 5.24 cm
5. 3 lb; 47 oz
6. 5.2 km; 5233 m

Determine the number of significant digits.

7. 4700
8. 16.005
9. 301,000
10. 0.1760
11. 7.0080
12. 0.000705

Use the following information for 13 and 14.

Marcel is measuring the volume of a liquid for chemistry class. He uses a beaker, a measuring cup, and a test tube. The teacher measures the liquid with a graduated cylinder, which gives the most accurate reading of 26.279 milliliters (mL). Marcel's measurements are shown below.

Measuring Device	Measurement (mL)
Beaker	26.3
Measuring Cup	25
Test Tube	26.21

13. Which device used by Marcel recorded the most precise measurement?

14. Which device used by Marcel recorded the most accurate measurement?

Problem Solving

Write the correct answer.

1. Rolondo is measuring the length of his lawn. Using a board that is 10 feet long, he measures his lawn to be 70 feet long. He then uses his foot, which is 12 inches long, to measure his lawn to be 864 inches. Which is the more precise measurement? Which is the more precise tool?

____

2. A bolt used to assemble a car must have a length of 37.5 mm or 3.75 cm. Which is the more precise measurement?

____

3. A bin contains 15 steel balls of various diameters. Give the number of significant digits in each measurement.

Ball	1	2	3	4	5
Diameter (in.)	1.062	1.100	0.072	0.802	2.010
Ball	6	7	8	9	10
Diameter (in.)	1.401	0.690	0.090	1.008	0.066
Ball	11	12	13	14	15
Diameter (in.)	0.810	2.100	0.068	0.590	0.009

____

____

____

____

Select the best answer.

4. Ann is measuring the capacity of a 16-oz water bottle. She first uses a measuring cup and finds that the water bottle holds 16.2 oz of water. She then uses a graduated cylinder and finds that the water bottle holds 16.18 oz of water. Which is the more precise measurement? Which is the more precise tool?

   A 16.2 oz; measuring cup

   B 16.2 oz; graduated cylinder

   C 16.18 oz; measuring cup

   D 16.18 oz; graduated cylinder

5. Ina added 32.155 milliliters (mL) of HCL to 64 mL of H_2O. How much solution does Ina have to the nearest milliliter?

   F 95 mL　　H 97 mL

   G 96 mL　　J 98 mL

6. Jesse mixed 8.24 oz of paprika with 12.23 oz of pepper. How much of the spice combination does Jesse have to the nearest tenth of an ounce?

   A 20.0 oz　　C 20.5 oz

   B 20.4 oz　　D 21.0 oz

7. An aquarium must be heated to 30.040°C. How many significant digits are there in this measurement?

   F two

   G three

   H four

   J five

Name ________________ Class ____________ Date ________

Performance Tasks

COMMON CORE

CC.9-12.N.Q.1
CC.9-12.A.SSE.1b
CC.9-12.A.CED.1
CC.9-12.A.CED.2
CC.9-12.A.CED.3
CC.9-12.A.CED.4
CC.9-12.A.REI.3

★ **1.** Astronomers talk about the *luminosity* of a star, which is a measure of how much energy the star puts out, and the *brightness* of a star, which is a measure of how intense the star's light is. The formula $b = \frac{L}{4\pi d^2}$ relates the brightness b of a star to its luminosity L and its distance from the Earth, d.

a. Solve the equation for L.

b. If d is measured in meters and b is measured in watts per meter squared, what units is L measured in?

★ **2.** A certain breakfast cereal has 9.0 g of protein in a 120-g serving. How many grams of protein are in a 200-oz serving? (1 oz $\approx$ 28.3 g)

3. A theater company put on a play, and charged the prices shown in the table for tickets.

Ticket Prices		
Child	**Adult**	**Senior**
\$2.50	\$6.00	\$3.50

a. Write an equation for the total revenue R for C children, A adults, and S seniors.

b. There were 4 times as many adults as children, and half as many seniors as adults. Write expressions for the number of children and the number of seniors in terms of the number of adults.

c. Rewrite your equation from part **a** in terms of A, the number of adults.

continued

d. If the company made a total of $301.50, how many children attended? Explain how you found your answer.

4. Ayn went to the hospital for a broken leg. Upon admission, she paid a co-payment of $150 to the hospital. Later she received a hospital bill for $714, the amount her insurance did not cover. Ayn's insurance policy covers 80% of her total hospital expenses minus the co-pay.

a. Write an equation that represents the amount of money Ayn pays the hospital if x is the total amount charged by the hospital. What was the total amount charged by the hospital?

b. Write an equation that represents the amount of money Ayn's insurance paid the hospital. Use the total charges from part **a** to find the amount the insurance paid. Does this make sense? Explain.

c. Ayn's policy is called an 80/20 policy because the insurance pays 80% and she pays 20%. Choose a policy with percentages that would be more favorable to Ayn, and use it to calculate how much she would have to pay for this visit under your plan, including the $150 co-payment. Show your work.

CHAPTER 1 COMMON CORE ASSESSMENT READINESS

Name ______________________ Class ______________ Date ________

MULTIPLE CHOICE

1. Evaluate $x^2 + 3x - 18$ for $x = 3$.

A. -6

B. 0

C. 6

D. 9

2. Simplify $4n + 2(3n - 5) - 8 + n$.

F. $8n - 13$

G. $9n - 8$

H. $10n - 2$

J. $11n - 18$

3. It costs \$75 per hour plus a \$65 service fee to have a home theater system set up for you. Let t represent the number of hours. Which expression represents the total cost?

A. $75t + 65$

B. $65t + 75$

C. $140t$

D. $75t$

4. Elizabeth and her friend purchase identical team shirts to wear to a football game. There is a 7% sales tax. If c represents the cost of the two shirts without tax, which algebraic expression represents the tax for one shirt?

F. $\frac{c}{2}$

G. $\frac{0.07c}{2}$

H. $\frac{1.07c}{2}$

J. $1.07c$

5. Which property of equality can be used to justify this step?

$$\begin{array}{rcr} 15 - 10x & = & 6x \\ + 10x & & + 10x \\ \hline 15 & = & 16x \end{array}$$

A. Substitution Property of Equality

B. Summation Property of Equality

C. Addition Property of Equality

D. Subtraction Property of Equality

6. Find the solution set for $8x - 3 = 2(x - \frac{1}{2})$.

F. $\left\{-\frac{1}{3}\right\}$ **H.** $\left\{\frac{1}{3}\right\}$

G. $\left\{\frac{1}{5}\right\}$ **J.** $\left\{\frac{2}{5}\right\}$

7. Tia spent \$15 on skating. This included a \$5 charge for renting skates and a \$2.50 per hour fee for skating. Which equation can be solved to find the number of hours t that Tia spent skating?

A. $5 = 2.5t + 15$

B. $5 = 15t + 2.5$

C. $15 = 2.5t + 5$

D. $15 = 5t + 2.5$

8. Solve $q = \frac{r}{2}(s + t)$ for t.

F. $t = \frac{qr}{2} - s$ **H.** $t = \frac{2q}{r} - s$

G. $t = \frac{2q - s}{r}$ **J.** $t = \frac{q}{2r} - s$

9. Solve $V = \frac{1}{3}\pi r^2 h$ for h.

A. $h = \frac{3V}{\pi r^2}$ **C.** $h = \frac{\pi V}{3r^2}$

B. $h = \frac{3\pi V}{r^2}$ **D.** $h = r\sqrt{\frac{3V}{\pi}}$

10. What solution(s) does the equation represented by the graph have in common with the equation $y = 1$?

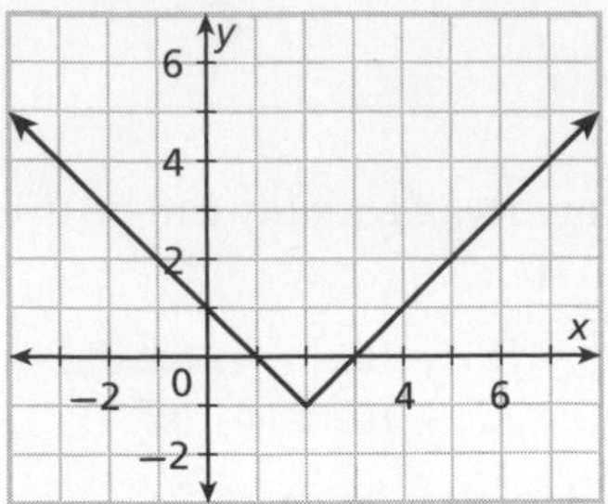

F. $x = 2$

G. $x = 1$ and $x = 3$

H. $x = 0$ and $x = 4$

J. No solutions

11. A student measures the length of a rectangular poster to the nearest centimeter and finds that the length is 75 cm. Another student measures the poster's width to the nearest tenth of a centimeter and finds that the width is 50.3 cm. How should the students report the area of the poster using the correct number of significant digits?

A. 3700 cm^2

B. 3770 cm^2

C. 3772.5 cm^2

D. 3800 cm^2

CONSTRUCTED RESPONSE

12. Student enrollment in a county's schools during a 16-year period is modeled by the equation $n = -0.3|t - 8| + 11$ where n is the number of students (in thousands) at time t (in number of years since 1990).

a. What was the enrollment in 1990? Show how you found your answer.

______

______

b. In what year(s) was the enrollment closest to 10,000? Explain how to find the answer.

______

______

______

______

13. The art club at Lily's school has had 300 calendars printed to sell as a fundraiser. It costs the art club \$4 per calendar to have the calendars printed and the club sells them for \$10 per calendar. The art club's profit $P(n)$ is given by the following function, where n represents the number of calendars sold.

$$P(n) = 10n - 1200$$

a. What does the term "$10n$" represent? What are its units? Explain your reasoning using unit analysis.

______

______

______

______

b. What does the term "1200" represent? Explain your reasoning.

______

______

______

______

c. What is the maximum profit the art club can earn? Explain.

______

______

______

______

Inequalities

Chapter Focus

In this chapter you will apply skills for solving linear equations to solving linear inequalities. You will justify your reasoning using appropriate properties and graph solutions on a number line. You will also solve compound inequalities where multiple conditions must be met at the same time. Finally, you will apply your skills with compound inequalities to solving inequalities involving absolute value.

Chapter at a Glance

COMMON CORE

Lesson		Standards for Mathematical Content
2-1	Graphing and Writing Inequalities	CC.9-12.A.CED.1
2-2	Solving Inequalities by Adding or Subtracting	CC.9-12.A.REI.3
2-3	Solving Inequalities by Multiplying or Dividing	CC.9-12.A.REI.3
2-4	Solving Two-Step and Multi-Step Inequalities	CC.9-12.A.REI.3
2-5	Solving Inequalities with Variables on Both Sides	CC.9-12.A.REI.3
2-6	Solving Compound Inequalities	CC.9-12.A.REI.3
2-7	Solving Absolute-Value Inequalities	CC.9-12.A.REI.3
	Performance Tasks	
	Assessment Readiness	

Unpacking the Standards

Understanding the standards and the vocabulary terms in the standards will help you know exactly what you are expected to learn in this chapter.

COMMON CORE **CC.9-12.A.CED.3**

Represent constraints by … inequalities … and interpret solutions as viable or nonviable options in a modeling context.

Key Vocabulary

inequality *(desigualdad)*
A statement that compares two expressions by using one of the following signs:
$<, >, \leq, \geq$, or $\neq$

solution of an inequality in one variable *(solución de una desigualdad en una variable)*
A value or values that make the inequality true.

What It Means For You Lesson 2-1

You can use inequalities to represent limits on the values in a situation so that the solutions make sense in a real-world context.

EXAMPLE

Anyone riding the large water slide at a park must be at least 40 inches tall.

Let h represent the heights that are allowed.

Height is at least 40 inches.		
h	$\geq$	40

CHAPTER 2

COMMON CORE **CC.9-12.N.Q.2**

Define appropriate quantities for the purpose of descriptive modeling.

What It Means For You Lesson 2-1

Defining quantities carefully helps guide your problem solving when you model a situation.

EXAMPLE

To find all sets of 3 consecutive even integers with sums from 60 to 70, let x be any integer. Then $2x$ is an even integer, and $2x + 2$ and $2x + 4$ are the next consecutive even integers.

$$60 \leq 2x + (2x + 2) + (2x + 4) \leq 70$$

$$60 \leq 6x + 6 \leq 70$$

$$54 \leq 6x \leq 64$$

$$9 \leq x \leq 10\tfrac{2}{3}$$

Because x can be 9 or 10, the first even integer is $2(9) = 18$ or $2(10) = 20$. The sets are 18, 20, 22, or 20, 22, 24.

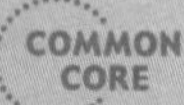

CC.9-12.A.REI.3

Solve linear … inequalities in one variable, …

Key Vocabulary

linear equation in one variable
(desigualdad lineal en una variable)
An inequality that can be written in one of the following forms: $ax < b$, $ax > b$, $ax \leq b$, $ax \geq b$, or $ax \neq b$, where a and b are constants and $a \neq 0$.

What It Means For You Lessons 2-2, 2-3, 2-4, 2-5, 2-6, 2-7

Solving inequalities lets you answer questions where a range of solutions is possible.

EXAMPLE

The final exam counts as two grades in calculating Cleo's course grade. Solve the inequality for t to find what grades on the final exam will give Cleo a course grade of "A."

$705 + 2t \geq 895$ *Cleo has 705 points and needs at least 895.*

$2t \geq 190$ *Subtract 705 from both sides.*

$t \geq 95$ *Divide both sides by 2.*

Cleo needs to earn a 95 or above on the final exam.

CC.9-12.A.CED.1

Create … inequalities … in one variable and use them to solve problems.

What It Means For You Lesson 2-1

You can write an inequality to represent a real-world problem and then solve the inequality to find the possible answers.

EXAMPLE

Amy uses $\frac{3}{4}$ cup of vanilla yogurt to make a smoothie. What are the possible whole numbers of smoothies that Amy can make using 1 quart of vanilla yogurt?

Let s represent the number of smoothies Amy can make.

cups per smoothie	•	number of smoothies	$\leq$	cups per quart
$\frac{3}{4}$	•	s	$\leq$	4
		$\frac{3}{4}s$	$\leq$	4
		s	$\leq$	$\frac{16}{3}$

Amy can make 0, 1, 2, 3, 4, or 5 smoothies.

CHAPTER 2

Key Vocabulary

absolute value *(valor absoluto)* The absolute value of x is the distance from zero to x on a number line, denoted $|x|$.

$$|x| = \begin{cases} x \text{ if } x \geq 0 \\ -x \text{ if } x < 0 \end{cases}$$

compound inequality *(desigualdad compuesta)* Two inequalities that are combined into one statement by the word *and* or *or*.

empty set *(conjunto vacío)* A set with no elements.

inequality *(desigualdad)* A statement that compares two expressions by using one of the following signs: $<$, $>$, $\leq$, $\geq$, or $\neq$.

intersection *(intersección de conjuntos)* The intersection of two sets is the set of all elements that are common to both sets, denoted by $\cap$.

linear inequality in one variable *(desigualdad lineal en una variable)* An inequality that can be written in one of the following forms: $ax < b$, $ax > b$, $ax \leq b$, $ax \geq b$, or $ax \neq b$, where a and b are constants and $a \neq 0$.

solution of an inequality in one variable *(solución de una desigualdad en una variable)* A value or values that make the inequality true.

union *(union)* The union of two sets is the set of all elements that are in either set, denoted by $\cup$.

CHAPTER 2

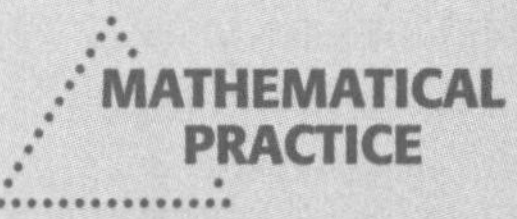

The Common Core Standards for Mathematical Practice describe varieties of expertise that mathematics educators at all levels should seek to develop in their students. Opportunities to develop these practices are integrated throughout this program.

1. **Make sense of problems and persevere in solving them.**
2. **Reason abstractly and quantitatively.**
3. **Construct viable arguments and critique the reasoning of others.**
4. **Model with mathematics.**
5. **Use appropriate tools strategically.**
6. **Attend to precision.**
7. **Look for and make use of structure.**
8. **Look for and express regularity in repeated reasoning**

Name ____________________ Class ____________ Date ________

2-1

Video Tutor

Graphing and Writing Inequalities

Going Deeper

Essential question: *How can you represent relationships using inequalities?*

An **inequality** is a statement that compares two expressions that are not strictly equal by using one of the following inequality signs.

Symbol	Meaning
$<$	is less than
$\leq$	is less than or equal to
$>$	is greater than
$\geq$	is greater than or equal to
$\neq$	is not equal to

A **solution of an inequality** is any value of the variable that makes the inequality true. You can find solutions by making a table.

CC.9–12.A.CED.1

1 EXAMPLE Writing and Solving Inequalities

Kristin can afford to spend at most $50 for a birthday dinner at a restaurant, including a 15% tip. Describe some costs that are within her budget.

A Which inequality symbol can be used to represent "at most"? ________

B Complete the verbal model for the situation.

Cost before tip (dollars)  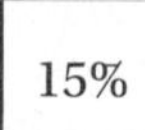

 Cost before tip (dollars)  Budget limit (dollars)

C Write and simplify an inequality for the model. ____________________

D Complete the table to find some costs that are within Kristin's budget.

Cost	Substitute	Compare	Solution?
\$47	$1.15(47) \leq 50$	$54.05 \leq 50$ ✗	No
\$45	$1.15(45) \leq 50$		
\$43			
\$41			

REFLECT

1a. Can Kristin spend \$40 on the meal before the tip? Explain.

1b. What whole dollar amount is the most Kristin can spend before the tip? Explain.

1c. The *solution set* of an equation or inequality consists of all values that make the statement true. Describe the whole dollar amounts that are in the solution set for this situation.

1d. Suppose Kristin also has to pay a 6% meal tax. Write an inequality to represent the new situation. Then identify two solutions.

PRACTICE

Tell whether each value of the variable is a solution of the inequality $4p < 64$. Show your reasoning.

1. $p = 40$

2. $p = 45$

3. $p = 5$

4. $p = 22$

Tell whether each value of the variable is a solution of the inequality $7p \geq 105$. Show your reasoning.

5. $p = 6$

6. $p = 21$

7. $p = 4$

8. $p = 15$

Tell whether the value is a solution of the inequality. Explain.

9. $x = 36$; $3x < 100$

10. $m = 12$; $5m + 4 > 50$

11. $b = 5$; $60 - 10b \leq 20$

12. $y = -4$; $7y + 6 < -20$

13. $n = -4$; $18 - 2n \geq 26$

14. $d = -6$; $27 + 8d > -14$

15. Brent is ordering books for a reading group. Each book costs \$11.95. If he orders at least \$200 worth of books, he will get free shipping.

a. Complete the verbal model for the situation.

Price per book	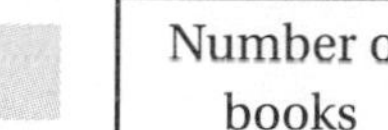	Number of books		Amount for free shipping

b. Choose a variable for the unknown quantity. Include units.

Let _______ represent the _______________________.

c. Write an inequality from the verbal model.

d. Complete the table to find some numbers of books Brent can order and receive free shipping.

Books	Substitute	Compare	Solution?
15	$11.95(15) \geq 200$	$179.25 \geq 200$ ✗	No
16			
17			
18			

16. Farzana has a prepaid cell phone that costs \$1 per day plus \$.10 per minute she uses. She has a daily budget of \$5 for phone costs.

a. Write an inequality to represent the situation.

b. What is the maximum number of minutes Farzana can use and still stay within her daily budget? Show your reasoning.

c. Describe the solution set of the inequality.

Name ______________________ Class ______________ Date ______________

2-1

Additional Practice

Tell whether the value is a solution of the inequality.

1. $m = 8$; $2m \geq 6$ ______________________

2. $t = 5$; $t + 3 < 8$ ______________________

3. $x = 2$; $1 < x - 5$ ______________________

4. $c = -28$; $-10 \geq \frac{1}{2}c$ ______________________

5. $n = 6$; $2n + 9 \geq 31$ ______________________

6. $d = -4$; $5d + 8 > -12$ ______________________

7. $h = -11$; $3h + 20 \leq -13$ ______________________

8. $y = 0$; $4y - 11 < 17$ ______________________

Define a variable and write an inequality for each situation.

9. Josephine sleeps more than 7 hours each night.

____

10. In 1955, the minimum wage in the U.S. was $0.75 per hour.

____

11. Sam can spend no more than $75 on school supplies. He has to spend $12 on paper and pencils. What is the maximum amount Sam can spend on a graphing calculator?

____

12. Sally and Tim need more than 24 bags of grass seed to reseed their lawn. The seed they want to buy is sold in cartons that contain 4 bags each. What is the minimum number of cartons of grass seed they need to buy?

____

Problem Solving

Write the correct answer.

1. A citizen must be at least 35 years old in order to run for the Presidency of the United States. Define a variable and write an inequality for this situation.

   ____

   ____

2. A certain elevator can hold no more than 2500 pounds. Define a variable and write an inequality for this situation.

   ____

   ____

3. Approximately 30% of the land on Earth is forested, but this percent is decreasing due to construction. Write an inequality for this situation.

   ____

   ____

4. Khalil weighed 125 pounds before he started to gain weight to play football. Write an inequality for this situation.

   ____

   ____

The Sanchez family is visiting an amusement park. When they enter the park, they receive a brochure which lists several requirements and restrictions. Select the best answer.

5. You must be at least 50 inches tall to ride The Wild Tornado roller coaster. Which of the following inequalities fits this situation?

   A $h \leq 50$ C $h \geq 50$

   B $h < 50$ D $h > 50$

6. Children less than 12 years old must be accompanied by an adult inside The Haunted House. Which of the following inequalities shows the ages of children who require an adult inside the house?

   F $y \leq 12$ H $y \geq 12$

   G $y < 12$ J $y > 12$

7. Totland is an area of the amusement park set aside for children who are 6 years old or younger. Which of the following inequalities represents the ages of children who are allowed in Totland?

   A $a \leq 6$ C $a \geq 6$

   B $a < 6$ D $a > 6$

8. The Bumpy Cars will not be turned on if there are 5 or more empty cars. Which of the following inequalities shows the possible numbers of empty cars if the ride is going to start?

   F $c \leq 5$ H $c \geq 5$

   G $c < 5$ J $c > 5$

Name ______________________ Class ______________ Date ________

2-2

Video Tutor

Solving Inequalities by Adding or Subtracting

Going Deeper

Essential question: *How can you use properties to justify solutions to inequalities that involve addition and subtraction?*

CC.9–12.A.REI.3

1 ENGAGE Properties of Inequality

You have solved addition and subtraction equations by performing inverse operations that isolate the variable on one side. The value on the other side is the solution. Inequalities involving addition and subtraction can be solved similarly using the following inequality properties. These properties are also true for $\geq$ and $\leq$.

Addition Property of Inequality	If $a > b$, then $a + c > b + c$. If $a < b$, then $a + c < b + c$.
Subtraction Property of Inequality	If $a > b$, then $a - c > b - c$. If $a < b$, then $a - c < b - c$.

REFLECT

1a. How do the Addition and Subtraction Properties of Inequality compare to the Addition and Subtraction Properties of Equality?

____

____

____

____

Most linear inequalities have infinitely many solutions. When using set notation, it is not possible to list all the solutions in braces. The solution $x \leq 1$ in set notation is $\{x \mid x \leq 1\}$. Read this as "the set of all x such that x is less than or equal to 1."

$\{x \mid x \leq 1\}$

the set of — all x — such that — x is less than or equal to 1

A number line graph can be used to represent the solution set of a linear inequality.

- To represent $<$ or $>$, mark the endpoint with an empty circle.
- To represent $\leq$ or $\geq$, mark the endpoint with a solid circle.
- Shade the part of the line that contains the solution set.

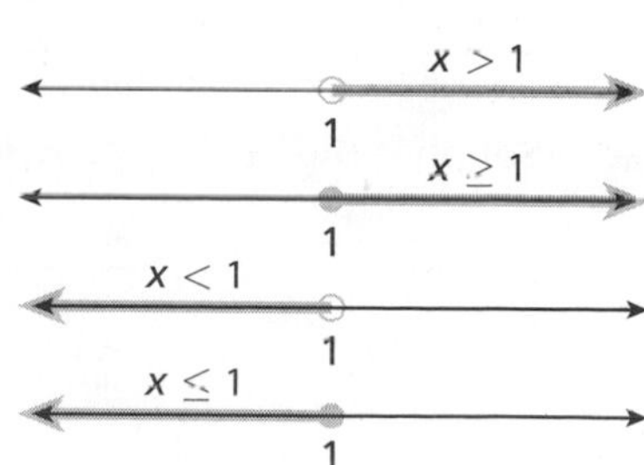

CC.9–12.A.REI.3

2 EXAMPLE Adding to Find the Solution Set

Solve. Write the solution using set notation. Graph your solution.

A $x - 3 < 2$

$x - 3 +$ ______ $< 2 +$ ______ ______________ Property of Inequality; add ______ to both sides.

$x <$ ______ Simplify.

Write the solution set using set notation.

____

Graph the solution set on a number line.

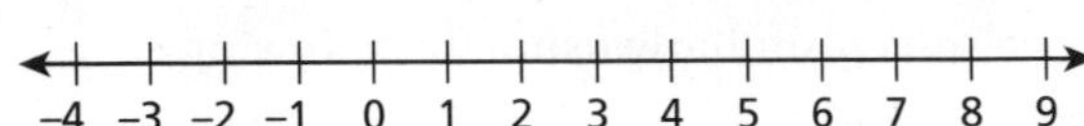

B $x - 5 \geq -3$

$x - 5 +$ ______ $\geq -3 +$ ______ ______________ Property of Inequality; add ______ to both sides.

$x \geq$ ______ Simplify.

Write the solution set using set notation.

____

Graph the solution set on a number line.

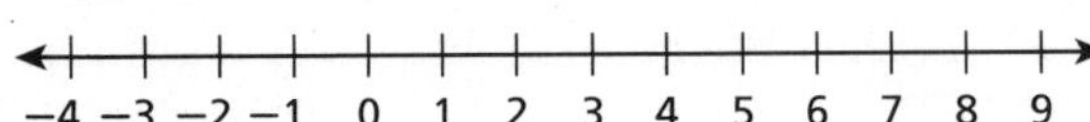

REFLECT

2a. Is 5 in the solution set of the inequality in Part A? Explain.

____

____

2b. Suppose the inequality symbol in Part A had been >. Describe the solution set.

____

2c. Suppose the inequality symbol in Part B had been ≤. Describe the solution set.

____

Subtracting to Find the Solution Set

Solve. Write the solution using set notation. Graph your solution.

A $x + 4 > 3$

$x + 4 - \square > 3 - \square$ __________ Property of Inequality

$x > \square$ Simplify.

Write the solution set using set notation.

____

Graph the solution set on a number line.

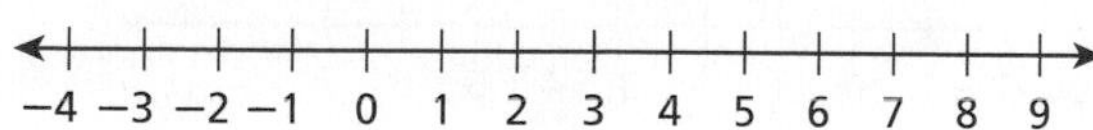

B $x + 2 \leq -1$

$x + 2 - \square \leq -1 - \square$ __________ Property of Inequality

$x \leq \square$ Simplify.

Write the solution set using set notation.

____

Graph the solution set on a number line.

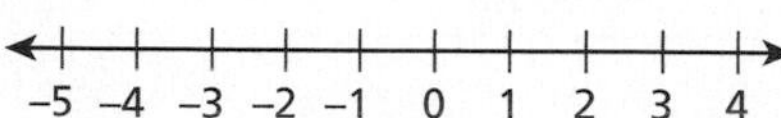

REFLECT

3a. Is -3 in the solution set of the inequality in Part B? Explain.

____

____

3b. Suppose the inequality symbol in Part A had been $\geq$. Describe the solution set.

____

3c. Suppose the inequality symbol in Part B had been $<$. Describe the solution set.

____

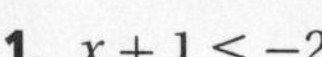

PRACTICE

Solve. Justify your steps. Write the solution in set notation. Graph your solution.

1. $x + 1 \leq -2$

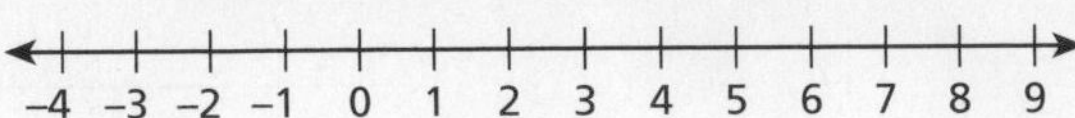

2. $x - 2 > 1$

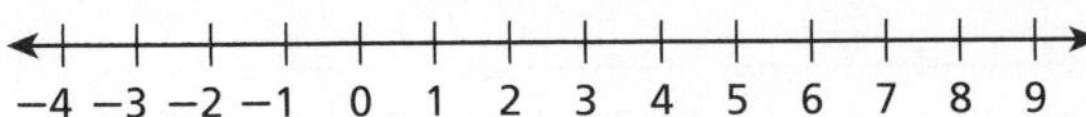

3. $x + 6 < 6$

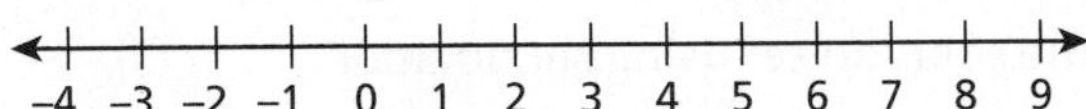

4. $x + 3 < 2$

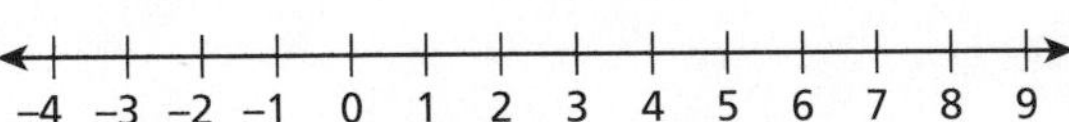

5. $x - 4 \geq -4$

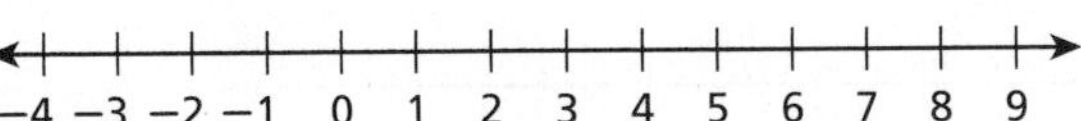

Name________________ Class________ Date________

2-2

Additional Practice

Solve each inequality and graph the solutions.

1. $b + 8 > 15$

____

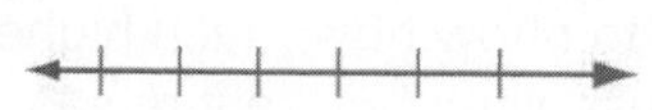

2. $t - 5 \geq -2$

____

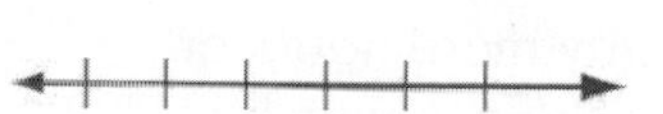

3. $-4 + x \geq 1$

____

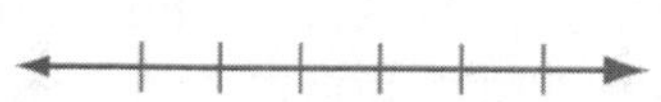

4. $g + 8 < 2$

____

5. $-9 \geq m - 9$

____

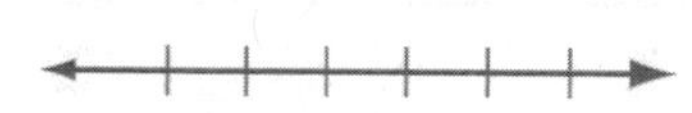

6. $15 > d + 19$

____

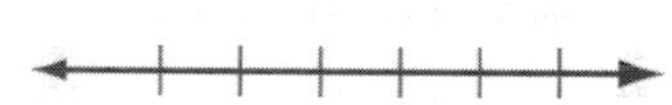

Answer each question.

7. Jessica makes overtime pay when she works more than 40 hours in a week. So far this week she has worked 29 hours. She will continue to work h hours this week. Write, solve, and graph an inequality to show the values of h that will allow Jessica to earn overtime pay.

____

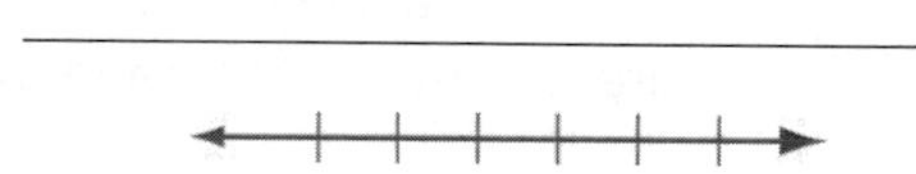

8. Henry's MP3 player has 512MB of memory. He has already downloaded 287MB and will continue to download m more megabytes. Write and solve an inequality that shows how many more megabytes he can download.

____

9. Eleanor needs to read at least 97 pages of a book for homework. She has read 34 pages already. Write and solve an inequality that shows how many more pages p she must read.

____

Problem Solving

Write the correct answer.

1. Sumiko is allowed to watch no more than 10 hours of television each week. She has watched 4 hours of television already. Write and solve an inequality to show how many more hours of television Sumiko can watch.

____

2. A satellite will be released into an orbit of more than 400 miles above the Earth. The rocket carrying it is currently 255 miles above Earth. Write and solve an inequality to show how much higher the rocket must climb before it releases the satellite.

____

3. Wayne's homework is to solve at least 20 questions from his textbook. So far, he has completed 9 of them. Write, solve, and graph an inequality to show how many more problems Wayne must complete.

____

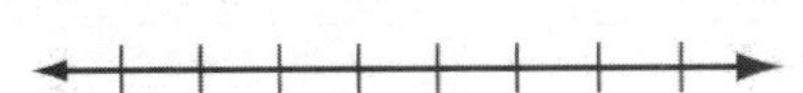

4. Felix wants to get at least one hour of exercise each day. Today, he has run for 40 minutes. Write, solve, and graph an inequality that shows how much longer Felix needs to exercise to reach his goal.

____

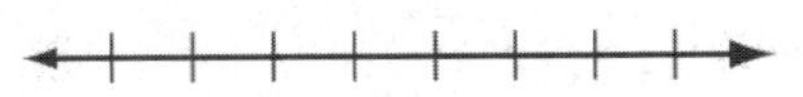

The high school has been raising money for charity and the class that raises the most will be awarded a party at the end of the year. The table below shows how much money each class has raised so far. Use this information to answer questions 5–7.

Class	Amount Raised ($)
Seniors	870
Juniors	650
Sophomores	675
First-Years	590

5. The school has a goal of raising at least $3000. Which inequality shows how much more money *m* they need to raise to reach their goal?

A $m \geq 215$ C $m \leq 215$

B $m < 215$ D $m > 2785$

6. The juniors would like to raise more money than the seniors. The seniors have completed their fundraising for the year. Which expression shows how much more money *j* the juniors must raise to overtake the seniors?

F $j \leq 220$ H $j \geq 220$

G $j < 220$ J $j > 220$

7. A local business has agreed to donate no more than half as much as the senior class raises. Which inequality shows how much money *b* the business will contribute?

A $\frac{1}{2}(870) \leq b$ C $\frac{1}{2}(870) \geq b$

B $870 \leq \frac{1}{2}b$ D $870 \geq \frac{1}{2}b$

Name________________________ Class________________ Date____________

2-3

Solving Inequalities by Multiplying or Dividing

Going Deeper

Essential question: *How can you use properties to justify solutions to inequalities that involve multiplication and division?*

Video Tutor

CC.9–12.A.REI.3

1 EXPLORE Multiplying or Dividing by a Negative Number

The following two inequalities are true.

$4 < 5$ $15 > 12$

What happens to the inequalities if you multiply both sides of the first inequality by 4 and divide both sides of the second inequality by 3?

$4 < 5$ $15 > 12$

________________ ________________

________________ ________________

Both statements are still true: 16 is less than 20, and 5 is greater than 4.

Now, multiply the first inequality by −4 and divide the second inequality by −3. Do not change the inequality symbol when you do these multiplications.

$4 < 5$ $15 > 12$

________________ ________________

________________ ________________

Is −16 less than −20? No, −16 is closer to 0 than −20 is, so it is greater than −20.
Is −5 greater than −4? No, −5 is farther from 0 than −4, so it is less than −4.

Repeat the multiplication by −4 and the division by −3, but this time reverse the inequality symbol when you do.

$4 < 5$ $15 > 12$

________________ ________________

________________ ________________

Do you get a true statement in each case? ________

REFLECT

1a. When solving inequalities, if you multiply by a negative number, you must

____

1b. When solving inequalities, if you divide by a negative number, you must

____

You can use the following inequality properties to solve inequalities involving multiplication and division. These properties are also true for $\geq$ and $\leq$.

Multiplication Property of Inequality	If $a > b$ and $c > 0$, then $ac > bc$. If $a < b$ and $c > 0$, then $ac < bc$. If $a > b$ and $c < 0$, then $ac < bc$. If $a < b$ and $c < 0$, then $ac > bc$.
Division Property of Inequality	If $a > b$ and $c > 0$, then $\frac{a}{c} > \frac{b}{c}$. If $a < b$ and $c > 0$, then $\frac{a}{c} < \frac{b}{c}$. If $a > b$ and $c < 0$, then $\frac{a}{c} < \frac{b}{c}$. If $a < b$ and $c < 0$, then $\frac{a}{c} > \frac{b}{c}$.

CC.9–12.A.REI.3

2 EXAMPLE Multiplying to Find the Solution Set

Solve. Write the solution using set notation. Graph your solution.

A $\frac{x}{2} > 3$

$\square\left(\frac{x}{2}\right) > \square(3)$ ____________ Property of Inequality

$x > \square$ Simplify.

Solution set: ____________

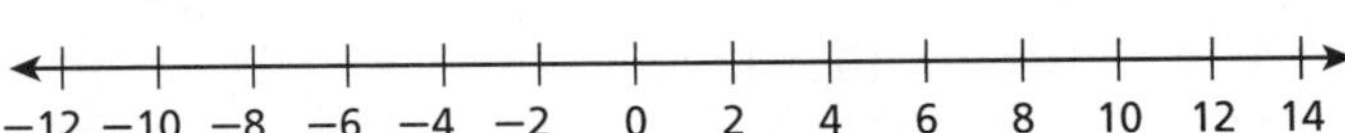

−12 −10 −8 −6 −4 −2 0 2 4 6 8 10 12 14

B $\frac{x}{-4} \leq -2$

$\square\left(\frac{x}{-4}\right) \geq \square(-2)$ ____________ Property of Inequality;

____________ $\leq$ symbol.

$x \geq \square$ Simplify.

Solution set: ____________

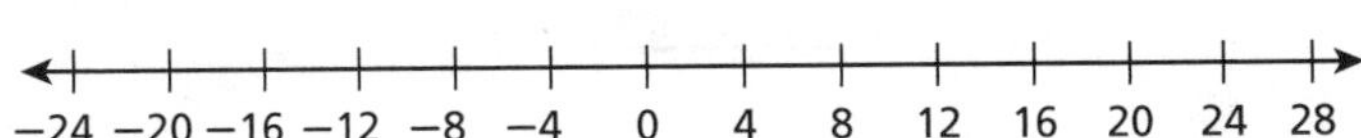

−24 −20 −16 −12 −8 −4 0 4 8 12 16 20 24 28

REFLECT

2a. Suppose the inequality symbol in Part A had been $\geq$. Describe the solution set.

____

2b. Suppose the inequality symbol in Part B had been $<$. Describe the solution set.

____

CC.9–12.A.REI.3

3 EXAMPLE Dividing to Find the Solution Set

Solve. Write the solution using set notation. Graph your solution.

A $3x \geq -9$

$\frac{3x}{\square} \geq \frac{-9}{\square}$ ____________ Property of Inequality

$x \geq \square$ Simplify.

Solution set: ____________

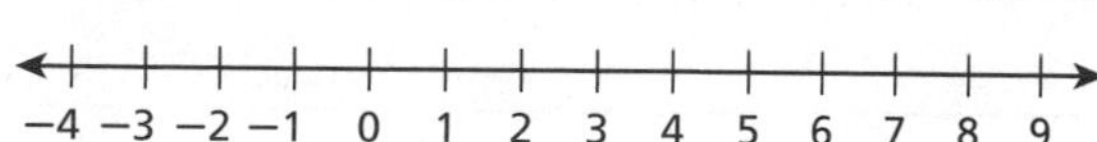

B $-5x < 20$

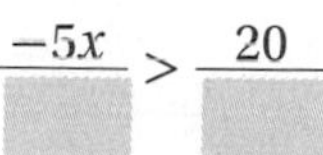

$\frac{-5x}{\square} > \frac{20}{\square}$ ____________ Property of Inequality;

____________ < symbol.

$x > \square$ Simplify.

Solution set: ____________

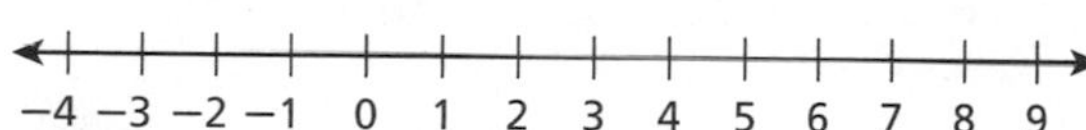

REFLECT

3a. There is a negative number in both Parts A and B. Why is the inequality symbol only reversed in Part B?

____

____

____

3b. Suppose the inequality symbol in Part A had been $>$. Describe the solution set.

____

3c. Suppose the inequality symbol in Part B had been $\leq$. Describe the solution set.

____

PRACTICE

Solve. Justify your steps. Write each solution using set notation. Graph your solution.

1. $4x < 32$

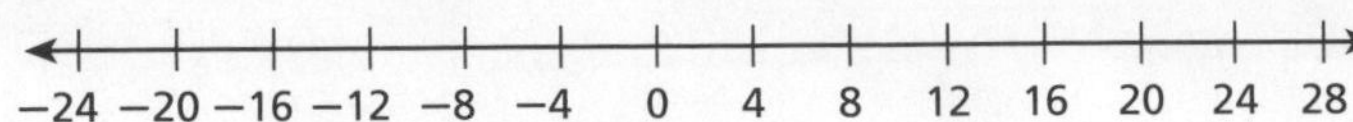

2. $\frac{x}{5} > -3$

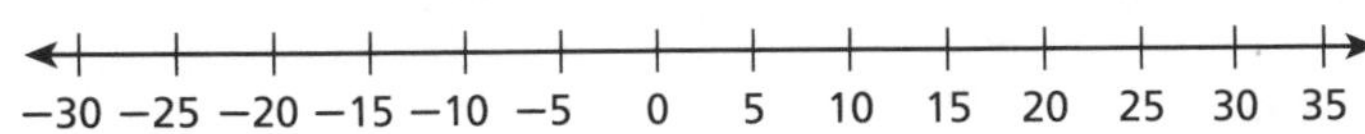

3. $\frac{x}{-4} \leq -4$

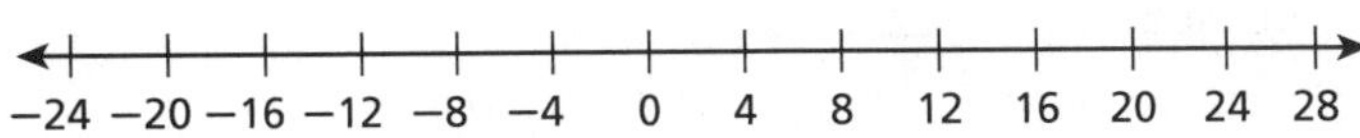

4. $-2x \geq -6$

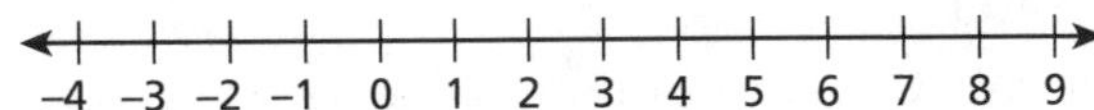

5. $\frac{x}{-6} < 3$

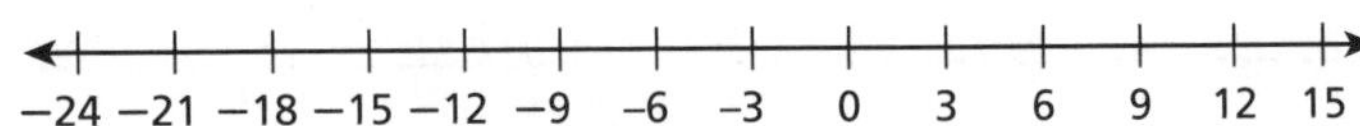

Name________________________ Class____________ Date__________ 2-3

Additional Practice

Solve each inequality and graph the solutions.

1. $4a > 32$

____

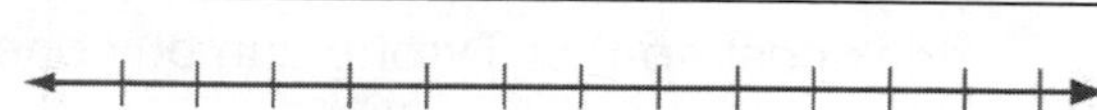

2. $-7y < 21$

____

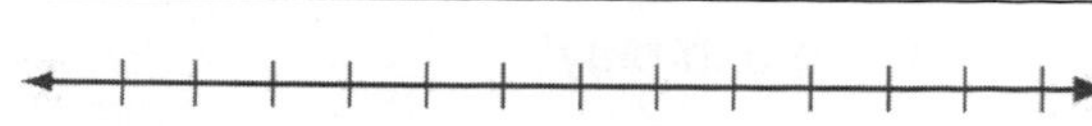

3. $1.5n \leq -18$

____

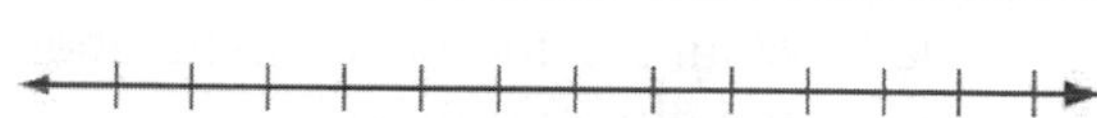

4. $-\frac{3}{8}c \geq 9$

____

5. $\frac{y}{5} > 4$

____

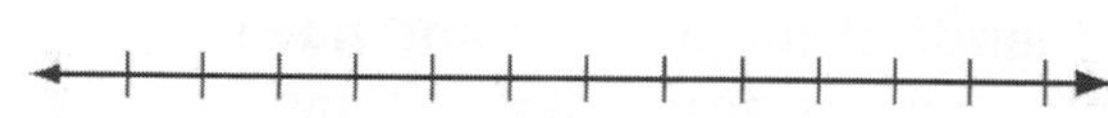

6. $2s \leq -3$

____

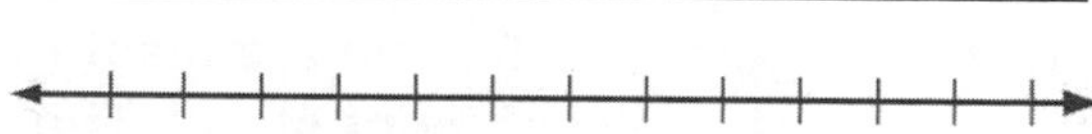

7. $-\frac{1}{3}b < -6$

____

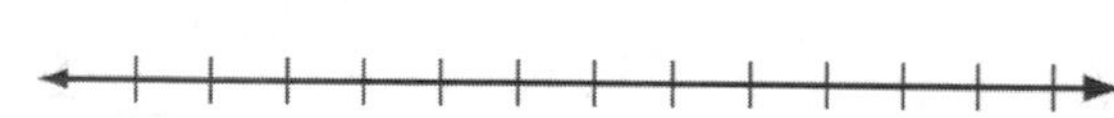

8. $\frac{z}{-8} \geq -0.25$

____

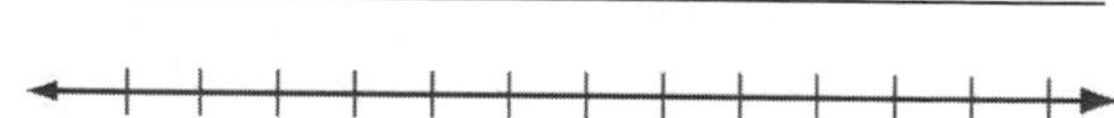

Write and solve an inequality for each problem.

9. Phil has a strip of wood trim that is 16 feet long. He needs 5-foot pieces to trim some windows. What are the possible numbers of pieces he can cut?

____

10. A teacher buys a 128-ounce bottle of juice and serves it in 5-ounce cups. What are the possible numbers of cups she can fill?

____

11. At an online bookstore, Kendra bought 4 copies of the same book for the members of her book club. She got free shipping because her total was at least $50. What was the minimum price of each book?

____

Problem Solving

Write and solve an inequality for each situation.

1. Karin has \$3 to spend in the arcade. The game she likes costs 50¢ per play. What are the possible numbers of times that she can play?

____

____

2. Tyrone has \$21 and wants to buy juice drinks for his soccer team. There are 15 players on his team. How much can each drink cost so that Tyrone can buy one drink for each person?

____

____

3. A swimming pool is 7 feet deep and is being filled at the rate of 2.5 feet per hour. How long can the pool be left unattended without the water overflowing?

____

____

4. Megan is making quilts that require 11 feet of cloth each. She has 50 feet of cloth. What are the possible numbers of quilts that she can make?

____

____

Alyssa, Reggie, and Cassie are meeting some friends at the movies and have stopped at the refreshment stand. The table below shows some of the items for sale and their prices. Use this information to answer questions 5–7.

Menu Item	Price(\$)
Popcorn	3.50
Drink	3.00
Hot Dog	2.50
Nachos	2.50
Fruit Snack	2.00

5. Alyssa has \$7 and would like to buy fruit snacks for as many of her friends as possible. Which inequality below can be solved to find the number of fruit snacks *f* she can buy?

   A $2f \leq 7$ C $7f \leq 2$
   B $2f < 7$ D $7f < 2$

6. Reggie brought \$13 and is going to buy popcorn for the group. Which answer below shows the possible numbers of popcorns *p* Reggie can buy for his friends?

   F 0, 1, or 2 H 0, 1, 2, 3, or 4
   G 0, 1, 2, or 3 J 0, 1, 2, 3, 4, or 5

7. The movie theater donates 12% of its sales to charity. From Cassie's purchases, the theater will donate at least \$2.15. Which inequality below shows the amount of money *m* that Cassie spent at the refreshment stand?

   A $m \geq 17.92$ C $m \geq 25.80$
   B $m \leq 17.92$ D $m \leq 25.80$

Name____________________ Class__________ Date__________

2-4

Video Tutor

Solving Two-Step and Multi-Step Inequalities

Going Deeper

Essential question: *How can you use properties to justify solutions to multi-step inequalities?*

You can use the properties of inequality you learned in the previous lessons, as well as other properties, to justify your solutions to multi-step inequalities.

CC.9–12.A.RE1.3

1 EXAMPLE Solving Inequalities With More Than One Step

Find the solution set. Justify each step and graph the solution set.

$4x - 3 + x + 8 > 20$

$4x + \square - \square + 8 > 20$ ____________ Property of Addition

$\square + \square > 20$ Combine like terms.

$5x + 5 - \square > 20 - \square$ ____________ Property of Inequality

$\square > \square$ Simplify.

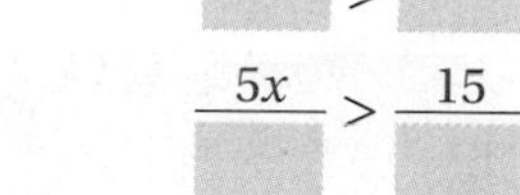

$\frac{5x}{\square} > \frac{15}{\square}$ ____________ Property of Inequality

$x > \square$ Simplify.

Solution set: __________

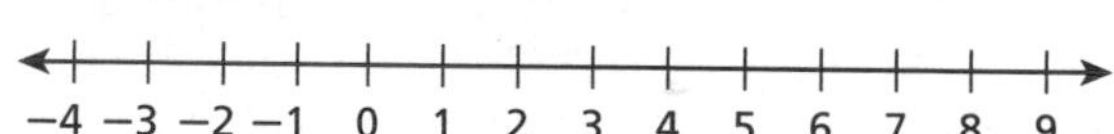

REFLECT

1a. How would the solution set change if the inequality symbol in the above inequality were $\geq$ rather than $>$?

____

1b. How would the above solution process be different if the first term were $-4x$?

____

____

You may need to use the Distributive Property before you can solve an inequality.

Distributive Property	If a, b, and c are real numbers, then $a(b + c) = ab + ac$.

CC.9-12.A.REI.3

2 EXAMPLE Using the Distributive Property

Find the solution set. Justify each step and graph the solution set.

$-2(3x - 8) < 10$

$\square + \square < 10$ ______________ Property

$-6x + 16 - \square < 10 - \square$ ______________ Property of Inequality

$\square < \square$ Simplify.

$\frac{6x}{\square} < \frac{-6}{\square}$ ______________ Property of Inequality

$x \ \square \ \square$ ______________ the inequality symbol; simplify.

Solution set: ______________

REFLECT

2a. Why was the inequality symbol not reversed when you multiplied by -2 using the Distributive Property?

____

____

PRACTICE

Find the solution set. Justify each step and graph the solution set.

1. $12 - 3x \leq 6$

____

____

____

____

Solution set: ______________

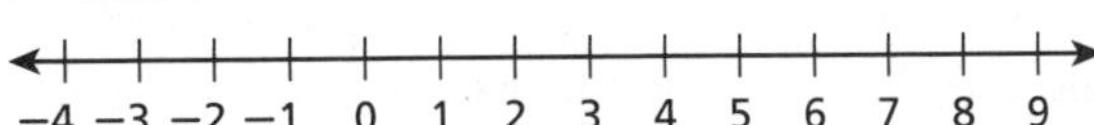

2. $2(x + 4) < 14$

____

____

____

____

____

Solution set: ______________

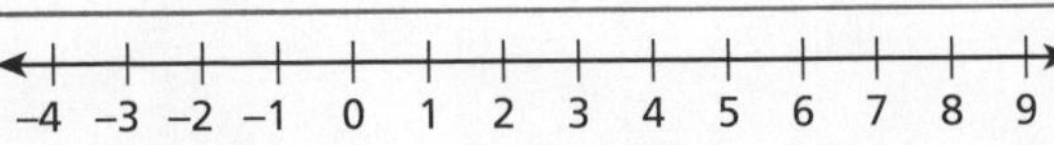

Name________________________ Class______________ Date____________

2-4

Additional Practice

Solve each inequality and graph the solutions.

1. $-3a + 10 < -11$

____

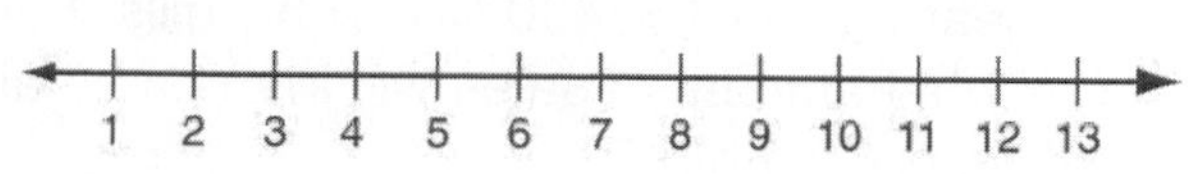

2. $4x - 12 \geq 20$

____

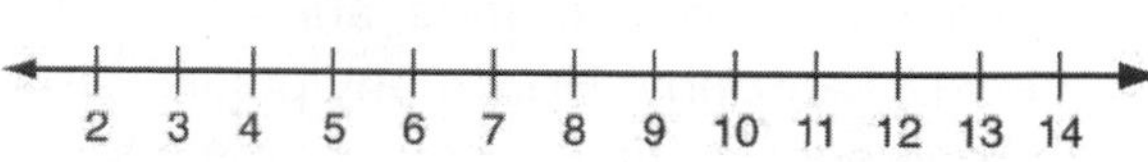

3. $\dfrac{2k - 3}{-5} > 7$

____

4. $-\dfrac{1}{5}z + \dfrac{2}{3} \leq 2$

____

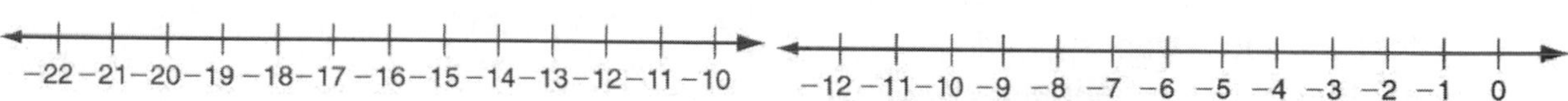

5. $6(n - 8) \geq -18$

____

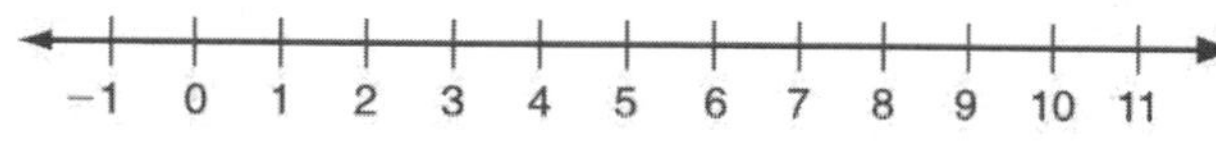

6. $10 - 2(3x + 4) < 11$

____

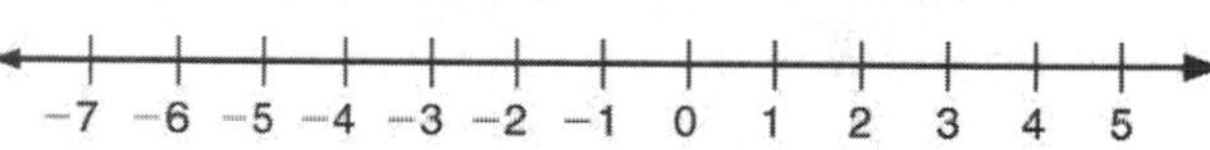

7. $7 + 2c - 4^2 \leq -9$

____

8. $15p + 3(p - 1) > 3\,(2^3)$

____

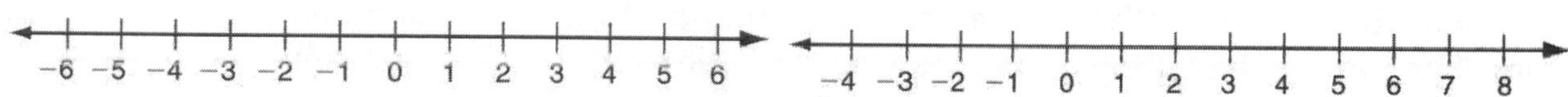

Write and solve an inequality for each problem.

9. A full-year membership to a gym costs $325 upfront with no monthly charge. A monthly membership costs $100 upfront and $30 per month. For what numbers of months is it less expensive to have a monthly membership?

____

10. The sum of the lengths of any two sides of a triangle must be greater than the length of the third side. What are the possible values of x for this triangle?

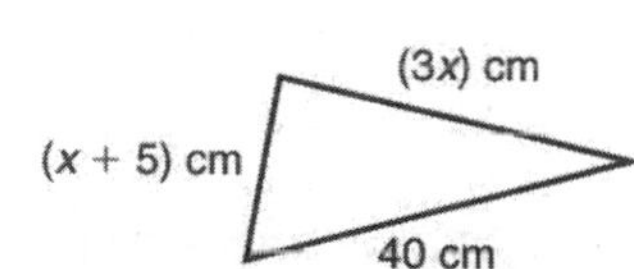

____

Problem Solving

Write and solve an inequality for each situation.

1. Jillene is playing in a basketball tournament and scored 24 points in her first game. If she averages over 20 points for both games, she will receive a trophy. How many points can Jillene score in the second game and receive a trophy?

____

____

2. Marcus has accepted a job selling cell phones. He will be paid \$1500 plus 15% of his sales each month. He needs to earn at least \$2430 to pay his bills. For what amount of sales will Marcus be able to pay his bills?

____

____

3. A 15-foot-tall cedar tree is growing at a rate of 2 feet per year beneath power lines that are 58 feet above the ground. The power company will have to prune or remove the tree before it reaches the lines. How many years can the power company wait before taking action?

____

____

4. Binh brought \$23 with her to the county fair. She purchased a \$5 T-shirt and now wants to buy some locally grown plants for \$2.50 each. What are the numbers of plants that she can purchase with her remaining money?

____

____

Benedict, Ricardo, and Charlie are considering opportunities for summer work. The table below shows the jobs open to them and the pay for each. Use this information to answer questions 5–7.

Job	Pay
Mowing Lawns	\$15 per lawn
Baby-Sitting	\$5.50 per hour
Tutoring	\$9 per session

5. Benedict has saved \$91 from last year and would like to baby-sit to earn enough to buy a mountain bike. A good quality bike costs at least \$300. What numbers of hours *h* can Benedict baby-sit to reach his goal?

   A $h \geq 14$ C $h \geq 38$

   B $h \geq 23$ D $h \geq 71$

6. Ricardo has agreed to tutor for the school. He owes his older brother \$59 and would like to end the summer with at least \$400 in savings. How many sessions *s* can Ricardo tutor to meet his goal?

   F $s \geq 31$ H $s \geq 51$

   G $s \geq 38$ J $s \geq 83$

7. Charlie has agreed to mow his neighbor's lawn each week and will also baby-sit some hours. If he makes \$100 or more each week, his parents will charge him rent. How many hours *h* should Charlie agree to baby-sit each week to avoid paying rent?

   A $h \leq 15$ C $h \leq 21$

   B $h \geq 15$ D $h \geq 21$

Name________________ Class__________ Date__________

2-5

Video Tutor

Solving Inequalities with Variables on Both Sides

Going Deeper

Essential question: *How can you use properties to justify solutions of inequalities with variables on both sides?*

You can use the Properties of Inequality and the Distributive Property to justify the steps in a solution when solving inequalities that have variables on both sides.

CC.9–12.A.REI.3

1 EXAMPLE Using Properties to Justify Solutions

Find the solution set. Justify each step and graph your solution.

$3(2x - 3) \leq x + 1$

$6x - 9 \leq x + 1$ ________________ Property

$6x$ ☐ $- 9 \leq x$ ☐ $+ 1$ ________________

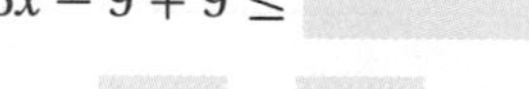 ☐ $\leq$ ☐ Simplify.

$5x - 9 + 9 \leq$ ☐ ________________

☐ $\leq$ ☐ Simplify.

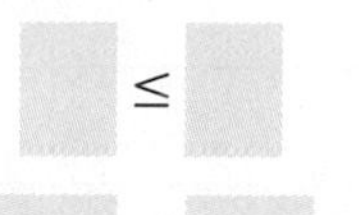 ☐ $\leq$ ☐ ________________

☐ $\leq$ ☐ Simplify.

Solution set: ________________

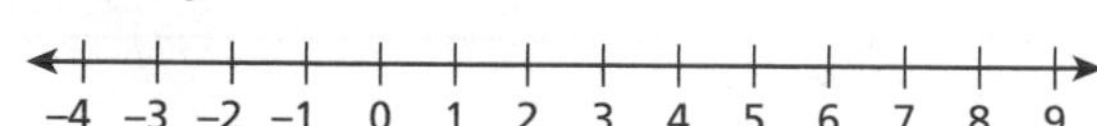

REFLECT

1a. Why is the Distributive Property applied first in the solution?

____

____

1b. Could the properties have been applied in a different order than shown above? If so, would this make finding the solution easier or more difficult? Explain.

____

____

____

1c. How would the solution change if the simplified coefficient of x were negative?

____

____

PRACTICE

Find the solution set. Justify each step and graph your solution.

1. $21x + 28 < 10 - 3x$

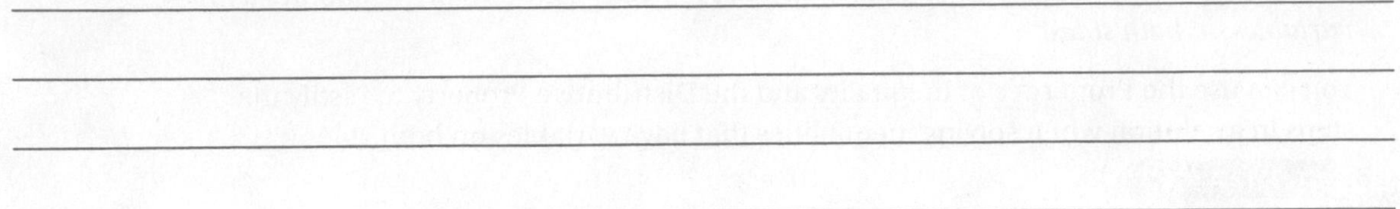

Solution set: ______________

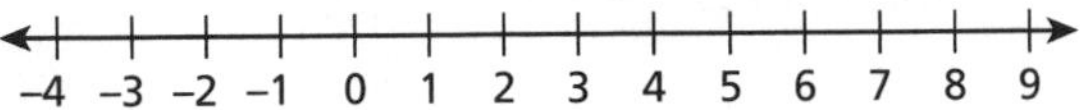

2. $-\frac{1}{3}(x + 2) \geq 7x + 3$

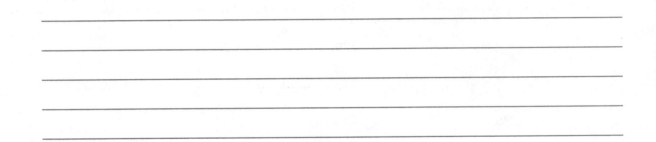

Solution set: ______________

–4 –3 –2 –1 0 1 2 3 4 5 6 7 8 9

3. $2(4 - 3x) \leq 4x - 2$

Solution set: ______________

–4 –3 –2 –1 0 1 2 3 4 5 6 7 8 9

Name____________________ Class__________ Date__________

Additional Practice

Solve each inequality and graph the solutions.

1. $2x + 30 \geq 7x$

____

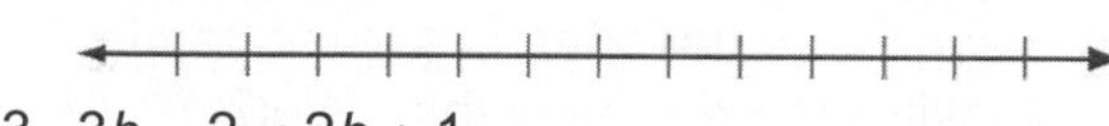

2. $2k + 6 < 5k - 3$

____

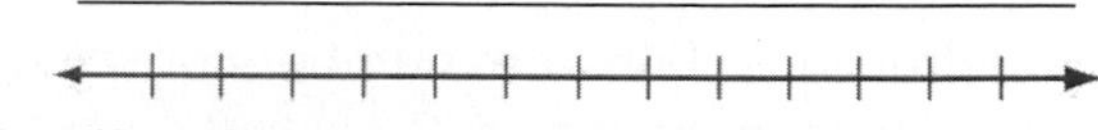

3. $3b - 2 \leq 2b + 1$

____

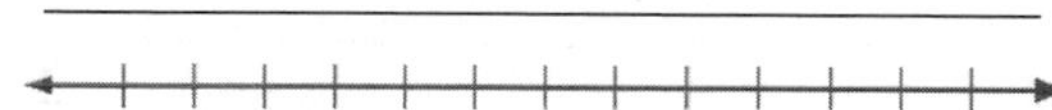

4. $2(3n + 7) > 5n$

____

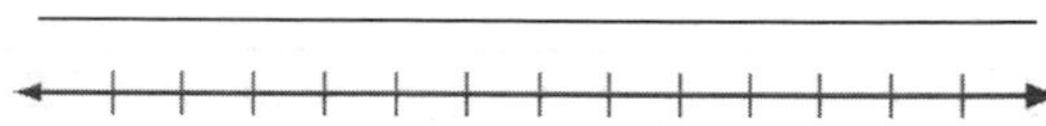

5. $5s - 9 < 2(s - 6)$

____

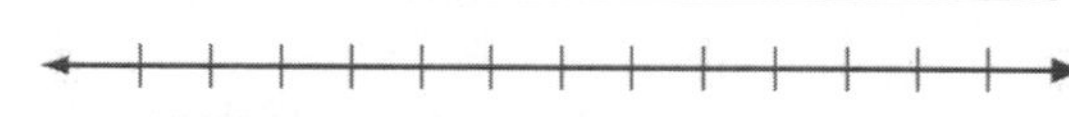

6. $-3(3x + 5) \geq -5(2x - 2)$

____

7. $1.4z + 2.2 > 2.6z - 0.2$

____

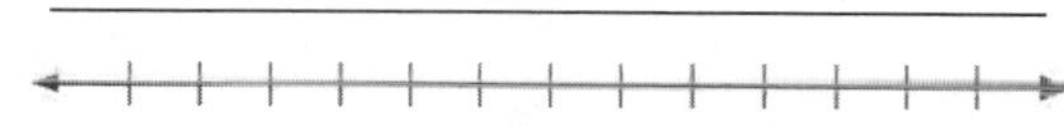

8. $\frac{7}{8}p - \frac{1}{4} \leq \frac{1}{2}p$

____

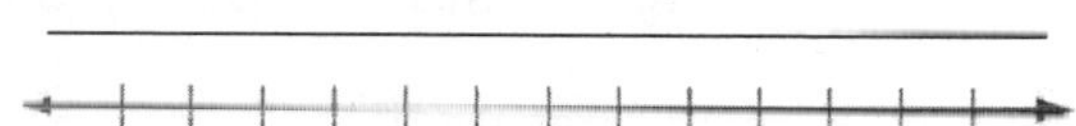

Solve each inequality.

9. $v + 1 > v - 6$ __________

10. $3(x + 4) \leq 3x$ __________

11. $-2(8 - 3x) \geq 6x + 2$ __________

Write and solve an inequality for each problem.

12. Ian wants to promote his band on the Internet. Site A offers website hosting for $4.95 per month with a $49.95 startup fee. Site B offers website hosting for $9.95 per month with no startup fee. For how many months would Ian need to keep the website for Site B to be less expensive than Site A?

____

13. For what values of x is the area of the rectangle greater than the perimeter?

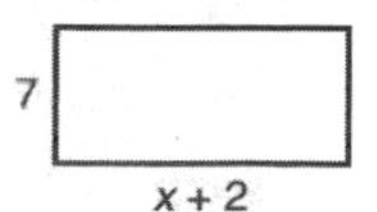

____

Problem Solving

Write and solve an inequality for each situation.

1. Rosa has decided to sell pet rocks at an art fair for \$5 each. She has paid \$50 to rent a table at the fair and it costs her \$2 to package each rock with a set of instructions. For what numbers of sales will Rosa make a profit?

____

____

2. Jamie has a job paying \$25,000 and expects to receive a \$1000 raise each year. Wei has a job paying \$19,000 a year and expects a \$1500 raise each year. For what span of time is Jamie making more money than Wei?

____

____

3. Sophia types 75 words per minute and is just starting to write a term paper. Patton already has 510 words written and types at a speed of 60 words per minute. For what numbers of minutes will Sophia have more words typed than Patton?

____

____

4. Keith is racing his little sister Pattie and has given her a 15 foot head start. She runs 5 ft/sec and he is chasing at 8 ft/sec. For how long can Pattie stay ahead of Keith?

____

____

The table below shows the population of four cities in 2004 and the amount of population change from 2003. Use this table to answer questions 5–6.

5. If the trends in this table continue, after how many years y will the population of Manchester, NH, be more than the population of Vallejo, CA? Round your answer to the nearest tenth of a year.

   A $y > 0.2$ C $y > 34.6$

   B $y > 6.4$ D $y > 78.6$

6. If the trends in this table continue, for how long x will the population of Carrollton, TX be less than the population of Lakewood, CO? Round your answer to the nearest tenth of a year.

   F $x < 11.7$ H $x < 20.1$

   G $x < 14.6$ J $x < 28.3$

City	Population (2004)	Population Change (from 2003)
Lakewood, CO	141,301	–830
Vallejo, CA	118,349	–1155
Carrollton, TX	117,823	+1170
Manchester, NH	109,310	+261

Name________________ Class__________ Date__________

2-6

Video Tutor

Solving Compound Inequalities

Extension: Solving Special Compound Inequalities

Essential question: *How can you solve special compound inequalities?*

Compound inequalities are two inequalities joined by AND ($\cap$) or OR ($\cup$).

To solve a compound inequality:

1. Solve each inequality independently.
2. Graph the solutions above the same number line.
3. Decide which parts of the graphs represent the solution. If AND is used, it's the common points. If OR is used, it's all points. Then graph the solution on the number line.

CC.9–12.A.REI.3

1 EXAMPLE Solving Compound Inequalities

Solve. Write the solution in set notation. Graph the solution.

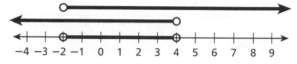

A $2x < 8$ AND $3x + 2 > -4$

$x < 4$ $\quad 3x > -6$

$x > -2$

−4 −3 −2 −1 0 1 2 3 4 5 6 7 8 9

Solution set: $\{x \mid x < \_\_\_\} \cap \{x \mid x < \_\_\_\}$ or $\{x \mid \_\_\_ < x < \_\_\_\}$

B $3x + 2 \geq -1$ OR $4 - x \geq 2$

$3x \geq -3$ $\quad -x \geq -2$

$x \geq -1$ $\quad x \leq 2$

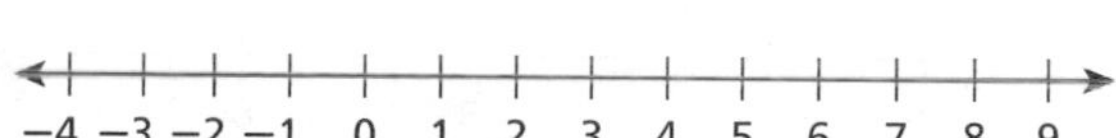

Solution set: $\{x \mid x \geq \_\_\_\} \cup \{x \mid x \leq \_\_\_\}$ or the set of all ________ numbers

C $2x - 3 > 3$ AND $x + 4 \leq 1$

$2x > 6$ $\quad x \leq -3$

$x > 3$

Solution set: $\{x \mid x > \_\_\_\} \cap \{x \mid x \leq \_\_\_\}$ or the ________ set or ___

D

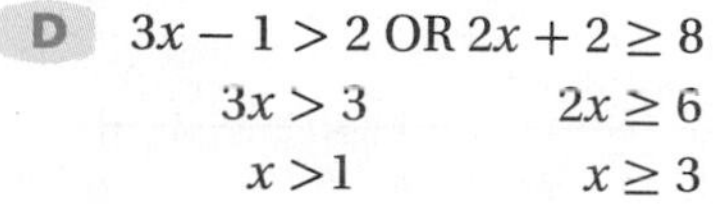

$3x - 1 > 2$ OR $2x + 2 \geq 8$

$3x > 3$ $\quad 2x \geq 6$

$x > 1$ $\quad x \geq 3$

Solution set: $\{x \mid x > \_\_\_\} \cup \{x \mid x \geq \_\_\_\}$ or $\{x \mid x > \_\_\_\}$

REFLECT

1a. In Part C, why is the solution set the empty set?

____

____

1b. In Part D, why is the solution set $\{x \mid x > 1\}$?

____

____

PRACTICE

Solve. Write the solution in set notation. Graph the solution.

1. $4x + 2 > 14$ AND $x + 6 \leq 4$

____

____

Solution set: ______________________

____

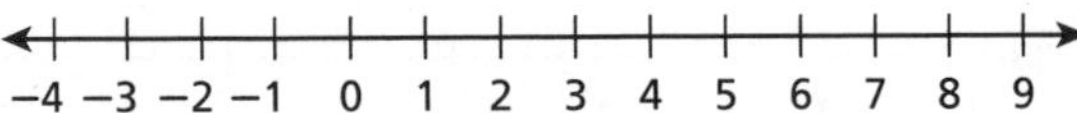

2. $-3x < 3$ OR $2x + 3 \geq 11$

____

____

Solution set: ______________________

____

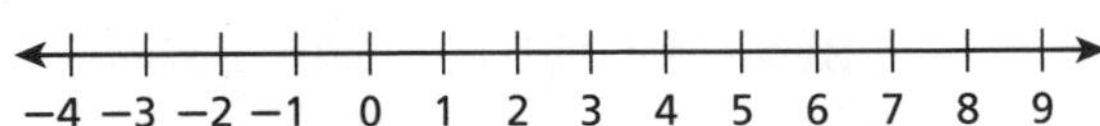

3. $2 + x < 1$ OR $-5x + 1 < 16$

____

____

Solution set: ______________________

____

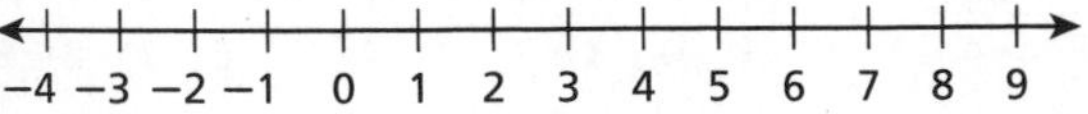

4. $4x - 3 > -7$ AND $3x - 2 \geq 7$

____

____

Solution set: ______________________

____

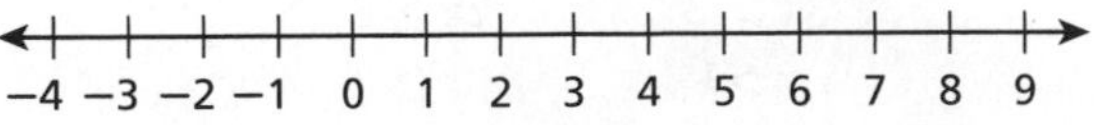

Name____________________ Class__________ Date__________

Additional Practice

Write the compound inequality shown by each graph.

1. 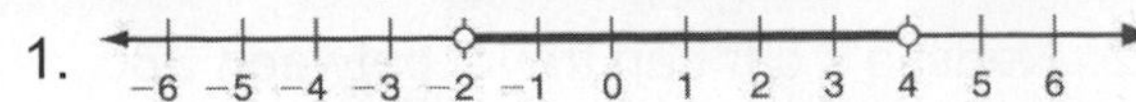

2. 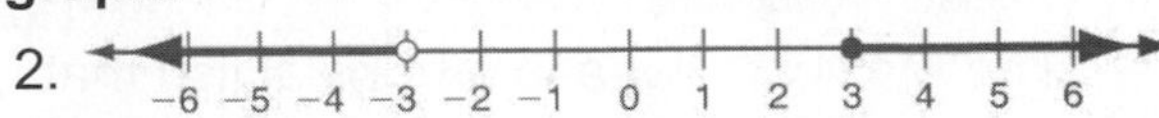

3. −18 −17 −16 −15 −14 −13 −12 −11 −10 −9 −8 −7 −6

4. 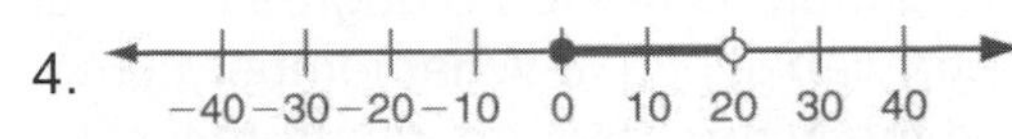

Solve each compound inequality and graph the solutions.

5. $-15 < x - 8 < -4$

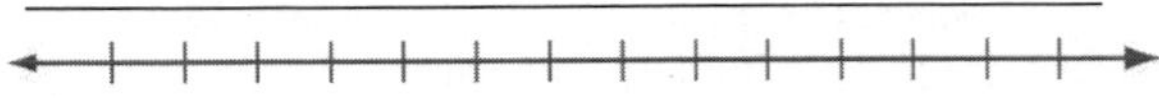

6. $12 \leq 4n < 28$

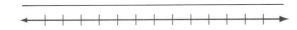

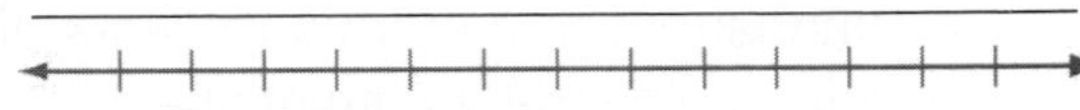

7. $-2 \leq 3b + 7 \leq 13$

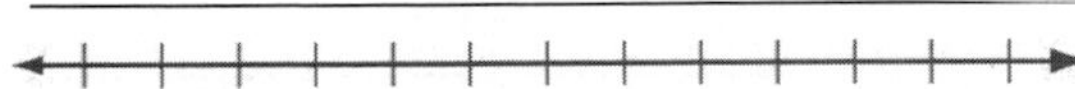

8. $x - 3 < -3$ OR $x - 3 \geq 3$

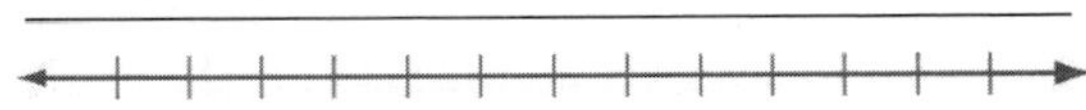

9. $5k \leq -20$ OR $2k \geq 8$

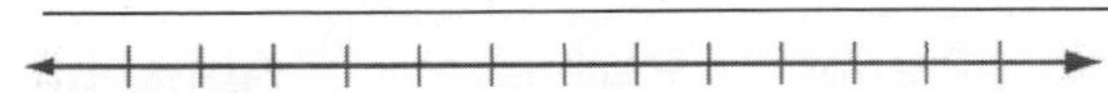

10. $2s + 3 \leq 7$ OR $3s + 5 > 26$

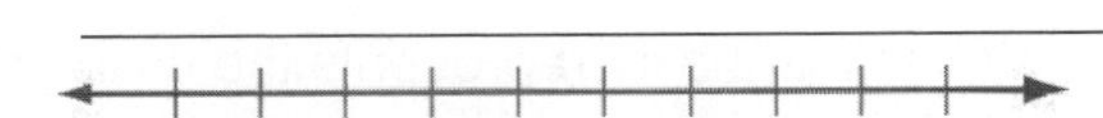

Write a compound inequality for each problem. Graph the solutions.

11. The human ear can distinguish sounds between 20 Hz and 20,000 Hz, inclusive.

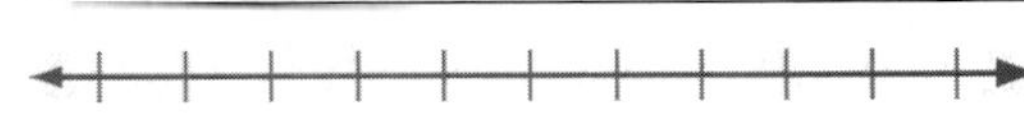

12. For a man to box as a welterweight, he must weigh more than 140 lbs, but at most 147 lbs.

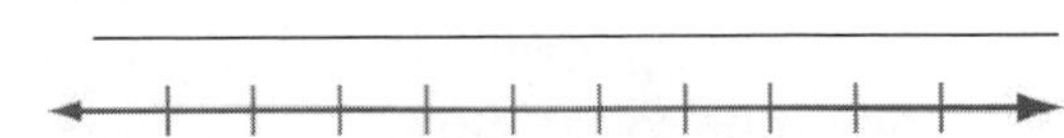

Problem Solving

Write and solve an inequality for each situation.

1. The Mexican Tetra is a tropical fish that requires a water temperature between 68 and 77 degrees Fahrenheit, inclusive. An aquarium is heated 8 degrees so that a Tetra can live in it. What temperatures could the water have been before the heating?

____

____

2. Nerissa's car can travel between 380 and 410 miles on a full tank of gas. She filled her gas tank and drove 45 miles. How many more miles can she drive without running out of gas?

____

____

3. A local company is hiring trainees with less than 1 year of experience and managers with 5 or more years of experience. Graph the solutions.

____

____

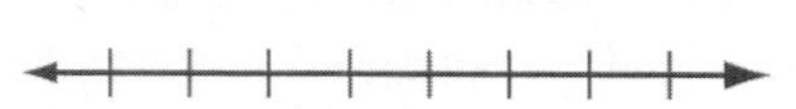

4. Marty's allowance is doubled and is now between \$10 and \$15, inclusive. What amounts could his allowance have been before the increase? Graph the solutions.

____

____

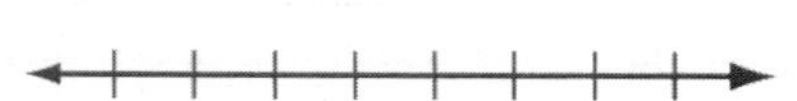

The elliptical orbits of planets bring them closer to and farther from the Sun at different times. The closest (perihelion) and furthest (aphelion) points are given for three planets below. Use this data to answer questions 5–7.

Planet	Perihelion (in 10^6 km)	Aphelion (in 10^6 km)
Uranus	2741.3	3003.6
Neptune	4444.5	4545.7
Pluto	4435.0	7304.3

5. Which inequality represents the distances d from the sun to Neptune?

   A $d \leq 4444.5$

   B $d \leq 4545.7$

   C $4444.5 \leq d \leq 4545.7$

   D $d = 4444.5$ OR $d \geq 4545.7$

6. A NASA probe is traveling between Uranus and Neptune. It is currently between their orbits. Which inequality shows the possible distance p from the probe to the Sun?

   F $1542.1 < p < 1703.2$

   G $2741.3 < p < 4545.7$

   H $3003.6 < p < 4444.5$

   J $7185.8 < p < 7549.3$

7. At what distances o do the orbits of Neptune and Pluto overlap?

   A $4435.0 \leq o \leq 4444.5$

   B $4435.0 \leq o \leq 4545.7$

   C $4444.5 \leq o \leq 7304.3$

   D $4545.7 \leq o \leq 7304.3$

Name________________________ Class________________ Date__________

2-7

Video Tutor

Solving Absolute-Value Inequalities

Connection: Connecting Absolute-Value and Compound Inequalities

Essential question: *How does solving absolute-value inequalities relate to solving compound inequalities?*

The **absolute value** of a number is its distance from 0 on a number line. To solve an absolute-value inequality, you rewrite the inequality as a compound inequality.

CC.9–12.A.REI.3

1 EXPLORE Solving Absolute-Value Inequalities with <

Solve the inequality $|x| + 2 < 5$.

A Use the Subtraction Property of Inequality to isolate the absolute-value expression.

$$|x| + 2 < 5$$

$$|x| + 2 - \square < 5 - \square$$

$$|x| < \square$$

B Write a description of the solution of the inequality.

All real numbers that are ____________ than ____________ units from 0

C Draw the graph of the solution on the number line.

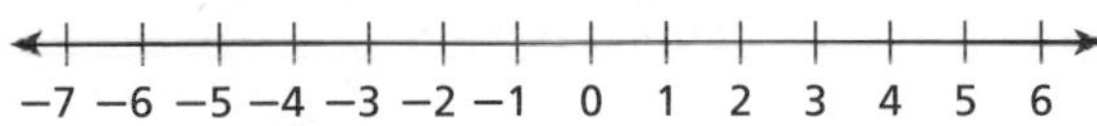

D Use the graph to rewrite $|x| < 3$ as a compound inequality.

$x > \square$ ____________ $x < \square$, or $\square < x < \square$

REFLECT

1a. How did you decide whether to use AND or OR in the compound inequality?

____

____

1b. Solve $|x + 2| \le 5$ by rewriting it as a compound inequality. Show your work.

____

____

____

____

CC.9–12.A.REI.3

2 EXPLORE Solving Absolute-Value Inequalities with >

Solve the inequality $|x| - 3 > 2$.

A Use the Addition Property of Inequality to isolate the absolute value expression.

$$|x| - 3 > 2$$
$$|x| - 3 + \square > 2 + \square$$
$$|x| > \square$$

B Write a description of the solution of the inequality.

All real numbers ____________ than _______ units from 0.

C Draw the graph of the solution on the number line.

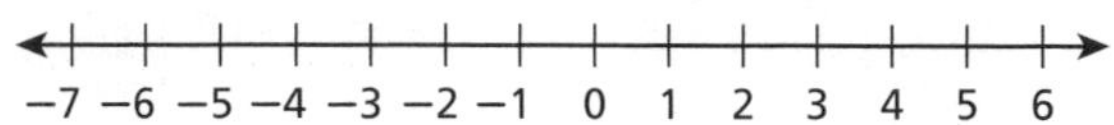

D Use the graph to rewrite $|x| > 5$ as a compound inequality.

$x < \square$ ____________ $x > \square$

REFLECT

2a. How did you decide whether to use AND or OR in the compound inequality?

2b. Solve $|x - 3| \geq 2$ by rewriting it as a compound inequality. Show your work.

2c. Write a generalization for absolute-value inequalities that relate the inequality symbol to the type of compound inequality that represents a solution.

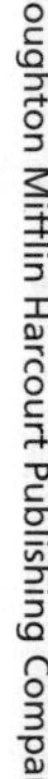

Additional Practice

Solve each inequality and graph the solutions.

1. $2x + 30 \geq 7x$

____

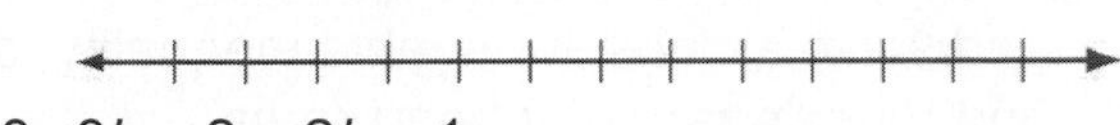

2. $2k + 6 < 5k - 3$

____

3. $3b - 2 \leq 2b + 1$

____

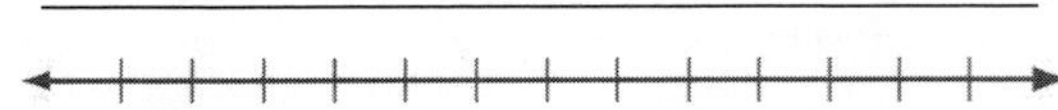

4. $2(3n + 7) > 5n$

____

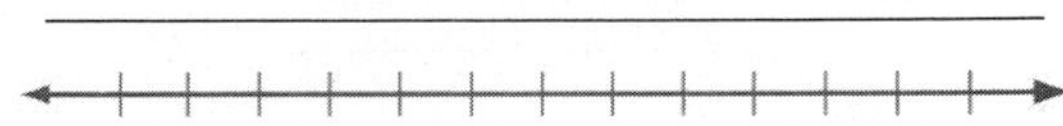

5. $5s - 9 < 2(s - 6)$

____

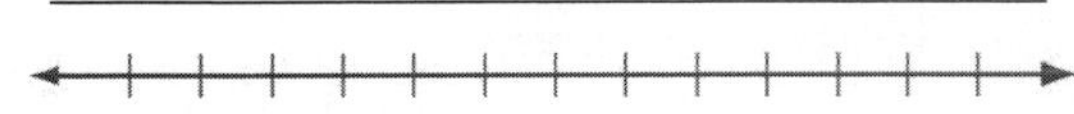

6. $-3(3x + 5) \geq -5(2x - 2)$

____

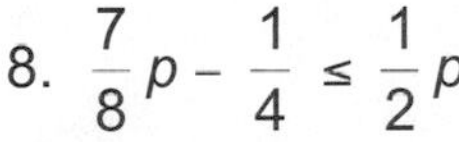

7. $1.4z + 2.2 > 2.6z - 0.2$

____

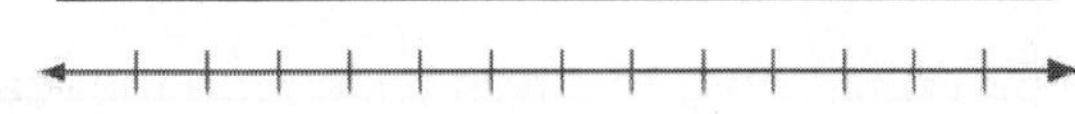

8. $\frac{7}{8}p - \frac{1}{4} \leq \frac{1}{2}p$

____

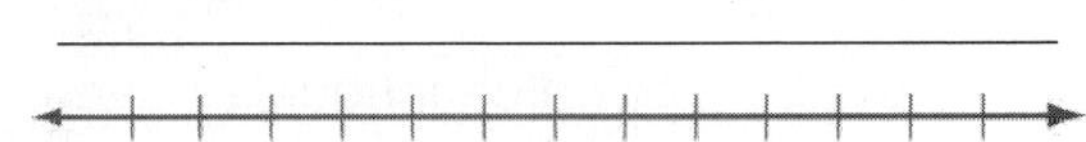

Solve each inequality.

9. $v + 1 > v - 6$ _______________

10. $3(x + 4) \leq 3x$ _______________

11. $-2(8 - 3x) \geq 6x + 2$ _______________

Write and solve an inequality for each problem.

12. Ian wants to promote his band on the Internet. Site A offers website hosting for $4.95 per month with a $49.95 startup fee. Site B offers website hosting for $9.95 per month with no startup fee. For how many months would Ian need to keep the website for Site B to be less expensive than Site A?

____

13. For what values of x is the area of the rectangle greater than the perimeter?

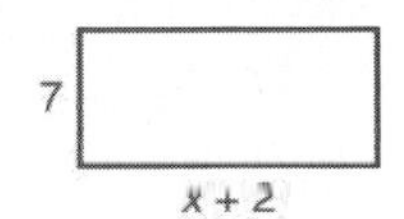

____

Problem Solving

Write the correct answer.

1. A carpenter cuts boards that are 2 meters long. It is acceptable for the length to differ from this value by at most 0.05 meters. Write and solve an absolute-value inequality to find the range of acceptable lengths.

____

____

2. During a workout, Vince tries to keep his heart rate at 134 beats per minute. His actual heart rate varies from this value by as much as 8 beats per minute. Write and solve an absolute-value inequality to find Vince's range of heart rates.

____

____

3. Mai thinks of a secret number. She says that her secret number is more than 11 units away from 50. Write an absolute-value inequality that gives the possible values of Mai's number.

____

4. Boxes of cereal are supposed to weigh 15.3 ounces each. A quality-control manager finds that the boxes are no more than 0.4 ounces away from this weight. Write an absolute-value inequality that gives the range of possible weights of the boxes.

____

The table gives the typical lifespan for several mammals. Use the table for questions 5-7. Select the best answer.

5. Which absolute-value inequality gives the number of years a goat may live?

   A $|x - 6| \leq 11$ C $|x - 24| \leq 6$

   B $|x - 15| \leq 9$ D $|x - 30| \leq 9$

6. Which mammal has a lifespan that can be represented by the absolute-value inequality $|x - 12.5| \leq 2.5$?

   F Antelope H Otter

   G Koala J Wolf

7. The inequality $|x - 17| \leq c$ gives the number of years a panda may live. What is the value of c?

   A 3 C 14

   B 6 D 20

Mammal	Lifespan (years)	Mammal	Lifespan (years)
Antelope	10 to 25	Otter	15 to 20
Goat	6 to 24	Panda	14 to 20
Koala	10 to 15	Wolf	13 to 15

Source:
http://www.sandiegozoo.org/animalbytes/a-mammal.html

Name_______________ Class_______________ Date_______________

CHAPTER 2

Performance Tasks

COMMON CORE

CC.9-12.A.CED.1
CC.9-12.A.REI.3

★ **1.** Sariq's last four test scores in history were 87, 85, 91, and 88. What scores on his next test will give him an average of 90 or above? Write and solve an inequality. Show your work.

★ **2.** Fernando is starting a new sales job, and needs to decide which of two salary plans to choose from. For plan A, he will earn $100/week plus 15% commission on all sales. For plan B, he will earn $150/week plus 10% commission on all sales.

a. Write an expression for each salary plan if s is Fernando's total weekly sales.

b. For what amount of weekly sales is plan B better than plan A?

★★ **3.** An electronics company has developed a new hand-held device. The company predicts that the start-up cost to manufacture the new product will be $125,000, and the cost to make one device will be $6.50.

a. If the company plans on selling the devices at a price of $9, write and solve an inequality to determine how many must be sold for the company to make a profit. Show your work.

b. The cost of one device is 10% more than the company predicted. What is the new cost of making one device? How many devices must they now sell at the same price to make a profit?

continued

c. Suppose the company wants to start making a profit after selling the same number of devices you found in part **a**. What is the lowest the new price can be? Explain how you found this price.

4. A machining company manufactures washers. The dimensions of the washer are shown in the figure, and the inner and outer radii can be ±2% of the indicated values. This range of acceptable values is called the *tolerance*.

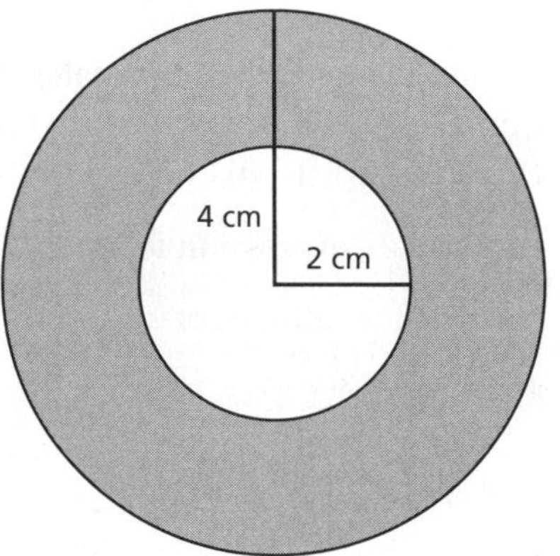

a. Write compound inequalities for the acceptable dimensions for the inner radius r and outer radius R.

b. Write an equation for the area of the face of the washer in terms of r, R, and π.

c. Write a compound inequality for the area, to the nearest tenth of a square centimeter, of the face of the washer. (*Hint*: Find the smallest possible area and the largest possible area.)

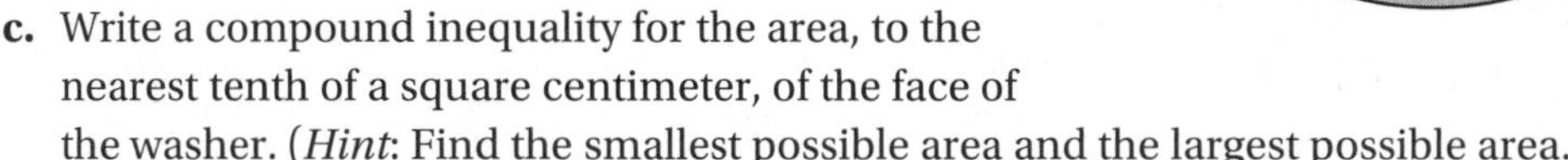

Name ______________________ Class ______________ Date __________

MULTIPLE CHOICE

1. What is the next and most efficient step in solving the inequality for x?

$$-4x > 12$$

A. $\frac{-4x}{-4} < \frac{12}{-4}$ C. $\frac{-4x}{-4} > \frac{12}{-4}$

B. $\frac{-4x}{4} > \frac{12}{4}$ D. $\frac{-4x}{4} < \frac{12}{4}$

2. Given $-\frac{1}{3}x - \frac{2}{3} \geq 7x + 3$, which property is used below?

$$3\left(-\frac{1}{3}x - \frac{2}{3}\right) \geq 3(7x + 3)$$

F. Distributive Property

G. Multiplication Property of Inequality

H. Subtraction Property of Inequality

J. Associative Property of Multiplication

3. A 130-pound woman burns 9.83 Calories per minute while running. She burns 3.25 Calories per minute while walking during her cool-down. She runs for t minutes and exercises for a total of 45 minutes. Write an inequality to represent the amount of time she has to run to burn at least 100 Calories.

A. $100 \leq = 9.83t + 3.25(45 - t)$

B. $100 \leq = 9.83t + 3.25(t - 45)$

C. $100 \leq = 9.83t + 3.25t$

D. $100 \leq = 9.83(t - 45) + 3.25t$

4. It costs \$5 to have a tote bag monogrammed with up to 12 letters and \$.50 for each additional letter. A club has a budget of \$8 maximum per tote bag. Write an inequality for the number of additional letters that the club can have monogrammed on a tote bag.

F. $5 + 0.5x > 8$ H. $5 + 0.5x < 8$

G. $5 + 0.5x \geq 8$ J. $5 + 0.5x \leq 8$

5. Solve the inequality for x, given $b < c$.

$$a + bx > cx - d$$

A. $x < \frac{a+d}{b-c}$

B. $x < \frac{a+d}{c-b}$

C. $x > \frac{a+d}{c-b}$

D. $x > \frac{-d-a}{b-c}$

6. Which inequality represents the situation: "Alex has at most \$45 to spend on a basketball, including 8% tax?"

F. $p + 0.08p < 45$

G. $p + 0.08p > 45$

H. $p + 0.08p \geq 45$

J. $p + 0.08p \leq 45$

7. Which graph represents the solution of the inequality $2x - 5 \leq -3$?

A. 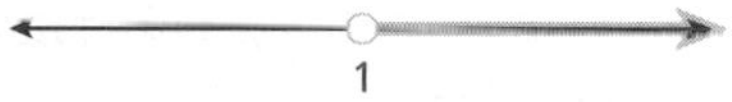

B. 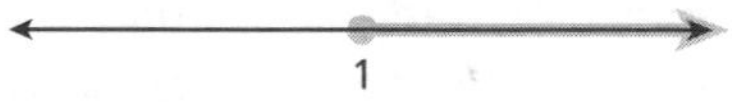

C. 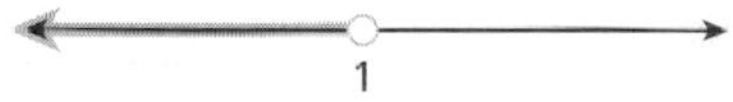

D. 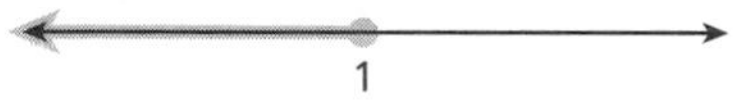

8. Which statement is equivalent to the inequality $|x - 3| > 5$?

F. $x - 3 > 5$ or $x - 3 < 5$

G. $x - 3 > 5$ or $x - 3 < -5$

H. $x - 3 > 5$ and $x - 3 < -5$

J. $x - 3 < 5$ and $x - 3 > -5$

9. Which compound inequality has the empty set as its solution?

A. $x + 1 > 3$ or $x + 6 < 4$

B. $x + 1 < 3$ or $x + 6 > 4$

C. $x + 1 > 3$ and $x + 6 < 4$

D. $x + 1 > 3$ and $x + 6 > 4$

10. What is the solution set of the inequality $3n > -6$?

F. All real numbers less than 2.

G. All real numbers less than -2.

H. All real numbers greater than 2.

J. All real numbers greater than -2.

11. Which number is a solution of the inequality $x + 8 < -4$?

A. -14

B. -12

C. -4

D. 4

CONSTRUCTED RESPONSE

12. Keira is asked to solve the inequality $4a + 7 < -3$ and $4a + 7 > 2$. Using number sense she immediately answers that there is no solution. How can she tell that there is no solution without solving algebraically?

13. Jim's distance (in yards) from shore as he rows a boat to an island and back to shore is given by the expression $-30|t - 4| + 120$ where t is the elapsed time (in minutes) of Jim's trip.

a. Write and solve an equation to find the elapsed times when Jim's distance from shore is 0.

b. Write and solve an absolute value inequality to find the elapsed times when Jim's distance from shore is greater than 30 yards.

c. Explain how you can use your answers to 13a and 13b to find the elapsed time intervals when Jim's distance from shore is less than or equal to 30 yards.

Functions

Chapter Focus

In this unit you will be introduced to mathematical relationships called functions, which pair data values. You will learn to recognize whether or not a relationship is a function, describe characteristics of functions, graphs functions, and write rules for functions and their inverses. You will also study special types of functions called arithmetic sequences.

Chapter at a Glance

COMMON CORE

Lesson		Standards for Mathematical Content
3-1	Graphing Relationships	CC.9-12.F.IF.4
3-2	Relations and Functions	CC.9-12.F.IF.1, CC.9-12.F.IF.2, CC.9-12.F.IF.5
3-3	Writing Functions	CC.9-12.F.BF.1b, CC.9-12.F.BF.4a
3-4	Graphing Functions	CC.9-12.A.CED.2, CC.9-12.F.IF.2, CC.9-12.F.IF.7b, CC.9-12.F.BF.1
3-5	Scatter Plots and Trend Lines	CC.9-12.S.ID.6a, CC.9-12.S.ID.6c, CC.9-12.S.ID.8, CC.9-12.S.ID.9
3-6	Arithmetic Sequences	CC.9-12.F.IF.3, CC.9-12.F.BF.2, CC.9-12.F.LE.2
	Performance Tasks	
	Assessment Readiness	

Unpacking the Standards

Understanding the standards and the vocabulary terms in the standards will help you know exactly what you are expected to learn in this chapter.

COMMON CORE **CC.9-12.F.IF.1**

Understand that a function from one set (called the domain) to another set (called the range) assigns to each element of the domain exactly one element of the range. …

Key Vocabulary

function *(función)* A relation in which every domain value is paired with exactly one range value.
domain *(dominio)* The set of all first coordinates (or *x*-values) of a relation or function.
range of a function or relation *(rango de una función o relación)* The set of all second coordinates (or *y*-values) of a function or relation.
element *(elemento)* Each member in a set.

What It Means For You — Lesson 3-2

A function model guarantees you that for any input value, you will get a unique output value.

EXAMPLE

$y = x^2$

One output for every input: When −2 is input, the output is always 4.

Relationship is a function

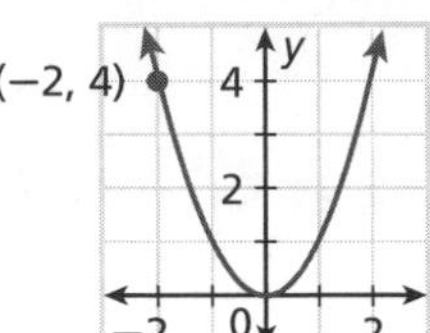

NON-EXAMPLE

$y^2 = x$

Two outputs for every input but 0: When 4 is input, the output can be −2 or 2.

Relationship is NOT a function

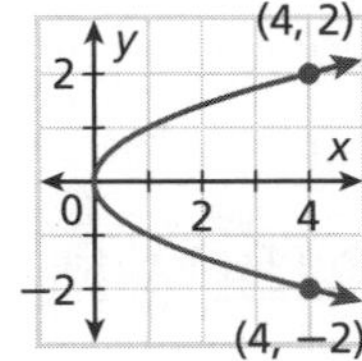

COMMON CORE **CC.9-12.F.IF.4**

For a function that models a relationship between two quantities, interpret key features of graphs and tables in terms of the quantities, and sketch graphs showing key features given a verbal description of the relationship.

What It Means For You — Lesson 3-1

Learning to interpret a graph enables a deep visual understanding of all sorts of relationships.

EXAMPLE

A group of friends walked to the town market, did some shopping there, then returned home

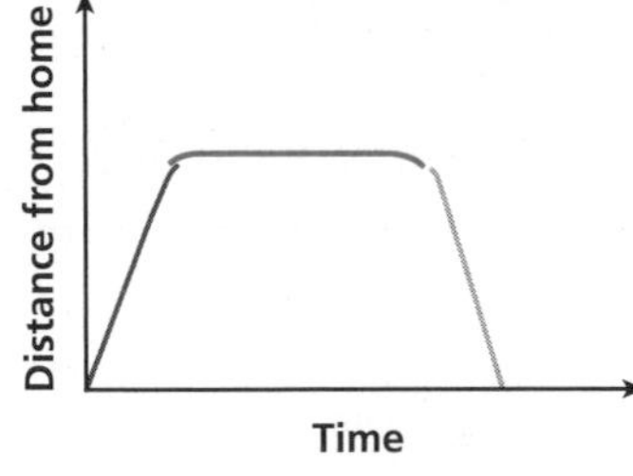

COMMON CORE **CC.9-12.F.IF.2**

Use function notation, evaluate functions for inputs in their domains, and interpret statements that use function notation in terms of a context.

Key Vocabulary

function notation *(notación de función)* If x is the independent variable and y is the dependent variable, then the function notation for y is $f(x)$, read "f of x," where f names the function.

What It Means For You

Lessons 3-2, 3-3, 3-4

Function notation keeps the input and output in a relationship clearly identified.

EXAMPLE

An account with a balance of \$800 has \$40 withdrawn weekly. The function $f(w) = 800 - 40w$ gives the balance after w weeks.

Input, w	1	2	3
Output, *f*(*w*)	$800 - 40(1)$ $= \$760$	$800 - 40(2)$ $= \$720$	$800 - 40(3)$ $= \$680$

COMMON CORE **CC.9-12.S.ID.6**

Represent data on two quantitative variables on a scatter plot, and describe how the variables are related.

Key Vocabulary

scatter plot *(diagrama de dispersion)* A graph with points plotted to show a possible relationship between two sets of data.

What It Means For You

Lesson 3-5

You can graph ordered pairs of data on a scatter plot to help you identify any pattern in the relationship between the data sets.

EXAMPLE

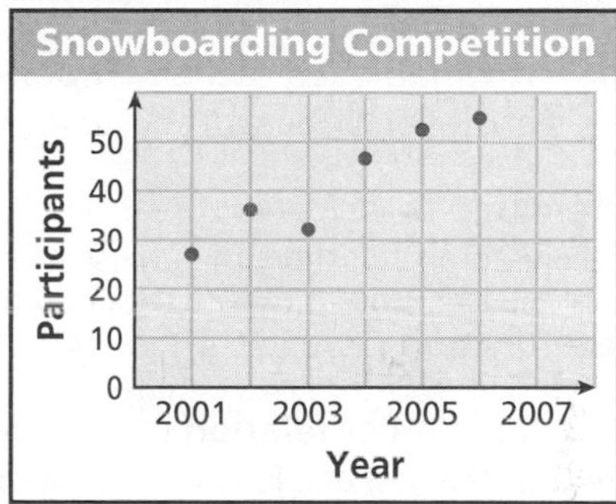

Participation in the snowboarding competition generally increased during the years shown.

Key Vocabulary

arithmetic sequence *(sucesión aritmética)* A sequence whose successive terms differ by the same nonzero number d, called the *common difference*.

common difference *(diferencia común)* In an arithmetic sequence, the nonzero constant difference of any term and the previous term.

correlation *(correlación)* A measure of the strength and direction of the relationship between two variables or data sets.

correlation coefficient *(coeficiente de correlación)* A number r, where $-1 \leq r \leq 1$, that describes how closely the points in a scatter plot cluster around the least-squares line.

dependent variable *(variable dependiente)* The output of a function; a variable whose value depends on the value of the input, or independent variable.

domain *(dominio)* The set of all first coordinates (or x-values) of a relation or function.

element *(elemento)* Each member in a set.

function *(función)* A relation in which every domain value is paired with exactly one range value.

function notation *(notación de función)* If x is the independent variable and y is the dependent variable, then the function notation for y is $f(x)$, read "f of x," where f names the function.

function rule *(regla de función)* An algebraic expression that defines a function.

independent variable *(variable independiente)* The input of a function; a variable whose value determines the value of the output, or dependent variable.

inverse function *(función inversa)* The function that results from exchanging the input and output values of a one-to-one function. The inverse of $f(x)$ is denoted $f^{-1}(x)$.

piecewise function *(función a trozos)* A function that is a combination of one or more functions.

range of a function or relation *(rango de una función o relación)* The set of all second coordinates (or y-values) of a function or relation.

recursive formula *(fórmula recurrente)* A formula for a sequence in which one or more previous terms are used to generate the next term.

scatter plot *(diagrama de dispersion)* A graph with points plotted to show a possible relationship between two sets of data.

sequence *(sucesión)* A list of numbers that often form a pattern.

step function *(función escalón)* A piecewise function that is constant over each interval in its domain.

term of a sequence *(término de una sucesión)* An element or number in the sequence.

Name ______________________ Class ______________ Date ________

3-1

Graphing Relationships
Going Deeper

Essential question: *How can you describe a relationship given a graph and sketch a graph given a description?*

Video Tutor

CC.9-12.F.IF.4

1 EXPLORE Interpreting Graphs

The outside temperature varies throughout the day. The graph shows the outside temperature for a day at one location from midnight to midnight.

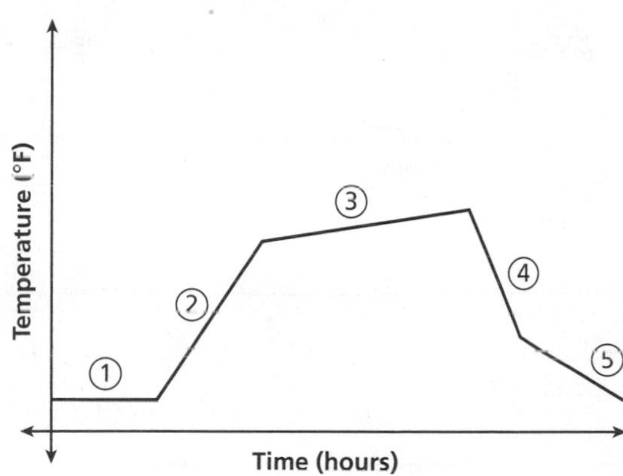

A Segment 1 shows that the temperature from midnight to sunrise stayed constant. Describe what Segment 2 shows.

____

B Based on the time frame, give a possible explanation for the change in temperature represented by Segment 2.

____

C Which segments of the graph show decreasing temperatures? Give a possible explanation.

____

REFLECT

1a. Explain how the slope of each segment of the graph is related to whether the temperature increases or decreases.

____

____

____

____

CC.9–12.F.IF.4

2 EXPLORE Match Graphs to Situations

On three days in September, Atlanta received the same amount of rainfall.

- On September 8, it rained very hard during the morning, but then rained less and less as the day went on.
- On September 19, it rained steadily all day.
- On September 27, it rained lightly during the morning, but then rained heavily for the rest of the day.

Match each day's rain with the correct graph.

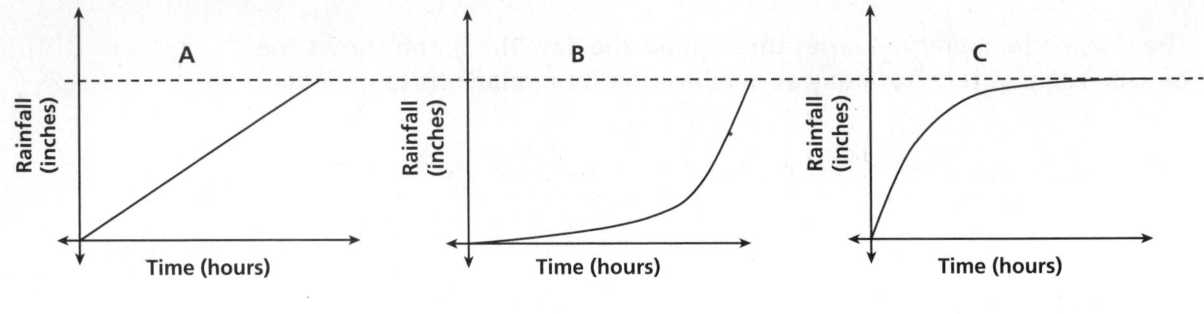

_______________ _______________ _______________

A Describe the rainfall represented by Graph A.

____

B Describe the rainfall represented by Graph B.

____

____

C Describe the rainfall represented by Graph C.

____

____

D Determine which graph represents each day's rainfall and write the dates under the appropriate graphs.

REFLECT

2a. Could a graph of rainfall throughout a day ever slant downward from left to right? Explain.

____

____

____

3 EXPLORE Sketching a Graph for a Situation

The pool in a community park is being filled for the summer. A water truck arrives early in the morning, but no water is put from it into the pool for one hour because a small repair must be made to the pool first. The spigot on the water truck is then opened partially to add water gradually to the pool during the next two hours.

A Sketch a graph showing the height of the water in the pool over the first three hours that the water truck is at the pool.

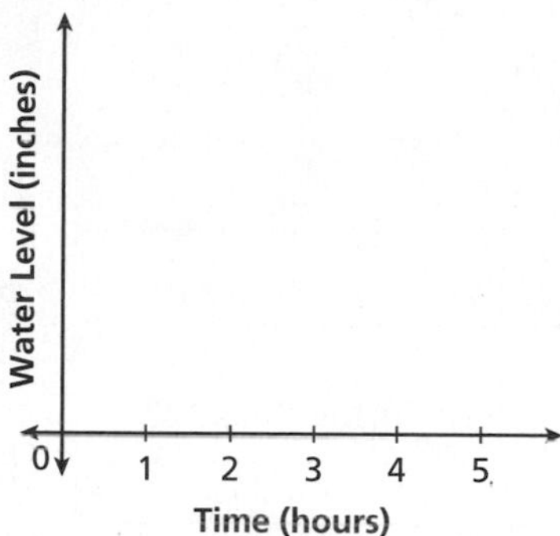

B The workers determine that the repair they made to the pool is working, so they completely open the spigot on the water truck to continue filling the pool. How do you think this will affect the water level in the pool?

____

C Considering your answer to **B**, sketch a graph showing the height of the water in the pool during the first six hours that the water truck is at the pool.

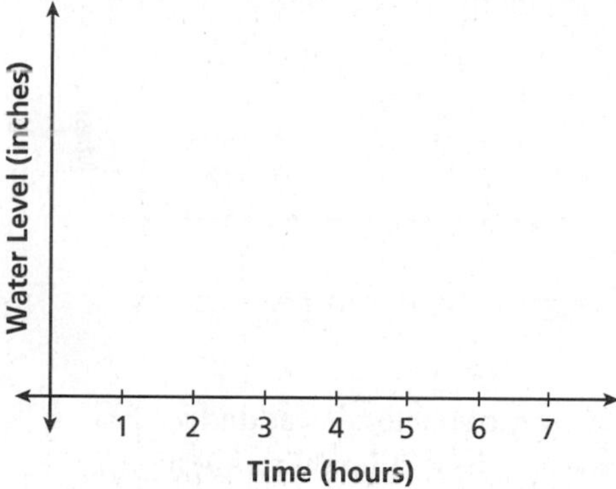

REFLECT

3a. Suppose a second water truck arrived at the end of 4 hours to also add water to the pool. How do you think this would affect the water level of the pool? How would it affect the water level if the second truck were the same type and size as the first truck?

____

____

3b. How would your answer to **3a** affect the graph?

____

____

PRACTICE

A hot air balloon rises as the air inside it is heated to a temperature greater than that of the surrounding air. During a balloon trip, the pilot controls the height of the balloon by adjusting the burning of propane fuel to change the temperature of the air inside the balloon. The graph shows the height of a balloon over time.

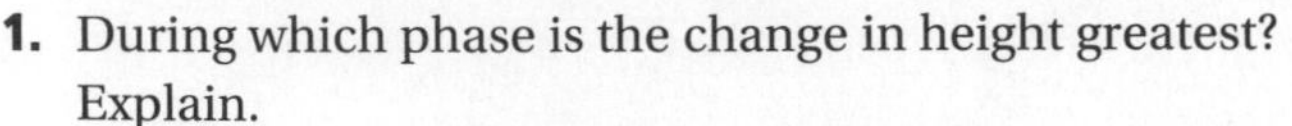

1. During which phase is the change in height greatest? Explain.

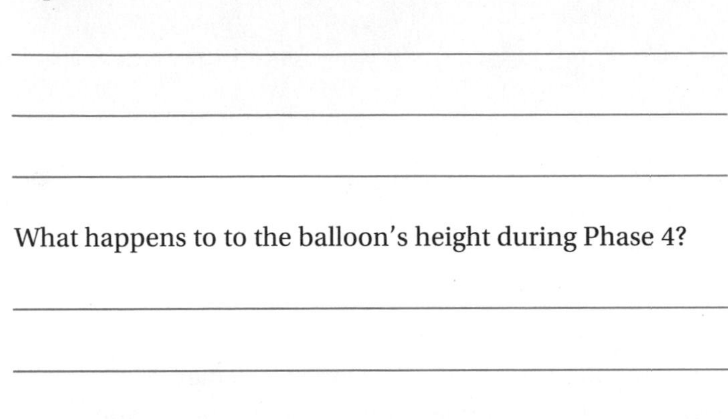

2. What happens to to the balloon's height during Phase 4?

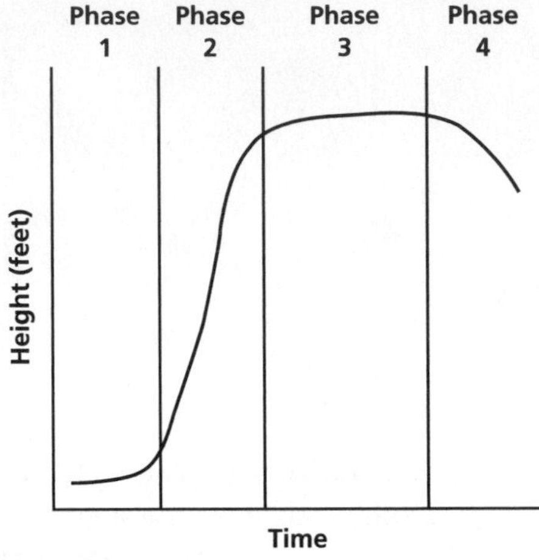

Scientists in a lab are conducting an experiment on a bacteria colony that causes its mass to fluctuate. The graph describes the changes in the colony's mass over time.

3. What happened to the bacteria colony's mass before time *t*?

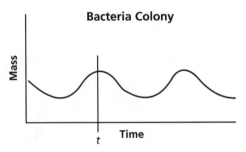

Bacteria Colony

Mass

Time

t

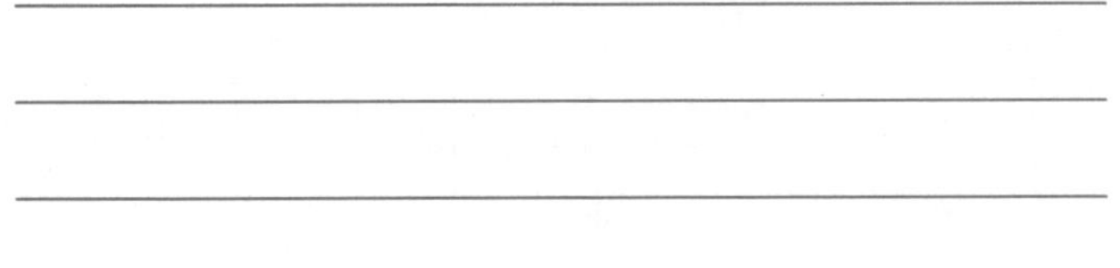

4. Suppose at time *t*, a second colony of bacteria is added to the first. Draw a new graph to show how this action might affect the mass of the bacteria colony after time *t*.

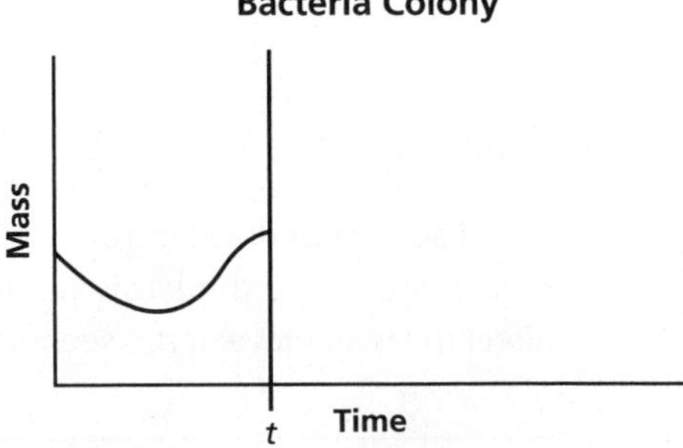

5. Suppose at some point after time *t*, scientists add a substance to the colony that destroys some of the bacteria. Describe how your graph from problem **4** might change.

Name________________________ Class______________ Date__________ 3-1

Additional Practice

Choose the graph that best represents each situation.

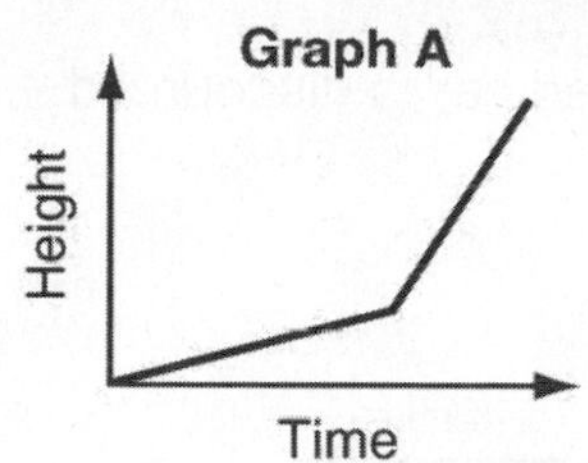

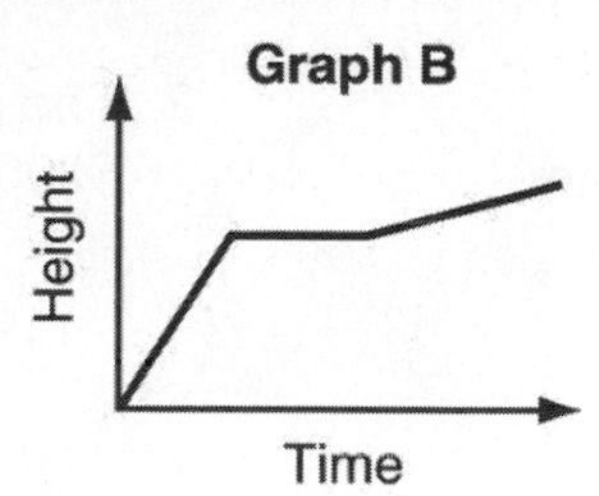

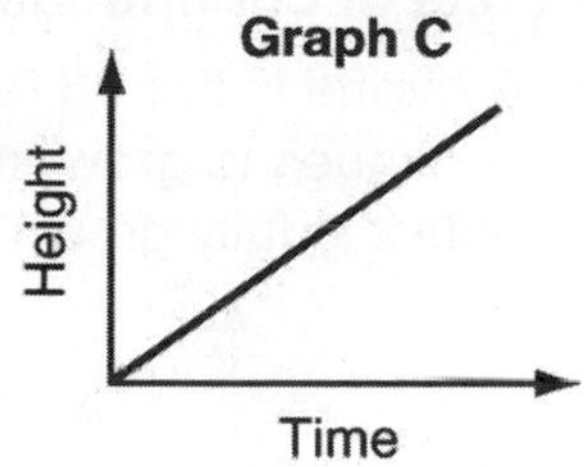

1. A tomato plant grows taller at a steady pace. ____________________

2. A tomato plant grows quickly at first, remains a constant height during a dry spell, then grows at a steady pace. ____________________

3. A tomato plant grows at a slow pace, then grows rapidly with more sun and water. ____________________

4. Lora has $15 to spend on movie rentals for the week. Each rental costs $3. Sketch a graph to show how much money she might spend on movies in a week. Tell whether the graph is continuous or discrete.

____

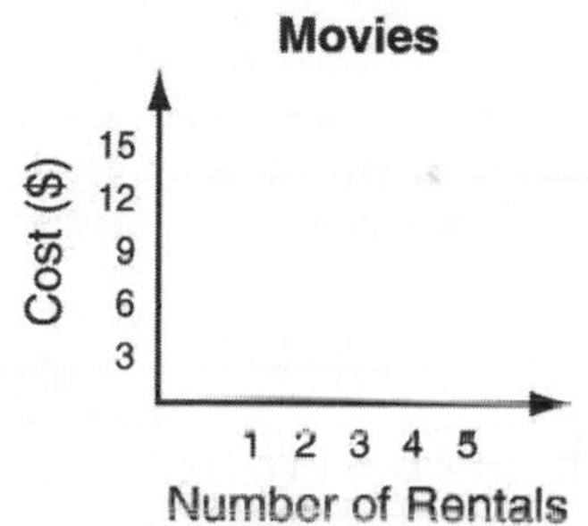

Write a possible situation for each graph.

5.

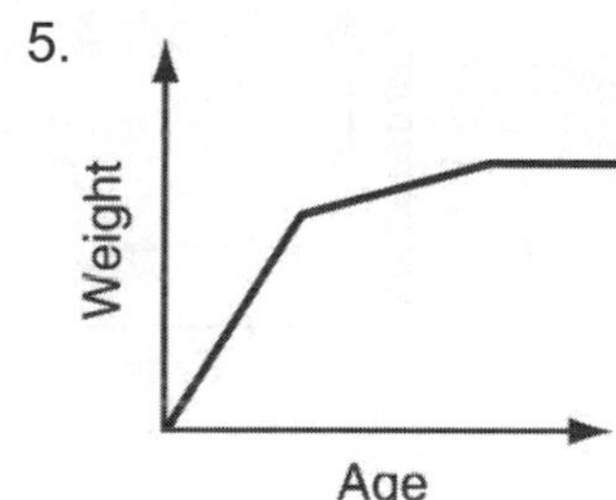

____

____

____

____

6.

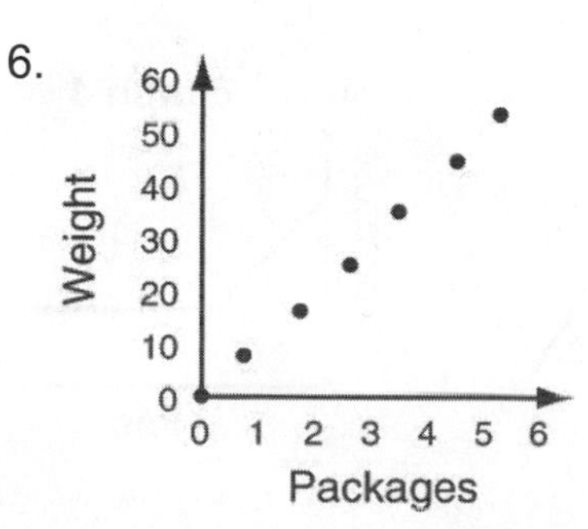

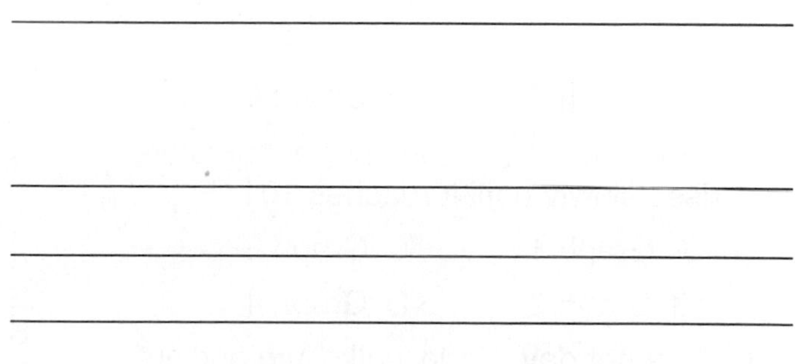

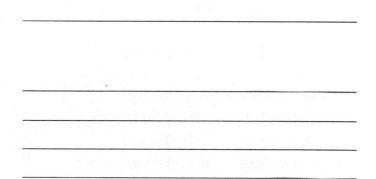

Problem Solving

Sketch a graph for the given situation. Tell whether the graph is discrete or continuous.

1. A giraffe is born 6 feet tall and continues to grow at a steady rate until it is fully grown.

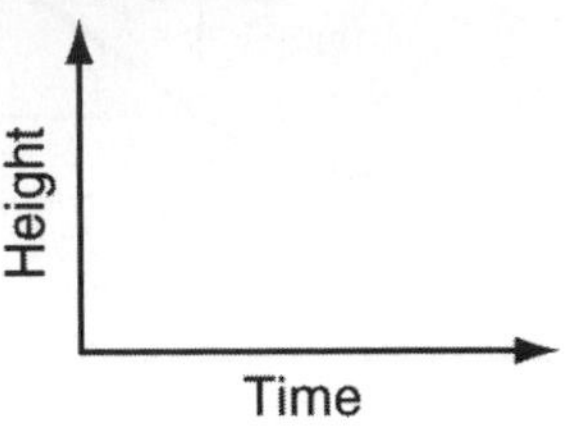

____

2. The price of a used car is discounted $200 each week.

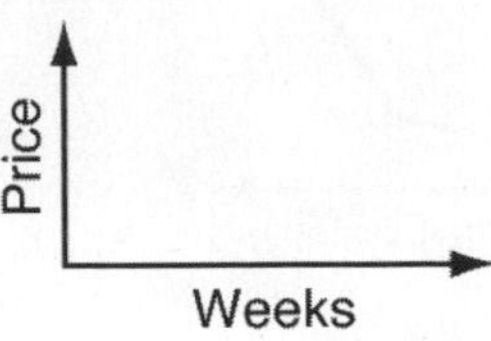

____

3. A city planner buys more buses as the population of her city grows.

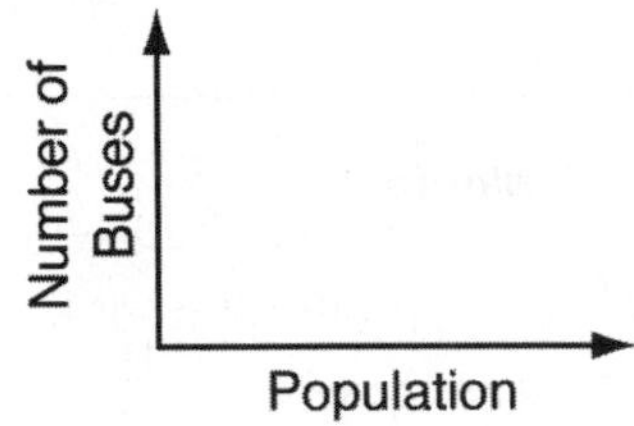

____

4. Joseph is sky-diving. At first, he is free-falling rapidly and then he releases his parachute to slow his descent until he reaches the ground.

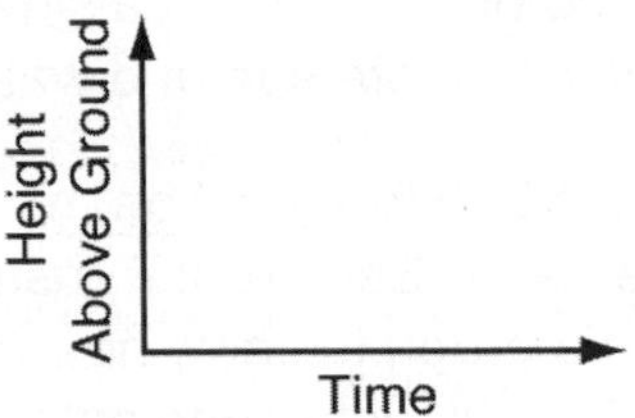

____

Choose the graph that best represents the situation.

5. Rebekah turns on the oven and sets it to 300 °F. She bakes a tray of cookies and then turns the oven off.

   A Graph 1 C Graph 3
   B Graph 2 D Graph 4

6. Leon puts ice cubes in his soup to cool it down before eating it.

   F Graph 1 H Graph 3
   G Graph 2 J Graph 4

7. Barlee has the flu and her temperature rises slowly until it reaches 101 °F.

   A Graph 1 C Graph 3
   B Graph 2 D Graph 4

8. On a hot day, Karin walks into and out of an air-conditioned building.

   F Graph 1 H Graph 3
   G Graph 2 J Graph 4

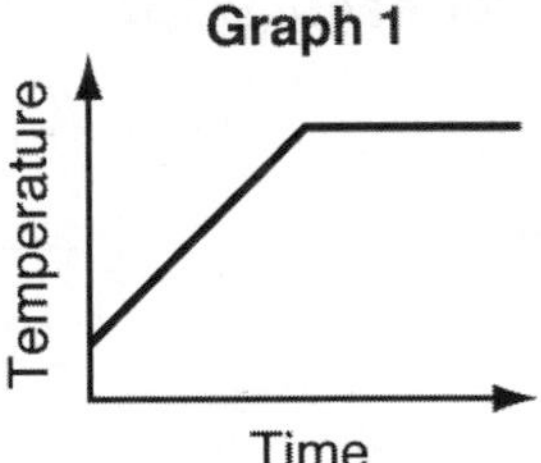

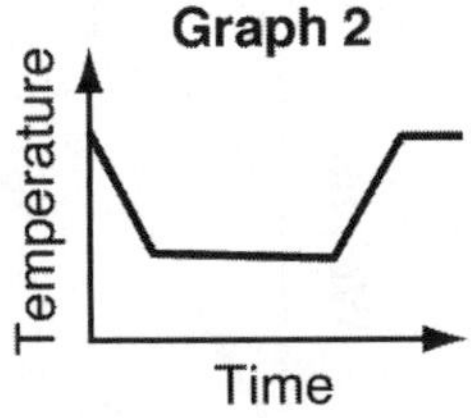

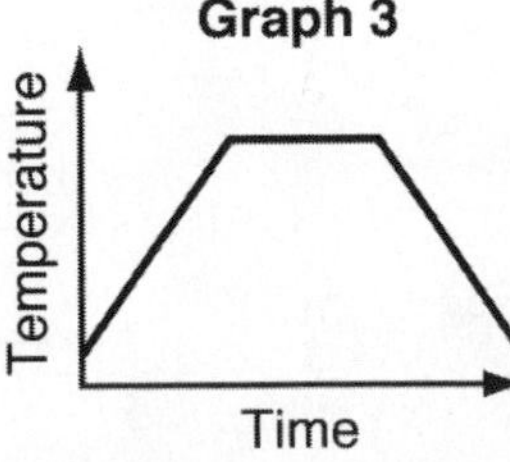

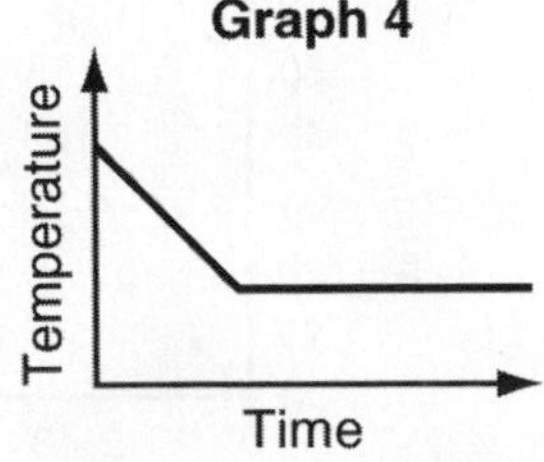

Name________________________ Class________________ Date__________

3-2

Relations and Functions

Going Deeper

Essential question: *How do you represent functions?*

Video Tutor

CC.9–12.F.IF.1

1 ENGAGE Understanding Functions

A *set* is a collection of items called *elements.* A **function** pairs each element in one set, called the **domain**, with exactly one element in a second set, called the **range**. For example, the function below pairs each element in the domain with its square.

Domain		Range
0	→	0
1	→	1
2	→	4
3	→	9
4	→	16

A function can be described using **function notation**. The function f assigns the *output* value $f(x)$ in the range to the corresponding *input* value x from the domain. The notation $f(x)$ is read as "f of x." (It does not indicate the product "f times x.") For the function shown above, $f(3) = 9$.

REFLECT

1a. The domain of the function can be written using *set notation* as $\{0, 1, 2, 3, 4\}$. Write the range of the function using set notation.

____

1b. Tell how to read the statement $f(4) = 16$. Then interpret what it means in terms of input and output values.

____

1c. Suppose the 3 were paired with the 4 instead of the 9. Would the pairing of the two sets still be a function? Why or why not?

____

1d. Suppose the 3 were paired with the 4 and the 9. Would the pairing of the two sets still be a function? Why or why not?

____

1e. If you pair each month with all the possible numbers of days in the month, will you get a function? Why or why not?

____

____

Functions are often used to describe a relationship between two variables. The **independent variable** represents an input value of the function and the **dependent variable** represents an output value.

An algebraic expression that defines a function is a **function rule**. For example, x^2 is the function rule for the squaring function $f(x) = x^2$. If you know a value for the independent variable, you can use a function rule to find the corresponding value for the dependent variable.

CC.9–12.F.IF.2

2 EXAMPLE Representing Discrete Linear Functions

The cost of sending m text messages at \$0.25 per message can be represented by the function $C(m) = 0.25m$.

A Complete the table for the given domain values. Write the results as ordered pairs in the form (independent variable, dependent variable).

Independent variable, m	Dependent variable, $C(m) = 0.25m$	$(m, C(m))$
0	$0.25(0) = 0$	(0, 0)
1		
2		
3		
4		

B Choose a beginning, an end, and a scale for the vertical axis.

C Graph the function by plotting the ordered pairs. The independent variable goes on the horizontal axis and the dependent variable on the vertical axis. Use scales that will make it easy to read points. Label the graph.

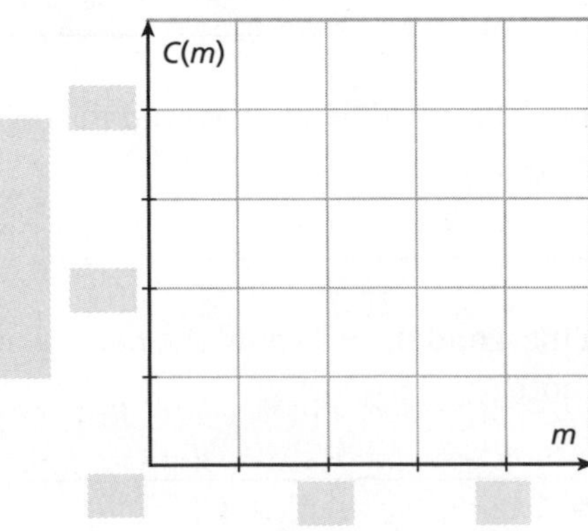

REFLECT

2a. Use function notation to represent the cost of sending 15 text messages. Evaluate the function for that value. Include units.

2b. Suppose that the domain of the function is not limited as in the Example. Describe a reasonable domain of the function.

2c. Suppose that the domain of the function is not limited as in the Example. Describe a reasonable range of the function.

2d. Is the independent variable represented by the *horizontal axis* or the *vertical axis*? Why does this make sense?

2e. Would it make sense to connect the points on the graph with a line? Why or why not?

2f. The figure below shows a representation of the function rule. Explain what is being shown in the context of the situation.

Input		Output
1 →	Rule: $C(m) = 0.25m$	→ 0.25

2g. Suppose the cost per text message were \$0.20 instead of \$0.25. Then the cost of sending m text messages could be represented by the function $C(m) = 0.2m$. Describe a reasonable domain and range for this function.

CC.9–12.F.IF.5

3 EXAMPLE Representing Discrete Nonlinear Functions

Ben wants to tile part of a floor with 36 square tiles. The tiles come in whole-number side lengths from 2 to 6 inches. If s is the side length of a tile, the area that he can cover is $A(s) = 36s^2$.

A Identify the domain of the function.

____

B Make a table of values for this domain. Write the results as ordered pairs in the form (independent variable, dependent variable).

Independent variable, s	Dependent variable, $A(s) = 36s^2$	$(s, A(s))$

C Choose a beginning, an end, and a scale for the vertical axis.

____

D Graph the function by plotting the ordered pairs.

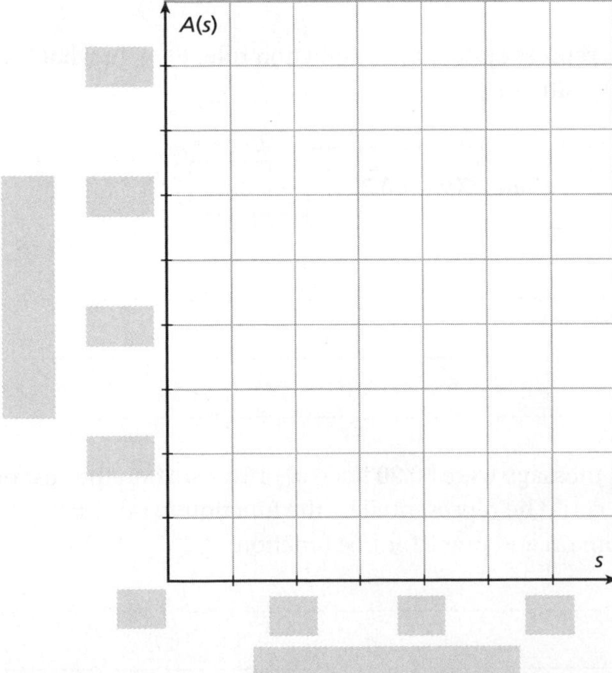

REFLECT

3a. Identify the range of the function.

3b. What does $A(3) = 324$ mean in this context?

3c. Describe another reasonable beginning, end, and scale for the vertical axis. Include units.

3d. Do the points appear to lie in a straight line?

PRACTICE

Tell whether each pairing of numbers describes a function. If so, identify the domain and the range. If not, explain why not.

1. Each whole number from 0 to 9 is paired with its opposite.

2. Each odd number from 3 to 9 is paired with the next greater whole number.

3. The whole numbers from 10 to 12 are paired with their factors.

4. Each even number from 2 to 10 is paired with half the number.

5. $\{(36, 6), (49, 7), (64, 8), (81, 9), (36, -6), (49, -7), (64, -8), (81, -9)\}$

6. $\{(-64, -4), (-27, -3), (-8, -2), (-1, -1), (0, 0), (1, 1), (8, 2), (27, 3), (64, 4)\}$

7. Whitley has a \$5 gift card for music downloads. Each song costs \$1 to download. The amount of money left on the card can be represented by the function $M(d) = 5 - d$, where d is the number of songs she has downloaded.

a. Make a table and graph the function.

d	*M*(*d*)	(*d*, *M*(*d*))

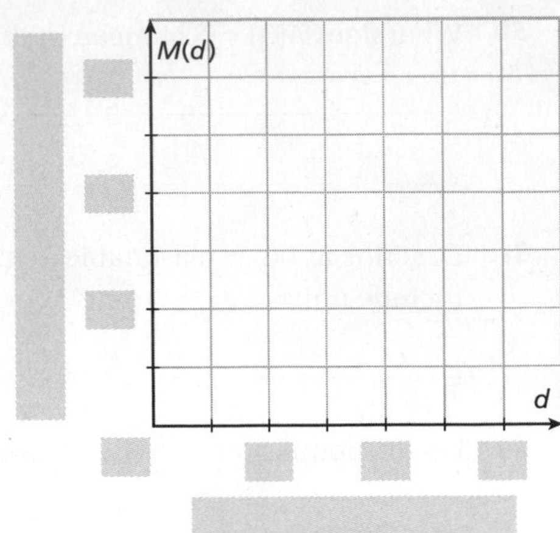

b. Identify the domain and range of the function and the units of the independent and dependent variables.

____

____

8. Ben wants to cover a table that has an area of 864 square inches. The function $T(s) = \frac{864}{s^2}$ gives the number of tiles he needs with side length s. The tiles come in side lengths of 1 in., 4 in., 6 in., and 12 in.

a. Make a table and graph the function.

s	*T*(*s*)	(*s*, *T*(*s*))

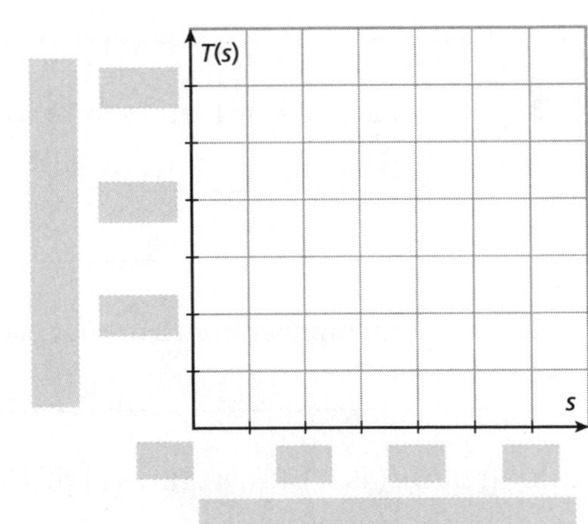

b. Identify the domain and range of the function and the units of the independent and dependent variables.

____

____

Name ______________________ Class ______________ Date __________

Additional Practice

Express each relation as a table, as a graph, and as a mapping diagram.

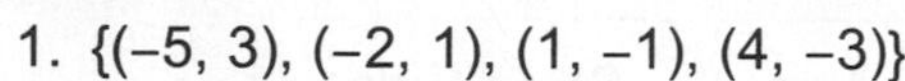

1. {(–5, 3), (–2, 1), (1, –1), (4, –3)}

x	y

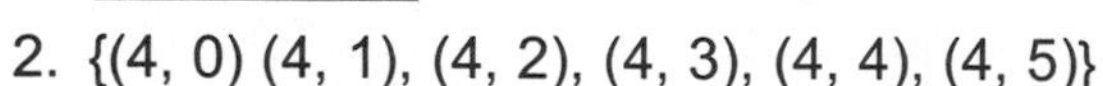

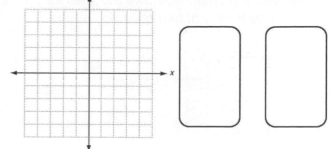

2. {(4, 0) (4, 1), (4, 2), (4, 3), (4, 4), (4, 5)}

x	y

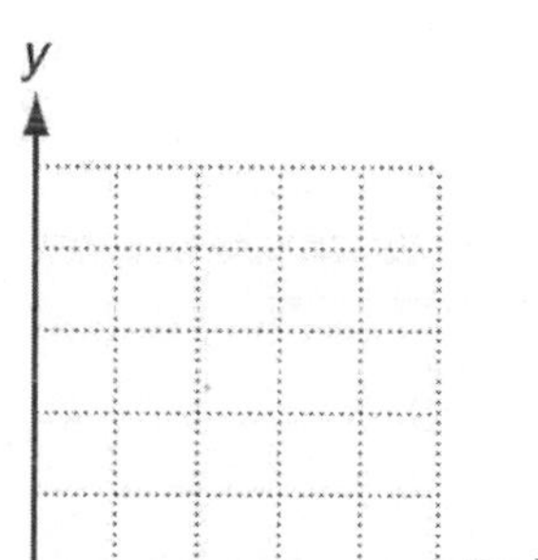

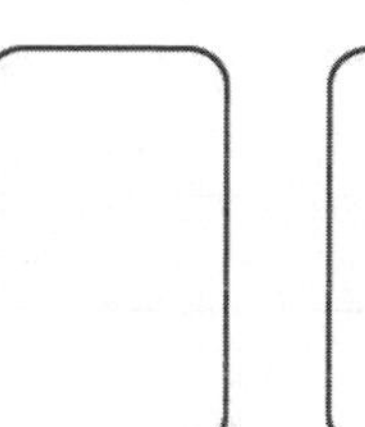

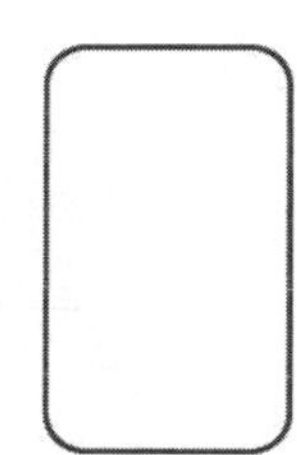

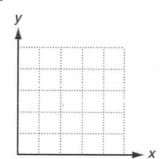

Give the domain and range of each relation. Tell whether the relation is a function. Explain.

3.

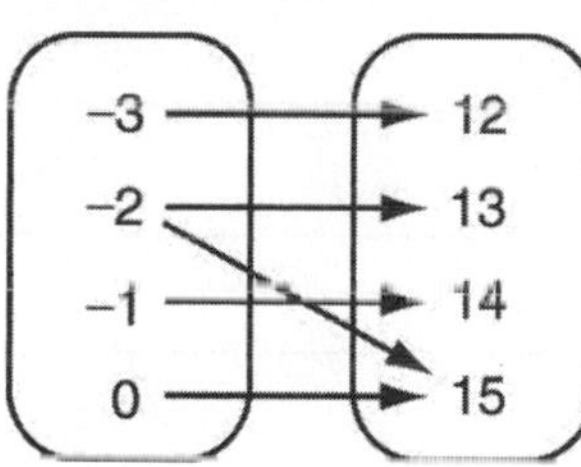

D: ______________

R: ______________

Function? ______________

Explain: ______________

4.

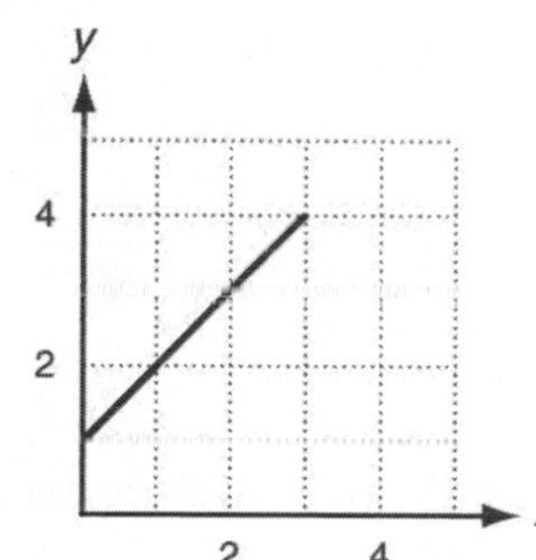

D: ______________

R: ______________

Function? ______________

Explain: ______________

5.

x	y
8	8
6	6
4	4
2	6
0	8

D: ______________

R: ______________

Function? ______________

Explain: ______________

Problem Solving

Give the domain and range of each relation and tell whether it is a function.

1. The mapping diagram shows the ages *x* and grade level *y* of four children.

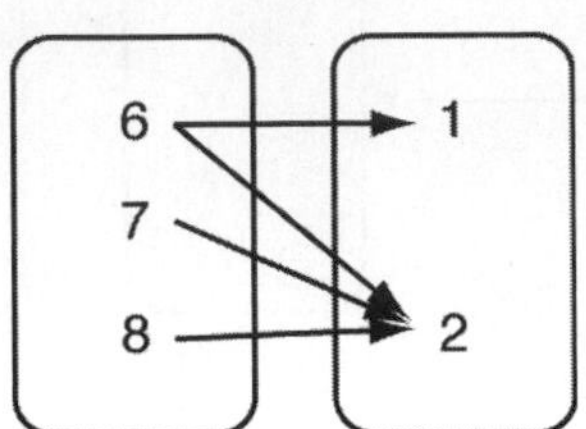

2.

Age *x*	Shoe Size *y*
6	8
9	10
12	10
15	10.5
18	11

3. The list represents the number of cars sold and the bonus received by the salespeople of a car dealership.

   {(1, 50), (2, 50), (3, 100), (4, 150)}

4. A 2-inch-tall plant grows at a rate of 2.5 inches every week for 5 weeks. Let *x* represent the number of weeks and *y* represent the height of the plant.

Use the graph below to answer questions 5–6. A conservation group has been working to increase the population of a herd of Asian elephants. The graph shows the results of their efforts. Select the correct answer.

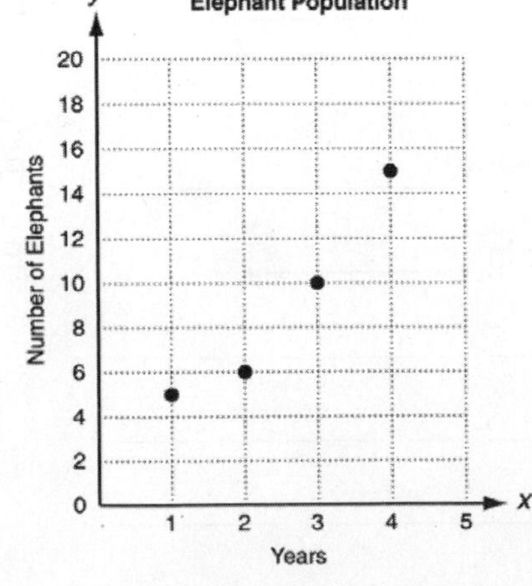

5. Which relation represents the information in the graph?

   A {(1, 4.5), (2, 6), (3, 10), (4, 14.5)}

   B {(1, 5), (2, 6), (3, 10), (4, 15)}

   C {(4.5, 1), (6, 2), (10, 3), (14.5, 4)}

   D {(5, 1), (6, 2), (10, 3), (15, 4)}

6. What is the range of the relation shown in the graph?

   F {0, 1, 2, 3, 4, 5}

   G {1, 2, 3, 4}

   H {4.5, 6, 10, 14.5}

   J {5, 6, 10, 15}

Name ________________ Class ________________ Date ________

3-3

Video Tutor

Writing Functions

Extension: Function Operations and Inverses

Essential question: *How can you use operations to combine functions and how can you find inverses of functions?*

Just as you can perform operations with numbers, you can perform operations with functions. In this lesson you will add and subtract linear functions as well as multiply a linear function by a nonzero constant function. Performing an operation on two functions $f(x)$ and $g(x)$ produces a new function $h(x)$.

CC.9–12.F.BF.1b

1 EXAMPLE Performing Operations with Functions

A **Given $f(x) = 3x - 1$ and $g(x) = -2x + 2$, find $h(x) = f(x) + g(x)$.**

$h(x) = f(x) + g(x)$ — Write the general form of $h(x)$.

$= (3x - 1) + (\quad)$ — Substitute the rules for $f(x)$ and $g(x)$.

$= (3x + \quad) + (-1 + \quad)$ — Collect like terms for adding.

$= \quad + \quad$ — Simplify.

B **Given $f(x) = x + 5$ and $g(x) = 4x - 2$, find $h(x) = f(x) - g(x)$.**

$h(x) = f(x) - g(x)$ — Write the general form of $h(x)$.

$= (x + 5) - (\quad)$ — Substitute the rules for $f(x)$ and $g(x)$.

$= (x - \quad) + (5 - \quad)$ — Collect like terms for subtracting.

$= \quad + \quad$ — Simplify.

C **Given $f(x) = 3$ and $g(x) = \frac{1}{3}x - 2$, find $h(x) = f(x) \cdot g(x)$.**

$h(x) = f(x) \cdot g(x)$ — Write the general form of $h(x)$.

$= \quad \left(\frac{1}{3}x - 2\right)$ — Substitute the rules for $f(x)$ and $g(x)$.

$= \quad - \quad$ — Multiply using the distributive property.

REFLECT

1a. The table shows the values of the sum $f(x) + g(x)$ for several values of x using the functions $f(x)$ and $g(x)$ from part A. Use the rule that you found for $h(x)$ in part A to complete the third column of the table. What do you notice?

____

x	$f(x) + g(x)$	$h(x)$
−2	−7 + 6 = −1	
−1	−4 + 4 = 0	
0	−1 + 2 = 1	
1	2 + 0 = 2	
2	5 + (−2) = 3	

1b. Error Analysis A student wrote the rule for $h(x)$ in part A as $5x + 1$. After letting $x = 0$ and observing that $f(0) + g(0) = -1 + 2 = 1$ and $h(0) = 1$, the student concluded that the rule must be correct. Describe what is incorrect about the student's reasoning, and describe what the student should have done to check the rule for $h(x)$.

____

____

____

Adding Linear Models

For the initial year of a soccer camp, 44 girls and 56 boys enrolled. Each year thereafter, 5 more girls and 8 more boys enrolled in the camp. Let *t* be the time (in years) since the camp opened. Write a rule for each of the following functions:

- **$g(t)$, the number of girls enrolled as a function of time t**
- **$b(t)$, the number of boys enrolled as a function of time t**
- **$T(t)$, the total enrollment as a function of time t**

A For the function $g(t)$, the initial value is ____________ and the rate of change is ____________. So, $g(t) =$ ____________.

B For the function $b(t)$, the initial value is ____________ and the rate of change is ____________. So, $b(t) =$ ____________.

C The total enrollment is the sum of the functions $g(t)$ and $b(t)$.

$T(t) = g(t) + b(t)$	Write the general form of $T(t)$.
$= \square + \square$	Substitute the rules for $g(t)$ and $b(t)$.
$= \square$	Simplify.

REFLECT

2a. Use unit analysis to show that the rule for $g(t)$ makes sense.

____

____

____

CC.9–12.F.BF.1b

3 EXAMPLE Multiplying Linear Models

For the soccer camp in the previous example, the cost per child each year was $200. Let t be the time (in years) since the camp opened. Write a rule for each of the following functions:

- **$C(t)$, the cost per child of the camp as a function of time t**
- **$R(t)$, the revenue generated by the total enrollment as a function of time t**

A For the function $C(t)$, the initial value is ______________ and the rate of change is ______________. So, $C(t) =$ ______________.

B The revenue generated by the total enrollment is the product of the cost function $C(t)$ and the total enrollment function $T(t)$, which was found in the previous example.

$R(t) = C(t) \cdot T(t)$	Write the general form of $R(t)$.
$= \square \cdot (\square)$	Substitute the rules for $C(t)$ and $T(t)$.
$= \square$	Multiply using the distributive property.

REFLECT

3a. Explain why $C(t)$ is a constant function.

____

3b. Use unit analysis to explain why you multiply the cost function $C(t)$ and the enrollment function $T(t)$ to get the revenue function $R(t)$.

____

____

____

3c. What was the initial revenue for the camp? What was the annual rate of change in the revenue?

____

3d. The camp's organizer had initial expenses of $18,000, which increased each year by $2,500. Write a rule for the expenses function $E(t)$. Then write a rule for the profit function $P(t)$ based on the fact that profit is the difference between revenue and expenses.

____

Recall that inverse operations are operations that undo each other. Similarly, the **inverse of a function** is another function that undoes everything that the original function does.

CC.9–12.F.BF.4a

4 EXPLORE Using Inverse Operations to Find Inverse Functions

Find the inverse of $f(x) = 2x + 1$ using inverse operations.

A List the operations that the function performs on an input value x in the order that the function performs them. Illustrate these steps using $x = 3$.

x ⟶ Multiply by 2. ⟶ ____________

3 ⟶ $2 \cdot 3 = 6$ ⟶ ____________

B List the *inverse operations* in the *reverse order*. Illustrate these steps using $x = 7$.

x ⟶ Subtract 1. ⟶ ____________

7 ⟶ $7 - 1 = 6$ ⟶ ____________

C Write a rule for the function $g(x)$ that performs the inverse operations in the reverse order. Check your rule by finding $g(7)$.

$g(x) = \frac{x - \square}{\square}$, so $g(7) = \frac{7 - \square}{\square} = \square$

REFLECT

4a. The first table at the right shows some input-output pairs for the function f. The outputs of f are then listed as inputs for the function g in the second table. Complete the second table.

x	$f(x)$
−2	−3
0	1
2	5

x	$g(x)$
−3	
1	
5	

4b. The function g is the inverse of the function f. If $f(a) = b$, then what is $g(b)$?

____

4c. Is it reasonable to describe f as the inverse of g? Explain.

____

To find the rule for the inverse of a linear function f, let $y = f(x)$ and solve for x in terms of y. Whatever sequence of operations f performs on x to obtain y, the process of solving for x will introduce the inverse operations in the reverse order. You now have a function g where $g(y) = x$. Since x is commonly used as a function's input variable and y as its output variable, as a final step switch x and y to obtain $g(x) = y$.

CC.9–12.F.BF.4a

5 EXAMPLE Finding the Inverse by Solving $y = f(x)$ for x

Find the inverse of $f(x) = \frac{1}{2}x - 1$.

A Let $y = f(x)$. Solve for x in terms of y.

$y = \square$ Write $y = f(x)$.

$y + \square = \square$ Add 1 to both sides.

$\square\left(y + \square\right) = \square$ Multiply both sides by 2.

$\square y + \square = \square$ Distribute.

B Switch x and y and then write the rule for the inverse function g.

$\square x + \square = \square$ Switch x and y.

The inverse of $f(x) = \frac{1}{2}x - 1$ is $g(x) =$ ____________.

REFLECT

5a. Find $f(4)$. Then use this value as the input x for $g(x)$. What output value do you get? Why is this expected?

____

____

5b. When solving $y = f(x)$ for x, you multiplied both sides by 2 instead of dividing both sides by $\frac{1}{2}$. In other words, instead of using an *inverse operation*, you used a *multiplicative inverse*. Why is this acceptable?

____

____

5c. When you switch x and y to find the inverse function, are you solving the function for y? Why or why not?

____

____

5d. The graph of $f(x) = \frac{1}{2}x - 1$ is shown. Graph the inverse function g. Also graph $y = x$ as a dashed line. How are the graphs of f and g related to the line $y = x$?

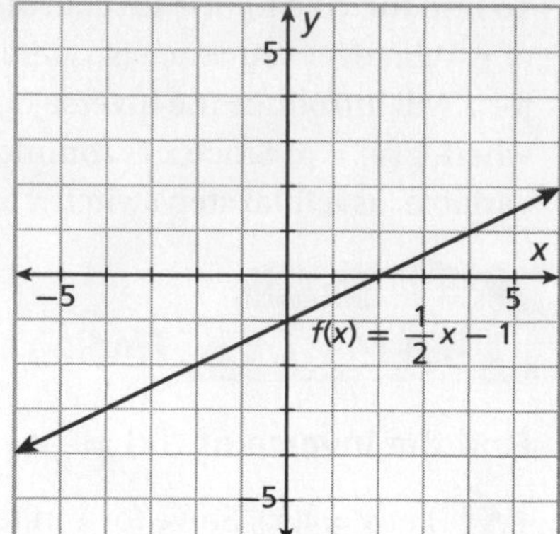

____

____

5e. The point (4, 1) is on the graph of f. What is the corresponding point on the graph of g? In general, if (a, b) is a point on the graph of f, what is the corresponding point on the graph of g?

____

CC.9–12.F.BF.4a

6 EXAMPLE Finding Inverses of Real-World Functions

The function $A(r) = 2r + 30$ gives the total amount A that you will spend at an amusement park if you spend \$30 on admission and food and you go on r rides that cost \$2 each. Find the inverse function.

$A = 2r + 30$	Write the function using A for $A(r)$.
$A - \square = \square$	Subtract 30 from both sides.
$\frac{A - \square}{\square} = r$	Divide both sides by 2.

REFLECT

6a. Write the inverse function using function notation.

____

6b. Explain how the inverse function would be useful if you have a fixed amount of money that you can spend at the amusement park.

____

____

____

6c. When finding the inverse of a real-world function, why shouldn't you switch the variables as the final step?

____

____

PRACTICE

1. Given $f(x) = -2x$ and $g(x) = 4x - 8$, find $h(x) = f(x) + g(x)$.

2. Given $f(x) = 3x - 5$ and $g(x) = -2x + 1$, find $h(x) = f(x) - g(x)$.

3. Given $f(x) = -2$ and $g(x) = 5x - 6$, find $h(x) = f(x) \cdot g(x)$.

4. Given $f(x) = 4$, $g(x) = x + 1$, and $h(x) = x$, find $j(x) = f(x) \cdot [g(x) + h(x)]$.

5. To raise funds, a club is publishing and selling a calendar. The club has sold \$500 in advertising and will sell copies of the calendar for \$20 each. The cost of printing each calendar is \$6. Let c be the number of calendars to be printed and sold.

   a. Write a rule for the function $R(c)$, which gives the revenue generated by the sale of the calendars.

   b. Write a rule for the function $E(c)$, which gives the expense of printing the calendars.

   c. Describe how the function $P(c)$, which gives the club's profit from the sale of the calendars, is related to $R(c)$ and $E(c)$. Then write a rule for $P(c)$.

6. The five winners of a radio station contest will spend a day at an amusement park with all expenses paid. The per-person admission cost is \$10, and each person can spend \$20 on food. The radio station will pay for all rides, which cost \$2 each. Assume that each person takes the same number r of rides.

   a. Write a rule for the function $C(r)$, which gives the cost per person.

   b. Write a rule for the function $P(r)$, which gives the number of people.

   c. Describe how the function $T(r)$, which gives the radio station's total cost, is related to $C(r)$ and $P(r)$. Then write a rule for $T(r)$.

Find the inverse $g(x)$ of each function.

7. $f(x) = x - 1$

8. $f(x) = -x + 4$

9. $f(x) = 2x - 3$

10. $f(x) = \frac{2}{3}x + 6$

11. $f(x) = 3x - \frac{3}{4}$

12. $f(x) = -\frac{5}{2}x - \frac{15}{2}$

13. The formula to convert a temperature F measured in degrees Fahrenheit to a temperature C measured in degrees Celsius is $C = \frac{9}{5}(F - 32)$. You can think of this formula as function $C(F)$. Find the inverse function $F(C)$ and describe what it does.

14. A cylindrical candle 10 inches tall burns at rate of 0.5 inch per hour.

a. Write a rule for the function $h(t)$, the height (in inches) of the candle at time t (in hours since the candle was lit). State the domain and range of the function.

b. Find the inverse function $t(h)$. State the domain and range of the function.

c. Explain how the inverse function is useful.

15. Prove that the inverse of a non-constant linear function is another non-constant linear function by starting with the general linear function $f(x) = mx + b$ where $m \neq 0$ and showing that the inverse function $g(x)$ is also linear. Identify the slope and y-intercept of the graph of $g(x)$.

16. Can a constant function have an inverse function? Why or why not?

Name____________________ Class__________ Date__________

Additional Practice

For each pair of functions, find $f(x) + g(x)$ and $f(x) - g(x)$.

1. $f(x) = 3x + 2$, $g(x) = 2x + 5$

2. $f(x) = 4x - 1$, $g(x) = 3x - 4$

3. $f(x) = -5x + 3$, $g(x) = 2x - 4$

4. $f(x) = 3x - 4$, $g(x) = -2x + 3$

For each pair of functions, find $f(x) \bullet g(x)$.

5. $f(x) = -x + 7$, $g(x) = -2$

6. $f(x) = -5$, $g(x) = 2x - 7$

Find the inverse of the function.

7. $f(x) = 3x + 9$

8. $f(x) = 5x - 2$

9. $f(x) = -x + 2$

10. $f(x) = -4x + 3$

11. $f(x) = 0.5x - 2$

12. $f(x) = -0.25x + 6$

Problem Solving

Write the correct answer.

1. Over time, the enrollment at one high school in a city can be modeled by $f(t) = 32t + 1255$. The enrollment at the city's other high school can be modeled by $g(t) = 27t + 1380$. Write a rule for the total enrollment as a function of time.

____

2. Use the functions from Problem 1 to find the difference in the enrollments between the two high schools. Write the answer using two different functions.

____

____

3. The function $f(x) = 50x + 6500$ represents the amount of money in a bank account over time. The function $g(x) = -25x + 9300$ represents the amount of money in another account over time. Write a rule for the total amount of money in the two accounts over time.

____

4. Use the functions from Problem 3 to find the difference in the amounts of money between the two accounts. Write the answer using two different functions.

____

____

Select the best answer.

5. The enrollment at a summer camp over time can be represented by $f(x) = 24x + 465$. The cost to attend the camp is \$500 per summer. Write a rule for the amount of money the camp makes over time.

   A $g(x) = 24x + 965$

   B $g(x) = 24x + 232{,}500$

   C $g(x) = 12{,}000x + 465$

   D $g(x) = 12{,}000x + 232{,}500$

6. Find the inverse of the function $f(x) = 0.25x + 12$.

   F $g(x) = -0.25x - 12$

   G $g(x) = -4x - 12$

   H $g(x) = 4x - 48$

   J $g(x) = 4x + 48$

7. Four friends go to an amusement arcade. The cost to get in is \$5 per person and the cost of each game is \$2. The cost per person can be represented by the function $c(x) = 2x + 5$. Write a rule for the total cost for the four friends if they all play the same number of games.

   A $T(x) = 5x + 8$

   B $T(x) = 8x + 20$

   C $T(x) = 2x + 20$

   D $T(x) = 20x + 5$

8. Find the inverse of the function $f(x) = -\frac{2}{3}x - 18$.

   F $g(x) = \frac{3}{2}x + 27$

   G $g(x) = -\frac{3}{2}x + 27$

   H $g(x) = -\frac{3}{2}x - 27$

   J $g(x) = \frac{3}{2}x - 27$

Name________________________ Class________________ Date__________

3-4

Video Tutor

Graphing Functions

Extension: Piecewise Functions

Essential question: *How are piecewise functions and their graphs different from other functions?*

A **piecewise function** has different rules for different parts of its domain. The **greatest integer function** is a piecewise function whose rule is denoted by $[\![x]\!]$, which represents the greatest integer less than or equal to x. To evaluate a piecewise function for a given value of x, substitute the value of x into the rule for the part of the domain that includes x.

CC.9–12.F.IF.2

1 EXAMPLE Evaluating Piecewise Functions

A **Find $f(-3)$, $f(-0.2)$, $f(0)$, and $f(2)$ for $f(x) = \begin{cases} -x & \text{if } x < 0 \\ x + 1 & \text{if } x \geq 0 \end{cases}$.**

$-3 < 0$, so use the rule $f(x) = -x$: $f(-3) = -(-3) =$ ________

$-0.2 < 0$, so use the rule ____________: $f(-0.2) = -(-0.2) =$ ________

$0 \geq 0$, so use the rule $f(x) = x + 1$: $f(0) = 0 + 1 =$ ________

$2 \geq 0$, so use the rule ____________: $f(2) =$ ________ $=$ ________

B **Find $f(-3)$, $f(-2.9)$, $f(0.7)$, and $f(1.06)$ for $f(x) = [\![x]\!]$.**

The greatest integer function $f(x) = [\![x]\!]$ can also be written as shown below. Complete the rules for the function before evaluating it.

$$f(x) = \begin{cases} \vdots & \\ -3 & \text{if } -3 \leq x < -2 \\ \square & \text{if } -2 \leq x < -1 \\ -1 & \text{if } \square \leq x < \square \\ \square & \text{if } 0 \leq x < 1 \\ 1 & \text{if } \square \leq x < \square \\ 2 & \text{if } \square \leq x < \square \\ \vdots & \end{cases}$$

← For any number x that is less than -2 and greater than or equal to -3, the greatest of the integers less than or equal to x is -3.

-3 is in the interval $-3 \leq x < -2$, so $f(-3) = -3$.

-2.9 is in the interval $-3 \leq x < -2$, so $f(-2.9) =$ ____________.

0.7 is in the interval ____________, so $f(0.7) =$ ____________.

1.06 is in the interval ____________, so $f(1.06) =$ ____________.

REFLECT

1a. Why should the parts of the domain of a piecewise function $f(x)$ have no common x-values?

1b. For positive numbers, how is applying the greatest integer function different from the method of rounding to the nearest whole number?

CC.9–12.F.IF.7b

2 EXAMPLE Graphing Piecewise Functions

Graph each function.

A $f(x) = \begin{cases} -x & \text{if } x < 0 \\ x + 1 & \text{if } x \geq 0 \end{cases}$

Complete the table. Use the values to help you complete the graph. Extend the pattern to cover the entire domain on the grid.

x	−3	−2	−1	−0.9	−0.1
f(x)	3	2		0.9	

x	0	0.1	0.9	1	2
f(x)	1	1.1			3

The transition from one rule, $-x$, to the other, $x + 1$, occurs at $x = 0$. Show an open dot at (0, 0) because the point is not part of the graph. Show a closed dot at (0, 1) because the point is part of the graph.

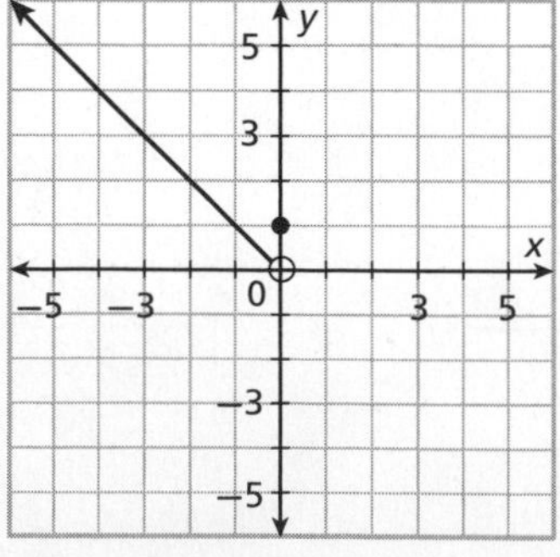

B $f(x) = [\![x]\!]$

Complete the table. Use the values to help you complete the graph. Extend the pattern to cover the entire domain on the grid.

x	−4	−3.9	−3.1	−3	−2.9
f(x)	−4	−4		−3	

x	−2.1	−2	−1.5	−1	0
f(x)		−2			0

x	1	1.5	2	3	4
f(x)					4

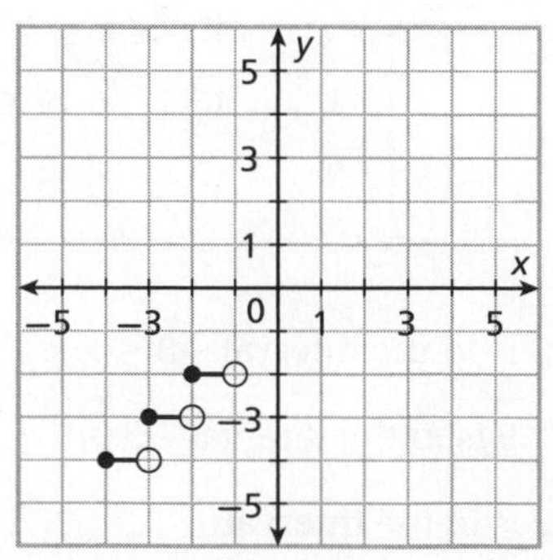

REFLECT

2a. Why does the first graph use rays and not lines?

2b. The greatest integer function is an example of a **step function**, a piecewise function that is constant for each rule. Use the graph of the greatest integer function to explain why such a function is called a step function.

2c. Does the greatest integer function have a maximum or minimum value? Explain.

CC.9–12.A.CED.2

3 EXAMPLE Writing and Graphing a Piecewise Function

On his way to class from his dorm room, a college student walks at a speed of 0.05 mile per minute for 3 minutes, stops to talk to a friend for 1 minute, and then to avoid being late for class, runs at a speed of 0.10 mile per minute for 2 minutes. Write a piecewise function for the student's distance from his dorm room during this time. Then graph the function.

A Express the student's distance traveled d (in miles) as a function of time t (in minutes). Write an equation for the function $d(t)$.

$$d(t) = \begin{cases} \_\_\_\_ \, t & \text{if } 0 \le t \le 3 \\ 0.15 & \text{if } 3 < t \le \_\_\_\_ \\ 0.15 + 0.10\,(t - 4) & \text{if } 4 < t \le \_\_\_\_ \end{cases}$$

← He travels at 0.05 mile per minute for 3 minutes.

← Distance traveled is constant for 1 minute.

← Add the distance traveled at 0.10 mile per minute to the distance already traveled.

B Complete the table.

t	0	1	2	3
d(t)				

t	4	5	6
d(t)			

C Complete the graph.

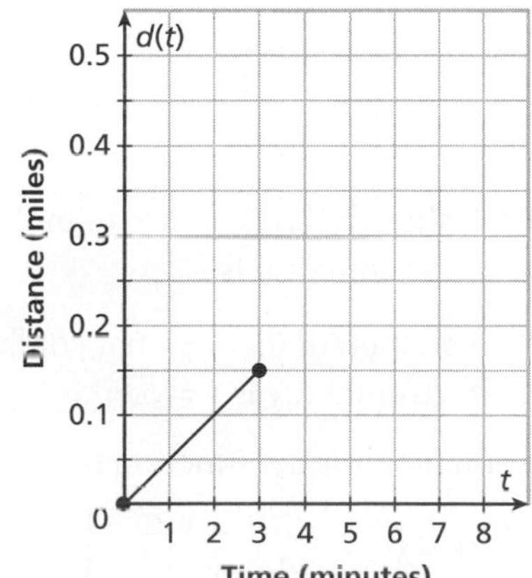

REFLECT

3a. Why is the second rule for the function $d(t) = 0.15$ instead of $d(t) = 0$?

____

3b. Why is the third rule for the function $d(t) = 0.15 + 0.10(t - 4)$?

____

____

CC.9–12.F.BF.1

4 EXAMPLE Writing a Function When Given a Graph

Write the equation for each function whose graph is shown.

A

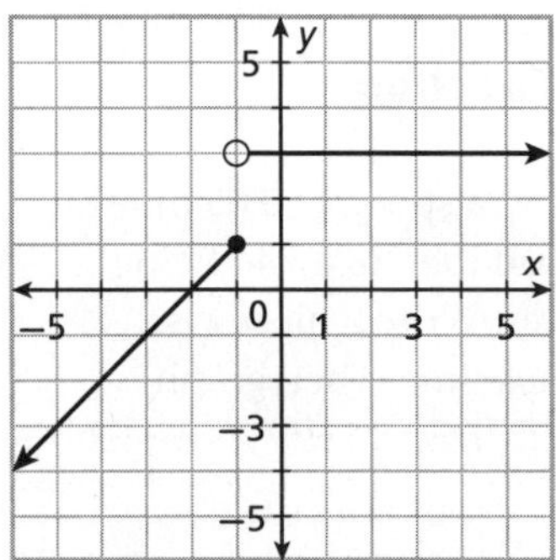

Find the equation for each ray:

- Make a table of values for the ray on the left.

x	y
−1	
−2	
−3	
−4	
−5	

The value of y is ____ more than the value of x. The equation is ________.

- The equation of the line that contains the horizontal ray is $y =$ ____.

The equation for the function is:

$$f(x) = \begin{cases} \quad & \text{if } x \le -1 \\ \quad & \text{if } x > -1 \end{cases}$$

B

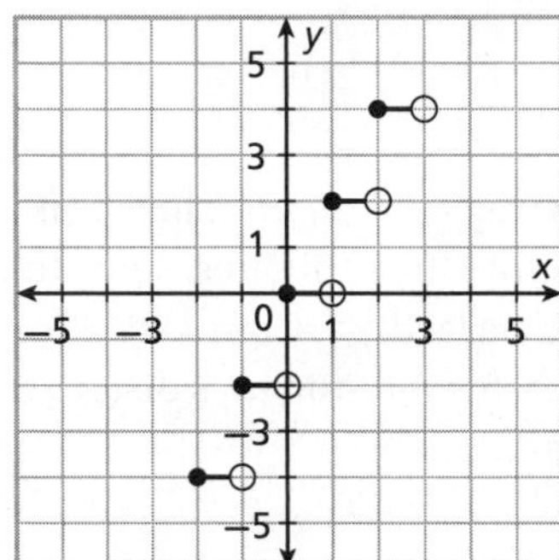

Write a rule for each horizontal line segment.

$$f(x) = \begin{cases} -4 & \text{if } -2 \le x < -1 \\ \quad & \text{if } -1 \le x < 0 \\ 0 & \text{if } 0 \le x < 1 \\ \quad & \text{if } 1 \le x < 2 \\ \quad & \text{if } 2 \le x < 3 \end{cases}$$

Although the graph shows the function's domain to be $-2 \le x < 3$, assume that the domain consists of all real numbers and that the graph continues its stair-step pattern for $x < -2$ and $x \ge 3$.

Notice that each function value is ________ times the corresponding value of the greatest integer function.

The equation for the function is:

$$f(x) = \quad [\![x]\!]$$

REFLECT

4a. When writing a piecewise function from a graph, how do you determine the domain of each rule?

____

____

4b. How can you use y-intercepts to check that your answer in part A is reasonable?

____

____

PRACTICE

Graph each function.

1. $f(x) = \begin{cases} -x + 1 & \text{if } x < 0 \\ x & \text{if } x \geq 0 \end{cases}$

2. $f(x) = \begin{cases} -1 & \text{if } x < 1 \\ 2x - 2 & \text{if } x \geq 1 \end{cases}$

3. $f(x) = [\![x]\!] + 1$

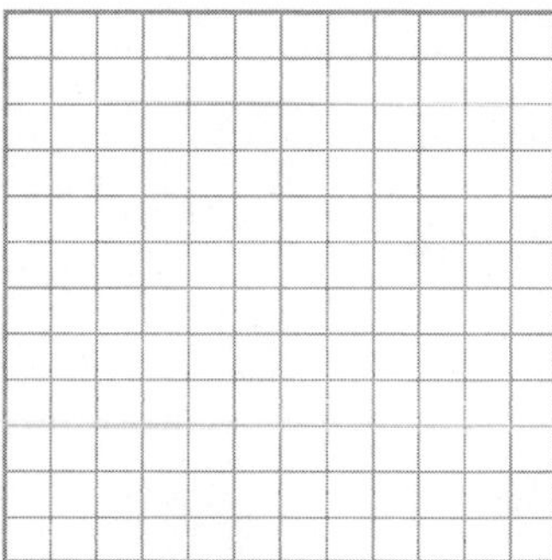

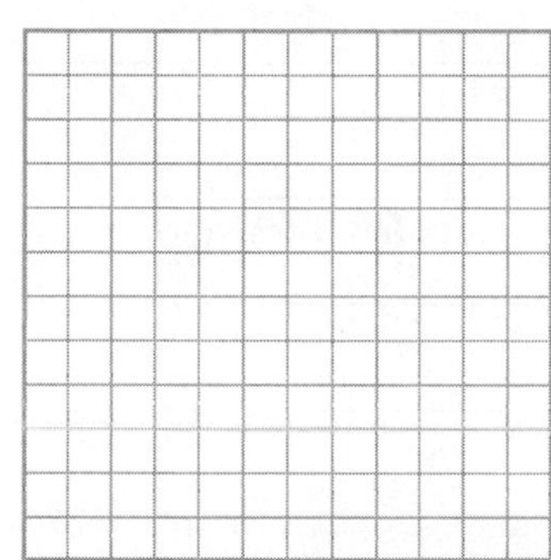

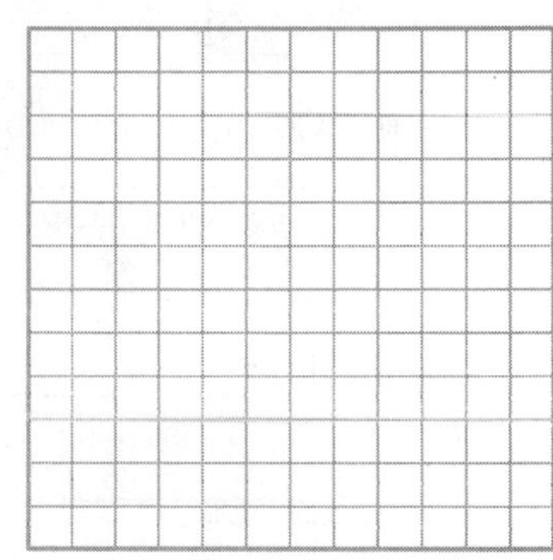

Write the equation for each function whose graph is shown.

4.

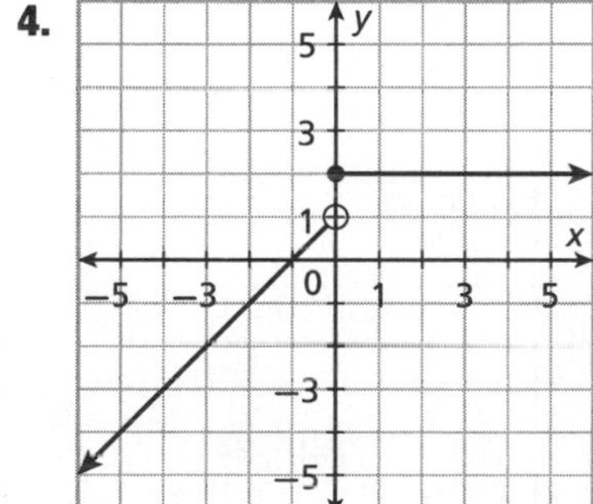

5.

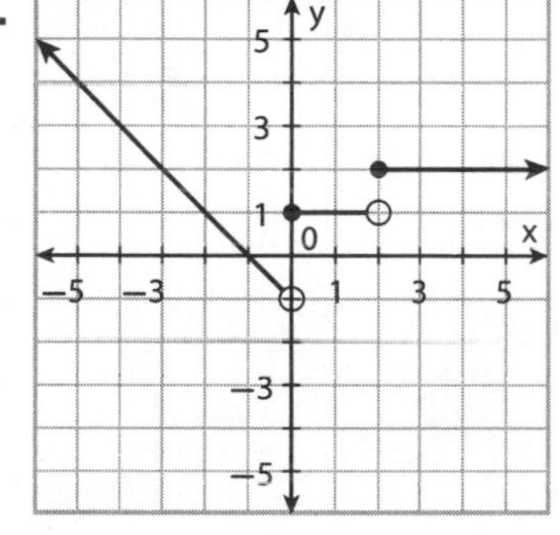

6.

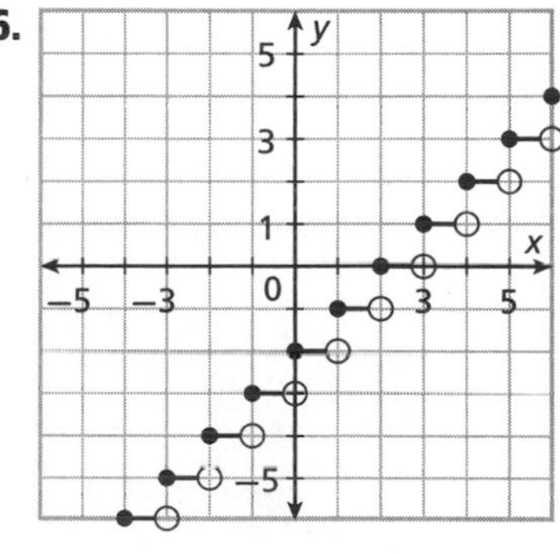

______________________ ______________________ ______________________

7. A garage charges the following rates for parking (with an 8 hour limit):

$3 per hour for the first 6 hours

No additional charge for the next 2 hours

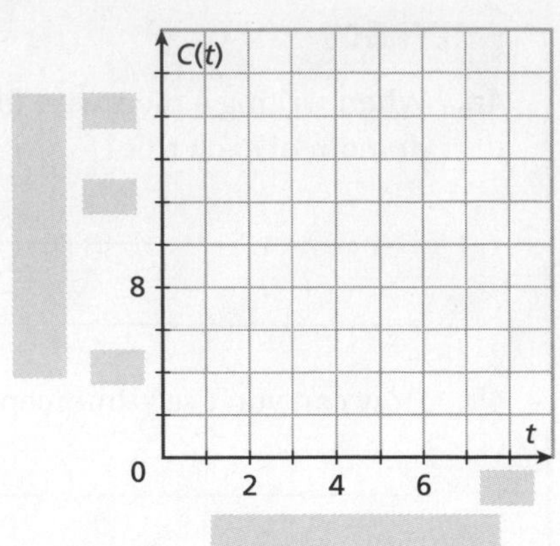

a. Write a piecewise function that gives the parking cost C (in dollars) in terms of the time t (in hours) that a car is parked in the garage.

____

b. Graph the function. Include labels to show what the axes represent and to show the scales on the axes.

8. The cost to send a package between two cities is $8.00 for any weight less than 1 pound. The cost increases by $4.00 when the weight reaches 1 pound and again each time the weight reaches a whole number of pounds after that.

a. For a package having weight w (in pounds), write a function in terms of $[\![w]\!]$ to represent the shipping cost C (in dollars).

____

b. Complete the table.

Weight (pounds) w	Cost (dollars) $C(w)$
0.5	
1	
1.5	
2	
2.5	

c. Graph the function. Show the costs for all weights less than 5 pounds.

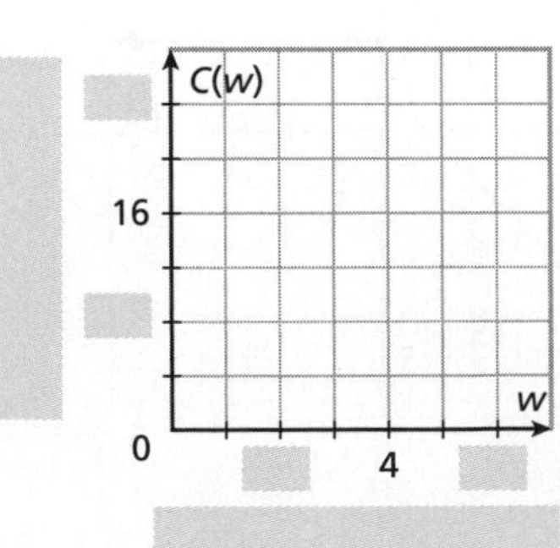

Name__________ Class__________ Date__________

Additional Practice

Graph the function for the given domain.

1. $f(x)=\begin{cases} 2x+1 \text{ if } x \le 0 \\ x-3 \text{ if } x>0 \end{cases}$

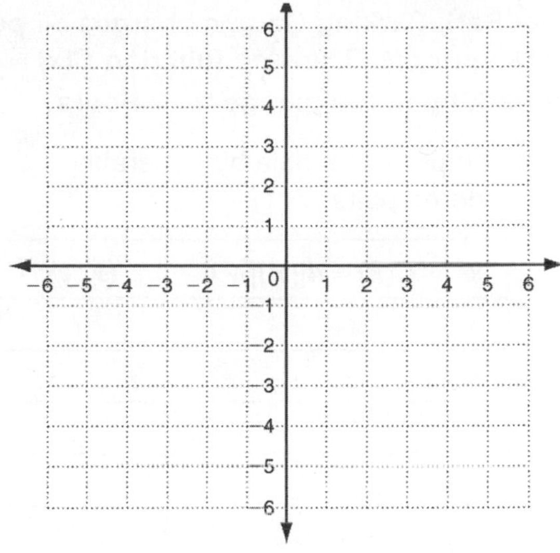

Graph the function.

2. $f(x)=\begin{cases} 3x-2 \text{ if } x \le 3 \\ -2x+5 \text{ if } x>3 \end{cases}$

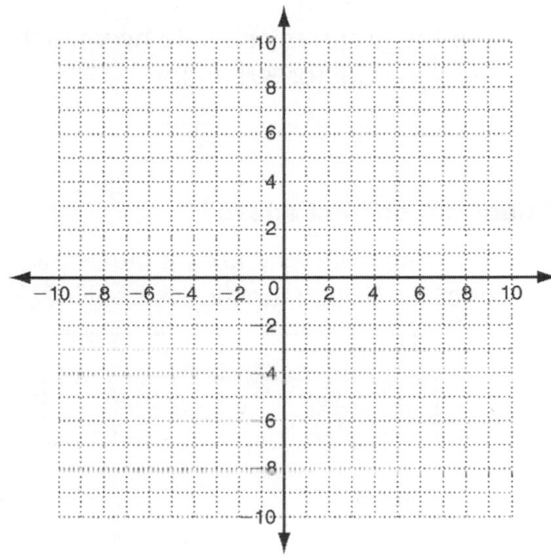

3. The cost for shipping a package is given by the step function $C(w) = [[\,w\,]] + 2$, where w is the weight of the package in pounds. Graph this function. Use the graph to find the cost of shipping a 6 pound package.

____

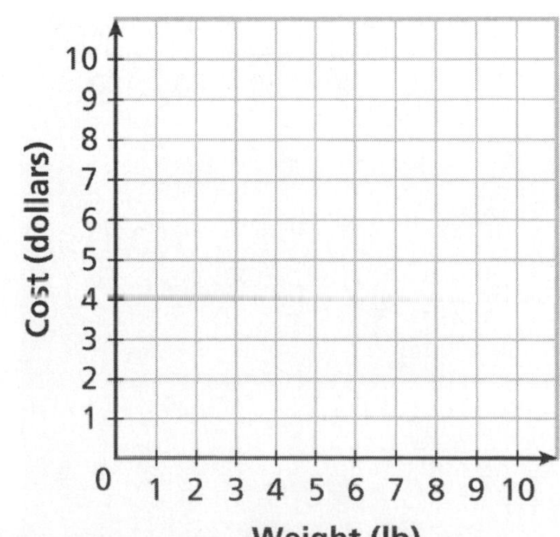

Problem Solving

City Park Parking Garage charges $4 per hour or part of an hour to park your car. The step function $C(x) = 4[[x]] + 4$ represents the cost of parking in the garage for x hours.

1. Complete the table by generating ordered pairs.

x	$C(x) = 4[[x]] + 4$	(x, y)
0		
1		
2		
3		
4		

2. Graph the function $C(x) = 4[[x]] + 4$.

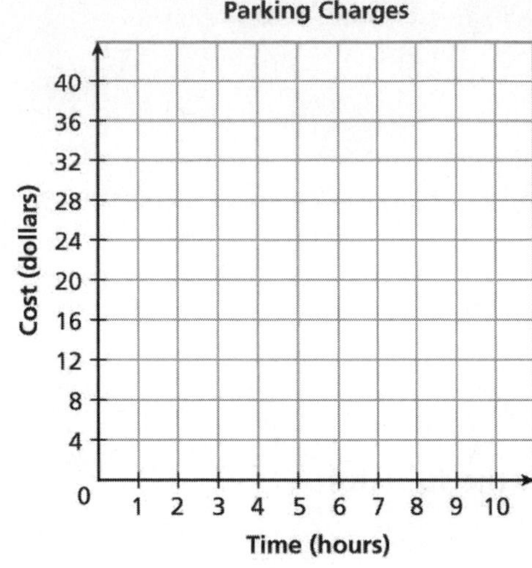

3. Use the graph to estimate how much it costs to park for 3.5 hours.

____

Select the correct answer.

4. The graph below shows a piecewise function. Which function is shown?

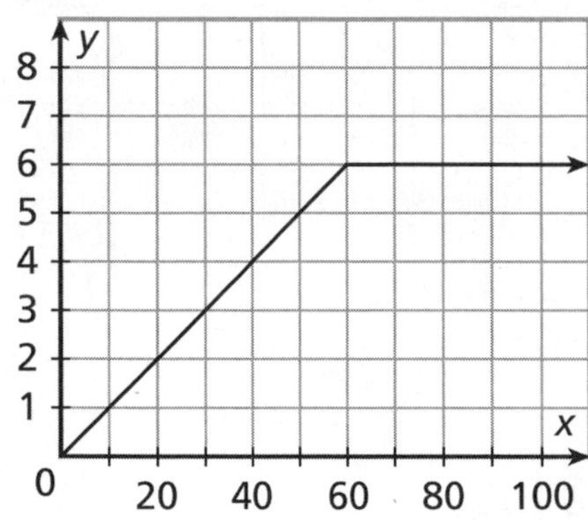

A $f(x) = \begin{cases} 0.1x \text{ if } 0 \le x < 6 \\ 6x \text{ if } x \ge 6 \end{cases}$

B $f(x) = \begin{cases} 0.1x \text{ if } 0 \le x < 6 \\ 6 \text{ if } x \ge 6 \end{cases}$

C $f(x) = \begin{cases} 10x \text{ if } 0 \le x < 6 \\ 6 \text{ if } x \ge 6 \end{cases}$

D $f(x) = \begin{cases} 10x \text{ if } 0 \le x < 6 \\ 6x \text{ if } x \ge 6 \end{cases}$

Name ____________________ Class ____________ Date ________

3-5

Scatter Plots and Trend Lines

Extension: Correlation, Lines of Fit, and Predictions

Essential question: *How can you decide whether a correlation exists between paired numerical data and, if so, what is the line of fit for that data?*

Video Tutor

CC.9–12.S.ID.8

1 ENGAGE Understanding Correlation

When two real-world variables (such as height and weight or latitude and average temperature) are measured from the same things (the same people, places, etc.), you obtain a set of paired numerical data that you can plot as points in the coordinate plane to create a data display called a *scatter plot.* Sometimes the scatter plot will show a linear pattern. When it does, the linear pattern may be tight (that is, the points lie very close to a line), or it may be loose (that is, the points are more dispersed about a line). The degree to which a scatter plot shows a linear pattern is an indicator of the strength of a **correlation** between the two variables.

Mathematicians have defined a measure of the direction and magnitude of a correlation. This measure is called the **correlation coefficient** and is denoted by r. When the points in a scatter plot all lie on a line that is not horizontal, r has a value of 1 if the line rises from left to right and a value of -1 if the line falls from left to right. The correlation coefficient takes on values between -1 and 1 in cases where the points are not perfectly linear.

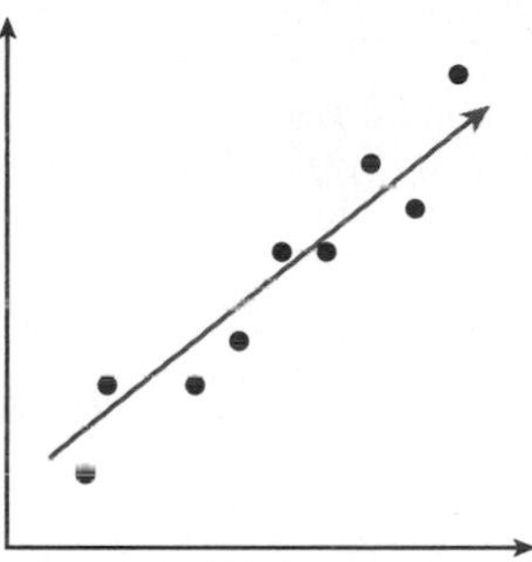

Strong positive correlation
r is close to 1.

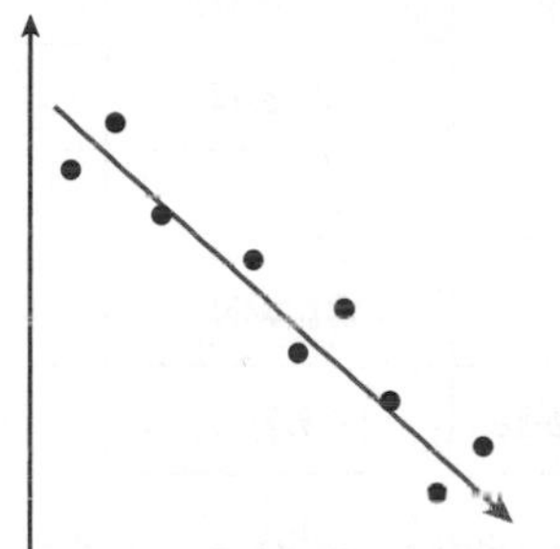

Strong negative correlation
r is close to –1.

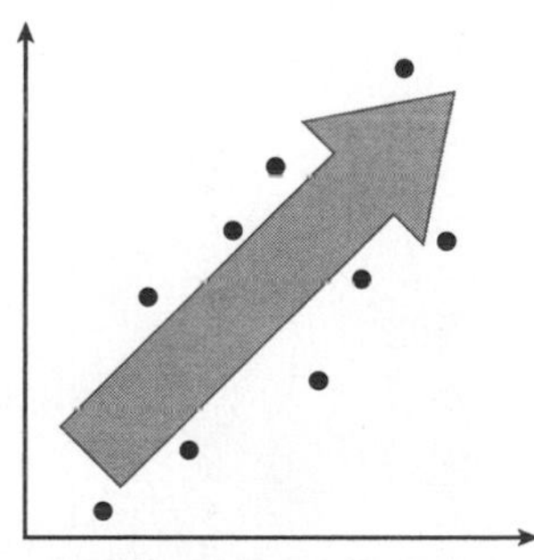

Weak positive correlation
r is closer to 0.5 than to 0 or 1.

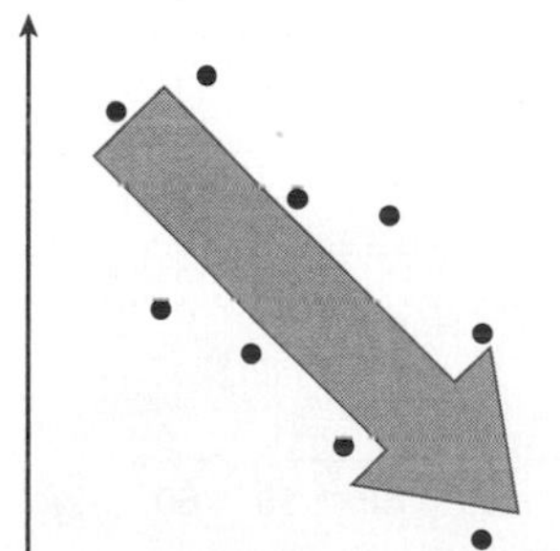

Weak negative correlation
r is closer to –0.5 than to 0 or –1.

REFLECT

1a. What conclusion would you draw about the value of r for the scatter plot shown at the right? Why?

____

____

1b. If the variables x and y have a strong positive correlation, what generally happens to y as x increases? What if x and y have a strong negative correlation?

____

CC.9–12.S.ID.8

2 EXAMPLE Estimating Correlation Coefficients

The table lists the latitude and average annual temperature for various cities in the Northern Hemisphere. Describe the correlation and estimate the correlation coefficient.

City	Latitude	Avg. Annual Temperature
Bangkok, Thailand	13.7°N	82.6°F
Cairo, Egypt	30.1°N	71.4°F
London, England	51.5°N	51.8°F
Moscow, Russia	55.8°N	39.4°F
New Delhi, India	28.6°N	77.0°F
Tokyo, Japan	35.7°N	58.1°F
Vancouver, Canada	49.2°N	49.6°F

A Make a scatter plot. The data pair for Bangkok has been plotted.

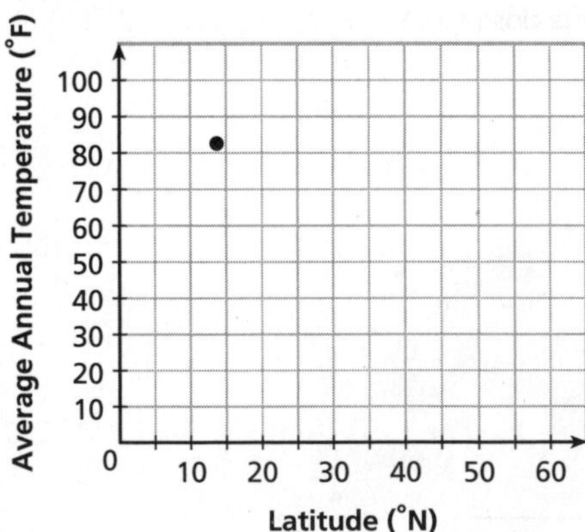

B Describe the correlation, and estimate the correlation coefficient.

Because the plotted points appear to lie very close to a line that slants __________ from left to right, the scatter plot shows a __________ correlation. So, the correlation coefficient is close to ______.

REFLECT

2a. Mexico City, Mexico, is at latitude 19.4°N and has an average annual temperature of 60.8°F. If you include this data pair in the data set, how would it affect the correlation? Why?

Correlation and Causation In the preceding example, you would expect that a city's latitude has an effect on the city's average annual temperature. While it does, there are other factors that contribute to a city's weather, such as whether a city is located on a coast or inland.

A common error when interpreting paired data is confusing correlation and causation. If a correlation exists between two variables, this does not necessarily mean that one variable causes the other. When one variable increases, the other variable may increase (or decrease) as a result of other variables not being considered. Such variables are sometimes called *lurking variables*.

CC.9–12.S.ID.9

3 EXAMPLE Distinguishing Causation from Correlation

Read the article. Decide whether correlation implies causation in this case.

A Identify the two variables that the scientists correlated. Was the correlation positive or negative?

B Decide whether correlation implies causation in this case. Explain your reasoning.

BRAIN'S AMYGDALA CONNECTED TO SOCIAL BEHAVIOR

An almond-shaped part of the brain called the amygdala has long been known to play a role in people's emotional states. Now scientists studying the amygdala have discovered a connection between its size and the size of a person's social network. The scientists used a brain scanner to determine the size of the amygdala in the brains of 58 adults. They also gave each person a survey that measured the size of the person's social network. Their analysis of the data found that there is a correlation between the two: People with larger amygdalas tend to have larger social networks.

REFLECT

3a. Suppose scientists study a group of people over time and find that those who increased the size of their social networks also had an increase in the size of their amygdalas. Does this result establish a cause-and-effect relationship? Explain.

____

____

When paired numerical data have a strong positive or negative correlation, you can find a linear model for the data. The process is called *fitting a line to the data* or *finding a line of fit for the data.*

CC.9–12.S.ID.6c

4 EXAMPLE Finding a Line of Fit for Data

The table lists the median age of females living in the United States based on the results of the U.S. Census over the past few decades. Determine whether a linear model is reasonable for the data. If so, find a linear model for the data.

Year	Median Age of Females
1970	29.2
1980	31.3
1990	34.0
2000	36.5
2010	38.2

A Identify the independent and dependent variables, and specify how you will represent them.

The independent variable is time, so use the variable t. Rather than let t take on the values 1970, 1980, and so on, define t as the number of years since 1970.

The dependent variable is the median age of females. Although you could simply use the variable a, you can use F as a subscript to remind yourself that only median *female* ages are being considered. So, the dependent variable is a_F.

B Make a table of paired values of t and a_F. Then draw a scatter plot.

t	a_F

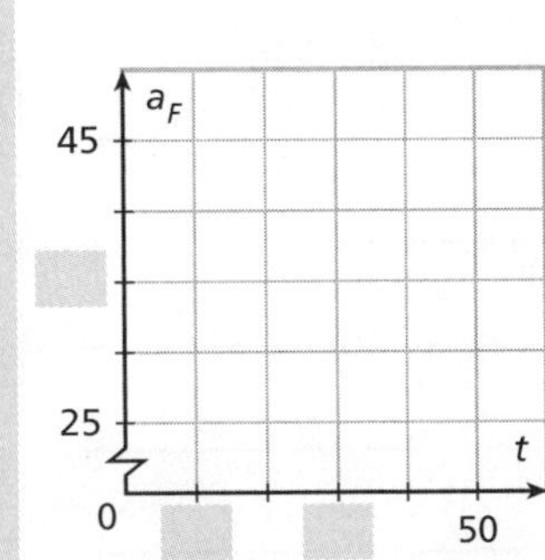

Time (years since 1970)

C Draw a line of fit on the scatter plot.

Using a ruler, draw a line that passes as close as possible to the plotted points. Your line does not necessarily have to pass through any of the points, but you should try to balance points above and below the line.

REFLECT

4a. What type of correlation does the scatter plot show?

____

4b. Before you placed a ruler on the scatter plot to draw a line of fit, you may have thought that the plotted points were perfectly linear. How does the table tell you that they are not?

____

____

____

____

Making Predictions A linear model establishes the dependent variable as a linear function of the independent variable, and you can use the function to make predictions. The accuracy of a prediction depends not only on the model's goodness of fit but also on the value of the independent variable for which you're making the prediction.

A model's domain is determined by the least and greatest values of the independent variable found in the data set. For instance, the least and greatest t-values for the median age data are 0 (for 1970) and 40 (for 2010), so the domain of any model for the data is $\{t \mid 0 \le t \le 40\}$. Making a prediction using a value of the independent variable from *within* the model's domain is called **interpolation**. Making a prediction using a value from *outside* the domain is called **extrapolation**. As you might expect, you can have greater confidence in an interpolation than in an extrapolation.

CC.9–12.S.ID.6a

5 EXAMPLE Making Predictions Using a Linear Model

A linear equation that models the data from the previous example is $a_F = 0.25t + 29$. Use this model to predict the median age of females in 1995 and in 2015. Identify each prediction as an interpolation or as an extrapolation.

A To make a prediction about 1995, let $t =$ _______________. Then to the nearest tenth, the predicted value of a_F is $a_F = 0.25(\quad) + 29 \approx$ _____.

Because the t-value falls _______________ the model's domain, the prediction is an _______________.

B To make a prediction about 2015, let $t =$ _______________. Then to the nearest tenth, the predicted value of a_F is $a_F = 0.25(\quad) + 29 \approx$ _____.

Because the t-value falls _______________ the model's domain, the prediction is an _______________.

REFLECT

5a. Use the linear model to predict the median age of females in 1995 and 2015.

5b. The Census Bureau gives 35.5 as the median age of females for 1995 and an estimate of 38.4 for 2015. Which of your predictions using the linear model was more accurate? Explain.

PRACTICE

1. The table lists the heights and weights of the six wide receivers who played for the New Orleans Saints during the 2010 football season.

Wide Receiver	Height (inches)	Weight (pounds)
Arrington	75	192
Colston	76	225
Henderson	71	200
Meachem	74	210
Moore	69	190
Roby	72	189

a. Make a scatter plot.

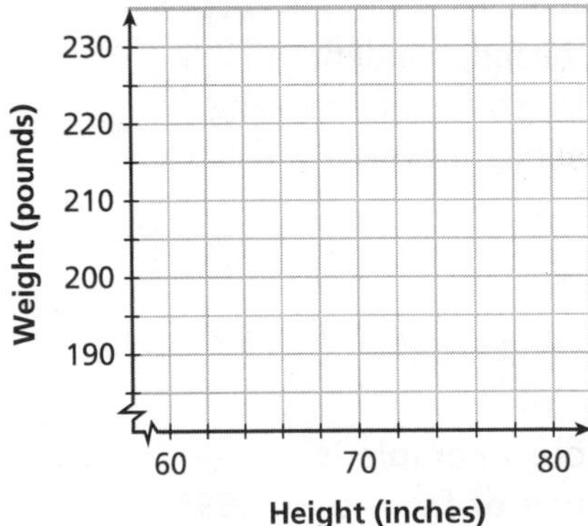

b. Describe the correlation, and estimate the correlation coefficient using one of these values: -1, -0.5, 0, 0.5, 1.

2. Read the article shown at the right. Describe the correlation and decide whether correlation implies causation in this case. Explain your reasoning.

WALKING SPEED MAY PREDICT LIFE SPAN

Researchers who looked at data from nearly 35,000 senior citizens discovered that an elderly person's walking speed is correlated to that person's chance of living 10 more years. For instance, the researchers found that only 19 percent of the slowest-walking 75-year-old men lived for 10 more years compared with 87 percent of the fastest-walking 75-year-old men. Similar results were found for elderly women.

3. The table lists the median age of males living in the United States based on the results of the U.S. Census over the past few decades.

Year	1970	1980	1990	2000	2010
Median Age of Males	26.8	28.8	31.6	34.0	35.5

a. Let t represent time (in years since 1970), and let a_M represent the median age of males. Make a table of paired values of t and a_M. Then draw a scatter plot.

t	a_M

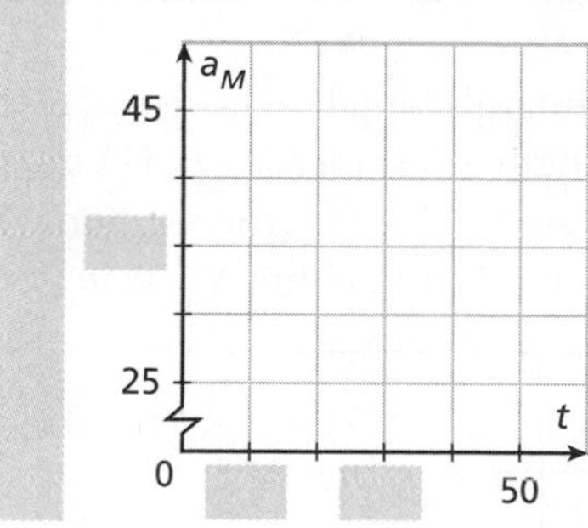

b. Draw a line of fit on the scatter plot.

c. A linear equation that models the data from parts (a) and (b) is $a_M = 0.24t + 26.6$. Use this model to predict the median age of males in 1995 and 2015. Identify each prediction as an interpolation or an extrapolation, and then compare the predictions with these median ages of males from the Census Bureau: 33.2 in 1995 and an estimated 35.9 in 2015.

4. Compare the equations of the lines of fit for the median age of females and the median age of males. When referring to any constants in those equations, be sure to interpret them in the context of the data.

5. Explain why it isn't reasonable to use linear models to predict the median age of females or males far into the future.

6. The table lists, for various lengths (in centimeters), the median weight (in kilograms) of male infants and female infants (ages 0–36 months) in the United States.

Length (cm)	50	60	70	80	90	100
Median Weight (kg) of Male Infants	3.4	5.9	8.4	10.8	13.0	15.5
Median Weight (kg) of Female Infants	3.4	5.8	8.3	10.6	12.8	15.2

a. Let l represent an infant's length in excess of 50 centimeters. (For instance, for an infant whose length is 60 cm, $l = 10$.) Let w_M represent the median weight of male infants, and let w_F represent the median weight of female infants. Make a table of paired values of l and either w_M or w_F (whichever you prefer).

l						
w						

b. Draw a scatter plot of the paired data.

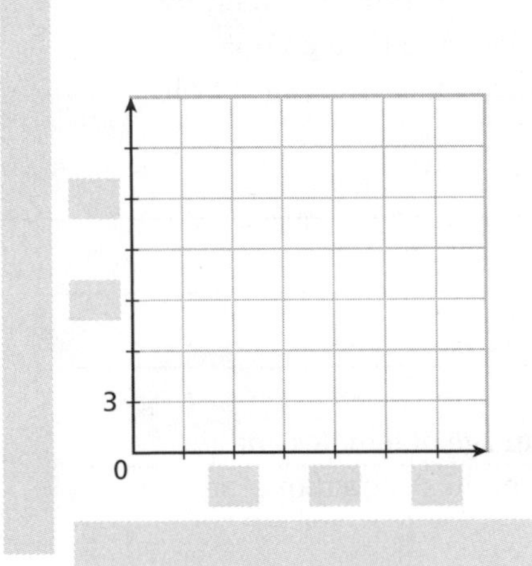

c. Draw a line of fit on the scatter plot.

d. A linear equation that models the data for the median weight of male infants is $w_M = 0.244l + 3.4$. A linear equation that models the data for the median weight of female infants is $w_F = 0.238l + 3.4$. According to these models, at what rate does weight change with respect to height?

Name ______________________ Class ______________ Date ____________

Additional Practice

Graph a scatter plot using the given data.

1. The table shows the percent of people ages 18–24 who reported they voted in the presidential elections. Graph a scatter plot using the given data.

Year	1988	1992	1996	2000	2004
% of 18-24 year olds	36	43	32	32	42

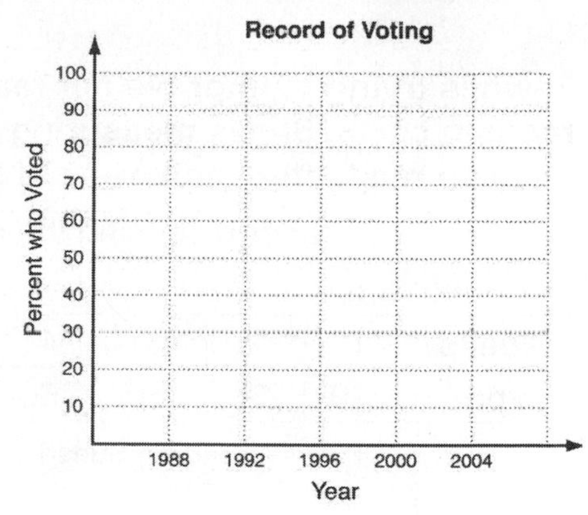

Write *positive, negative,* or *none* to describe the correlation illustrated by each scatter plot.

2. 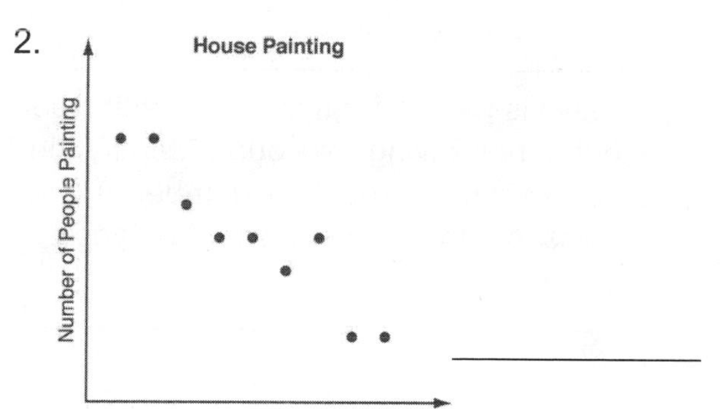

____

3. 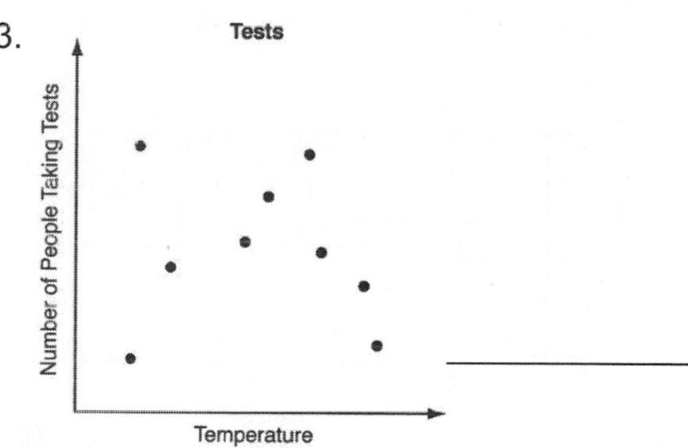

____

4. Identify the correlation you would expect to see between the number of pets a person has and the number of times they go to a pet store. Explain.

____

____

Neal kept track of the number of minutes it took him to assemble sandwiches at his restaurant. The information is in the table below.

Number of sandwiches	1	2	4	6	7
Minutes	3	4	5	6	7

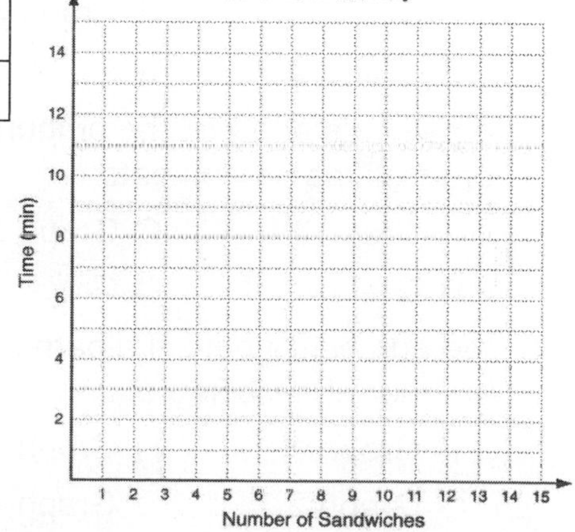

5. Graph a scatter plot of the data.
6. Draw a trend line.
7. Describe the correlation.

____

8. Based on the trend line you drew, predict the amount of time it will take Neal to assemble 12 sandwiches.

____

Problem Solving

Fawn is trying to improve her reading skills by taking a speed-reading class. She is measuring how many words per minute (wpm) she can read after each week of the class.

1. Graph a scatter plot using the given data.

Weeks	1	2	3	4	5
wpm	220	230	260	260	280

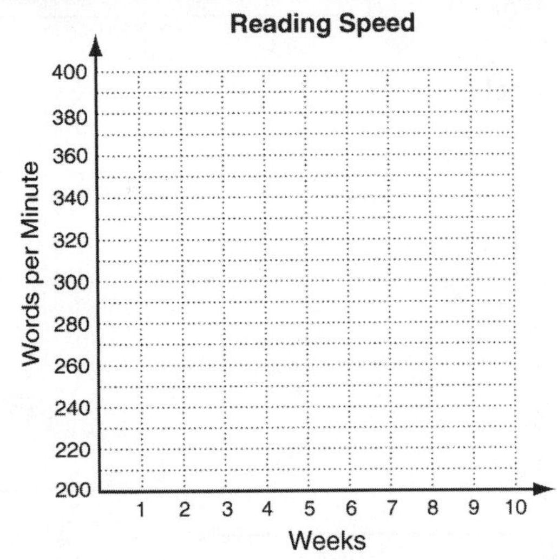

2. Describe the correlation illustrated by the scatter plot.

____

____

3. Draw a trend line and use it to predict the number of words per minute that Fawn will read after 8 weeks of this class.

____

4. Fawn is paying for this class each week out of her savings account. Identify the correlation between the number of classes and Fawn's account balance.

____

____

Choose the scatter plot that best represents the described relationship.

5. the distance a person runs and how physically tired that person is

   A Graph 1 C Graph 3
   B Graph 2 D Graph 4

6. the price of a new car and the number of hours in a day

   F Graph 1 H Graph 3
   G Graph 2 J Graph 4

7. a person's age and the amount of broccoli the person eats

   A Graph 1 C Graph 3
   B Graph 2 D Graph 4

8. the number of cats in a barn and the number of mice in that barn

   F Graph 1 H Graph 3
   G Graph 2 J Graph 4

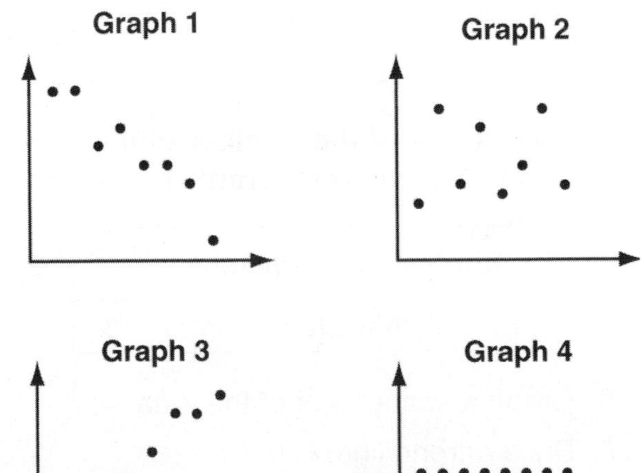

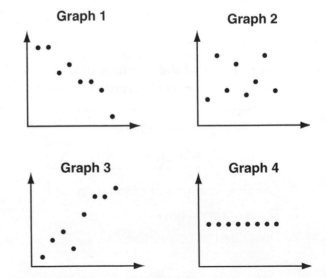

Name ____________________ Class ____________ Date ____________

3-6

Arithmetic Sequences

Going Deeper

Essential question: *Why is a sequence a function and how can you write a rule for an arithmetic sequence?*

Video Tutor

CC.9–12.F.IF.3

1 ENGAGE Understanding Sequences

A **sequence** is an ordered list of numbers or other items. Each element in a sequence is called a **term**. For instance, in the sequence 1, 3, 5, 7, 9, …, the second term is 3.

Each term in a sequence can be paired with a position number, and these pairings establish a function whose domain is the set of position numbers and whose range is the set of terms, as illustrated below. The position numbers are consecutive integers that typically start at either 1 or 0.

Position number	n	1	2	3	4	5	Domain
Term of sequence	$f(n)$	1	3	5	7	9	Range

For the sequence shown in the table, you can write $f(4) = 7$, which can be interpreted as "the fourth term of the sequence is 7."

REFLECT

1a. The domain of the function f defining the sequence 2, 5, 8, 11, 14, … is the set of consecutive integers starting with 0. What is $f(4)$? Explain how you determined your answer.

____

____

1b. How does your answer to Question 1a change if the domain of the function is the set of consecutive integers starting with 1?

____

1c. Predict the next term in the sequence 48, 42, 36, 30, 24, …. Explain your reasoning.

____

____

1d. Why is the relationship between the position numbers and the terms of a sequence a function?

____

1e. Give an example of a sequence from your everyday life. Explain why your example represents a sequence.

____

____

Some numerical sequences can be described by using algebraic rules. An **explicit rule** for a sequence defines the *n*th term as a function of *n*.

CC.9–12.F.BF.2

2 EXAMPLE Using an Explicit Rule to Generate a Sequence

Write the first 4 terms of the sequence $f(n) = n^2 + 1$. Assume that the domain of the function is the set of consecutive integers starting with 1.

n	$n^2 + 1$	$f(n)$
1	$\square^2 + 1 = \square + 1$	
2	$\square^2 + 1 = \square + 1$	
3	$\square^2 + 1 = \square + 1$	
4	$\square^2 + 1 = \square + 1$	

The first 4 terms are ________________________.

REFLECT

2a. How could you use a graphing calculator to check your answer?

____

2b. Explain how to find the 20th term of the sequence.

____

A **recursive rule** for a sequence defines the *n*th term by relating it to one or more previous terms.

CC.9–12.F.BF.2

3 EXAMPLE Using a Recursive Rule to Generate a Sequence

Write the first 4 terms of the sequence with $f(1) = 3$ and $f(n) = f(n - 1) + 2$ for $n \geq 2$. Assume that the domain of the function is the set of consecutive integers starting with 1.

The first term is given: $f(1) = 3$. Use $f(1)$ to find $f(2)$, $f(2)$ to find $f(3)$, and so on. In general, $f(n - 1)$ refers to the term that precedes $f(n)$.

n	$f(n - 1) + 2$	$f(n)$
2	$f(2 - 1) + 2 = f(1) + 2 = 3 + 2$	
3	$f(\square - 1) + 2 = f(\square) + 2 = \square + 2$	
4	$f(\square - 1) + 2 = f(\square) + 2 = \square + 2$	

The first 4 terms are ________________________.

REFLECT

3a. Describe how to find the 12th term of the sequence.

____

3b. Suppose you want to find the 50th term of a sequence. Would you rather use a recursive rule or an explicit rule? Explain your reasoning.

____

____

____

In an **arithmetic sequence**, the difference between consecutive terms is constant. The constant difference is called the **common difference**, often written as d.

CC.9–12.F.BF.2

4 EXAMPLE Writing Rules for an Arithmetic Sequence

The table shows end-of-month balances in a bank account that does not earn interest. Write a recursive and an explicit rule for the arithmetic sequence described by the table.

Month	n	1	2	3	4	5
Account Balance ($)	$f(n)$	60	80	100	120	140

A Find the common difference by calculating the differences between consecutive terms.

$80 - 60 =$ ____

$100 - 80 =$ ____

$120 - 100 =$ ____

$140 - 120 =$ ____

The common difference, d, is ________.

B Write a recursive rule for the sequence.

$f(1) =$ ____ and — The first term is ________.

$f(n) =$ ________ $+$ ____ for $n \geq 2$ — Every other term is the ________ of the previous term and the common difference.

C Write an explicit rule for the sequence by writing each term as the sum of the first term and a multiple of the common difference.

n	$f(n)$
1	$60 + 20(0) = 60$
2	$60 + 20(1) = 80$
3	$60 + 20(\square) = 100$
4	$60 + 20(\square) = 120$
5	$60 + 20(\square) = 140$

Generalize the results from the table: $f(n) = \square + 20(n - \square)$

REFLECT

4a. Explain how you know that the sequence 1, 2, 4, 8, 16, ... is not an arithmetic sequence.

____

4b. An arithmetic sequence has a common difference of 3. If you know that the third term of the sequence is 15, how can you find the fourth term?

____

CC.9–12.F.BF.2

5 EXPLORE Writing General Rules for Arithmetic Sequences

Use the arithmetic sequence 6, 9, 12, 15, 18, ... to help you write a recursive rule and an explicit rule for any arithmetic sequence. For the general rules, the values of *n* are consecutive integers starting with 1.

A Find the common difference.

Numbers

6, 9, 12, 15, 18, ...

Common difference = $\square$

Algebra

$f(1), f(2), f(3), \square, \square, \ldots$

Common difference = d

B Write a recursive rule.

Numbers

$f(1) = \square$ and

$f(n) = f(n - 1) + \square$ for $n \geq 2$

Algebra

Given $f(1)$,

$f(n) = f(n - 1) + \square$ for $n \geq 2$

C Write an explicit rule.

Numbers

$f(n) = \square + \square(n - 1)$

Algebra

$f(n) = \square + \square(n - 1)$

REFLECT

5a. The first term of an arithmetic sequence is 4 and the common difference is 10. Explain how you can find the 6th term of the sequence.

____

____

5b. What information do you need to know in order to find the 8th term of an arithmetic sequence by using its recursive rule?

____

5c. What is the recursive rule for the sequence $f(n) = 2 + (-3)(n - 1)$?

____

CC.9–12.F.LE.2

6 EXAMPLE Relating Arithmetic Sequences and Functions

The graph shows how the cost of a rafting trip depends on the number of passengers. Write an explicit rule for the sequence of costs.

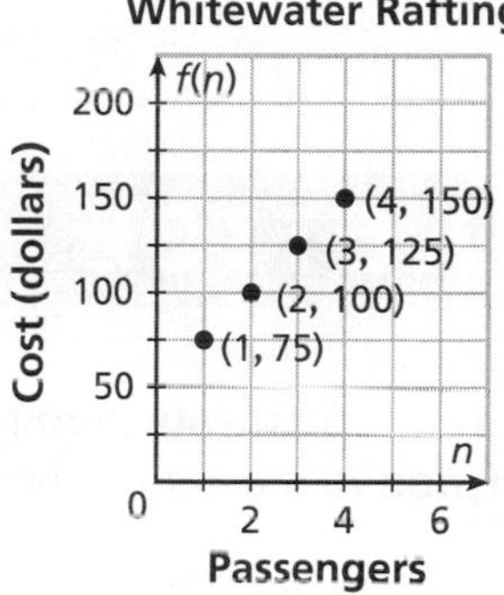

A Represent the sequence in a table.

n	1	2	3	4
f(n)				

B Examine the sequence.

Is the sequence arithmetic? Explain how you know.

____

What is the common difference? ________

C Write an explicit rule for the sequence.

$f(n) = f(1) + d(n - 1)$ Write the general rule.

$f(n) = \square + \square(n - 1)$ Substitute ________ for $f(1)$ and ________ for d.

So, the sequence has the rule ________________, where n is the number of passengers and $f(n)$ is the ________________.

REFLECT

6a. An arithmetic sequence is equivalent to a function with a restricted domain. On the graph above, draw the line that passes through the given points. Then write a function of the form $f(n) = mn + b$ for the line that you drew and give the function's domain.

____

6b. Show that the explicit rule for the sequence is equivalent to the function. Justify the steps you take.

____

____

____

6c. A function of the form $f(n) = mn + b$ is called a *linear function* because its graph is a line. Using the line you drew, what is the relationship between m and the common difference of the arithmetic sequence?

____

PRACTICE

Write the first four terms of each sequence. Assume that the domain of the function is the set of consecutive integers starting with 1.

1. $f(n) = (n - 1)^2$ ______________

2. $f(n) = \dfrac{n+1}{n+3}$ ______________

3. $f(n) = 4(0.5)^n$ ______________

4. $f(n) = \sqrt{n-1}$ ______________

5. $f(1) = 2$ and $f(n) = f(n - 1) + 10$ for $n \geq 2$ ______________

6. $f(1) = 16$ and $f(n) = \frac{1}{2} f(n - 1)$ for $n \geq 2$ ______________

7. $f(1) = 1$ and $f(n) = 2f(n - 1) + 1$ for $n \geq 2$ ______________

8. $f(1) = f(2) = 1$ and $f(n) = f(n - 2) - f(n - 1)$ for $n \geq 3$ ______________

Write the 12th term of each sequence. Assume that the domain of the function is the set of consecutive integers starting with 1.

9. $f(n) = 3n - 2$ ______________

10. $f(n) = 2n(n + 1)$ ______________

Write an explicit rule for each sequence. Assume that the domain of the function is the set of consecutive integers starting with 1.

11.

n	$f(n)$
1	6
2	7
3	8
4	9
5	10

____

12.

n	$f(n)$
1	3
2	6
3	9
4	12
5	15

____

13.

n	$f(n)$
1	1
2	$\frac{1}{2}$
3	$\frac{1}{3}$
4	$\frac{1}{4}$
5	$\frac{1}{5}$

____

Write a recursive rule for each sequence. Assume that the domain of the function is the set of consecutive integers starting with 1.

14.

n	$f(n)$
1	8
2	9
3	10
4	11
5	12

____

____

15.

n	$f(n)$
1	2
2	4
3	8
4	16
5	32

____

____

16.

n	$f(n)$
1	27
2	24
3	21
4	18
5	15

____

____

Write a recursive rule and an explicit rule for each arithmetic sequence.

17. $3, 7, 11, 15, \ldots$

____

18. $19, 9, -1, -11, \ldots$

____

19. $1, \frac{5}{2}, 4, \frac{11}{2}, \ldots$

____

20. Carrie borrowed money interest-free to pay for a car repair. She is repaying the loan in equal monthly payments.

Monthly Payment Number	n	1	2	3	4	5
Loan Balance ($)	$f(n)$	840	720	600	480	360

a. Explain how you know that the sequence of loan balances is arithmetic.

b. Write recursive and explicit rules for the sequence of loan balances.

c. How many months will it take Carrie to pay off the loan? Explain.

d. How much did Carrie borrow? Explain.

21. The graph shows the lengths of the rows formed by various numbers of grocery carts when they are nested together.

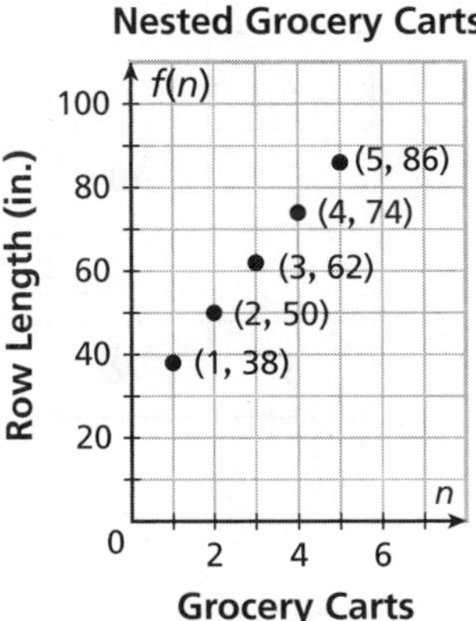

a. Write an explicit rule for the sequence of row lengths.

b. What is the length of a row of 25 nested carts?

22. Each stair on a staircase has a height of 7.5 inches.

a. Write an explicit rule for an arithmetic sequence that gives the height (in inches) of the nth stair above the base of the staircase.

b. What is the fourth term of the sequence, and what does it represent in this situation?

Name________________ Class________________ Date________________

3-6

Additional Practice

Determine whether each sequence is an arithmetic sequence. If so, find the common difference and the next three terms.

1. –10, –7, –4, –1, ...

2. 0, 1.5, 3, 4.5, ...

3. 5, 8, 12, 17, ...

4. –20, –20.5, –21, –21.5, ...

Find the indicated term of each arithmetic sequence.

5. 28th term: 0, –4, –8, –12, ...

6. 15th term: 2, 3.5, 5, 6.5, ...

7. 37th term: $a_1 = -3$; $d = 2.8$

8. 14th term: $a_1 = 4.2$; $d = -5$

9. 17th term; $a_1 = 2.3$; $d = -2.3$

10. 92nd term; $a_1 = 1$; $d = 0.8$

11. A movie rental club charges $4.95 for the first month's rentals. The club charges $18.95 for each additional month. How much is the total cost for one year?

12. A carnival game awards a prize if Kasey can shoot a basket. The charge is $5.00 for the first shot, then $2.00 for each additional shot. Kasey needed 11 shots to win a prize. What is the total amount Kasey spent to win a prize?

Problem Solving

Find the indicated term of each arithmetic sequence.

1. Darnell has a job and his saving his paychecks each week.

Weeks	1	2	3	4
Savings	$130	$260	$390	$520

How much will Darnell have saved after 11 weeks?

____

2. A tube containing 3 ounces of toothpaste is being used at a rate of 0.15 ounces per day. How much toothpaste will be in the tube after one week?

____

3. A new car costs $13,000 and is depreciating by $900 each year. How much will the car be worth after 4 years?

____

4. Jessie is playing an arcade game that costs 50¢ for the first game and 25¢ to continue if she loses. How much will she spend on the game if she continues 9 times?

____

Use the graph below to answer questions 5–9. The graph shows the size of Ivor's ant colony over the first four weeks. Assume the ant population will continue to grow at the same rate. Select the best answer.

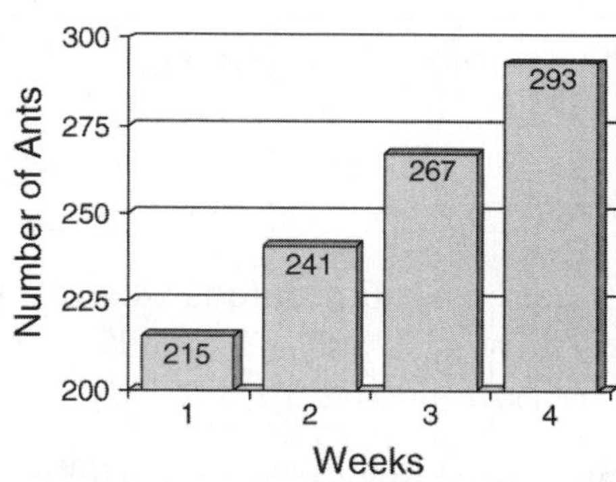

5. Which of the following shows how many ants Ivor will have in the next three weeks?

   A 315, 341, 367

   B 317, 343, 369

   C 318, 334, 350

   D 319, 345, 371

6. Which rule can be used to find how large the colony will be in *n* weeks?

   F $a_n = 215 + 26n$

   G $a_n = 215n + 26$

   H $a_n = 215(n - 1) + 26$

   J $a_n = 215 + 26(n - 1)$

7. How many ants will Ivor have in 27 weeks?

   A 891   C 5616

   B 917   D 5831

8. Ivor's ants weigh 1.5 grams each. How many grams do all of his ants weigh in 13 weeks?

   F 660.5   H 722

   G 683   J 790.5

9. When the colony reaches 1385 ants, Ivor's ant farm will not be big enough for all of them. In how many weeks will the ant population be too large?

   A 45   C 47

   B 46   D 48

Name_______________ Class_______________ Date_______________

CHAPTER 3

Performance Tasks

COMMON CORE

CC.9-12.F-IF.2, 4, 5, 7
CC.9-12.F-BF.1
CC.9-12.F-LE.2, 5
CC.9-12.S-ID.6a

★ **1.** A construction company's cost to build a new home is $35,000 plus $95 for each square foot of floor space.

a. Write an equation for a function where the cost c to build a house is a function of f square feet of floor space.

b. Use your function to determine how much it will cost to build a house with an area of 1600 square feet.

★ **2.** The relationship between the number of hours students spend watching TV every week and the number of hours they spend playing video games is shown in the scatter plot. Based on the data, what is the approximate number of hours of video games for a student who watches 5 hours of TV per week? Explain how you found your answer.

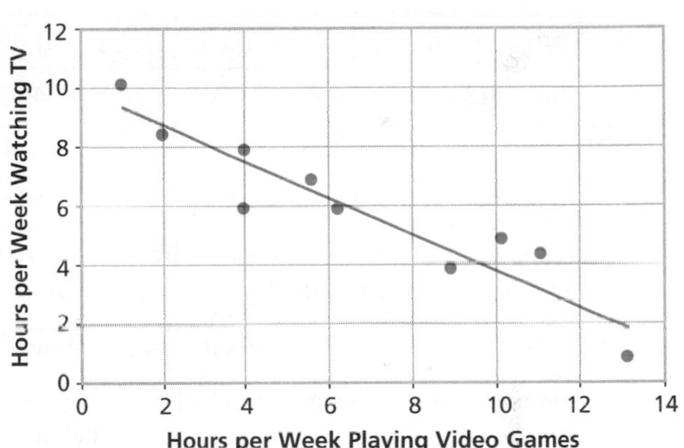

★★ **3.** The weight in pounds that can be supported by a diving board is given by the function $w(x) = \frac{5000}{x}$, where x is the distance in feet from the base of the diving board to a point along the length of the board.

a. What is the domain of the function? Can the domain include zero? Explain.

b. Make a table of values and generate five ordered pairs to represent the function.

c. Plot the ordered pairs and draw a smooth curve connecting the points.

continued

4. The results of a test of a metal are shown in the table, with strain in meters per meter, and stress in units called *megapascals*, or MPa. Stress is a measure of how much force is applied to the metal, and strain is a measure of how far the metal bends under that force.

Strain (m/m)	0.01	0.02	0.03	0.04	0.05	0.06	0.07	0.08	0.09
Stress (MPa)	100	200	300	400	500	540	560	550	525

a. Make a graph of the data with strain on the horizontal axis.

b. Hooke's law states that stress is directly proportional to strain. Does the metal obey Hooke's law for in any part of its domain? Explain your reasoning.

c. Write a function that models this material over the domain you found in part **b**.

d. The ultimate tensile strength is the maximum value on the stress-strain curve. What are the stress and strain values for this material's ultimate tensile strength?

Name ______________________ Class ____________ Date ________

MULTIPLE CHOICE

1. Which set of ordered pairs represents a function?

   A. $\{(-1, 1), (0, 0), (1, 1), (2, 2)\}$

   B. $\{(3, -3), (2, -2), (1, -1), (1, 1)\}$

   C. $\{(4, 2), (4, -2), (9, 3), (9, -3)\}$

   D. $\{(-2, -1), (-2, 0), (-2, 1), (-2, 2)\}$

2. You and three friends plan to split the cost b (in dollars) of a large bag of popcorn at a movie. Which function describes the cost for each person as a function of the cost per bag?

   F. $P(b) = 3b$

   G. $P(b) = \frac{3}{b}$

   H. $P(b) = 4b$

   J. $P(b) = \frac{b}{4}$

3. Jorge bought a mechanical pencil for \$8. A lead and eraser refill pack costs \$2. Write a linear function to describe the cost of using the pencil as a function of the number of refill packs.

   A. $C(r) = 8r - 2$ C. $C(r) = 2r$

   B. $C(r) = 2r + 8$ D. $C(r) = 8r + 2$

4. Gary works no more than 9 hours on weekends and gets paid \$10 per hour. He works whole-hour shifts. His pay P is a function of the number of hours he works n. What is the range of this function?

   F. $0 \leq n \leq 9$

   G. $0 \leq P \leq 90$

   H. $\{0, 1, 2, 3, 4, 5, 6, 7, 8, 9\}$

   J. $\{0, 10, 20, 30, 40, 50, 60, 70, 80, 90\}$

5. Given $f(x) = 3x + 2$ and $g(x) = -2x - 4$, find $h(x) = f(x) - g(x)$.

   A. $h(x) = x - 2$

   B. $h(x) = x + 6$

   C. $h(x) = 5x + 6$

   D. $h(x) = 5x - 2$

6. The cost to ship a package is $C(w) = 0.23w + 7$ where w is the weight in pounds. Write the inverse function to find the weight of a package as a function $w(C)$ of the cost.

   F. $w(C) = \frac{C - 7}{0.23}$

   G. $w(C) = \frac{C + 7}{0.23}$

   H. $w(C) = 0.23C + 7$

   J. $w(C) = -0.23C - 7$

7. Which number best approximates the correlation coefficient for the data below?

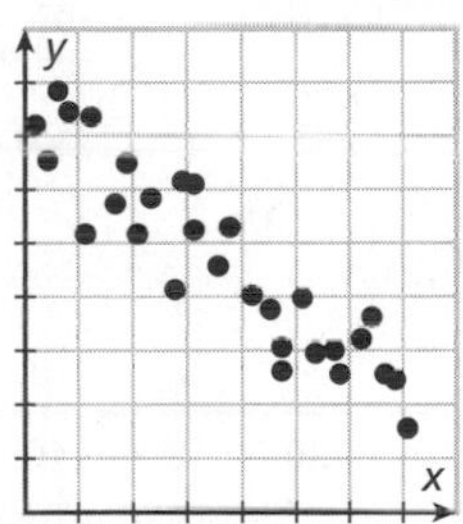

   A. -0.8 C. 0.2

   B. -0.2 D. 0.8

8. The function $C(t)$ gives the cost C of buying t tickets to a museum exhibit when a group discount is offered.

$$C(t) = \begin{cases} 20t \text{ if } 0 \leq t < 10 \\ 18t \text{ if } t \geq 10 \end{cases}$$

   Which statement describes what $C(10)$ represents?

   F. 10 tickets cost \$200.

   G. 10 tickets cost \$180.

   H. 10 tickets cost \$20.

   J. 10 tickets cost \$18.

CONSTRUCTED RESPONSE

9. A taxicab driver charges \$6.00 for any distance less than 1 mile. For distances of 1 mile or more, he charges \$6.00 plus \$3.00 for each complete mile.

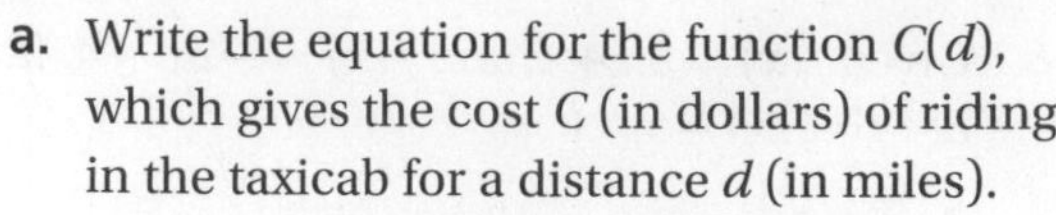

   a. Write the equation for the function $C(d)$, which gives the cost C (in dollars) of riding in the taxicab for a distance d (in miles).

   ____

   b. Graph the function to show the costs for all distances less than 5 miles. Include labels and scales on your graph.

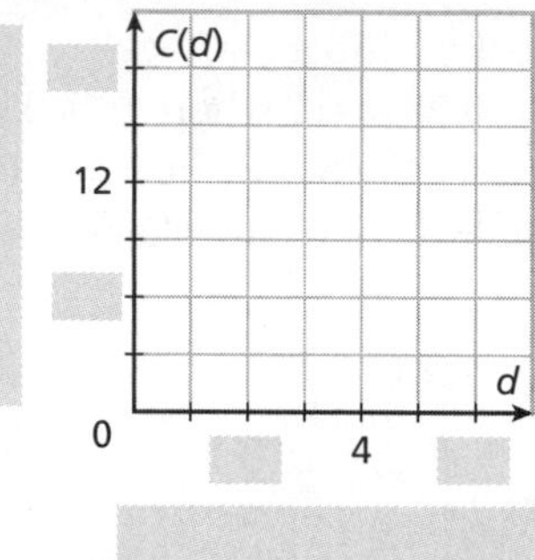

10. Emily walks to meet her brother and one of his classmates after kindergarten and walks them home.

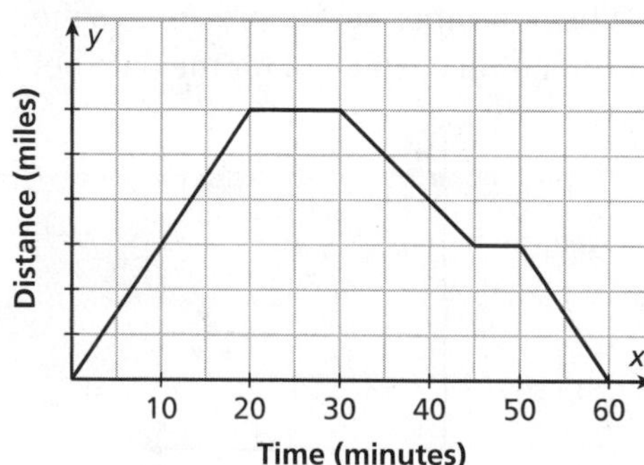

   a. During which interval(s) is Emily's distance from home increasing?

   ____

   b. During which interval(s) is Emily's distance from home decreasing?

   ____

   ____

   c. Which interval do you think represents the time when Emily is dropping her brother's classmate at his house? Justify your answer.

   ____

   ____

   ____

   ____

   ____

   ____

11. Henry purchased a roll of 100 stamps. He uses 5 stamps each week.

   a. The number of stamps at the end of each week is a function $S(w)$ of the number of weeks. Write an equation for the function.

   ____

   b. What types of numbers are reasonable for the domain and the range?

   ____

   ____

   ____

   c. Complete the table using selected domain values. Then graph the function.

w	*S(w)*	*(w, S(w))*

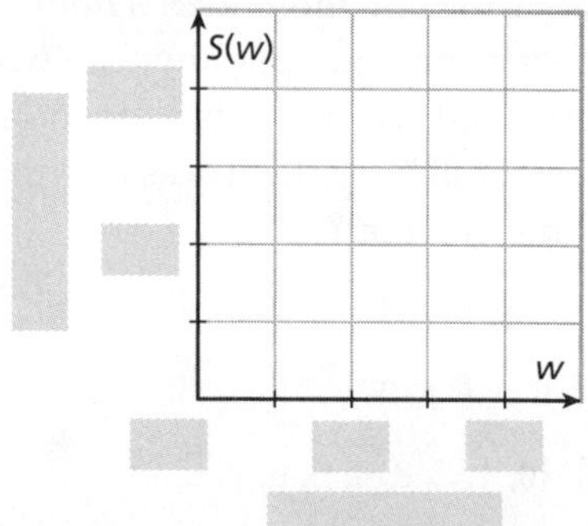

   d. At the end of how many weeks will Henry have one quarter of the stamps left? Explain your reasoning.

   ____

   ____

CHAPTER 4

Linear Functions

Chapter Focus

In this unit you will examine the characteristics of linear functions and their graphs. You will learn to recognize linear functions by their constant rate of change. You will learn to write linear functions based on given values, using paper-and-pencil techniques as well as technology. You will also learn how to transform the graph of a linear function in the coordinate plane.

Chapter at a Glance

COMMON CORE

Lesson		Standards for Mathematical Content
4-1	Identifying Linear Functions	CC.9-12.F.IF.2, CC.9-12.F.IF.3, CC.9-12.F.IF.5, CC.9-12.F.IF.9
4-2	Using Intercepts	CC.9-12.A.REI.10
4-3	Rate of Change and Slope	CC.9-12.F.IF.6
4-4	The Slope Formula	CC.9-12.F.IF.6
4-5	Direct Variation	CC.9-12.A.CED.2, CC.9-12.F.IF.7b, CC.9-12.F.BF.1, CC.9-12.F.BF.3
4-6	Slope-Intercept Form	CC.9-12.A.REI.11, CC.9-12.F.IF.7a, CC.9-12.F.LE.2
4-7	Point-Slope Form	CC.9-12.F.IF.8, CC.9-12.F.LE.2
4-8	Line of Best fit	CC.9-12.S.ID.6b, CC.9-12.S.ID.6c
4-9	Slopes of Parallel and Perpendicular Lines	CC.9-12.A.CED.2, CC.9-12.A.CED.3
4-10	Transforming Linear Functions	CC.9-12.F.BF.1, CC.9-12.F.BF.3
	Performance Tasks	
	Assessment Readiness	

CHAPTER 4

Unpacking the Standards

Understanding the standards and the vocabulary terms in the standards will help you know exactly what you are expected to learn in this chapter.

COMMON CORE **CC.9-12.F.IF.6**

Calculate and interpret the average rate of change of a function (presented symbolically or as a table) over a specified interval. Estimate the rate of change from a graph.

Key Vocabulary

rate of change *(tasa de cambio)*
A ratio that compares the amount of change in a dependent variable to the amount of change in an independent variable.

What It Means For You — Lessons 4-1, 4-3, 4-4

Average rate of change measures the change in the dependent variable against the change in the independent variable over a specific interval. This helps you understand how quickly the values in a function change.

EXAMPLE

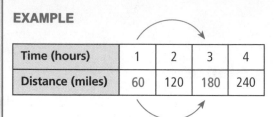

Time (hours)	1	2	3	4
Distance (miles)	60	120	180	240

Average rate of change $= \frac{180 - 60}{3 - 1} = 60$ mi/h

CHAPTER 4

COMMON CORE **CC.9-12.F.IF.7a**

Graph linear … functions and show intercepts, …

Key Vocabulary

linear function *(función lineal)*
A function that can be written in the form $y = mx + b$, where x is the independent variable and m and b are real numbers. Its graph is a line.

x-intercept *(intersección con el eje x)* The x-coordinate(s) of the point(s) where a graph intersects the x-axis.

y-intercept *(intersección con el eje y)* The y-coordinate(s) of the point(s) where a graph intersects the y-axis.

What It Means For You — Lessons 4-1, 4-2, 4-6

The graph of a linear function is a line. If you know two points on a line, you can graph it by drawing a straight line through the two points. You can use intercepts to help you locate two points.

EXAMPLE **Graph of a linear function**

$2x - 4y = 8$

$y = \frac{1}{2}x - 2$

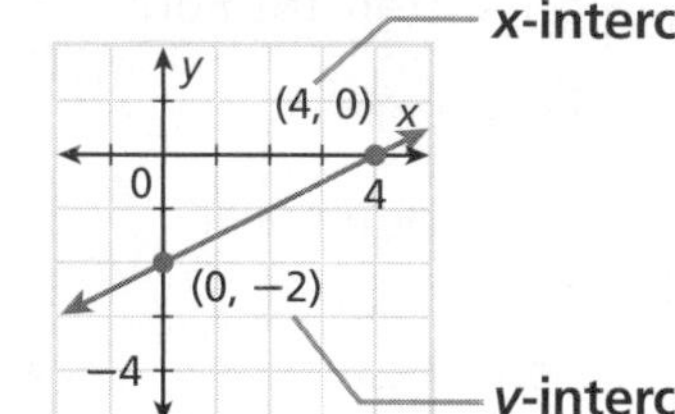

NON-EXAMPLE **Graph of a nonlinear function**

$y = x^2 - 4x + 4$

y-intercept
y
4
(0, 4)
2
x
0
(2, 0)
4
x-intercept

COMMON CORE **CC.9-12.A.CED.2**

Create equations in two … variables to represent relationships between quantities; graph equations on coordinate axes with labels and scales.

Key Vocabulary

equation *(ecuación)* A mathematical statement that two expressions are equivalent.

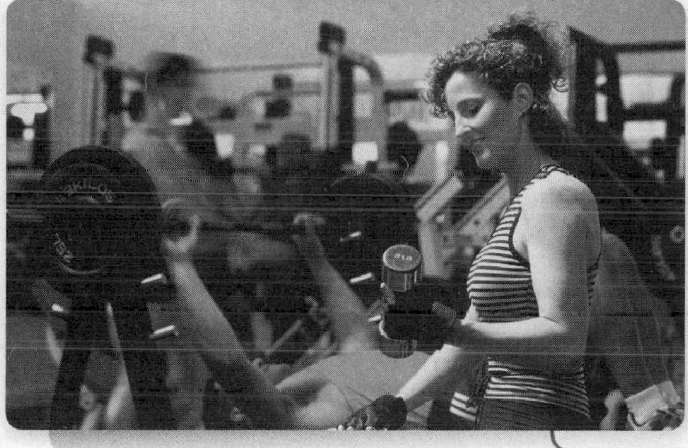

What It Means For You — Lessons 4-5, 4-6, 4-8, 4-9

You can represent mathematical relationships with words, equations, tables, and graphs.

EXAMPLE

Membership costs \$150 plus \$75 per month.

$$y = 75x + 150$$

Months	0	1	2	3	4
Cost (\$)	150	225	300	375	450

CHAPTER 4

COMMON CORE **CC.9-12.F.BF.3**

Identify the effect on the graph of replacing $f(x)$ by $f(x) + k$, $k\,f(x)$, $f(kx)$, and $f(x + k)$ for specific values of k (both positive and negative); …

Key Vocabulary

function notation *(notación de función)* If x is the independent variable and y is the dependent variable, then the function notation for y is $f(x)$, read "f of x," where f names the function.

What It Means For You — Lessons 4-5, 4-10

You can change a function by adding or multiplying by a constant. The result will be a new function that is a transformation of the original function.

EXAMPLE **Vertical translations of the function $f(x) = x$**

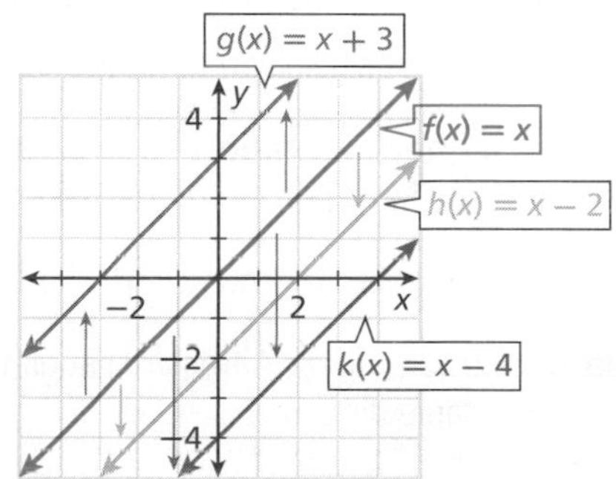

CHAPTER 4

Key Vocabulary

constant of variation *(constante de variación)* The constant k in direct and inverse variation equations.

correlation coefficient *(coeficiente de correlación)* A number r, where $-1 \leq r \leq 1$, that describes how closely the points in a scatter plot cluster around the least-squares line.

direct variation *(variación directa)* A linear relationship between two variables, x and y, that can be written in the form $y = kx$, where k is a nonzero constant.

least-squares line *(línea de mínimos cuadrados)* The line of fit for which the sum of the squares of the residuals is as small as possible.

line of best fit *(línea de mejor ajuste)* The line that comes closest to all of the points in a data set.

linear equation in two variables *(ecuación lineal en dos variables)* An equation that can be written in the form $Ax + By = C$ where A, B, and C are constants and A and B are not both 0.

linear function *(función lineal)* A function that can be written in the form $y = mx + b$, where x is the independent variable and m and b are real numbers. Its graph is a line.

linear regression *(regresión lineal)* A statistical method used to fit a linear model to a given data set.

parent function *(función madre)* The simplest function with the defining characteristics of the family. Functions in the same family are transformations of their parent function.

rate of change *(tasa de cambio)* A ratio that compares the amount of change in a dependent variable to the amount of change in an independent variable.

reflection *(reflexión)* A transformation that reflects, or "flips," a graph or figure across a line, called the line of reflection.

residual *(residuo)* The signed vertical distance between a data point and a line of fit.

rotation *(rotación)* A transformation that rotates or turns a figure about a point called the center of rotation.

slope *(pendiente)* A measure of the steepness of a line. If (x_1, y_1) and (x_2, y_2) are any two points on the line, the slope of the line, known as m, is represented by the equation $m = \frac{y_2 - y_1}{x_2 - x_1}$.

solution of a linear equation in two variables *(solución de una ecuación lineal en dos variables)* An ordered pair or ordered pairs that make the equation true.

transformation *(transformación)* A change in the position, size, or shape of a figure or graph.

translation *(traslación)* A transformation that shifts or slides every point of a figure or graph the same distance in the same direction.

x-intercept *(intersección con el eje x)* The x-coordinate(s) of the point(s) where a graph intersects the x-axis.

y-intercept *(intersección con el eje y)* The y-coordinate(s) of the point(s) where a graph intersects the y-axis.

Name ______________________ Class ______________ Date __________

4-1

Video Tutor

Identifying Linear Functions

Extension: Discrete and Continuous Functions

Essential question: *What is a discrete linear function and how are discrete and continuous linear functions alike and how are they different?*

CC.9–12.F.IF.5

1 EXPLORE Analyzing a Discrete Real-World Function

You buy a printer for \$80 and then pay \$15 for each ink cartridge that you use. A function relating the cost, C (in dollars), of operating the printer to the number of cartridges used, n, is $C(n) = 15n + 80$.

A Complete the table to represent the total cost for 0 to 4 cartridges.

Number of cartridges, n	Cost, C (dollars)
0	
1	
2	
3	
4	

B Graph the function from Part A. Specify the scale you use.

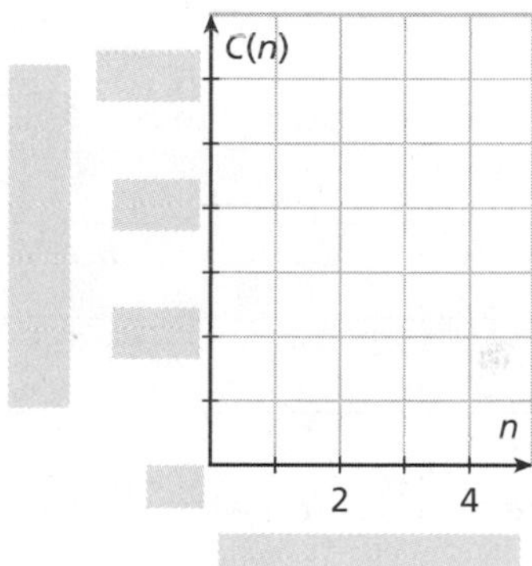

C What is the initial value of the cost function? What does it represent? What number of cartridges corresponds to the initial cost?

____

D Compare the differences in cost with each unit increase in the number of cartridges purchased.

____

____

REFLECT

1a. Identify the domain and range for the function $C(n)$ using set notation.

Domain: ______________ Range: ______________

1b. Describe the pattern formed by the points in the graph.

____

1c. How do your answers change if the price of the printer is $90?

CC.9–12.F.IF.3

2 ENGAGE Recognizing Linear Functions

A function whose output values have a *common difference* for each unit increase in the input values is a *linear function.* A **linear function** can be represented by the equation $f(x) = mx + b$, where m and b are constants. The graph of a linear function forms a straight line.

When a linear function is *discrete,* its graph consists of isolated points along a straight line. If a discrete linear function has inputs that are a set of equally spaced integers, then its outputs form an arithmetic sequence.

REFLECT

2a. Give three reasons why the cost function in the Explore is linear.

2b. What are m and b and what do they represent for the cost function?

CC.9–12.F.IF.2

3 EXPLORE Comparing Linear Functions

A Avocados cost $1.50 each. Green beans cost $1.50 per pound. The total cost of a avocados is $C(a) = 1.5a$ and the total cost of g pounds of green beans is $C(g) = 1.5g$. Complete the tables to find a few values.

Cost of Avocados		
a	**C(a) = 1.5a**	**(a, C(a))**
0	0	(0, 0)
1		
2		
3		

Cost of Green Beans		
g	**C(g) = 1.5g**	**(g, C(g))**
0	0	(0, 0)
1		
2		
3		

B What is a reasonable domain for $C(a)$? for $C(g)$? Explain.

C Graph the two cost functions for all appropriate domain values from the given scales below.

C(a)
2
0
2
4
a

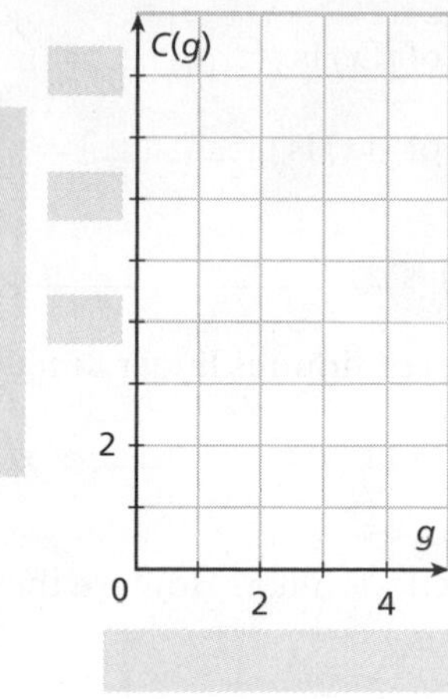

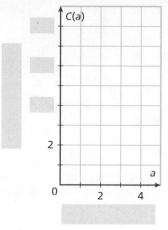

D Compare the graphs. How are they alike? How are they different?

____

____

____

____

REFLECT

3a. Describe the range for $C(a)$ and for $C(g)$.

____

____

3b. How do the units of a and g imply that their graphs will be different?

____

____

____

3c. A function whose graph is unbroken is a *continuous* function. Tell which cost function is *continuous* and which is *discrete*.

____

CC.9–12.F.IF.9

4 EXAMPLE Comparing Functions Given a Table and a Rule

The functions $f(x)$ and $g(x)$ below are linear. Find the initial value and the range of each function. Then compare the functions.

- The table gives the values of the function $f(x)$. The domain of $f(x)$ is $\{4, 5, 6, 7\}$.
- Let the domain of the function $g(x) = 2x + 3$ be all real numbers such that $4 \le x \le 7$.

x	f(x)
4	8
5	10
6	12
7	14

A The initial value is the output that is paired with the least input.

The initial value of $f(x)$ is f(________) = ________.

The initial value of $g(x)$ is g(________) = ________.

B The range of $f(x)$ is ____________________.

Because $g(x)$ is a continuous linear function the range is

$g(4) \le g(x) \le g(7)$, or $\{g(x) \mid$ ________ $\le g(x) \le$ ________$\}$.

C How are the functions alike? How are they different? Consider their domains, initial values, and ranges.

____

____

____

____

____

____

REFLECT

4a. Find and compare the common differences per unit increase in the input values for the functions $f(x)$ and $g(x)$ in the Example.

____

____

4b. How can you tell that $f(x)$ and $g(x)$ in the Example are linear?

____

____

____

CC.9–12.F.IF.9

5 EXAMPLE Comparing Descriptions and Graphs of Functions

Compare the following functions.

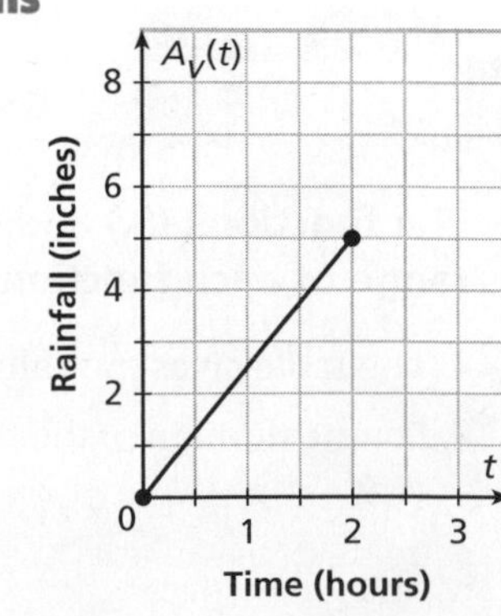

- A heavy rainstorm lasted for 2.5 hours during which time it rained at a steady rate of 0.5 inches per hour. The function $A_h(t)$ represents the amount of rain that fell in t hours.
- The graph at the right shows the amount of rain that fell during a violent rainstorm $A_v(t)$ (in inches) as a function of time t (in hours).

A How long did each storm last? Explain your reasoning.

____

____

B Calculate the amount of rainfall during the heavy storm. Then compare the amounts of rainfall for the two storms.

Heavy rainfall: (______ inches per hour) • (______ hours) = ______ inches of rain

____

____

C Calculate how many inches of rain fell per hour during the violent rainstorm. Then compare the rainfall rates for the two storms.

Violent rainfall rate: (______ inches) ÷ (______ hours) = ______ inches per hour

____

REFLECT

5a. How would the graphs of $A_h(t)$ and $A_v(t)$ compare with one another?

____

____

PRACTICE

1. Andrea receives a $40 gift card to use a town pool. It costs her $8 per visit to swim. A function relating the value of the gift card, v, to the number of visits, n, is $v(n) = 40 - 8n$.

a. Graph the function. Label axes and scales.

b. What is the initial value?

____

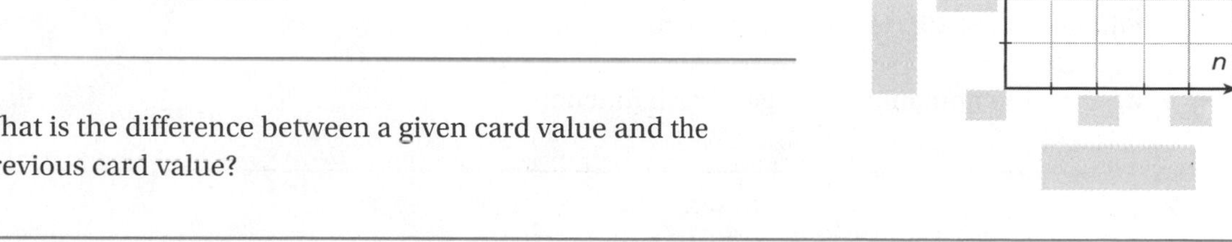

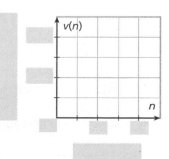

c. What is the difference between a given card value and the previous card value?

____

d. Identify the domain and the range of the function using set notation.

____

e. Is the function a discrete linear function? Are its outputs an arithmetic sequence? Why or why not?

2. The functions $f(x)$ and $g(x)$ are defined by the table and graph below.

x	$f(x)$
0	−2
1	1
2	4
3	7
4	10
5	13

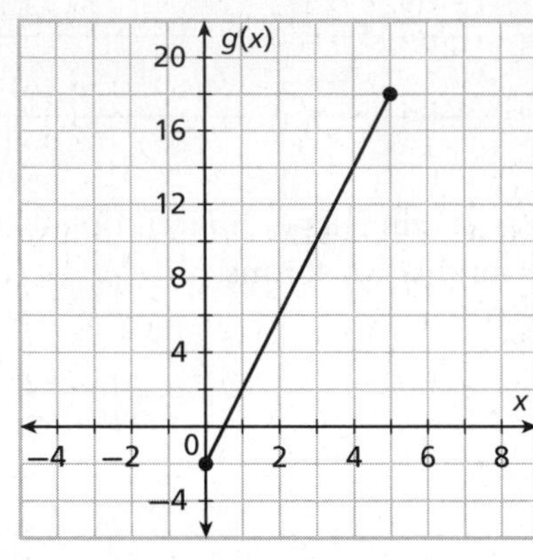

a. Compare the domains, initial values, and ranges of the functions.

b. Explain why the functions are linear. Tell whether each function is *discrete* or *continuous.*

3. Grace works between 10 and 20 hours per week while attending college. She earns \$9.00 per hour. Her hours are rounded to the nearest quarter hour. Her roommate Frances also has a job. Her pay for t hours is given by the function $f(t) = 10t$, where $5 \leq t \leq 15$. Her hours are not rounded.

a. Find the domain and range of each function.

b. Compare their hourly wages and the amount they each earn per week.

Name____ Class____________________ Date______________

4-1

Additional Practice

Identify whether each graph represents a function. Explain. If the graph does represent a function, is the function linear?

1. ____

____

____

2. 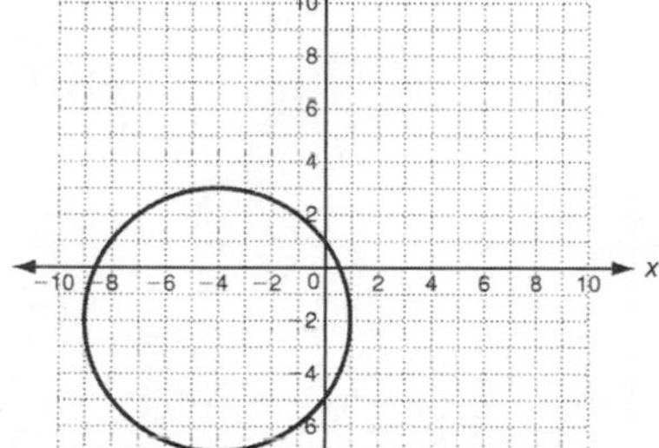

____

____

____

3. Compare the functions represented by the ordered pairs.

Set A: {(5, 1), (4, 4), (3, 9), (2, 16), (1, 25)} ________________________

Set B: {(1, –5), (2, –3), (3, –1), (4, 1), (5, 3)} ________________________

4. Graph $y = -2x$. Give the domain and range. Is the function discrete or continuous?

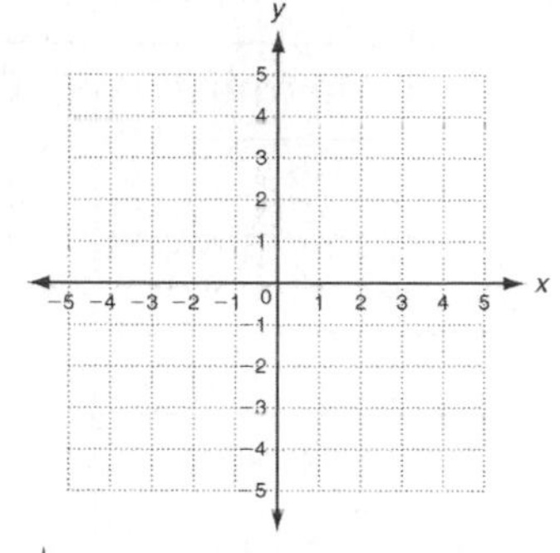

____

____

5. In 2005, the Shabelle River in Somalia rose an estimated 5.25 inches every hour for 15 hours. The increase in water level is represented by the function $f(x) = 5.25x$, where x is the number of hours. Graph this function and give its domain and range. Is the function discrete or continuous?

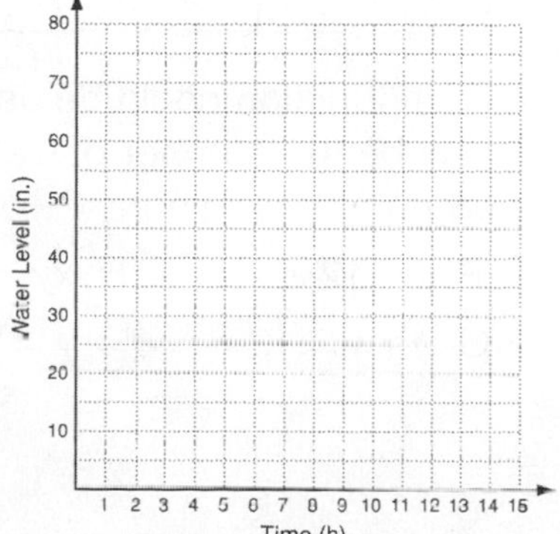

____

____

Problem Solving

Write the correct answer.

1. A daycare center charges a $75 enrollment fee plus $100 per week. The function $f(x) = 100x + 75$ gives the cost of daycare for x weeks. Graph this function and give its domain and range. Is the function discrete or continuous?

____

____

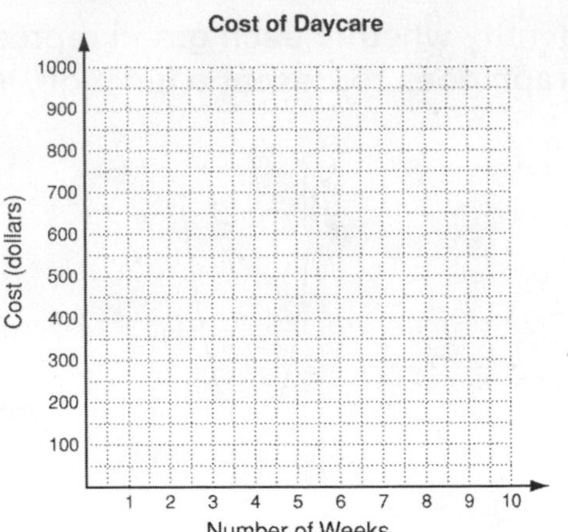

2. A family swimming pool holds 60 m^3 of water. The function $f(x) = 60 - 0.18x$ gives the cubic meters of water in the pool, taking into account water lost to evaporation over x days. Graph this function and give its domain and range. Is the function discrete or continuous?

____

____

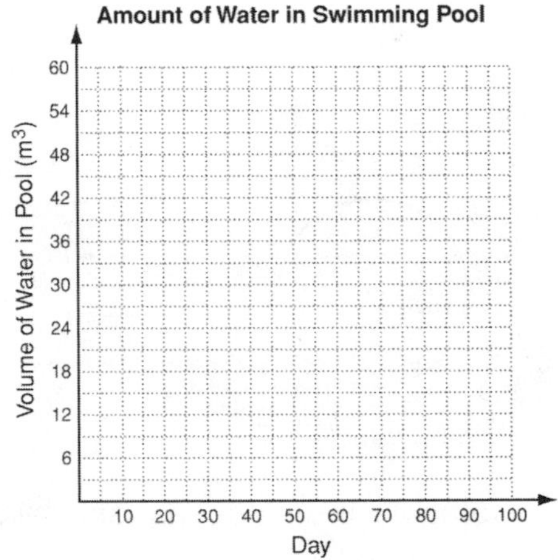

Elijah is using a rowing machine. The table shows how many Calories he can burn for certain lengths of time. Select the best answer.

Time (min)	Calories
2	24
4	48
6	72
8	96
10	120

3. Which function could be used to describe the number of Calories burned after x minutes?

   F $y = 12 + x$ H $xy = 12$

   G $x + y = 12$ J $y = 12x$

4. What is the domain of the function?

   A {0, 1, 2, 3, ...} C $x \geq 0$

   B {2, 4, 6, ...} D $x \geq 2$

5. What is the range of the function?

   F {0, 12, 24, 36, ...} H $y \geq 0$

   G {24, 48, 72, ...} J $y \geq 24$

6. Elijah graphed the function in problem 3. Which best describes the graph?

   A Line increasing from left to right.

   B Line decreasing from left to right.

   C Five points increasing from left to right.

   D Five points decreasing from left to right.

Name_______________ Class_______________ Date_______________

4-2

Video Tutor

Using Intercepts

Going Deeper

Essential question: *How can you use intercepts to graph the solutions to a linear equation in two variables?*

An equation in two variables x and y that can be written in the form $Ax + By = C$ for real numbers A, B, and C is a **linear equation in two variables.**

The form $Ax + By = C$ where A and B are not both 0 is called the **standard form of a linear equation.**

A **solution of an equation in two variables** x and y is any ordered pair (x, y) that makes the equation true.

CC.9–12.A.REI.10

1 EXPLORE Definition of a Linear Equation in Two Variables

A Complete the table of values to find solutions of the linear equation $x + y = 5$.

B Plot the ordered pairs on a coordinate grid.

x_1	y_1	(x_1, y_1)
−2		
−1		
0		
1		
2		
3		
4		
5		
6		
7		

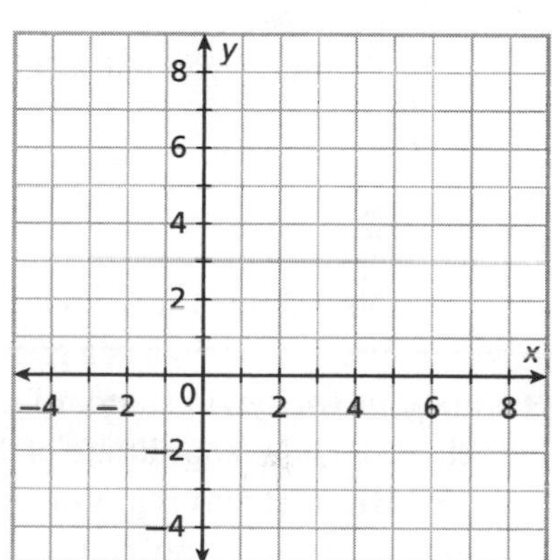

REFLECT

1a. What appears to be true about the points that are solutions of a linear equation?

____

1b. What is the minimum number of points you would need to plot to graph a linear equation? Explain. Why should you graph more than the minimum number of points?

____

____

____

To determine whether an ordered pair (x_1, y_1) is a solution of a linear equation, substitute the values of x_1 and y_1 into the linear equation. If the two sides of the equation are equal, then the ordered pair is a solution.

CC.9–12.A.REI.10

2 EXAMPLE Determining Whether an Ordered Pair is a Solution

Which ordered pair is a solution to $3x + 5y = 15$?

A $(0, 3)$

$3(0) + 5(3) = 15$

____

B $(8, 1)$

____

____

$(0, 3)$______ a solution to $3x + 5y = 15$.

$(8, 1)$______ a solution to $3x + 5y = 15$.

REFLECT

2a. What do you know about the point $(0, 3)$ and its relationship to the graph of $3x + 5y = 15$?

____

2b. Explain how you know that $3x + 5y = 15$ is a linear equation.

____

The graph of a linear equation is a line. To graph a line, it is necessary to plot only two points. However, it is a good idea to plot a third point as a check. For linear equations written in standard form, two good points to plot are where the line crosses each axis. The x-coordinate of the point where the line crosses the x-axis is called the **x-intercept** and is found by substituting 0 for y in the equation of the line. The y-coordinate of the point where the line crosses the y-axis is called the **y-intercept** and is found by substituting 0 for x in the equation of the line.

CC.9–12.A.REI.10

3 EXAMPLE Graphing a Linear Equation in Standard Form

Graph $2x + y = 4$.

A Make a table of values. Each row in the table of values makes an ordered pair (x, y).

x	y
0	
	0
1	

B Substitute 0 for x in the equation and solve for y.

$2(0) + y = 4$

$y =$

Write the value for y next to the 0 in the first row of the table.

C Next substitute 0 for y in the equation and solve for x.

$2x + (0) = 4$

$2x = 4$

$x =$ ☐

Write the value for x before the 0 in the second row of the table.

D Choose another value for x and solve for y. It is usually easiest to choose a simple value such as 1.

$2(1) + y = 4$

☐ $+ y = 4$

$y =$ ☐

Write the value for y after the 1 in the third row of the table.

E Plot the first two points on the coordinate grid. Then plot the third point. If you have done your calculations correctly, all three points should lie on a straight line. Draw a line through the points.

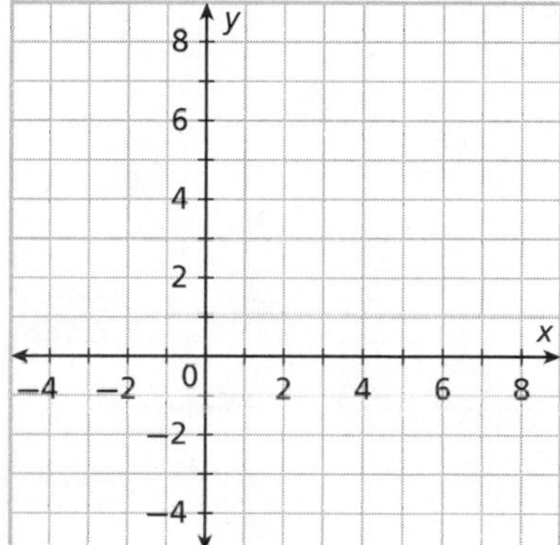

REFLECT

3a. List three other solutions to $2x + y = 4$.

____

3b. Why should you find the x- and y-intercepts when making a table of values to graph a linear equation?

____

____

3c. Suppose that in part E the three points did not lie on a straight line. What would this tell you and what should you do?

____

____

CC.9–12.A.REI.10

4 EXAMPLE Vertical and Horizontal Lines

Graph $x = 3$ and $y = -4$.

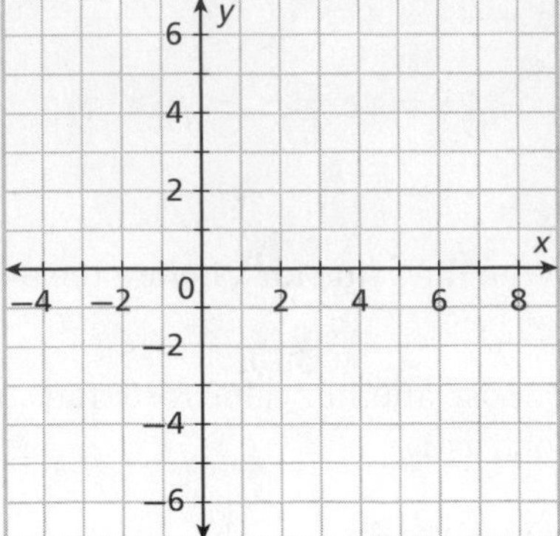

Note that the equation $x = 3$ can be written as $1x + 0y = 3$. All points with an x-value of 3 are solutions to the equation. These points lie on a vertical line that passes through (3, 0).

Note that the equation $y = -4$ can be written as $0x + 1y = -4$. All points with a y-value of -4 are solutions to the equation. These points lie on a horizontal line that passes through (0, -4).

REFLECT

4a. Describe the graph of the line $y = 1$.

____

4b. Describe the graph of the line $x = -2$.

____

A linear equation in the form $Ax + By = C$ where $C = 0$ has a special property. To see what this property is, look below at the table and graph of the equation $-4x + 3y = 0$.

x	y
0	0
0	0
3	4

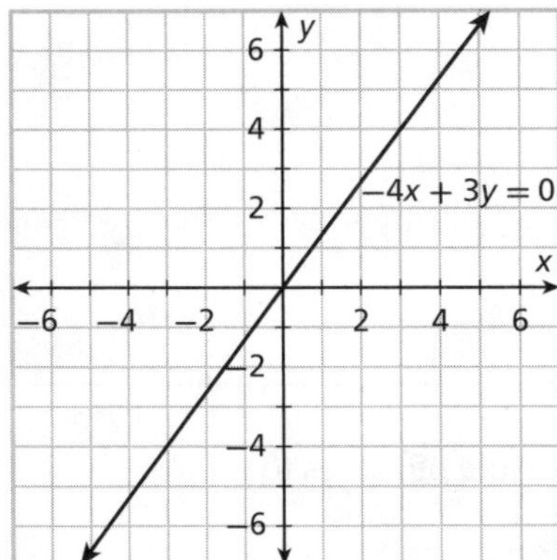

Notice that the table gives the same point for the x-intercept and for the y-intercept, namely the point (0, 0). Notice also that the graph passes through the origin. This is true for any linear equation of the form $Ax + By = C$ where $C = 0$. Consequently, you cannot use the x- and y-intercepts to draw their graphs. For these equations, first plot a point at the origin. Then substitute two other values for x to locate two more points.

CC.9–12.A.REI.10

5 EXAMPLE Lines Through the Origin

Graph $2x - 3y = 0$.

A Complete the table of values.

B Plot the points on the coordinate grid.

C Check that all three points are collinear.

D Draw a line through the points.

x	y
0	0
1	
2	

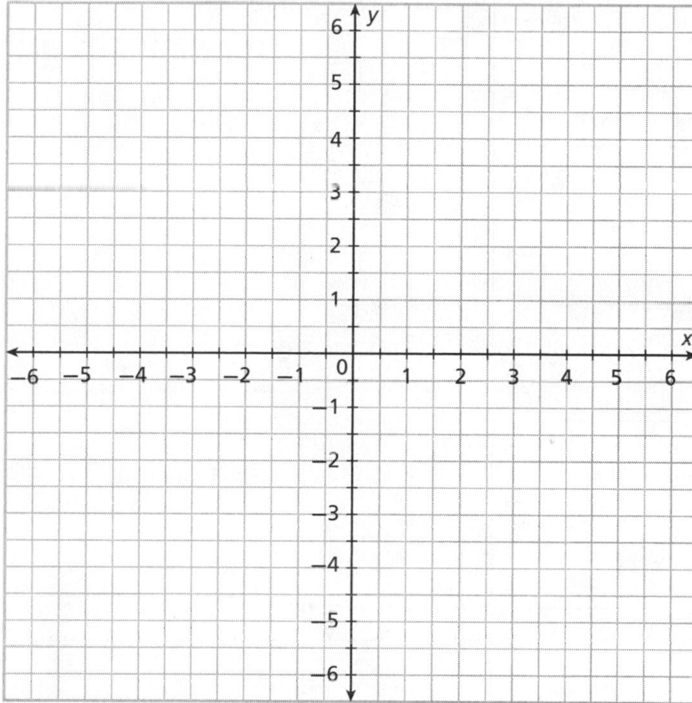

REFLECT

5a. Would it have been easier to use x-values of 3 and -3 to graph the line? Why or why not?

____

____

5b. If C does not equal 0, can the graph of $Ax + By = C$ pass through the origin? Why or why not?

____

____

PRACTICE

Tell whether the ordered pair is a solution to the equation.

1. $-5x + 2y = 4$; $(4, 8)$

2. $2x - 7y = 1$; $(11, 3)$

Complete the table and graph the equation.

3. $-2x + y = 3$

x	*y*

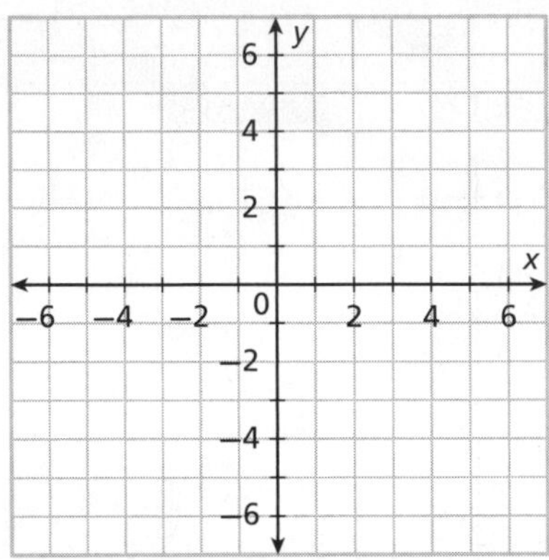

4. $3x = -6$

x	*y*

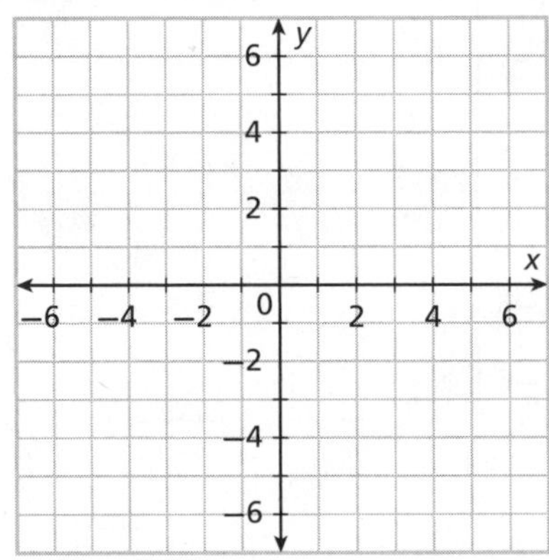

5. $4x + 5y = 0$

x	*y*
0	
	−4
−5	

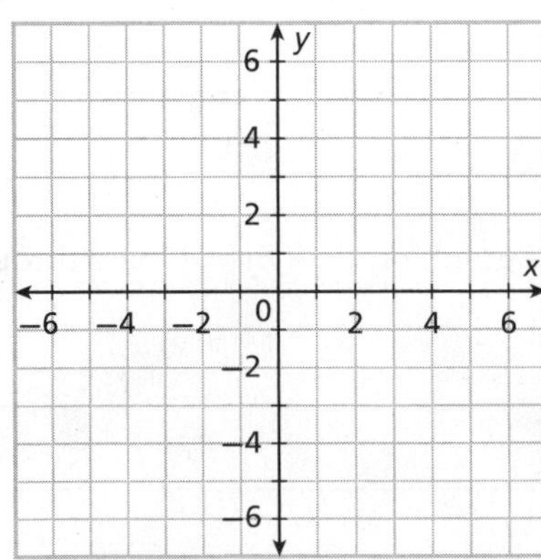

Name ______________________ Class ______________ Date ______________

4-2

Additional Practice

Find the *x*- and *y*-intercepts.

1.

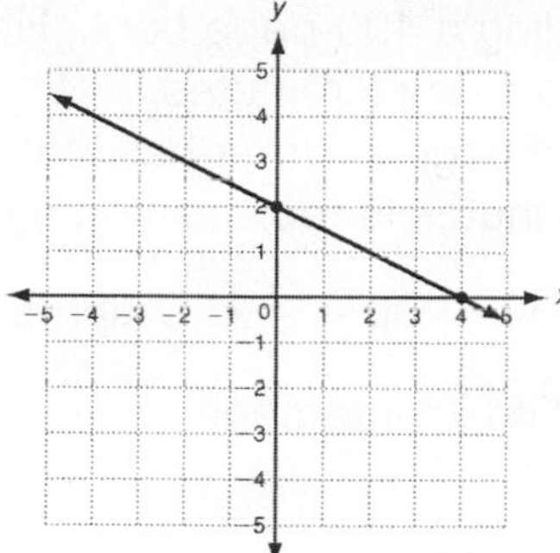

____

____

2.

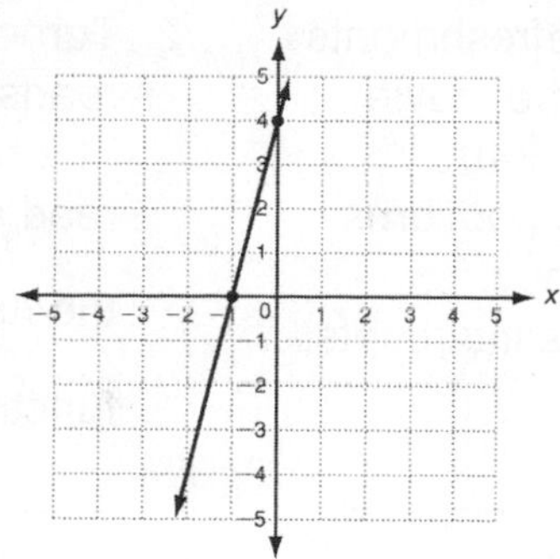

____

____

3.

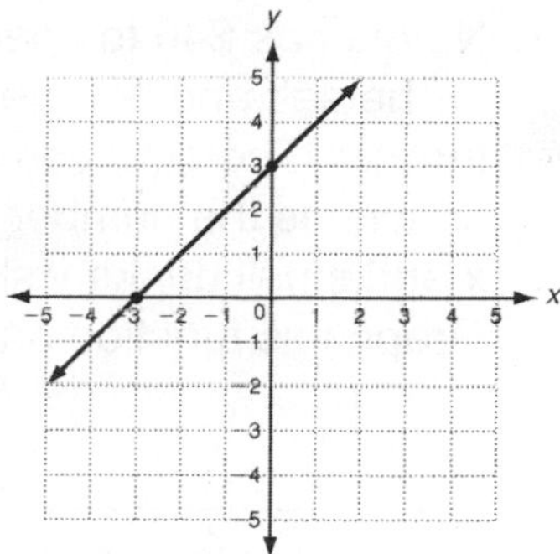

____

____

Use intercepts to graph the line described by each equation.

4. $3x + 2y = -6$

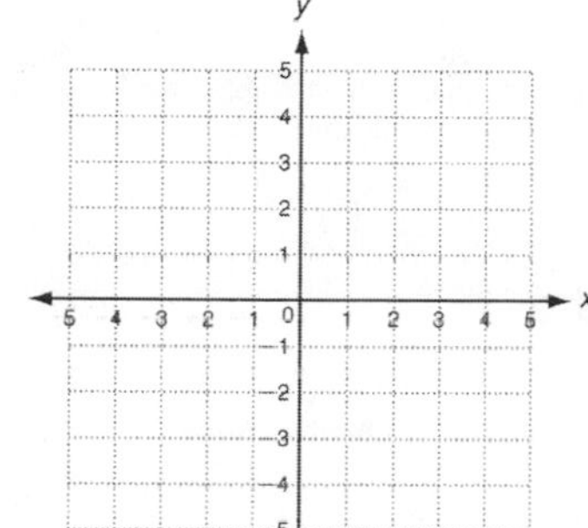

5. $x - 4y = 4$

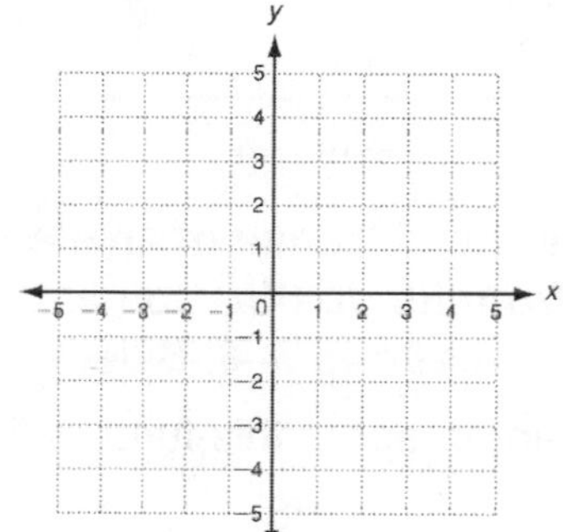

6. At a fair, hamburgers sell for \$3.00 each and hot dogs sell for \$1.50 each. The equation $3x + 1.5y = 30$ describes the number of hamburgers and hot dogs a family can buy with \$30.

   a. Find the intercepts and graph the function.

   ____

   b. What does each intercept represent?

   ____

   ____

   ____

   ____

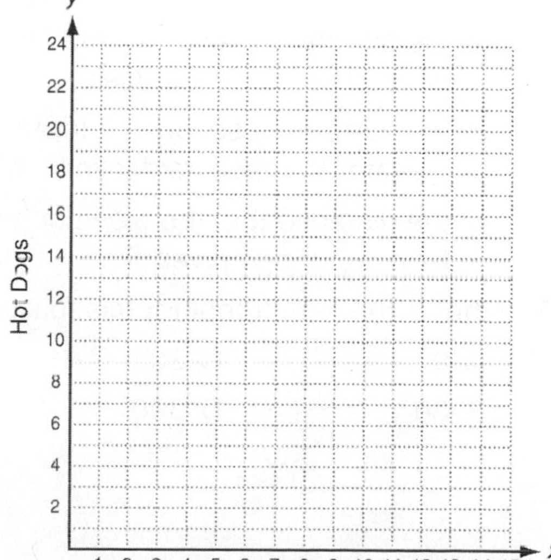

Problem Solving

Write the correct answer.

1. Naima has \$40 to spend on refreshments for herself and her friends at the movie theater. The equation $5x + 2y = 40$ describes the number of large popcorns x and small drinks y she can buy. Graph this function and find its intercepts.

____

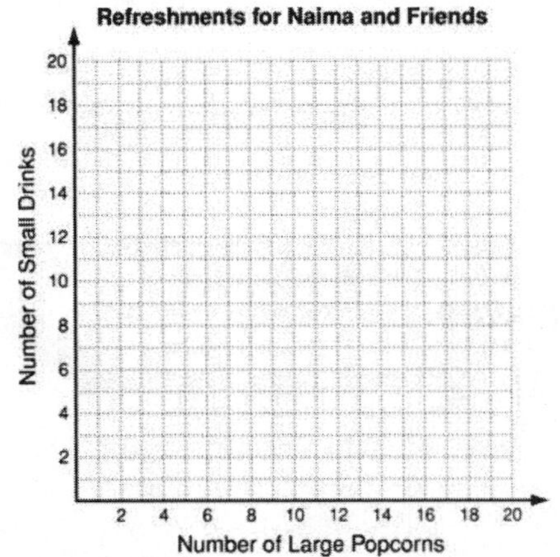

2. Turner is reading a 400-page book. He reads 4 pages every 5 minutes. The number of pages Turner has left to read after x minutes is represented by the function $f(x) = 400 - \frac{4}{5}x$. Graph this function and find its intercepts.

____

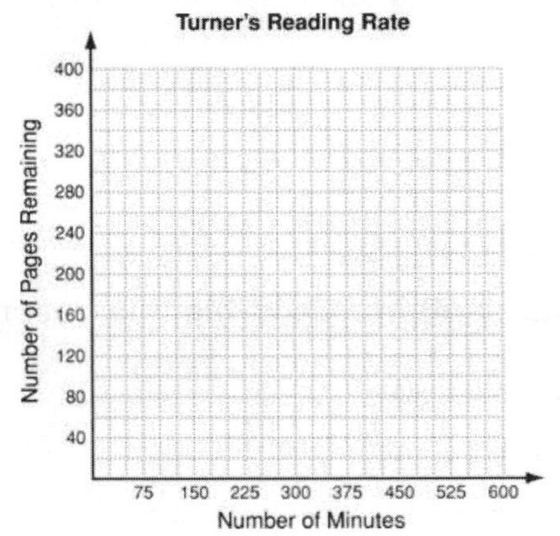

The graph shows the distance of an elevator at Chimney Rock, North Carolina, from its destination as a function of time. Use the graph to answer questions 3–6. Select the best answer.

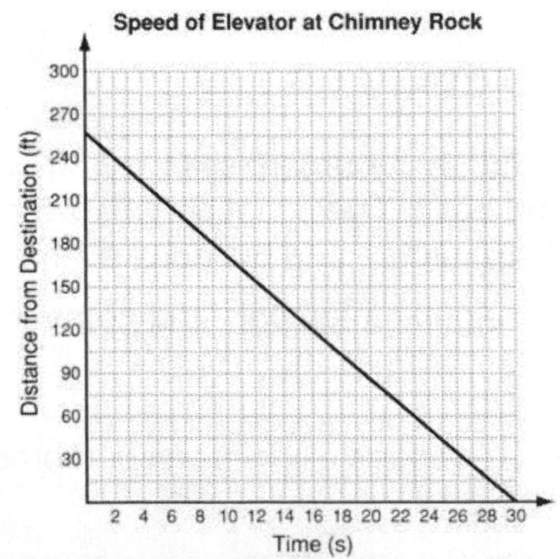

3. What is the x-intercept of this function?

A 0 C 258

B 30 D 300

4. What does the x-intercept represent?

F the total distance the elevator travels

G the number of seconds that have passed for any given distance

H the number of seconds it takes the elevator to reach its destination

J the distance that the elevator has traveled at any given time

5. What is the y-intercept for this function?

A 0 C 258

B 30 D 300

6. What does the y-intercept represent?

F the total distance the elevator travels

G the number of seconds that have passed for any given distance

H the number of seconds it takes the elevator to reach its destination

J the distance that the elevator has traveled at any given time

Name_______________ Class_______________ Date_______________

4-3

Video Tutor

Rate of Change and Slope

Going Deeper

Essential question: *What is the slope of a linear function and how can you use it to graph the function?*

If $f(x)$ is a linear function, then its graph is a line. The ordered pairs $(x_1, f(x_1))$ and $(x_2, f(x_2))$ can be used to name two points on the line. The change in the independent variables between these points is $x_2 - x_1$. The change in the dependent variables is $f(x_2) - f(x_1)$.

CC.9–12.F.IF.6

1 EXPLORE Changes in Independent and Dependent Variables

A Use the function $f(x) = 2x + 1$ to complete the table for each interval.

Interval	From $x = 1$ to $x = 2$	From $x = 1$ to $x = 3$	From $x = 1$ to $x = 4$
Change in x, the independent variable	$2 - 1 = 1$		
Change in $f(x)$, the dependent variable	$f(2) - f(1) =$ $5 - 3 = 2$		
$\frac{\text{Change in } f(x)}{\text{Change in } x}$	$\frac{2}{1} = 2$	$\frac{\square}{\square} = \square$	$\frac{\square}{\square} = \square$

B The ratio $\frac{f(x_2) - f(x_1)}{x_2 - x_1}$ over each interval simplifies to _______.

REFLECT

1a. What is the relationship between the ratio of $f(x_2) - f(x_1)$ to $x_2 - x_1$ and the function rule?

____

1b. Is the ratio of $f(x_2) - f(x_1)$ to $x_2 - x_1$ the same over the interval from $x = 2$ to $x = 4$? Explain.

____

1c. Suppose the function rule was $f(x) = 2x + 5$ instead of $f(x) = 2x + 1$. Would the ratio of $f(x_2) - f(x_1)$ to $x_2 - x_1$ remain the same? Explain.

____

____

____

CC.9-12.F.IF.6

2 ENGAGE Understanding Slope of a Linear Function

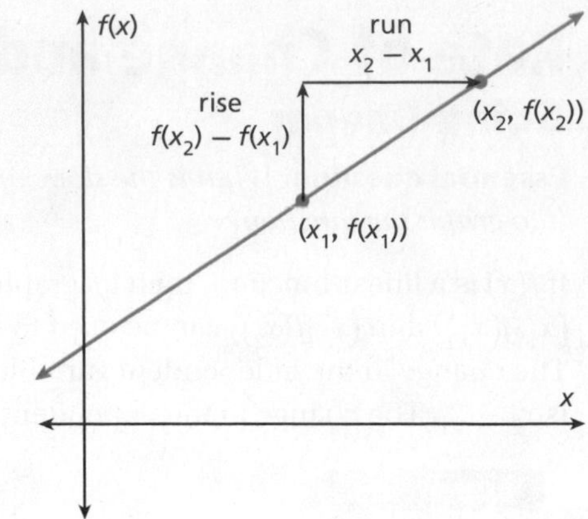

The ratio of $f(x_2) - f(x_1)$ to $x_2 - x_1$ for a linear function $f(x)$ is the **rate of change** of $f(x)$ with respect to x. The rate of change is the same for any two points on the graph of a given linear function.

You can interpret the rate of change of a linear function $f(x)$ geometrically as the *slope* of its graph. The diagram at the right shows the graph of $f(x)$, where the vertical axis represents the function values. The **rise** is the change in function values, $f(x_2) - f(x_1)$, and the **run** is the change in x-values, $x_2 - x_1$. The **slope** of the line is the ratio of the rise to the run.

Several ways of expressing the slope of a line are given below.

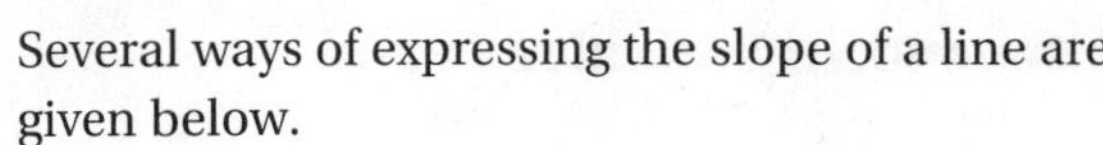

$$\text{slope} = \frac{\text{rise}}{\text{run}} = \frac{f(x_2) - f(x_1)}{x_2 - x_1} = \frac{\text{change in } f(x)}{\text{change in } x}$$

REFLECT

2a. Complete the following to show that the y-intercept of the graph of a linear function $f(x)$ is the value of b in the equation $f(x) = mx + b$.

The y-intercept of the graph of an equation occurs where $x = 0$.

So, the y-intercept of the graph of $f(x) = mx + b$ is as follows.

$$f(0) = m \cdot \square + b$$

$$f(0) = \square + b$$

$$f(0) = b$$

2b. Complete the following to show that the slope of the graph of a linear function $f(x)$ is the value of m in the equation $f(x) = mx + b$.

To find the slope of the graph of $f(x) = mx + b$, choose any two points on the line. Two convenient points are $(x_1, f(x_1)) = (0, b)$ and $(x_2, f(x_2)) = (1, m + b)$.

$$\frac{f(x_2) - f(x_1)}{x_2 - x_1} = \frac{\square - \square}{\square - \square} = \frac{\square}{\square} = m$$

2c. Show that the y-intercept of the graph of the function $f(x) = 4x + 1$ is 1 and that the rate of change of $f(x)$ with respect to x is 4.

CC.9–12.F.IF.6

3 ENGAGE Classifying Slopes of Lines

The slope of a line, can be positive, negative, 0, or undefined. If the slope is undefined, the line is not the graph of a function.

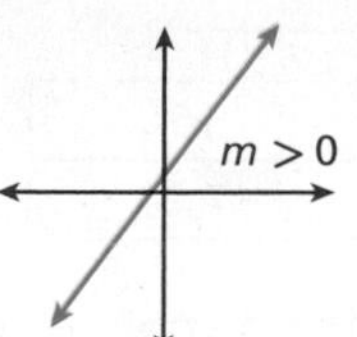

The line rises from left to right.

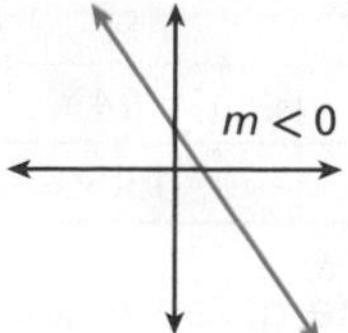

The line falls from left to right.

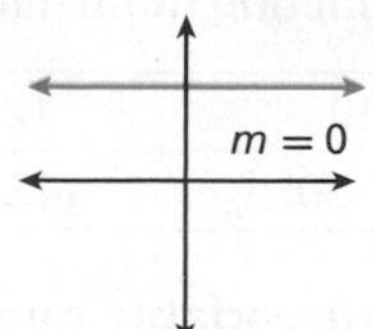

The line is horizontal.

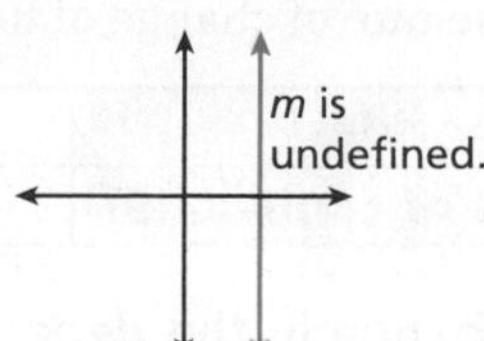

The line is vertical.

REFLECT

3a. When you move from left to right between two points on a line with a positive slope, is the rise *positive, negative,* or 0? Is the run *positive, negative,* or 0? Use your answers to explain why the slope of a line that rises from left to right is positive.

3b. When you move from left to right between two points on a line with a negative slope, is the rise *positive, negative,* or 0? Is the run *positive, negative,* or 0? Use your answers to explain why the slope of a line that falls from left to right is negative.

3c. When you move from left to right between two points on a horizontal line, is the rise *positive, negative,* or 0? Is the run *positive, negative,* or 0? Use your answers to explain why the slope of a horizontal line is 0.

3d. When you move up from one point to another on a vertical line, is the rise *positive, negative,* or 0? Is the run *positive, negative,* or 0? Use your answers to explain why the slope of a vertical line is undefined.

3e. A **constant function** is a function that has a rate of change of 0. Describe the graph of a constant function and the form of its equation.

PRACTICE

1. Calculate the rate of change of the function in the table. ______________

Tickets for rides	10	12	14	16
Total cost of carnival ($)	12.50	14.00	15.50	17.00

Estimate the change in the dependent variable over the given interval from the domain of the independent variable. Estimate the rate of change.

2.

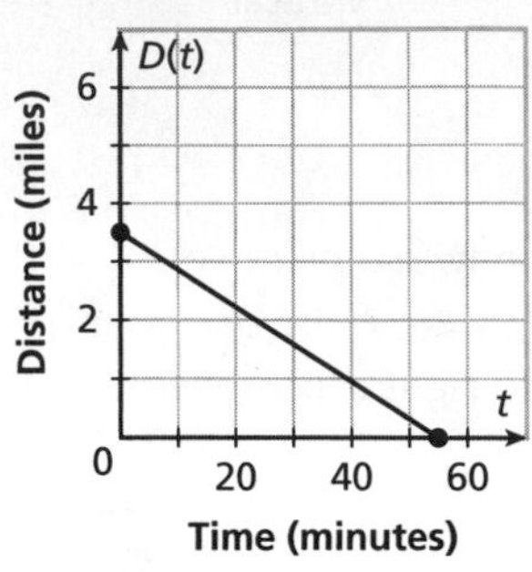

Given interval: $20 \leq t \leq 40$

Change in $D(t)$: ______________

Rate of change: ______________

3.

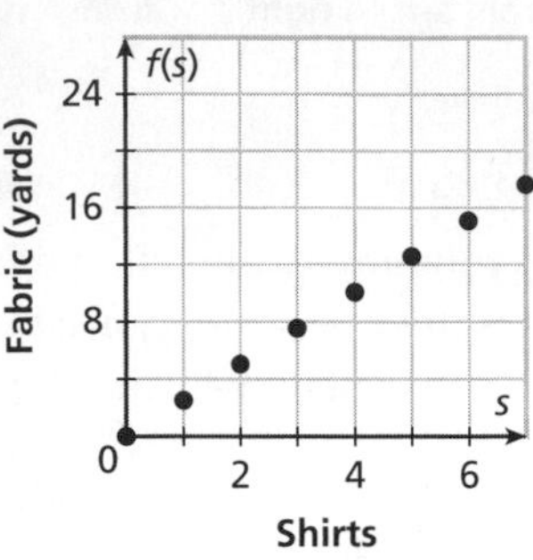

Given interval: $3 \leq s \leq 5$

Change in $f(s)$: ______________

Rate of change: ______________

Find the slope of the line that passes through the two given points. Classify each slope and tell whether the line represents a function.

4. $(-3, 2)$ and $(5, -3)$

____

5. $(0, -4)$ and $(7, 5)$

____

6. $(-4, 5)$ and $(-4, -8)$

____

7. $(-3, 0)$ and $(7, 0)$

____

8. $(-5, 0)$ and $(0, -10)$

____

9. $(-2, -7)$ and $(4, -1)$

____

Name ______________________ Class ____________ Date __________

Additional Practice

Find the rise and run between each set of points. Then, write the slope of the line.

1. 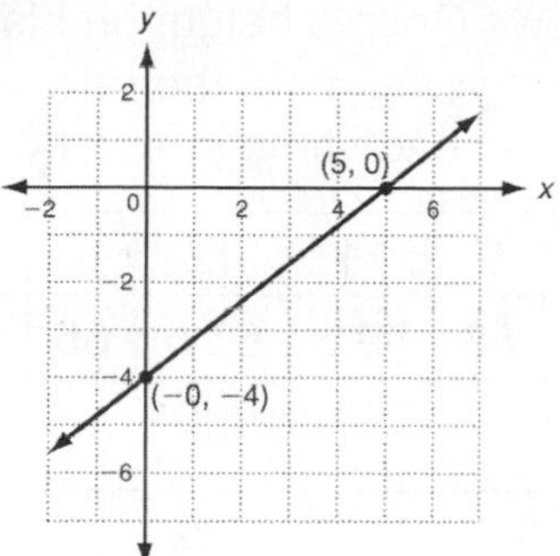

rise = _____ run = _____

slope = ____________

2. 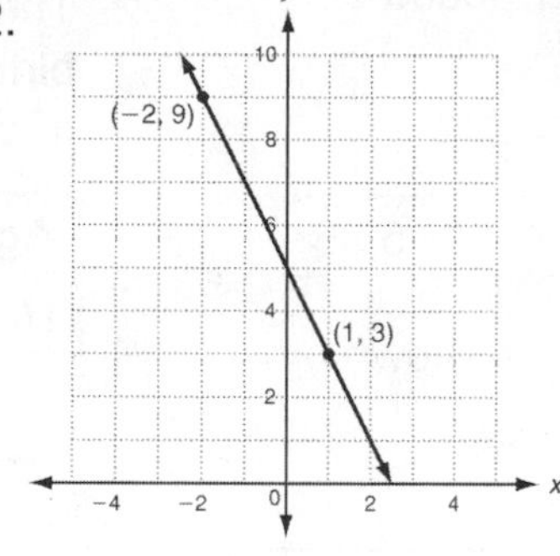

rise = _____ run = _____

slope = ____________

3. 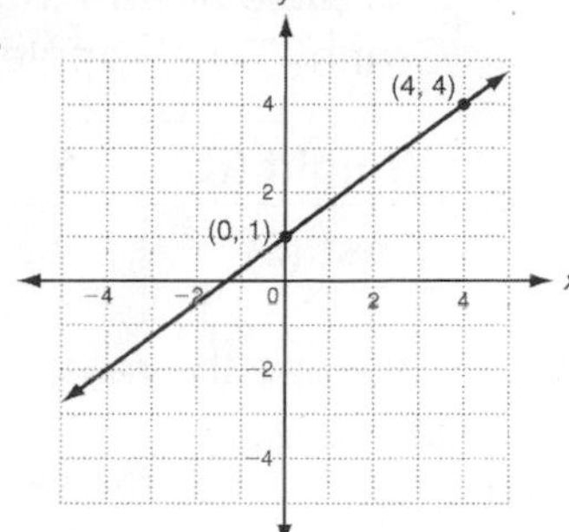

rise = _____ run = _____

slope = ____________

4. 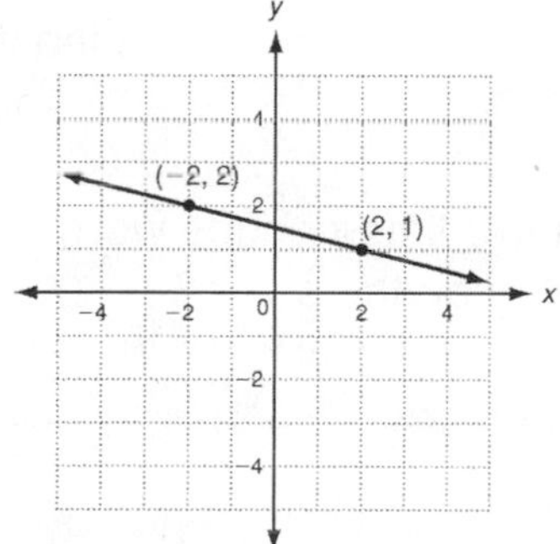

rise = _____ run = _____

slope = ____________

5. 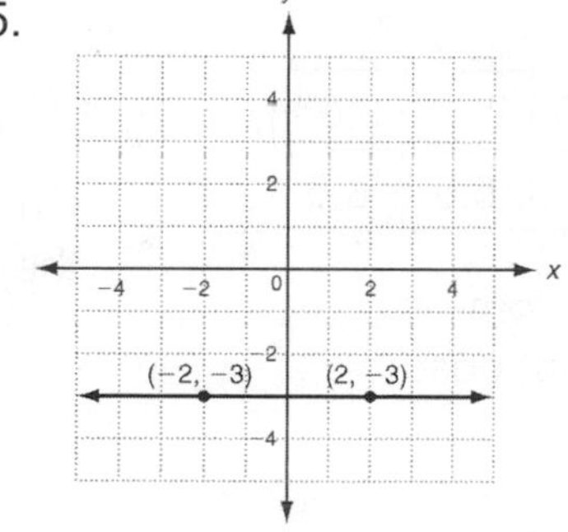

rise = _____ run = _____

slope = ____________

6. 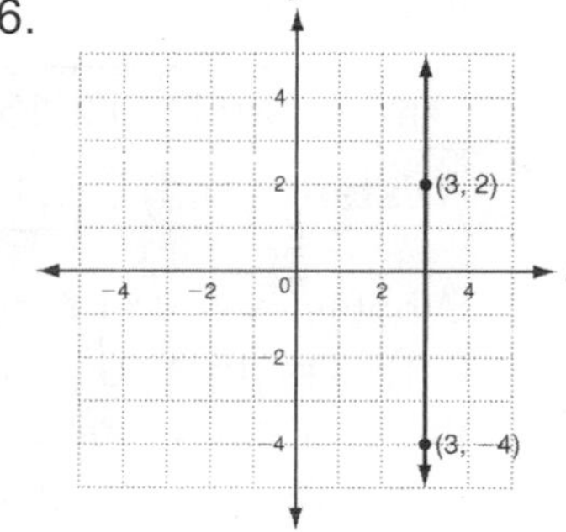

rise = _____ run = _____

slope = ____________

Tell whether the slope of each line is positive, negative, zero, or undefined.

7. 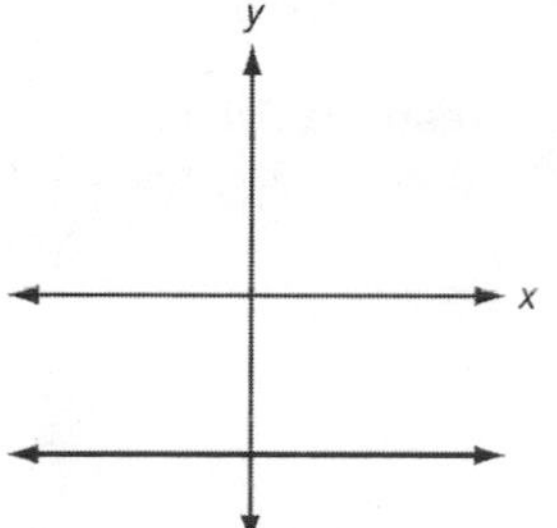

____

8. 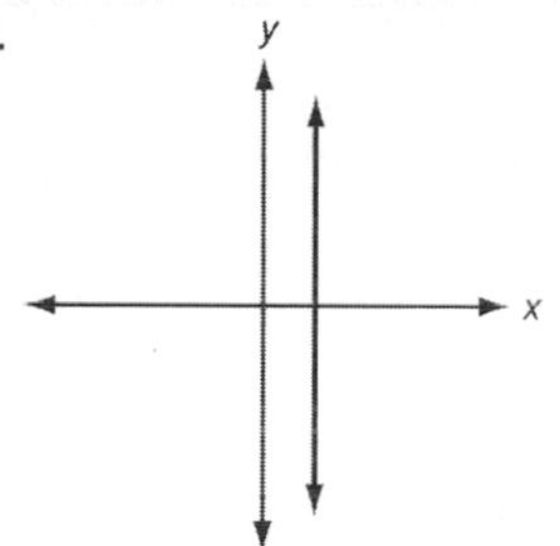

____

9. 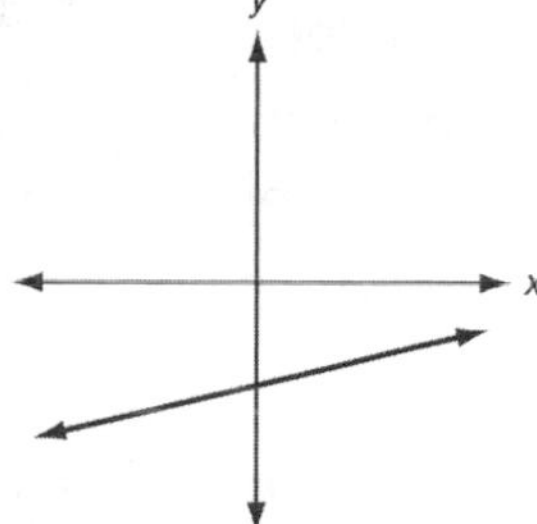

____

10. The table shows the amount of water in a pitcher at different times. Graph the data and show the rates of change. Between which two hours is the rate of change the greatest? ____________

Time (h)	0	1	2	3	4	5	6	7
Amount (oz)	60	50	25	80	65	65	65	50

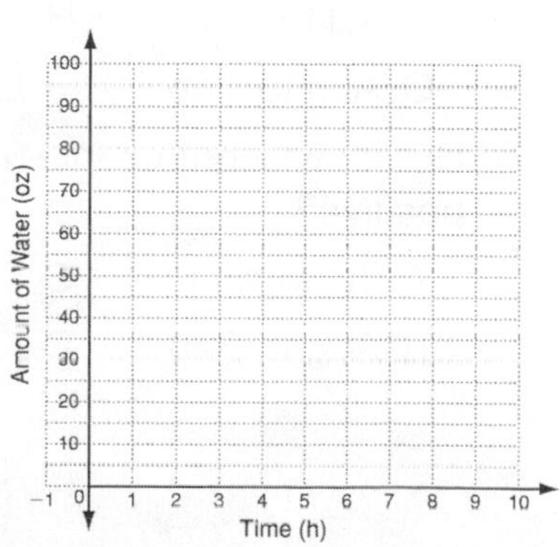

Problem Solving

Write the correct answer.

1. The table shows the cost per pound of Granny Smith apples.

Weight (lb)	1	2	3	4
Cost ($)	1.49	2.98	4.47	5.96

Describe the rate(s) of change shown by the data.

____

____

2. The table shows Gabe's height on his birthday for five years. Find the rate of change during each time interval.

Age	9	11	12	13	15
Height (in.)	58	59.5	61.5	65	69

____

____

When did the greatest rate of change occur? ____________________

When was the rate of change the least?

____

During which two time periods were the rates of change the same?

____

3. The table shows the distance of a courier from her destination.

Time (p.m.)	2:15	2:30	2:45	3:00
Distance (mi)	5.4	5.4	5.0	0.5

What is the rate of change from 2:15 p.m. to 2:30 p.m.? What does this rate of change mean?

____

____

The graph below tracks regular gasoline prices from July 2004 to December 2004. Use the graph to answer questions 5–7. Select the best answer.

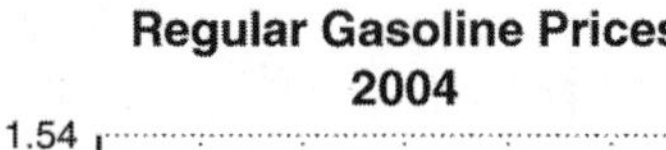

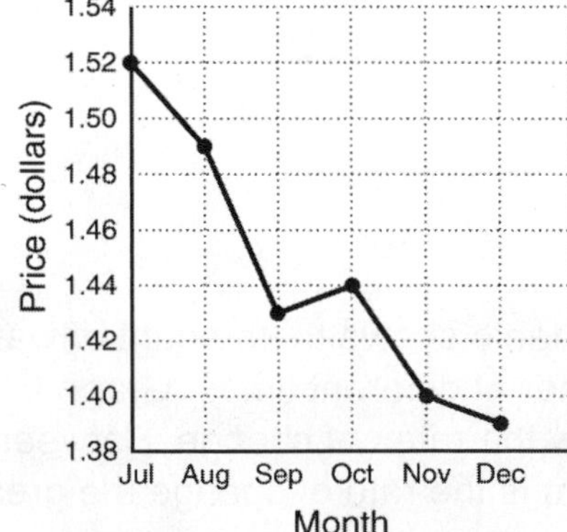

4. What is the slope of the line from November to December?

   A –4 C –0.04
   B –1 D –0.01

5. During which time interval did the cost decrease at the greatest rate?

   F Jul to Aug H Sep to Oct
   G Aug to Sep J Oct to Nov

6. During which time interval was the slope positive?

   A Jul to Aug C Sep to Oct
   B Aug to Sep D Oct to Nov

7. What was the rate of change from October to December?

   F –0.05 H 0.025
   G –0.025 J 0.05

Name ____________________ Class ____________ Date ________

4-4

Video Tutor

The Slope Formula
Extension: Estimating Average Rate of Change

Essential Question: *How can you estimate the average rate of change of a function from a graph?*

The slope of a line is the ratio of the difference in y-values to the difference in x-values between any two points on the line. This is represented by $m = \frac{y_2 - y_1}{x_2 - x_1}$.

CC.9-12.F.IF.6

1 EXPLORE Finding the Slope of a Linear Function

Find the slope of the linear function represented by the graph.

A (−3, −5)
B (1, 3)
C (2, 5)

A Use points A and B to find the slope of the line.
Let the coordinates of A be (x_1, y_1) and the coordinates of B be (x_2, y_2).

$m = \frac{y_2 - y_1}{x_2 - x_1}$ Use the slope formula.

$m = \frac{\square - (\square)}{\square - (\square)}$ Substitute.

$m = \frac{\square}{\square} = \square$ Simplify.

B Use points A and C to find the slope of the line.
Let the coordinates of A be (x_1, y_1) and the coordinates of C be (x_2, y_2).

$m = \frac{y_2 - y_1}{x_2 - x_1}$ Use the slope formula.

$m = \frac{\square - (\square)}{\square - (\square)}$ Substitute.

$m = \frac{\square}{\square} = \square$ Simplify.

C Use points B and C to find the slope of the line.
Let the coordinates of B be (x_1, y_1) and the coordinates of C be (x_2, y_2).

$m = \frac{y_2 - y_1}{x_2 - x_1}$ Use the slope formula.

$m = \frac{\square - \square}{\square - \square}$ Substitute.

$m = \frac{\square}{\square} = \square$ Simplify.

REFLECT

1a. Is the slope of the linear function constant? Explain.

CC.9–12.F.IF.6

2 EXPLORE Estimating the Slope of Sections of a Quadratic Function

Estimate the average slope of particular sections of the quadratic function $y = x^2$ represented by the graph at the right.

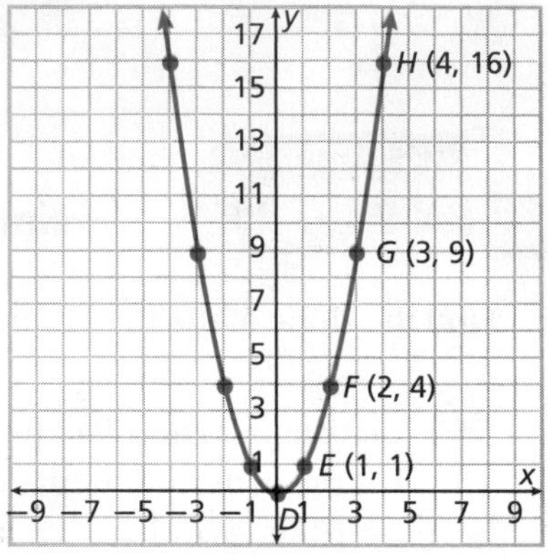

A Use the slope formula to complete the table below.

x-coordinate of *D*	*x*-coordinate of *E*	*x*-coordinate of *F*	*x*-coordinate of *G*
y*-coordinate of *D	***y*-coordinate of *E***	***y*-coordinate of *F***	***y*-coordinate of *G***
average slope between *D* and *E*	**average slope between *E* and *F***	**average slope between *F* and *G***	**average slope between *G* and *H***

B How are the *x*-coordinates of each pair of points given in the table related?

C For $y = x^2$, make a conjecture about how the average slope between two points whose *x*-coordinates are 1 unit apart is related to the *x*-coordinate of the point with the lesser *x*-coordinate. [*Hint*: Write and simplify an algebraic expression for the slope between (x, x^2) and $(x + 1, (x + 1)^2)$.] Is the slope of a quadratic function constant?

D Use your conjecture to estimate the average slope between (8, 64) and (9, 81) in $y = x^2$. Explain your work. Then use the slope formula to check your estimate.

REFLECT

2a. Will your conjecture hold for negative x-coordinates? Give an example or counterexample to support your answer.

____

____

2b. Find the average slopes of pairs of points with negative x-coordinates that are 1 unit apart. Arrange them in order from least to greatest with the slopes from Part A. What do you notice about the average slopes as the x-coordinates increase? Will the average slope ever be zero? Why or why not?

____

____

CC.9–12.F.IF.6

3 EXPLORE Estimating the Slope of Sections of an Exponential Function

Estimate the average slope of particular sections of the exponential function $y = 2^x$ represented by the graph at the right.

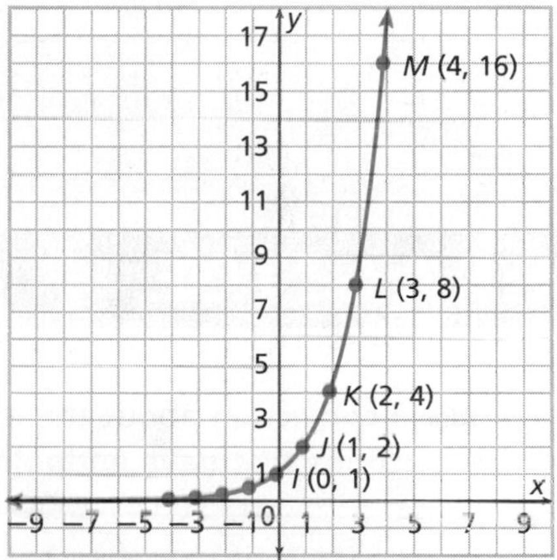

A Use the slope formula to complete the table below.

x-coordinate of I	x-coordinate of J	x-coordinate of K	x-coordinate of L
average slope between I and J	**average slope between J and K**	**average slope between K and L**	**average slope between L and M**

B How are the x-coordinates of each pair of points given in the table related?

____

____

C For $y = 2^x$, make a conjecture about how the average slope between two points whose x-coordinates are 1 unit apart is related to the x-coordinate of the point with the lesser x-coordinate?

____

____

D Use your conjecture to estimate the average slope between (8, 256) and (9, 512) in $y = 2^x$. Explain your work. Then use the slope formula to check your estimate.

REFLECT

3a. Will your conjecture hold for negative x-coordinates? Give an example or counterexample to support your answer.

3b. Find the average slopes of pairs of points with negative x-coordinates that are 1 unit apart. Arrange them in order from least to greatest with the slopes from Part A. What do you notice about the average slopes as the x-coordinates increase? Do you think the average slope will ever be negative? Why or why not?

PRACTICE

Make a conjecture about the average slope of various sections of each graph. Use sections that have endpoints in which the x-coordinates are 1 unit apart.

1. $y = 2x^2$

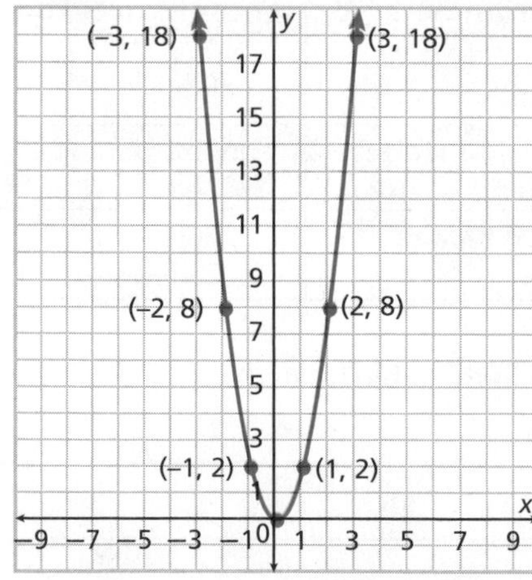

2. $y = 3^x$

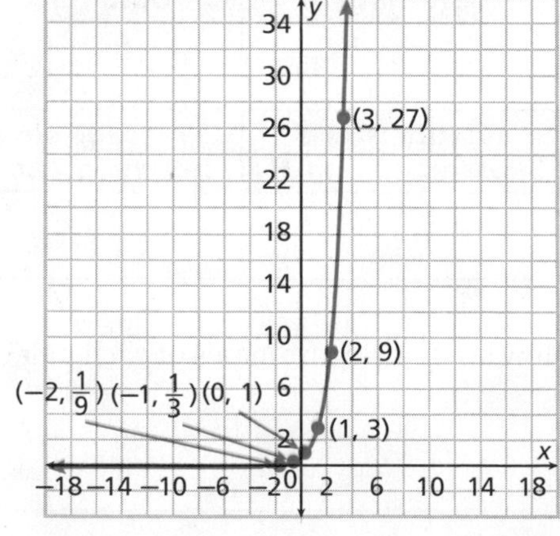

Name ______________________ Class ______________ Date ____________ 4-4

Additional Practice

Find the slope of the line that contains each pair of points.

1. (2, 8) and (1, –3)

$m = \frac{y_2 - y_1}{x_2 - x_1}$

$= \frac{\square - \square}{\square - \square}$

$= \frac{\square}{\square} = \square$

2. (–4, 0) and (–6, –2)

$m = \frac{y_2 - y_1}{x_2 - x_1}$

$= \frac{\square - \square}{\square - \square}$

$= \frac{\square}{\square} = \square$

3. (0, –2) and (4, –7)

$m = \frac{y_2 - y_1}{x_2 - x_1}$

$= \frac{\square - \square}{\square - \square}$

$= \frac{\square}{\square}$

Each graph or table shows a linear relationship. Find the slope.

4.

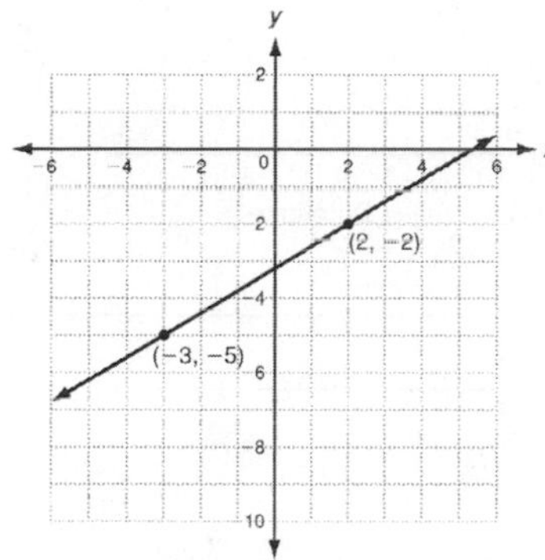

____

5.

x	y
1	3.75
2	5
3	6.25
4	7.50
5	8.75

____

6.

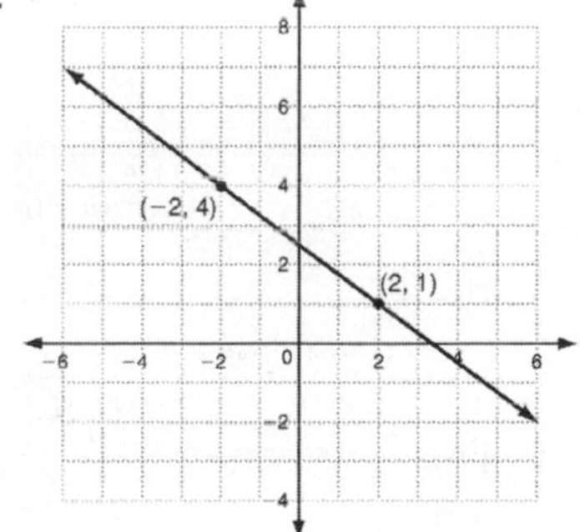

____

Find the slope of each line.

7.

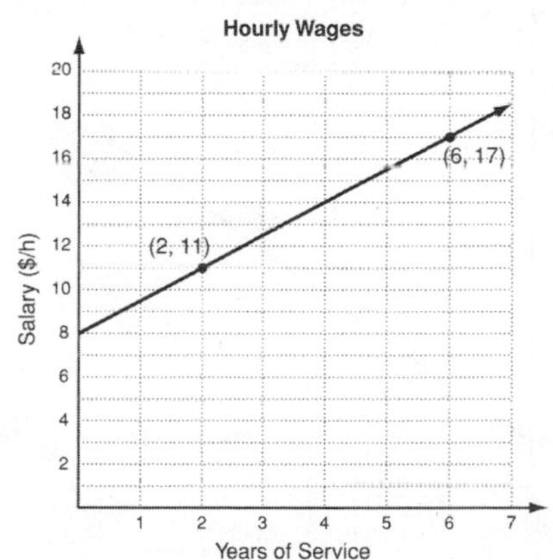

____

____

8.

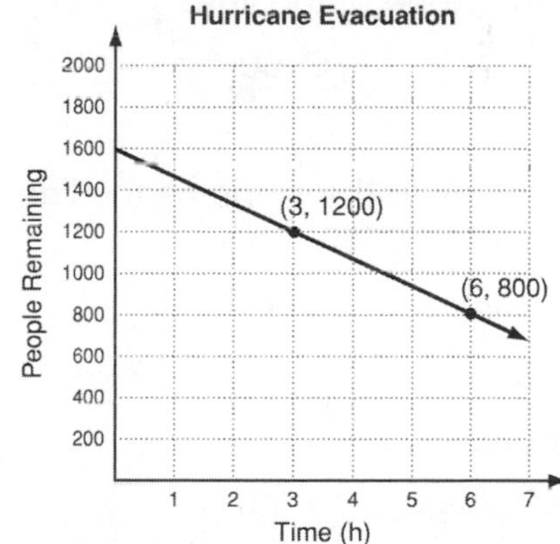

____

____

For each equation, find the slope between the given points.

9. $y = 3x^2$; (0, 0) and (1, 3); (1, 3) and (2, 12)

____

10. $y = 4^x$; (0, 1) and (1, 4); (1, 4) and (2, 16)

____

Problem Solving

Write the correct answer.

1. The graph shows the number of emergency kits assembled by volunteers over a period of days. Find the slope of the line.

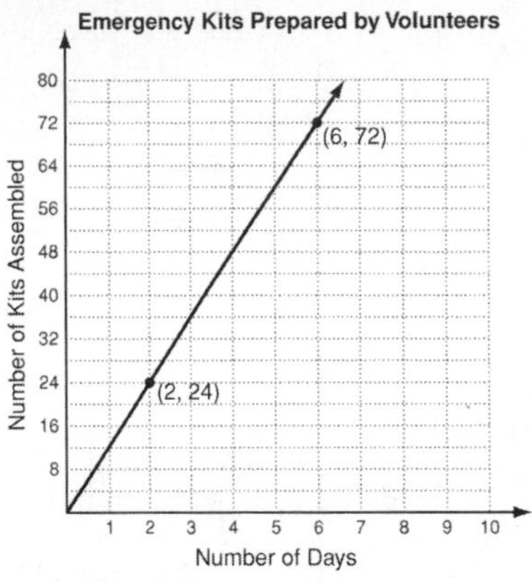

____

____

2. The graph shows how much flour is in a bag at different times. Find the slope of the line.

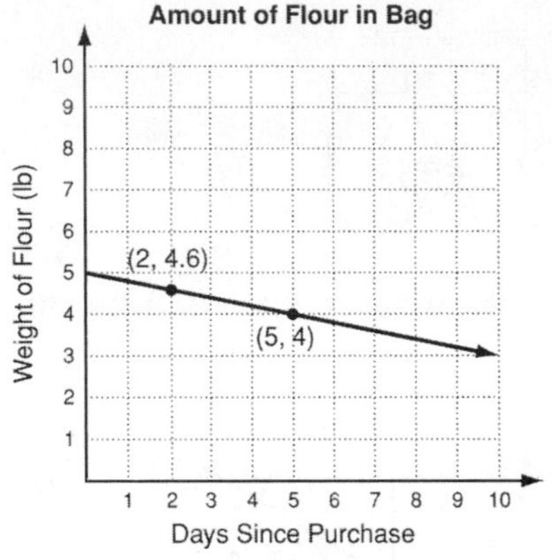

____

____

3. The function $y = 10^x$ represents a population of amoebas each day. Is the slope of this function increasing or decreasing as x increases?

____

The graph below shows the cost of membership at Fabulously Fit. Use the graph to answer questions 4–7. Select the best answer.

Membership at Fabulously Fit

Cost ($)

Number of Months

(7, 295)

(2, 120)

4. What is the slope of the line?

   A 24   C 50

   B 35   D 70

5. What happens to the slope as the line rises?

   F It increases.

   G It decreases.

   H It becomes 0.

   J It remains constant.

6. A second line is graphed that shows the cost of membership at The Fitness Studio. The line contains (0, 35) and (5, 85). What is the slope of this line?

   A 10   C 45

   B 20   D 50

7. How much greater is the monthly fee at Fabulously Fit than The Fitness Studio?

   F $15   H $35

   G $25   J $40

Name ______________________ Class ______________ Date __________

4-5

Exploring Direct Variation

Extension: Transformations of $f(x) = mx$ and $g(x) = a|x|$

Essential question: *How does changing the values of m and a affect the graphs of $f(x) = mx$ and $g(x) = a|x|$?*

Video Tutor

CC.9–12.F.BF.3

1 EXPLORE Changing the Value of m in $f(x) = mx$

Investigate what happens to the graph of $f(x) = mx$ when you change the value of m.

A Use a graphing calculator. Start with the standard viewing window, which you can obtain by pressing ZOOM and selecting ZStandard. Because the distances between consecutive tick marks on the x-axis and on the y-axis are not equal, you can make them equal by pressing ZOOM again and selecting ZSquare.

What interval on each axis does the viewing window now show? (Press WINDOW to find out.)

____

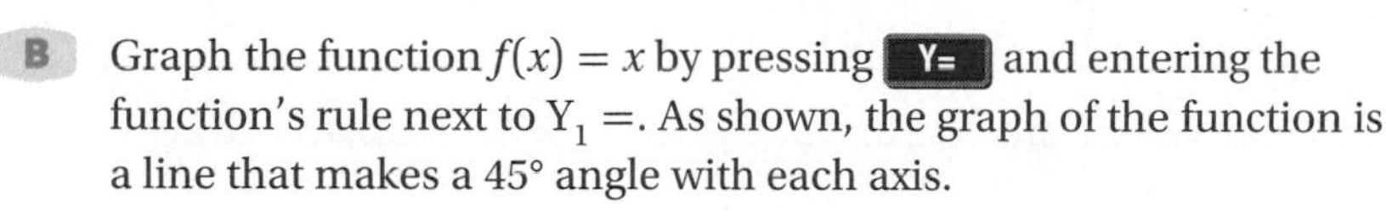

B Graph the function $f(x) = x$ by pressing Y= and entering the function's rule next to $Y_1 =$. As shown, the graph of the function is a line that makes a 45° angle with each axis.

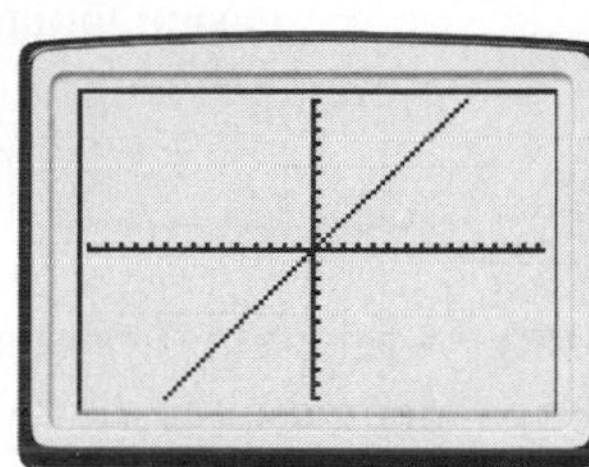

What are the slope and y-intercept of the graph of $f(x) = x$?

____

C Press Y= and graph other functions of the form $f(x) = mx$ by entering their rules next to $Y_2 =$, $Y_3 =$, and so on. Use only values of m that are greater than 1. For instance, graph $f(x) = 2x$ and $f(x) = 6x$.

What do the graphs have in common? How are they different?

____

As the value of m increases from 1, does the graph become more vertical or more horizontal?

____

D Again press Y= and clear out all but the function $f(x) = x$. Then graph other functions of the form $f(x) = mx$ by entering their rules next to $Y_2 =$, $Y_3 =$, and so on. This time use only values of m that are less than 1 but greater than 0. For instance, graph $f(x) = 0.5x$ and $f(x) = 0.2x$.

As the value of m decreases from 1 toward 0, does the graph become more vertical or more horizontal?

____

E Again press **Y=** and clear out all but the function $f(x) = x$. Then graph the function $f(x) = -x$ by entering its rule next to $Y_2 =$.

What are the slope and y-intercept of the graph of $f(x) = -x$?

____

How are the graphs of $f(x) = x$ and $f(x) = -x$ geometrically related?

____

F Again press **Y=** and clear out all the functions. Graph $f(x) = -x$ by entering its rule next to $Y_1 =$. Then graph other functions of the form $f(x) = mx$ where $m < 0$ by entering their rules next to $Y_2 =$, $Y_3 =$, and so on. Be sure to choose values of m less than -1 as well as values of m between -1 and 0.

Describe what happens to the graph of $f(x) = mx$ as the value of m decreases from -1 and as it increases from -1 to 0.

____

REFLECT

1a. A function $f(x)$ is called an *increasing function* when the value of $f(x)$ always increases as the value of x increases. For what values of m is the function $f(x) = mx$ an increasing function? How can you tell from the graph of a linear function that it is an increasing function?

____

1b. A function $f(x)$ is called a *decreasing function* when the value of $f(x)$ always decreases as the value of x increases. For what values of m is the function $f(x) = mx$ a decreasing function? How can you tell from the graph of a linear function that is a decreasing function?

____

1c. When $m > 0$, increasing the value of m results in an increasing linear function that increases *faster*. What effect does increasing m have on the graph of the function?

____

1d. When $m > 0$, decreasing the value of m toward 0 results in an increasing linear function that increases *slower*. What effect does decreasing m have on the graph of the function?

____

1e. When $m < 0$, decreasing the value of m results in a decreasing linear function that decreases *faster*. What effect does decreasing m have on the graph of the function?

____

1f. When $m < 0$, increasing the value of m toward 0 results in a decreasing linear function that decreases *slower*. What effect does increasing m have on the graph of the function?

____

1g. The *steepness* of a line refers to the absolute value of its slope. A steeper line is more vertical; a less steep line is more horizontal. Complete the table to summarize, in terms of steepness, the effect of changing the value of m on the graph of $f(x) = mx$.

How the Value of m Changes	Effect on the Graph of $f(x) = mx$
Increase m when $m > 0$.	
Decrease m toward 0 when $m > 0$.	
Decrease m when $m < 0$.	
Increase m toward 0 when $m < 0$.	

As you have seen, changing the value of m in the function $f(x) = mx$ makes the graph more or less steep compared to the graph of $f(x) = x$ and reflects it over the x-axis if $m < 0$. Changing the value of a in the *absolute value function* $g(x) = a|x|$ has a similar effect on its graph compared to the graph of the parent function $g(x) = |x|$.

CC.9–12.F.IF.7b

2 ENGAGE Understanding the Parent Absolute Value Function

The most basic **absolute value function** is a piecewise function given by the following rule.

$$f(x) = |x| = \begin{cases} x & \text{if } x \geq 0 \\ -x & \text{if } x < 0 \end{cases}$$

This function is sometimes called the *parent* absolute value function.

To graph the function, you can make a table of values like the one shown below, plot the ordered pairs, and draw the graph.

x	$f(x) = \|x\|$
−3	3
−2	2
−1	1
0	0
1	1
2	2
3	3

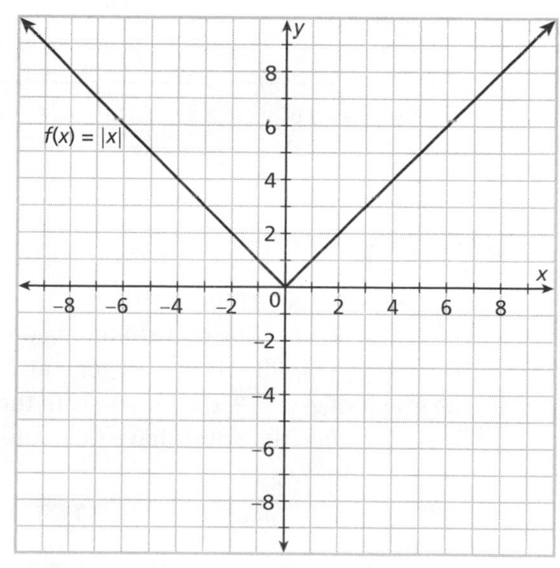

As shown at the right, the function's V-shaped graph consists of two rays with a common endpoint at (0, 0). This point is called the *vertex* of the graph.

REFLECT

2a. What is the domain of $f(x) = |x|$? What is the range?

2b. If you fold the graph of $f(x) = |x|$ over the y-axis, the two halves of the graph match up perfectly. The graph is said to be *symmetric* about the y-axis. Explain why it makes sense that the graph of $f(x) = |x|$ is symmetric about the y-axis.

2c. For what values of x is the function $f(x) = |x|$ increasing? decreasing?

To understand the effect of the constant a on the graph of $g(x) = a|x|$, you will graph the function using various values of a.

CC.9–12.F.BF.3

3 EXAMPLE Graphing $g(x) = a|x|$ when $|a| > 1$

Graph each absolute value function using the same coordinate plane. (The graph of the parent function $f(x) = |x|$ is shown in gray.)

A $g(x) = 2|x|$

x	−3	−2	−1	0	1	2	3
$g(x) = 2\|x\|$							

B $g(x) = -2|x|$

x	−3	−2	−1	0	1	2	3
$g(x) = -2\|x\|$							

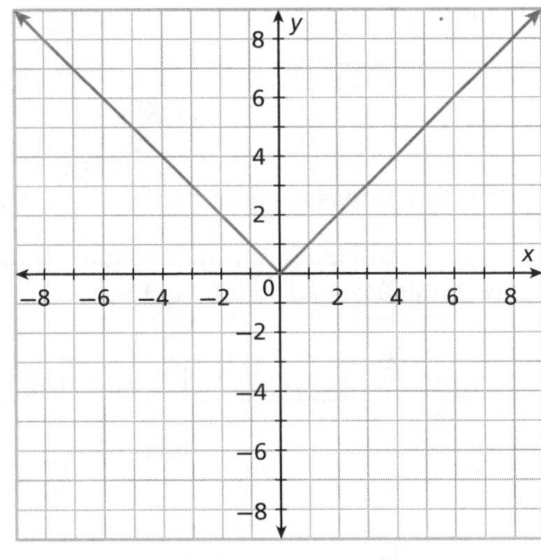

REFLECT

3a. The graph of the parent function $f(x) = |x|$ includes the point $(-1, 1)$ because $f(-1) = |-1| = 1$. The corresponding point on the graph of $g(x) = 2|x|$ is $(-1, 2)$ because $g(-1) = 2|-1| = 2$. In general, how does the y-coordinate of a point on the graph of $g(x) = 2|x|$ compare with the y-coordinate of a point on the graph of $f(x) = |x|$ when the points have the same x-coordinate?

3b. Describe how the graph of $g(x) = 2|x|$ compares with the graph of $f(x) = |x|$. Use either the word *stretch* or *shrink*, and include the direction of the movement.

3c. What other transformation occurs when the value of a in $g(x) = a|x|$ is negative?

____

CC.9–12.F.BF.3

4 EXAMPLE Graphing $g(x) = a|x|$ when $|a| < 1$

Graph each absolute value function using the same coordinate plane. (The graph of the parent function $f(x) = |x|$ is shown in gray.)

A $g(x) = \frac{1}{4}|x|$

x	−8	−4	0	4	8
$g(x) = \frac{1}{4}|x|$					

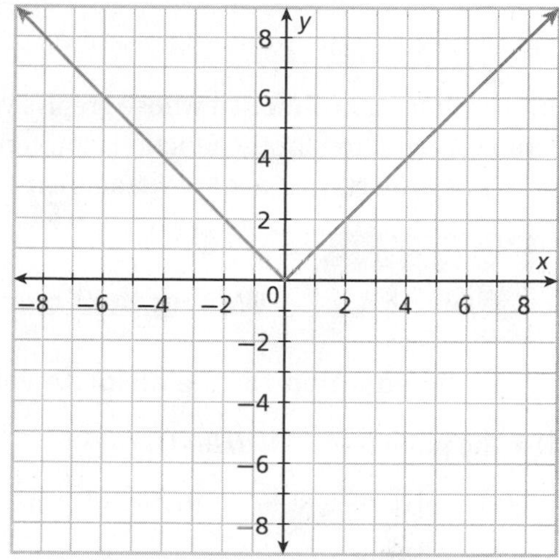

B $g(x) = -\frac{1}{4}|x|$

x	−8	−4	0	4	8
$g(x) = -\frac{1}{4}|x|$					

REFLECT

4a. How does the y-coordinate of a point on the graph of $g(x) = \frac{1}{4}|x|$ compare with the y-coordinate of a point on the graph of $f(x) = |x|$ when the points have the same x-coordinate?

____

____

4b. Describe how the graph of $g(x) = \frac{1}{4}|x|$ compares with the graph of $f(x) = |x|$. Use either the word *stretch* or *shrink*, and include the direction of the movement.

____

4c. What other transformation occurs when the value of a in $g(x) = a|x|$ is negative?

____

4d. Compare the domain and range of $g(x) = a|x|$ when $a > 0$ and when $a < 0$.

____

____

____

4e. Summarize your observations about the graph of $g(x) = a|x|$.

Value of a	Vertical stretch or shrink?	Reflection across x-axis?
$a > 1$	Vertical stretch	No
$0 < a < 1$		
$-1 < a < 0$		
$a < -1$		

An absolute value function whose graph's vertex is at (0, 0) has the form $g(x) = a|x|$. To write the equation for the function, you can use the coordinates of a point (x_1, y_1) on the graph to write $g(x_1) = a|x_1| = y_1$ and then solve for a.

CC.9-12.F.BF.1

5 EXAMPLE Writing the Equation for an Absolute Value Function

Write the equation for the absolute value function whose graph is shown.

Use the point $(-4, -3)$ to find a.

$g(x) = a|x|$	Function form
$g(-4) = a|\ \ \	= \ \ \ $	Substitute.
$a(\ \ \ ) = \ \ \ $	Simplify.
$a = \frac{\ \ }{\ \ }$	Solve for a.

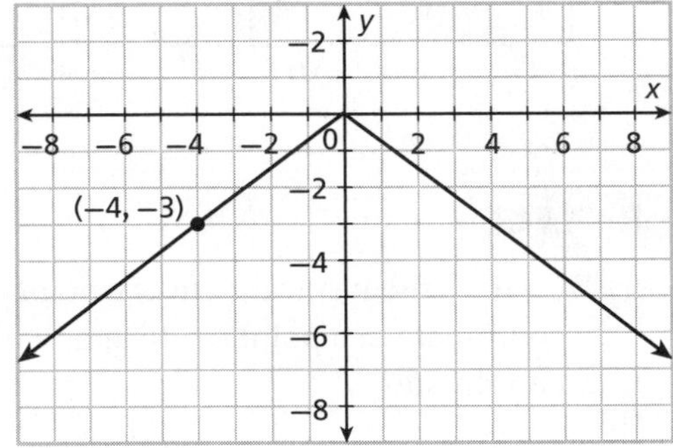

The equation for the function is ______________.

REFLECT

5a. The fact that the given graph lies on or below the x-axis tells you what about the value of a? Does this agree with the value of a that you found? Explain.

____

5b. The angle between the two rays that make up the graph of the parent function $f(x) = |x|$ is a right angle. What happens to this angle when the graph is vertically stretched? When the graph is vertically shrunk?

____

5c. Based on your answer to Question 5b, does the given graph represent a vertical stretch or a vertical shrink of the graph of the parent function? Does this fact agree with the value of a that you found? Explain.

____

Modeling with Absolute Value Functions When a rolling ball, such as a billiard ball, strikes a flat surface, such as an edge of the billiard table, the ball bounces off the surface at the same angle at which the ball hit the surface. (The angles are measured off a line perpendicular to the surface, as shown in the diagram.) A ray of light striking a mirror behaves in the same way.

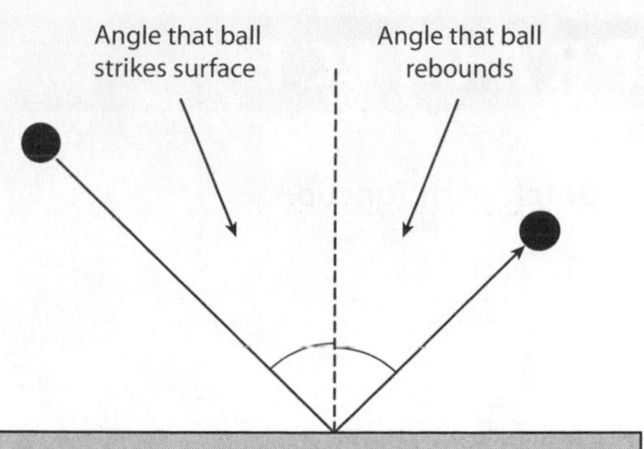

The symmetry of the graph of an absolute value function makes the graph a perfect model for the path of a rolling ball or a ray of light.

CC.9–12.A.CED.2

6 EXAMPLE Modeling a Real-World Situation

Inez is playing miniature golf. Her ball is at point $A(-4, 6)$. She wants to putt the ball into the hole at $C(2, 3)$ with a bank shot, as shown. If the ball hits the edge at $B(0, 0)$, find the equation for the absolute value function whose graph models the path of the ball. How does the equation tell you whether the ball will go into the hole (if the ball is hit with sufficient force)?

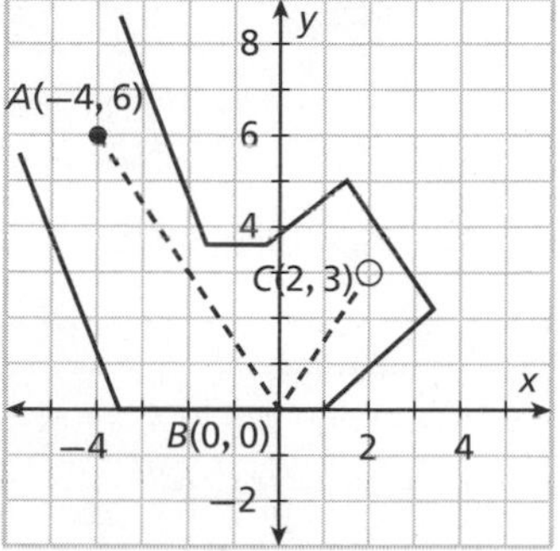

A Use the point $A(-4, 6)$ to write the equation for a function of the form $g(x) = a|x|$.

$g(x) = a\lvert x\rvert$	Function form
$g(-4) = a\lvert\square\rvert = \square$	Substitute.
$a(\square) = \square$	Simplify.
$a = \dfrac{\square}{\square}$	Solve for a.

So, the equation for the function is________________.

B Check to see whether the point $C(2, 3)$ lies on the path of the ball.

$g(2) = \frac{3}{2}|2| = \square$, so the ball__________ go into the hole.

REFLECT

6a. If you reflect point C in the x-axis, what do you notice about points A, B, and the reflection of C? Explain why this is so.

PRACTICE

Graph each function.

1. $g(x) = 3x$

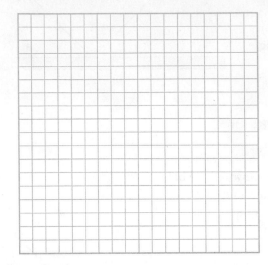

2. $g(x) = -2.5|x|$

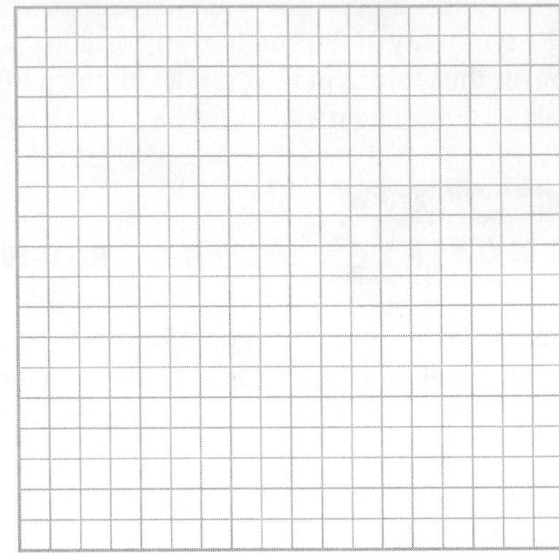

3. $g(x) = \frac{1}{2}|x|$

4. $g(x) = -\frac{2}{3}|x|$

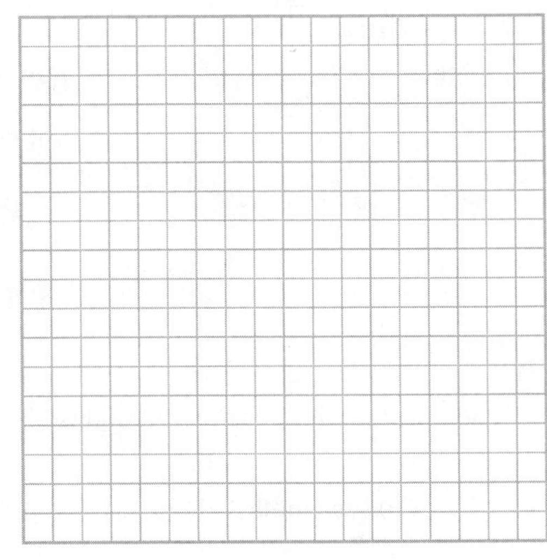

5. a. Complete the table and graph all the functions on the same coordinate plane.

x	-6	-3	0	3	6
$g(x) = \frac{1}{3}\|x\|$					
$g(x) = \left\|\frac{1}{3}x\right\|$					
$g(x) = -\frac{1}{3}\|x\|$					
$g(x) = \left\|-\frac{1}{3}x\right\|$					

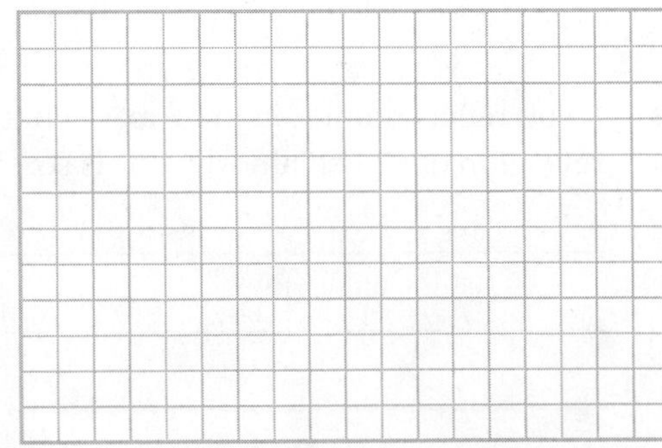

b. How do the graphs of $f(x) = a|x|$ and $g(x) = |ax|$ compare?

Write the equation of each function whose graph is shown.

6.

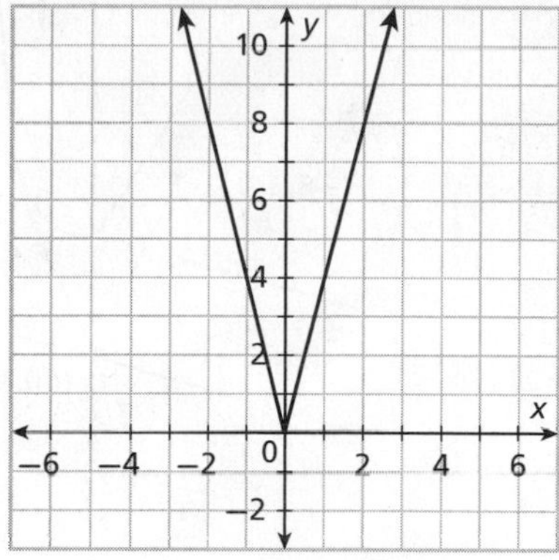

7.

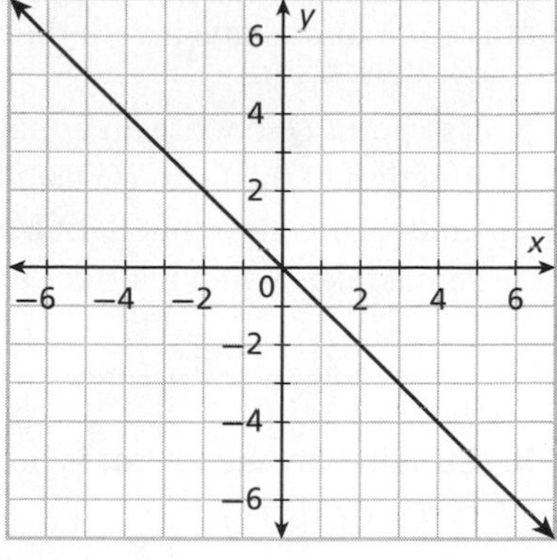

8.

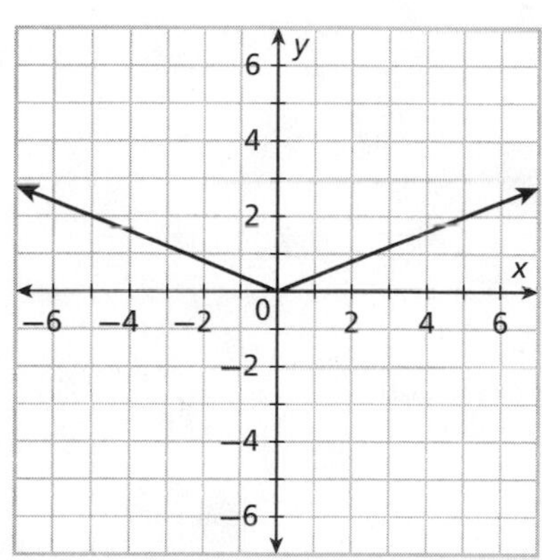

9.

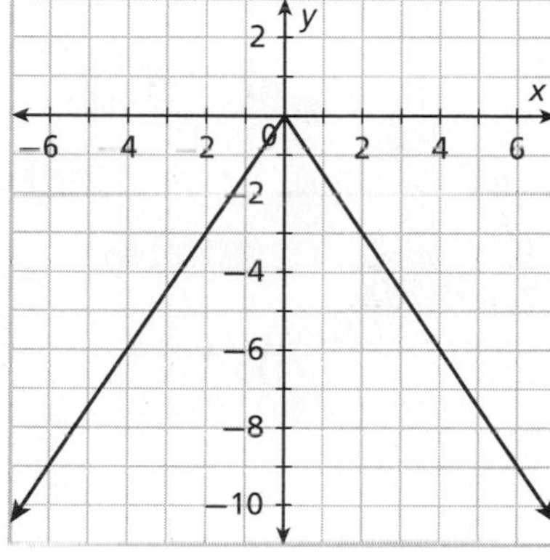

10.

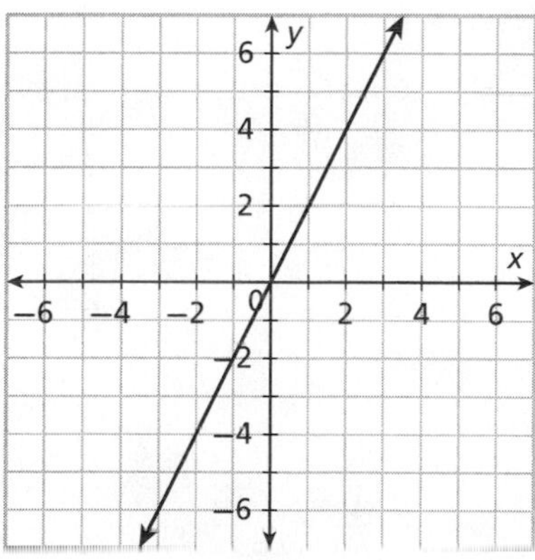

11.

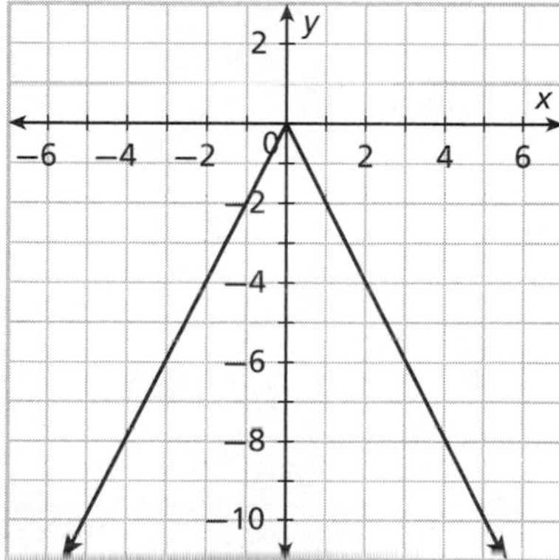

12. From his driveway at point P, Mr. Carey's direct view of the traffic signal at point Q is blocked. In order to see the traffic signal, he places a mirror at point R and aligns it with the x-axis as shown.

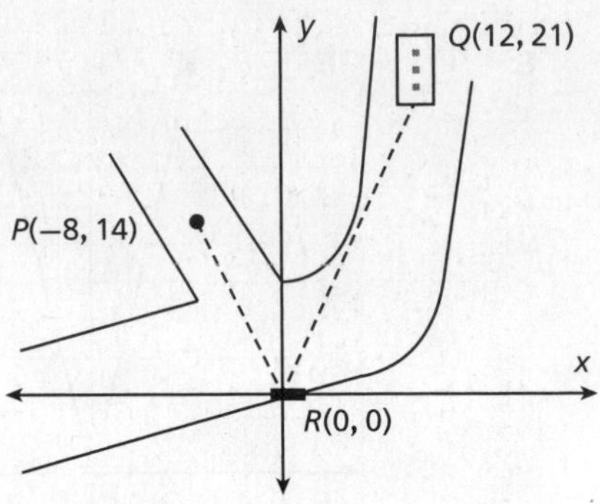

a. Use point Q to write an equation for a function of the form $g(x) = a|x|$ whose graph models the path that light from the traffic signal takes when it strikes the mirror at R.

____

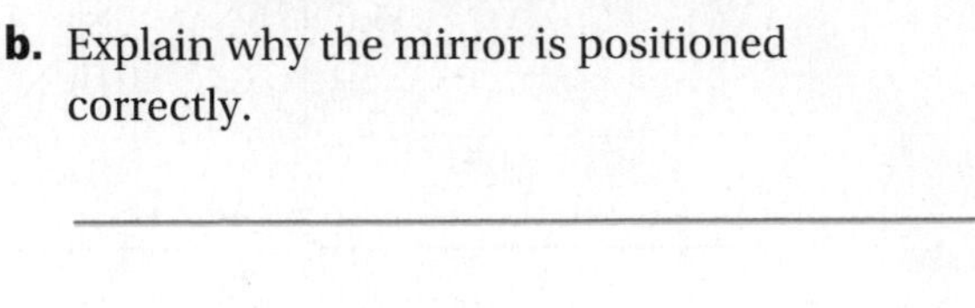

b. Explain why the mirror is positioned correctly.

____

____

Name________________________ Class________________ Date______________

4-5

Additional Practice

Graph $f(x)$ and $g(x)$. Then describe the transformation from the graph of $f(x)$ to the graph of $g(x)$.

1. $f(x) = x$; $g(x) = 0.25x$

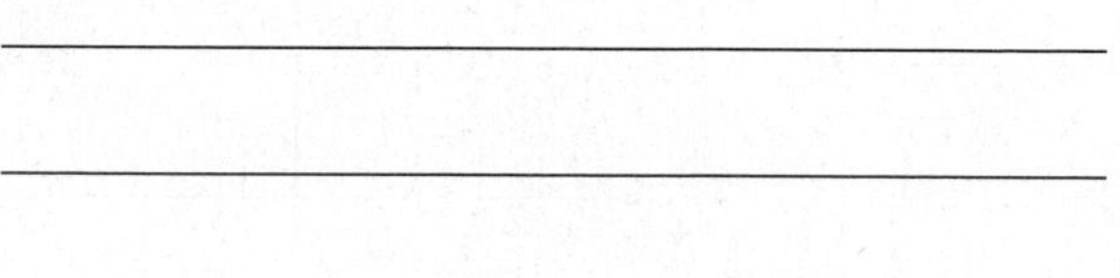

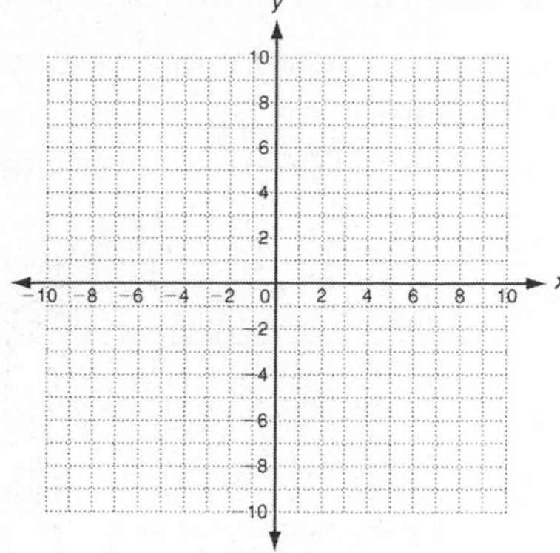

2. $f(x) = x$; $g(x) = -5x$

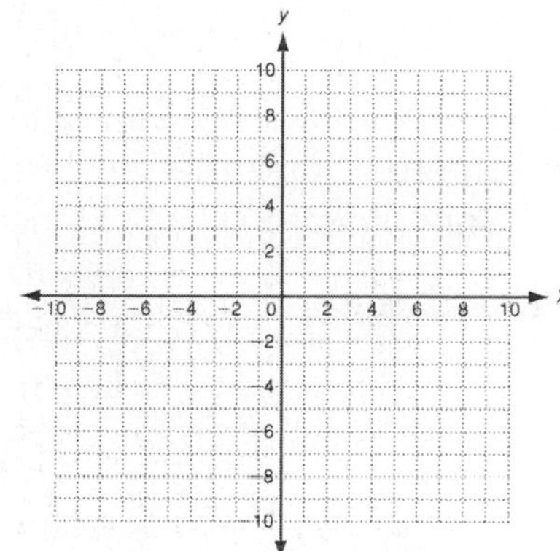

3. $f(x) = |x|$; $g(x) = 2|x|$

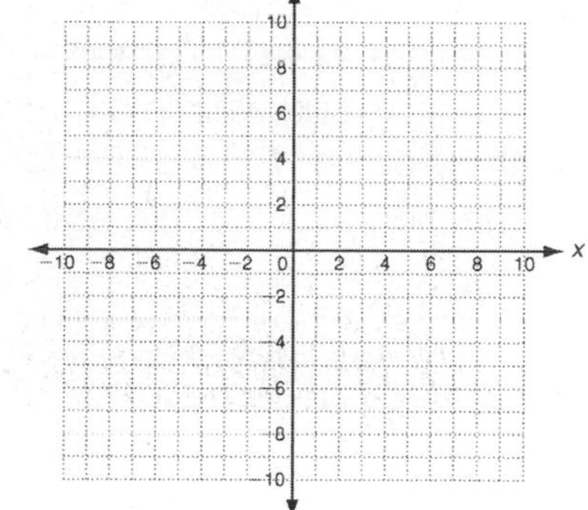

4. $f(x) = |x|$; $g(x) = -3|x|$

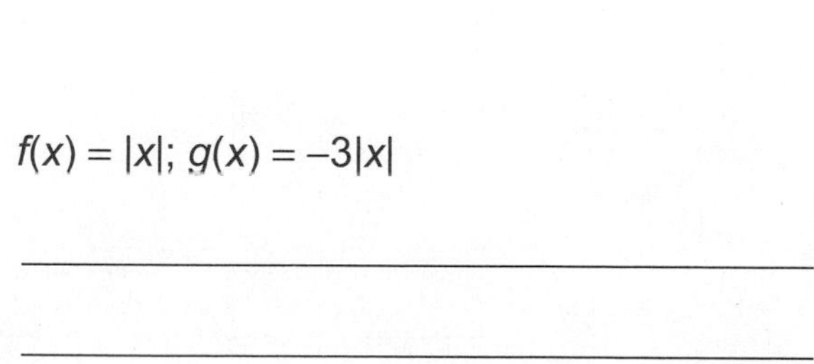

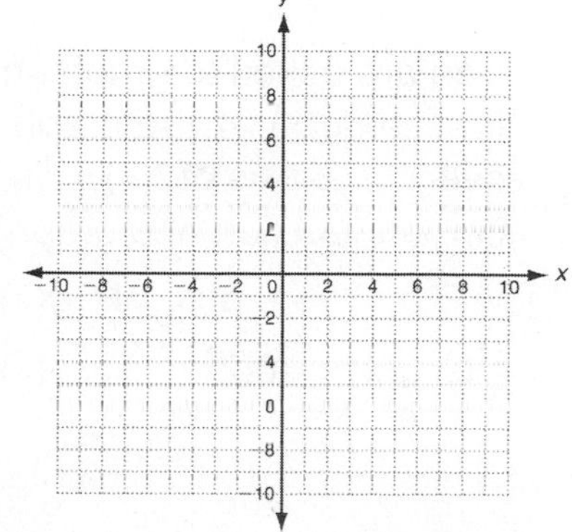

Problem Solving

Graph *f*(*x*) and *g*(*x*) given in Problems 1 and 2. Then describe the transformation from the graph of *f*(*x*) to the graph of *g*(*x*).

1. Sam is designing a target for a game called X Marks the Spot. One line of the X is given by $f(x) = 2x$. The other line is given by $g(x) = -2x$.

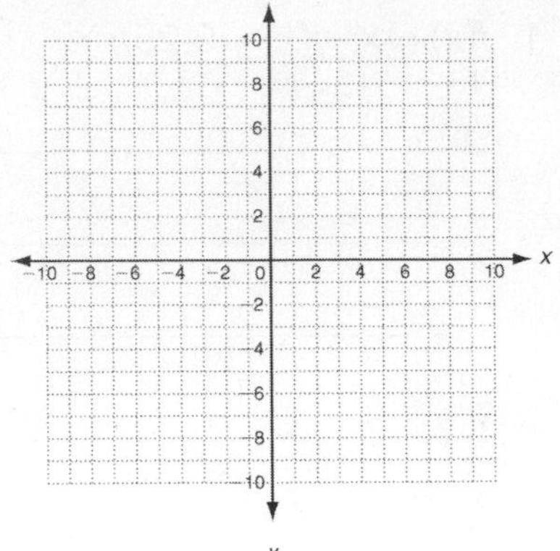

2. The X Marks the Spot game needs two different X's for targets. For the second X Sam uses $f(x) = 0.5|x|$ and $g(x) = -0.5|x|$.

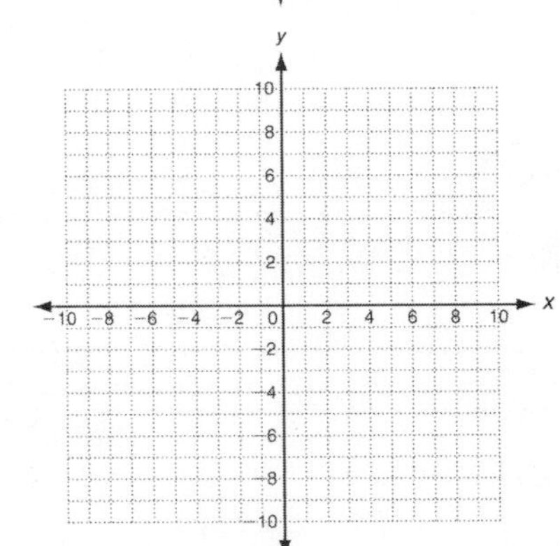

3. You are asked to graph an increasing linear function $g(x)$ whose slope is steeper than the slope of $f(x) = x$. Choose the correct function and graph it at the right.

   A $g(x) = 0.3x$ C $g(x) = 3x$

   B $g(x) = -0.3x$ D $g(x) = -3x$

4. You are asked to graph an absolute value function $g(x)$ whose graph is a reflection over the x-axis of $f(x) = 5|x|$. Choose the correct function and graph it at the right.

   F $g(x) = -0.5|x|$ H $g(x) = 0.2|x|$

   G $g(x) = -0.2|x|$ J $g(x) = -5|x|$

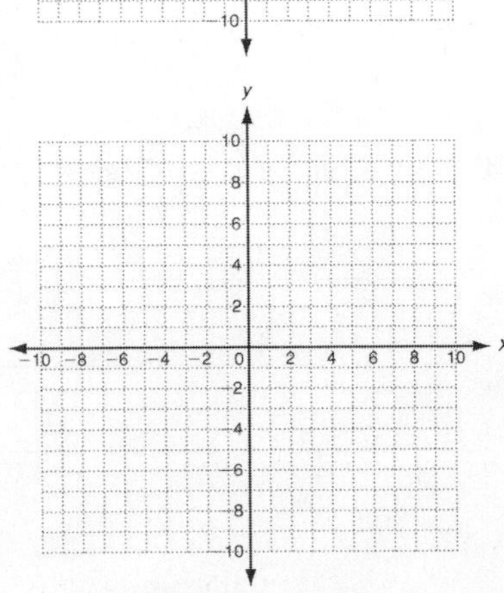

Name________________________ Class______________ Date__________

4-6

Video Tutor

Graphing and Writing Linear Functions

Going Deeper

Essential question: *How can you represent relationships using linear functions?*

Graphing Lines You can graph the linear function $f(x) = mx + b$ using only the slope m and the y-intercept b. First, locate the point $(0, b)$ on the y-axis. Next, use the rise and run of the slope to locate another point on the line. Draw the line through the two points.

When using m to locate a second point, bear in mind that m is a ratio, so many values of rise and run are possible. For instance, if $m = \frac{1}{2}$, then you could use a rise of $\frac{1}{2}$ and a run of 1, a rise of 1 and run of 2, a rise of -2 and a run of -4, and so on. Your choice of rise and run often depends on the scales used on the coordinate plane's axes.

CC.9–12.F.IF.7a

1 EXAMPLE Graphing a Line Using the Slope and y-Intercept

Graph each function.

A $f(x) = -\frac{2}{3}x + 4$

- The y-intercept is ________. Plot the point that corresponds to the y-intercept.
- The slope is ________. If you use -2 as the rise, then the run is ________.
- Use the slope to move from the first point to a second point. Begin by moving down ________ units, because the rise is negative. Then move right ________ units, because the run is positive. Plot a second point.
- Draw the line through the two points.
- The domain is the set of ____________ numbers.

  The range is the set of ____________ numbers.

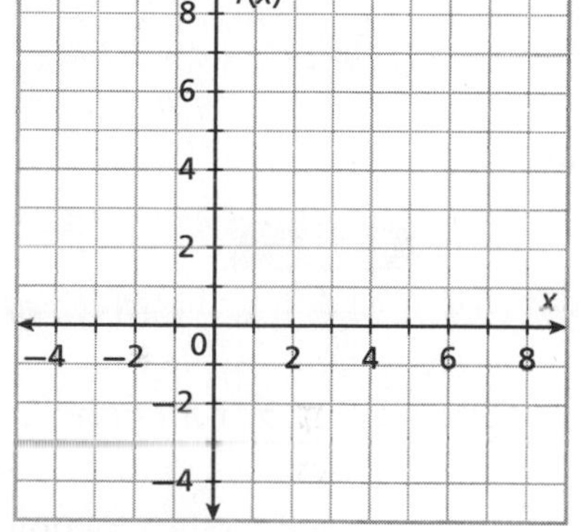

B A pitcher with a maximum capacity of 4 cups contains 1 cup of apple juice concentrate. A faucet is turned on filling the pitcher at a rate of 0.25 cup per second. The amount of liquid in the pitcher (in cups) is a function $A(t)$ of the time t (in seconds) that the water is running.

- The y-intercept is the initial amount in the pitcher at time 0, or ________ cup. Plot the point that corresponds to the y-intercept.
- The slope is the rate of change: ________ cup per second, or 1 cup in ________ seconds. So, the rise is ________ and the run is ________.
- Use the rise and run to move from the first point to a second point on the line by moving up ________ unit and right ________ units. Plot a second point.

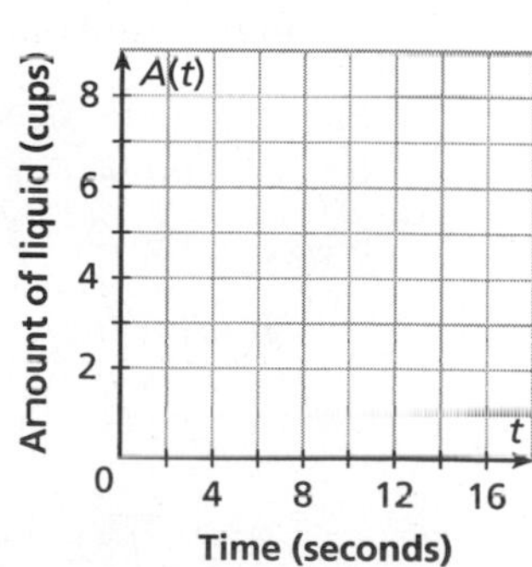

continued

- Connect the points and extend the line to the maximum value of the function, where $A(t) =$ ________ cups.

- The domain is the set of numbers ________ $\le t \le$ ________.

  The range is the set of numbers ________ $\le A(t) \le$ ________.

REFLECT

1a. How could you use the slope and y-intercept to graph the function $f(x) = 3$?

____

____

1b. What are the units of the rise in Part B? What are the units of the run?

____

1c. How long does it take to fill the pitcher? Explain.

____

1d. Why is the function rule $A(t) = \frac{1}{4}t + 1$? Use units to justify your answer.

____

____

____

____

CC.9–12.F.LE.2

2 EXAMPLE Writing a Linear Function

Write the linear function *f* using the given information.

A The graph of the function has a slope of 3 and a y-intercept of -1.

A linear function has the form $f(x) = mx + b$ where m is the slope and b is the y-intercept. Substitute ________ for m and ________ for b.

So, the function is $f(x) =$ ________.

B A different function has the values shown in the table.

x	$f(x)$
−1	5
3	−3
7	−11

First calculate the slope using any two ordered pairs from the table. For instance, let $(x_1, f(x_1)) = (-1, 5)$ and $(x_2, f(x_2)) = (3, -3)$.

$m = \dfrac{f(x_2) - f(x_1)}{x_2 - x_1}$ Write the slope formula.

$= \dfrac{\square - \square}{\square - (\square)}$ Substitute values.

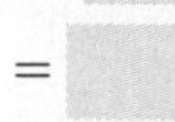

$= \frac{\square}{\square}$ Simplify numerator and denominator.

$= \square$ Simplify fraction.

Then find the value of b using the fact that $m =$ _______ and $f(-1) = 5$.

$f(x) = \square\, x + b$ Write the function with the known value of m.

$\square = \square(\square) + b$ Substitute −1 for x and 5 for $f(x)$.

$\square = \square + b$ Simplify the right side of the equation.

$\square = b$ Solve for b.

So, the function is $f(x) = \square$.

REFLECT

2a. In Part B, use the ordered pair (7, −11) to check your answer.

____

CC.9–12.F.LE.2

3 EXAMPLE Writing a Linear Function from a Graph

The graph shows the increase in pressure (measured in pounds per square inch) as a scuba diver descends from a depth of 10 feet to a depth of 30 feet.

Pressure is the result of the weight of the column of water above the diver as well as the weight of the column of Earth's atmosphere above the water. Pressure is a linear function of depth.

What is the pressure on the diver at the water's surface?

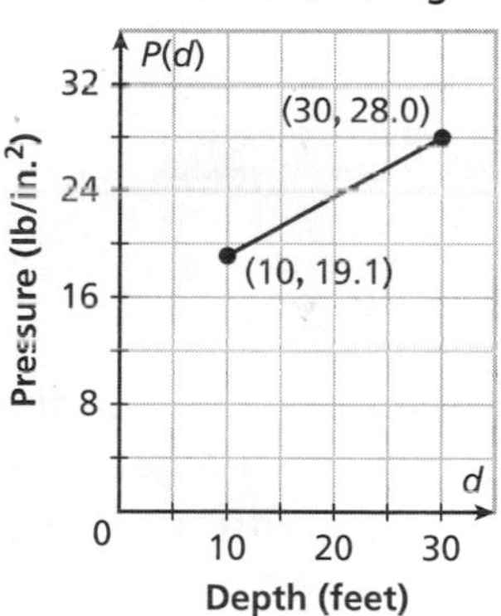

A Interpret the question.

Let d represent depth and P represent pressure. At the water's surface,

$d =$ _______. For this value of d, what meaning does $P(d)$ have in terms of the line that contains the line segment shown on the graph?

____

B Find the value of m in $P(d) = md + b$. Use the fact that $P(10) = 19.1$ and $P(30) = 28.0$.

$m = \frac{P(d_2) - P(d_1)}{d_2 - d_1}$ Write the slope formula.

$= \frac{\square - \square}{30 - 10}$ Substitute values.

continued

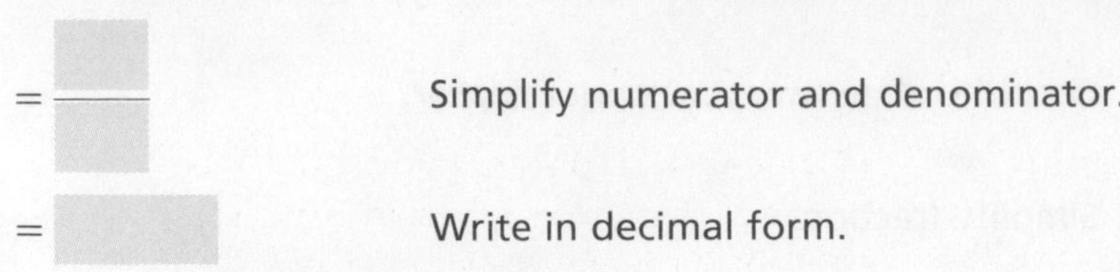

Simplify numerator and denominator.

Write in decimal form.

C Find the value of b in $P(d) = md + b$. Use the value of m from Part B as well as the fact that $P(10) = 19.1$.

$P(d) = \_\_\_ d + b$ — Write the function with the known value of m.

$\_\_\_ = \_\_\_(\_\_\_) + b$ — Substitute 10 for d and 19.1 for $P(d)$.

$\_\_\_ = \_\_\_ + b$ — Simplify the right side of the equation.

$\_\_\_ \approx b$ — Solve for b. Round to the nearest tenth.

So, the pressure at the water's surface is $P(0) = b \approx$ ______ lb/in.^{2}

REFLECT

3a. Interpret the value of m in the context of the problem.

____

3b. Write the function $P(d) = md + b$ using the calculated values of m and b. Use the function to find the pressure on the diver at a depth of 20 feet.

____

CC.9–12.A.REI.11

4 EXAMPLE Writing and Solving a System of Equations

Mr. Jackson takes a commuter bus from his suburban home to his job in the city. He normally gets on the bus in the town where he lives, but today he is running a little late. He gets to the bus stop 2 minutes after the bus has left. He wants to catch up with the bus by the time it gets to the next stop in a neighboring town 5 miles away.

The speed limit on the road connecting the two stops is 40 miles per hour, but Mr. Jackson knows that the bus travels the road at 30 miles per hour. He decides to drive at 40 miles per hour to the next stop. Does he successfully catch the bus there?

A Identify the independent and dependent variables, how they are measured, and how you will represent them.

The independent variable is __________, measured in minutes. Let t represent the time since Mr. Jackson began driving to the next bus stop.

The dependent variable is __________, measured in miles. Let d represent the distance traveled. Since you need to track the distances traveled by both Mr. Jackson and the bus, use subscripts: d_J will represent the distance traveled by Mr. Jackson, and d_B will represent the distance traveled by the bus.

B Write a distance-traveled function for Mr. Jackson and for the bus.

Each function has the form $d(t) = rt + d_0$ where r is the rate of travel and d_0 is any initial distance. Although you know the rates of travel, they are given in miles per hour, which is incompatible with the unit of time (minutes). So, you need to convert miles per hour to miles per minute. In the conversions below, express the miles as simplified fractions.

Mr. Jackson: $\frac{40 \text{ miles}}{\cancel{\text{hour}}} \cdot \frac{1 \cancel{\text{hour}}}{60 \text{ minutes}} = \square$ mile per minute

Bus: $\frac{30 \text{ miles}}{\cancel{\text{hour}}} \cdot \frac{1 \cancel{\text{hour}}}{60 \text{ minutes}} = \square$ mile per minute

At the moment Mr. Jackson begins driving to the next bus stop, the bus has traveled for 2 minutes. If you use Mr. Jackson's position as the starting point, then the initial distance for Mr. Jackson is 0 miles, and the initial distance for the bus is $\square \cdot 2 = \square$.

So, the distance-traveled functions are:

Mr. Jackson: $d_J(t) = \square\, t + \square$ Bus: $d_B(t) = \square\, t + \square$

C Determine the value of t for which $d_J(t) = d_B(t)$. You can do this by graphing the two functions and seeing where the graphs intersect. Carefully draw the graphs on the coordinate plane below, and label the intersection point.

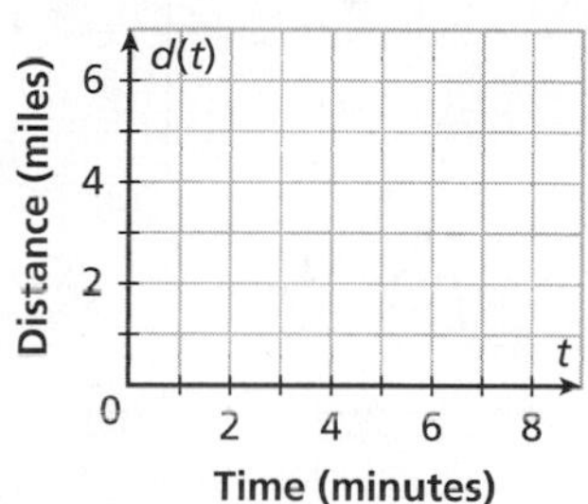

The t-coordinate of the point of intersection is ________, so

Mr. Jackson catches up with the bus in ____________.

D Check the result against the conditions of the problem, and then answer the problem's question.

The problem states that the next bus stop is ________ miles away, and the

graph shows that Mr. Jackson catches up with the bus in ________ miles.

So, does Mr. Jackson successfully catch the bus? ________

REFLECT

4a. Explain how you can use algebra rather than a graph to find the time when Mr. Jackson catches up with the bus. Then show that you get the same result.

4b. In terms of the context of the problem, explain why the t-coordinate of the intersection point (and not some other point) determines how long it takes Mr. Jackson to catch up with the bus.

____

____

____

PRACTICE

Graph each linear function.

1. $f(x) = 3x - 4$

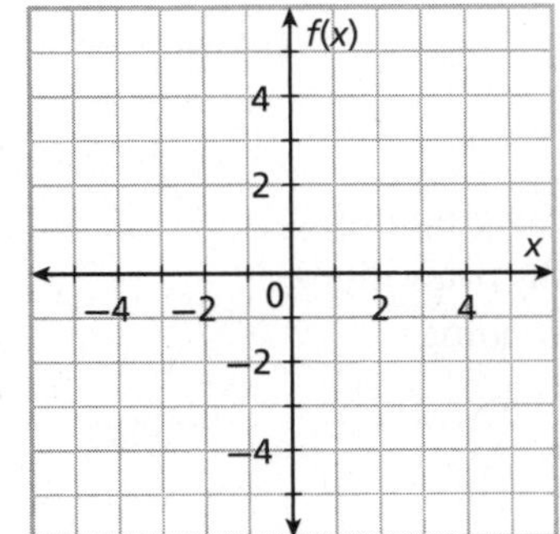

2. $f(x) = \frac{1}{2}x + 2$

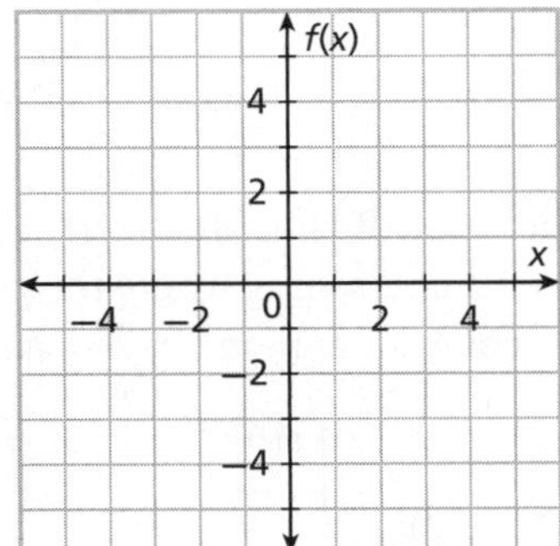

3. $f(x) = -1$

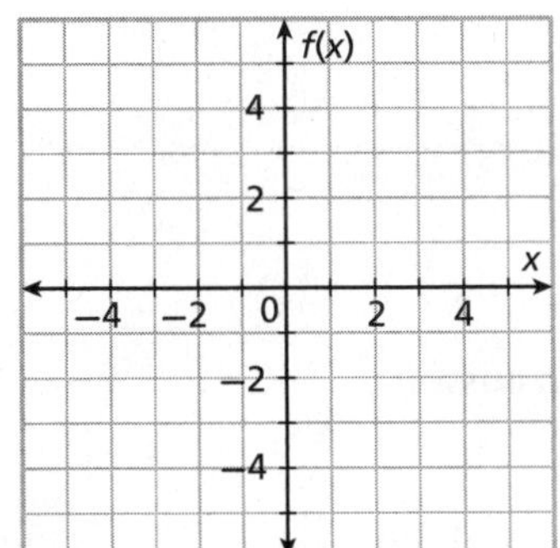

4. $f(x) = \frac{4}{3}x$

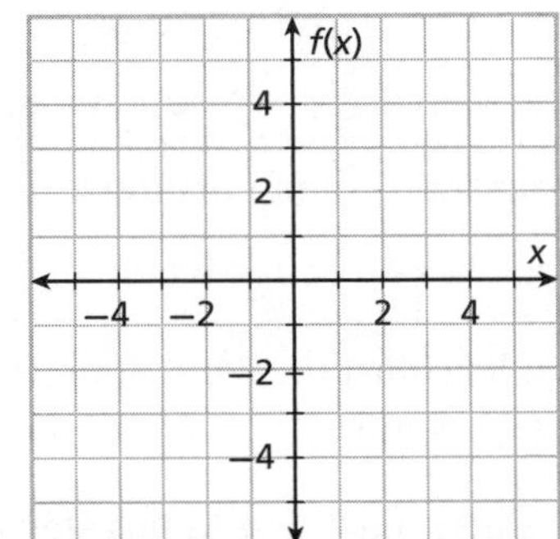

5. $f(x) = \frac{1}{4}x - 3$

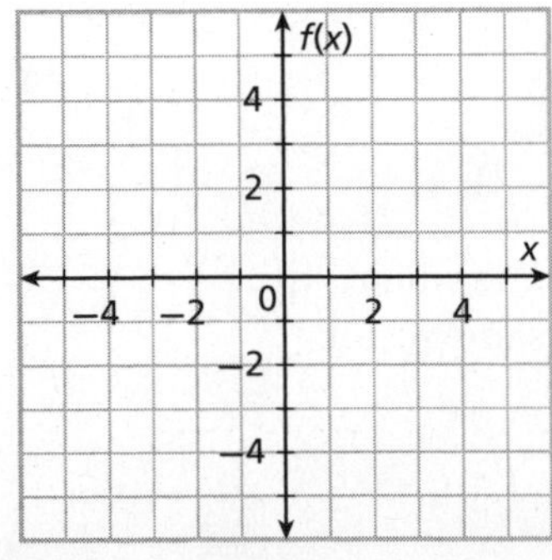

6. $f(x) = -5x + 1$

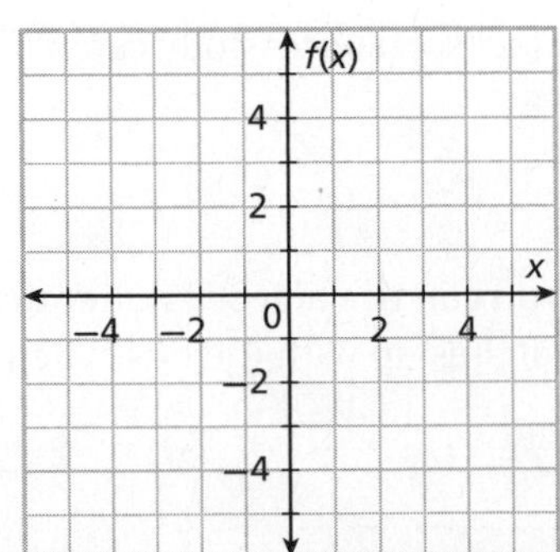

Graph each linear function and answer the question. Explain your answer.

7. A plumber charges \$50 for a service call plus \$75 per hour. The total of these costs (in dollars) is a function $C(t)$ of the time t (in hours) on the job. For how many hours will the cost be \$200? \$300?

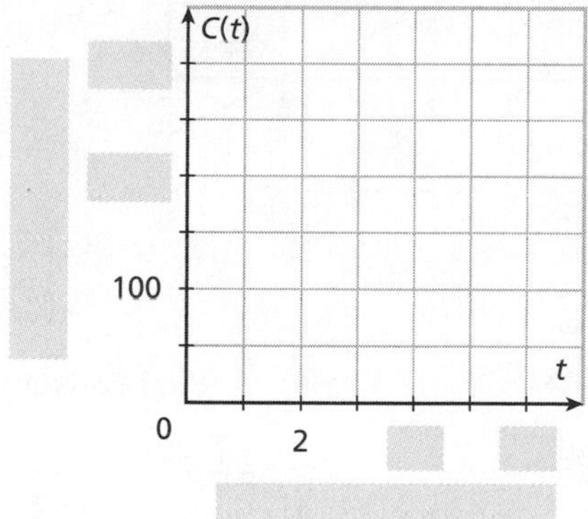

8. A bamboo plant is 10 centimeters tall at noon and grows at a rate of 5 centimeters every 2 hours. The height (in centimeters) is a function $h(t)$ of the time t it grows. When will the plant be 20 centimeters tall?

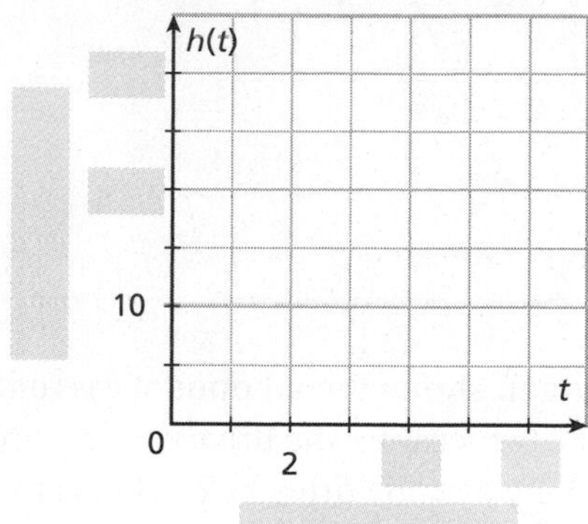

Write the linear function *f* using the given information.

9. The graph of the function has a slope of 4 and a y-intercept of 1.

10. The graph of the function has a slope of 0 and a y-intercept of 6.

11. The graph of the function has a slope of $-\frac{2}{3}$ and a y-intercept of 5.

12. The graph of the function has a slope of $\frac{7}{4}$ and a y-intercept of 0.

13.

x	$f(x)$
–3	8
0	5
3	2

14.

x	$f(x)$
0	–3
2	0
4	3

15.

x	$f(x)$
1	–1
2	5
3	11

16.

x	$f(x)$
5	–2
10	–6
15	–10

Write the linear function *f* using the given information.

17.

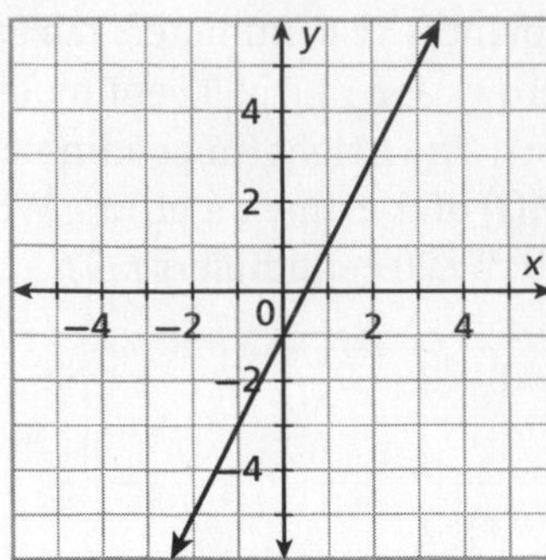

____

18.

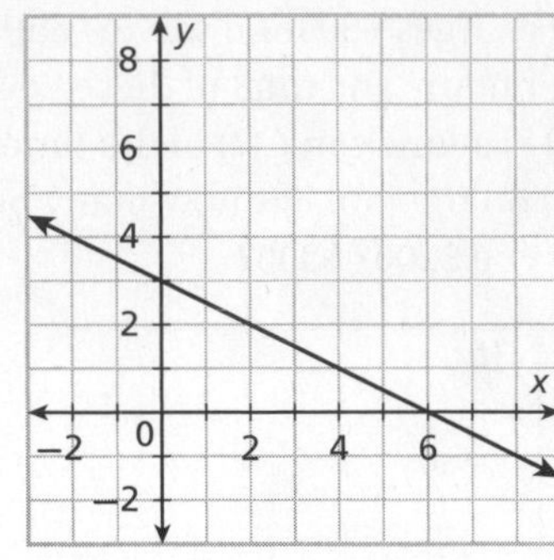

____

19. The graph shows the amount of gas remaining in the gas tank of Mrs. Liu's car as she drives at a steady speed for 2 hours. How long can she drive before her car runs out of gas?

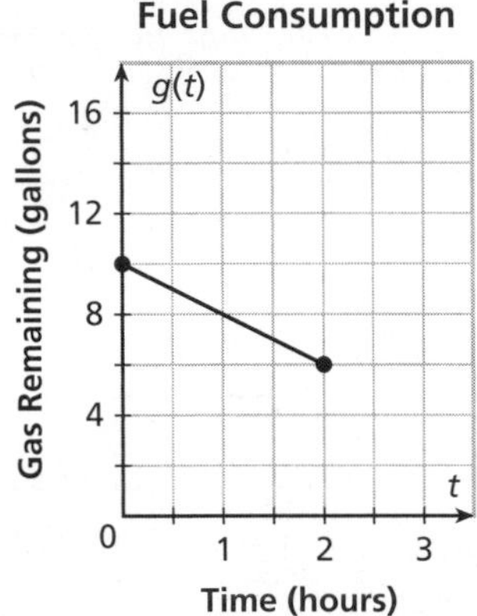

a. Interpret the question by describing what aspect of the graph would answer the question.

____

____

b. Write a linear function whose graph includes the segment shown.

____

c. Tell how to use the function to answer the question; then find the answer.

____

20. Jamal and Nathan exercise by running one circuit of a basically circular route that is 5 miles long and takes them past each other's home. The two boys run in the same direction, and Jamal passes Nathan's home 12 minutes into his run. Jamal runs at a rate of 7.5 miles per hour while Nathan runs at a rate of 6 miles per hour. If the two boys start running at the same time, when, if ever, will Jamal catch up with Nathan before completing his run?

a. Identify the independent and dependent variables, how they are measured, and how you will represent them.

____

____

____

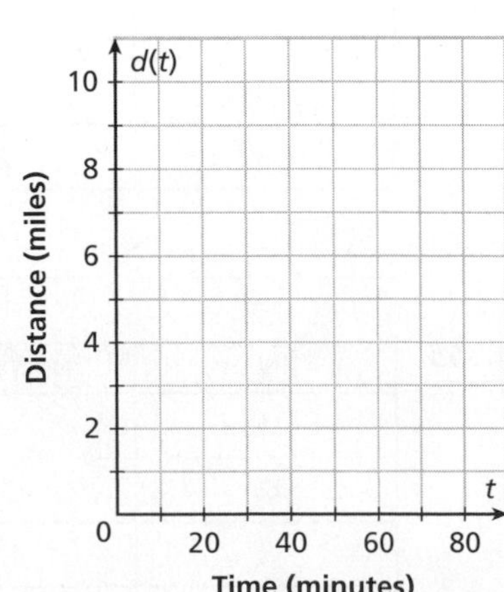

b. Write distance-run functions for Jamal and Nathan.

____

c. Graph the functions, find the intersection point, and check the point against the conditions of the problem to answer the question.

____

Name ______________________ Class ______________ Date ____________

4-6

Additional Practice

Write the equation that describes each line in slope-intercept form.

1. slope = 4; y-intercept = −3

   y = ____________

2. slope = −2; y-intercept = 0

   y = ____________

3. slope = $-\frac{1}{3}$; y-intercept = 6

   y = ____________

4. slope = $\frac{2}{5}$, (10, 3) is on the line.

   Find the y-intercept $y = mx + b$

   ____ = (____)____ + b

   ____ = ____ + b

   ____ = b

   Write the equation: y = ____________

Write each equation in slope-intercept form. Then graph the line described by the equation.

5. $y + x = 3$

____

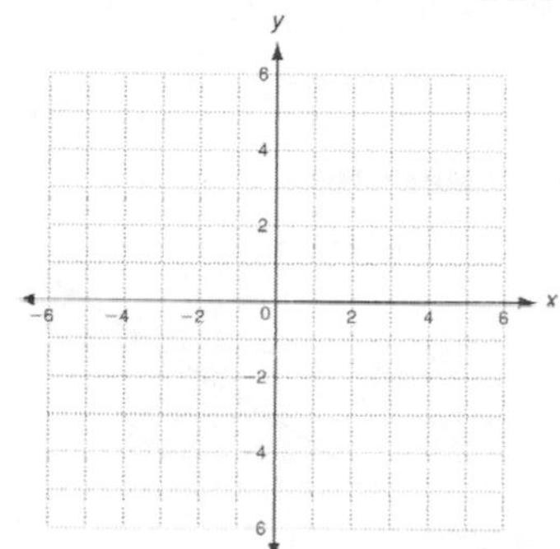

6. $y + 4 = \frac{4}{3}x$

____

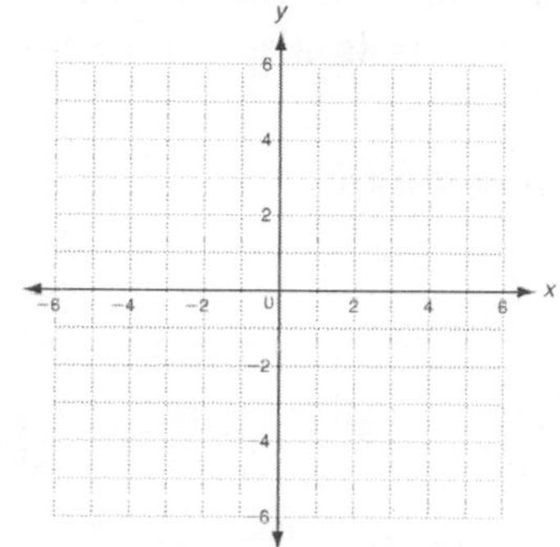

7. $5x - 2y = 10$

____

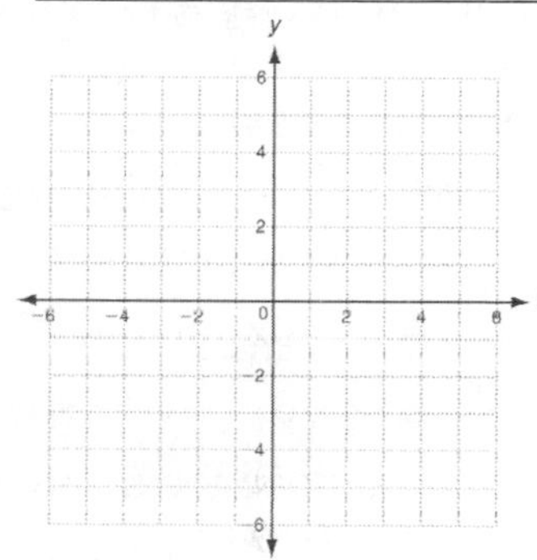

8. Daniel works as a volunteer in a homeless shelter. So far, he has worked 22 hours, and he plans to continue working 3 hours per week. His hours worked as a function of time is shown in the graph.

   a. Write an equation that represents the hours Daniel will work as a function of time. ____________

   b. Identify the slope and y-intercept and describe their meanings. ____________

   ____

   c. Find the number of hours worked after 16 weeks.

   ____

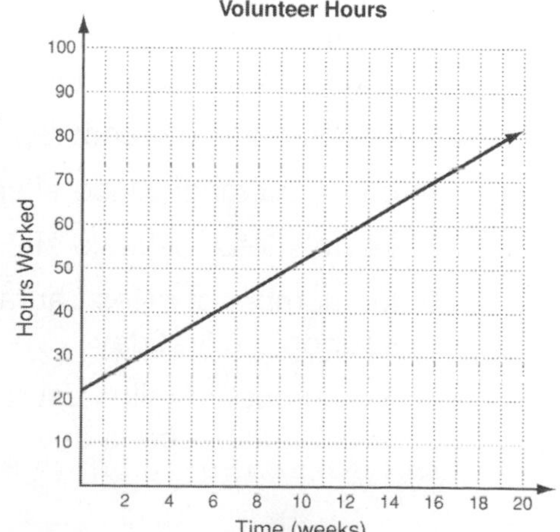

Problem Solving

The cost of food for an honor roll dinner is $300 plus $10 per student. The cost of the food as a function of the number of students is shown in the graph. Write the correct answer.

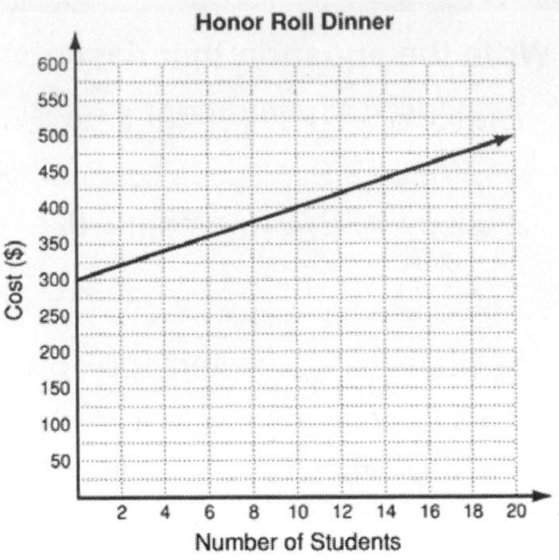

1. Write an equation that represents the cost as a function of the number of students.

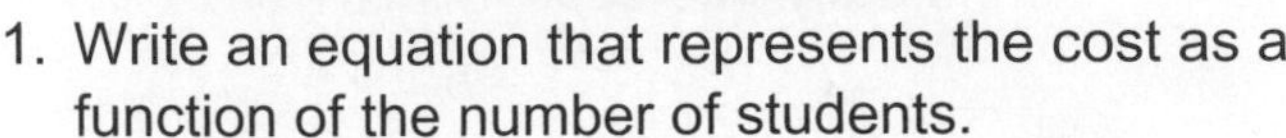

____

2. Identify the slope and y-intercept and describe their meanings.

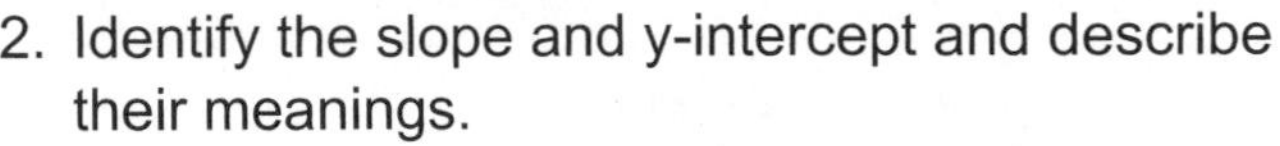

____

____

3. Find the cost of the food for 50 students. ______________________________

Laura is on a two-day hike in the Smoky Mountains. She hiked 8 miles on the first day and is hiking at a rate of 3 mi/h on the second day. Her total distance as a function of time is shown in the graph. Select the best answer.

4. Which equation represents Laura's total distance as a function of time?

   A $y = 3x$ C $y = 3x + 8$

   B $y = 8x$ D $y = 8x + 3$

5. What does the slope represent?

   F Laura's total distance after one day

   G Laura's total distance after two days

   H the number of miles Laura hiked per hour on the first day

   J the number of miles Laura hikes per hour on the second day

6. What does the *y*-intercept represent?

   A Laura's total distance after one day

   B Laura's total distance after two days

   C the number of miles Laura hiked per hour on the first day

   D the number of miles Laura hikes per hour on the second day

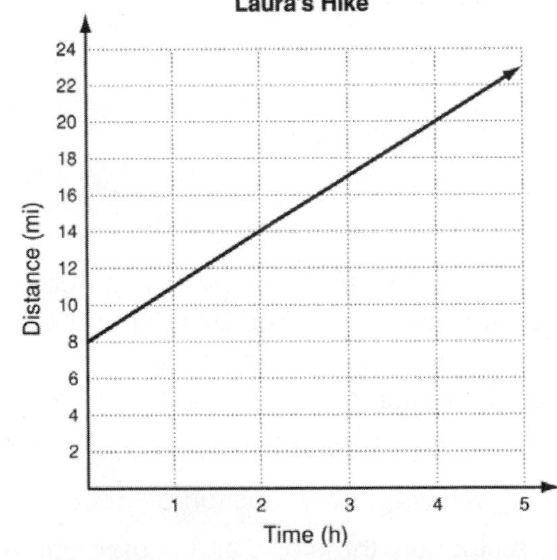

7. What will be Laura's total distance if she hikes for 6 hours on the second day?

   F 14 miles   H 26 miles

   G 18 miles   J 28 miles

Name______________________________ Class______________ Date__________

4-7

Video Tutor

Point-Slope Form

Connection: Relating Slope-Intercept, Point-Slope, and Standard Forms

Essential question: *What properties of linear functions does each linear function form illustrate?*

CC.9–12.F.IF.8

1 EXAMPLE Writing Equations in Slope-Intercept Form

Write an equation for $-4x + 5y = 10$ in slope-intercept form. Then use that form to identify the slope and y-intercept.

A Rewrite the equation in slope-intercept form by solving for y.

$-4x + 5y = 10$	Standard form of the equation
$5y = \square + 10$	Add $4x$ to each side.
$y = \square + \frac{10}{5}$	Divide each side by 5.
$y = \square$	Simplify.

B Identify the slope and y-intercept of the line.

The equation is in the form $y = mx + b$, where m is the slope and b is the y-intercept. So, the slope of the line is ______ and the y-intercept is ______.

REFLECT

1a. In the Example, which equation form would you use to graph the equation? Explain.

____

____

____

1b. Rewrite $Ax + By = C$ in slope-intercept form. Explain how you can use this form to identify the slope and y-intercept of a line when its equation is given in standard form.

____

____

____

CC.9–12.F.IF.8

2 EXAMPLE Writing Equations in Standard Form

Write an equation for $y - 4 = \frac{2}{3}(x - 9)$ in standard form. Then use that form to identify the x- and y-intercepts.

A Rewrite the equation in standard form by collecting the x- and y-terms on one side of the equation.

$y - 4 = \frac{2}{3}(x - 9)$	Point-slope form of the equation
$\_\_\_\_ = \_\_\_\_ \bullet \frac{2}{3}(x - 9)$	Multiply each side by 3.
$3y - 12 = \_\_\_\_$	Simplify.
$3y = \_\_\_\_$	Add 12 to each side.
$\_\_\_\_ = \_\_\_\_$	Subtract $2x$ from each side.

B Find the x-intercept by substituting 0 for y and solving for x.

$-2x + 3(\_\_\_\_) = -6$	Substitute 0 for y.
$\_\_\_\_ = -6$	Simplify.
$x = \_\_\_\_$	Solve for x.

The x-intercept is ____.

C Find the y-intercept by substituting 0 for x and solving for y.

$-2(\_\_\_\_) + 3y = -6$	Substitute 0 for x.
$\_\_\_\_ = -6$	Simplify.
$y = \_\_\_\_$	Solve for y.

The y-intercept is ____.

REFLECT

2a. Find the x-intercept of the line in the Example by substituting 0 for y and solving for x in the point-slope form of the equation. Is it easier to find the x-intercept using the standard form or the point-slope form? Explain your answer.

____

____

2b. Explain why you substitute 0 for x in the equation to find the y-intercept.

____

____

____

CC.9–12.F.LE.2

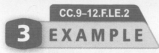

3 EXAMPLE Choosing an Appropriate Form of a Linear Equation

Determine which form of a linear equation to use to write an equation for the line that passes through (–4, 9) and (8, 6). Then write an equation for the line.

A To determine which form to use, identify the given information.

Two points on the line are given, and neither of them is the y-intercept. So, write the equation using ______________ form.

B Find the slope of the line using the two points.

$$m = \frac{y_2 - y_1}{x_2 - x_1} = \frac{6 - \square}{\square - (-4)} = \square = \square$$

C Write the equation in ______________ form using the point (8, 6).

$y - y_1 = m(x - x_1)$ General form of the equation

$y - \square = \square(x - \square)$ Substitute values for x_1, y_1, and m.

REFLECT

3a. Could (–4, 9) have been used to write an equation of the line in Part C? Explain.

____

____

3b. Suppose you are given the y-intercept and the slope of a line. Which linear equation form would you use to write an equation for the line? Explain your reasoning.

____

____

The following table provides a summary of the information presented in the Examples above.

Form	Equation	Information	When to Use
slope-intercept	$y = mx + b$	• m is the slope. • b is the y-intercept.	• When given the slope and the y-intercept
point-slope	$y - y_1 = m(x - x_1)$	• m is the slope. • (x_1, y_1) lies on the line.	• When given the slope and one point on the line • When given two points on the line
standard	$Ax + By = C$	• A, B, and C are real numbers. • A and B are not both 0.	• When given a horizontal or vertical line and one point on the line

PRACTICE

Rewrite the equation to find the characteristics of the line.

1. Rewrite $y = -\frac{3}{2}x + 6$ in standard form. Identify the x-intercept of the line.

2. Rewrite $-7x + 9y = 18$ in slope-intercept form. Identify the slope and y-intercept of the line.

3. Rewrite $y + 1 = 4(x + 3)$ in slope-intercept form. Identify the y-intercept of the line.

4. Rewrite $y + 25 = -\frac{5}{3}(x - 12)$ in standard form. Identify the x- and y-intercepts of the line.

Determine which form of a linear equation to use to write an equation for the line with the given characteristics. Then write an equation for the line in that form.

5. passes through $(-5, -4)$, $(7, 5)$

6. slope $= -\frac{2}{7}$; y-intercept $= 9$

7. vertical line through $(8, 1)$

8. slope $= \frac{11}{13}$; passes through $(-3, 6)$

9. You are asked to rewrite $-9x + 4y = 14$ to find the slope of the line. Would you rewrite the equation in slope-intercept form or point-slope form? Explain.

10. Find the x- and y-intercepts of the graph of $Ax + By = C$. Explain how you can use these intercepts to find the x- and y-intercepts of any line in standard form.

Name________________________ Class______________ Date____________

Additional Practice

Write an equation in point-slope form for the line with the given slope that contains the given point.

1. slope = 3; (–4, 2)

____

2. slope = –1; (6, –1)

____

Graph the line described by each equation.

3. $y + 2 = -\frac{2}{3}(x - 6)$

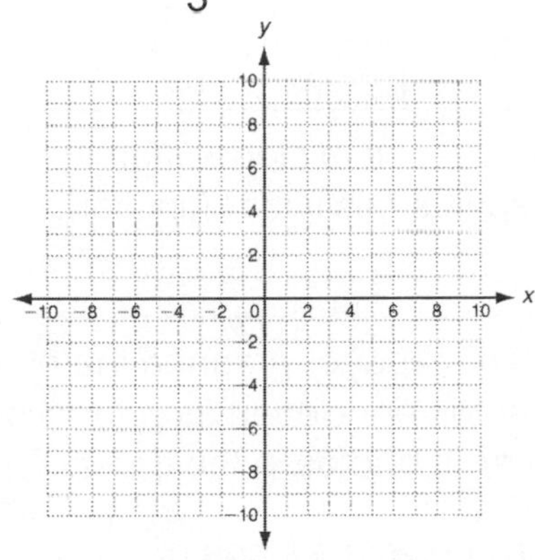

4. $y + 3 = -2(x - 4)$

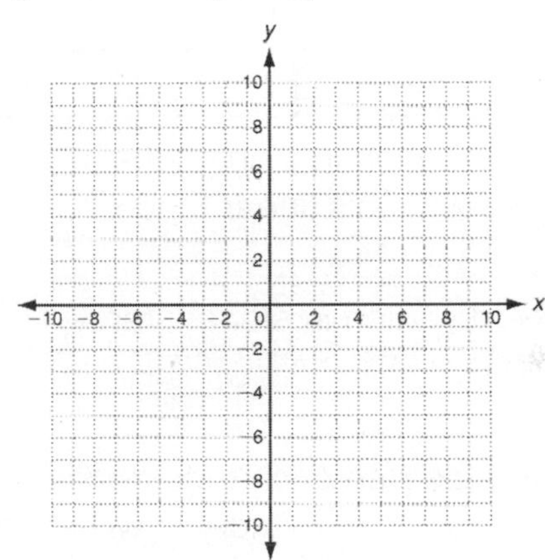

Write the equation that describes the line in slope-intercept form.

5. slope = –4; (1, –3) is on the line

____

6. slope = $\frac{1}{2}$; (–8, –5) is on the line

____

7. (2, 1) and (0, –7) are on the line

____

8. (–6, –6) and (2, –2) are on the line

____

Find the intercepts of the line that contains each pair of points.

9. (–1, –4) and (6, 10) __________________

10. (3, 4) and (–6, 16) __________________

11. The cost of internet access at a cafe is a function of time. The costs for 8, 25, and 40 minutes are shown. Write an equation in slope-intercept form that represents the function. Then find the cost of surfing the web at the cafe for one hour.

Time (min)	8	25	40
Cost ($)	4.36	7.25	9.80

____

Problem Solving

Write the correct answer.

1. The number of students in a school has been increasing at a constant rate. The table shows the number of students in the school for certain numbers of years since 1995.

Years Since 1995	Number of Students
0	118
5	124
10	130

Write an equation in point-slope form that represents this linear function.

____

Write the equation in slope-intercept form.

____

Assuming the rate of change remains constant, how many students will be in the school in 2010?

____

2. Toni is finishing a scarf at a constant rate. The table shows the number of hours Toni has spent knitting this week and the corresponding number of rows in the scarf.

Toni's Knitting	
Hours	**Rows of Knitting**
2	38
4	44
6	50

Write an equation in slope-intercept form that represents this linear function.

____

3. A photo lab manager graphed the cost of having photos developed as a function of the number of photos in the order. The graph is a line with a slope of $\frac{1}{10}$ that passes through (10, 6). Write an equation in slope-intercept form that describes the cost to have photos developed. How much does it cost to have 25 photos developed?

____

The cost of a cell phone for one month is a linear function of the number of minutes used. The total cost for 20, 35, and 40 additional minutes are shown. Select the best answer.

Cell-Phone Costs			
Number of Additional Minutes	20	35	40
Total Cost	$48	$54	$56

4. What is the slope of the line represented in the table?
   - A 0.1
   - B 0.4
   - C 2
   - D 2.5

5. What would be the monthly cost if 60 additional minutes were used?
   - F $64
   - G $72
   - H $84
   - J $150

6. What does the *y*-intercept of the function represent?
   - A total cost of the bill
   - B cost per additional minute
   - C number of additional minutes used
   - D cost with no additional minutes used

Name________________________ Class______________ Date__________

4-8

Residuals and Linear Regression

Going Deeper

Video Tutor

Essential question: *How can you use residuals and linear regression to fit a line to data?*

Residuals You can evaluate a linear model's goodness of fit using *residuals*. A **residual** is the difference between an actual value of the dependent variable and the value predicted by the linear model. After calculating residuals, you can draw a **residual plot**, which is a scatter plot of points whose *x*-coordinates are the values of the independent variable and whose *y*-coordinates are the corresponding residuals.

Whether the fit of a line to data is suitable and good depends on the distribution of the residuals, as illustrated below.

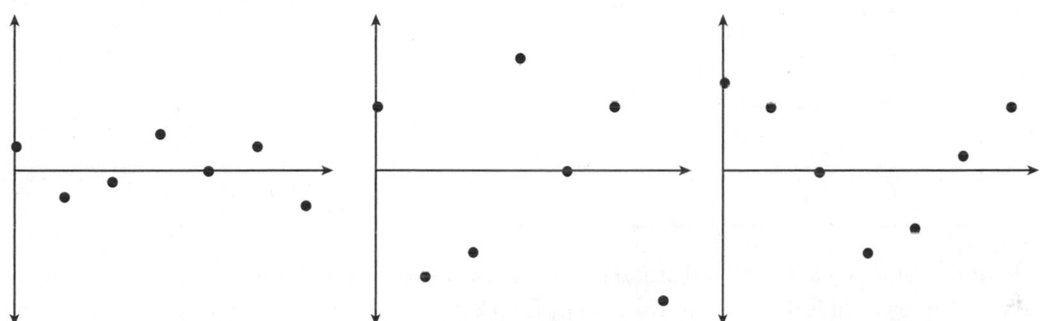

Distribution of residuals about the *x*-axis is random and tight. A linear fit to the data is suitable and strong.

Distribution of residuals about the *x*-axis is random but loose. A linear fit to the data is suitable but weak.

Distribution of residuals about the *x*-axis is not random. A linear fit to the data may not be suitable.

CC.9–12.S.ID.6b

1 EXAMPLE Creating a Residual Plot and Evaluating Fit

Using t as the years since 1970 and a_F as the median age of females, a student fit the line $a_F = 0.25t + 29$ to the data shown in the table. Make a residual plot and evaluate the goodness of fit.

Year	Median Age of Females
1970	29.2
1980	31.3
1990	34.0
2000	36.5
2010	38.2

A Calculate the residuals. Substitute each value of t into the equation to find the value predicted for a_F by the linear model. Then subtract predicted from actual to find the residual.

t	a_F actual	a_F predicted	Residual
0	29.2	29.0	0.2
10	31.3		
20	34.0		
30	36.5		
40	38.2		

B Plot the residuals.

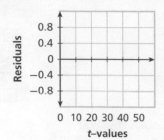

Residuals: 0.8, 0.4, 0, −0.4, −0.8

t-values: 0 10 20 30 40 50

C Evaluate the suitability of a linear fit and the goodness of the fit.

- Is there a balance between positive and negative residuals?

- Is there a pattern to the residuals? If so, describe it.

- Is the absolute value of each residual small relative to a_F (actual)? For instance, when $t = 0$, the residual is 0.2 and the value of a_F is 29.2, so the relative size of the residual is $\frac{0.2}{29.2} \approx 0.7\%$, which is quite small.

- What is your overall evaluation of the suitability and goodness of the linear fit?

REFLECT

1a. Suppose the line of fit with equation $a_F = 0.25t + 29$ is changed to $a_F = 0.25t + 28.8$. What effect does this change have on the residuals? On the residual plot? Is the new line a better fit to the data? Explain.

You can use a graphing calculator to fit a line to a set of paired numerical data that have a strong positive or negative correlation. The calculator uses a method called **linear regression**, which involves minimizing the sum of the squares of the residuals.

CC.9–12.S.ID.6c

2 EXPLORE Comparing Sums of Squared Residuals

Suppose in the first Example one person came up with the equation $a_F = 0.25t + 29.0$ while another came up with $a_F = 0.25t + 28.8$ where, in each case, t is the time in years since 1970 and a_F is the median age of females.

A Complete each table below in order to calculate the squares of the residuals for each line of fit.

Table for $a_F = 0.25t + 29.0$

$a_F = 0.25t + 29.0$				
t	a_F (actual)	a_F (predicted)	Residuals	Square of Residuals
0	29.2	29.0	0.2	0.04
10	31.3			
20	34.0			
30	36.5			
40	38.2			

Table for $a_F = 0.25t + 28.8$

$a_F = 0.25t + 28.8$				
t	a_F (actual)	a_F (predicted)	Residuals	Square of Residuals
0	29.2	28.8	0.4	0.16
10	31.3			
20	34.0			
30	36.5			
40	38.2			

B Find the sum of the squared residuals for each line of fit.

Sum of squared residuals for $a_F = 0.25t + 29.0$: ____________________

Sum of squared residuals for $a_F = 0.25t + 28.8$: ____________________

C Identify the line that has the smaller sum of the squared residuals.

____

____

____

REFLECT

2a. If you use a graphing calculator to perform linear regression on the data, you obtain the equation $a_F = 0.232t + 29.2$. Complete the table to calculate the squares of the residuals and then the sum of the squares for this line of fit.

$a_F = 0.232t + 29.2$				
t	a_F (actual)	a_F (predicted)	Residuals	Square of Residuals
0	29.2	29.2	0	0
10	31.3			
20	34.0			
30	36.5			
40	38.2			

Sum of squared residuals: __________

2b. Explain why the model $a_F = 0.232t + 29.2$ is a better fit to the data than $a_F = 0.25t + 29.0$ or $a_F = 0.25t + 28.8$.

____

____

____

Because linear regression produces an equation for which the sum of the squared residuals is as small as possible, the line obtained from linear regression is sometimes called the *least-squares regression line.* It is also called the *line of best fit.* Not only will a graphing calculator automatically find the equation of the line of best fit, but it will also give you the correlation coefficient and display the residual plot.

CC.9–12.S.ID.6c

3 EXAMPLE Performing Linear Regression on a Graphing Calculator

The table gives the distances (in meters) that a discus was thrown by men to win the gold medal at the Olympic Games from 1920 to 1964. (No Olympic Games were held during World War II.) Use a graphing calculator to find the line of best fit, to find the correlation coefficient, and to evaluate the goodness of fit.

Year of Olympic Games	Men's Gold Medal Discus Throw (meters)
1920	44.685
1924	46.155
1928	47.32
1932	49.49
1936	50.48
1940	No Olympics
1944	No Olympics
1948	52.78
1952	55.03
1956	56.36
1960	59.18
1964	61.00

A Identify the independent and dependent variables, and specify how you will represent them.

The independent variable is time. Since the graphing calculator uses the variables x and y, let x represent time. To simplify the values of x, define x as years since 1920 so that, for instance, $x = 0$ represents 1920 and $x = 44$ represents 1964. Then $x =$ ________ represents 1924, $x =$ ________ represents 1928, $x =$ ________ represents 1932, and so on.

The dependent variable is the distance that won the gold medal for the men's discus throw. Let y represent that distance.

B Enter the paired data into two lists, L_1 and L_2, on your graphing calculator after pressing STAT.

Do the distances increase or decrease over time? What does this mean for the correlation?

____

____

C Create a scatter plot of the paired data using STAT PLOT. The calculator will choose a good viewing window and plot the points automatically if you press ZOOM and select ZoomStat.

Describe the correlation.

____

____

____

D Perform linear regression by pressing STAT and selecting LinReg ($ax + b$) from the CALC menu. The calculator reports the slope a and y-intercept b of the line of best fit. It also reports the correlation coefficient r.

```
LinReg
 y=ax+b
 a=.3461140351
 b=44.63349123
 r²=.9792416093
 r=.9895663744
```

Does the correlation coefficient agree with your description of the correlation in Part C? Explain.

____

____

____

E Graph the line of best fit by pressing Y= , entering the equation of the line of best fit, and then pressing GRAPH. You should round the values of a and b when entering them so that each has at most 4 significant digits.

What is the equation of the line of best fit?

____

F Create a residual plot by replacing L_2 with RESID in STAT PLOT as the choice for Ylist. (You can select RESID from the NAMES menu after pressing 2nd STAT.)

Evaluate the suitability and goodness of the fit.

____

____

____

REFLECT

3a. Interpret the slope and *y*-intercept of the line of best fit in the context of the data.

3b. Use the line of best fit to make predictions about the distances that would have won gold medals if the Olympic Games had been held in 1940 and 1944. Are the predictions interpolations or extrapolations?

3c. Several Olympic Games were held prior to 1920. Use the line of best fit to make a prediction about the distance that would have won a gold medal in the 1908 Olympics. What value of *x* must you use? Is the prediction an interpolation or an extrapolation? How does the prediction compare with the actual value of 40.89 meters?

PRACTICE

Throughout these exercises, use a graphing calculator.

1. The table gives the distances (in meters) that a discus was thrown by men to win the gold medal at the Olympic Games from 1968 to 2008.

Year of Olympic Games	Men's Gold Medal Discus Throw (meters)
1968	64.78
1972	64.40
1976	67.50
1980	66.64
1984	66.60
1988	68.82
1992	65.12
1996	69.40
2000	69.30
2004	69.89
2008	68.82

a. Find the equation of the line of best fit.

b. Find the correlation coefficient.

c. Evaluate the suitability and goodness of the fit.

d. Does the slope of the line of best fit for the 1968–2008 data equal the slope of the line of best fit for the 1920–1964 data? If not, speculate about why this is so.

2. Women began competing in the discus throw in the 1928 Olympic Games. The table gives the distances (in meters) that a discus was thrown by women to win the gold medal at the Olympic Games from 1928 to 1964.

Year of Olympic Games	Women's Gold Medal Discus Throw (meters)
1928	39.62
1932	40.58
1936	47.63
1940	No Olympics
1944	No Olympics
1948	41.92
1952	51.42
1956	53.69
1962	55.10
1964	57.27

a. Find the equation of the line of best fit.

____

b. Find the correlation coefficient.

____

c. Evaluate the suitability and goodness of the fit.

____

____

____

3. Research the distances that a discus was thrown by women to win the gold medal at the Olympic Games from 1968 to 2008. Explain why a linear model is not appropriate for the data.

____

4. The table lists the median heights (in centimeters) of girls and boys from age 2 to age 10. Choose either the data for girls or the data for boys.

Age (years)	Median Height (cm) of Girls	Median Height (cm) of Boys
2	84.98	86.45
3	93.92	94.96
4	100.75	102.22
5	107.66	108.90
6	114.71	115.39
7	121.49	121.77
8	127.59	128.88
9	132.92	133.51
10	137.99	138.62

a. Identify the real-world variables that x and y will represent.

____

b. Find the equation of the line of best fit.

____

____

c. Find the correlation coefficient.

____

d. Evaluate the suitability and goodness of the fit.

____

____

Additional Practice

1. The data in the table are graphed at right along with two lines of fit.

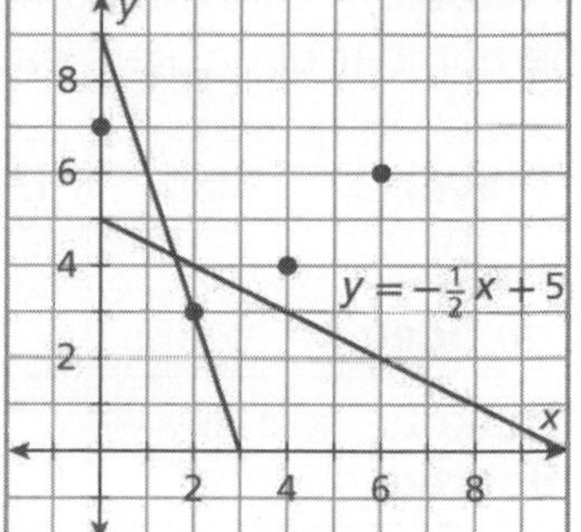

x	0	2	4	6
y	7	3	4	6

   a. Find the sum of the squares of the residuals for $y = -3x + 9$. _______________

   b. Find the sum of the squares of the residuals for $y = -\frac{1}{2}x + 5$. _______________

   c. Which line is a better fit for the data? _______________

2. Use the data in the table to answer the questions that follow.

x	5	6	6.5	7.5	9
y	0	–1	3	–2	4

   a. Find an equation for a line of best fit. _______________

   b. What is the correlation coefficient? _______________

   c. How well does the line represent the data? _______________

   d. Describe the correlation. _______________

3. Use the data in the table to answer the questions that follow.

x	10	8	6	4	2
y	1	1.1	1.2	1.3	1.5

   a. Find an equation for a line of best fit. _______________

   b. What is the correlation coefficient? _______________

   c. How well does the line represent the data? _______________

   d. Describe the correlation. _______________

4. The table shows the number of pickles four students ate during the week versus their grades on a test. The equation of the least-squares line is $y \approx 2.11x + 79.28$, and $r \approx 0.97$. Discuss correlation and causation for the data set.

Pickles Eaten	0	2	5	10
Test Score	77	85	92	99

____

____

Problem Solving

1. The table shows the number of hours different players practice basketball each week and the number of baskets each player scored during a game.

Player	Alan	Brenda	Caleb	Shawna	Fernando	Gabriela
Hours Practiced	5	10	7	2	0	21
Baskets Scored	6	11	8	4	2	19

a. Find an equation for a line of best fit. Round decimals to the nearest tenth.

____

b. Interpret the meaning of the slope and y-intercept.

____

____

c. Find the correlation coefficient. ______________________

Select the best answer.

2. Use your equation above to predict the number of baskets scored by a player who practices 40 hours a week. Round to the nearest whole number.

A 32 baskets

B 33 baskets

C 34 baskets

D 35 baskets

3. Which is the best description of the correlation?

F strong positive

G weak positive

H weak negative

J strong negative

4. Given the data, what advice can you give to a player who wants to increase the number of baskets he or she scores during a game?

A Practice more hours per week.

B Practice fewer hours per week.

C Practice the same hours per week.

D There is no way to increase baskets.

5. Do the data support causation, correlation, or chance?

F correlation

G causation

H chance

J chance and correlation

Name ______________________ Class ____________ Date ________

4-9

Slopes of Parallel and Perpendicular Lines

Focus on Modeling

Essential question: *How can you use linear equations to model the results of a fundraiser?*

COMMON CORE

CC.9-12.N.Q.1*, CC.9-12.N.Q.2*, CC.9-12.A.SSE.1*, CC.9-12.A.SSE.1a*, CC.9-12.A.CED.2*, CC.9-12.A.CED.3*

The Band Booster Club is selling T-shirts and blanket wraps to raise money for a trip. The band director has asked the club to raise at least $1000 in sales. So, the booster club has set a fundraising goal of $2000 in sales.

The booster club president wants to know how many T-shirts and how many blankets wraps the club needs to sell to meet their goal of $2000. The T-shirts cost $10 each and the blanket wraps cost $25 each. How can the booster club president use the sales price of each item to help the fundraiser meet its goal?

1 Write a linear equation to show the amount of money raised.

A Let x equal the number of T-shirts sold. Write an expression for the amount of money raised from T-shirt sales. Interpret the expression.

____

B Let y equal the number of blanket wraps sold. Write an expression for the amount of money raised from blanket wrap sales. Interpret the expression.

____

C Combine the expressions and the sales goal in a linear equation.

____

REFLECT

1a. Determine whether the booster club will meet their goal if they sell 50 T-shirts and 50 blanket wraps. Explain.

____

1b. Determine whether the booster club will meet their goal if they sell 100 T-shirts and 40 blanket wraps. Explain.

____

2 Graph the linear equation.

A Calculate three pairs of values for x and y. Enter your results in the table.

x	y
0	
	0
50	

B Plot the ordered pairs on the coordinate grid. Connect the points to graph the equation.

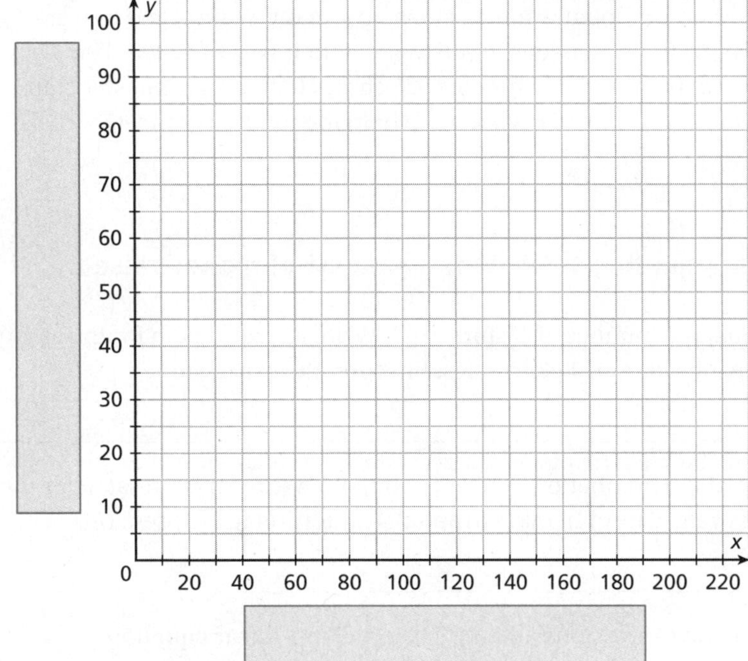

C Label the x- and y-axes in the boxes provided.

REFLECT

2a. What does the point where the line intersects the x-axis represent?

2b. Explain what the point (100, 40) represents on this graph.

2c. Suppose the Band Booster Club sells 25 blanket wraps during a chilly football game. Use the graph to determine about how many T-shirts they need to sell.

---

3 Write and graph a linear equation that shows the sales required to raise the minimum of $1000.

A Use the expressions for the amount of money raised from T-shirts and blanket wraps and the minimum goal of $1000 to write a linear equation.

B Calculate three pairs of values for x and y. Enter your results in the table. Then, graph the linear equation.

x	y
0	
	0
50	

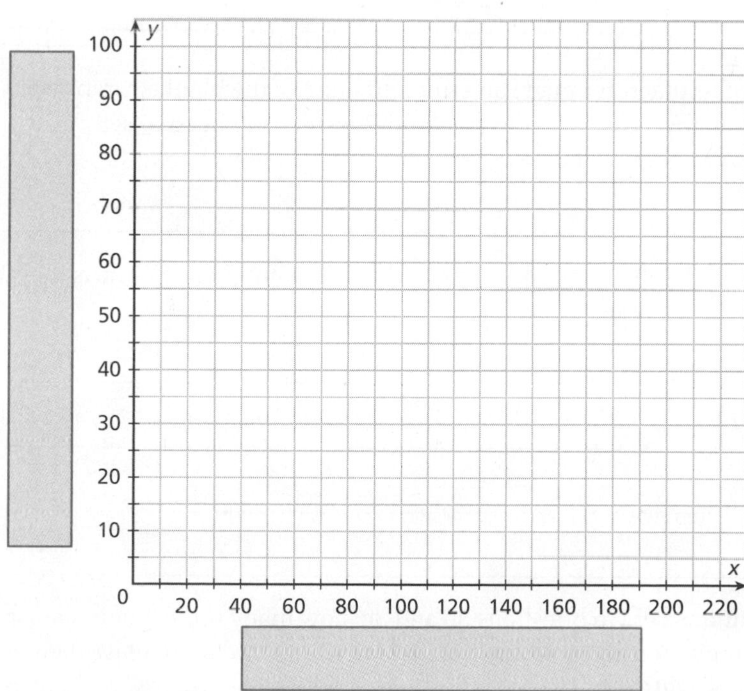

C Graph the linear equation you found in part 1 that represents the sales goal of \$2000 on the same axes.

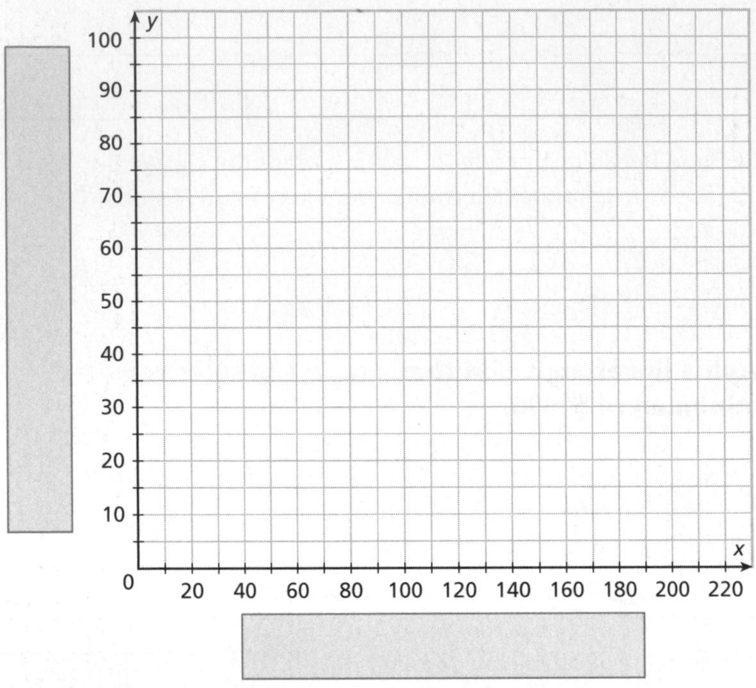

REFLECT

3a. Make a conjecture about the graphs of the two linear equations. How could you show your conjecture is true?

____

____

3b. Suppose the manufacturer made an error and none of the blanket wraps were sellable. How many T-shirts would the Band Booster Club need to sell to raise \$1000? to raise \$2000?

____

3c. If the booster club sells 18 blanket wraps, what is the number of T-shirts they need to sell to raise \$1000? to raise \$2000?

____

____

____

____

3d. Based on your answers to questions 3b and 3c, how many more T-shirts must the Booster Club sell for a given number of blanket wraps sold to increase their total from \$1000 to \$2000?

____

EXTEND

1. Use unit analysis to determine the unit of measurement for the expression $10x + 25y$.

2. Describe where the lines were in relation to each other when you graphed them both on the same coordinate grid.

3. The booster club sold 30 more T-shirts than blanket wraps at a fundraising event and made exactly $1000. How many of each did they sell?

4. If the booster club orders 100 blanket wraps, they get a reduced price on them. Does it make sense for the booster club to order 100 blanket wraps if the goal is to raise $2000? Explain your answer.

5. The booster club will earn $5 profit for every T-shirt sold and $10 profit for every blanket wrap sold. Write an equation to show how many T-shirts and blanket wraps the club would need to sell to make a profit of $1000.

6. Find a solution to the linear equation you wrote in Problem 5. How much money would the booster club raise in *sales* if they sold that many T-shirts and blanket wraps?

Name________________________ Class______________ Date______________

4-9

Additional Practice

Identify which lines are parallel.

1. $y = 3x + 4$; $y = 4$; $y = 3x$; $y = 3$

____

2. $y = \frac{1}{2}x + 4$; $x = \frac{1}{2}$; $2x + y = 1$; $y = \frac{1}{2}x + 1$

____

3. Find the slope of each segment.

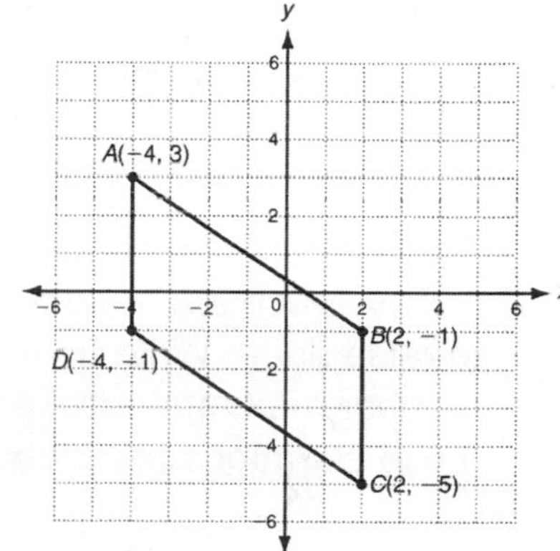

slope of $\overline{AB}$: ______________

slope of $\overline{AD}$: ______________

slope of $\overline{DC}$: ______________

slope of $\overline{BC}$: ______________

Explain why *ABCD* is a parallelogram.

____

____

The Math Club is doing a fundraiser to raise money to attend a math competition. The club was told by their advisor to raise \$2000, but they decided to raise \$4000. The club is selling "I like π" T-shirts for \$10 and "I like π" sweatshirts for \$20. Let *x* equal the number of T-shirts sold and let *y* equal the number of sweatshirts sold.

4. Write a linear equation to represent raising \$2000.

____

5. Write a linear equation to represent raising \$4000.

____

6. Are the graphs of the equations parallel? How can you tell?

____

7. What are the values of the *y*-intercepts of both equations? What do these numbers represent in terms of the situation?

____

8. What are the values of the *x*-intercepts of both equations? What do these numbers represent in terms of the situation?

____

Problem Solving

Write the correct answer.

1. Hamid is making a stained-glass window. He needs a piece of glass that is a perfect parallelogram. Hamid lays a piece of glass that he has cut on a coordinate grid. Show that the glass is in the shape of a parallelogram.

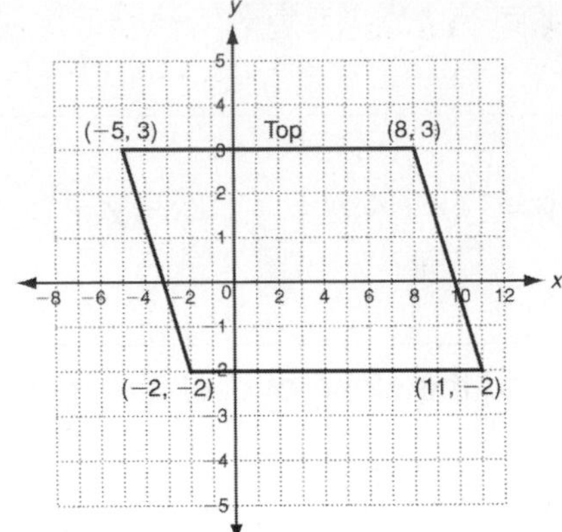

____

____

____

2. The cheer leading squad is selling bumper stickers and school pennants. Bumper stickers cost \$5 each and pennants cost \$10 each. Write a linear equation if the cheerleaders want to raise \$500. Write an equation if the cheerleaders want to raise \$1000. Let x equal the number of bumper stickers sold and y equal the number of pennants sold. If you graph these equations are these lines parallel? Why or why not?

____

____

____

The graph shows a street map. Use it to answer Problems 3–5.

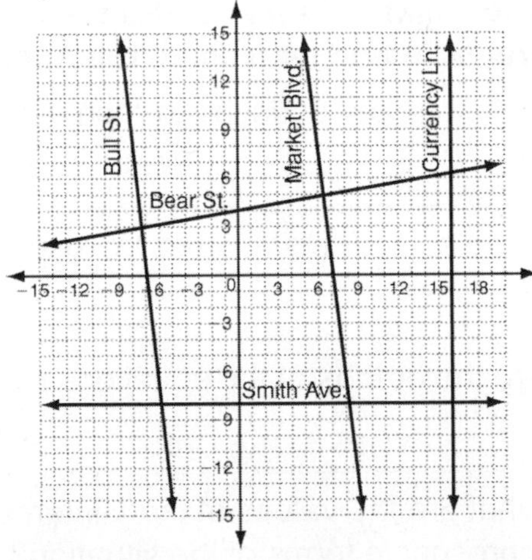

3. The district plans to add Industrial Road next year. It will run parallel to Currency Lane and pass through (–14, 2). What equation will describe the location of Industrial Road?

   A $y = 14 - x$ C $y = -14$

   B $y = x - 14$ D $x = -14$

4. In two years, the business district plans to add Stock Street. It will run parallel to Market Blvd. and pass through (–1, 5). What equation will describe the location of Stock Street?

   F $y = -7x + 12$ H $y = \frac{1}{7}x + \frac{34}{7}$

   G $y = -7x - 2$ J $y = \frac{1}{7}x + \frac{36}{7}$

5. What is the slope of a street parallel to Bear Street?

   A –7 C 7

   B $-\frac{1}{7}$ D $\frac{1}{7}$

Name________________________ Class________________ Date__________

4-10

Video Tutor

Transforming Linear Functions

Extension: Transforming Linear and Absolute-Value Functions

Essential question: *How do the values of the constants affect the graphs of $f(x) = mx + b$ and $g(x) = a|x - h| + k$?*

CC.9-12.F.BF.3

1 EXPLORE Changing the Value of b in $f(x) = x + b$

Investigate what happens to the graph of $f(x) = x + b$ when you change the value of b.

A Use a graphing calculator. Start with the standard viewing window, which you can obtain by pressing ZOOM and selecting ZStandard. Because the distances between consecutive tick marks on the x-axis and on the y-axis are not equal, you can make them equal by pressing ZOOM again and selecting ZSquare.

What interval on each axis does the viewing window now show? (Press WINDOW to find out.)

____

B Graph the function $f(x) = x$ by pressing Y= and entering the function's rule next to Y_1 =. As shown, the graph of the function is a line that makes a 45° angle with each axis.

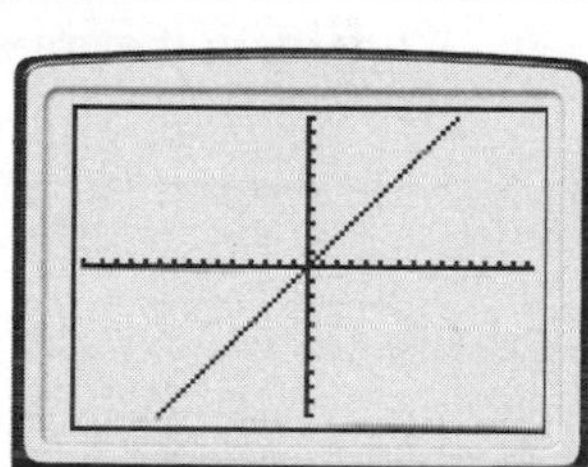

What are the slope and y-intercept of the graph of $f(x) = x$?

____

C Graph other functions of the form $f(x) = x + b$ by entering their rules next to Y_2 =, Y_3 =, and so on. Be sure to choose both positive and negative values of b. For instance, graph $f(x) = x + 2$ and $f(x) = x - 3$. What do the graphs have in common? How are they different?

____

REFLECT

1a. A *vertical translation* moves all points on a figure the same distance either up or down. Use the idea of a vertical translation to describe what happens to the graph of $f(x) = x + b$ when you increase the value of b and when you decrease the value of b.

____

____

CC.9–12.F.BF.3

2 EXAMPLE Modeling with Changes in *m* and *b*

A gym charges a one-time joining fee of \$50 and then a monthly membership fee of \$25. The total cost *C* of being a member of the gym is given by the function $C(t) = 25t + 50$ where *t* is the time (in months) since joining the gym. For each situation described below, *sketch* a graph using the given graph of $C(t) = 25t + 50$ as a reference.

A The gym decreases its one-time joining fee. (Remember: You are not graphing a specific function for this situation. Rather, you are sketching a representative graph of a function related to $C(t) = 25t + 50$, whose graph is shown.)

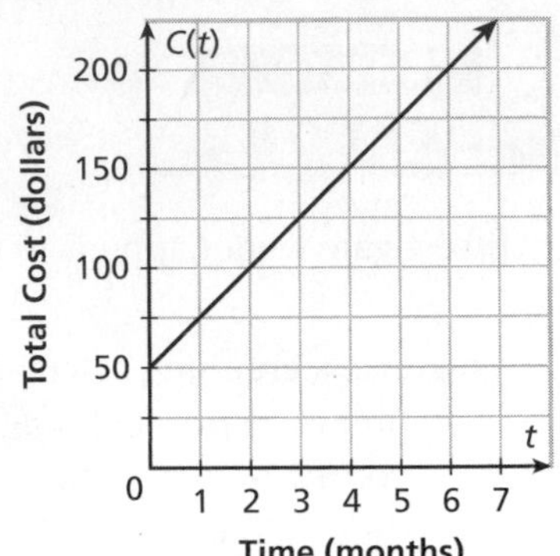

What change did you make to the graph of $C(t) = 25t + 50$ to obtain the graph that you drew?

____

____

B The gym increases its monthly membership fee.

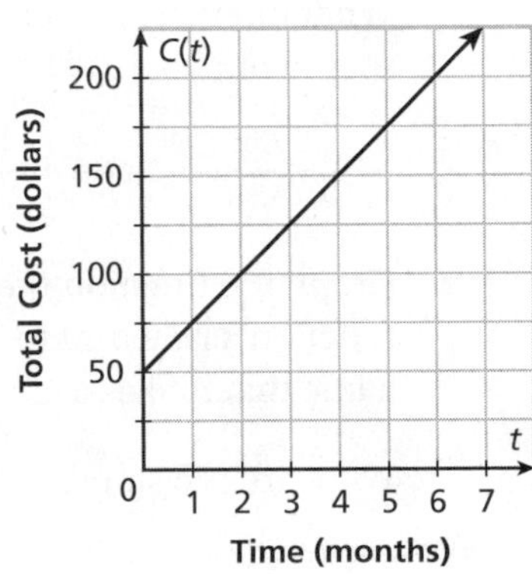

What change did you make to the graph of $C(t) = 25t + 50$ to obtain the graph that you drew?

____

____

REFLECT

2a. Suppose the gym increases its one-time joining fee *and* decreases its monthly membership fee. Describe how you would alter the graph of $C(t) = 25t + 50$ to illustrate the new cost function.

____

____

____

2b. Suppose the gym increases its one-time joining fee *and* decreases its monthly membership fee, as in Question 3a. Does this have any impact on the domain of the function? Does this have any impact on the range of the function? Explain your reasoning.

____

____

Changing the values of *a*, *h*, and *k* in the absolute value function $g(x) = a|x - h| + k$ creates effects on its graph similar to those of changing *m* and *b* in $f(x) = mx + b$. The graph may move up or down, left or right, become more or less steep, and may reflect over the *x*-axis.

Graphing Functions of the Form $g(x) = |x - h| + k$

Graph each absolute value function. (The graph of the parent function $f(x) = |x|$ is shown in gray.)

A $g(x) = |x| + 2$

x	$g(x) = |x| + 2$
−3	
−2	
−1	
0	
1	
2	
3	

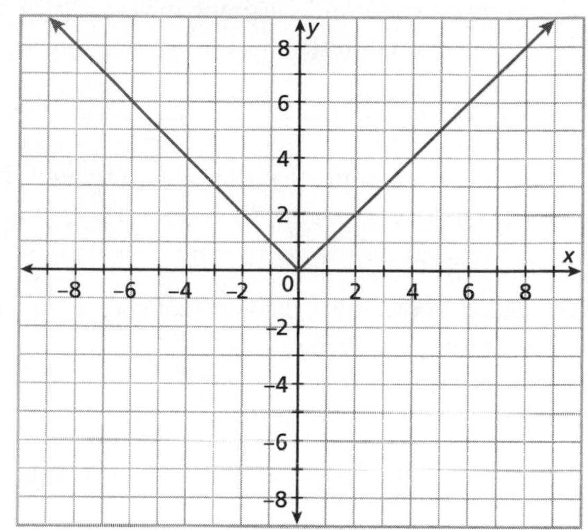

B $g(x) = |x - 4|$

x	$g(x) = |x - 4|$

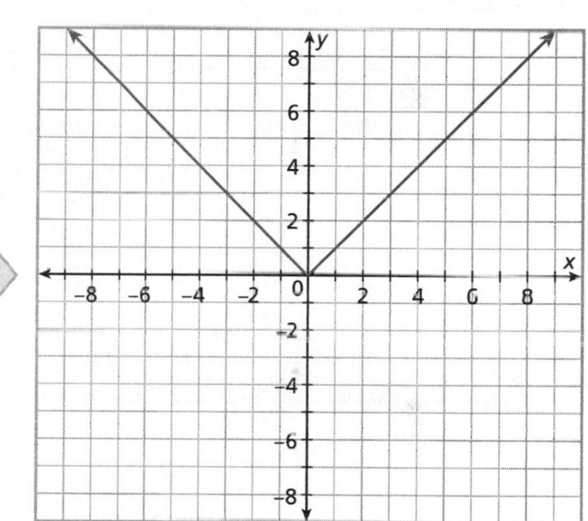

C $g(x) = |x - 4| + 2$

x	$g(x) = |x - 4| + 2$

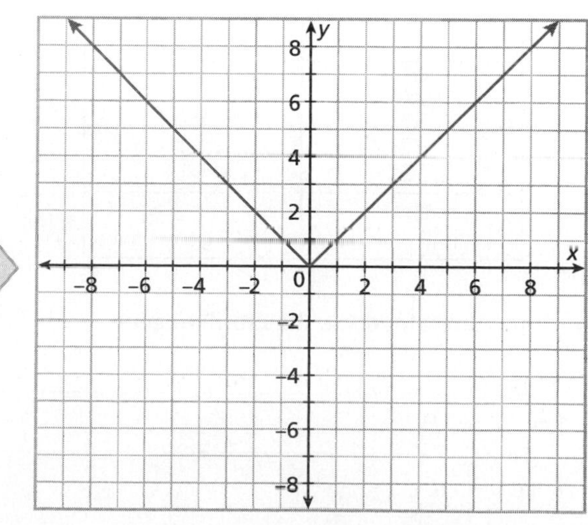

REFLECT

3a. How is the graph of $g(x) = |x| + 2$ related to the graph of the parent function $f(x) = |x|$?

3b. How do you think the graph of $g(x) = |x| - 2$ would be related to the graph of the parent function $f(x) = |x|$?

3c. How is the graph of $g(x) = |x - 4|$ related to the graph of the parent function $f(x) = |x|$?

3d. How do you think the graph of $g(x) = |x + 4|$ would be related to the graph of the parent function $f(x) = |x|$?

3e. How is the graph of $g(x) = |x - 4| + 2$ related to the graph of the parent function $f(x) = |x|$?

3f. Predict how the graph of $g(x) = |x + 3| - 5$ is related to the graph of the parent function $f(x) = |x|$. Then check your prediction by making a table of values and graphing the function. (The graph of $f(x) = |x|$ is shown in gray.)

x	$g(x) = \|x + 3\| - 5$

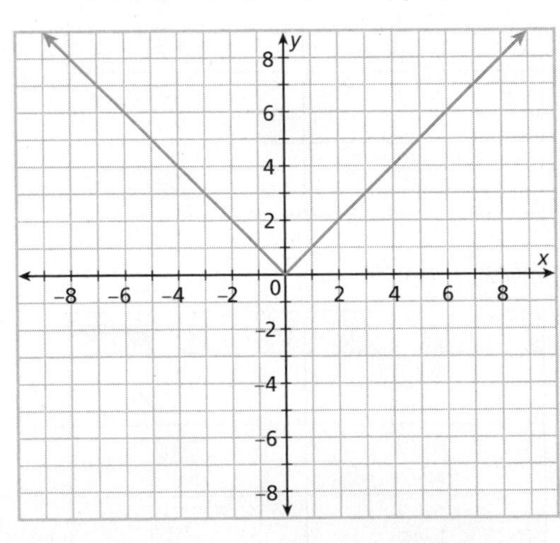

3g. In general, how is the graph of $g(x) = |x - h| + k$ related to the graph of $f(x) = |x|$?

CC.9–12.F.BF.1

4 EXAMPLE Writing Equations for Absolute Value Functions

Write the equation for the absolute value function whose graph is shown.

A Compare the given graph to the graph of the parent function $f(x) = |x|$.

Complete the table to describe how the parent function must be translated to get the graph shown here.

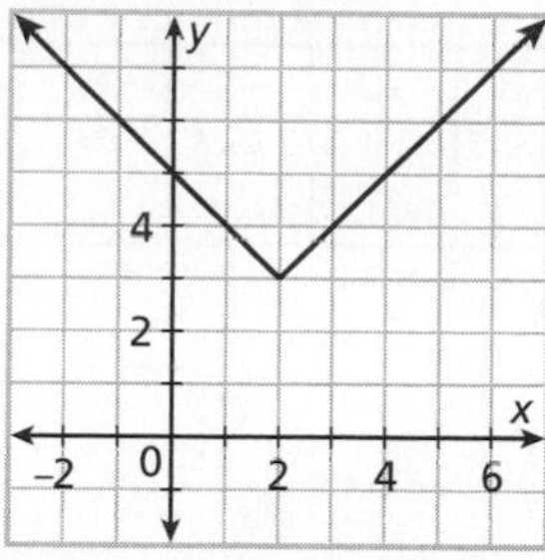

Type of Translation	Number of Units	Direction
Horizontal Translation		
Vertical Translation		

B Determine the values of h and k for the function $g(x) = |x - h| + k$.

- h is the number of units that the parent function is translated horizontally. For a translation to the right, h is positive; for a translation to the left, h is negative.
- k is the number of units that the parent function is translated vertically. For a translation up, k is positive; for a translation down, k is negative.

So, $h =$ ________ and $k =$ ________. The function is ____________.

REFLECT

4a. What can you do to check that your equation is correct?

____

____

4b. If the graph of an absolute value function is a translation of the graph of the parent function, explain how you can use the vertex of the translated graph to help you determine the equation for the function.

____

____

4c. Suppose the graph in the Example is shifted left one unit so that the vertex is at (1, 3). What will be the equation of that absolute value function?

____

CC.9–12.F.BF.3

5 EXAMPLE Graphing $g(x) = a|x - h| + k$

Graph $g(x) = -2|x + 1| + 3$. (The graph of the parent function $f(x) = |x|$ is shown in gray.)

x	−4	−3	−2	−1	0	1	2
y							

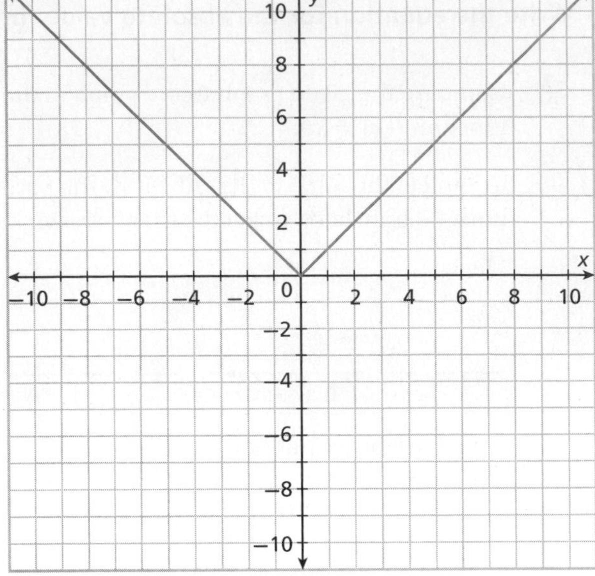

REFLECT

5a. How is the graph of $g(x) = -2|x + 1| + 3$ related to the graph of $f(x) = |x|$?

____

____

5b. How is the graph of $g(x) = -2|x + 1| + 3$ affected if you replace 3 with -3?

____

5c. Complete the table to summarize how you can obtain the graph of $g(x) = a|x - h| + k$ from the graph of the parent function $f(x) = |x|$.

Obtaining the graph of $g(x) = a\|x - h\| + k$ from the graph of $f(x) = \|x\|$
Vertically stretch or shrink the graph by a factor of $\|a\|$. Also reflect the graph across the x-axis if the value of a is negative. • If $\|a\| > 1$, __________ the graph of $f(x) = \|x\|$ vertically by a factor of $\|a\|$. • If $\|a\| < 1$, __________ the graph of $f(x) = \|x\|$ vertically by a factor of $\|a\|$. • If $a <$ __________, reflect the graph across the x-axis.
Translate the graph h units horizontally. • If $h > 0$, translate __________. • If $h < 0$, translate __________.
Translate the graph k units vertically. • If k is positive, translate __________. • If k is negative, translate __________.

CC.9–12.F.BF.1

6 EXAMPLE Writing the Equation for an Absolute Value Function

Write the equation for the absolute value function whose graph is shown.

To write the equation in the form $g(x) = a|x - h| + k$, you need to find the values of a, h, and k.

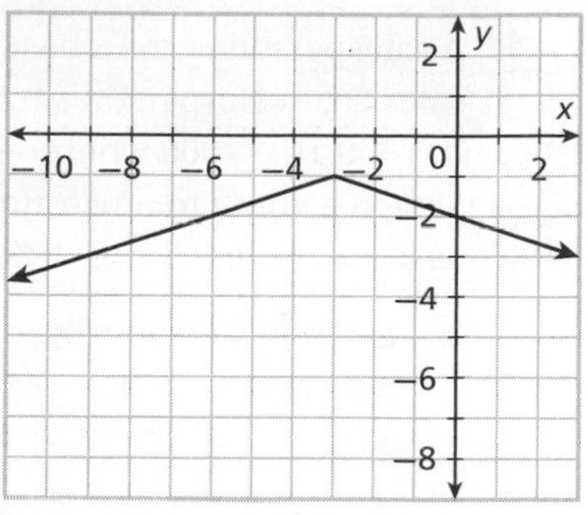

A Use the coordinates of the vertex to determine the values of h and k.

The vertex is at ________, so $h =$ ________ and $k =$ ________. Substituting these values into the general equation for $g(x)$ gives $g(x) = a|x - \square| + \square$.

B Use the coordinates of another point on the graph to determine the value of a.

From the graph you can see that $g(0) =$ ________. Substituting 0 for x and ________ for $g(x)$ into the equation from part A and solving for a gives:

$$\square = a|\square - \square| + \square$$

$$\square = a$$

C Write the simplified equation for the function: ________________

REFLECT

6a. The graph of $g(x)$ opens down. In what way does this fact help you check that your equation is reasonable?

____

6b. The graph of $g(x)$ passes through the point $(-9, -3)$. Show how you can use this fact to check the accuracy of your equation.

____

____

6c. If you know the coordinates of the vertex of the graph of an absolute value function, then you know how the graph of the parent function has been translated. Explain why this is so.

____

____

____

PRACTICE

1. A salesperson earns a base monthly salary of $2000 plus a 10% commission on sales. The salesperson's monthly income I (in dollars) is given by the function $I(s) = 0.1s + 2000$ where s is the sales (in dollars) that the salesperson makes. Sketch a graph to illustrate each situation using the graph of $I(s) = 0.1s + 2000$ as a reference.

   a. The salesperson's base salary is increased.

   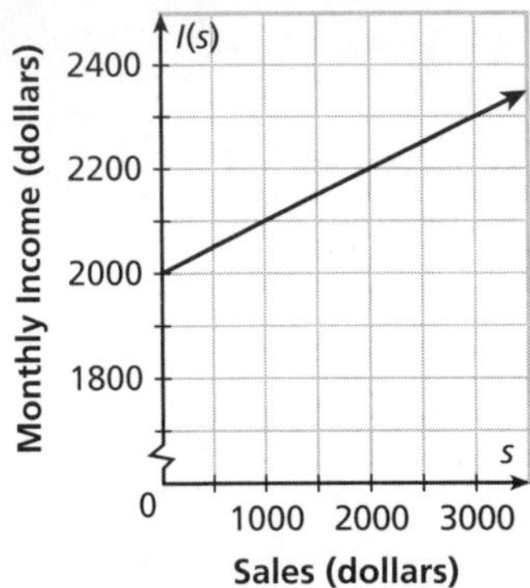

   b. The salesperson's commission rate is decreased.

   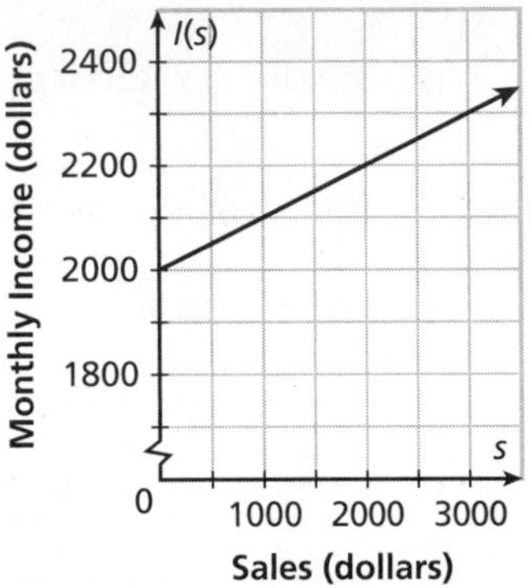

2. Mr. Resnick is driving at a speed of 40 miles per hour to visit relatives who live 100 miles away from his home. His distance d (in miles) from his destination is given by the function $d(t) = 100 - 40t$ where t is the time (in hours) since his trip began. Sketch a graph to illustrate each situation.

   a. He increases his speed to get to his destination sooner.

   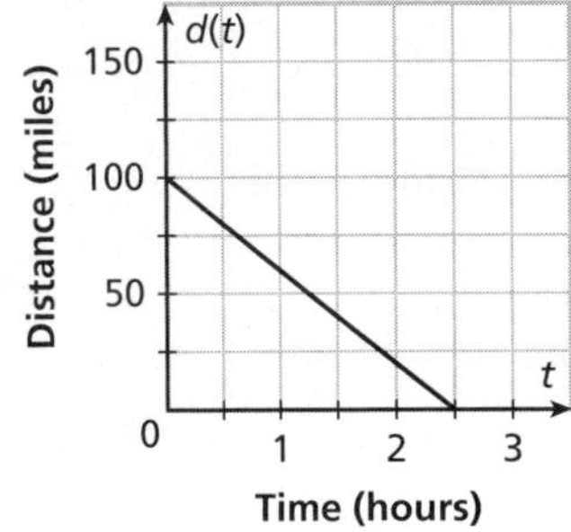

   b. He encounters a detour that increases the driving distance.

   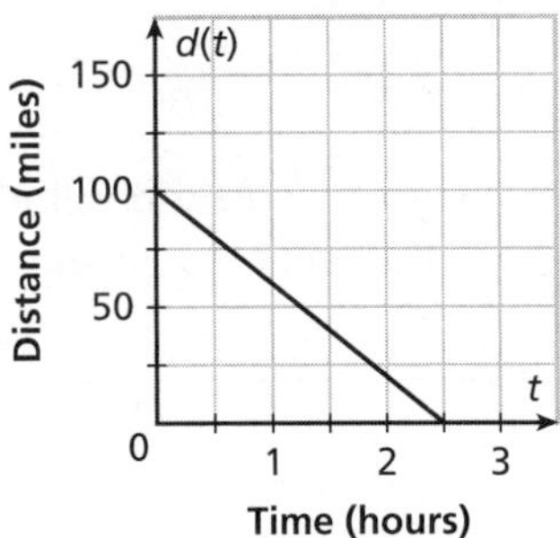

3. Use the graph of $d(t) = 100 - 40t$ in Exercise 2 to identify the domain and range of the function. Then tell whether the domain, the range, neither, or both are affected by the changes described in each part.

____

____

Graph each absolute value function.

4. $g(x) = |x| + 5$

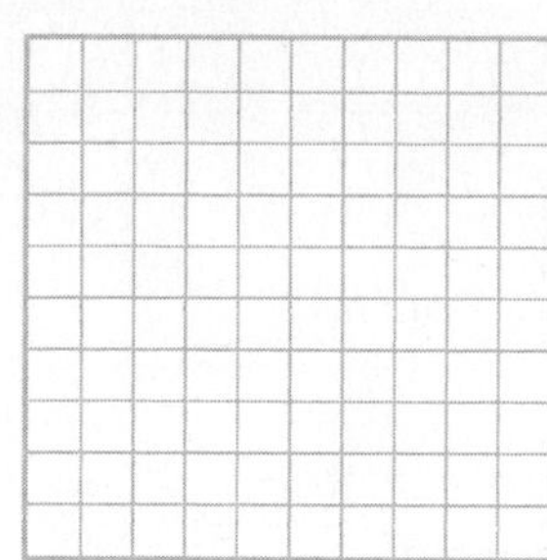

5. $g(x) = |x| - 4$

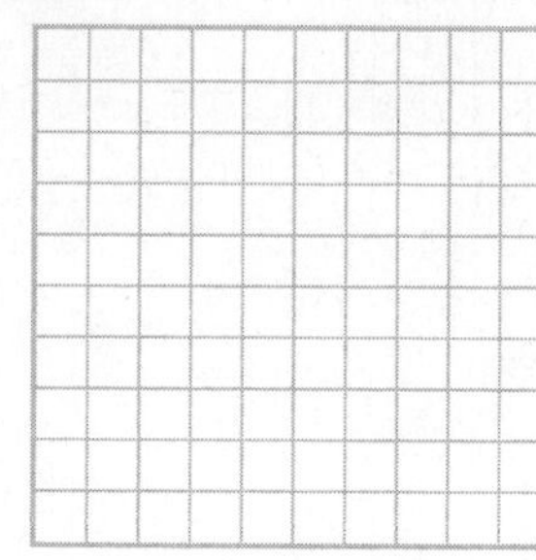

6. $g(x) = |x + 3|$

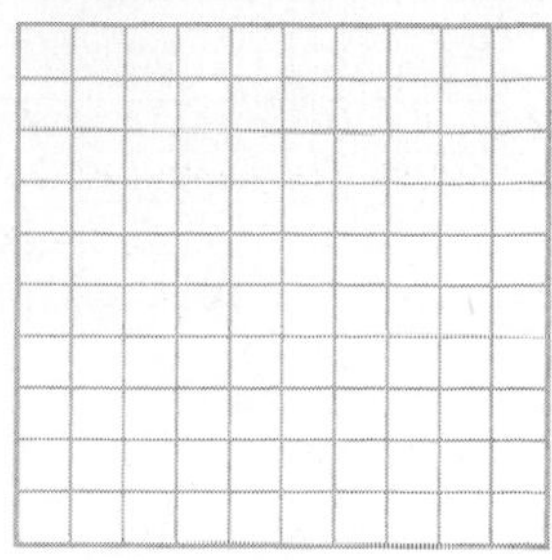

7. $g(x) = |x - 2|$

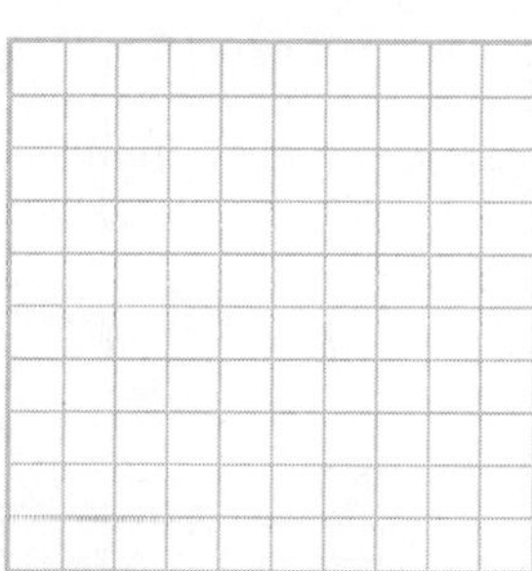

8. $g(x) = |x + 1| + 1$

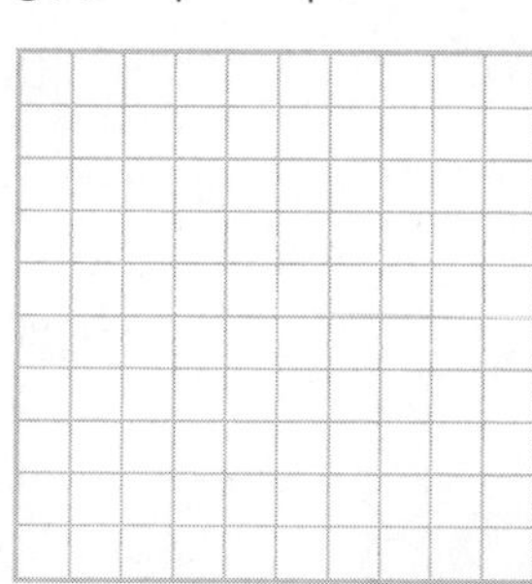

9. $g(x) = |x - 3| - 5$

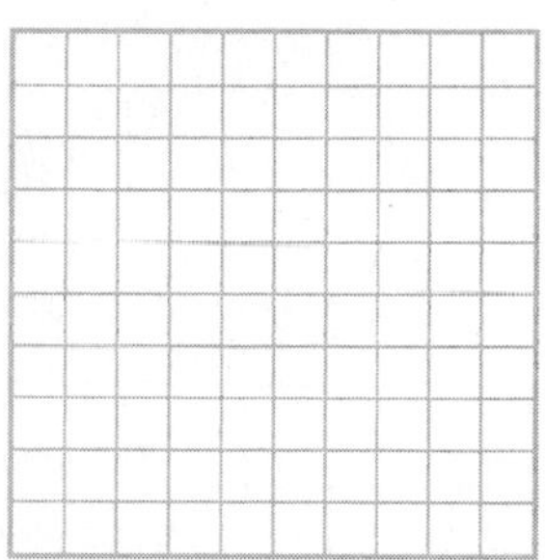

Write the equation of each absolute value function whose graph is shown.

10.

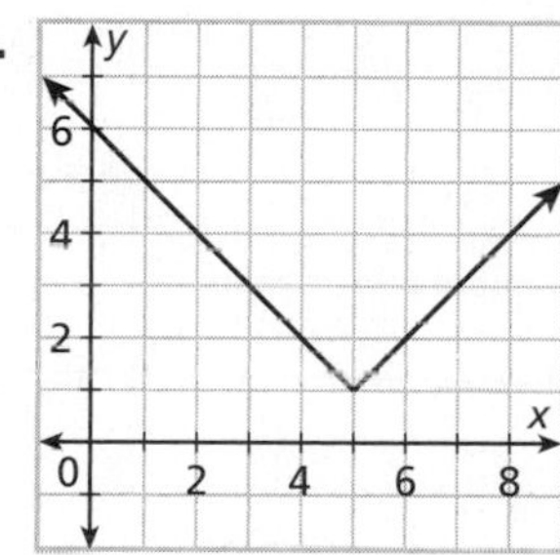

____

11.

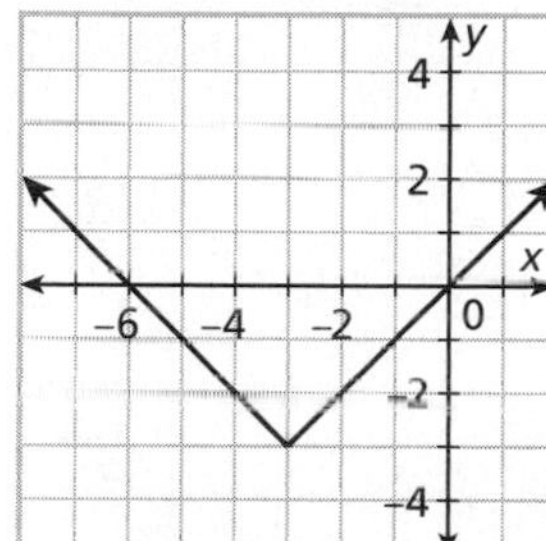

____

12.

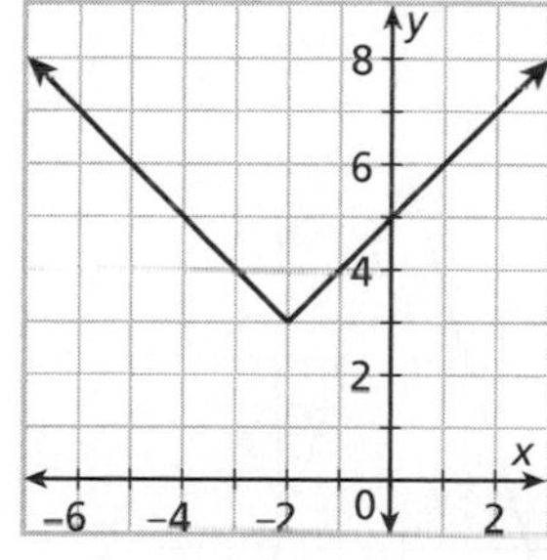

____

13.

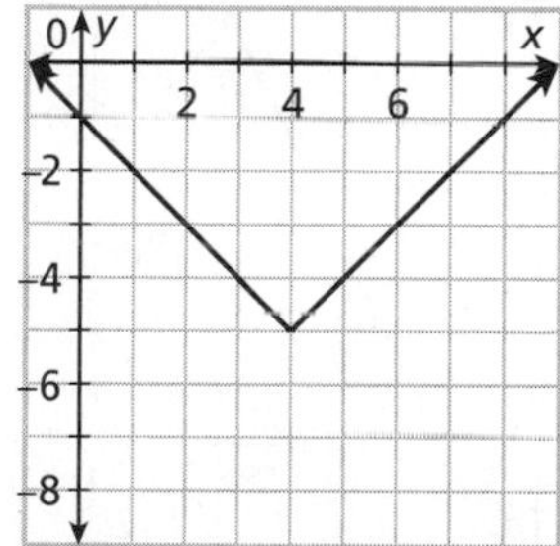

____

Graph each absolute value function.

14. $g(x) = \frac{3}{4}|x + 2|$

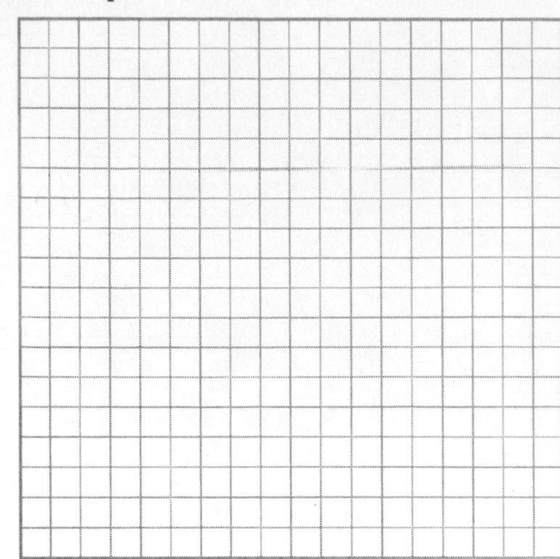

15. $g(x) = 2|x| - 4$

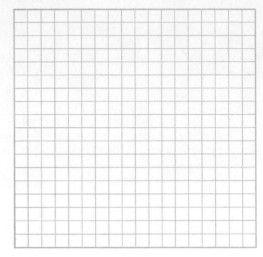

16. $g(x) = -3|x - 3| + 5$

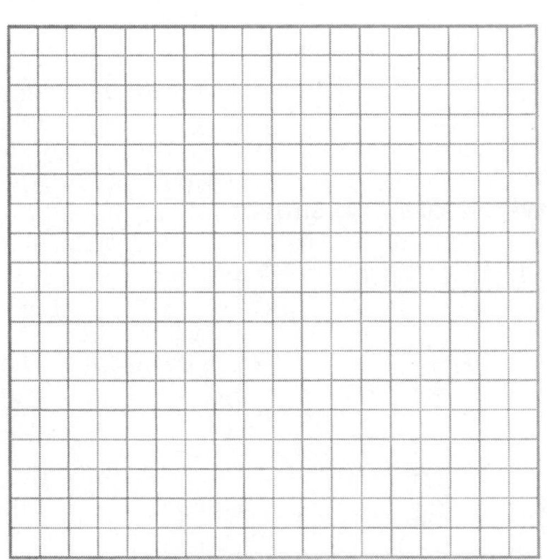

17. $g(x) = 1.5|x - 2| - 3$

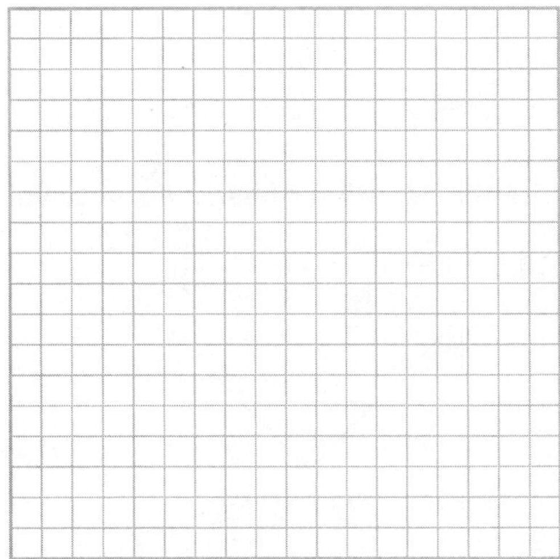

Write the equation for each absolute value function whose graph is shown.

18.

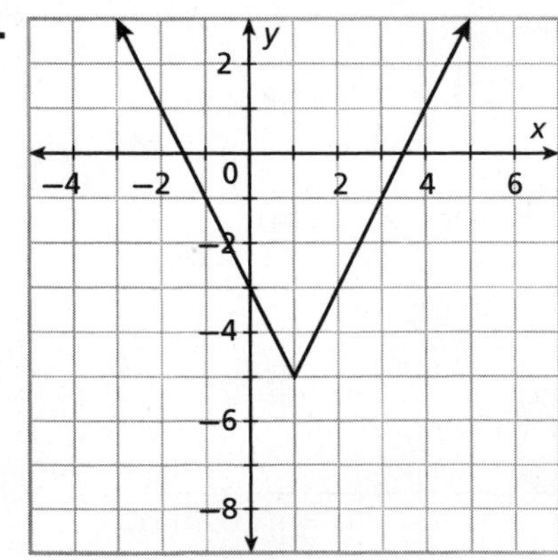

____

19.

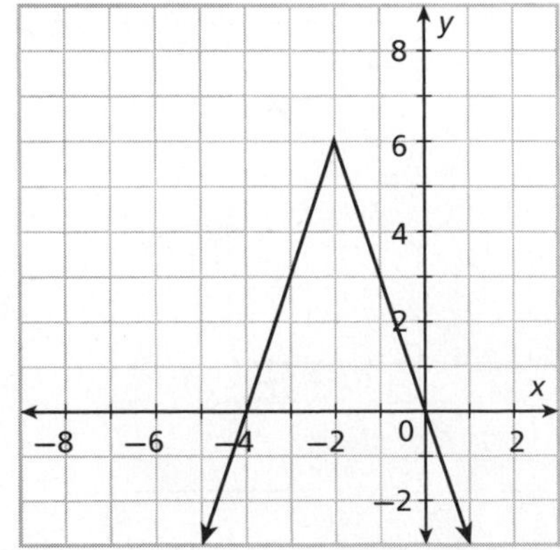

____

Name _______________ Class _______________ Date _______________

Additional Practice

Graph *f*(*x*) and *g*(*x*). Then describe the transformation from the graph of *f*(*x*) to the graph of *g*(*x*).

1. $f(x) = x$; $g(x) = x + 3$

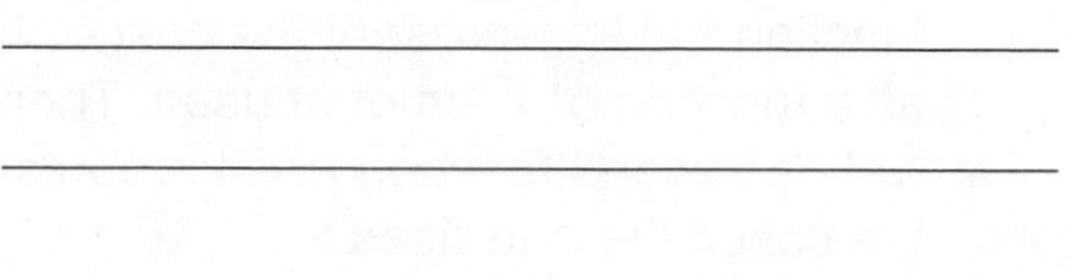

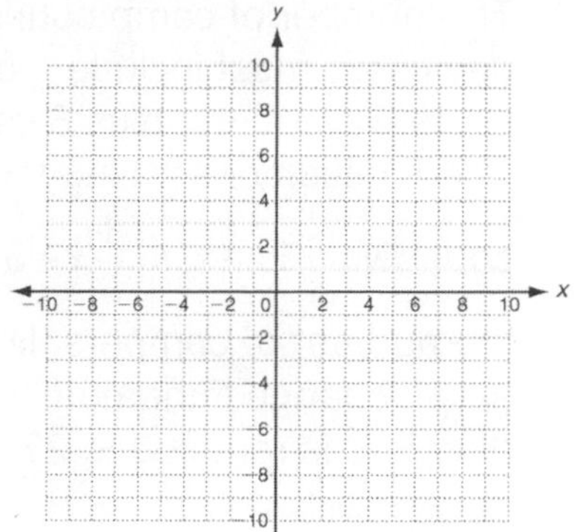

2. $f(x) = x$; $g(x) = \frac{1}{4}x - 4$

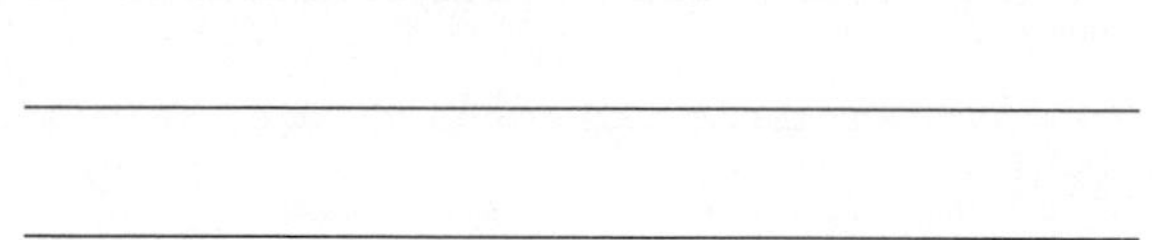

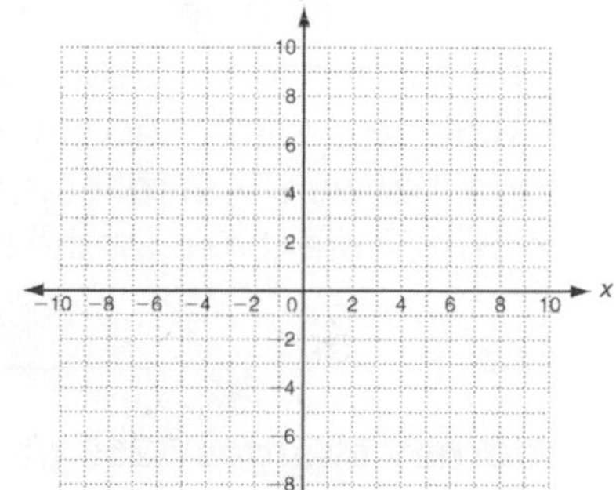

3. $f(x) = |x|$; $g(x) = |x + 4| - 3$

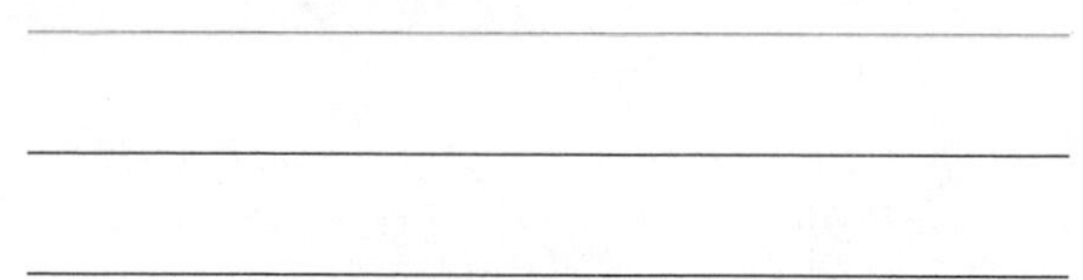

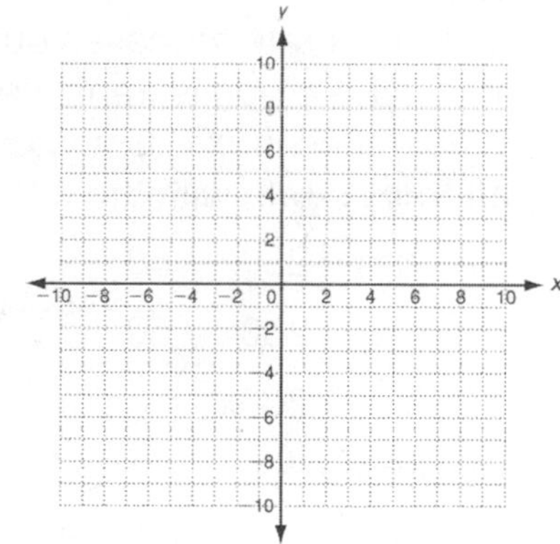

4. $f(x) = |x|$; $g(x) = |x - 6| + 2$

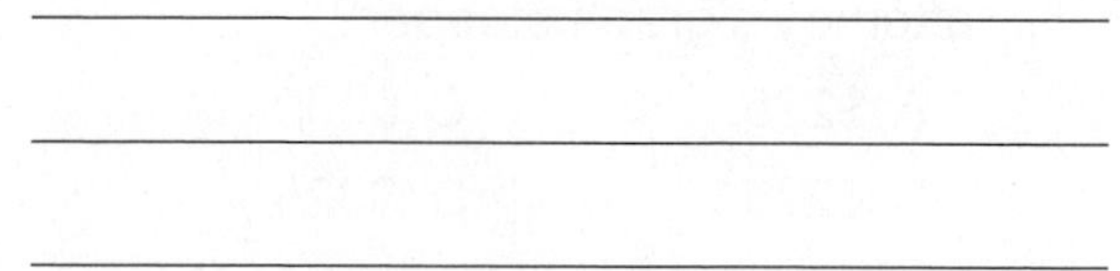

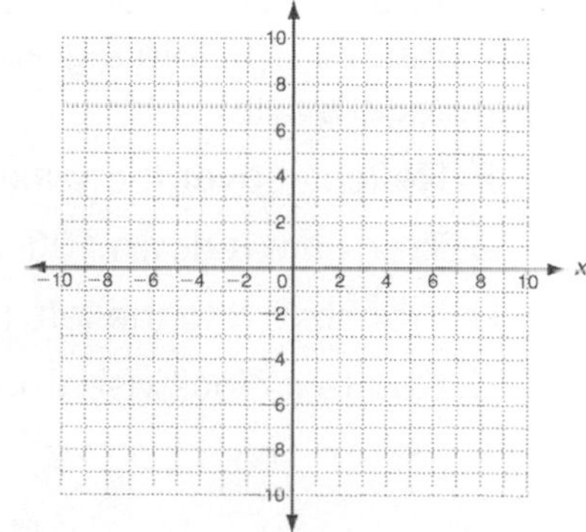

Problem Solving

Write the correct answer.

1. The number of camp counselors at a day camp must include 1 counselor for every 8 campers, plus 3 camp directors. The function describing the number of counselors is $f(x) = \frac{1}{8}x + 3$ where x is the number of campers. How will the graph change if the number of camp directors is reduced to 2?

____

2. A city water service has a base cost of \$12 per month plus \$1.50 per hundred cubic feet (HCF) of water. Write a function $f(x)$ to represent the cost of water as a function of x, amount used. Then write a second function $g(x)$ to represent the cost if the rate rises to \$1.60 per HCF.

____

____

How would the graph of $g(x)$ compare to the graph of $f(x)$?

____

____

3. You have the graph of $f(x) = 3|x + 4| - 6$. You are told to translate it 2 units up and 5 units to the left. These translations are then followed by a reflection over the x-axis. Write a rule for the new function.

____

An attorney charges \$250 per hour. The graph represents the cost of the attorney as a function of time. Select the best answer.

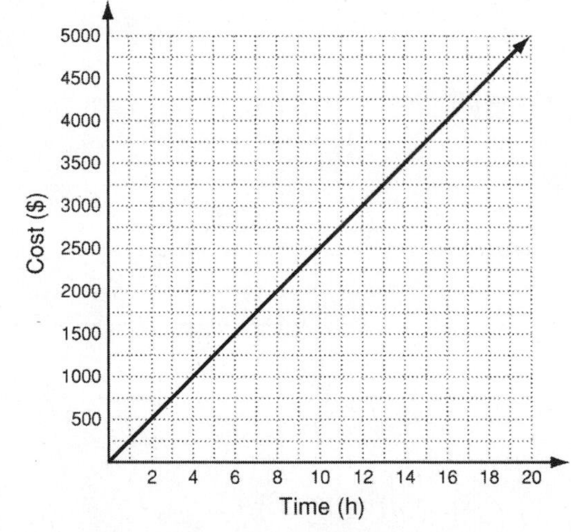

4. When a traveling fee is added to the attorney's rate for cases outside the city limits, the graph is translated up 50 units. What function $h(x)$ would describe the attorney's rate with the traveling fee?

   A $h(x) = 250x - 50$

   B $h(x) = 250x + 50$

   C $h(x) = 200x$

   D $h(x) = 300x$

5. The attorney's paralegal has an hourly rate of \$150. How would you transform the graph of $f(x)$ into a graph for the paralegal's rate?

   F Reflect it over the y-axis.

   G Translate it down 100 units.

   H Translate it to the left 100 units.

   J Rotate it clockwise about (0, 0).

6. Which hourly rate would NOT make the attorney's graph steeper?

   A \$225   C \$300

   B \$275   D \$325

Name________________ Class________________ Date________

CHAPTER 4

Performance Tasks

COMMON CORE

CC.9-12.A.CED.2
CC.9-12.F.IF.6
CC.9-12.F.BF.1
CC.9-12.F.LE.5
CC.9-12.S.ID.6a
CC.9-12.S.ID.6c

★ **1.** A gym charges a one-time sign-up fee and then a regular monthly fee. The cost of a membership as a function of the number of months as a member is shown for 2010 and 2011 on the graph.

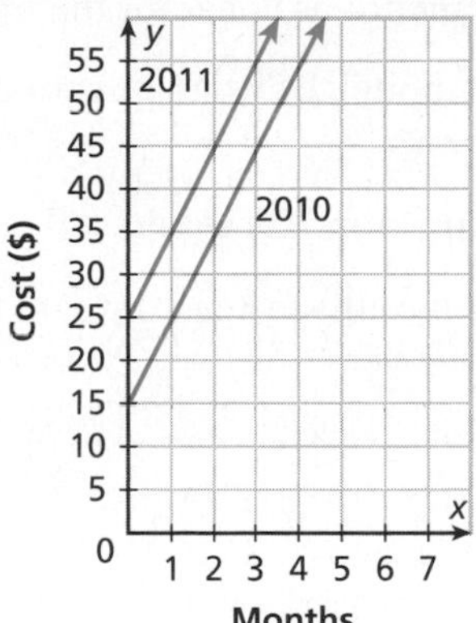

a. What characteristics of the graph represent the sign-up fee and the monthly fee? What are those values for the 2010 line?

b. How did the membership costs change from 2010 to 2011? Explain how you can tell from the graphs.

★ **2.** A bicycle computer records each wheel rotation to calculate the total distance traveled. To set up the computer, you select a calibration constant based on the bicycle's wheel size. The computer multiplies this constant times the number of wheel rotations to find the total distance in miles. Write an equation where distance d in miles is a function of rotations n if the calibration constant is 1382. If the function is incorrect and your wheel is actually slightly smaller, how should the function change?

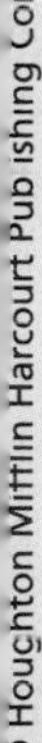

3. High demand cars that are also in low supply tend to retain their value better than other cars. The data in the table is for a car that won a resale value award.

Year	1	3	5
Value (%)	84	64	44

a. Write a function to represent the change in the percentage of the car's value over time. Assume that the function is linear for the first 5 years.

b. According to your model, by what percent did the car's value drop the day it was purchased and driven off the lot?

c. Do you think the linear model would still be useful after 10 years? Explain why or why not.

d. Suppose you used months instead of years to write a function. How would your model change?

4. A scientist theorizes that you can estimate the temperature by counting how often crickets chirp. The scientist gathers the data in the table shown.

Number of chirps in a 14-second interval	37	32	42	37	46	35	34
Temperature (°F)	78	72	81	77	88	75	76

a. How many cricket chirps would you expect to indicate a temperature of 85 degrees? Include a graph and an equation as part of the justification of your answer.

b. What might be the lowest temperature to which your model could be applied? Explain your reasoning.

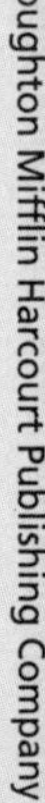

CHAPTER 4 COMMON CORE ASSESSMENT READINESS

Name ______________________ Class ______________ Date ________

MULTIPLE CHOICE

1. Which function is represented by the graph?

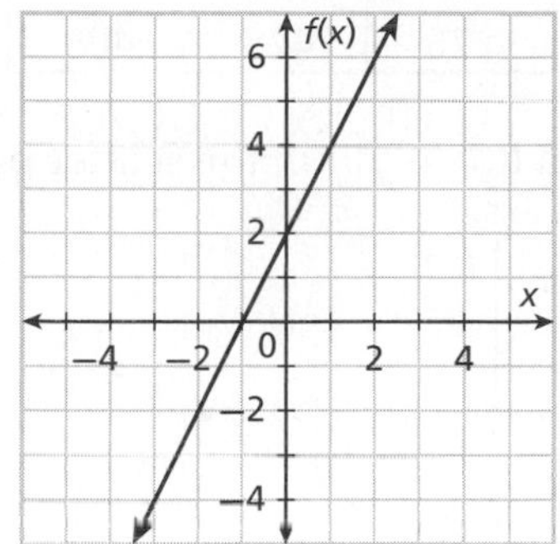

A. $f(x) = -x + 2$ **C.** $f(x) = 2x - 1$

B. $f(x) = x - 1$ **D.** $f(x) = 2x + 2$

2. Which ordered pair is *not* a solution to $2x + 3y = 12$?

F. (0, 4) **H.** (2, 3)

G. (3, 2) **J.** (6, 0)

3. The function $A(t) = 99t$ describes the cost of Cell Phone Plan A (in dollars) for t months. The table shows the cost of Cell Phone Plan B for t months. Which plan will cost more for 6 months, and which function describes the cost of Plan B?

t	1	2	3
B(t)	\$150	\$200	\$250

A. Plan B; $B(t) = 100t + 50$

B. Plan B; $B(t) = 50t + 100$

C. Plan A; $B(t) = 100t + 50$

D. Plan A; $B(t) = 50t + 100$

4. Pat pays \$250 to be a gym member for 2 months and \$550 to be a member for 6 months. What is the monthly cost of a gym membership?

F. \$50 **H.** \$150

G. \$75 **J.** \$300

5. For $f(x) = -\frac{2}{5}x + 3$, find the slope and y-intercept, and determine whether the graph is increasing or decreasing.

A. $m = -\frac{2}{5}$, $b = 3$, decreasing

B. $m = -\frac{2}{5}$, $b = 3$, increasing

C. $m = 3$, $b = -\frac{2}{5}$, decreasing

D. $m = 3$, $b = -\frac{2}{5}$, increasing

6. The graph shows the distance Tiana walks as a function of time. How would the graph change if she walked 1 mi/h faster?

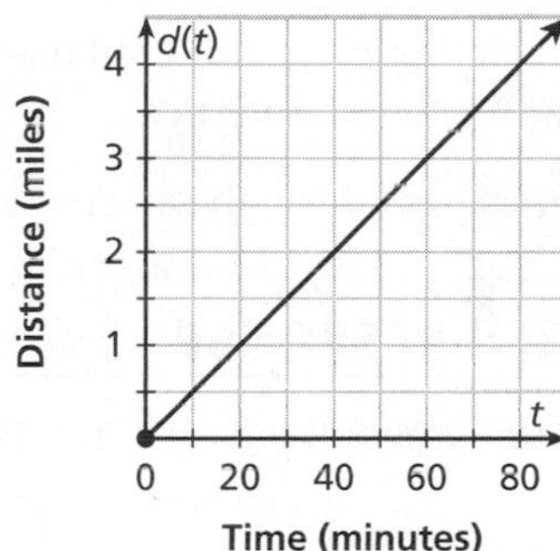

F. The line in the graph would not change.

G. The line would be less steep.

H. The line would be steeper.

J. The line would shift up on the y-axis.

7. How would the graphs of $f(x) = 2x + 6$ and $g(x) = 2x + 3$ compare if graphed on the same coordinate plane?

A. The graphs would intersect at (0, 2).

B. The graph of $f(x)$ would be twice as steep as the graph of $g(x)$.

C. The graph of $f(x)$ would be 3 units above the graph of $g(x)$.

D. The graph of $f(x)$ would be 6 units above the graph of $g(x)$.

8. Which of the following describes a way to graph the function $g(x) = -2|x|$?

F. Stretch the graph of $f(x) = |x|$ vertically by a factor of 2. Then reflect the result across the x-axis.

G. Shrink the graph of $f(x) = |x|$ vertically by a factor of $\frac{1}{2}$. Then reflect the result across the x-axis.

H. Translate the graph of $f(x) = |x|$ down 2 units.

J. Translate the graph of $f(x) = |x|$ right 2 units.

9. Which statement about the graphs of $x = 2$ and $y = 4$ is true?

A. The two lines intersect at (2, 4).

B. The two lines intersect at (4, 2).

C. The graph of $x = 2$ is horizontal and the graph of $y = 4$ is vertical.

D. Both lines pass through the origin (0, 0).

CONSTRUCTED RESPONSE

10. a. Graph the function $g(x) = \frac{1}{2}|x + 1| - 4$.

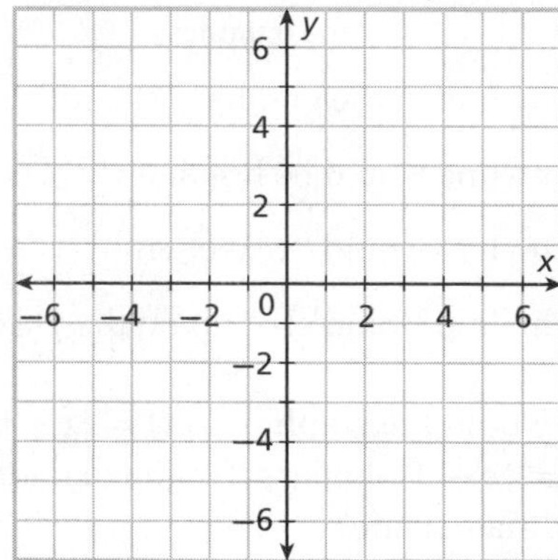

b. Describe how to transform the graph of $f(x) = |x|$ to obtain the graph of $g(x) = \frac{1}{2}|x + 1| - 4$.

____

____

____

____

11. The table shows the temperature T displayed on an oven while it was heating as a function of the amount of time a since it was turned on.

a (sec)	T (°F)	a (sec)	T (°F)
31	175	250	300
61	200	285	325
104	225	327	350
158	250	380	375
202	275	428	400

a. Draw a line of fit on the scatter plot.

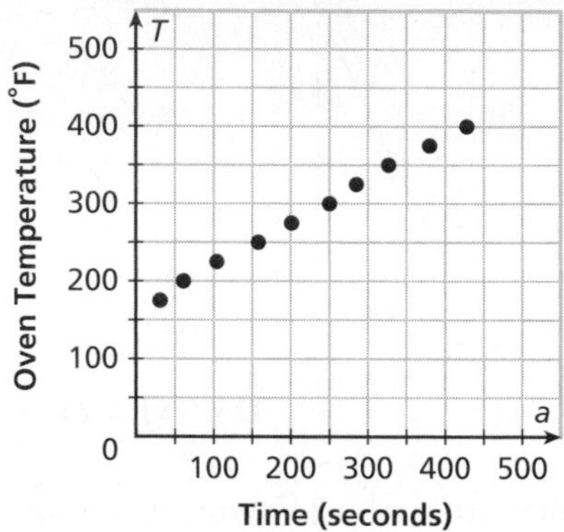

b. Find an equation of your line of fit.

____

c. Perform linear regression to find the equation of the line of best fit and the correlation coefficient.

____

d. Create a residual plot on a graphing calculator. Evaluate the suitability and goodness of fit of the regression equation.

____

____

____

____

e. Is the model a good predictor of the initial value? Why or why not?

____

____

____

Systems of Equations and Inequalities

Chapter Focus

In this chapter, you will learn how to solve systems of linear equations and inequalities. You will begin by graphing two equations of a linear system and seeing how the solution of the system can be determined by looking at the graph. Then, you will explore different ways to solve linear systems algebraically. You will extend those skills to learn how to graph systems of linear inequalities and interpret the solutions. Finally, you will apply your knowledge to a real-world situation in which you will write and solve systems of equations and inequalities to model a shopping trip.

Chapter at a Glance

Lesson		Standards for Mathematical Content
5-1	Solving Systems by Graphing	CC.9-12.A.REI.6
5-2	Solving Systems by Substitution	CC.9-12.A.REI.6
5-3	Solving Systems by Elimination	CC.9-12.A.REI.5, CC.9-12.A.REI.6
5-4	Solving Special Systems	CC.9-12.A.REI.6
5-5	Solving Linear Inequalities	CC.9-12.A.REI.12
5-6	Solving Systems of Linear Inequalities	CC.9-12.N.Q.2, CC.9-12.A.CED.3, CC.9-12.A.REI.6
	Performance Tasks	
	Assessment Readiness	

Unpacking the Standards

Understanding the standards and the vocabulary terms in the standards will help you know exactly what you are expected to learn in this chapter.

CC.9-12.A.CED.2

Create equations in two or more variables to represent relationships between quantities; graph equations on coordinate axes with labels and scales.

Key Vocabulary

equation *(ecuación)*
A mathematical statement that two expressions are equivalent.

What It Means For You — Lesson 5-6

Creating equations in two variables to describe relationships gives you access to the tools of graphing and algebra to solve the equations.

EXAMPLE

A customer spent \$29 on a bouquet of roses and daisies.

r = number of roses in bouquet
d = number of daises in bouquet

$2.5r + 1.75d = 29$

CHAPTER 5

COMMON CORE **CC.9-12.A.REI.6**

Solve systems of linear equations exactly and approximately (e.g., with graphs), focusing on pairs of linear equations in two variables.

Key Vocabulary

system of linear equations *(sistema de ecuaciones lineales)* A system of equations in which all of the equations are linear.

What It Means For You — Lessons 5-1, 5-2, 5-3, 5-4, 5-6

You can solve systems of equations to find out when two relationships involving the same variables are true at the same time.

EXAMPLE

The cost of bowling at bowling alley **A** or **B** is a function of the number of games g.

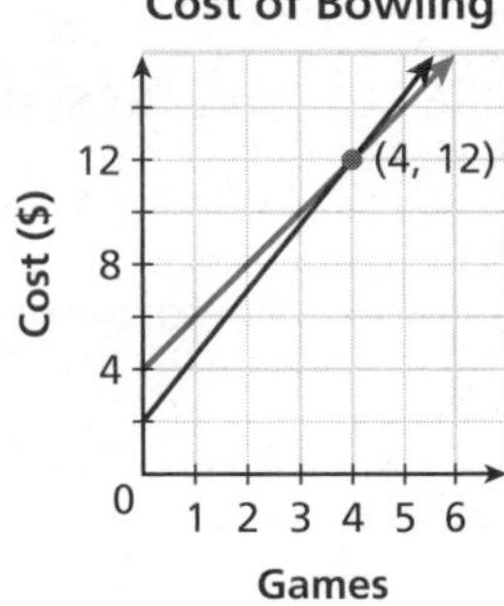

$$\text{Cost } \mathbf{A} = 2.5g + 2$$
$$\text{Cost } \mathbf{B} = 2g + 4$$

When are the costs the same?

$$\text{Cost } \mathbf{A} = \text{Cost } \mathbf{B}$$
$$2.5g + 2 = 2g + 4$$

The cost is \$12 at both bowling alleys when g is 4.

CC.9-12.A.REI.12

Graph the solutions to a linear inequality in two variables as a half-plane (excluding the boundary in the case of a strict inequality), and graph the solution set to a system of linear inequalities in two variables as the intersection of the corresponding half-planes.

Key Vocabulary

half-plane *(semiplano)* The part of the coordinate plane on one side of a line, which may include the line.

solution of a linear inequality in two variables *(solución de una desigualdad lineal en dos variables)* An ordered pair or ordered pairs that make the inequality true.

system of linear inequalities *(sistema de desigualdades lineales)* A system of inequalities in which all of the inequalities are linear.

What It Means For You

Lessons 5-5, 5-6

Systems of linear inequalities model many real-life situations where you want to know when one or more conditions are met, but where there are many possible solutions.

EXAMPLE **Linear Inequality**

$y > \frac{2}{3}x - 1$

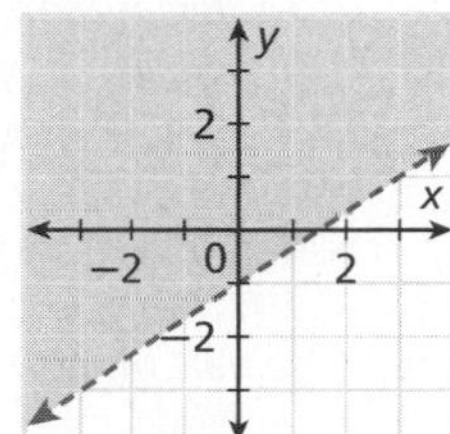

EXAMPLE **System of Two Linear Inequalities**

$$\begin{cases} y > \frac{2}{3}x - 1 \\ y \leq -2x - 2 \end{cases}$$

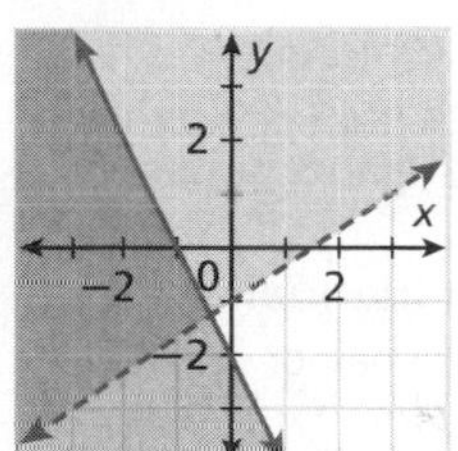

EXAMPLE **System of Three Linear Inequalities**

Tracy works at least 5 hours per week as a cashier: $c \geq 5$

Tracy works at least 10 hours per week at a library: $p \geq 10$

Tracy works at most 24 hours per week: $c + p \leq 24$

How can Tracy divide her time between the two jobs?

Sample Solutions	
Cashier (hours)	Page (hours)
5	10
5	16
8	12
8	16
10	12
12	12

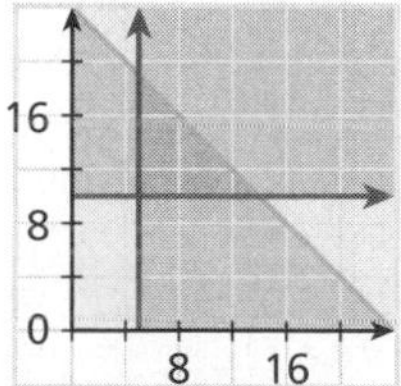

CHAPTER 5

Key Vocabulary

consistent system *(sistema consistente)* A system of equations or inequalities that has at least one solution.

dependent system *(sistema dependiente)* A system of equations that has infinitely many solutions.

elimination method *(eliminación)* A method used to solve systems of equations in which one variable is eliminated by adding or subtracting two equations of the system.

equation *(ecuación)* A mathematical statement that two expressions are equivalent.

half-plane *(semiplano)* The part of the coordinate plane on one side of a line, which may include the line.

inconsistent system *(sistema inconsistente)* A system of equations or inequalities that has no solution.

independent system *(sistema independiente)* A system of equations that has exactly one solution.

linear inequality in two variables *(desigualdad lineal en dos variables)* An inequality that can be written in one of the following forms: $Ax + By < C$, $Ax + By > C$, $Ax + By \leq C$, $Ax + By \geq C$, or $Ax + By \neq C$, where A, B, and C are constants and A and B are not both 0.

solution of a linear inequality in two variables *(solución de una desigualdad lineal en dos variables)* An ordered pair or ordered pairs that make the inequality true.

solution of a system of linear equations *(solución de un sistema de ecuaciones lineales)* Any ordered pair that satisfies all the equations in a system.

solution of a system of linear inequalities *(solución de un sistema de desigualdades lineales)* Any ordered pair that satisfies all the inequalities in a system.

substitution method *(sustitución)* A method used to solve systems of equations by solving an equation for one variable and substituting the resulting expression into the other equation(s).

system of linear equations *(sistema de ecuaciones lineales)* A system of equations in which all of the equations are linear.

system of linear inequalities *(sistema de desigualdades lineales)* A system of inequalities in which all of the inequalities are linear.

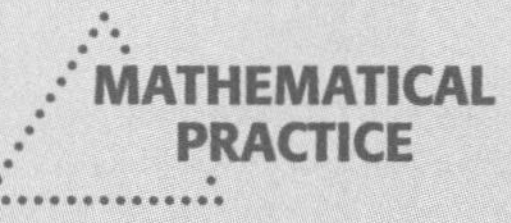

The Common Core Standards for Mathematical Practice describe varieties of expertise that mathematics educators at all levels should seek to develop in their students. Opportunities to develop these practices are integrated throughout this program.

1. **Make sense of problems and persevere in solving them.**
2. **Reason abstractly and quantitatively.**
3. **Construct viable arguments and critique the reasoning of others.**
4. **Model with mathematics.**
5. **Use appropriate tools strategically.**
6. **Attend to precision.**
7. **Look for and make use of structure.**
8. **Look for and express regularity in repeated reasoning**

CHAPTER 5

Name_________________________ Class_______________ Date_________

5-1

Solving Systems by Graphing

Going Deeper

Essential question: *How do you approximate the solution of a system of linear equations by graphing?*

Video Tutor

A **system of linear equations** consists of two or more linear equations that have the same variables. A **solution of a system of linear equations** with two variables is an ordered pair that satisfies both equations in the system. The values of the variables in the ordered pair make each equation in the system true.

Systems of linear equations can be solved by graphing and by using algebra. In this lesson you will learn to solve linear systems by graphing the equations of the system and analyzing how those graphs are related.

CC.9–12.A.REI.6

1 EXAMPLE Solving a Linear System by Graphing

Solve the system of equations below by graphing. Check your answer.

$$\begin{cases} -x + y = 3 \\ 2x + y = 6 \end{cases}$$

A Graph each equation.

Step 1: Find the intercepts for $-x + y = 3$, plus a third point for a check. Graph the line.

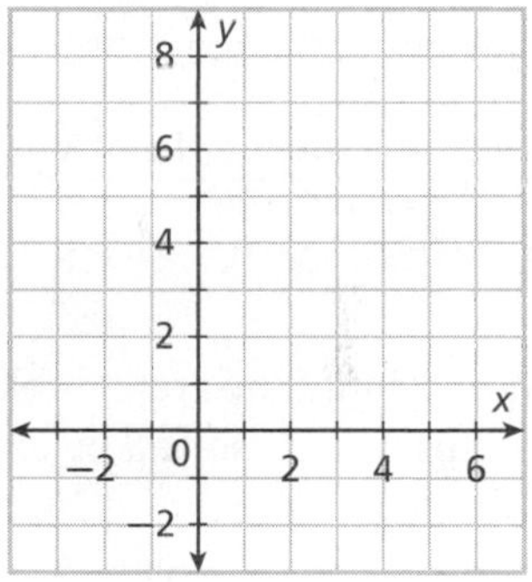

***x*-intercept:** _________ ***y*-intercept:** _________

Check: The y-value for $x = 2$ is $y =$ _________.

Is that point (x, y) on the line? _________

Step 2: Find the intercepts for $2x + y = 6$ and graph the line.

***x*-intercept:** _________ ***y*-intercept:** _________

Check: The y-value for $x = 2$ is $y =$ _________.

Is that point (x, y) on the line? _________

B Find the point of intersection.

The two lines appear to intersect at _________.

How is the point of intersection related to the solution of the linear system?

____

____

C Check if the ordered pair is a solution.

The solution of the system appears to be ________.

To check, substitute the ordered pair (x, y) into each equation.

$-x + y = 3$	
$-\square + \square$	3
$\square$	3 ✓

$2x + y = 6$	
$2(\square) + \square$	6
$\square + \square$	6
$\square$	6 ✓

The ordered pair ________ makes both equations ________.

So, ________ is a solution of the system.

REFLECT

1a. How is the graph of each equation related to the solutions of the equation?

____

____

1b. Explain why the solution of a linear system with two equations is represented by the point where the graphs of the two equations intersect.

____

____

1c. Describe the graphs of $x = 4$ and $y = 2$. Explain how to solve the linear system by graphing.

$$\begin{cases} x = 4 \\ y = 2 \end{cases}$$

What would the graph look like? What is the solution of the linear system? Can systems of this type be solved by examining the equations without graphing them?

____

____

____

____

____

____

CC.9–12.A.REI.6

2 EXAMPLE Estimating a Solution by Graphing

Estimate the solution for the linear system by graphing.

$$\begin{cases} x + 2y = 2 \\ 2x - 3y = 12 \end{cases}$$

A Graph each equation by finding intercepts.

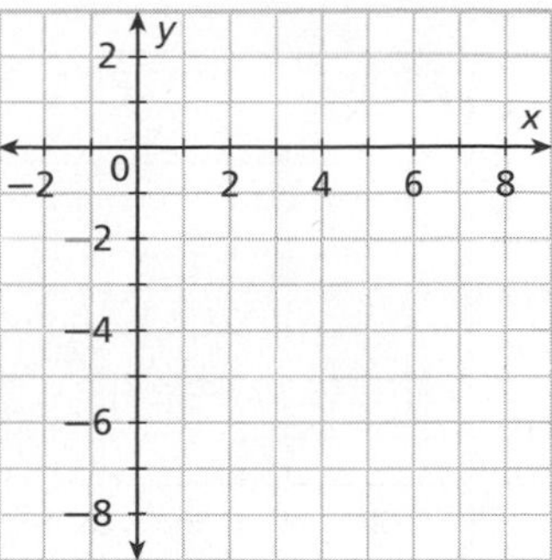

$x + 2y = 2$	$2x - 3y = 12$
***x*-intercept:** ________	***x*-intercept:** ________
***y*-intercept:** ________	***y*-intercept:** ________

B Find the point of intersection.

The two lines appear to intersect at __________.

C Check if the ordered pair is an approximate solution.

$x + 2y$	$= 2$
___ $+ 2($___$)$	2
___ $+$ ___	2
___	2 ✓

$2x - 3y$	$= 12$
$2($___$) - 3($___$)$	12
___ $-$ ___	12
___	12 ✓

Does the approximate solution make both equations true? If not, explain why not and whether the approximate solution is acceptable.

____

____

____

REFLECT

2a. How could you adjust the graph to make your estimate more accurate?

____

____

2b. Can an approximate solution make both equations true? Explain.

____

PRACTICE

Solve each system by graphing. Check your answer.

1. $\begin{cases} x - y = -2 \\ 2x + y = 8 \end{cases}$

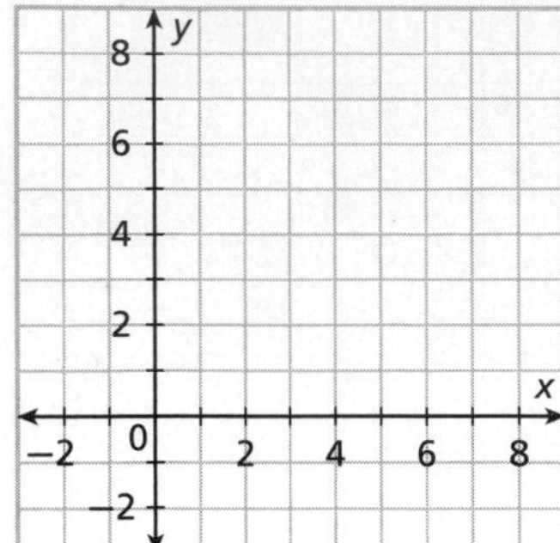

Solution: ______________________

2. $\begin{cases} x - y = -5 \\ 2x + 4y = -4 \end{cases}$

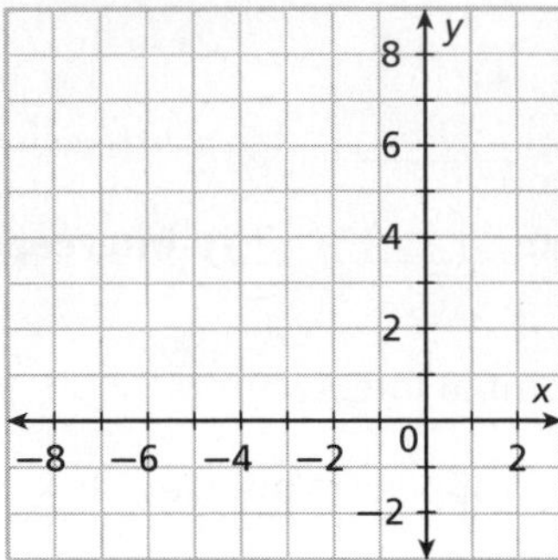

Solution: ______________________

Estimate the solution for the linear system by graphing. Check your answer.

3. $\begin{cases} x + y = 5 \\ x - 3y = 3 \end{cases}$

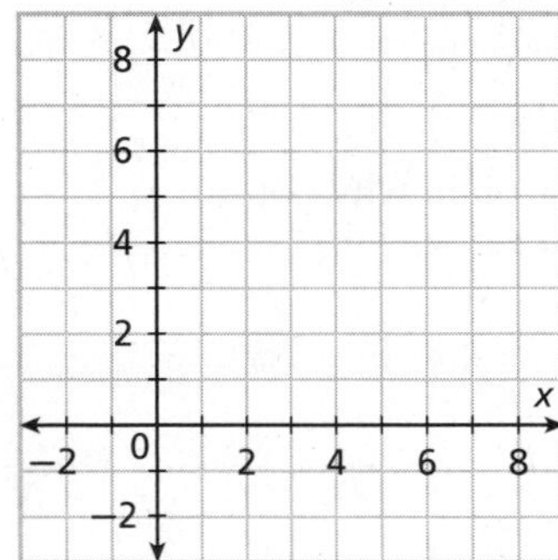

Approximate solution: ______________________

4. $\begin{cases} 3x = 8 \\ 2x - 2y = -3 \end{cases}$

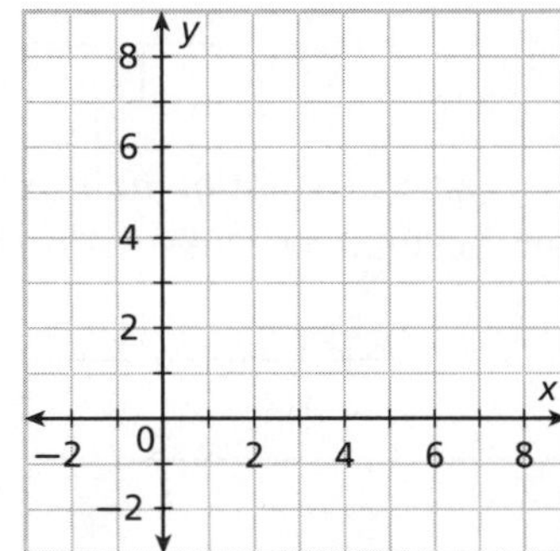

Approximate solution: ______________________

5. $\begin{cases} 3x - 2y = 12 \\ 2x - 6y = 9 \end{cases}$

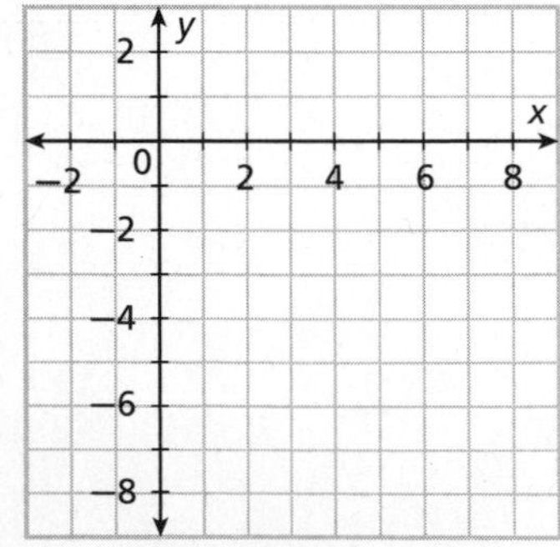

Approximate solution: ______________________

6. $\begin{cases} x + 2y = -6 \\ 2x + y = -4 \end{cases}$

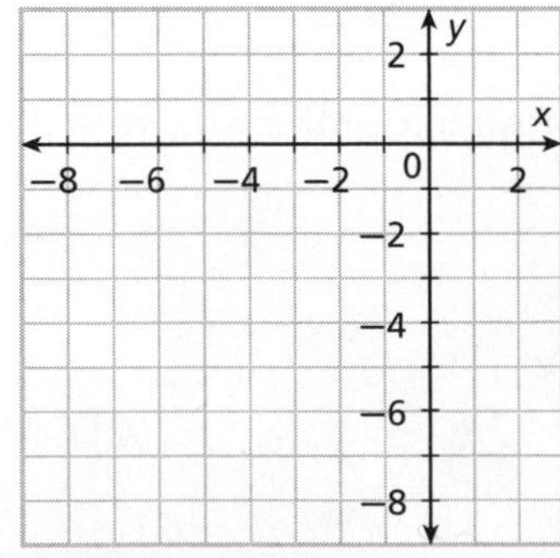

Approximate solution: ______________________

Name________________________ Class______________ Date__________

Additional Practice

Tell whether the ordered pair is a solution of the given system.

1. (3, 1); $\begin{cases} x+3y=6 \\ 4x-5y=7 \end{cases}$ ________

$x+3y=6$	

$4x-5y=7$	

2. (6, –2); $\begin{cases} 3x-2y=14 \\ 5x-y=32 \end{cases}$ ________

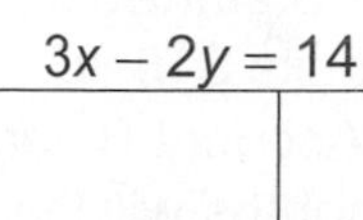

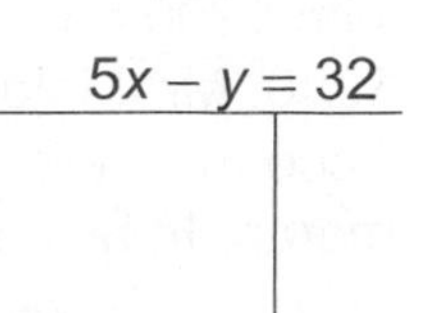

Solve each system by graphing. Check your answer.

3. $\begin{cases} y=x+4 \\ y=-2x+1 \end{cases}$ Solution: ________

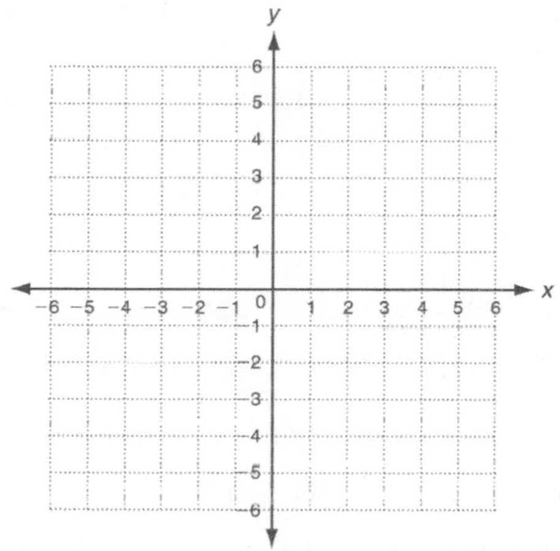

4. $\begin{cases} y=x+6 \\ y=-3x+6 \end{cases}$ Solution: ________

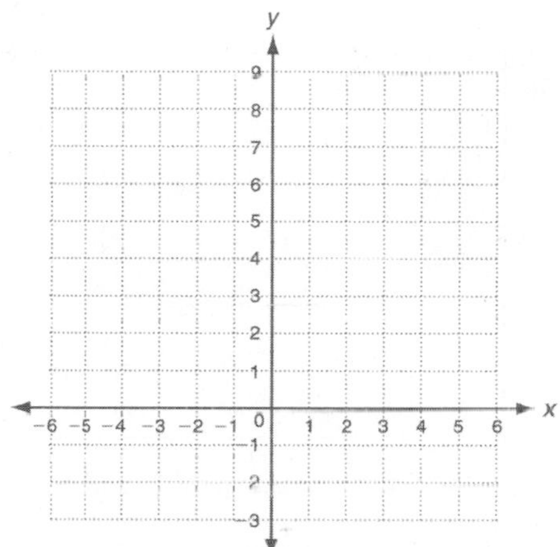

5. Maryann and Carlos are each saving for new scooters. So far, Maryann has $9 saved, and can earn $6 per hour babysitting. Carlos has $3 saved, and can earn $9 per hour working at his family's restaurant. After how many hours of work will Maryann and Carlos have saved the same amount? What will that amount be?

____

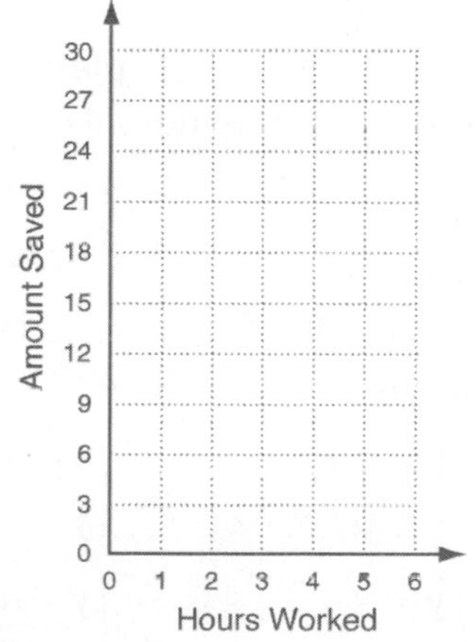

Problem Solving

Write the correct answer.

1. Mr. Malone is putting money in two savings accounts. Account A started with $200 and Account B started with $300. Mr. Malone deposits $15 in Account A and $10 in Account B each month. In how many months will the accounts have the same balance? What will that balance be?

____

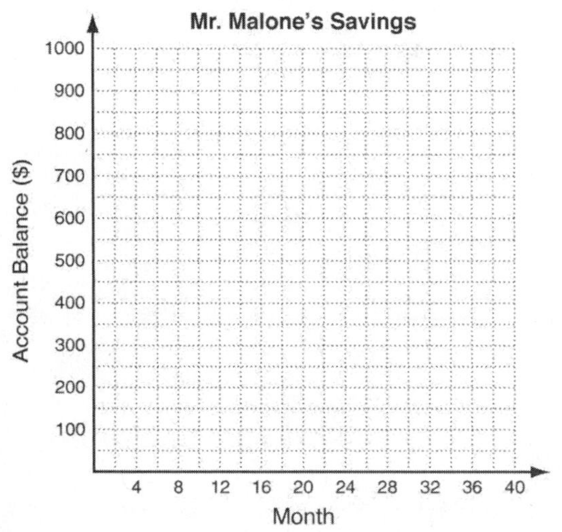

2. Tom currently has 5 comic books in his collection and has subscribed to receive 5 new comic books each month. His uncle has 145 comic books, but sends 5 to each of his 3 nieces each month. In how many months will they have the same number of comic books? How many books will that be?

____

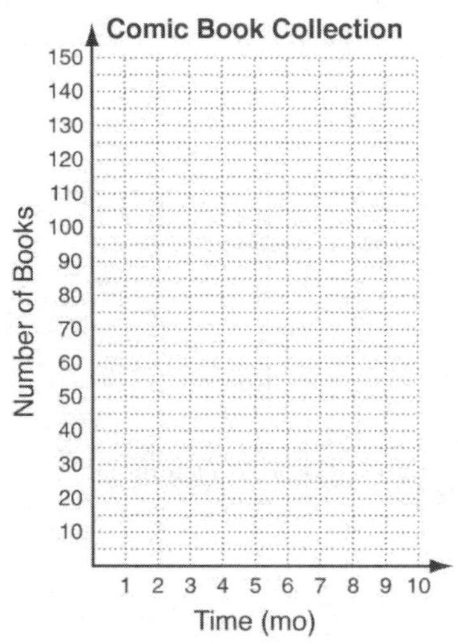

The graph below compares the heights of two trees. Use the graph to answer questions 3–6. Select the best answer.

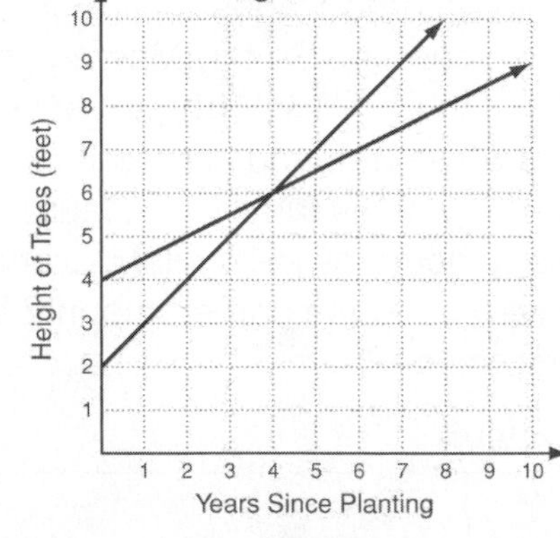

3. How many years after planting will the trees be the same height?

   A 1 years C 4 years

   B 2 years D 6 years

4. Which system of equations is represented by the graph?

   F $\begin{cases} y = x + 2 \\ y = 0.5x + 2 \end{cases}$ H $\begin{cases} y = 2x + 4 \\ y = x + 4 \end{cases}$

   G $\begin{cases} y = x + 2 \\ y = 0.5x + 4 \end{cases}$ J $\begin{cases} y = 4x - 2 \\ y = 2x + 2 \end{cases}$

5. How fast does the tree that started at 2 feet tall grow?

   A 0.5 ft/yr C 1.5 ft/yr

   B 1 ft/yr D 2 ft/yr

6. How fast does the tree that started at 4 feet tall grow?

   F 0.5 ft/yr H 1.5 ft/yr

   G 1 ft/yr J 2 ft/yr

Name______________________ Class______________ Date__________

5-2

Video Tutor

Solving Systems by Substitution

Going Deeper

Essential question: *How do you use substitution to solve a system of linear equations?*

The **substitution method** is used to solve systems of linear equations by solving an equation for one variable and then substituting the resulting expression for that variable into the other equation. The steps for this method are as follows:

1. Solve one of the equations for one of its variables.
2. Substitute the expression from step 1 into the other equation and solve for the other variable.
3. Substitute the value from step 2 into either original equation and solve to find the value of the variable in step 1.

CC.9–12.A.REI.6

1 EXAMPLE Solving a Linear System by Substitution

Solve the system of linear equations by substitution. Check your answer.

$$\begin{cases} -3x + y = 1 \\ 4x + y = 8 \end{cases}$$

A Solve an equation for one variable.

$-3x + y = 1$	Select one of the equations.
$y = \underline{\quad\quad}$	Solve for the variable y. Isolate y on one side.

B Substitute the expression for y in the other equation and solve.

$4x + (\underline{\quad\quad}) = 8$	Substitute the expression for the variable y.
$\underline{\quad} + 1 = 8$	Combine like terms.
$\underline{\quad} = 7$	Subtract _____ from each side.
$x = \underline{\quad}$	Divide each side by _____.

C Substitute the value of x you found into one of the equations and solve for the other variable, y.

$-3(\underline{\quad}) + y = 1$	Substitute the value of x into the first equation.
$\underline{\quad} + y = 1$	Simplify.
$y = \underline{\quad}$	Add _____ to each side.

So, _______ is the solution of the system.

D Check the solution by graphing.

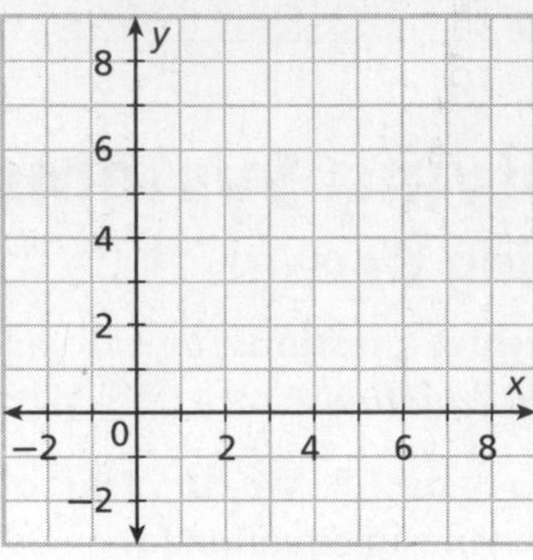

$-3x + y = 1$

x-intercept: _____

y-intercept: _____

$4x + y = 8$

x-intercept: _____

y-intercept: _____

The point of intersection is ________.

REFLECT

1a. Is it more efficient to solve $-3x + y = 1$ for x? Why or why not?

____

1b. Is there another way to solve the system?

____

1c. What is another way to check your solution?

____

PRACTICE

Solve each system by substitution. Check your answer.

1. $\begin{cases} x + y = 3 \\ 2x + 4y = 8 \end{cases}$

Solution: _______________

2. $\begin{cases} x + 2y = 7 \\ 4x + 3y = 3 \end{cases}$

Solution: _______________

3. $\begin{cases} -4x + y = 3 \\ 5x - 2y = -9 \end{cases}$

Solution: _______________

4. $\begin{cases} 8x - 7y = -2 \\ -2x - 3y = 10 \end{cases}$

Solution: _______________

5. $\begin{cases} 2x + 7y = 2 \\ 4x + 2y = -2 \end{cases}$

Solution: _______________

6. $\begin{cases} 2x - y = 7 \\ 2x + 7y = 31 \end{cases}$

Solution: _______________

Tell whether it is more efficient to solve for *x* and then substitute for *x* or to solve for *y* and then substitute for *y*. Explain your reasoning. Then solve the system.

7. $\begin{cases} 6x - 3y = 15 \\ x + 3y = -8 \end{cases}$

____

____

Solution: ________________________

Name________________ Class__________ Date__________

5-2

Additional Practice

Solve each system by substitution. Check your answer.

1. $\begin{cases} y=x-2 \\ y=4x+1 \end{cases}$

2. $\begin{cases} y=x-4 \\ y=-x+2 \end{cases}$

3. $\begin{cases} y=3x+1 \\ y=5x-3 \end{cases}$

4. $\begin{cases} 2x-y=6 \\ x+y=-3 \end{cases}$

5. $\begin{cases} 2x+y=8 \\ y=x-7 \end{cases}$

6. $\begin{cases} 2x+3y=0 \\ x+2y=-1 \end{cases}$

7. $\begin{cases} 3x-2y=7 \\ x+3y=-5 \end{cases}$

8. $\begin{cases} -2x+y=0 \\ 5x+3y=-11 \end{cases}$

9. $\begin{cases} \frac{1}{2}x+\frac{1}{3}y=5 \\ \frac{1}{4}x+y=10 \end{cases}$

Write a system of equations to represent the situation. Then, solve the system by substitution.

10. The length of a rectangle is 3 more than its width. The perimeter of the rectangle is 58 cm. What are the rectangle's dimensions?

11. Carla and Benicio work in a men's clothing store. They earn commission from each suit and each pair of shoes they sell. For selling 3 suits and one pair of shoes, Carla has earned \$47 in commission. For selling 7 suits and 2 pairs of shoes, Benicio has earned \$107 in commission. How much do the salespeople earn for the sale of a suit? for the sale of a pair of shoes?

Problem Solving

Write the correct answer.

1. Maribel has \$1.25 in her pocket. The money is in quarters and dimes. There are a total of 8 coins. How many quarters and dimes does Maribel have in her pocket?

____

____

2. Fabulously Fit offers memberships for \$35 per month plus a \$50 enrollment fee. The Fitness Studio offers memberships for \$40 per month plus a \$35 enrollment fee. In how many months will the fitness clubs cost the same? What will the cost be?

____

____

3. Vong grilled 21 burgers at a block party. He grilled the same number of pounds of turkey burgers as hamburgers. Each turkey burger weighed $\frac{1}{4}$ pound and each hamburger weighed $\frac{1}{3}$ pound. How many of each did Vong grill?

____

____

4. Kate bought 3 used CDs and 1 used DVD at the bookstore. Her friend Joel bought 2 used CDs and 2 used DVDs at the same store. If Kate spent \$20 and Joel spent \$22, determine the cost of a used CD and a used DVD.

____

____

Use the chart below to answer questions 5–8. Select the best answer. The chart compares the quotes that the Masons received from four different flooring contractors to tear out and replace a floor.

Contractor	Cost to tear out old floor	Cost of new floor per square foot
Smith & Son	\$250	\$8.00
V.I.P. Inc.	\$350	\$7.75
Dad's Floors	\$150	\$8.00
Floorshop	\$300	\$8.25

5. Which expression shows the total cost if the work is done by Dad's Floors?

A $8 + 150x$ C $150(8x)$

B $150 + 8x$ D $158x$

6. How many square feet would the Masons need to have installed to make the total cost of V.I.P. Inc. the same as the total cost of Floorshop?

F 10 sq ft H 100 sq ft

G 200 sq ft J 350 sq ft

7. When the total costs of V.I.P. Inc. and Floorshop are the same, what is the total cost?

A \$1125.00 C \$1950.00

B \$1900.00 D \$3187.50

8. How many square feet would the Masons need to have installed to make the total cost of Smith & Son the same as the total cost of V.I.P. Inc.?

F 80 sq ft H 400 sq ft

G 100 sq ft J 1000 sq ft

Name________________________ Class______________ Date__________

5-3

Video Tutor

Solving Systems by Elimination
Going Deeper

Essential question: *How do you solve a system of linear equations by adding or subtracting?*

The **elimination method** is another method used to solve a system of linear equations. In this method, one variable is *eliminated* by adding or subtracting the two equations of the system to obtain a single equation in one variable. The steps for this method are as follows:

1. Add or subtract the equations to eliminate one variable.
2. Solve the resulting equation for the other variable.
3. Substitute the value into either original equation to find the value of the eliminated variable.

CC.9-12.A.REI.6

1 EXAMPLE Solving a Linear System by Adding

Solve the system of equations by adding. Check your answer.

$$\begin{cases} 4x - 2y = 12 \\ x + 2y = 8 \end{cases}$$

A Add the equations.

$4x - 2y = 12$	Write the equations so that like terms are aligned.
$+ x + 2y = 8$	Notice that the terms ______ and ______ are opposites.
$5x + 0 = 20$	Add to eliminate the variable ______.
$5x = 20$	Simplify and solve for *x*.
$\frac{5x}{5} = \frac{20}{5}$	Divide both sides by 5.
$x = $ ☐	Simplify.

B Substitute the solution into one of the equations and solve for *y*.

$x + 2y = 8$	Use the second equation.
$(\quad) + 2y = 8$	Substitute ______ for the variable ______.
$2y = $ ☐	Subtract ______ from each side.
$y = $ ☐	Divide each side by ______.

C Write the solution as an ordered pair: ______

D Check the solution by graphing.

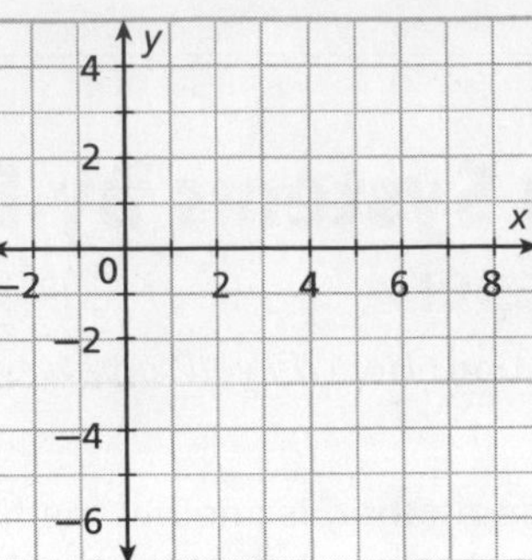

$4x - 2y = 12$ | $x + 2y = 8$

***x*-intercept:** _______ ***x*-intercept:** _______

***y*-intercept:** _______ ***y*-intercept:** _______

The point of intersection is _______.

REFLECT

1a. Can this linear system be solved by subtracting one of the original equations from the other? Why or why not?

____

____

1b. What is another way to check your solution?

____

CC.9–12.A.REI.6

2 EXAMPLE Solving a Linear System by Subtracting

Solve the system of equations by subtracting. Check your answer.

$$\begin{cases} 2x + 6y = 6 \\ 2x - y = -8 \end{cases}$$

A Subtract the equations.

$2x + 6y = 6$	Write the equations so that like terms are aligned.
$-(2x - y = -8)$	Notice that both equations contain the term _______.
$0 \ + 7y = 14$	Subtract to eliminate the variable _______.
$7y = 14$	Simplify and solve for y.
$\frac{7y}{7} = \frac{14}{7}$	Divide both sides by 7.
$y = \square$	Simplify.

B Substitute the solution into one of the equations and solve for x.

$2x - y = -8$	Use the second equation.
$2x - (\square) = -8$	Substitute _______ for the variable _______.
$2x = \square$	Add _______ to each side.
$x = \square$	Divide each side by _______.

C Write the solution as an ordered pair: _______

D Check the solution by graphing.

$2x + 6y = 6$ $2x - y = -8$

x-intercept: ________ **x-intercept:** ________

y-intercept: ________ **y-intercept:** ________

The point of intersection is ________.

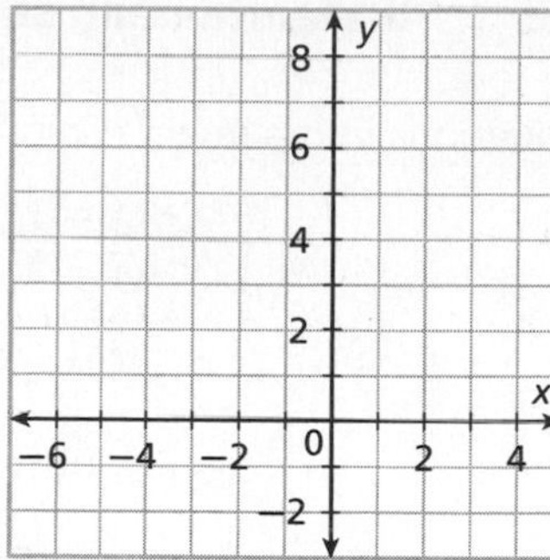

REFLECT

2a. What would happen if you added the original equations instead of subtracting?

____

____

2b. Instead of subtracting $2x - y = -8$ from $2x + 6y = 6$, what equation can you add to get the same result? Explain.

____

____

2c. How can you decide whether to add or subtract to eliminate a variable in a linear system? Explain your reasoning.

____

____

____

In some linear systems, neither variable can be eliminated by adding or subtracting the equations directly. In systems like these, you need to multiply one or both of the equations by a constant so that adding or subtracting the equations will eliminate one variable. The steps for this method are as follows:

1. Decide which variable to eliminate.
2. Multiply one or both equations by a constant so that adding or subtracting will eliminate that variable.
3. Solve the system using the elimination method.

CC.9-12.A.REI.5

3 EXPLORE Understanding Linear Systems and Multiplication

A Use the equations in the linear system below to write a third equation.

$$\begin{cases} 2x - y = 1 \\ x + y = 2 \end{cases}$$

$x + y = 2$	Write the second equation in the system.
$2(x + y = 2)$	Multiply each term in the equation by 2.
$2x + 2y = 4$	Simplify.
$+ \quad 2x - y = 1$	Write the first equation in the system.
 $\_\_\_ x + \_\_\_ y = \_\_\_$	Add the equations to write a third equation.

B Graph and label each equation in the original linear system.

The solution of the system is ________.

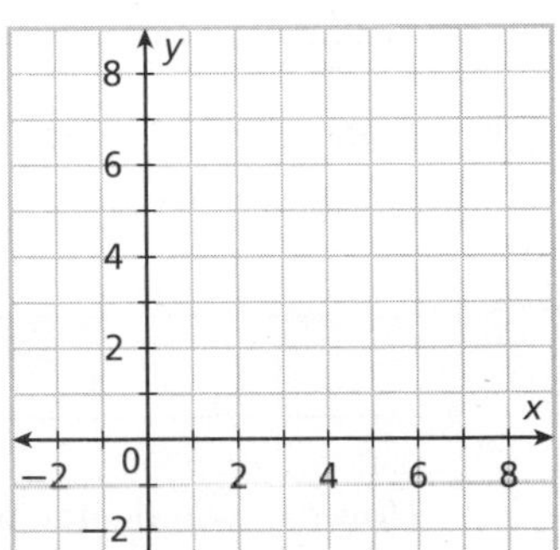

C Graph and label the third equation.

How is the graph of the third equation related to the graphs of the two equations in the original system?

____

____

Is the solution of the original system also a solution of the system formed by the equation $2x - y = 1$ and the third equation? Explain.

____

REFLECT

3a. Examine your results from the Explore. Does it appear that a new linear system composed of one of the equations from the original system and a new equation created by adding a multiple of one original equation to the other equation will have the same solution as the original system? Explain.

____

____

____

3b. If the two equations in the original system are represented by $Ax + By = C$ and $Dx + Ey = F$, where A, B, C, D, E, and F are constants, then the third equation you wrote can be represented by doing the following:

Multiply the second equation by a nonzero constant k to get $kDx + kEy = kF$.

Then add this equation to the first equation to get the third equation.

$$\begin{array}{rrrr} & Ax + & By = & C \\ + & kDx + & kEy = & kF \\ \hline \multicolumn{4}{l}{(A + kD)x + (B + kE)y = C + kF} \end{array}$$

Complete the proof below to show that if (x_1, y_1) is a solution of the original system, then it is also a solution of the new system below.

$$\begin{cases} Ax + By = C \\ (A + kD)x + (B + kE)y = C + kF \end{cases}$$

$Ax_1 + By_1 = C$	(x_1, y_1) is a solution of $Ax + By = C$.
$Dx_1 + Ey_1 = F$	(x_1, y_1) is a solution of $Dx + Ey = F$.
$\_\_\_\_(Dx_1 + Ey_1) = kF$	Multiplication Property of ________
$kDx_1 + kEy_1 = kF$	________ Property
$C + kDx_1 + kEy_1 = \_\_\_\_ + kF$	________ Property of Equality
$Ax_1 + \_\_\_\_ + kDx_1 + kEy_1 = C + kF$	Substitute $Ax_1 + By_1$ for C on the left side.
$Ax_1 + kDx_1 + \_\_\_\_ + kEy_1 = C + kF$	________ Property of Addition
$(Ax_1 + kDx_1) + (By_1 + kEy_1) = C + kF$	Associative Property of Addition
$(A + kD)x_1 + (\_\_\_\_ + kE)y_1 = C + kF$	Distributive Property

Since $(A + kD)x_1 + (B + kE)y_1 = C + kF$, (x_1, y_1) is a solution of the new system.

CC.9–12.A.REI.6

4 EXAMPLE Solving a Linear System by Multiplying One Equation

Solve the system of equations by multiplying.

$$\begin{cases} 3x + 8y = 7 \\ 2x - 2y = -10 \end{cases}$$

A Explain how to multiply one of the equations by a number so that the coefficients for one of the variables are opposites.

____

____

B Multiply the second equation by the constant you found in part A and add this new equation to the first equation.

☐ $(2x - 2y = -10)$	Multiply each term in the second equation by ______ to get opposite coefficients for the y-terms.
$8x - 8y = -40$ $+\ 3x + 8y = 7$	Simplify. Add the first equation to the new equation.
$11x + 0y = -33$	Add to eliminate the variable ______.
$11x = -33$	Simplify and solve for x.
$\frac{11x}{11} = \frac{-33}{11}$	Divide both sides by 11.
$x =$ ☐	Simplify.

C Substitute the solution into one of the equations and solve.

$3x + 8y = 7$	Use the first equation.
$3(\ \square\ ) + 8y = 7$	Substitute ______ for the variable ______.
☐ $+ 8y = 7$	Simplify.
$8y =$ ☐	Add ______ to each side.
$y =$ ☐	Divide each side by ______.

D Write the solution as an ordered pair: __________

REFLECT

4a. How can you solve this linear system by subtracting? Which is more efficient, adding or subtracting? Explain your reasoning.

4b. Can this linear system be solved by adding or subtracting without multiplying? Why or why not?

4c. What would you need to multiply the second equation by to eliminate x by adding? Why might you choose to eliminate y instead of x?

CC.9–12.A.REI.6

5 EXAMPLE Solving a Linear System by Multiplying Both Equations

Solve the system of equations by multiplying.

$$\begin{cases} -3x + 9y = -3 \\ 4x - 13y = 5 \end{cases}$$

A Explain how to multiply both of the equations by different integers so that the coefficients for one of the variables are opposites.

____

____

B Multiply both of the equations and add.

$\square(-3x + 9y = -3)$	Multiply the first equation by ____.
$\square(4x - 13y = 5)$	Multiply the second equation by ____.
$-12x + 36y = -12$	Simplify the multiple of the first equation.
$+\ 12x - 39y = 15$	Simplify the multiple of the second equation.
$-3y = 3$	Add to eliminate the variable ____.
$\frac{-3y}{-3} = \frac{3}{-3}$	Divide both sides by −3.
$y = \square$	Simplify.

C Substitute the solution into one of the equations and solve.

$4x - 13y = 5$	Use the second equation.
$4x - 13(\square) = 5$	Substitute ____ for the variable ____.
$4x - (\square) = 5$	Simplify.
$4x = \square$	Add ____ to each side.
$\frac{4x}{4} = \frac{-8}{4}$	Divide each side by ____.
$x = \square$	Simplify.

D Write the solution as an ordered pair: ________

REFLECT

5a. What numbers would you need to multiply both equations by to eliminate y? Why might you choose to eliminate x instead?

____

____

____

____

5b. Describe how to find the numbers by which you would multiply both equations to eliminate a variable.

____

____

____

____

____

5c. If both equations must be multiplied in order to eliminate a variable, how can you decide which variable will be easier to eliminate?

____

____

____

PRACTICE

Solve each system by adding or subtracting. Check your answer.

1. $\begin{cases} -5x + y = -3 \\ 5x - 3y = -1 \end{cases}$

Solution: ______________________________

2. $\begin{cases} 2x + y = -6 \\ -5x + y = 8 \end{cases}$

Solution: ______________________________

3. $\begin{cases} 2x - 3y = -2 \\ 2x + y = 14 \end{cases}$

Solution: ______________________________

4. $\begin{cases} 6x - 3y = 15 \\ 4x + 3y = -5 \end{cases}$

Solution: ______________________________

5. **Error Analysis** Which solution is incorrect? Explain the error.

A

$$\begin{cases} x + y = -4 \\ 2x + y = -3 \end{cases} \qquad \begin{array}{r} x + y = -4 \\ -(2x + y = -3) \\ \hline -x = -7 \\ x = 7 \end{array}$$

$7 + y = -4$

$y = -11$

Solution is $(7, -11)$.

B

$$\begin{cases} x + y = -4 \\ 2x + y = -3 \end{cases} \qquad \begin{array}{r} x + y = -4 \\ -(2x + y = -3) \\ \hline -x = -1 \\ x = 1 \end{array}$$

$1 + y = -4$

$y = -5$

Solution is $(1, -5)$.

____

____

6. Is it possible to solve the system in the first Example by using substitution? If so, explain how. Which method is easier to use? Why?

____

____

____

____

____

Solve each system by multiplying. Check your answer.

7. $\begin{cases} -2x + 2y = 2 \\ 5x - 6y = -9 \end{cases}$

Solution: ____________________

8. $\begin{cases} 3x + 3y = 12 \\ -6x - 11y = -14 \end{cases}$

Solution: ____________________

9. $\begin{cases} 4x + 3y = 11 \\ 2x - 2y = -12 \end{cases}$

Solution: ____________________

10. $\begin{cases} 6x + 3y = -24 \\ 7x - 5y = 6 \end{cases}$

Solution: ____________________

11. $\begin{cases} 3x + 8y = 17 \\ -2x + 9y = 3 \end{cases}$

Solution: ____________________

12. $\begin{cases} 11x + 6y = -20 \\ 15x + 9y = -33 \end{cases}$

Solution: ____________________

13. $\begin{cases} 12x - 6y = 12 \\ 8x - 16y = -16 \end{cases}$

Solution: ____________________

14. $\begin{cases} 5x + 9y = -3 \\ -4x - 7y = 3 \end{cases}$

Solution: ____________________

15. Error Analysis A linear system has two equations, $Ax + By = C$ and $Dx + Ey = F$. A student multiplies the x- and y-coefficients in the second equation by a constant k to get $kDx + kEy = F$. The student then adds the result to $Ax + By = C$ to write a new equation.

a. What is the new equation that the student wrote?

____

b. If the ordered pair (x_1, y_1) is a solution of the original system, will it also be a solution of $Ax + By = C$ and the new equation? Why or why not?

____

____

____

Name____________________ Class____________ Date____________

5-3

Additional Practice

Follow the steps to solve each system by elimination.

1. $\begin{cases} 2x - 3y = 14 \\ 2x + y = -10 \end{cases}$

Subtract the second equation:

$2x - 3y = 14$
$-\ (2x + y = -10)$

____

Solve the resulting equation:

$y =$ __________

Use your answer to find the value of x:

$x =$ __________

Solution: (____, ____)

2. $\begin{cases} 3x + y = 17 \\ 4x + 2y = 20 \end{cases}$

Multiply the first equation by –2. Then, add the equations:

___ x – ___ y = ____
$+\ 4x + 2y = 20$

____

Solve the resulting equation:

$x =$ __________

Use your answer to find the value of y:

$y =$ __________

Solution: (____, ____)

Solve each system by elimination. Check your answer.

3. $\begin{cases} x + 3y = -7 \\ -x + 2y = -8 \end{cases}$ ____________

4. $\begin{cases} 3x + y = -26 \\ 2x - y = -19 \end{cases}$ ____________

5. $\begin{cases} x + 3y = -14 \\ 2x - 4y = 32 \end{cases}$ ____________

6. $\begin{cases} 4x - y = -5 \\ -2x + 3y = 10 \end{cases}$ ____________

7. $\begin{cases} y - 3x = 11 \\ 2y - x = 2 \end{cases}$ ____________

8. $\begin{cases} -10x + y = 0 \\ 5x + 3y = -7 \end{cases}$ ____________

Solve.

9. Brianna's family spent $134 on 2 adult tickets and 3 youth tickets at an amusement park. Max's family spent $146 on 3 adult tickets and 2 youth tickets. What is the price of a youth ticket? ____________

10. Carl bought 19 apples of 2 different varieties to make a pie. The total cost of the apples was $5.10. Granny Smith apples cost $0.25 each and Gala apples cost $0.30 each. How many of each type of apple did Carl buy? ____________

Problem Solving

Write the correct answer.

1. Mr. Nguyen bought a package of 3 chicken legs and a package of 7 chicken wings. Ms. Dawes bought a package of 3 chicken legs and a package of 6 chicken wings. Mr. Nguyen bought 45 ounces of chicken. Ms. Dawes bought 42 ounces of chicken. How much did each chicken leg and each chicken wing weigh?

____

____

2. Jayce bought 2 bath towels and returned 3 hand towels. His sister Jayna bought 3 bath towels and 3 hand towels. Jayce's bill was $5. Jayna's bill was $45. What are the prices of a bath towel and a hand towel?

____

____

3. The Lees spent $31 on movie tickets for 2 adults and 3 children. The Macias spent $26 on movie tickets for 2 adults and 2 children. What are the prices for adult and child movie tickets?

____

____

4. Last month Stephanie spent $57 on 4 allergy shots and 1 office visit. This month she spent $9 after 1 office visit and a refund for 2 allergy shots from her insurance company. How much does an office visit cost? an allergy shot?

____

____

Use the chart below to answer questions 5–6. Select the best answer. The chart shows the price per pound for dried fruit.

Dried Fruit Price List			
Pineapple	Apple	Mango	Papaya
$7.50/lb	$7.00/lb	$8.00/lb	$7.25/lb

5. A customer bought 5 pounds of mango and papaya for $37.75. How many pounds of each fruit did the customer buy?
   A 2 lbs mango and 3 lbs papaya
   B 3 lbs mango and 2 lbs papaya
   C 1 lb mango and 4 lbs papaya
   D 4 lbs mango and 1 lb papaya

6. A store employee made two gift baskets of dried fruit, each costing $100. The first basket had 12 pounds of fruit x and 2 pounds of fruit y. The second basket had 4 pounds of fruit x and 9 pounds of fruit y. Which two fruits did the employee use in the baskets?
   F pineapple and apple
   G apple and mango
   H mango and papaya
   J papaya and pineapple

Name______________________ Class______________ Date__________

5-4

Video Tutor

Solving Special Systems
Going Deeper

Essential question: *How do you solve systems with no or infinitely many solutions?*

CC.9-12.A.REI.6

1 EXAMPLE **Solving Special Systems by Graphing**

Use the graph to solve each system of linear equations.

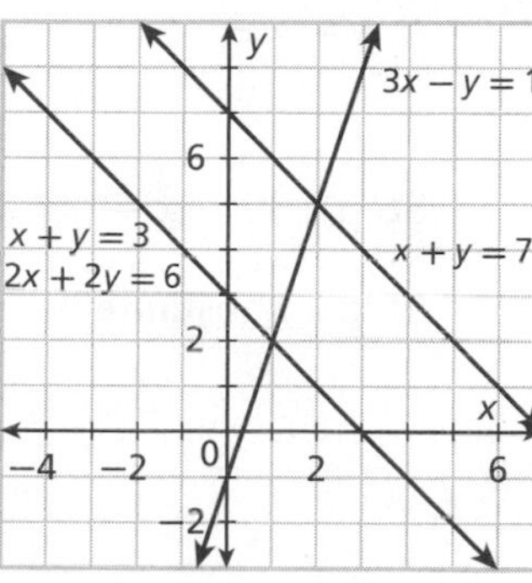

A $\begin{cases} x + y = 7 \\ 2x + 2y = 6 \end{cases}$

Is there a point of intersection? Explain.

___

___

Does this linear system have a solution? Use the graph to explain.

___

___

B $\begin{cases} 2x + 2y = 6 \\ x + y = 3 \end{cases}$

Is there a point of intersection? Explain.

___

Does this linear system have a solution? Use the graph to explain.

___

___

REFLECT

1a. Use the graph to identify two lines that represent a linear system with exactly one solution. What are the equations of the lines? Explain your reasoning.

___

1b. If each equation in a system of two linear equations is represented by a different line when graphed, what is the greatest number of solutions the system can have? Explain your reasoning.

___

___

1c. Identify the three possible numbers of solutions for a system of linear equations. Explain when each type of solution occurs.

____

____

CC.9–12.A.REI.6

2 EXAMPLE Solving Special Systems Algebraically

A Solve the system of linear equations by substitution.

$$\begin{cases} x - y = -2 \\ -x + y = 4 \end{cases}$$

Step 1 Solve $x - y = -2$ for x: $x = $ ______

Step 2 Substitute the resulting expression into the other equation and solve.

$-($ ______ $) + y = 4$ Substitute the expression for the variable *x*.

______ $= 4$ Simplify.

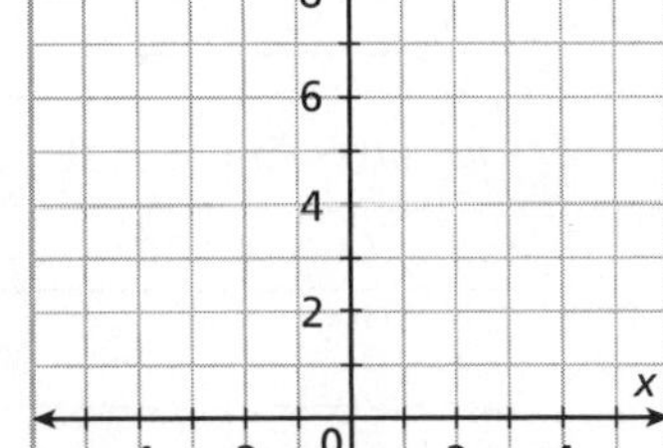

Step 3 Interpret the solution. Graph the equations to provide more information.

What does the graph tell you about the solution?

____

How is this solution represented algebraically when the system is solved using substitution?

____

B Solve the system of linear equations by elimination.

$$\begin{cases} 2x + y = -2 \\ 4x + 2y = -4 \end{cases}$$

Step 1 Multiply the first equation by -2.

$-2(2x + y = -2) \rightarrow -4x + (-2y) = 4$

Step 2 Add the new equation from Step 1 to the original second equation.

$$\begin{array}{rrcr} & -4x + (-2y) & = & 4 \\ + & 4x + \quad 2y & = & -4 \\ \hline & 0x + \quad 0y & = & 0 \\ & 0 & = & 0 \end{array}$$

Step 3 Interpret the solution. Graph the equations to provide more information.

What does the graph tell you about the solution?

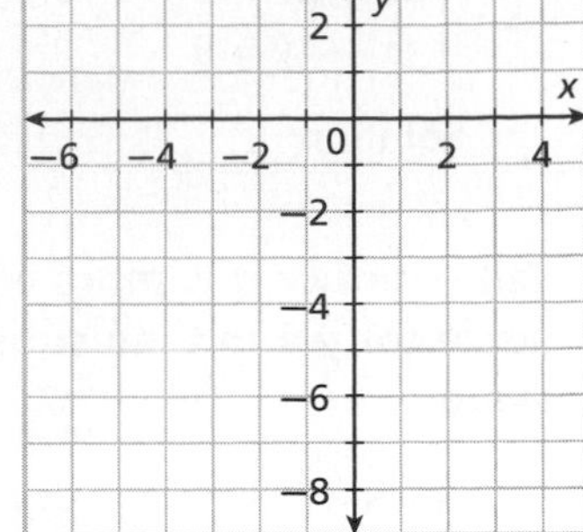

____

____

How is this solution represented algebraically when the linear system is solved using substitution?

____

____

____

REFLECT

2a. If x represents a variable and a and b represent constants such that $a \neq b$, interpret what each result means when solving a system of linear equations by substitution.

$x = a$ ______________________________

$a = b$ ______________________________

$a = a$ ______________________________

2b. In part B of Example 2, why is it more efficient to solve and substitute for y than to solve and substitute for x?

____

____

2c. Give two possible solutions of the system in part B of Example 2. How are all the solutions of this system related to one another?

____

PRACTICE

Solve each system by graphing. Check your answer.

1. $\begin{cases} x + 2y = -8 \\ -2x - 4y = 4 \end{cases}$

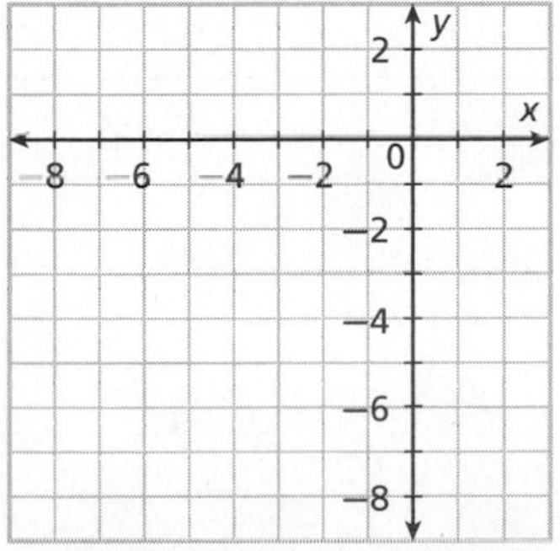

Solution: ______________________________

2. $\begin{cases} 2x - y = -6 \\ 4x - 2y = -12 \end{cases}$

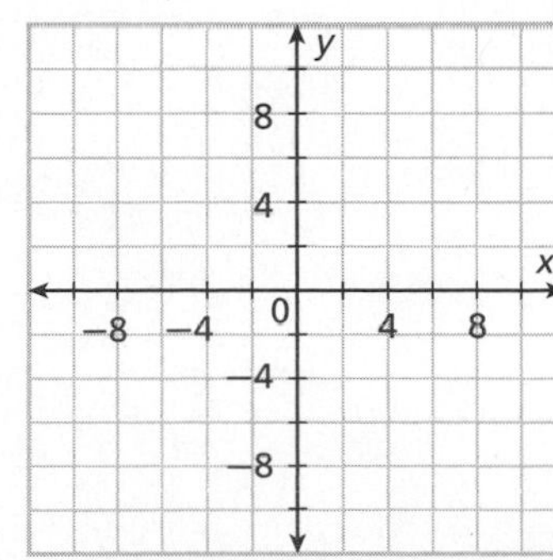

Solution: ______________________________

Solve each system by substitution. Check your answer.

3. $\begin{cases} 2x - 2y = 5 \\ 4x - 4y = 9 \end{cases}$

Solution: ______________________

4. $\begin{cases} x - 2y = -4 \\ 4y = 2x + 8 \end{cases}$

Solution: ______________________

Tell whether it is more efficient to solve for *x* and then substitute for *x* or to solve for *y* and then substitute for *y*. Explain your reasoning. Then solve the system.

5. $\begin{cases} \frac{x}{2} + y = 6 \\ \frac{x}{4} + \frac{y}{2} = 3 \end{cases}$

____

____

Solution: ______________________

Solve each system by adding or subtracting. Check your answer.

6. $\begin{cases} -4x + y = -3 \\ 4x - y = -2 \end{cases}$

Solution: ______________________

7. $\begin{cases} x - 6y = 7 \\ -x + 6y = -7 \end{cases}$

Solution: ______________________

8. If a linear system has no solution, what happens when you try to solve the system by adding or subtracting?

____

____

9. If a linear system has infinitely many solutions, what happens when you try to solve the system by adding or subtracting?

____

____

Solve each system by multiplying. Check your answer.

10. $\begin{cases} 2x + 3y = -6 \\ 10x + 15y = -30 \end{cases}$

Solution: ______________________

11. $\begin{cases} 3x - 4y = -1 \\ -6x + 8y = 3 \end{cases}$

Solution: ______________________

Name________________________ Class________________ Date______________

5-4

Additional Practice

Solve each system of linear equations.

1. $\begin{cases} y = 2x - 3 \\ y - 2x = -3 \end{cases}$

____

2. $\begin{cases} 3x + y = 4 \\ -3x = y - 7 \end{cases}$

____

3. $\begin{cases} y = -4x + 1 \\ 4x = -y - 6 \end{cases}$

____

4. $\begin{cases} y - x + 3 = 0 \\ x = y + 3 \end{cases}$

____

Classify each system. Give the number of solutions.

5. $\begin{cases} y = 3(x - 1) \\ -y + 3x = 3 \end{cases}$

____

____

6. $\begin{cases} y - 2x = 5 \\ x = y - 3 \end{cases}$

____

____

7. Sabina and Lou are reading the same book. Sabina reads 12 pages a day. She had read 36 pages when Lou started the book, and Lou reads at a pace of 15 pages per day. If their reading rates continue, will Sabina and Lou ever be reading the same page on the same day? Explain.

____

____

____

____

8. Brandon started jogging at 4 miles per hour. After he jogged 1 mile, his friend Anton started jogging along the same path at a pace of 4 miles per hour. If they continue to jog at the same rate, will Anton ever catch up with Brandon? Explain.

____

____

____

____

Problem Solving

Write the correct answer.

1. Tyra and Charmian are training for a bike race. Tyra has logged 256 miles so far and rides 48 miles per week. Charmian has logged 125 miles so far and rides 48 miles per week. If these rates continue, will Tyra's distance ever equal Charmian's distance? Explain.

2. Metroplexpress and Local Express are courier companies. Metroplexpress charges \$15 to pick up a package and \$0.50 per mile. Local Express charges \$10 to pick up a package and \$0.55 per mile. Classify this system and find its solution, if any.

3. The Singhs start savings accounts for their twin boys. The accounts earn 5% annual interest. The initial deposit in each account is \$200. Classify this system and find its solution, if any.

4. Frank earns \$8 per hour. Madison earns \$7.50 per hour. Frank started working after Madison had already earned \$300. If these rates continue, will Frank's earnings ever equal Madison's earnings? If so, when?

Select the best answer.

5. A studio apartment at The Oaks costs \$400 per month plus a \$350 deposit. A studio apartment at Crossroads costs \$400 per month plus a \$300 deposit. How many solutions does this system have?
   - A no solutions
   - B 1 solution
   - C 2 solutions
   - D an infinite number of solutions

6. Jane and Gary are both landscape designers. Jane charges \$75 for a consultation plus \$25 per hour. Gary charges \$50 for a consultation plus \$30 per hour. For how many hours will Jane's charges equal Gary's charges?
   - F never
   - G after 2 hours
   - H after 5 hours
   - J always

7. A tank filled with 75 liters of water loses 0.5 liter of water per hour. A tank filled with 50 liters of water loses 0.1 liter of water per hour. How would this system be classified?
   - A inconsistent
   - B dependent
   - C consistent and independent
   - D consistent and dependent

8. Simon is 3 years older than Renata. Five years ago, Renata was half as old as Simon is now. How old are Simon and Renata now?
   - F Simon is 13 and Renata is 10.
   - G Simon is 15 and Renata is 10.
   - H Simon is 16 and Renata is 8.
   - J Simon is 16 and Renata is 13.

Name ______________________ Class ______________ Date __________

5-5

Solving Linear Inequalities

Going Deeper

Video Tutor

Essential question: *How do you graph a linear inequality in two variables?*

A **linear inequality in two variables**, such as $2x - 3y \geq 6$, results when you replace the = sign in an equation by <, >, ≤, or ≥. A **solution of an inequality in two variables** x and y is any ordered pair (x, y) that makes the inequality true.

CC.9–12.A.REI.12

1 EXAMPLE Graphing a Linear Inequality

Graph the solution set for $2x - 3y \geq 6$.

A Start by graphing $2x - 3y = 6$. The inequality is true for every point on this line because the inequality symbol is less than or equal to. The line is called the *boundary line* of the solution set.

x	y
0	
	0

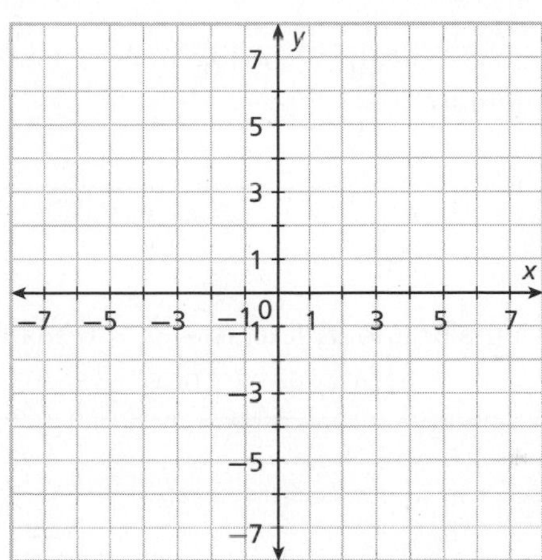

B Test several other points in the plane that are not on the boundary line to determine whether the inequality is true.

Point	Above or Below the Line?	Inequality	True or False?
(0, 0)	Above	$2(0) - 3(0) \geq 6$	False
(5, 0)			
(0, 3)			
(4, 2)			
(6, 1)			

The solutions of $2x - 3y \geq 6$ lie on or ______________ $2x - 3y = 6$.

C Shade the set of solutions to the inequality $2x - 3y \geq 6$. The shaded region and the boundary line make up the graph of $2x - 3y \geq 6$. This area is referred to as a *half-plane.*

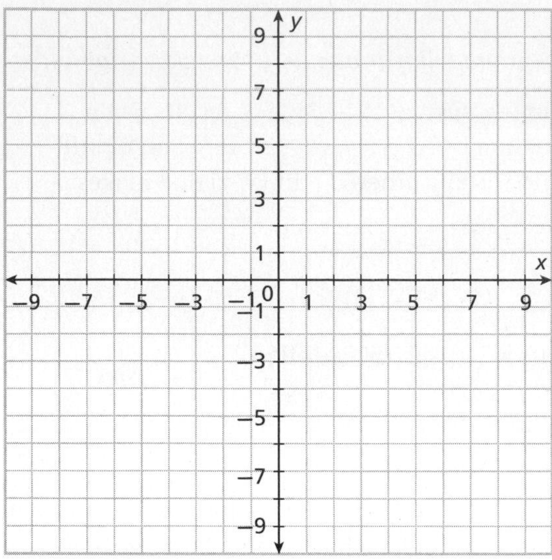

REFLECT

1a. How would the graph of $2x - 3y \leq 6$ be like the graph of $2x - 3y \geq 6$? How would it be different?

1b. Would the points on the boundary line $2x - 3y = 6$ be included in the graph of the inequality $2x - 3y > 6$? Why or why not?

1c. **Error Analysis** A student says that you shade above the boundary line when the inequality is > or ≥ and you shade below it when the inequality is < or ≤. Use the example to explain why this is not always true.

To graph a linear inequality in the coordinate plane:

1. Graph the boundary line. If the symbol is ≤ or ≥, draw a solid line. If the symbol is < or >, draw a dashed line.
2. Choose a test point (x, y) that is not on the line. Substitute the values of x and y into the inequality and determine whether it is true or false.
3. If the inequality is true for the test point, shade the half-plane on the side of the boundary line that contains the test point. If not, shade the half-plane on the opposite side of the line.

CC.9–12.A.REI.12

2 EXAMPLE Graphing a Linear Inequality in Two Variables

Graph the inequality $7x - y < 13$.

A Write the equation of the boundary line. ____________

B Graph the boundary line. The inequality symbol is >, so the line will be dashed.

C Test a point that is not on the line, such as (0, 0).

$7(\quad) - \quad < 13$ True or false? ____________

Shade the part of the plane on the correct side of the line.

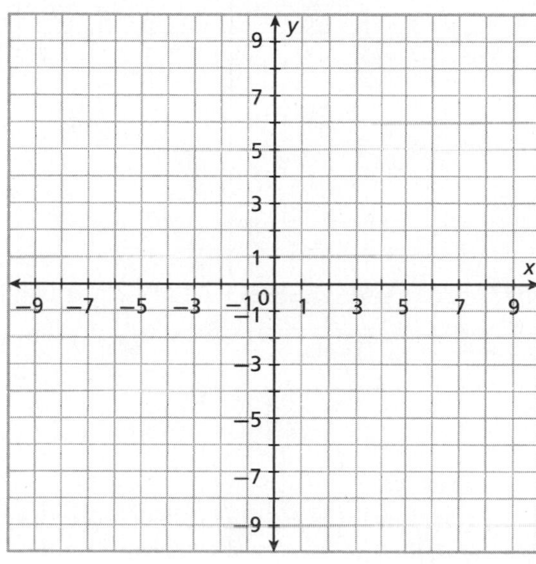

REFLECT

2a. Why is (0, 0) a good choice for a test point? When could you not use (0, 0)?

____

____

2b. For the graph of $x \geq 4$, the boundary line is the vertical line $x = 4$. Would you shade to the left or right of the boundary? Explain.

____

____

____

____

PRACTICE

Graph the inequality.

1. $y \geq 2$

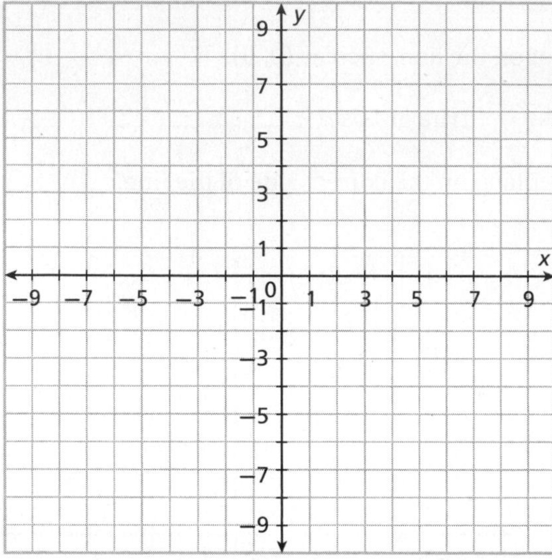

2. $x < -3$

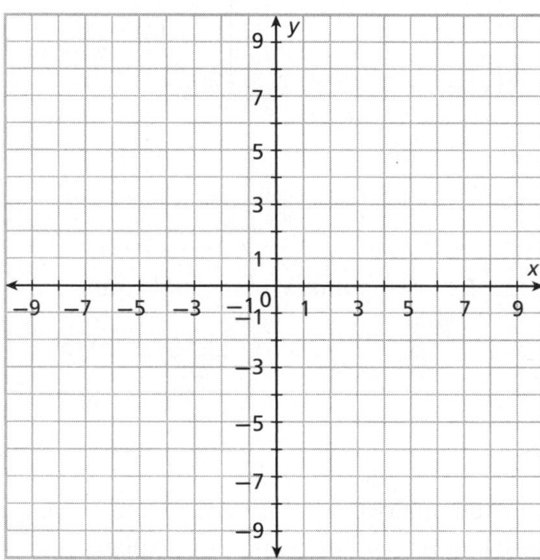

3. $x + 4y < 9$

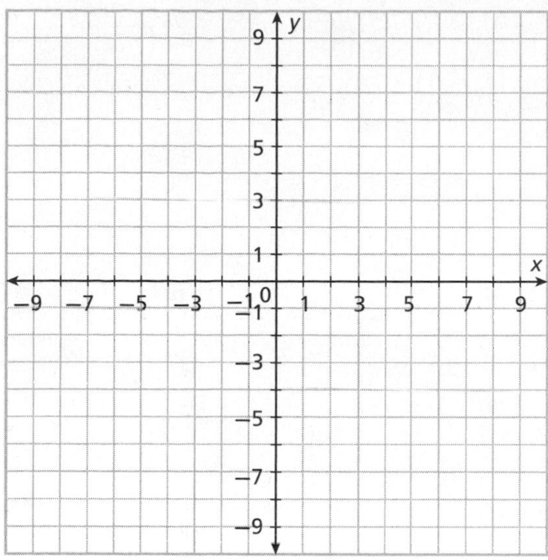

4. $2x - 2y \geq 5$

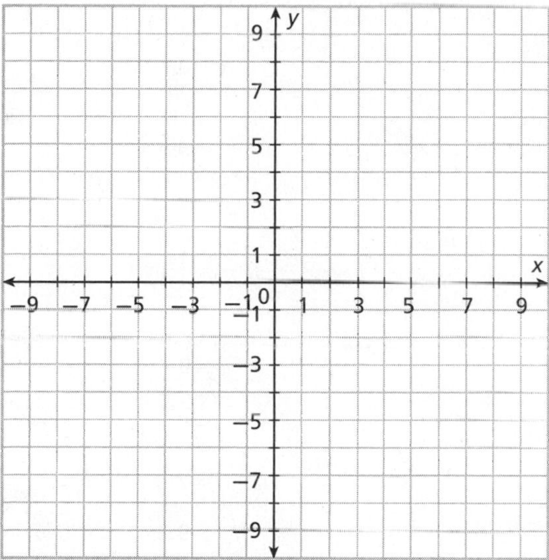

5. $-3x + 6y \geq 2$

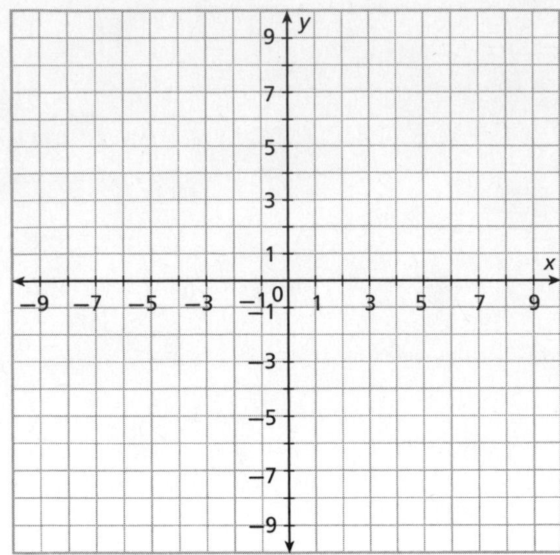

6. $7x - y > 13$

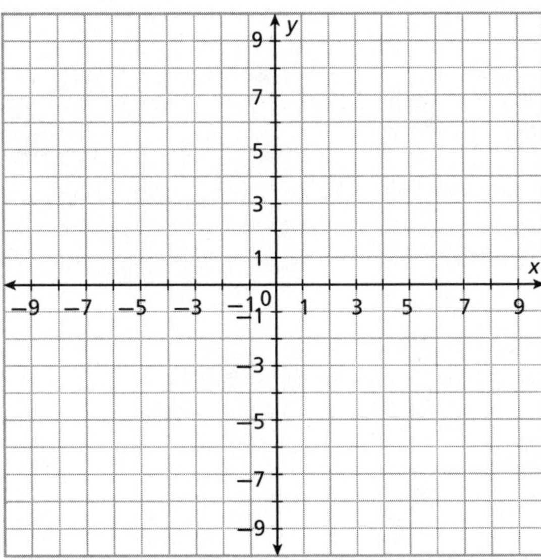

Name ____________________ Class ____________ Date ____________

5-5

Additional Practice

Tell whether the ordered pair is a solution of the given inequality.

1. $(1, 6); y < x + 6$
2. $(-3, -12); y \geq 2x - 5$
3. $(5, -3); y \leq -x + 2$

Graph the solutions of each linear inequality.

4. $y \leq x + 4$

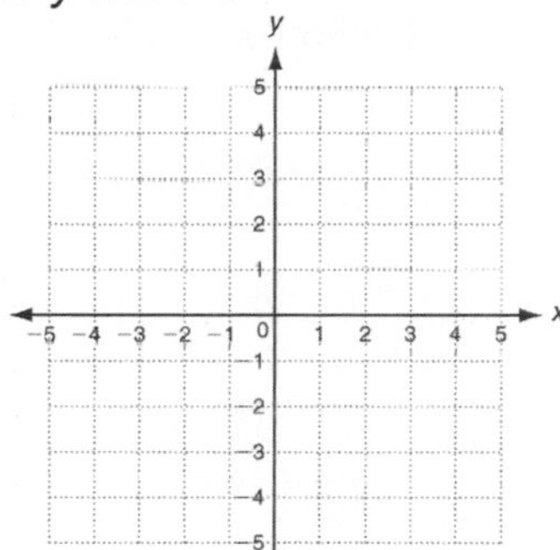

5. $2x + y > -2$

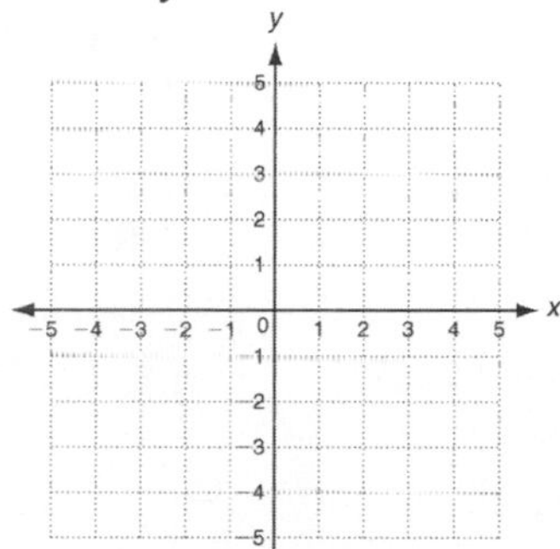

6. $x + y - 1 < 0$

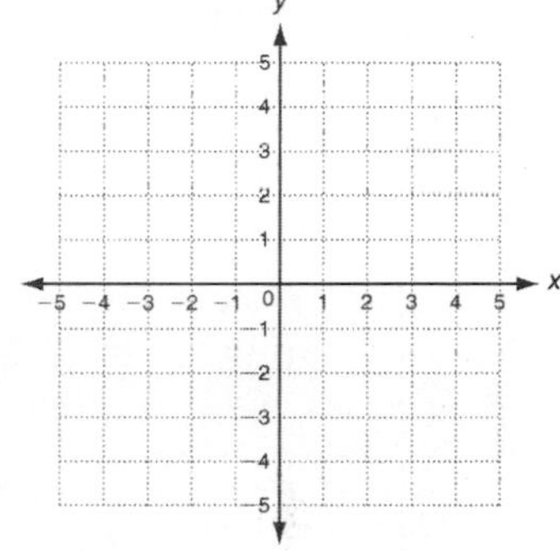

7. Clark is having a party at his house. His father has allowed him to spend at most \$20 on snack food. He'd like to buy chips that cost \$4 per bag, and pretzels that cost \$2 per bag.
   a. Write an inequality to describe the situation.
   b. Graph the solutions.
   c. Give two possible combinations of bags of chips and pretzels that Clark can buy.

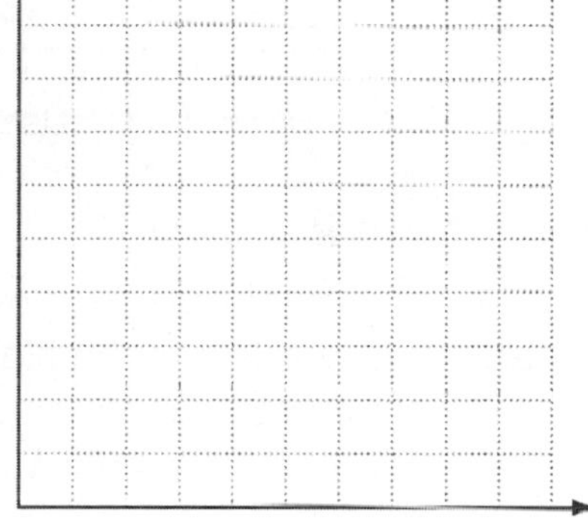

Write an inequality to represent each graph.

8.

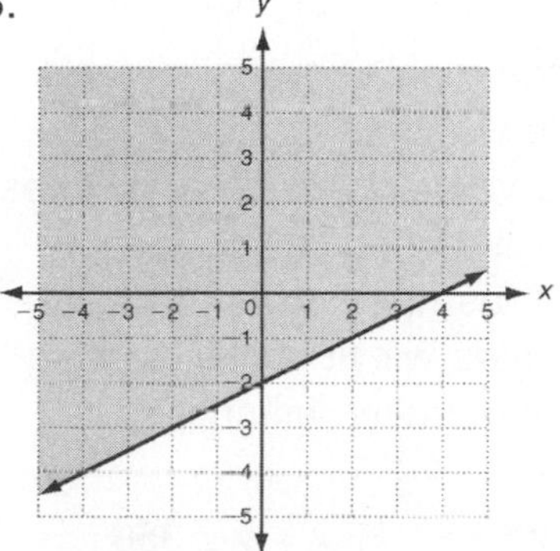

9.

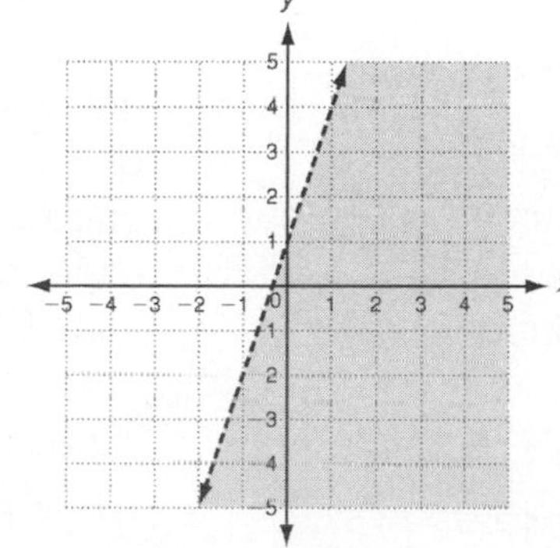

10.

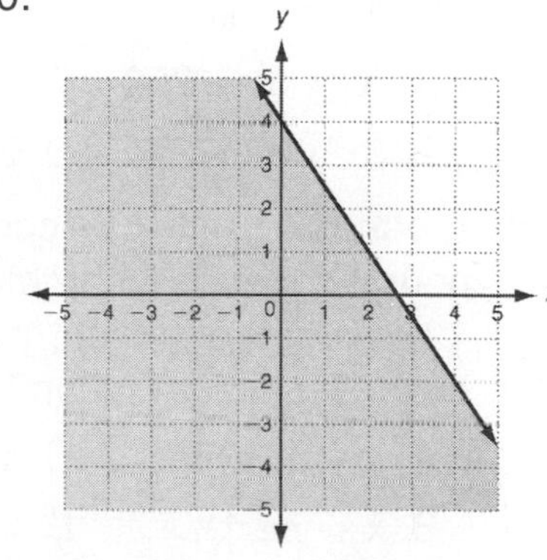

Problem Solving

Write the correct answer.

1. Shania would like to give \$5 gift cards and \$4 teddy bears as party favors. Sixteen people have been invited to the party. Shania has \$100 to spend on party favors. Write and graph an inequality to find the number of gift cards x and teddy bears y Shania could purchase.

____

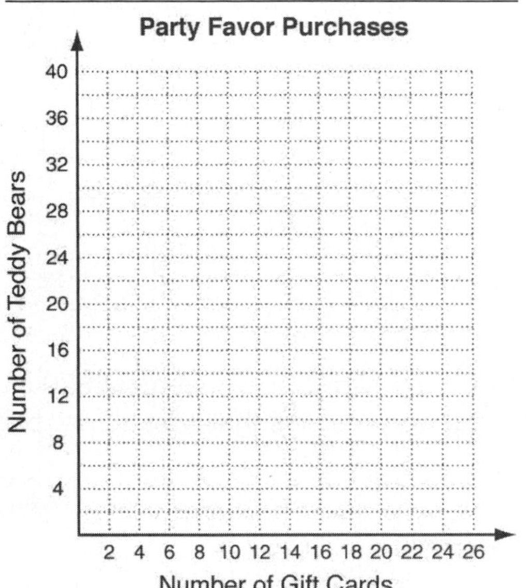

2. Hank has 20 yards of lumber that he can use to build a raised garden. Write and graph a linear inequality that describes the possible lengths and widths of the garden. If Hank wants the dimensions to be whole numbers only, what dimensions would produce the largest area?

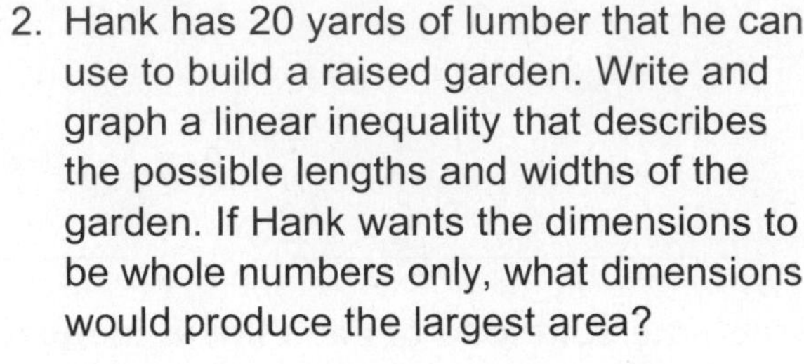

____

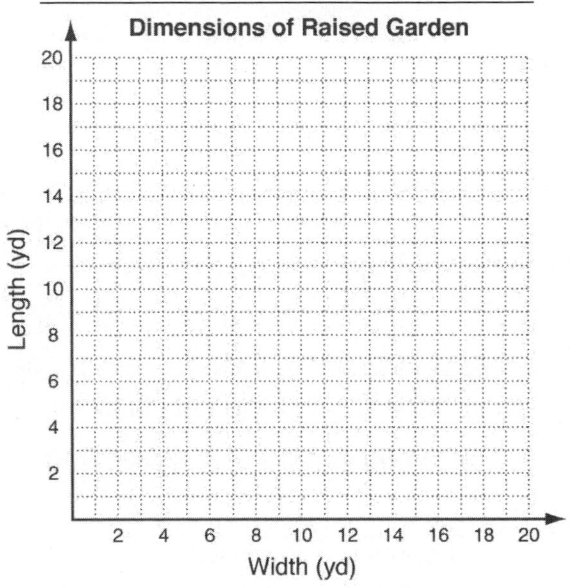

Select the best answer.

3. The royalties for the high school play are \$250. Tickets to the play cost \$5 for students and \$8 for nonstudents. What linear inequality describes the number of student and nonstudent tickets that need to be sold so that the drama class can pay the royalties?

   A $5x + 8y \geq 250$　　C $5xy + 8 < 250$

   B $5x + 8y > 250$　　D $5xy + 8 \geq 250$

4. The inequality $x + y \leq 8$ describes the amounts of two juices Annette combines to make a smoothie. Which is a solution to the inequality?

   F (3, 6)　　H (7, 2)

   G (6, 1)　　J (0, 10)

5. A baker is making chocolate and lemon pound cakes. He can make at most 12 cakes at one time. Which inequality describes the situation?

   A $x + y > 12$　　C $x + y \leq 12$

   B $x + y \geq 12$　　D $x + y < 12$

6. Erasmus is the master gardener for a university. He wants to plant a mixture of purple and yellow pansies at the west entrance to the campus. From past experience, Erasmus knows that fewer than 350 pansies will fit in the planting area. Which inequality describes the situation?

   F $x + y \geq 350$　　H $x + y \leq 350$

   G $x + y > 350$　　J $x + y < 350$

Name________________ Class________ Date________

5-6

Solving Systems of Linear Inequalities

Focus on Modeling

Essential question: *How can you use systems of linear equations or inequalities to model and solve contextual problems?*

COMMON CORE

CC.9-12.N.Q.1*, CC.9-12.N.Q.2*, CC.9-12.A.CED.2*, CC.9-12.A.CED.3*, CC.9-12.A.REI.6, CC.9-12.A.REI.12

You are purchasing jeans and T-shirts. Jeans cost \$35 and T-shirts cost \$15. You plan on spending \$115 and purchasing a total of 5 items. How many pairs of jeans and how many T-shirts can you buy?

1 Write a system of linear equations to model the situation.

A Write an expression to represent the amount you will pay for x pairs of jeans at \$35 per pair.

____

B Write an expression to represent the amount you will pay for y T-shirts at \$15 per shirt.

____

C The total amount spent for jeans and T-shirts is given below in words. Use this verbal model and your expressions from Steps 1A and 1B to write an equation for the total amount you will spend.

Amount Spent for Jeans	+	Amount Spent for T-shirts	=	Total Amount Spent
	+		=	

D What variable represents the number of pairs of jeans purchased?

____

E What variable represents the number of T-shirts purchased?

____

F Write an equation to represent the total number of items purchased.

____

G Write a system of linear equations to model the situation.

____

REFLECT

1a. What units are associated with the expressions that you wrote in 1A and 1B?

1b. When you add the units for the expressions representing the amounts spent on jeans and T-shirts, what units do you get for total amount spent? Are they the units you expect?

2 Solve the system algebraically.

A Solve an equation for one variable.

$x + y = 5$ Select one of the equations.

$y =$ ____ Isolate the variable y on one side.

B Substitute the expression for y into the other equation and solve.

$35x + 15($ ____ $) = 115$ Substitute the expression for the variable y.

$35x +$ ____ $+ 75 = 115$ Use the Distributive Property.

____ $+ 75 = 115$ Combine like terms.

____ $= 40$ Subtract ____ from each side.

$x =$ ____ Divide each side by ______.

C Substitute the value of the variable you found in Part B into one of the equations and solve for the other variable.

____ $+ y = 5$ Substitute the value you found into an equation.

$y =$ ____ Subtract ____ from each side.

So, ______ is the solution of the system.

REFLECT

2a. In the solution, what does the x-value of the ordered pair represent in the context of the situation? What does the y-value represent?

2b. Explain why substitution is a good method to use to solve this system.

3 Check the solution by graphing.

A Graph each equation.

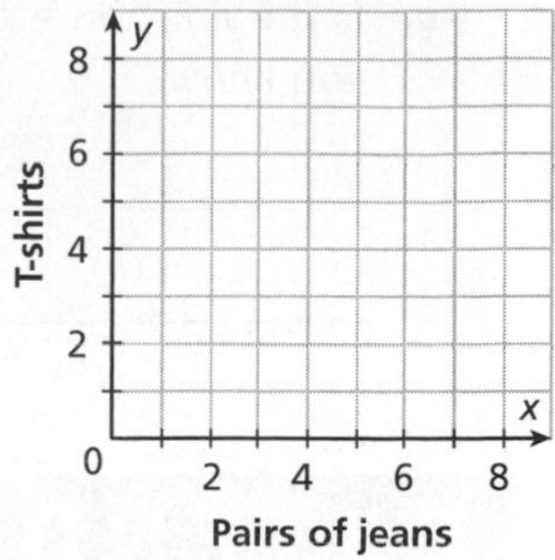

Step 1: Find the intercepts for $35x + 15y = 115$ and graph the line.

***x*-intercept:** ______ ***y*-intercept:** ______

Step 2: Find the intercepts for $x + y = 5$ and graph the line.

***x*-intercept:** ______ ***y*-intercept:** ______

B Find the point of intersection.

The two lines appear to intersect at ______.

REFLECT

3a. What units are represented on the x-axis?

____

3b. What units are represented on the y-axis?

____

3c. Does the solution you found by graphing confirm that the solution you found algebraically was correct? Explain.

____

____

3d. Was it easier to solve the system algebraically or by graphing? Explain your reasoning.

____

____

4 Interpret the solution.

A What does the solution tell you about the number of pairs of jeans and the number of T-shirts you can purchase?

____

B In the context of the problem, what could be the values of x and y?

____

C Is the solution reasonable? Explain your reasoning.

____

____

____

REFLECT

4a. Is the solution you found the only solution for this linear system? Explain how you know.

EXTEND

1. Suppose you want to buy at least 5 items and spend no more than $115. How can you modify the system of linear equations you wrote to model this new situation?

2. Write an inequality to represent buying at least 5 items.

3. Write an inequality to represent spending no more than $115.

4. Are there any other conditions on the system, based on the context of the problem? If so, what are they?

5. Write a system of linear inequalities to model the situation. Include any new conditions from Question 4.

6. What constraints do the additional conditions based on the context of the problem place on where in the plane the solution region will be located?

7. Graph the system of inequalities.

Step 1 Graph $x + y \geq 5$.

The equation of the boundary line is ____________.

***x*-intercept:** ______ ***y*-intercept:** ______

The inequality symbol is $\geq$, use a __________ line.

Shade ________ the boundary line, because (0, 0) is *not* a solution of the inequality.

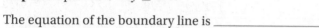

Step 2 Graph $35x + 15y \leq 115$.

The equation of the boundary line is ________________.

***x*-intercept:** ______ ***y*-intercept:** ______

The inequality symbol is $\leq$, use a __________ line.

Shade ________ the boundary line line, because (0, 0) *is* a solution of the inequality.

Step 3 Identify the solutions.

The solutions of the system are represented by the ____________ shaded regions that form a __________ to the __________ of the y-axis.

8. In the context of the situation, are all points in the overlapping shaded region possible solutions? Why or why not? Explain.

____

____

9. Is the ordered pair that was the solution of the system of linear equations for this situation a solution of this system of inequalities?

____

____

10. If you buy at least 5 items and spend no more than $115, what is the greatest number of jeans you can buy? Explain your reasoning.

____

____

11. If you buy at least 5 items and spend no more than $115, what is the greatest number of T-shirts you can buy? Explain your reasoning.

____

____

12. Use the graph to make a list of all the possible solutions for the number of pairs of jeans and number of T-shirts you can purchase if you buy at least 5 items and spend no more than $115.

Pairs of Jeans	T-Shirts	Total Items	Total Cost

Name_______________________ Class_______________ Date_____________

5-6

Additional Practice

Tell whether the ordered pair is a solution of the given system.

1. $(2, -2); \begin{cases} y < x - 3 \\ y > -x + 1 \end{cases}$ ________________

2. $(2, 5); \begin{cases} y > 2x \\ y \geq x + 2 \end{cases}$ ________________

3. $(1, 3); \begin{cases} y \leq x + 2 \\ y > 4x - 1 \end{cases}$ ________________

Graph the system of linear inequalities. a. Give two ordered pairs that are solutions. b. Give two ordered pairs that are not solutions.

4. $\begin{cases} y \leq x + 4 \\ y \geq -2x \end{cases}$

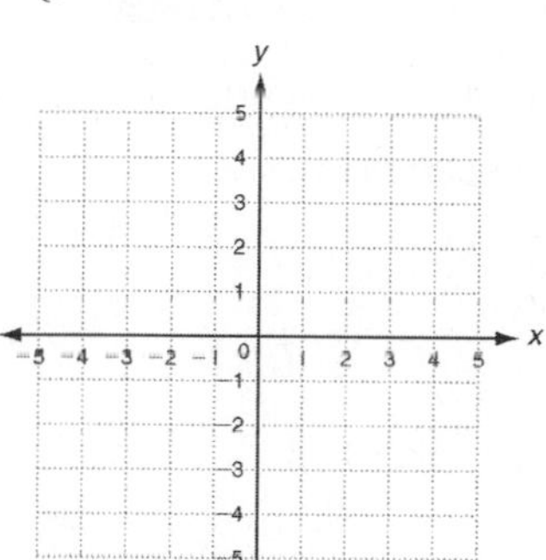

a. ________________

b. ________________

5. $\begin{cases} y \leq \frac{1}{2}x + 1 \\ x + y < 3 \end{cases}$

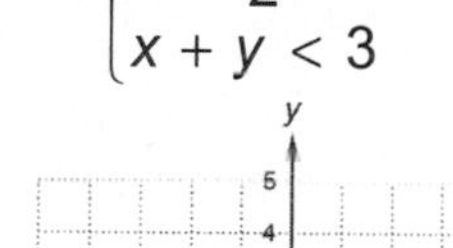

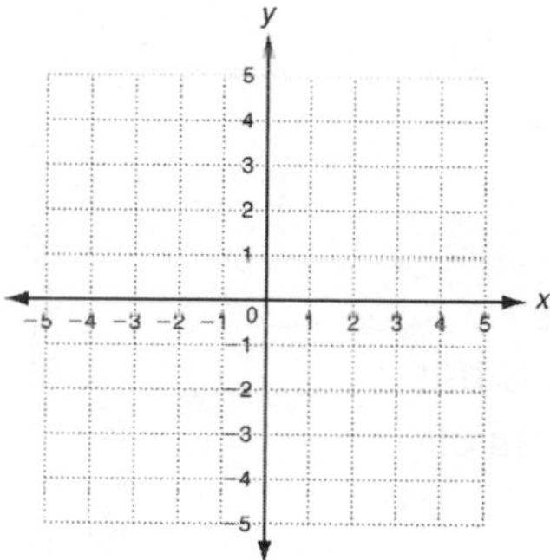

a. ________________

b. ________________

6. $\begin{cases} y > x - 4 \\ y < x + 2 \end{cases}$

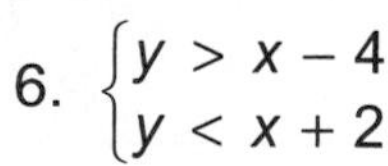

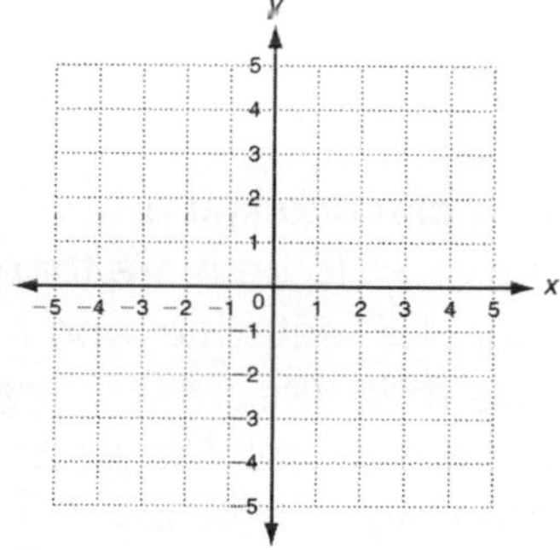

a. ________________

b. ________________

7. Charlene makes \$10 per hour babysitting and \$5 per hour gardening. She wants to make at least \$80 a week, but can work no more than 12 hours a week.

   a. Write a system of linear equations.

   ____

   b. Graph the solutions of the system.

   c. Describe all the possible combinations of hours that Charlene could work at each job.

   ____

   ____

   d. List two possible combinations. ________________________________

   ____

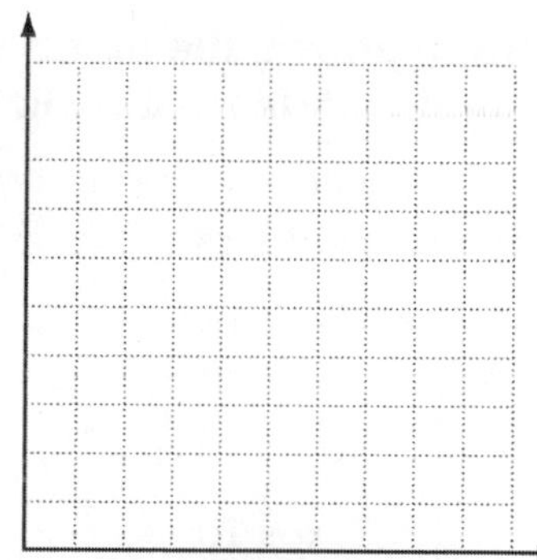

Problem Solving

Write the correct answer.

1. Paul earns \$7 per hour at the bagel shop and \$12 per hour mowing lawns. Paul needs to earn at least \$120 per week, but he must work less than 30 hours per week. Write and graph the system of linear inequalities that describes this situation.

   ____

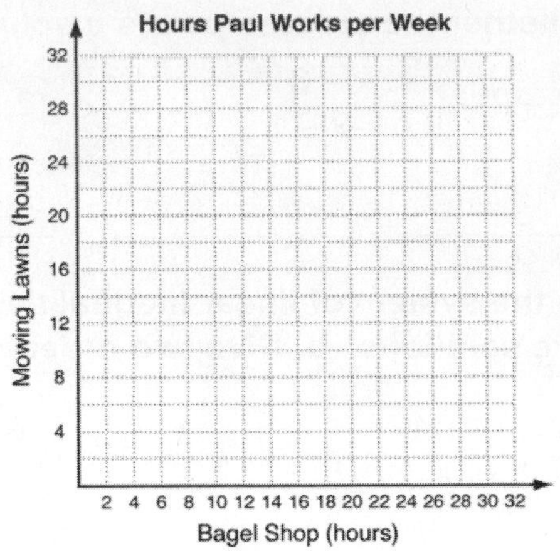

2. Zoe plans to knit a scarf. She wants the scarf to be more than 1 but less than 1.5 feet wide, and more than 6 but less than 8 feet long. Graph all possible dimensions of Zoe's scarf. List two possible combinations.

   ____

   ____

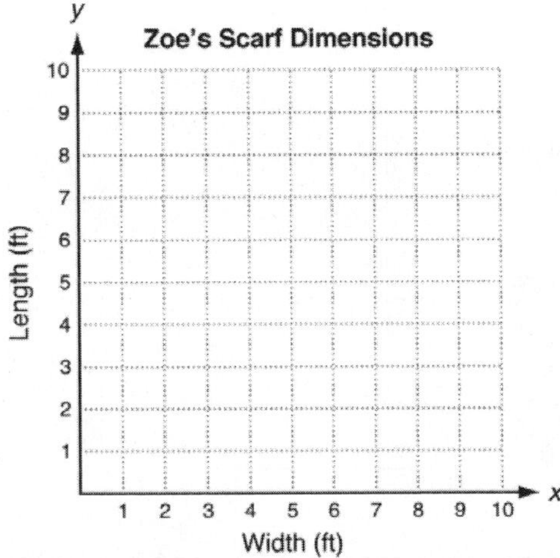

The graph shows the numbers of two types of custom wood tables that can be made to fit a client's needs. Select the best answer.

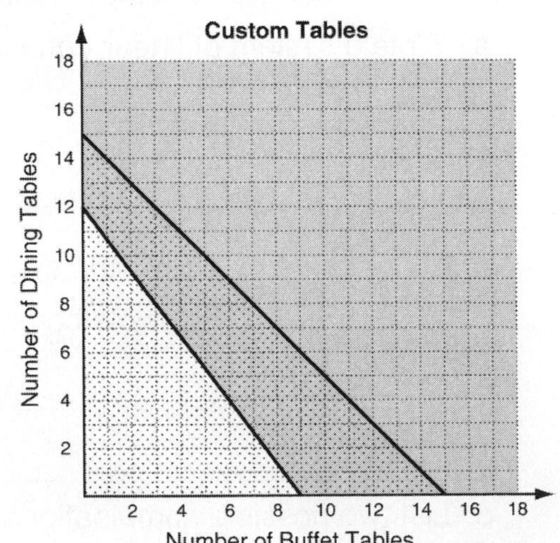

3. Which system of linear inequalities represents the graph?

   A $\begin{cases} x + y \le 15 \\ y \ge 12 - \dfrac{4}{3}x \end{cases}$ C $\begin{cases} x + y \ge 15 \\ y \ge \dfrac{4}{3}x - 12 \end{cases}$

   B $\begin{cases} y \le x + 15 \\ y \ge 12 - \dfrac{4}{3}x \end{cases}$ D $\begin{cases} y \le 15 - x \\ y \le \dfrac{4}{3}x - 12 \end{cases}$

4. If 6 buffet tables are built, which can NOT be the number of dining tables built?

   F 4 H 8

   G 6 J 10

Name________________ Class____________ Date________

Performance Tasks

COMMON CORE

CC.9-12.A.CED.2
CC.9-12.A.CED.3
CC.9-12.A.REI.6
CC.9-12.A.REI.12

1. A model for the number of pounds of kiwis consumers are willing to buy, called the demand, is given by $q = -400p + 1500$, where p is the price per pound and q is the quantity in pounds. The amount of kiwis producers are willing to supply is given by $q = 200p$. Find the price for kiwis when supply and demand are equal..

2. Owners of a coffee shop purchased 60 pounds of Guatemalan coffee beans and 90 pounds of Nicaraguan coffee beans. The total purchase price was $180. The next week they purchased 80 pounds of Guatemalan coffee and 20 pounds of Nicaraguan coffee, and the cost was $100. Write and solve a system of equations to find the cost per pound for both the Guatemalan and Nicaraguan coffee beans.

3. A boat takes 6.5 hours to make a 70-mile trip upstream and 5 hours on the 70-mile return trip. Let v be the speed of the boat in still water, and c be the speed of the current. The upstream speed of the boat is $v - c$ and the downstream boat speed is $v + c$.

   a. Write two equations, one for the upstream part of the trip and one for the downstream part, relating boat speed, distance, and time.

   b. Solve the equations in part **a** for the speed of the current. Round your answer to the nearest tenth of a mile per hour and show your work.

continued

c. How long would it take the boat to travel the 70 miles if there were no current? Round your answer to the nearest minute and show your work.

★★★ **4.** Students are raising money for a field trip by selling scented candles and specialty soap. The candles cost $0.75 each and will be sold for $1.75, and the soap costs $1.25 per bar and will be sold for $3.25. The students need to raise at least $200 to cover their trip costs.

a. Write an inequality that relates the number of candles *c* and the number of bars of soap *s* to the needed income.

b. The wholesaler can supply no more than 80 bars of soap and no more than 140 candles. Graph the inequality from part **a** and these constraints, using number of candles for the vertical axis.

c. What does the shaded area of your graph represent?

Name ______________________ Class ______________ Date ________

MULTIPLE CHOICE

1. Which system of linear equations is represented by the graph shown below?

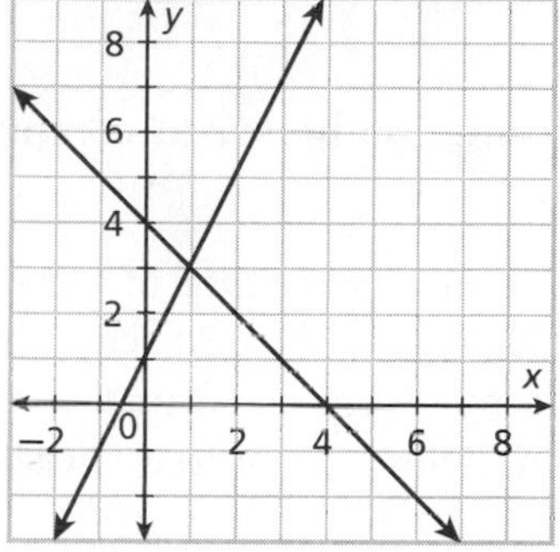

A. $\begin{cases} x + y = 4 \\ 2x + y = 1 \end{cases}$

B. $\begin{cases} x + y = 4 \\ 2x - y = -1 \end{cases}$

C. $\begin{cases} x - y = 4 \\ 2x - y = -1 \end{cases}$

D. $\begin{cases} x + y = 4 \\ x - 2y = 1 \end{cases}$

2. Katy is solving the linear system below by substitution.

$$\begin{cases} 2x + y = 7 \\ 3x - 2y = -7 \end{cases}$$

Which of the following would be a step in solving the system?

F. Substitute $y + 7$ for x in $3x - 2y = -7$.

G. Substitute $-y + 7$ for x in $3x - 2y = -7$.

H. Substitute $-2x + 7$ for y in $3x - 2y = -7$.

J. Substitute $2x - 7$ for y in $3x - 2y = -7$.

3. Which step can be taken to eliminate a variable from the linear system below?

$$\begin{cases} -4x + 2y = -2 \\ 4x - 3y = -1 \end{cases}$$

A. Add to eliminate the variable x.

B. Subtract to eliminate the variable x.

C. Add to eliminate the variable y.

D. Subtract to eliminate the variable y.

4. Frank wants to eliminate the variable y from the system below by adding.

$$\begin{cases} 7x - 6y = 8 \\ 2x + 2y = 6 \end{cases}$$

First, he will have to multiply one of the equations by a number. Which step will enable him to eliminate y by adding?

F. Multiply each term in $7x - 6y = 8$ by 3.

G. Multiply each term in $7x - 6y = 8$ by -3.

H. Multiply each term in $2x + 2y = 6$ by 3.

J. Multiply each term in $2x + 2y = 6$ by -3.

5. Which ordered pair is *not* a solution of the system of linear inequalities graphed below?

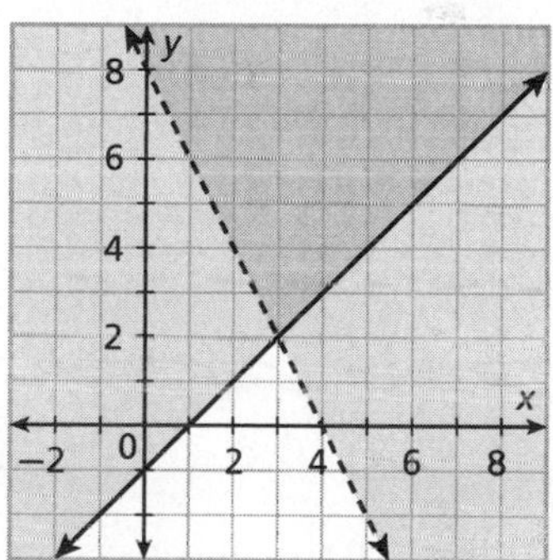

A. (1, 7)

B. (2, 5)

C. (3, 2)

D. (4, 3)

6. You are purchasing paint and paintbrushes for an art project. Tubes of paint cost $6 each and paintbrushes cost $8 each. You plan on spending $60 and purchasing a total of 9 items. Which linear system best represents the situation?

F. $\begin{cases} 6x + 8y = 9 \\ x + y = 60 \end{cases}$

G. $\begin{cases} 6x + 9y = 60 \\ 9x + 8y = 60 \end{cases}$

H. $\begin{cases} 9x + 9y = 60 \\ 6x + 8y = 60 \end{cases}$

J. $\begin{cases} x + y = 9 \\ 6x + 8y = 60 \end{cases}$

7. Which description fits the graph of $x > 4$?

A. Vertical solid line shaded to the right

B. Horizontal dashed line shaded above

C. Horizontal solid line shaded above

D. Vertical dashed line shaded to the right

CONSTRUCTED RESPONSE

8. A system of two linear equations has no solution. Describe the graph of the system.

____

____

____

9. Solve the linear system below. Describe the steps you used to solve it.

$$\begin{cases} 2x + 3y = 13 \\ x - 2y = 3 \end{cases}$$

____

____

____

____

____

10. Pilar says that the two linear systems below have the same solution.

$$\begin{cases} 3x + 2y = 2 \\ 5x + 4y = 6 \end{cases} \qquad \begin{cases} 3x + 2y = 2 \\ 11x + 8y = 10 \end{cases}$$

Is she correct? Explain.

____

____

____

____

____

____

____

11. Graph the solution to $3x - 4y \leq 1$.

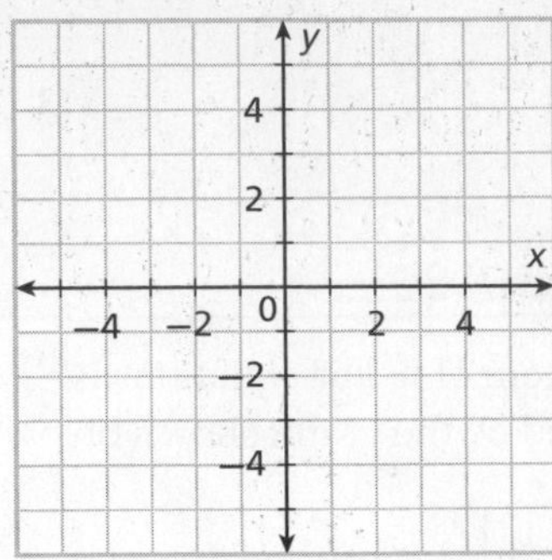

Use the information below to complete Items 12–14.

Terrance purchased a total of 10 pens and pencils for \$4. Pens cost 50 cents and pencils cost 25 cents. Terrance wrote the system of equations below to represent the situation.

$$\begin{cases} x + y = 10 \\ \frac{1}{2}x + \frac{1}{4}y = 4 \end{cases}$$

12. What units are associated with the expressions in the second equation?

____

____

____

____

13. Describe the constraint that each equation places on the system.

____

____

____

____

14. Are there any other constraints on the system? If so, what are they?

____

____

____

Exponents and Polynomials

Chapter Focus

In this chapter you will learn the relationship between rational exponents and radicals. You will apply rules of exponents for integers to rational exponents in order to simplify expressions. You will also perform operations with polynomials.

Chapter at a Glance

COMMON CORE

Lesson		Standards for Mathematical Content
6-1	Integer Exponents	CC.9-12.N.RN.1
6-2	Rational Exponents	CC.9-12.N.RN.1, CC.9-12.N.RN.2, CC.9-12.N.RN.3
6-3	Polynomials	CC.9-12.A.SSE.1, CC.9-12.A.SSE.1a, CC.9-12.A.SSE.1b
6-4	Adding and Subtracting Polynomials	CC.9-12.A.APR.1, CC.9-12.F.BF.1a
6-5	Multiplying Polynomials	CC.9-12.A.SSE.2, CC.9-12.A.APR.1
6-6	Special Products of Binomials	CC.9-12.A.SSE.2
	Performance Tasks	
	Assessment Readiness	

Unpacking the Standards

Understanding the standards and the vocabulary terms in the standards will help you know exactly what you are expected to learn in this chapter.

COMMON CORE **CC.9-12.N.RN.2**

Rewrite expressions involving radicals and rational exponents using the properties of exponents.

Key Vocabulary

expression *(expresión)* A mathematical phrase that contains operations, numbers, and/or variables.

radical *(radical)* An indicated root of a quantity.

rational exponent *(exponente racional)* An exponent that can be expressed as $\frac{m}{n}$ such that if m and n are integers, then $b^{\frac{m}{n}} = \sqrt[n]{b^m} = \left(\sqrt[n]{b}\right)^m$.

exponent *(exponente)* The number that indicates how many times the base in a power is used as a factor.

What It Means For You — Lesson 6-2

You can translate between radical expressions and expressions with rational exponents in order to simplify them.

EXAMPLE

A 16 kilogram (35 pound) dog needs about $72(16)^{\frac{3}{4}}$ Calories per day. You can simplify this expression as shown.

$$72(16)^{\frac{3}{4}} = 72\left(\sqrt[4]{16}\right)^3 \qquad b^{\frac{m}{n}} = \sqrt[n]{b^m} = \left(\sqrt[n]{b}\right)^m$$

$$= 72\left(\sqrt[4]{2^4}\right)^3 \qquad 16 = 2^4$$

$$= 72(2)^3 \qquad \text{The 4th root of } 2^4 \text{ is 2.}$$

$$= 72(8), \text{ or } 576$$

CHAPTER 6

COMMON CORE **CC.9-12.A.SSE.1a**

Interpret parts of an expression, such as terms, factors, and coefficients.

Key Vocabulary

term of an expression *(término de una expresión)* The parts of the expression that are added or subtracted.

factor *(factor)* A number or expression that is multiplied by another number or expression to get a product.

coefficient *(coeficiente)* A number that is multiplied by a variable.

What It Means For You — Lesson 6-3

In an expression that models a real-world context, the different parts of the expression represent different aspects of the situation.

EXAMPLE

The expression below represents the height in feet of a firework t seconds after being fired.

$$\underbrace{-16t^2}_{\text{1st term}} + \underbrace{200t}_{\text{2nd term}} + \underbrace{6}_{\text{3rd term}}$$

The terms and coefficients each represent something different.

−16: This accounts for Earth's gravity.
200: This is the speed at which the firework was shot.
6: This is the height from which the firework was shot.

CC.9-12.A.APR.1

Understand that polynomials form a system analogous to the integers, namely, they are closed under the operations of addition, subtraction, and multiplication; add, subtract, and multiply polynomials.

Key Vocabulary

polynomial *(polinomio)* A monomial or a sum or difference of monomials.
closure *(cerradura)* A set of numbers is said to be closed, or have closure, under a given operation if the result of the operation on any two numbers in the set is also in the set.

What It Means For You Lessons 6-4, 6-5, 6-6

When you add, subtract, or multiply two integers, the result is always another integer. The same is true for polynomials. The sum, difference, or product of two polynomials is always a polynomial.

EXAMPLE

The method of multiplying two binomials called FOIL actually relies on the distributive property. The letters stand for the First, Outer, Inner, and Last terms of the expression.

$$(x+3)(x+2) = x^2 + 2x + 3x + 6$$

F O I L

Adding the like terms **$2x$** and **$3x$** gives the final result:

$$(x+3)(x+2) = x^2 + 5x + 6$$

CC.9-12.A.CED.2

Create equations in two or more variables to represent relationships between quantities; graph equations on coordinate axes with labels and scales.

Key Vocabulary

equation *(ecuación)* A mathematical statement that two expressions are equivalent.

What It Means For You Lesson 6-4

You can use formulas and other equations in many real-world contexts to model known relationships between different quantities.

EXAMPLE

The shape of the dulcimer in the diagram is a trapezoid. The base lengths are expressed in terms of the height. You can use the formula for the area of a trapezoid to express the relationship between the height h of the dulcimer and its area A.

$b_2 = h + 1$

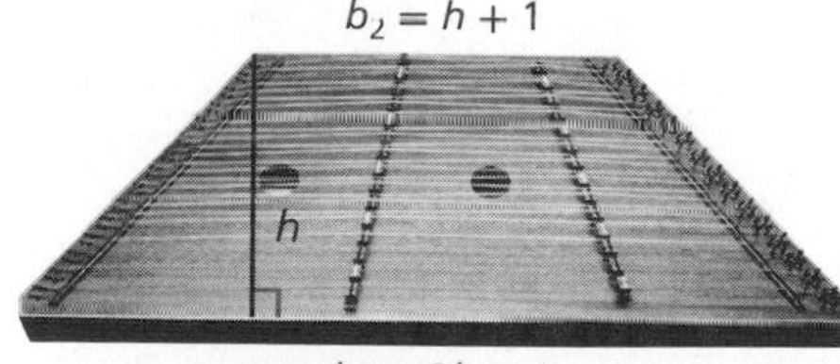

$b_1 = 2h - 1$

$$A = \frac{1}{2}h(b_1 + b_2) = \frac{1}{2}h[(2h-1) + (h+1)]$$

Simplifying the expression gives $A = \frac{3}{2}h^2$.

CHAPTER 6

CHAPTER 6

Key Vocabulary

binomial *(binomio)* A polynomial with two terms.

closure *(cerradura)* A set of numbers is said to be closed, or have closure, under a given operation if the result of the operation on any two numbers in the set is also in the set.

coefficient *(coeficiente)* A number that is multiplied by a variable.

constant *(constante)* A value that does not change.

equation *(ecuación)* A mathematical statement that two expressions are equivalent.

exponent *(exponente)* The number that indicates how many times the base in a power is used as a factor.

expression *(expresión)* A mathematical phrase that contains operations, numbers, and/or variables.

factor *(factor)* A number or expression that is multiplied by another number or expression to get a product.

monomial *(monomio)* A number or a product of numbers and variables with whole-number exponents, or a polynomial with one term.

polynomial *(polinomio)* A monomial or a sum or difference of monomials.

radical *(radical)* An indicated root of a quantity.

radical expression *(expresión radical)* An expression that contains a radical sign.

rational exponent *(exponente racional)* An exponent that can be expressed as $\frac{m}{n}$ such that if m and n are integers, then $b^{\frac{m}{n}} = \sqrt[n]{b^m} = \left(\sqrt[n]{b}\right)^m$.

term of an expression *(término de una expresión)* The parts of the expression that are added or subtracted.

variable *(variable)* A symbol used to represent a quantity that can change.

Name_____________ Class_____________ Date_________

6-1

Integer Exponents

Going Deeper

Essential question: *How can you develop and use the properties of integer exponents?*

Video Tutor

PREP FOR CC.9-12.N.RN.1

1 EXPLORE Using Patterns of Integer Exponents

The table below shows powers of 5, 4, and 3.

$5^4 = 625$	$5^3 = 125$	$5^2 = 25$	$5^1 = 5$	$5^0 =$	$5^{-1} =$	$5^{-2} =$
$4^4 = 256$	$4^3 = 64$	$4^2 = 16$	$4^1 = 4$	$4^0 =$	$4^{-1} =$	$4^{-2} =$
$3^4 = 81$	$3^3 = 27$	$3^2 = 9$	$3^1 = 3$	$3^0 =$	$3^{-1} =$	$3^{-2} =$

A What pattern do you see in the powers of 5?

____

____

B What pattern do you see in the powers of 4?

____

____

C Complete the table for the values of 5^0, 5^{-1}, 5^{-2}.

D Complete the table for the values of 4^0, 4^{-1}, 4^{-2}.

E Complete the table for the values of 3^0, 3^{-1}, 3^{-2}.

F **Conjecture** Write a general rule for the values of a^0 and a^{-n} based on the patterns in the table.

____

REFLECT

1a. Do the general rules you wrote in Part F for a^0 and a^{-n} apply when $a = 0$? Explain.

____

____

____

PREP FOR CC.9-12.N.RN.1

2 EXPLORE Applying Properties of Integer Exponents

A Complete the following equations.

$3 \cdot 3 \cdot 3 \cdot 3 \cdot 3 = 3^{\square}$

$(3 \cdot 3 \cdot 3 \cdot 3) \cdot 3 = 3^{\square} \cdot 3^{\square} = 3^{\square}$

$(3 \cdot 3 \cdot 3) \cdot (3 \cdot 3) = 3^{\square} \cdot 3^{\square} = 3^{\square}$

What pattern do you see when multiplying two powers with the same base?

____

____

Use your pattern to complete this equation: $5^2 \cdot 5^5 = 5^{\square}$.

Conjecture Write a general rule for the result of $a^m \cdot a^n$. ____________________

B Complete the following equation: $\frac{4^5}{4^3} = \frac{4 \cdot 4 \cdot 4 \cdot 4 \cdot 4}{4 \cdot 4 \cdot 4} = \frac{\overset{1}{\cancel{4}} \cdot \overset{1}{\cancel{4}} \cdot \overset{1}{\cancel{4}} \cdot 4 \cdot 4}{\underset{1}{\cancel{4}} \cdot \underset{1}{\cancel{4}} \cdot \underset{1}{\cancel{4}}} = 4 \cdot 4 = 4^{\square}$

What pattern do you see when dividing two powers with the same base?

____

____

Use your pattern to complete this equation: $\frac{6^8}{6^3} = 6^{\square}$.

Conjecture Write a general rule for the result of $\frac{a^m}{a^n}$. ____________________

C Complete the following equations:

$(5^3)^2 = (5 \cdot 5 \cdot 5)^{\square}$

$= (5 \cdot 5 \cdot 5) \cdot (5 \cdot 5 \cdot 5)$

$= 5^{\square}$

What pattern do you see when raising a power to a power?

____

____

Use your pattern to complete this equation: $(7^2)^4 = 7^{\square}$.

Conjecture Write a general rule for the result of $(a^m)^n$. ____________________

REFLECT

2a. Do the general rules you wrote in Parts A, B, and C apply if $a = 0$? Explain. (Assume m and n are not 0.)

____

____

____

PREP FOR CC.9-12.N.RN.1

3 EXAMPLE Applying Properties of Integer Exponents

Simplify each expression.

A $(5-2)^5 \cdot 3^{-8} + (5+2)^0$

$(5-2)^5 \cdot 3^{-8} + (5+2)^0$ Follow the order of operations.

$(\quad)^5 \cdot 3^{-8} + (\quad)^0$ Simplify within parentheses.

$3^{\square} + \square$ Use properties of exponents.

$3^{\square} + \square$ Simplify.

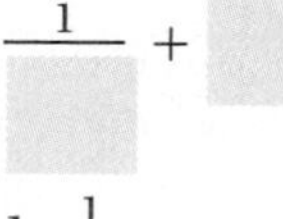

$\frac{1}{\square} + \square$ Add.

$1\frac{1}{\square}$

B $(10-6)^3 \cdot 4^2 + (10+2)^2$

$(10-6)^3 \cdot 4^2 + (10+2)^2$ Follow the order of operations.

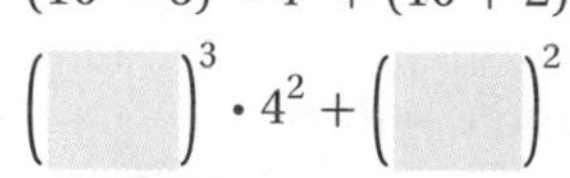

$(\quad)^3 \cdot 4^2 + (\quad)^2$ Simplify within parentheses.

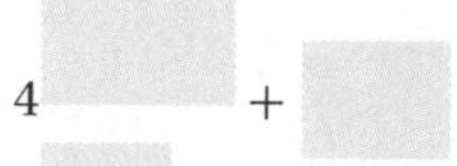

$4^{\square} + \square$ Use properties of exponents.

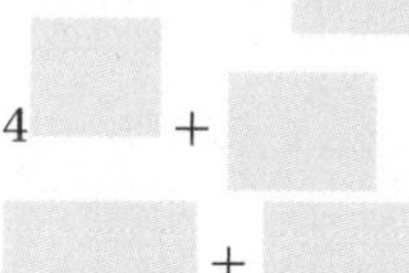

$4^{\square} + \square$ Simplify.

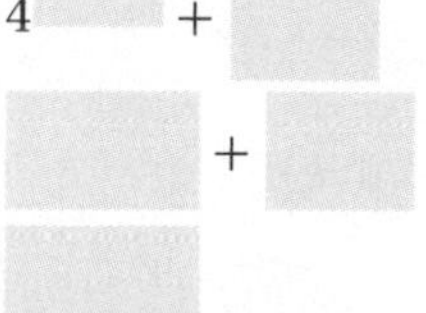

$\square + \square$ Add.

$\square$

REFLECT

3a. Describe a different method you could use to simplify each expression above that does not use properties of exponents.

____

____

____

PRACTICE

Find the value of each power.

1. 7^{-2} ______

2. 15^{0} ______

3. 10^{-3} ______

4. 2^{-5} ______

5. 5^{-3} ______

6. 7^{3} ______

Use properties of integers to write an equivalent expression.

7. $15^{2} \cdot 15^{-5}$ ______

8. $\frac{20^{13}}{20^{10}}$ ______

9. $\frac{14^{4}}{14^{9}}$ ______

10. $(8^{3})^{16}$ ______

11. $(12^{-5})^{3}$ ______

12. $4^{-8} \cdot 4^{-16}$ ______

13. $m \cdot m^{4}$ ______

14. $\frac{r^{9}}{r^{6}}$ ______

15. $(a^{3})^{-3}$ ______

Find the missing exponent.

16. $b^{\square} \cdot b^{2} = b^{8}$

17. $\frac{x^{5}}{x^{\square}} = x^{-2}$

18. $\left(n^{\square}\right)^{4} = n^{0}$

Simplify each expression.

19. $(2 + 4)^{2} + 8^{-6} \times (12 - 4)^{10}$ ______

20. $(3^{3})^{2} \times \left(\frac{(5-2)^{3}}{3^{4}}\right) + (10 - 4)^{2} \times 6^{10}$ ______

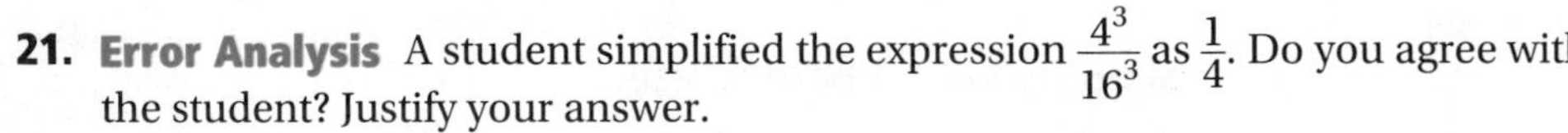

21. **Error Analysis** A student simplified the expression $\frac{4^{3}}{16^{3}}$ as $\frac{1}{4}$. Do you agree with the student? Justify your answer.

______

22. Find the values of $x^{5} \cdot x^{-3}$ and $\frac{x^{5}}{x^{3}}$. What do you notice about the two values? Explain why your results make sense based on the properties you learned in this lesson.

______

Name ____________ Class ________ Date ________

6-1

Additional Practice

Simplify.

1. $5^{-3} = \frac{1}{\_\_\_\_\_\_} = \frac{1}{\_\_\_\_\_\_}$

2. $2^{-6} = \frac{1}{\_\_\_\_\_\_} = \frac{1}{\_\_\_\_\_\_}$

3. $(-5)^{-2}$ ________

4. $-(4)^{-3}$ ________

5. -6^{0} ________

6. $(7)^{-2}$ ________

Evaluate each expression for the given value(s) of the variable(s).

7. d^{-3} for $d = -2$ ________

8. a^5b^{-6} for $a = 3$ and $b = 2$ ________

9. $(b - 4)^{-2}$ for $b = 1$ ________

10. $5z^{-x}$ for $z = -3$ and $x = 2$ ________

11. $(5z)^{-x}$ for $z = -3$ and $x = 2$ ________

12. $c^{-3}(16^{-2})$ for $c = 4$ ________

Simplify.

13. t^{-4} ________

14. $3r^{-5}$ ________

15. $\frac{s^{-3}}{t^{-5}}$ ________

16. $\frac{h^0}{3}$ ________

17. $\frac{2x^{-3}y^{-2}}{z^4}$ ________

18. $\frac{4fg^{-5}}{5h^{-3}}$ ________

19. $\frac{14a^{-4}}{20bc^{-1}}$ ________

20. $\frac{a^4c^2e^0}{b^{1}d^{-3}}$ ________

21. $\frac{-3g^{-2}hk^{-2}}{-6h^0}$ ________

22. A cooking website claims to contain 10^5 recipes. Evaluate this expression. ________

23. A ball bearing has diameter 2^{-3} inches. Evaluate this expression. ________

Problem Solving

Write the correct answer.

1. At the 2005 World Exposition in Aichi, Japan, tiny mu-chips were embedded in the admissions tickets to prevent counterfeiting. The mu-chip was developed by Hitachi in 2003. Its area is $4^2(10)^{-2}$ square millimeters. Simplify this expression.

2. Despite their name, Northern Yellow Bats are commonly found in warm, humid areas in the southeast United States. An adult has a wingspan of about 14 inches and weighs between $3(2)^{-3}$ and $3(2)^{-2}$ ounces. Simplify these expressions.

3. Saira is using the formula for the area of a circle to determine the value of π. She is using the expression Ar^{-2} where $A = 50.265$ and $r = 4$. Use a calculator to evaluate Saira's expression to find her approximation of the value of π to the nearest thousandth.

4. The volume of a freshwater tank can be expressed in terms of x, y, and z. Expressed in these terms, the volume of the tank is $x^3y^{-2}z$ liters. Determine the volume of the tank if $x = 4$, $y = 3$, and $z = 6$.

Alison has an interest in entomology, the study of insects. Her collection of insects from around the world includes the four specimens shown in the table below. Select the best answer.

Insect	Mass
Emperor Scorpion	2^{-5} kg
African Goliath Beetle	11^{-1} kg
Giant Weta	2^{-4} kg
Madagascar Hissing Cockroach	5^{-3} kg

5. Cockroaches have been found on every continent, including Antarctica. What is the mass of Alison's Madagascar Hissing Cockroach expressed as a quotient?

   A $-\frac{1}{125}$ kg
   C $\frac{1}{15}$ kg
   B $\frac{1}{125}$ kg
   D 125 kg

6. Many Giant Wetas are so heavy that they cannot jump. Which expression is another way to show the mass of the specimen in Alison's collection?

   F $-(2)4$ kg
   H $\frac{1}{2 \cdot 2 \cdot 2 \cdot 2}$ kg
   G $\left(\frac{1}{2}\right)^{-4}$ kg
   J $4\frac{1}{2}$ kg

7. Scorpions are closely related to spiders and horseshoe crabs. What is the mass of Alison's Emperor Scorpion expressed as a quotient?

   A $-\frac{1}{32}$ kg
   C $\frac{1}{32}$ kg
   B $\frac{1}{25}$ kg
   D 32 kg

Name ______________________ Class ______________ Date ________

6-2

Rational Exponents

Connection: Relating Radicals and Rational Exponents

Essential question: *What are rational and irrational numbers and how are radicals related to rational exponents?*

Video Tutor

CC.9–12.N.RN.3

1 ENGAGE Understanding Real Numbers and Their Properties

The Venn diagram shows the relationship between the set of real numbers and its subsets.

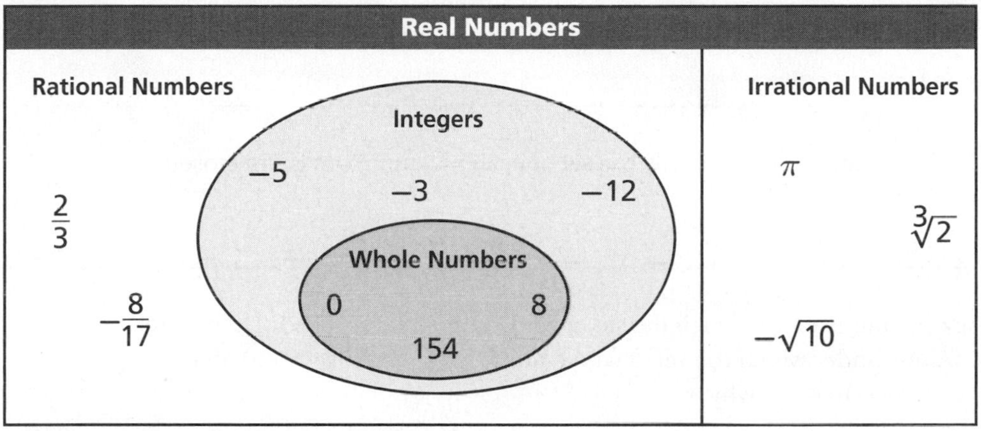

Real Numbers

Rational Numbers: $\frac{2}{3}$, $-\frac{8}{17}$

Integers: -5, -3, -12

Whole Numbers: 0, 8, 154

Irrational Numbers: π, $\sqrt[3]{2}$, $-\sqrt{10}$

A rational number can be expressed in the form $\frac{p}{q}$ where p and q are integers and $q \neq 0$. The decimal form a rational number either terminates or repeats. For instance, $\frac{3}{4} = 0.75$ and $-\frac{5}{6} = -0.8333\ldots$.

An irrational number cannot be written as the quotient of two integers, and its decimal form is nonrepeating and nonterminating. For instance, the decimal form of $\sqrt{3}$, $1.7320508\ldots$, neither repeats nor terminates.

Real numbers, regardless of whether they are rational or irrational, have the following properties with respect to addition and multiplication.

Properties of Real Numbers	
Commutative Property of Addition	$a + b = b + a$
Associative Property of Addition	$(a + b) + c = a + (b + c)$
Additive Identity	The additive identity is 0, because $a + 0 = a$.
Additive Inverse	The additive inverse of a is $-a$, because $a + (-a) = 0$.
Commutative Property of Multiplication	$a \cdot b = b \cdot a$
Associative Property of Multiplication	$(a \cdot b) \cdot c = a \cdot (b \cdot c)$
Multiplicative Identity	The multiplicative identity is 1, because $1(a) = a$.
Multiplicative Inverse	The multiplicative inverse of a for $a \neq 0$ is $\frac{1}{a}$, because $a\left(\frac{1}{a}\right) = 1$.
Distributive Property	$a(b + c) = ab + ac$

A set of numbers is **closed** under an operation if the result of the operation on any two numbers in the set (provided the operation is defined for those two numbers) is another number in that set. To prove that a set is not closed under an operation, you need to find only one counterexample.

Closure of Sets Under the Four Basic Operations				
Set	**Addition**	**Subtraction**	**Multiplication**	**Division**
Real numbers	Yes	Yes	Yes	Yes
Irrational numbers	No	No	No	No
Rational numbers	Yes	Yes	Yes	Yes
Integers	Yes	Yes	Yes	No

REFLECT

1a. Give a counterexample to show why the set of integers is not closed under division.

____

1b. Give a counterexample to show why the set of irrational numbers is not closed under multiplication.

____

1c. State the operations under which the set of whole numbers is closed. Then state the operations under which the set of whole numbers is not closed, and give counterexamples to show why.

____

____

CC.9–12.N.RN.3

2 EXAMPLE Proving That a Set Is Closed

Given that the set of integers is closed under addition and multiplication, prove that the set of rational numbers is closed under addition.

Let a and b be rational numbers.

$a + b = \frac{p}{q} + \frac{r}{s}$ p, q, r, and s are integers with q and s nonzero.

$= \frac{s}{s}\left(\frac{p}{q}\right) + \frac{q}{q}\left(\frac{r}{s}\right)$ Find a common denominator.

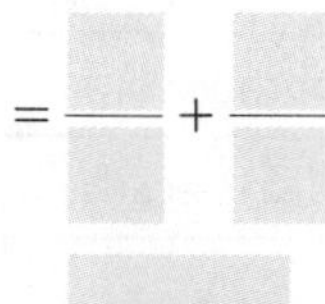

$= \frac{\square}{\square} + \frac{\square}{\square}$ Multiply.

$= \frac{\square}{\square}$ Add the numerators.

Because $ps + qr$ and qs are integers, $\frac{ps + qr}{qs}$ is a rational number.

REFLECT

2a. How do you know that $ps + qr$ and qs are integers?

2b. Why does $a + b = \frac{ps + qr}{qs}$ prove that the set of rational numbers is closed under addition?

2c. Given that the set of rational numbers is closed under addition, how can you prove that the set of rational numbers is closed under subtraction?

An **indirect proof** starts by assuming that what you want to prove is *not* true. If the assumption leads to a contradiction, then the original statement must be true.

CC.9–12.N.RN.3

3 EXAMPLE Proving That the Sum of a Rational Number and an Irrational Number Is Irrational

Given that the set of rational numbers is closed under addition, prove that the sum of a rational number and an irrational number is an irrational number.

Let a be a rational number, let b be an irrational number, and let $a + b = c$. Assume that c is rational.

Rewrite $a + b = c$ as $b = -a + c$ by adding $-a$ to both sides. Because $-a$ and c are both

________ and the set of rational numbers is closed under addition, $-a + c$ must

be ________, which means that b is ________.

This contradicts the condition that b be irrational. So, the assumption that c is rational must be false, which means that c, the sum of a rational number and an irrational number, is ________.

REFLECT

3a. Indirect proof is also called *proof by contradiction.* What is the contradiction in the preceding proof?

3b. Compare an indirect proof to a counterexample.

4 ENGAGE Understanding Radicals and Rational Exponents

A **radical expression** is an expression that is written using the radical sign, $\sqrt{}$. A radical expression has an *index* and a *radicand* as identified below.

Index (a positive integer) → $\sqrt[n]{a}$ ← Radicand (a nonnegative number when n is even; not restricted when n is odd)

Read the expression as "the nth root of a." It represents the number whose nth power is a. (When n is even, a positive number a has two nth roots, one positive and one negative, and $\sqrt[n]{a}$ represents the positive nth root.) When the index is not shown, it is understood to be 2, and the radical is a *square root*. For example, the positive square root of 25, written $\sqrt{25}$, represents 5 because $5^2 = 25$. If the index is 3, then the root is called a *cube root*. For example, the cube root of −8, written $\sqrt[3]{-8}$, is −2 because $(-2)^3 = -8$.

You can write a radical as a power by extending the properties of integer exponents. For instance, you can write $\sqrt{a}$ as a power, a^k, as follows:

$(\sqrt{a})^2 = a$	Definition of square root
$(a^k)^2 = a$	Substitute a^k for $\sqrt{a}$.
$a^{2k} = a^1$	Power of a power property
$2k = 1$	Equate exponents.
$k = \frac{1}{2}$	Solve for k.

So, $\sqrt{a} = a^{\frac{1}{2}}$. This result can be generalized to any nth root of a and any nth root of a power of a.

Converting Between Radical and Rational Exponent Form

If the nth root of a is a real number and m is an integer, then

$$\sqrt[n]{a} = a^{\frac{1}{n}} \text{ and } \sqrt[n]{a^m} = a^{\frac{m}{n}}.$$

REFLECT

4a. Explain why it makes sense that $\sqrt[3]{a} = a^{\frac{1}{3}}$ and $\sqrt[3]{a^2} = a^{\frac{2}{3}}$.

____

____

If radical expressions are rewritten in rational exponent form, you can then apply the following properties to simplify them.

Properties of Rational Exponents	
Let a and b be real numbers and m and n be integers.	
Product of Powers Property	$a^m \cdot a^n = a^{m+n}$
Quotient of Powers Property	$\frac{a^m}{a^n} = a^{m-n}$, $a \neq 0$
Power of a Product Property	$(a \cdot b)^n = a^n \cdot b^n$
Power of a Quotient Property	$\left(\frac{a}{b}\right)^n = \frac{a^n}{b^n}$, $b \neq 0$
Power of a Power Property	$(a^m)^n = a^{mn}$
Negative Exponent Property	$a^{-n} = \frac{1}{a^n}$, $a \neq 0$

CC.9–12.N.RN.2

5 EXAMPLE Using Exponent Properties to Simplify Radical Expressions

Simplify each expression. Assume all variables are positive.

A $\sqrt[3]{(xy)^6} = (xy)^{\frac{6}{3}}$ Rewrite using a rational exponent.

$= (xy)$ Simplify the exponent.

$= x \quad y$ Power of a product property

B $\sqrt{x} \cdot \sqrt[3]{x} = x^{\frac{1}{2}} \cdot x^{\frac{1}{3}}$ Rewrite using rational exponents.

$= x$  Product of powers property

$= x$ Simplify the exponent.

$= \sqrt[6]{x}$ Rewrite the expression in radical form.

C $\frac{\sqrt{x}}{\sqrt[4]{x}} = \frac{x^{\frac{1}{2}}}{x^{\frac{1}{4}}}$ Rewrite using rational exponents.

$= x$ Quotient of powers property

$= x$ Simplify the exponent.

$= \sqrt{x}$ Rewrite the expression in radical form.

REFLECT

5a. In parts B and C, you started with an expression in radical form, converted to rational exponent form, and then converted back to radical form to record the answer. Explain the purpose of each conversion.

5b. Can $\sqrt{a} \cdot \sqrt[3]{b}$ be simplified? Refer to the properties of exponents to support your answer.

5c. Use the properties of exponents to prove that $\sqrt[n]{a} \cdot \sqrt[n]{b} = \sqrt[n]{ab}$.

CC.9–12.N.RN.2

6 EXAMPLE Simplifying Expressions Involving Rational Exponents

$(27x^9)^{\frac{2}{3}} = (3^3)^{\square}(x^9)^{\square}$ Power of a product property

$= 3^{\square} x^{\square}$ Power of a power property

$= 3^{\square} x^{\square}$ Simplify exponents.

$= \square x^{\square}$ Evaluate the numerical power.

REFLECT

6a. Show that you get the same simplified form of $(27x^9)^{\frac{2}{3}}$ if you simplify $[(27x^9)^2]^{\frac{1}{3}}$. That is, square $27x^9$ and then raise to the $\frac{1}{3}$ power.

6b. What is the simplified form of $(27x^9)^{-\frac{2}{3}}$? How is it related to the simplified form of $(27x^9)^{\frac{2}{3}}$?

PRACTICE

1. Given that the set of integers is closed under multiplication, prove that the set of rational numbers is closed under multiplication.

2. Given that the set of rational numbers is closed under multiplication, how can you prove that the set of rational numbers is closed under division?

3. Given that the set of rational numbers is closed under multiplication, prove that the product of a nonzero rational number and an irrational number is an irrational number.

4. Given that 3 is a rational number and $\sqrt{3}$ is an irrational number, classify each number below as either rational or irrational. Explain your reasoning.

   a. $3 + \sqrt{3}$

   b. $3 - \sqrt{3}$

   c. $(3 + \sqrt{3})(3 - \sqrt{3})$
   Hint: Use the distributive property to carry out the multiplication.

Write each radical expression in rational exponent form. Assume all variables are positive.

5. $\sqrt[5]{d}$ ________ **6.** $\sqrt[3]{b^2}$ ________ **7.** $\sqrt[4]{m^3}$ ________

Simplify each expression. Assume all variables are positive.

8. $\sqrt[3]{y^3z}$ ________ **9.** $\sqrt{x^4y}$ ________ **10.** $\sqrt{49x^2y^4}$ ________

11. $\sqrt[3]{x} \cdot \sqrt[4]{x}$ ________ **12.** $\sqrt{(3x)(12x^3)}$ ________ **13.** $\sqrt{xy} \cdot \sqrt{x^3y^5}$ ________

14. $\frac{\sqrt[3]{x}}{\sqrt[6]{x}}$ ________ **15.** $\sqrt[3]{\frac{8x^6}{y^9}}$ ________ **16.** $\sqrt[4]{\frac{x}{y^8}}$ ________

17. $(8x^3)^{\frac{2}{3}}$ ________ **18.** $\left(\frac{x^{\frac{3}{4}}}{y^{-\frac{1}{4}}}\right)^{12}$ ________ **19.** $\left(\frac{4x^2}{y^6}\right)^{\frac{1}{2}}$ ________

20. $(216a^9)^{\frac{1}{3}}$ ________ **21.** $(a^4b^{-8})^{-\frac{3}{4}}$ ________ **22.** $(16b^{-2})^{-\frac{1}{2}}$ ________

23. Explain why the expression $x^{\frac{1}{2}}$ is undefined when $x < 0$.

____

____

24. Use the properties of exponents to show that $\sqrt[n]{\frac{a}{b}} = \frac{\sqrt[n]{a}}{\sqrt[n]{b}}$.

____

____

25. Show that $\sqrt[n]{a^m} = (\sqrt[n]{a})^m$.

____

26. **Error Analysis** A student simplified the expression $\sqrt[3]{x^2} \cdot \sqrt{x}$ by writing $\sqrt[3]{x^2} \cdot \sqrt{x} = x^{\frac{3}{2}} \cdot x^{\frac{1}{2}} = x^{\frac{3}{2}+\frac{1}{2}} = x^{\frac{4}{2}} = x^2$. Describe and correct the student's error.

____

27. In the expression $\sqrt[n]{a^m}$, suppose m is a multiple of n. That is, $m = kn$ where k is an integer. Show how to obtain the simplified form of $\sqrt[n]{a^m}$. If a is a nonzero rational number, is $\sqrt[n]{a^m}$ rational or irrational? Explain.

____

____

____

____

Name________________________ Class________________ Date____________

6-2

Additional Practice

Simplify each expression. All variables represent nonnegative numbers.

1. $27^{\frac{1}{3}}$ ______

2. $121^{\frac{1}{2}}$ ______

3. $0^{\frac{1}{3}}$ ______

4. $64^{\frac{1}{2}} + 27^{\frac{1}{3}}$ ______

5. $16^{\frac{1}{4}} + 8^{\frac{1}{3}}$ ______

6. $100^{\frac{1}{2}} - 64^{\frac{1}{6}}$ ______

7. $1^{\frac{1}{5}} + 49^{\frac{1}{2}}$ ______

8. $25^{\frac{3}{2}}$ ______

9. $32^{\frac{3}{5}}$ ______

10. $16^{\frac{3}{4}}$ ______

11. $1^{\frac{5}{6}}$ ______

12. $121^{\frac{3}{2}}$ ______

13. $\sqrt[5]{y^5}$ ______

14. $\sqrt{x^4 y^{12}}$ ______

15. $\sqrt[3]{a^6 b^3}$ ______

16. $(x^{\frac{1}{2}})^4 \sqrt{x^6}$ ______

17. $(x^{\frac{1}{3}} y)^3 \sqrt{x^2 y^2}$ ______

18. $\dfrac{(x^{\frac{1}{4}})^8}{\sqrt[3]{x^3}}$ ______

19. Given a cube with volume V, you can use the formula $P = 4V^{\frac{1}{3}}$ to find the perimeter of one of the cube's square faces. Find the perimeter of a face of a cube that has volume 125 m^3.

____

Problem Solving

Write the correct answer.

1. For a pendulum with a length of L meters, the time in seconds that it takes the pendulum to swing back and forth is approximately $2L^{\frac{1}{2}}$. About how long does it take a pendulum that is 9 meters long to swing back and forth?

   ____

2. The Beaufort Scale is used to measure the intensity of tornados. For a tornado with Beaufort number B, the formula $v = 1.9B^{\frac{3}{2}}$ may be used to estimate the tornado's wind speed in miles per hour. Estimate the wind speed of a tornado with Beaufort number 9.

   ____

3. Given a cube whose faces each have area A, the volume of the cube is given by the formula $V = A^{\frac{3}{2}}$. Find the volume of a cube whose faces each have an area of 64 in^2.

   ____

4. At a factory that makes cylindrical cans, the formula $r = \left(\frac{V}{12}\right)^{\frac{1}{2}}$ is used to find the radius of a can with volume V. What is the radius of a can whose volume is 192 cm^3?

   ____

Given an animal's body mass *m*, in grams, the formula $B = 1.8m^{\frac{3}{4}}$ may be used to estimate the mass *B*, in grams, of the animal's brain. The table shows the body mass of several birds. Use the table for questions 5–7. Select the best answer.

5. Which is the best estimate for the brain mass of a macaw?

   A 9 g　　C 125 g
   B 45 g　　D 225 g

6. How much larger is the brain mass of a barn owl compared to the brain mass of a cockatiel?

   F 189 g　　H 388.8 g
   G 340.2 g　　J 1215 g

7. An animal has a body mass given by the expression x^4. Which expression can be used to estimate the animal's brain mass?

   A $B = 1.8x^3$　　C $B = 1.8x^{12}$
   B $B = 1.8x^{\frac{3}{4}}$　　D $B = 1.8x$

Typical Body Masses of Birds

Bird	Body Mass (g)
Cockatiel	81
Guam Rail	256
Macaw	625
Barn Owl	1296

Sources:
http://www.beyondveg.com/billings-t/comp-anat/comp-anat-appx2.shtml
http://www.sandiegozoo.org/animalbytes/index.html

Name ________________ Class ________ Date ______

6-3

Video Tutor

Polynomials
Going Deeper

Essential question: *What parts of a polynomial represent terms, factors, and coefficients?*

CC.9-12.A.SSE.1a

1 ENGAGE Investigating Parts of a Polynomial

The parts of a polynomial that are added are called the *terms* of the polynomial. Each term is either a **constant term** (a number) or a **variable term** (a variable, or a product of one or more variables with whole number exponents). Terms may have factors that are numbers, variables, or combinations of both. To identify the terms of the polynomial $4x^3 + 2x - 9$, first rewrite the subtraction as addition.

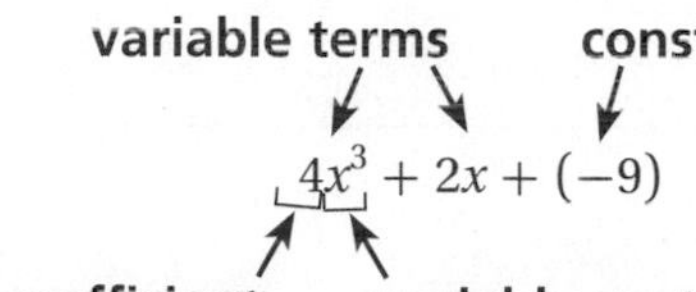

factors of $4x^3$: 1, 2, 4, x, x^2, x^3, $2x$, $2x^2$, $2x^3$, $4x$, $4x^2$, $4x^3$
factors of $2x$: 1, 2, x, $2x$

Variable terms in a polynomial can be broken down into a coefficient and a variable part, as shown above for the first term, $4x^3$. For the second term, $2x$, 2 is the coefficient and x is the variable part. The *degree* of a polynomial in one variable is the greatest power of the variable. For the polynomial above, the degree is 3. Notice that the variable terms have the common factors 2, x, and $2x$, but there are no common factors greater than 1 of all three terms.

You can also have a polynomial in a variable other than x. Below is a polynomial in the variable q.

$$9q + 6 - 3q^2$$

Variable terms: $9q$, $-3q^2$ Constant term: 6   Degree: 2

REFLECT

1a. What is the degree of the polynomial $8y^3 + 6y - 4y^5 + 2y^2$? Do the coefficients of the terms have any common factors? Do the variable parts of the terms have any common factors? What is the greatest common factor of all four of the terms of the polynomial?

____

____

____

1b. The polynomial $x^4 + x^3y^4 + xy^5$ has two variables. The degree of any term is the sum of the exponents of its variables. The degree of the polynomial is the degree of the term with the greatest degree. Find the degree of each term of this polynomial and the degree of the polynomial.

____

____

Writing polynomials in *standard form* lets you easily identify the characteristics of and compare different polynomials. Polynomials in one variable are written in standard form when the terms are in order from greatest degree to least degree. Standard form also makes it easy to compare the *leading coefficients* of two polynomials, or the coefficients of their first terms.

CC.9-12.A.SSE.1b

2 EXAMPLE Writing Polynomials in Standard Form

Consider the polynomial $16y + 2y^4 + 11 - 3y^2$.

A The polynomial has ________ terms. The terms and their degrees are

$16y$ (degree ________), ________ (degree 4), ________ (degree 0), and $-3y^2$

(degree ________). The term with the highest degree is ________, so the

polynomial has degree ________.

B The polynomial written in standard form is ________________________

The leading coefficient of the polynomial is ________.

REFLECT

2a. Notice that the number of terms is the same as the degree of the polynomial in the Example. Is this true for any polynomial? Explain.

____

____

____

2b. A *trinomial* is a polynomial that has three terms. What possible degrees can a trinomial have (consider that each term has a different exponent and that the exponents are whole numbers)? Explain.

____

____

____

Polynomials often contain letters other than the variable(s) that take specific values depending on the particular situation. These values are often referred to as *parameters*. For $ax + b$, a general linear polynomial in the variable x, the letters a and b are parameters. The parameters $a = 50$ and $b = 100$ give $50x + 100$. This might represent, for example, the total cost of a gym that has a monthly cost of \$50 and a membership fee of \$100.

The quadratic polynomial $-\frac{1}{2}at^2 + v_0t + h_0$ is a polynomial in the variable t, for time. It represents the height of a projectile launched upward in the presence of gravity. The parameters a, v_0, and h_0 represent the acceleration caused by gravity in a location, the initial upward velocity, and the initial height. Once you know the parameters for a given situation, you can find the heights for different values of the variable t.

CC.9–12.A.SSE.1

3 EXAMPLE Interpreting Polynomials

A compressed air model rocket is launched straight into the air from a platform 3 feet above the ground at an initial upward velocity of 350 feet per second. The height of the rocket in feet t seconds after being launched is modeled by $-16t^2 + 350t + 3$. Interpret each term in the polynomial. Then use unit analysis to show how the value of the polynomial is a distance in feet.

A The terms of the polynomial are ______________________.

The term ________ depends on the acceleration of gravity times the ______________ of the time in seconds after the rocket is launched.

The term ________ is the ______________________ times

____.

The term ________ is the

____.

B To use unit analysis, write the polynomial with its units. Then divide out any common units.

$$-16\frac{\text{ft}}{\text{s}^2}\bullet\left(t\ \square\right)^2 + 350\frac{\text{ft}}{\text{s}}\bullet t\ \square + 3\ \square = -16t^2\left(\frac{\square\bullet\square}{\square}\right) + 350t\left(\frac{\square\bullet\square}{\square}\right) + 3\ \square$$

$$= -16t^2\ \square + 350t\ \square + 3\ \square$$

The simplified expression shows that the polynomial gives a distance in feet.

REFLECT

3a. Suppose the model rocket in the Example is launched from a platform 10 feet above the ground at the same initial upward velocity. Explain how the polynomial that models the height in feet of this rocket t seconds after the rocket is launched differs from the polynomial in the Example.

____

____

3b. Suppose the model rocket in the Example is launched from a platform 9 inches above the ground. Does the polynomial $-16t^2 + 350t + 9$ correctly model the height of the rocket in feet t seconds after it is launched? Explain.

____

____

____

PRACTICE

For each polynomial, find the variable terms and their coefficients, any constant terms, and the degree of the polynomial. If all the terms of a polynomial have any common factors greater than 1, find the greatest common factor of the terms.

1. $6x - 4x^3 + 14$

2. $-12t - 24t^3 + 18t^2 - 30t^4$

3. $x^3 + 3x^2y + 3xy^2 + y^3$

Write each polynomial in standard form. Identify the degree and leading coefficient of the polynomial.

4. $16z + 30z^3 - 1 + 2z^6$

5. $x - x^4 + x^8 - x^6 + x^2$

6. $2.2y^3 - 1.6 - y^5 + 3.4y^4$

7. A compressed air model rocket is launched straight up into the air from a platform 1.4 meters above the ground with an initial upward velocity of 107 meters per second. The height of the rocket in meters t seconds after the rocket is launched is modeled by $-4.9t^2 + 107t + 1.4$.

a. Interpret each term in the polynomial.

b. Use unit analysis to show how the value of the polynomial is a distance in meters.

Additional Practice

Find the degree and number of terms of each polynomial.

1. $14h^3 + 2h + 10$
2. $7y - 10y^2$
3. $2a^2 - 5a + 34 - 6a^4$

Write each polynomial in standard form. Then, give the leading coefficient.

4. $3x^2 - 2 + 4x^8 - x$
5. $7 - 50j + 3j^3 - 4j^2$
6. $6k + 5k^4 - 4k^3 + 3k^2$

Classify each polynomial by its degree and number of terms.

7. $-5t^2 + 10$
8. $8w - 32 + 9w^4$
9. $b - b^3 - 2b^2 + 5b^4$

Evaluate each polynomial for the given value.

10. $3m + 8 - 2m^3$ for $m = -1$
11. $4y^5 - 6y + 8y^2 - 1$ for $y = -1$
12. $2w + w^3 - \frac{1}{2}w^2$ for $w = 2$
13. An egg is thrown off the top of a building. Its height in meters above the ground can be approximated by the polynomial $300 + 2t - 4.9t^2$, where t is the time since it was thrown in seconds.
    a. How high is the egg above the ground after 5 seconds?
    b. How high is the egg above the ground after 6 seconds?

Problem Solving

Write the correct answer.

1. The surface area of a cylinder is given by the polynomial $2\pi r^2 + 2\pi rh$. A cylinder has a radius of 2 centimeters and a height of 5 centimeters. Find the surface area of the cylinder. Use 3.14 for π.

____

2. A firework is launched from the ground at a velocity of 180 feet per second. Its height after t seconds is given by the polynomial $-16t^2 + 180t$. Find the height of the firework after 2 seconds and after 5 seconds.

____

____

3. In the United Kingdom, transportation authorities use the polynomial $\frac{1}{20}v^2 + v$ for calculating the number of feet needed to stop on dry pavement. In the United States, many use the polynomial $0.096v^2$. Both formulas are based on speed v in miles per hour. Calculate the stopping distances for a car traveling 45 miles per hour in both the U.S. and the UK.

____

____

4. A piece of cardboard that measures 2 feet by 3 feet can be folded into a box if notches are cut out of the corners. The length of the side of the notch will be the same as the height h of the resulting box. The volume of the box is given by $4h^3 - 10h^2 + 6h$. Find the volume of the box for $h = 0.25$ and $h = 0.5$.

____

____

The height of a rocket in meters *t* seconds after it is launched is approximated by the polynomial $0.5at^2 + vt + h$ where *a* is always –9.8, *v* is the initial velocity, and *h* is the initial height. Use this information with the data in the chart for questions 5 – 7. Select the best answer.

Model Number	Initial Velocity (m/s)
300X	250
Q99	90
4400*i*	125

5. A 300X was launched from a height of 10 meters. What was its height after 3 seconds?

   A 715.9 m C 755.5 m

   B 745.3 m D 760 m

6. Marie and Bob launched their rockets at the same time from a platform 5 meters above the ground. Marie launched the 4400*i* and Bob launched the Q99. How much higher was Marie's rocket after 2 seconds?

   F 35 meters H 140 meters

   G 70 meters J 320 meters

7. The 4400*i* was launched from the ground at the same time the Q99 was launched from 175 meters above the ground. After how many seconds were the rockets at the same height?

   A 2 s C 5 s

   B 4 s D 6 s

Name________________________ Class______________ Date__________

6-4

Video Tutor

Adding and Subtracting Polynomials

Going Deeper

Essential question: *How do you add and subtract polynomials?*

To add or subtract polynomials, you combine like terms. You can add or subtract horizontally or vertically.

CC.9–12.A.APR.1

1 EXAMPLE Adding Polynomials

Add.

A $(4x^3 + 12x^2 + 8x + 6) + (5x^2 - 6x + 9)$

Use a vertical arrangement.

$4x^3 + 12x^2 + 8x + 6$ Write the polynomials, aligning like terms.

$\underline{\qquad\quad 5x^2 - 6x + 9}$

$\_\_\_x^3 + \_\_\_x^2 + \_\_\_x + \_\_\_$ Add the coefficients of like terms.

B $(2x - 7x^2) + (x^2 - 2x + 5)$

Use a horizontal arrangement.

$(-7x^2 + 2x) + (x^2 - 2x + 5)$ Write the polynomials in standard form.

$= (-7x^2 + \_\_\_) + (2x - \_\_\_) + \_\_\_$ Group like terms.

$= \_\_\_ + 0x + \_\_\_$ Add the coefficients of like terms.

$= \_\_\_ + \_\_\_$ Simplify.

REFLECT

1a. Do you get the same results whether you add polynomials vertically or horizontally? Why or why not?

____

____

1b. Is the sum of two polynomials always another polynomial? Explain.

____

____

1c. Is the sum of two polynomials of degree 5 always a polynomial of degree 5? Give an example to explain your answer.

____

To subtract polynomials, you add the opposite of the subtracted polynomial. The following example shows how to use this method with the vertical and horizontal formats.

CC.9–12.A.APR.1

2 EXAMPLE Subtracting Polynomials

Subtract.

A $(2 + 9x^2) - (-6x^2 - 3x + 1)$

Use a vertical arrangement.

$9x^2 \qquad\qquad + 2$	Write the first polynomial in standard form.
$6x^2 + \quad 3x \; - \; 1$	Add the opposite of the second polynomial.
$\_\_\_x^2 + \_\_\_x + \_\_\_$	Add the coefficients of like terms.

B $(6x^3 + 3x^2 + 2x + 9) - (4x^3 + 6x^2 - 2x + 7)$

Use a horizontal arrangement.

$(6x^3 + 3x^2 + 2x + 9) - (4x^3 + 6x^2 - 2x + 7)$	Write the polynomials.
$= (6x^3 + 3x^2 + 2x + 9) + (-4x^3 - 6x^2 + 2x - 7)$	Add the opposite.
$= (6x^3 - \_\_\_) + (3x^2 - \_\_\_) + (\_\_\_ + 2x) + (\_\_\_ - 7)$	Group like terms.
$= \_\_\_x^3 - \_\_\_x^2 + \_\_\_x + \_\_\_$	Add the coefficients of like terms.

REFLECT

2a. How is subtracting polynomials similar to subtracting integers?

____

____

2b. In part A, you leave a gap in the polynomial $9x^2 + 2$ when you write the subtraction problem vertically. Why?

____

____

2c. Is the difference of two polynomials always another polynomial? Explain.

____

____

____

3 EXAMPLE Modeling High School Populations

According to data from the U.S. Census Bureau for the period 2000–2007, the number of male students enrolled in high school in the United States can be approximated by the function $M(x) = -0.004x^3 + 0.037x^2 + 0.049x + 8.11$ where x is the number of years since 2000 and $M(x)$ is the number of male students in millions. The number of female students enrolled in high school in the United States can be approximated by the function $F(x) = -0.006x^3 + 0.029x^2 + 0.165x + 7.67$ where x is the number of years since 2000 and $F(x)$ is the number of female students in millions. Estimate the total number of students enrolled in high school in the United States in 2007.

A Make a plan. The problem asks for the total number of students in 2007. First find $T(x) = M(x) + F(x)$ to find a model for the total enrollment. Then evaluate $T(x)$ at an appropriate value of x to find the total enrollment in 2007.

B Add the polynomials.

$-0.004x^3 + \quad 0.037x^2 + \quad 0.049x + 8.11$ Write the polynomials, aligning like terms.

$-0.006x^3 + \quad 0.029x^2 + \quad 0.165x + 7.67$

$\_\_\_\_ x^3 + \_\_\_\_ x^2 + \_\_\_\_ x + \_\_\_\_$ Add the coefficients of like terms.

$T(x) =$ ______________________

C Evaluate $T(x)$.

For 2007, $x = 7$. Use a calculator to evaluate $T(7)$. Round to one decimal place.

$T(7) \approx$ ______________

So, there were approximately ______________ high school students in 2007.

REFLECT

3a. Is it possible to solve this problem without adding the polynomials? Explain.

____

____

3b. Explain how you can use the given information to estimate how many more male high school students than female high school students there were in the United States in 2007.

____

____

____

____

PRACTICE

Add or subtract.

1. $(2x^4 - 6x^2 + 8) + (-x^4 + 3x^2 - 12)$

2. $(7x^2 - 2x + 1) + (8x^3 + 2x^2 + 7x - 4)$

3. $(5x^2 - 6x^3 + 11) + (9x^3 + 3x + 7x^4)$

4. $(-3x^3 - 7x^5 - 3) + (5x^2 + 3x^3 + 7x^5)$

5. $(2x^4 - 6x^2 + 8) - (-x^4 + 5x^2 - 12)$

6. $(x^3 + 25) - (-x^2 - 18x - 12)$

7. $(2x^2 + 3x + 1) - (7x^2 - 2x + 7x^3)$

8. $(10x^2 + 3) - (15x^2 - 4x + 9x^4 + 7)$

9. $(14x^4 - x^3 + 2x^2 + 5x + 15) - (10x^4 + 3x^3 - 5x^2 - 6x + 4)$

10. $(-6x^3 + 10x + 26) + (5x^2 - 6x^5 + 7x) + (3 - 22x^4)$

11. According to data from the U.S. Census Bureau, the total number of people in the United States labor force can be approximated by the function $T(x) = -0.011x^2 + 2x + 107$, where x is the number of years since 1980 and $T(x)$ is the number of workers in millions. The number of women in the United States labor force can be approximated by the function $W(x) = -0.012x^2 + 1.26x + 45.5$.

a. Write a polynomial function $M(x)$ that models the number of men in the labor force.

b. Estimate the number of men in the labor force in 2008. Explain how you made your estimate.

12. Error Analysis A student was asked to find the difference $(4x^5 - 3x^4 + 6x^2) - (7x^5 - 6x^4 + x^3)$. The student's work is shown at right. Identify the student's error and give the correct difference.

$$\begin{array}{r} 4x^5 - 3x^4 \qquad\quad + 6x^2 \\ -7x^5 - 6x^4 + x^3 \qquad\quad \\ \hline -3x^5 - 9x^4 + x^3 + 6x^2 \end{array}$$

Name________________________ Class______________ Date______________

6-4

Additional Practice

Add or subtract.

1. $3m^3 + 8m^3 - 3 + m^3 - 2m^2$ ______________

2. $2pg - p^5 - 12pg + 5g - 6p^5$ ______________

Add.

3. $\begin{array}{r} 3k^2 - 2k + 7 \\ + \quad\quad k - 2 \\ \hline \end{array}$ ______________

4. $\begin{array}{r} 5x^2 - 2x + 3y \\ + 6x^2 + 5x + 6y \\ \hline \end{array}$ ______________

5. $\begin{array}{r} 11hz^3 + 3hz^2 + 8hz \\ + 9hz^3 + hz^2 - 3hz \\ \hline \end{array}$ ______________

6. $(ab^2 + 13b - 4a) + (3ab^2 + a + 7b)$ ______________

7. $(4x^3 - x^2 + 4x) + (x^3 - x^2 - 4x)$ ______________

Subtract.

8. $\begin{array}{r} 12d^2 + 3dx + x \\ -(-4d^2 + 2dx - 8x) \\ \hline \end{array}$ ______________

9. $\begin{array}{r} 2v^5 - 3v^4 - 8 \\ -(3v^5 + 2v^4 - 8) \\ \hline \end{array}$ ______________

10. $\begin{array}{r} -y^4 + 6ay^2 - y + a \\ -(-6y^4 - 2ay^2 + y) \\ \hline \end{array}$ ______________

11. $(-r^2 + 8pr - p) - (-12r^2 - 2pr + 8p)$ ______________

12. $(un - n^2 + 2un^3) - (3un^3 + n^2 + 4un)$ ______________

13. Antoine is making a banner in the shape of a triangle. He wants to line the banner with a decorative border. How long will the border be?

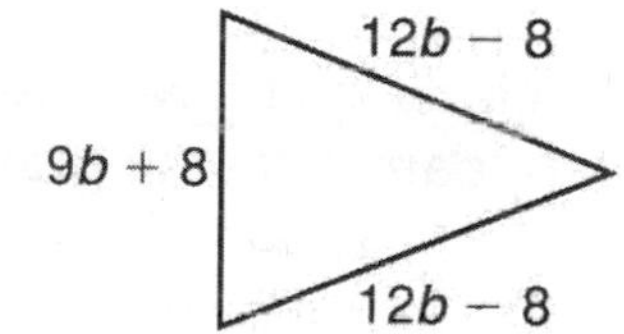

____

14. Darnell and Stephanie have competing refreshment stand businesses. Darnell's profit can be modeled with the polynomial $c^2 + 8c - 100$, where c is the number of items sold. Stephanie's profit can be modeled with the polynomial $2c^2 - 7c - 200$.

    a. Write a polynomial that represents the difference between Stephanie's profit and Darnell's profit.

    ____

    b. Write a polynomial to show how much they can expect to earn if they decided to combine their businesses.

    ____

Problem Solving

Write the correct answer.

1. There are two boxes in a storage unit. The volume of the first box is $4x^3 + 4x^2$ cubic units. The volume of the second box is $6x^3 - 18x^2$ cubic units. Write a polynomial for the total volume of the two boxes.

____

____

2. The recreation field at a middle school is shaped like a rectangle with a length of $15x$ yards and a width of $10x - 3$ yards. Write a polynomial for the perimeter of the field. Then calculate the perimeter if $x = 2$.

____

____

3. Two cabins on opposite banks of a river are $12x^2 - 7x + 5$ feet apart. One cabin is $9x + 1$ feet from the river. The other cabin is $3x^2 + 4$ feet from the river. Write the polynomial that represents the width of the river where it passes between the two cabins. Then calculate the width if $x = 3$.

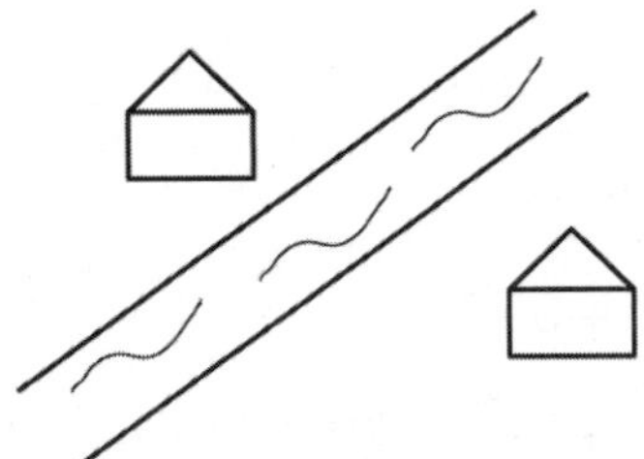

____

The circle graph represents election results for the president of the math team. Use the graph for questions 4–6. Select the best answer.

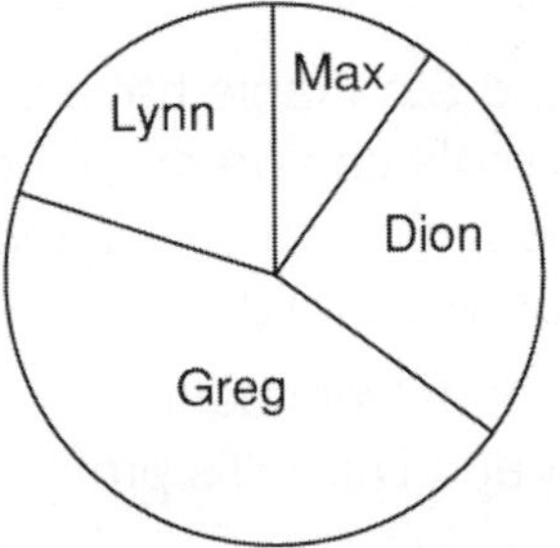

4. The angle value of Greg's sector can be modeled by $x^2 + 6x + 2$. The angle value of Dion's sector can be modeled by $7x + 20$. Which polynomial represents both sectors combined?

   A $x^2 + x + 18$ C $6x^2 + 7x + 18$

   B $x^2 + 13x + 22$ D $7x^2 + 6x + 22$

5. The sum of Greg and Lynn's sectors is $2x^2 + 4x - 6$. The sum of Max and Dion's sectors is $10x + 26$. Which polynomial represents how much greater Greg and Lynn's combined sectors are than Max and Dion's?

   F $2x^2 + 6x + 32$ H $2x^2 - 6x - 32$

   G $2x^2 - 6x + 20$ J $2x^2 + 14x + 20$

6. The sum of Lynn's sector and Max's sector is $2x^2 - 9x - 2$. Max's sector can be modeled by $3x + 6$. Which polynomial represents the angle value of Lynn's sector?

   A $2x^2 - 6x + 4$ C $2x^2 - 12x + 8$

   B $2x^2 - 6x - 4$ D $2x^2 - 12x - 8$

Name ______________________ Class ______________ Date ________

6-5

Video Tutor

Multiplying Polynomials

Going Deeper

Essential question: *How do you multiply polynomials?*

A **monomial** is a number, a variable, or the product of a number and one or more variables raised to whole number powers, such as 5, x, $-8y$, and $3x^2y^4$. A **polynomial** is a monomial or a sum of monomials. Each monomial in the expression is called a **term**. A polynomial with two terms is a **binomial**. You can multiply two binomials by using algebra tiles.

CC.9–12.A.SSE.2

1 EXPLORE Multiplying Two Binomials Using Algebra Tiles

To use algebra tiles to multiply $(2x + 1)(x + 3)$, first represent $2x + 1$ vertically along the left side of an algebra tile diagram and $x + 3$ horizontally along the top. Then use x^2-tiles, x-tiles, and 1-tiles to complete the diagram, as shown below.

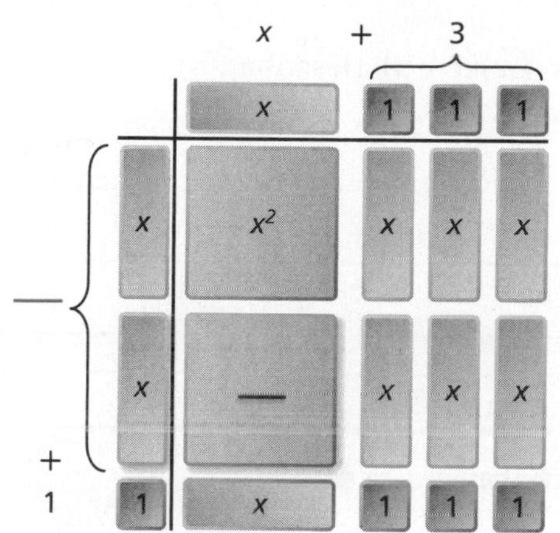

$2x(x + 3) =$ ____ $x^2 +$ ____ x

$1(x + 3) =$ ____ $x +$ ____

____ $x^2 +$ ____ $x +$ ____

$(2x + 1)(x + 3) =$ ____ $x^2 +$ ____ $x +$ ____

The product is a **trinomial**, a polynomial with three terms.

REFLECT

1a. Look at the algebra tile diagram. What two terms in the original binomials combine to form the x^2-term in the trinomial? How do they combine (by multiplying, by adding, or by subtracting)?

____

1b. Look at the algebra tile diagram. What two terms in the original binomials combine to form the constant term in the trinomial? How do they combine (by multiplying, by adding, or by subtracting)?

____

1c. Look at the algebra tile diagram. Show how the terms of the original binomials combine to form the x-term in the trinomial.

____

1d. You can verify that the expressions are equivalent by substituting a value for x into both expressions and simplifying to show that they are equal. Verify that the expressions are equivalent. Use $x = 4$.

____

____

____

____

1e. Suppose you want to use algebra tiles to find the product $(2x + 1)(x + 2)$. Describe how you can modify the algebra tile diagram to find the product.

____

____

1f. Suppose you want to use algebra tiles to find the product $(2x + 2)(x + 3)$. Describe how you can modify the algebra tile diagram to find the answer.

____

____

____

CC.9–12.A.APR.1

2 ENGAGE Multiplying Binomials Using the Distributive Property

Using algebra tiles to multiply two binomials is a useful tool for understanding how the two binomials are being multiplied. However, it is not a very practical method for everyday use. Using the distributive property is.

To multiply $(2x + 1)(x + 3)$ using the distributive property, you distribute the binomial $x + 3$ to each term of $2x + 1$. Then you distribute the monomial $2x$ to each term of $x + 3$ as well as the monomial 1 to each term of $x + 3$.

$$\begin{aligned}(\mathbf{2x} + \mathbf{1})(x + 3) &= \mathbf{2x}(x + 3) + \mathbf{1}(x + 3)\\ &= 2x^2 + 6x + x + 3\\ &= 2x^2 + 7x + 3\end{aligned}$$

Notice that the product found using algebra tiles in the Explore is the same as the product found here using the distributive property. Thus, the two methods are equivalent.

To multiply $(4x - 7)(3x + 6)$ using the distributive property, you should think of $4x - 7$ as $4x + (-7)$ and therefore keep the negative sign with the 7.

$$\begin{aligned}(\mathbf{4x} - \mathbf{7})(3x + 6) &= \mathbf{4x}(3x + 6) - \mathbf{7}(3x + 6)\\ &= 12x^2 + 24x - 21x - 42\\ &= 12x^2 + 3x - 42\end{aligned}$$

This method of using the distributive property to multiply two binomials is referred to as the FOIL method. The letters of the word FOIL stand for **F**irst, **O**uter, **I**nner, and **L**ast and will help you remember how to use the distributive property to multiply binomials.

You apply the FOIL method by multiplying each of the four pairs of terms described below and then simplifying the resulting polynomial.

- **F**irst refers to the first terms of each binomial.
- **O**uter refers to the two terms on the outside of the expression.
- **I**nner refers to the two terms on the inside of the expression.
- **L**ast refers to the last terms of each binomial.

Now multiply $(7x - 1)(3x - 5)$ using FOIL. Again, think of $7x - 1$ as $7x + (-1)$ and $3x - 5$ as $3x + (-5)$. This results in a positive constant term of 5 because $(-1)(-5) = 5$.

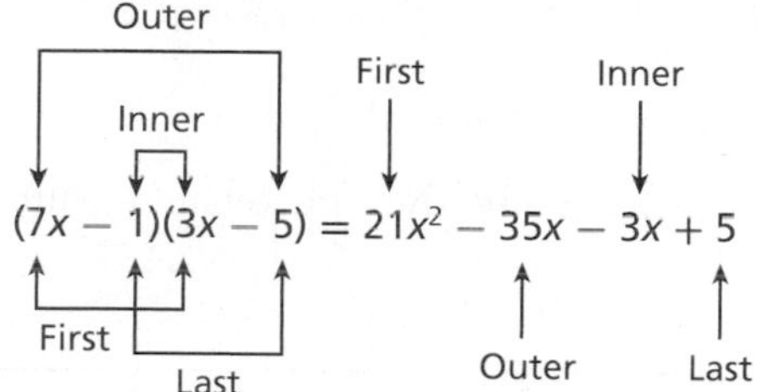

$$(7x - 1)(3x - 5) = 21x^2 - 38x + 5$$

Notice that the trinomials are written with variable terms in descending order of exponents and with the constant term last. This is a standard form for writing polynomials: Starting with the variable term with the greatest exponent, write the other variable terms in descending order of their exponents, and put the constant term last.

REFLECT

2a. Refer back to the Explore. Using the tiles, you multiplied $2x$ by $\left(x + \square\right)$ and then multiplied 1 by $\left(x + \square\right)$. You are using the ________ property.

2b. In FOIL, which of the products combine to form the x-term?

____

2c. In FOIL, which of the products combine to form the constant term?

____

2d. In FOIL, which of the products combine to form the x^2-term?

____

2e. Two binomials are multiplied to form a trinomial. When is the constant term of the trinomial positive? When is it negative?

____

____

CC.9–12.A.APR.1

3 EXAMPLE Multiplying Two Binomials Using FOIL

Multiply (12*x* – 5)(3*x* + 6) using the FOIL method.

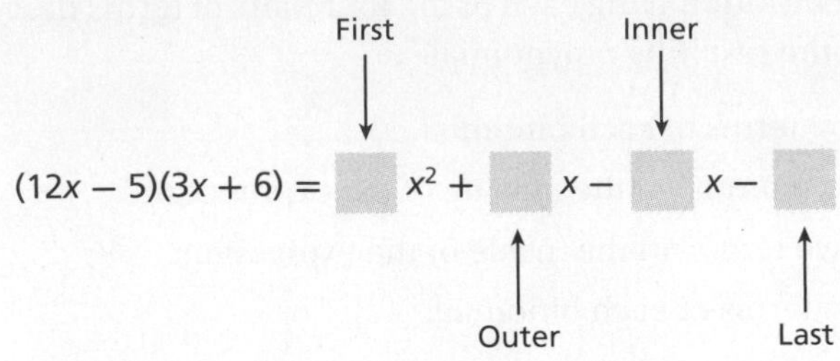

$(12x - 5)(3x + 6) =$ ______________________

REFLECT

3a. How does the final x-term in the answer to the Example relate to your answer to Question 2b? Explain.

____

____

3b. How does the final constant in the answer to the Example relate to your answer to Question 2c? Explain.

____

3c. How does the final x^2-term in the answer to the Example relate to your answer to Question 2d? Explain.

____

3d. Suppose the problem in the example were $(12x - 5)(3x + 2)$. Would the x^2-term in the product change? Would the x-term change? Would the constant term change? Explain your reasoning.

____

____

____

____

____

____

3e. Multiply $(12x - 5)(3x + 2)$.

____

As with binomials, you can multiply two polynomials by using the distributive property so that every term in the first factor is multiplied by every term in the second factor. You also use the product of powers property ($a^m \cdot a^n = a^{m+n}$) each time you multiply two terms.

CC.9–12.A.APR.1

4 EXAMPLE Multiplying Polynomials

Find the product.

A $(4x^2)(2x^3 - x^2 + 5)$

$= (4x^2)(2x^3) + (4x^2)(-x^2) + (4x^2)(5)$ Distributive property

$= 8x^5 -$ ______ $+$ ______ Multiply monomials.

B $(x - 3)(-x^2 + 2x + 1)$

Method 1: Use a horizontal arrangement.

$(x - 3)(-x^2 + 2x + 1)$

$= x(-x^2) + x(2x) + x(1) - 3(-x^2) - 3(2x) - 3(1)$ Distribute x and then -3.

$= -x^3 +$ ______ $+ x +$ ______ $-$ ______ $- 3$ Multiply monomials.

$= -x^3 +$ ______ $-$ ______ $-$ ______ Combine like terms.

Method 2: Use a vertical arrangement.

$-x^2 + 2x + 1$ Write the polynomials vertically.

$x - 3$

$3x^2 - 6x - 3$ Multiply $(-x^2 + 2x + 1)$ by -3.

$-x^3 +$ ______ $+$ ______ Multiply $(-x^2 + 2x + 1)$ by x.

$-x^3 +$ ______ $-$ ______ $-$ ______ Add.

REFLECT

4a. Is the product of two polynomials always another polynomial? Explain.

______

______

4b. If one polynomial has m terms and the other has n terms, how many terms does the product of the polynomials have before it is simplified?

______

PRACTICE

Find each product.

1. $(x + 2)(x + 3)$

2. $(x + 7)(x + 11)$

3. $(2x + 13)(x - 6)$

4. $(2x - 5)(3x + 1)$

5. $(2x^3)(2x^2 - 9x + 3)$

6. $(x + 5)(3x^2 - x + 1)$

7. $(2x^4 - 5x^2)(6x + 4x^2)$

8. $(x + y)(2x - y)$

9. $(x + 2y)(x^2 + xy + y^2)$

10. $(x^3)(x^2 - 3)(3x + 1)$

11. The *vertex form* of a quadratic function is $f(x) = a(x - h)^2 + k$. Use your knowledge about multiplying binomials to complete the following.

$f(x) = a(x - h)(\square - \square) + k$ Write as a product of two binomials.

$= a\left(x^2 - \square x + \square^2\right) + k$ Multiply the binomials.

$= ax^2 - \square x + \square + k$ Distribute the constant *a*.

Compare this rewritten form to the standard form of a quadratic function, $f(x) = ax^2 + bx + c$. Discuss how *b* and *c* relate to the rewritten function. How can you rewrite a quadratic function in vertex form so that it is in standard form?

12. The set of polynomials is analogous to a set of numbers you have studied. To determine this set of numbers, consider the following questions about closure.

a. Under which operations is the set of polynomials closed?

b. Which set of the numbers discussed in the lesson on Rational Exponents is closed under the same set of operations?

Name________________________ Class________________ Date______________ 6-5

Additional Practice

Multiply.

1. $(6m^4)(8m^2)$ ______
2. $(5x^3)(4xy^2)$ ______
3. $(10s^5t)(7st^4)$ ______
4. $4(x^2 + 5x + 6)$ ______
5. $2x(3x - 4)$ ______
6. $7xy(3x^2 + 4y + 2)$ ______
7. $(x + 3)(x + 4)$ ______
8. $(x - 6)(x - 6)$ ______
9. $(x - 2)(x - 5)$ ______
10. $(2x + 5)(x + 6)$ ______
11. $(m^3 + 3)(5m + n)$ ______
12. $(a^2 + b^2)(a + b)$ ______
13. $(x + 4)(x^2 + 3x + 5)$ ______
14. $(3m + 4)(m^2 - 3m + 5)$ ______
15. $(2x - 5)(4x^2 - 3x + 1)$ ______

16. **The length of a rectangle is 3 inches greater than the width.**
    a. Write a polynomial that represents the area of the rectangle. ______
    b. Find the area of the rectangle when the width is 4 inches. ______

17. **The length of a rectangle is 8 centimeters less than 3 times the width.**
    a. Write a polynomial that represents the area of the rectangle. ______
    b. Find the area of the rectangle when the width is 10 centimeters. ______

18. Write a polynomial to represent the volume of the rectangular prism.

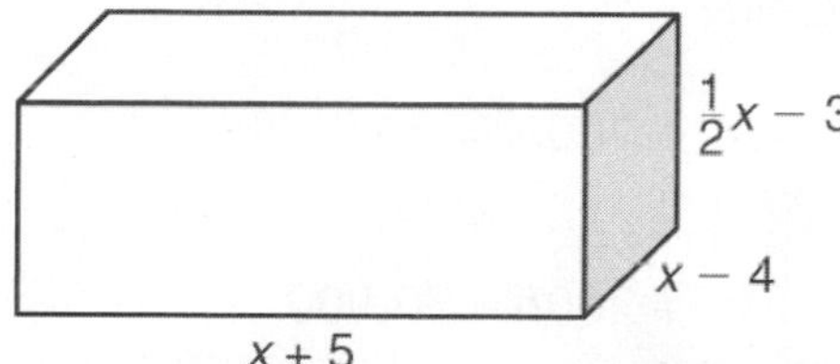

______

Problem Solving

Write the correct answer.

1. A bedroom has a length of $x + 3$ feet and a width of $x - 1$ feet. Write a polynomial to express the area of the bedroom. Then calculate the area if $x = 10$.

____

____

2. The length of a classroom is 4 feet longer than its width. Write a polynomial to express the area of the classroom. Then calculate the area if the width is 22 feet.

____

____

3. Nicholas is determining if he can afford to buy a car. He multiplies the number of months m by $i + p + 30f$ where i represents the monthly cost of insurance, p represents the monthly car payment, and f represents the number of times he fills the gas tank each month. Write the polynomial that Nicholas can use to determine how much it will cost him to own a car both for one month and for one year.

____

4. A seat cushion is shaped like a trapezoid. The shorter base of the cushion is 3 inches greater than the height. The longer base is 2 inches shorter than twice the height. Write the polynomial that can be used to find the area of the cushion. (The area of a trapezoid is represented by $\frac{1}{2}h(b_1+b_2)$.)

____

The volume of a pyramid can be found by using $\frac{1}{3}Bh$ where B is the area of the base and h is the height of the pyramid. The Great Pyramid of Giza has a square base, and each side is about 300 feet longer than the height of the pyramid. Select the best answer.

5. Which polynomial represents the approximate area of the base of the Great Pyramid?

   A $h + 90{,}000$

   B $2h + 90{,}000$

   C $h^2 + 600h + 90{,}000$

   D $2h^2 + 600h + 90{,}000$

6. Which polynomial represents the approximate volume of the Great Pyramid?

   F $\frac{1}{3}h^3 + 200h^2 + 30{,}000h$

   G $\frac{1}{3}h^2 + 200h + 30{,}000$

   H $h^3 + 600h^2 + 90{,}000h$

   J $3h^3 + 600h^2 + 90{,}000h$

7. The original height of the Great Pyramid was 485 feet. Due to erosion, it is now about 450 feet. Find the approximate volume of the Great Pyramid today.

   A 562,500 ft^3

   B 616,225 ft^3

   C 84,375,000 ft^3

   D 99,623,042 ft^3

Name________________________ Class________________ Date__________

6-6

Video Tutor

Special Products of Binomials

Going Deeper

Essential question: *How can you find special products of binomials?*

The special products $(ax + b)^2$, $(ax - b)^2$, and $(ax + b)(ax - b)$ can all be found using the FOIL method. The products $(ax + b)^2$ and $(ax - b)^2$ are called *squares of binomials* and the product $(ax + b)(ax - b)$ is called the *sum and difference product.*

CC.9–12.A.SSE.2

1 EXAMPLE Multiplying Special Cases

A Multiply $(2x + 5)^2$ using FOIL.

$(2x + 5)^2 = (2x + 5)(2x + 5) =$ ______________________

$=$ ______________________

B Multiply $(2x - 5)^2$ using FOIL.

$(2x - 5)^2 = (2x - 5)(2x - 5) =$ ______________________

$=$ ______________________

C Multiply $(2x - 5)(2x + 5)$ using FOIL.

$(2x - 5)(2x + 5) =$ ______________________

$=$ ______________________

REFLECT

1a. In the final answer of Part A, which two terms of the trinomial are perfect squares? How can you use the coefficients 2 and 5 to produce the coefficient of x in the product? Generalize these results to write a rule for the product $(ax + b)^2$ in terms of a, b, and x.

____

1b. In the final answer of Part B, which two terms of the trinomial are perfect squares? How can you use the coefficients 2 and 5 to produce the coefficient of x in the product? Generalize these results to write a rule for the product $(ax - b)^2$ in terms of a, b, and x.

____

1c. In the final answer of Part C, which two terms of the trinomial are perfect squares? What is the coefficient of the x-term and how was it created? Generalize these results to write a rule for the product $(ax - b)(ax + b)$ in terms of a, b, and x.

____

____

1d. In Part C, suppose the product had been $(2x + 5)(2x - 5)$. Would the answer have been different? Explain.

____

The squares of binomials and the sum and difference product occur so frequently that it is helpful to recognize their patterns and develop rules for them. These rules, along with the rules for the cubes of binomials, are summarized in the table.

Special Product Rules	
Sum and Difference	$(a+b)(a-b) = a^2 - b^2$
Square of a Binomial	$(a+b)^2 = a^2 + 2ab + b^2$ $(a-b)^2 = a^2 - 2ab + b^2$
Cube of a Binomial	$(a+b)^3 = a^3 + 3a^2b + 3ab^2 + b^3$ $(a-b)^3 = a^3 - 3a^2b + 3ab^2 - b^3$

CC.9–12.A.SSE.2

2 EXAMPLE Justifying and Applying a Special Product Rule

Justify the sum and difference rule. Then use it to find the product $(4x^2 + 15)(4x^2 - 15)$.

A Justify the rule.

$(a+b)(a-b) = a \cdot a + a(-b) +$ ______ $+$ ______ Distribute a and then b.

$= a^2 \quad - ab \quad +$ ______ $+$ ______ Multiply monomials.

$=$ ______ $-$ ______ Combine like terms.

B Find the product $(4x^2 + 15)(4x^2 - 15)$.

$(4x^2 + 15)(4x^2 - 15) = ($______$)^2 - ($______$)^2$ Sum and difference rule

$=$ __________ Simplify.

REFLECT

2a. Error Analysis A student was asked to find the square of $7x + 3$. The student quickly wrote $(7x + 3)^2 = 49x^2 + 9$. Identify the student's error and provide the correct answer.

____

____

2b. Show how to justify the rule for the cube of a binomial, $(a + b)^3$.

____

____

____

____

PRACTICE

Find each product.

1. $(x + 4)^2$

2. $(x - 1)(x + 1)$

3. $(3x - 8)^2$

4. $(6x + 1)^2$

5. $(9x - 7)(9x + 7)$

6. $(4x - 5)(4x + 5)$

7. $(2x + 9)(2x - 9)$

8. $(10x + 3)(10x - 3)$

9. $(8x + 7)^2$

10. $(5x - 4)^2$

11. $(4 + 3x)(4 - 3x)$

12. $(1 - 5x)^2$

13. Justify the rule for the square of a binomial, $(a + b)^2 = a^2 + 2ab + b^2$. Then use it to expand $(2x^3 + 6y)^2$.

Use a special product rule to find each product.

14. $(9x + 5y)^2$

15. $(6x - 4y)^2$

16. $(2x^2 - 5y)(2x^2 + 5y)$

17. $(4x - 3y^3)(4x + 3y^3)$

18. $(8x^2 + 3y)^2$

19. $(4x - 7y^3)^2$

20. The sum and difference rule is useful for mental-math calculations. Explain how you can use the rule and mental math to calculate $32 \cdot 28$. (*Hint:* $32 \cdot 28 = (30 + 2)(30 - 2)$.)

____

____

____

Write each product using the sum and difference rule. Then find the product using mental math.

21. $37 \cdot 43$

____

22. $26 \cdot 34$

____

23. $22 \cdot 18$

____

24. $27 \cdot 13$

____

25. $45 \cdot 55$

____

26. $99 \cdot 101$

____

Name ______________________ Class ____________ Date ____________

6-6

Additional Practice

Multiply.

1. $(x+2)^2$ ____________
2. $(m+4)^2$ ____________
3. $(3+a)^2$ ____________
4. $(2x+5)^2$ ____________
5. $(3a+2)^2$ ____________
6. $(6+5b)^2$ ____________
7. $(b-3)^2$ ____________
8. $(8-y)^2$ ____________
9. $(a-10)^2$ ____________
10. $(3x-7)^2$ ____________
11. $(4m-9)^2$ ____________
12. $(6-3n)^2$ ____________
13. $(x+3)(x-3)$ ____________
14. $(8+y)(8-y)$ ____________
15. $(x+6)(x-6)$ ____________
16. $(5x+2)(5x-2)$ ____________
17. $(10x+7y)(10x-7y)$ ____________
18. $(x^2+3y)(x^2-3y)$ ____________

19. Write a simplified expression that represents the...

    a. area of the large rectangle.

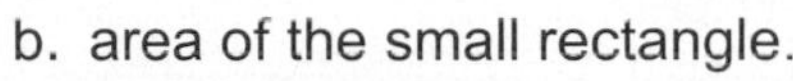

    b. area of the small rectangle.

    ____

    c. area of the shaded area.

    ____

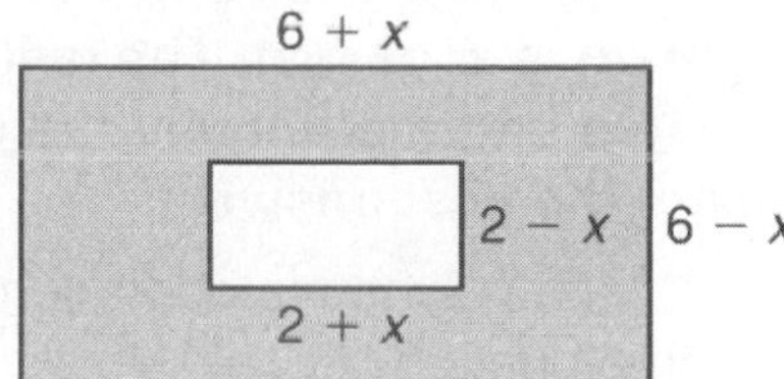

20. The small rectangle is made larger by adding 2 units to the length and 2 units to the width.

    a. What is the new area of the smaller rectangle?

    ____

    b. What is the area of the new shaded area?

    ____

Problem Solving

Write the correct answer.

1. This week Kyara worked $x + 4$ hours. She is paid $x - 4$ dollars per hour. Write a polynomial for the amount that Kyara earned this week. Then calculate her pay if $x = 12$.

____

____

2. A museum set aside part of a large gallery for a special exhibit.

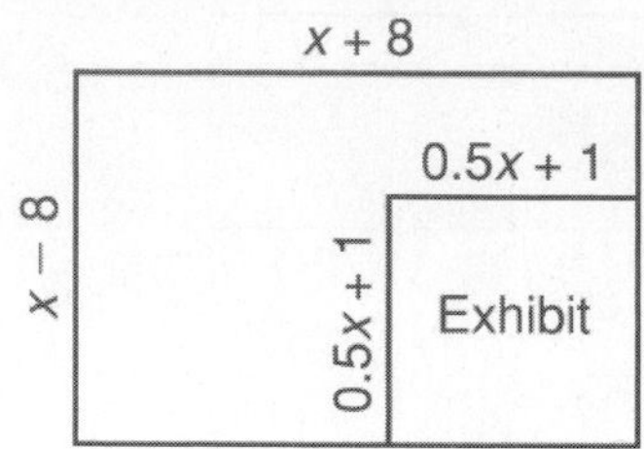

Write a polynomial for the area of the gallery that is not part of the exhibit. Then calculate the area of that section if $x = 60$.

____

____

3. Gary is building a square table for a kitchen. In his initial sketch, each side measured x inches. After rearranging some furniture, he realized he would have to add one foot to the length and remove one foot from the width and have a rectangular table instead. Write a polynomial to represent the area of the rectangular table.

____

A fountain is in the center of a square garden. The radius of the fountain is $x - 2$ feet. The length of the garden is $2x + 4$ feet. Use this information and the diagram for questions 4 – 7. Select the best answer.

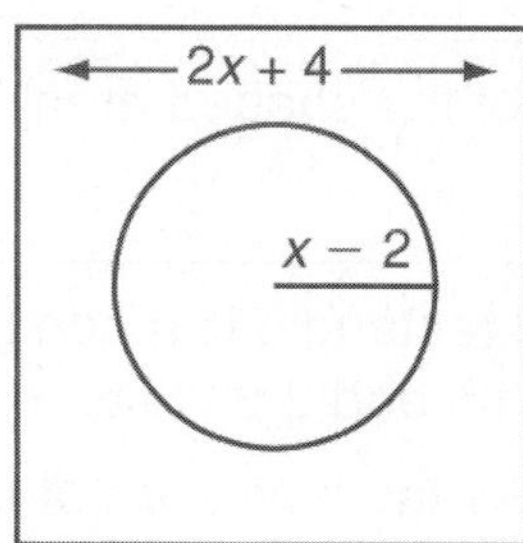

4. Which polynomial represents the area of the fountain?

   A $2\pi x - 4\pi$ C $\pi x^2 - 4\pi$

   B $\pi x^2 - 4\pi x - 4\pi$ D $\pi x^2 - 4\pi x + 4\pi$

5. Which polynomial represents the area of the garden, including the fountain?

   F $4x^2 + 8$ H $4x^2 + 16$

   G $4x^2 + 16x + 16$ J $4x^2 + 8x + 16$

6. Which polynomial represents the area of the garden *outside* the fountain? (Use 3.14 for π.)

   A $0.86x^2 + 28.56x + 3.44$

   B $0.86x^2 + 3.44x + 28.56$

   C $7.14x^2 + 28.56x + 3.44$

   D $7.14x^2 + 3.44x + 28.56$

7. A 3-ft wide path is built around the garden. Which expression represents the area of the path?

   F $12x + 33$ H $4x^2 + 28x + 29$

   G $24x + 84$ J $4x^2 + 40x + 100$

Name _______________ Class _______________ Date _______________

CHAPTER 6

Performance Tasks

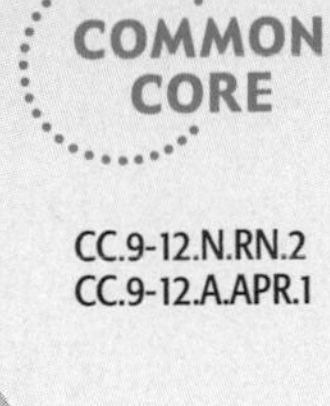

CC.9-12.N.RN.2
CC.9-12.A.APR.1

★ **1.** The box at the right is a cube with edges that measure 2 feet. The sides of the triangle inside the cube are a diagonal of a face, an edge, and a segment with endpoints at opposite corners of the cube. The triangle is a right triangle with leg lengths 2 and $\sqrt{2^3}$. Write the area of the triangle as the number 2 with a rational exponent.

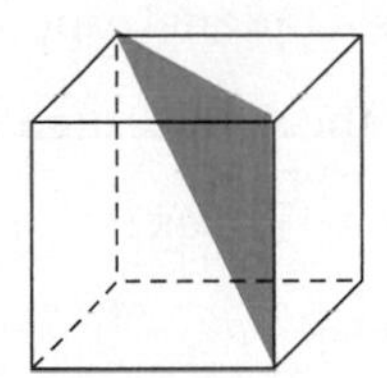

★ **2.** A movie theater sells 3 sizes of popcorn as described in the table.

Popcorn Sizes		
Small	**Medium**	**Large**
\$2	\$3	\$4

a. Write a polynomial with 3 terms to represent the total sales in dollars of all popcorn. Define the variables you use.

b. Pam says that the expression $9p$ represents the total sales of popcorn, where p is the total number of all sizes of popcorn sold. Does this make sense? Explain.

3. Linda is wrapping gifts at a toy store. The gifts are in boxes of various sizes, and each box is a cube.

a. Linda writes $s = \sqrt[3]{V}$, where s is the side length of a square face of a box and V is the volume. Rewrite this formula using a rational exponent.

b. The area of one face of a box is $A = s^2$. Use the answer from part **a** and this formula to write A in terms of V. Use a rational exponent.

c. Write a formula for the surface area of a box in terms of V.

d. Find the surface area of a box that has a volume of 64 cubic inches.

4. A rectangular parking space is m feet wide and n feet long. In the new design for the parking lot, each space will have its width increased by 1 foot and its length increased by 20%.

a. Write a polynomial to represent the area of the new parking space.

b. Shoshanna says that the area of each new parking space is 20% larger than the area of the old parking space. Is this correct? Use the polynomial you wrote in part **a** to explain why or why not.

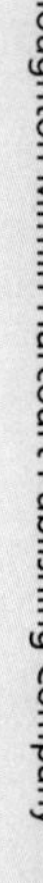

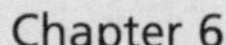

Name ______________________ Class ______________ Date ________

MULTIPLE CHOICE

1. Which set of numbers is *not* closed under multiplication?
   A. Real numbers
   B. Rational numbers
   C. Integers
   D. Irrational numbers

2. If a, b, c, and d are integers with $b \neq 0$ and $d \neq 0$, what conclusion can you draw from the statement $\frac{a}{b} + \frac{c}{d} = \frac{ad + bc}{bd}$ given that the set of integers is closed under addition and multiplication?
   F. The set of rational numbers is closed under multiplication.
   G. The set of irrational numbers is closed under multiplication.
   H. The set of rational numbers is closed under addition.
   J. The set of irrational numbers is closed under addition.

3. Which of the following statements shows that the set of irrational numbers is *not* closed under addition?
   A. $\sqrt{2} + \sqrt{2} = 2\sqrt{2}$
   B. $-\sqrt{2} + \sqrt{2} = 0$
   C. $\sqrt{4} + \sqrt{1} = 3$
   D. $1 + \sqrt{1} = 2$

4. What is the simplified form of $8^{-\frac{1}{3}}$?
   F. $\frac{1}{2}$
   H. -2
   G. $\frac{1}{512}$
   J. -512

5. What is $\sqrt[3]{a^2}$ in rational exponent form?
   A. $a^{\frac{3}{2}}$
   C. a^6
   B. $a^{\frac{2}{3}}$
   D. a^5

6. Sue began simplifying the expression $\sqrt{x} \cdot \sqrt[4]{x}$ by writing $\sqrt{x} \cdot \sqrt[4]{x} = x^{\frac{1}{2}} \cdot x^{\frac{1}{4}}$. What is the next step that she should take?
   F. Write $x^{\frac{1}{2}} \cdot x^{\frac{1}{4}}$ as $x^{\frac{1}{2} \cdot \frac{1}{4}}$.
   G. Write $x^{\frac{1}{2}} \cdot x^{\frac{1}{4}}$ as $\frac{1}{x^{2 \cdot 4}}$.
   H. Write as $x^{\frac{1}{2}} \cdot x^{\frac{1}{4}}$ as $x^{\frac{1}{2} + \frac{1}{4}}$.
   J. Write $x^{\frac{1}{2}} \cdot x^{\frac{1}{4}}$ as $\frac{1}{x^{2+4}}$.

7. What is the product $(2x - 9)(3x + 5)$?
   A. $6x^2 - 17x - 45$
   B. $6x^2 - 21x + 45$
   C. $6x^2 + 10x - 45$
   D. $6x^2 + 37x + 45$

8. Under which operation(s) is the set of polynomials closed?
   F. addition only
   G. addition and multiplication only
   H. addition, subtraction, and multiplication only
   J. addition, subtraction, multiplication, and division

9. Which expression is the expansion of $(x - 4)^3$?
   A. $x^3 + 3x^2 + 3x + 4$
   B. $x^3 - 3x^2 + 3x - 4$
   C. $x^3 + 12x^2 + 48x + 64$
   D. $x^3 - 12x^2 + 48x - 64$

10. What is the standard form of the polynomial $(x^2 + 5x - 1) - (8x^2 - 5x + 9)$?

F. $-7x^2 + 8$

G. $9x^2 + 8$

H. $-7x^2 + 10x - 10$

J. $-7x^4 + 10x^2 - 10$

11. What is $\sqrt{x^5}\,\sqrt[3]{x^2}$ in simplified radical form? (Assume all variables are positive.)

A. $x^2\sqrt{x}\,\sqrt[3]{x^2}$

B. $x^3\sqrt[6]{x}$

C. $x^{\frac{19}{6}}$

D. $\sqrt[6]{x^{19}}$

12. What is the simplified form of $(16a^8)^{\frac{3}{2}}$?

F. $8a^6$

G. $16a^8$

H. $96a^{18}$

J. $64a^{12}$

CONSTRUCTED RESPONSE

13. Describe how to use the general pattern for finding the square of a binomial $(a + b)^2$ to write the expansion of $(3m + 5n)^2$.

____

____

____

____

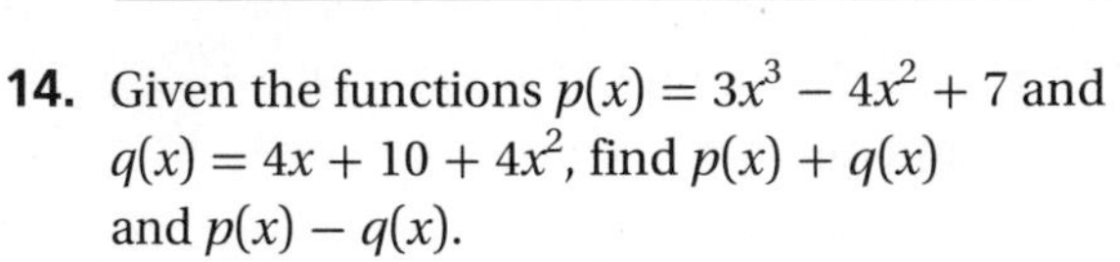

14. Given the functions $p(x) = 3x^3 - 4x^2 + 7$ and $q(x) = 4x + 10 + 4x^2$, find $p(x) + q(x)$ and $p(x) - q(x)$.

____

____

15. You make a box by cutting out a square from each corner of a rectangular sheet of cardboard and folding up the flaps as shown below.

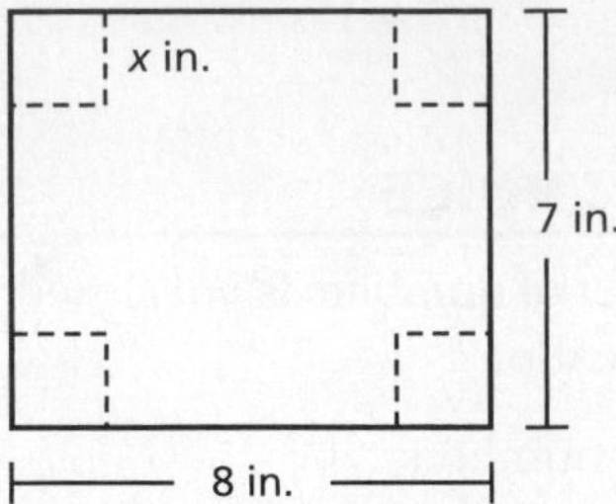

Write a function $V(x)$ to represent the volume of the box. Explain how you wrote $V(x)$.

____

____

____

____

16. **a.** Explain why you can write $\sqrt{a}$ as $a^{\frac{1}{2}}$.

____

____

____

b. Complete the simplification of the product $\sqrt{a} \cdot \sqrt[6]{a}$.

$\sqrt{a} \cdot \sqrt[6]{a} = a^{\square} \cdot a^{\square}$	Rational exponent form
$= a^{\square}$	Product of powers property
$= a^{\square}$	Simplify the exponent.
$= \sqrt[\square]{a^{\square}}$	Radical form

CHAPTER 7

Factoring Polynomials

Chapter Focus

In this chapter you will examine the structures of polynomials in order to find ways to rewrite them using various factoring techniques.

COMMON CORE

Chapter at a Glance

Lesson		Standards for Mathematical Content
7-1	Factors and Greatest Common Factors	CC.9-12.A.SSE.1a, CC.9-12.A.SSE.1b
7-2	Factoring by GCF	CC.9-12.A.SSE.1b, CC.9-12.A.SSE.2
7-3	Factoring $x^2 + bx + c$	CC.9-12.A.SSE.2
7-4	Factoring $ax^2 + bx + c$	CC.9-12.A.SSE.2
7-5	Factoring Special Products	CC.9-12.A.SSE.2
7-6	Choosing a Factoring Method	CC.9-12.A.SSE.1b, CC.9-12.A.SSE.2
	Performance Tasks	
	Assessment Readiness	

CHAPTER 7

Unpacking the Standards

Understanding the standards and the vocabulary terms in the standards will help you know exactly what you are expected to learn in this chapter.

COMMON CORE **CC.9-12.A.SSE.2**

Use the structure of an expression to identify ways to rewrite it.

Key Vocabulary

expression *(expresión)* A mathematical phrase that contains operations, numbers, and/or variables.

CHAPTER 7

What It Means For You Lessons 7-1, 7-2, 7-3, 7-4, 7-5, 7-6

You will learn to *factor* expressions, which means you will rewrite them as a product of two or more expressions. Being able to recognize patterns will help you decide which method to use.

EXAMPLE **Factor $x^2 + 7x + 6$**

The algebra tiles below show that $x^2 + 7x + 6 = (x + 1)(x + 6)$.

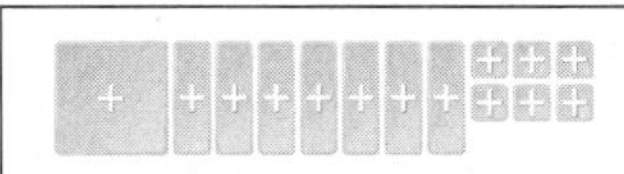

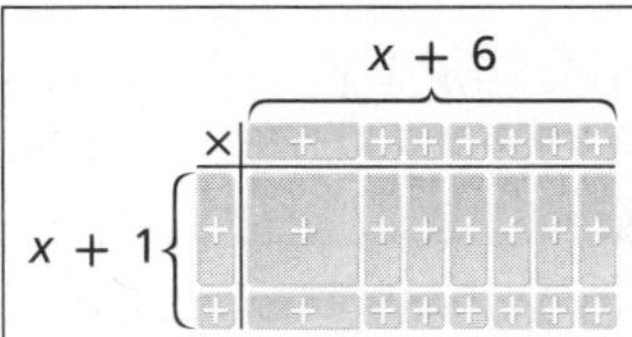

EXAMPLE **Factor $6x^2 - 11x + 3$**

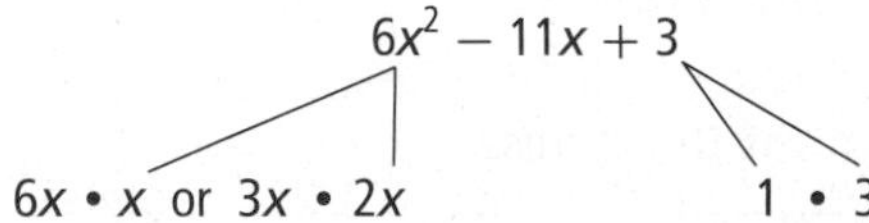

Guess and check: $(6x - 1)(x - 3) = 6x^2 - 18x - x + 3$

$= 6x^2 - 19x + 3$ ✗

Guess and check: $(3x - 1)(2x - 3) = 6x^2 - 9x - 2x + 3$

$= 6x^2 - 11x + 3$ ✓

EXAMPLE **Factor $x^2 - 49$**

Use the difference of two squares pattern:

$$a^2 - b^2 = (a + b)(a - b)$$

$$x^2 - 49 = (x + 7)(x - 7)$$

COMMON CORE **CC.9-12.A.SSE.1b**

Interpret complicated expressions by viewing one or more of their parts as a single entity.

Key Vocabulary

expression *(expresión)* A mathematical phrase that contains operations, numbers, and/or variables.

What It Means For You

Lessons 7-1, 7-2, 7-5, 7-6

You will learn to recognize when the terms of an expression share common factors. You will also learn to recognize when an expression fits a certain pattern based on the structure of its parts.

EXAMPLE **Factor Out the Greatest Common Factor**

$$8x^3y^2 + 6x^2y + 10xy =$$

$$2xy(4x^2y) + 2xy(3x) + 2xy(5) =$$

$$2xy(4x^2y + 3x + 5)$$

EXAMPLE **Factor by Grouping**

$$3x^2 + 6x + 5x + 10 =$$

$$3x(x) + 3x(2) + 5(x) + 5(2) =$$

$$3x(x + 2) + 5(x + 2) =$$

$$(3x + 5)(x + 2)$$

EXAMPLE **Factor a Perfect-Square Trinomial**

A square quilt is made up of squares sewn together in a grid pattern with a one-foot border on all sides. The side length of each square is x feet. The area in square feet is given by the expression $100x^2 + 40x + 4$. Write an expression for the side length of the quilt.

Use a formula: Area of square = Side length squared

Factor: $100x^2 + 40x + 4 = (10x + 2)^2$

The side length in feet is given by the expression $10x + 2$.

CHAPTER 7

Key Vocabulary

binomial *(binomio)* A polynomial with two terms.

difference of two squares *(diferencia de dos cuadrados)* A polynomial of the form $a^2 - b^2$, which may be written as the product $(a + b)(a - b)$.

expression *(expresión)* A mathematical phrase that contains operations, numbers, and/or variables.

factor *(factor)* A number or expression that is multiplied by another number or expression to get a product. *See also* factoring.

factoring *(factorización)* The process of writing a number or algebraic expression as a product.

greatest common factor (monomials) (GCF) *(máximo común divisor (monomios) (MCD))* The product of the greatest integer and the greatest power of each variable that divide evenly into each monomial.

monomial *(monomio)* A number or a product of numbers and variables with whole-number exponents, or a polynomial with one term.

perfect-square trinomial *(trinomio cuadrado perfecto)* A trinomial whose factored form is the square of a binomial. A perfect-square trinomial has the form $a^2 - 2ab + b^2 = (a - b)^2$ or $a^2 + 2ab + b^2 = (a + b)^2$.

polynomial *(polinomio)* A monomial or a sum or difference of monomials.

trinomial *(trinomio)* A polynomial with three terms.

CHAPTER 7

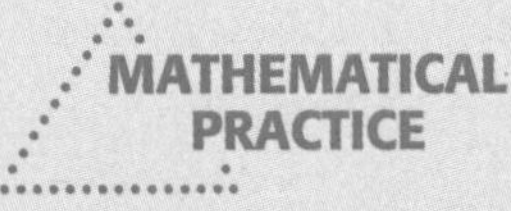

The Common Core Standards for Mathematical Practice describe varieties of expertise that mathematics educators at all levels should seek to develop in their students. Opportunities to develop these practices are integrated throughout this program.

1. **Make sense of problems and persevere in solving them.**
2. **Reason abstractly and quantitatively.**
3. **Construct viable arguments and critique the reasoning of others.**
4. **Model with mathematics.**
5. **Use appropriate tools strategically.**
6. **Attend to precision.**
7. **Look for and make use of structure.**
8. **Look for and express regularity in repeated reasoning**

Name ______________________ Class ______________ Date __________

7-1

Video Tutor

Factors and Greatest Common Factor
Going Deeper

Essential question: *How can you find the GCF of monomials?*

CC.9–12.A.SSE.1a

1 EXPLORE — Finding the Greatest Common Factor (GCF) of Two Monomials

Find the GCF of $8y^2$ and $4y^4$.

A Use the prime factorization of each coefficient and the powers of each variable.

$8y^2 = 2 \bullet \square \bullet \square \bullet y \bullet \square$

$4y^4 = \square \bullet \square \bullet \square \bullet \square \bullet \square \bullet \square$

Circle the common factors above.

Find the product of the common factors: $2 \bullet \square \bullet y \bullet \square = \square$

The GCF of $8y^2$ and $4y^4$ is ______.

B Use another method.

Write each monomial as the prime factorization of each coefficient and the variable raised to its power.

$8y^2 = \square \bullet \square \bullet \square \bullet y^2$

$4y^4 = \square \bullet \square \bullet \square$

Find the product of the common factors of the coefficients and the variable that is raised to the lower power.

$2 \bullet \square \bullet y^{\square} = \square$

How does this product compare to the GCF you found in Step A?

____

C Another way to find the GCF of two monomials with the same variable is to multiply the ______ of the coefficients times the variable that is raised to the ________ power.

REFLECT

1a. Two whole numbers are *relatively prime* if the only common factor they have is 1. Give an example of two monomials that each have a coefficient and a variable and that could be described as relatively prime. Explain your thinking.

____

____

1b. How could you apply the method you described in Step C to find the GCF of $6x^2y^5$ and $9x^3y^3$? Show its application.

____

____

____

1c. How many variables are in the GCF of $4a^2b$ and $6a^3$? Explain. Find the GCF.

____

CC.9–12.A.SSE.1a

2 EXAMPLE Finding the GCF of Three Monomials

Find the GCF of $9a^2b^2$, $6ab^3$, and $12b$.

The coefficients are ______________, so the GCF of the coefficients is ______.

Is a a common factor of all of the monomials? ______

Is b a common factor of all of the monomials? ______

So, write b to its lowest power. ______

What is the product of the GCF of the coefficients and any common variables raised to their lowest powers? ______

The GCF of $9a^2b^2$, $6ab^3$, and $12b$ is ______.

REFLECT

2a. How could you change the monomials in the Example so that they are relatively prime? Give an example.

____

____

____

2b. Suppose you were asked to find the GCF of four or more monomials. How would your method compare to the method used in the Example?

____

The expression $3(x + 5)^2$ can be factored as $3 \bullet (x + 5) \bullet (x + 5)$. The coefficient 3 and the binomial $(x + 5)$ are factors of the expression. x and 5 are **not** factors of the expression. This is important when you are finding the GCF of expressions involving binomials.

CC.9–12.A.SSE.1b

3 EXAMPLE Finding the GCF of Expressions with Binomial Factors

Find the GCF of $6(x - 2)^3$ and $8(x - 2)^4$.

The coefficients are ___________, so the GCF of the coefficients is ________.

Is the binomial $(x - 2)$ a common factor of both expressions? ________

Write $(x - 2)$ with its lower power. __________

What is the product of the GCF of the coefficients and the common binomial raised to its lower power? ___________

The GCF of $6(x - 2)^3$ and $8(x - 2)^4$ is ___________.

REFLECT

3a. Suppose the expressions in the Example had been $6(2x - 4)^3$ and $8(x - 2)^4$. What additional steps would you take to find the GCF?

____

____

____

3b. What is the GCF of $6(2x - 4)^3$ and $8(x - 2)^4$? Explain your work.

____

____

____

3c. How would the GCF be different in the Example if the expression $5(x - 2)^2$ had also been included in the set of expressions? Explain.

____

____

____

____

PRACTICE

Find the GCF of each pair of monomials.

1. $3e^5$ and $9e^2$

2. $4f^6$ and $3f^4$

3. $7m^2p$ and $8p^2q$

4. $2a^3b^6$ and $5a^4b^2$

5. $5h^3k^3$ and $6s^3t^3$

6. $12x^5y^5$ and $9x^7y^5$

Find the GCF of each set of monomials.

7. x^5y^3, x^4y^4, x^3y^5

8. $6s^5t^2, 4st^4, 8s^2t$

9. $10c^4d^4, 20d^2e^3, 15c^2e^2$

10. $9a^4b^2, 3a^3b^4, 12a^4b^3$

11. $4g^2h, 8fg, 5f^4h^3, 6g^3h^2$

12. $t^3v^2w^4, t^5w^2, v^3w^4, t^2vw^5$

Find the GCF of each pair of expressions.

13. $2(y-3)^4$ and $5(y-3)^5$

14. $6(x+4)^3$ and $3(x+4)^2$

15. $8(c+2)^3$ and $6(c+2)^4$

16. $3(2d-6)$ and $4(d-3)^2$

Find the GCF of each set of expressions.

17. $5(s+5)^6, 7(x+5)^2, 6(s+5)^4$

18. $12(w-1)^2, 4(w-1), 9(w-1)^3$

19. $6(z+3)^4, 16(z+3)^3, 8(z+3)^4$

20. $8(h-5)^3, (h-5)^5, 4(h-5)^2$

Name ________________ Class ________ Date ________

7-1

Additional Practice

Find the GCF of each pair of monomials.

1. $15x^4$ and $35x^2$ ________
2. $12p^2$ and $30q^5$ ________
3. $-6t^3$ and $9t$ ________
4. $27y^3z$ and $45x^2y$ ________
5. $12ab$ and 12 ________
6. $-8d^3$ and $14d^4$ ________
7. $-m^8n^4$ and $3m^6n$ ________
8. $10gh^2$ and $5h$ ________

Find the GCF of each set of monomials.

9. $5x^3$, $15x^2$, $45x^5$ ________
10. $2p^2$, $-8q^5$, $10q^7$ ________
11. $6st^3$, $18s^2t$, $24st$ ________
12. $24x^2y^3$, $42x^2y$, $6x^4y^2$ ________
13. $12ab$, $12a^2b$, $12ab^2$ ________
14. $-8c^2d^3$, $4cd^4$, $-4c^3d$ ________
15. $-6m^4n^3$, $3m^2n$, $-3mn^2$ ________
16. $10g^2h^2$, $5g^3h$, $15g^4h^5$ ________

Find the GCF of each pair of expressions.

17. $5(x-3)$ and $25(x-3)^3$ ________
18. $-2(p+7)^2$ and $8(p+7)^4$ ________
19. $-8(t+1)^3$ and $8(t+1)^6$ ________
20. $-7(z-9)^8$ and $14(z-9)^2$ ________
21. $12(a-4)^5$ and $2(a-4)^4$ ________
22. $4(d+3)^9$ and $-4(d+3)^4$ ________
23. $9(m+7)^2$ and $3(m+7)^5$ ________
24. $10(g-5)^2$ and $5(g-5)^5$ ________

Find the GCF of each set of expressions.

25. $5(x+7)^4$, $35(x+7)^2$, $15(x+7)^3$ ________
26. $6(t-5)^3$, $9(t-5)^5$, $15(t-5)^7$ ________
27. $-4(a-2)$, $12(a-2)^5$, $20(a-2)^3$ ________
28. $-(n+6)^4$, $-3(n+6)^3$, $-3(n+6)^6$ ________

Problem Solving

Write the correct answer.

1. Eloise was taking a quiz on factoring monomials. Exercise 5 asked her to find the GCF of $18a^3b^4$ and $27a^5b^2$. She gave an answer of $6a^5b^4$. Is this correct? If not, give the correct answer.

   ____

   ____

2. Exercise 9 on the quiz asked for the GCF of $36(x - 5)^4$ and $48(x - 5)^9$. Eloise gave an answer of $12(x - 5)^4$. Is this correct? If not, give the correct answer.

   ____

   ____

3. Matias was taking a test on factoring. Exercise 11 asked him to find the GCF of $72x^8y^5$, $80x^4y^3$, and $64x^2y^3$. He gave an answer of $8x^4y^3$. Is this correct? If not, give the correct answer.

   ____

   ____

4. Exercise 15 on the test asked students to find the GCF of $36(a + 3)^3$, $90(a + 3)^9$, and $72(x + 3)^6$. Matias gave an answer of $6(a + 3)^3$. Is this correct? If not, give the correct answer.

   ____

   ____

Select the best answer.

5. Lamar is asked to find the GCF of $24m^6n^3$ and $60m^3n^6$. Which answer should he give?

   A $60m^6n^6$

   B $24m^3n^3$

   C $12m^3n^3$

   D $12m^6n^6$

6. A teacher is writing a test on factoring. The teacher wants students to find the GCF of $45x^4y^8$, $120x^2y^6$, and $75x^6y^4$. What is the correct answer?

   F $15x^2y^4$

   G $15x^6y^8$

   H $45x^2y^4$

   J $120x^6y^8$

7. Another question on the test from Problem 6 asks students to find the GCF of $24(x - 9)^2$ and $54(x - 9)^4$. What is the correct answer?

   A $6(x - 3)(x + 3)$

   B $6(x - 9)^2$

   C $6(x - 9)^4$

   D $24(x - 9)^2$

8. On a test, Maria is asked to find the GCF of $21(k + 4)^{18}$, $84(k + 4)^3$, and $28(k + 4)^6$. Which answer should she give?

   F $21(k + 4)^3$

   G $7(k + 4)^3$

   H $84(k + 4)^{18}$

   J $21(k + 4)^{18}$

Name________________________ Class________________ Date__________

7-2

Video Tutor

Factoring by GCF

Going Deeper

Essential question: *How can you factor polynomials completely by grouping?*

When a polynomial has four terms, you may be able to make two groups of terms and factor out the GCF from each group. Before doing this, however, you should check if there is a GCF for all the terms that can be factored out first.

CC.9–12.A.SSE.2

1 EXAMPLE Factoring out a GCF and Grouping

Factor $-2x^4 - 2x^3 - 6x^2 - 6x$.

( ) Factor out ______, the GCF of all the terms.

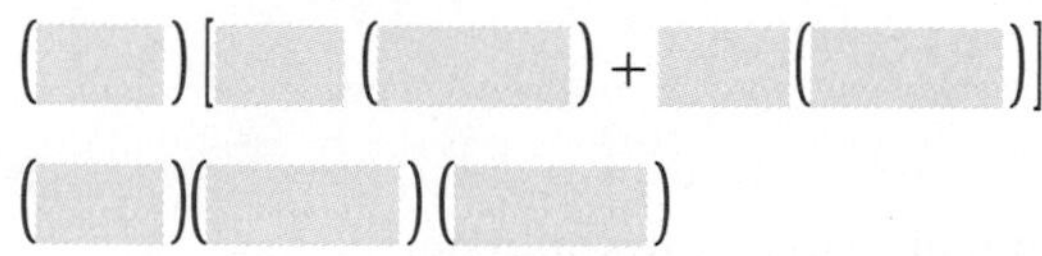

Group terms that have a common factor. The common factor of x^3 and x^2 is ______. The common factor of $3x$ and 3 is ______.

( )[( ) + ( )] Factor out the GCF of each group.

( )( )( ) Factor out ________, the common factor of the products inside the brackets.

REFLECT

1a. Why did the operation signs change when $-2x$ was factored out of each term?

____

____

____

____

1b. Does performing grouping before factoring out $-2x$ change the factorization? Explain.

____

____

____

____

____

____

Binomials have opposites. For example, $(3 - x)$ and $-(3 - x)$ are opposites. The expression $-(3 - x)$ can be rewritten as $(-3 + x)$ or $(x - 3)$. So, $(3 - x)$ and $(x - 3)$ are opposites.

CC.9–12.A.SSE.1b

2 EXAMPLE Factoring with Binomial Opposites

Factor $4x^3 - 8x^2 + 6 - 3x$.

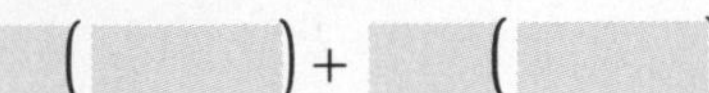

Group terms in the order in which they appear.

The GCF of the terms in the first group is ______. The GCF of the terms in the second group is ______. Factor out the GCF of each group.

The polynomial contains the binomial opposites (______) and (______).

Write $(2 - x)$ as $(-1)(x -$ ___$)$.

Simplify.

Factor out ________, the common factor of the products.

REFLECT

2a. How could you have rearranged the terms of the polynomial so that you would not have encountered binomial opposites when factoring? Show how you would have factored the polynomial if you had first rearranged the terms.

PRACTICE

Factor each polynomial by grouping.

1. $-3a^3 - 9a^2 - 6a - 18$

2. $-2c^3 + 4c^2 - 8c + 16$

3. $5s^3 - 5s^2 + 2 - 2s$

4. $4z^3 - 16z^2 + 40 - 10z$

Name ____________ Class ____________ Date ____________

7-2

Additional Practice

Factor each polynomial. Check your answer.

1. $8c^2 + 7c$
2. $3n^3 + 12n^2$
3. $15x^5 - 18x$
4. $-8s^4 + 20t^3 - 28$
5. $6n^6 + 18n^4 - 24n$
6. $-5m^4 - 5m^3 + 5m^2$
7. A ball is hit vertically into the air using a paddle at a speed of 32 ft/sec. The expression $-16t^2 + 32t$ gives the ball's height after t seconds. Factor this expression.
8. The area of Margo's laptop computer screen is $12x^2 + 3x$ in^2. Factor this polynomial to find expressions for the dimensions of her computer screen.

Factor each expression.

9. $3m(m + 5) + 4(m + 5)$
10. $16b(b - 3) + (b - 3)$

Factor each polynomial by grouping.

11. $2x^3 + 8x^2 + 3x + 12$
12. $4n^3 + 3n^2 + 4n + 3$
13. $10d^2 - 6d + 35d - 21$
14. $12n^3 - 15n^2 - 8n + 10$
15. $5b^4 - 15b^3 + 3 - b$
16. $t^3 - 5t^2 + 10 - 2t$

Problem Solving

Write the correct answer.

1. The area of a rug, which is shaped like a rectangle, is $4x^2 + 4x$ square feet. Factor this polynomial to find expressions for the dimensions of the rug.

   ____

2. The number of customers visiting a local museum since the year 2000 can be modeled by the expression $-3x^2 - 27x + 825$, where x is the number of years since 2000. Factor this polynomial.

   ____

3. The perimeter of a rhombus is $12x + 28$ feet. Factor this expression. Then find the length of one side if $x = 8$. (*Hint:* A rhombus is a parallelogram with four congruent sides.)

   ____

4. The foundation for a new high school building is rectangular in shape, and the area is $5x^3 + 4x^2 - 10x - 8$ square meters. Factor by grouping to find expressions for the dimensions of the building.

   ____

The diagram shows four sections of an herb garden. Use the figure to answer questions 5–8. Select the best answer.

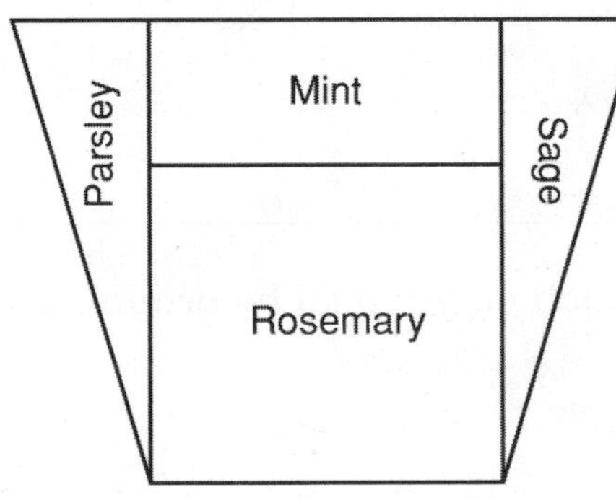

5. The section where rosemary grows is square and has an area of $4x^2$ square feet. What is the length of one side?

   A x feet C $2x$ feet
   B x^2 feet D $4x$ feet

6. Rosemary and mint cover $6x^2 - 2x$ square feet. Assuming the length is adjacent to rosemary, what is the width of the mint section?

   F $2x$ feet H $2x - 2$ feet
   G $x - 1$ feet J $3x - 1$ feet

7. The parsley and sage sections each have an area of $\frac{1}{2}(3x^2 - 6x - x + 2)$ square feet. Factor $3x^2 - 6x - x + 2$. What are the base and height of each triangular section?

   A $2x - 3$ feet; $x + 1$ feet
   B $2x - 3$ feet; $x^2 + 1$ feet
   C $3x - 1$ feet; $x - 2$ feet
   D $3x - 1$ feet; $x^2 - 2$ feet

8. Assuming the side adjacent to mint and rosemary is the base, what is the height of each triangle on which parsley and sage grow?

   F $x - 2$ feet
   G $x + 1$ feet
   H $x^2 + 1$ feet
   J $2x$ feet

Name________________________ Class________________ Date__________

7-3

Factoring $x^2 + bx + c$

Going Deeper

Essential question: *How can you factor $x^2 + bx + c$?*

Video Tutor

CC.9-12.A.SSE.2

1 ENGAGE Factoring Trinomials

You know how to multiply binomials: for example, $(x + 3)(x - 5) = x^2 - 2x - 15$. In this lesson, you will learn how to reverse this process and factor trinomials.

There are several important things you should remember from multiplying binomials.

- Using FOIL, the constant term in the trinomial is a result of multiplying the *last* terms in the two binomials.
- Using FOIL, the x-term results from adding the products of the *outside* terms and *inside* terms.

You can factor $x^2 + 10x + 21$ by working FOIL backward. Both signs in the trinomial are plus signs, so you know both binomials are of the form *x plus something.* Therefore, you can set up the factoring as shown below.

$$x^2 + 10x + 21 = (x + \boxed{?})(x + \boxed{?})$$

To find the constant terms in the binomials, use the information above and follow the steps below.

1) The constant term in the trinomial, 21, is the product of the last terms in the two binomials. Factor 21 into pairs. The factor pairs are shown in the table at the right.
2) The correct factor pair is the one whose sum is the coefficient of x in the trinomial.
3) Complete the binomial expression with the appropriate numbers.

$$x^2 + 10x + 21 = \left(x + \boxed{}\right)\left(x + \boxed{}\right)$$

Factors of 21	Sum of Factors
1 and 21	22
3 and 7	10 ✓

REFLECT

1a. You want to factor $x^2 - 6x + 8$. What factoring pattern would you set up to begin the process? Explain.

____

____

1b. You want to factor $x^2 - 2x - 15$. What factoring pattern would you set up to begin the process? Explain. Would this pattern also work for $x^2 + 2x - 15$? Explain.

1c. Use factoring patterns to factor $x^2 + 8x + 16$ and $x^2 - 6x + 9$. What do you notice about the factored forms? What special type of trinomials are $x^2 + 8x + 16$ and $x^2 - 6x + 9$?

CC.9–12.A.SSE.2

2 EXAMPLE Factoring Trinomials

A **Factor $x^2 + 3x - 10$.**

The constant is negative, so you know one binomial will have a subtraction sign.

$$x^2 + 3x - 10 = (x + \boxed{?})(x - \boxed{?})$$

Complete the table at the right. Note that you are finding the factors of −10, not 10. Since the coefficient of x is positive, the factor with the greater absolute value will be positive (and the other factor will be negative).

Factors of −10	Sum of Factors
−1 and 10	

$$x^2 + 3x - 10 = \left(x + \quad\right)\left(x - \quad\right)$$

B **Factor $x^2 - 8x - 48$.**

The constant is negative, so you know one binomial will have a subtraction sign.

$$x^2 - 8x - 48 = (x + \boxed{?})(x - \boxed{?})$$

Complete the table at the right. Since the coefficient of x is negative, the factor with the greater absolute value will be negative (and the other factor will be positive).

Factors of −48	Sum of Factors
1 and −48	
2 and	

$$x^2 - 8x - 48 = \left(x + \quad\right)\left(x - \quad\right)$$

REFLECT

2a. Complete the table below. Assume that *b*, *c*, *p*, and *q* are positive numbers.

Trinomial	Form of Binomial Factors
$x^2 + bx + c$	$(x \ \square \ p)(x \ \square \ q)$
$x^2 - bx + c$	$(x \ \square \ p)(x \ \square \ q)$
$x^2 - bx - c$ or $x^2 + bx - c$	$(x \ \square \ p)(x \ \square \ q)$

For the last row in the table, explain how to determine which factor contains a + sign and which factor contains a − sign.

____

____

____

PRACTICE

Complete the factorization of the polynomial.

1. $t^2 + 6t + 5 = (t + 5)(t + \square)$

2. $z^2 - 121 = (z + 11)(z \ \square \ \square)$

3. $d^2 + 5d - 24 = (d + \square)(d - \square)$

4. $x^4 - 4 = (x^2 + \square)(\square - 2)$

Factor the polynomial.

5. $y^2 + 3y - 4$

____

6. $x^2 - 2x + 1$

____

7. $p^2 - 2p - 24$

____

8. $g^2 - 100$

____

9. $z^2 - 7z + 12$

____

10. $q^2 + 25q + 100$

____

11. $m^2 + 8m + 16$

____

12. $n^2 - 10n - 24$

____

13. $x^2 + 25x$

____

14. $y^2 - 13y - 30$

____

Factor the polynomial.

15. $z^2 - 9$

____

16. $p^2 + 3p - 54$

____

17. $x^2 + 11x - 42$

____

18. $g^2 - 14g - 51$

____

19. $n^2 - 81$

____

20. $y^2 - 25y$

____

21. $x^2 + 11x + 30$

____

22. $x^2 - x - 20$

____

23. $x^2 + 6x - 7$

____

24. $x^2 + 2x + 1$

____

Name________________ Class__________ Date__________

Additional Practice

Factor each trinomial.

1. $x^2 + 7x + 10$ ________
2. $x^2 + 9x + 8$ ________
3. $x^2 + 13x + 36$ ________
4. $x^2 + 9x + 14$ ________
5. $x^2 + 7x + 12$ ________
6. $x^2 + 9x + 18$ ________
7. $x^2 - 9x + 18$ ________
8. $x^2 - 5x + 4$ ________
9. $x^2 - 9x + 20$ ________
10. $x^2 - 12x + 20$ ________
11. $x^2 - 11x + 18$ ________
12. $x^2 - 12x + 32$ ________
13. $x^2 + 7x - 18$ ________
14. $x^2 + 10x - 24$ ________
15. $x^2 + 2x - 3$ ________
16. $x^2 + 2x - 15$ ________
17. $x^2 + 5x - 6$ ________
18. $x^2 + 5x - 24$ ________
19. $x^2 - 5x - 6$ ________
20. $x^2 - 2x - 35$ ________
21. $x^2 - 7x - 30$ ________
22. $x^2 - x - 56$ ________
23. $x^2 - 2x - 8$ ________
24. $x^2 - x - 20$ ________
25. Factor $n^2 + 5n - 24$. Show that the original polynomial and the factored form describe the same sequence of numbers for $n = 0, 1, 2, 3,$ and 4.

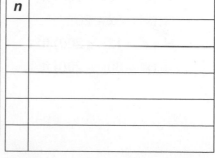

____

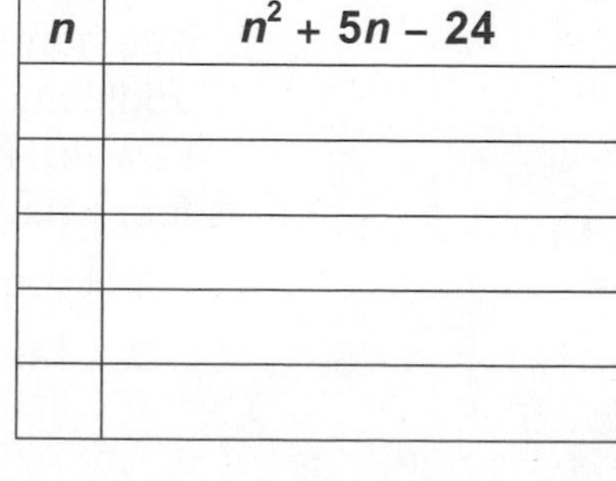

n	$n^2 + 5n - 24$

n	

Problem Solving

Write the correct answer.

1. A plot of land is rectangular and has an area of $x^2 - 5x - 24$ m^2. The length is $x + 3$ m. Find the width of the plot.

____

____

2. An antique Persian carpet has an area of $(x^2 + x - 20)$ ft^2 and a length of $(x + 5)$ feet. The rug is displayed on a wall in a museum. The wall has a width of $(x + 2)$ feet and an area of $(x^2 + 17x + 30)$ ft^2. Write expressions for the length and width of both the rug and wall. Then find the dimensions of the rug and the wall if $x = 20$ feet.

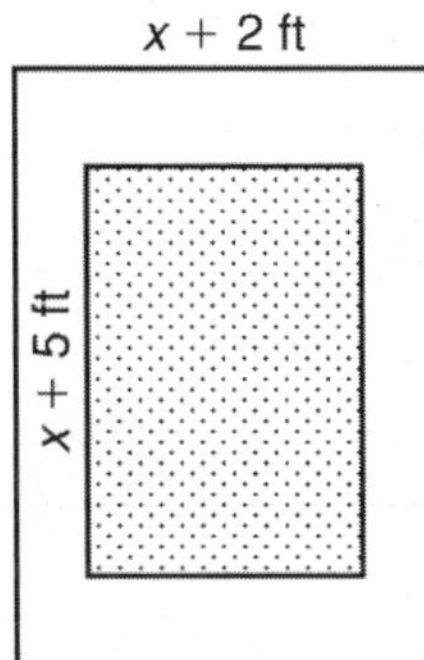

____

____

3. The area of a poster board is $x^2 + 3x - 10$ inches. The width is $x - 2$ inches.

   a. Write an expression for the length of the poster board.

   ____

   b. Find the dimensions of the poster board when $x = 14$.

   ____

   c. Write a polynomial for the area of the poster board if one inch is removed from each side.

   ____

The figure shows the plans for an addition on the back of a house. Use the figure to answer questions 4–6. Select the best answer.

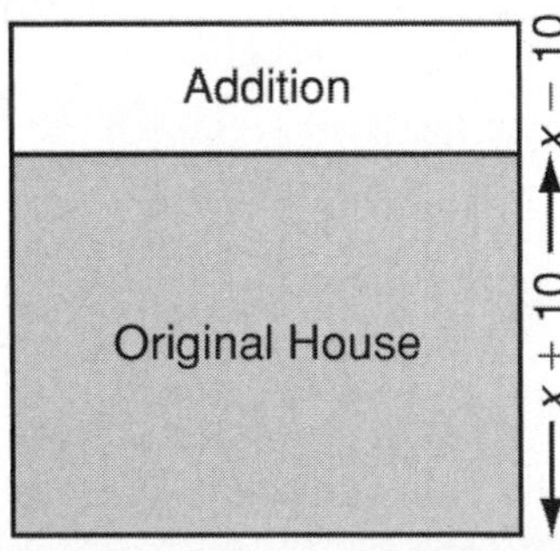

4. The area of the addition is $(x^2 + 10x - 200)$ ft^2. What is its length?

   A $(x - 20)$ feet

   B $(x - 2)$ feet

   C $(x + 2)$ feet

   D $(x + 20)$ feet

5. What is the area of the original house?

   F $(x^2 - 10x - 200)$ ft^2

   G $(x^2 + 8x - 20)$ ft^2

   H $(x^2 + 12x + 200)$ ft^2

   J $(x^2 + 30x + 200)$ ft^2

6. The homeowners decide to extend the addition. The area with the addition is now $(x^2 + 12x - 160)$ ft^2. By how many feet was the addition extended?

   A 1 foot

   B 2 feet

   C 3 feet

   D 4 feet

Name________________________ Class______________ Date__________

7-4

Video Tutor

Factoring $ax^2 + bx + c$

Going Deeper

Essential question: *How can you factor $ax^2 + bx + c$?*

You have learned how to factor $ax^2 + bx + c$ when $a = 1$ by identifying the correct pair of factors of c whose sum is b. But what if the coefficient of x^2 is not 1?

First, review binomial multiplication. The product $(2x + 5)(3x + 2)$ is found by using FOIL.

$$(2x + 5)(3x + 2) = \underset{\textbf{F}}{6x^2} + \underset{\textbf{O}}{4x} + \underset{\textbf{I}}{15x} + \underset{\textbf{L}}{10} = 6x^2 + 19x + 10$$

F The product of the coefficients of the **first** terms is a.

O, **I** } The sum of the coefficients of the **outer** and **inner** products is b.

L The product of the **last** terms is c.

To factor $ax^2 + bx + c$, you need to reverse this process. Start by listing the possible factor pairs of a and c. Then use trial and error to find a sum of b for the outer and inner products.

CC.9–12.A.SSE.2

1 EXAMPLE Factoring $ax^2 + bx + c$

Factor $5n^2 + 11n + 2$.

A First list the possible factor pairs for both a and c. All of the signs of the terms are positive, so the factors of a and c must all be positive.

The only factor pair for a is_____, _____. The only factor pair for c is_____, _____.

B Choose the arrangement of the factor pairs that makes $b = 11$. Check your result by multiplying.

$$5n^2 + 11n + 2 = (\square n + \square)(\square n + \square)$$

REFLECT

1a. What other arrangement of factor pairs is possible for a and c? What is the resulting product, and how is it different from $5n^2 + 11n + 2$?

____

1b. If a is positive, b is negative, and c is positive, what are the signs of the factors of a and c that you are looking for?

____

1c. If a is positive, b is negative, and c is negative, what are the signs of the factors of a and c that you are looking for?

If a and c have a lot of factors, there are many possible arrangements. One way to quickly check each arrangement is shown below, using the trinomial $5n^2 + 11n + 2$. List the factor pairs of a and c vertically, then multiply diagonally, and add.

Factors of a	Factors of c		Inner and Outer products
1	2	=	10
5	1	=	1
			11 ← Sum

If the sum is correct, the factors are read across: $(1n + 2)$ and $(5n + 1)$.

CC.9–12.A.SSE.2

2 EXAMPLE Factoring $ax^2 + bx + c$

Factor $6x^2 - 13x - 8$.

A First list the possible factor pairs for both a and c. Because c is negative, one of the factors of c must be positive, and the other must be negative.

The factor pairs for a are: ____, ____ and ____, ____.

The factor pairs for c are: ____, ____; ____, ____; ____, ____; ____, ____.

B Choose the arrangement of factor pairs that makes $b = -13$. Each factor pair of a can be arranged in two ways with each factor pair of c, so there are 16 possible arrangements. Three are shown below.

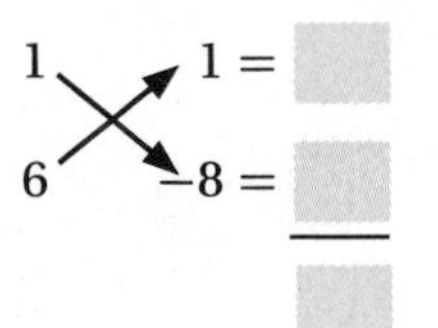

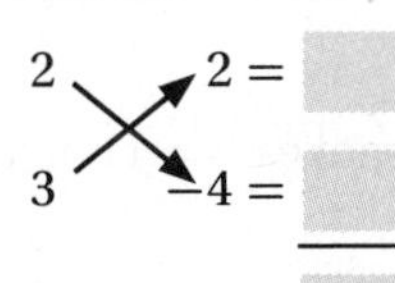

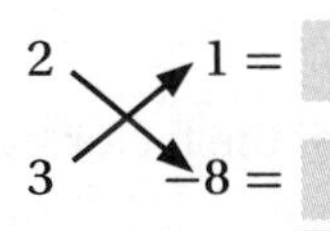

$6x^2 - 13x - 8 = (\ \ x + \ \ )(\ \ x - \ \ )$

REFLECT

2a. If you know the factors of $6x^2 - 13x - 8$, how could you easily factor $6x^2 + 13x - 8$?

2b. What fact about the sign of the sum can you use so that you need to test at most half of the possible arrangements?

PRACTICE

Factor.

1. $2x^2 + 15x + 7$

2. $7z^2 - 30z + 27$

3. $8x^2 - 10x - 3$

4. $30d^2 + 7d - 15$

5. $10g^2 + 23g + 12$

6. $5y^2 - 2y - 7$

7. $2n^2 - 11n + 15$

8. $6a^2 + 7a - 10$

9. $12x^2 - x$

10. $9z^2 - 25$

11. $36h^2 - 12h + 1$

12. $3n^2 - 20n + 12$

13. $9x^2 + 12x + 4$

14. $4y^2 + y - 18$

To factor a polynomial of the form $ax^2 + bx + c$ where a is negative, you first factor out −1 from all the terms. Factor each polynomial.

15. $-6x^2 + 11x + 10$

16. $-3x^2 + 5x + 22$

17. $-4x^2 - 12x + 7$

18. $-8x^2 + 6x + 9$

19. $-6x^2 + 7x + 5$

20. $-6x^2 - 25x + 9$

21. $-5x^2 + 17x - 6$

22. $-15x^2 + 2x + 8$

23. A dolphin bounces a ball off its nose at an initial upward velocity of 6 m/s to a trainer lying on a 1-meter high platform. The polynomial $-5t^2 + 6t - 1$ models the ball's height (in meters) above the platform.

a. Factor the polynomial.

____

b. When $t = 0$, what is the value of the polynomial? What does this value mean in the context of the situation?

____

____

c. For what values on t does the polynomial equal 0?

$t =$ _______ or $t =$ _______

d. Explain the two values for t in the context of the situation.

____

____

____

Additional Practice

Factor each trinomial.

1. $2x^2 + 13x + 15$ ________
2. $3x^2 + 10x + 8$ ________
3. $4x^2 + 24x + 27$ ________
4. $5x^2 + 21x + 4$ ________
5. $4x^2 + 11x + 7$ ________
6. $6x^2 - 23x + 20$ ________
7. $7x^2 - 59x + 24$ ________
8. $3x^2 - 14x + 15$ ________
9. $8x^2 - 73x + 9$ ________
10. $2x^2 + 11x - 13$ ________
11. $3x^2 + 2x - 16$ ________
12. $2x^2 + 17x - 30$ ________
13. $8x^2 + 29x - 12$ ________
14. $11x^2 + 25x - 24$ ________
15. $9x^2 - 3x - 2$ ________
16. $12x^2 - 7x - 12$ ________
17. $9x^2 - 49x - 30$ ________
18. $6x^2 + x - 40$ ________
19. $-12x^2 - 35x - 18$ ________
20. $-20x^2 + 29x - 6$ ________
21. $-2x^2 + 5x + 42$ ________
22. The area of a rectangle is $20x^2 - 27x - 8$. The length is $4x + 1$. What is the width? ________

Problem Solving

Write the correct answer.

1. A rectangular painting has an area of $(2x^2 + 8x + 6)$ cm^2. Its length is $(2x + 2)$ cm. Find the width of the painting.

____

2. A ball is kicked straight up into the air. The height of the ball in feet is given by the expression $-16t^2 + 12t + 4$, where t is time in seconds. Factor the expression. Then find the height of the ball after 1 second.

____

____

3. Instructors led an exercise class from a raised rectangular platform at the front of the room. The width of the platform was $(3x - 1)$ feet and the area was $(9x^2 + 6x - 3)$ ft^2. Find the length of this platform. After the exercise studio is remodeled, the area of the platform will be $(9x^2 + 12x + 3)$ ft^2. By how many feet will the width of the platform change?

____

____

4. A clothing store has a rectangular clearance section with a length that is twice the width w. During a sale, the section is expanded to an area of $(2w^2 + 19w + 35)$ ft^2. Find the amount of the increase in the length and width of the clearance section.

____

____

Select the best answer.

5. The area of a soccer field is $(24x^2 + 100x + 100)$ m^2. The width of the field is $(4x + 10)$ m. What is the length?

   A $(3x + 10)$ m C $(6x + 10)$ m

   B $(6x + 1)$ m D $(8x + 2)$ m

6. A square parking lot has an area of $(4x^2 + 20x + 25)$ ft^2. What is the length of one side of the parking lot?

   F $(2x + 5)$ ft H $(5x + 4)$ ft

   G $(2x + 10)$ ft J $(5x + 2)$ ft

7. For a certain college, the number of applications received after x recruiting seminars is modeled by the polynomial $3x^2 + 490x + 6000$. What is this expression in factored form?

   A $(3x - 40)(x - 150)$

   B $(3x + 40)(x + 150)$

   C $(3x - 30)(x - 200)$

   D $(3x - 30)(x + 200)$

8. Jin needs to fence in his rectangular backyard. The fence will have one long section away from, but parallel to, the length of his house and two shorter sides connecting that section to the house. The length of Jin's house is $(3x + 4)$ yd and the area of his backyard is $(9x^2 + 15x + 4)$ yd^2. How many yards of fencing will Jin need?

   F $(6x + 2)$ yd H $(9x + 9)$ yd

   G $(9x + 6)$ yd J $(12x + 10)$ yd

Name________________________ Class______________ Date__________

7-5

Factoring Special Products
Connection: Area

Video Tutor

Essential question: *How can you represent factoring special products geometrically?*

Recall that perfect square trinomials and the difference of two squares are special polynomials.

CC.9–12.A.SSE.2

1 EXPLORE Representing the Factoring of a Perfect Square Trinomial

Use area models to factor $a^2 + 2ab + b^2$.

A Finish labeling this model of $a^2 + 2ab + b^2$. Use a and b.

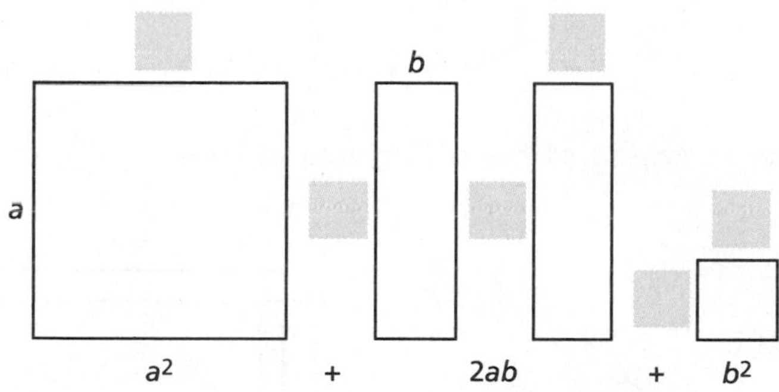

B Draw dashed lines inside the square below to show how the squares and rectangles from Step A could be placed together to form a larger square. Label the dimension of each part of the length and width of the larger square.

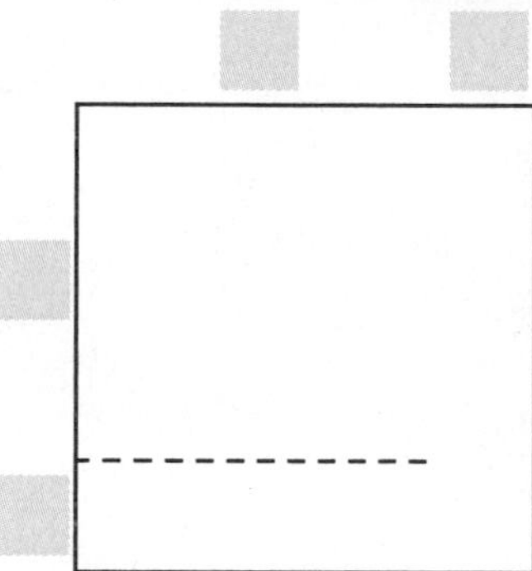

C Use the dimensions of the square in Step B to write the area of the square in Step B.

$A = (\_\_\_\_\_\_\_\_)(\_\_\_\_\_\_\_\_)$

D Because the square has the same area as the model of the polynomial, the factorization of $a^2 + 2ab + b^2$ is ____________.

REFLECT

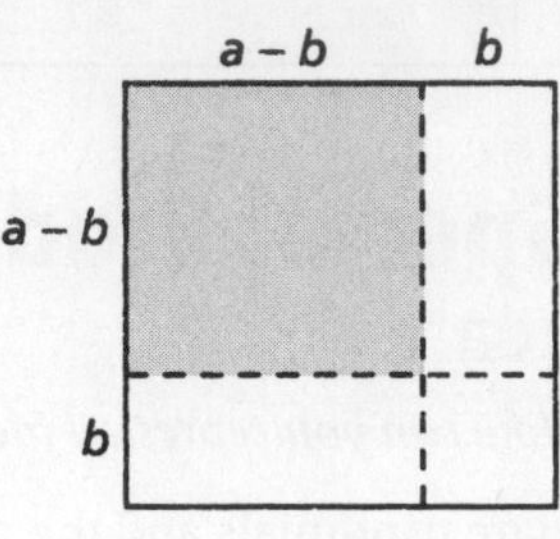

1a. How does the model at the right show that the factorization of $a^2 - 2ab + b^2$ is $(a - b)(a - b)$?

____

____

____

____

____

CC.9–12.A.SSE.2

2 EXPLORE Representing the Factoring of the Difference of Two Squares

Use area models to factor $a^2 - b^2$.

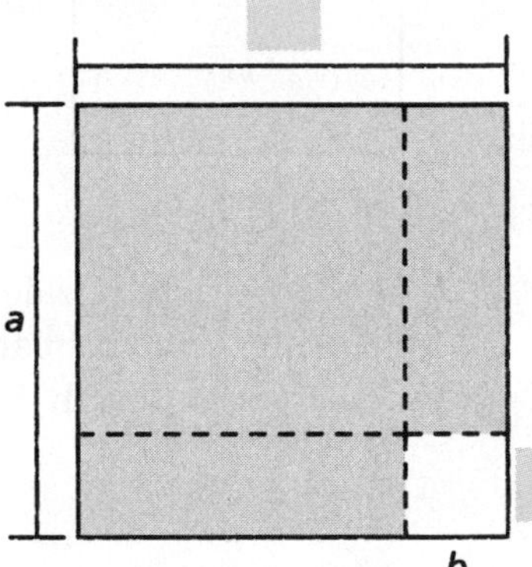

A Finish labeling this model of $a^2 - b^2$. Use a and b.

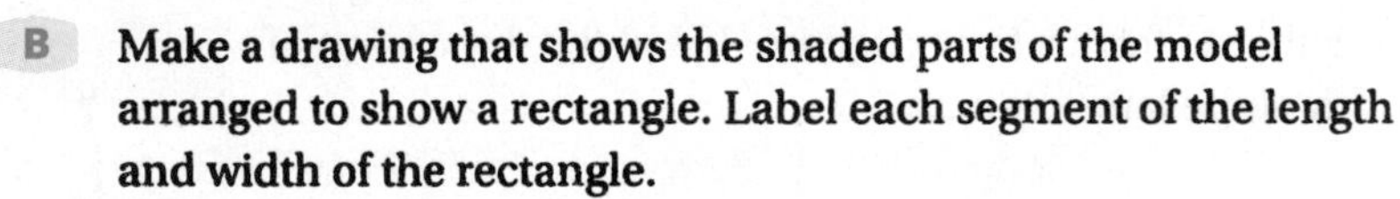

B Make a drawing that shows the shaded parts of the model arranged to show a rectangle. Label each segment of the length and width of the rectangle.

C What is the length of the longer side of the rectangle? Explain.

____

What is the length of the shorter side of the rectangle? __________

What is the area of the rectangle? (__________)(__________)

D Because the rectangle has the same area as the model of the polynomial, the factorization of $a^2 - b^2$ is __________________.

Name________________________ Class______________ Date______________

7-5

Additional Practice

Determine whether each trinomial is a perfect square. If so, factor it. If not, explain why.

1. $x^2 + 6x + 9$

____

2. $4x^2 + 20x + 25$

____

3. $36x^2 - 24x + 16$

____

4. $9x^2 - 12x + 4$

____

5. A rectangular fountain in the center of a shopping mall has an area of $(4x^2 + 12x + 9)$ ft^2. The dimensions of the fountain are of the form $cx + d$, where c and d are whole numbers. Find an expression for the perimeter of the fountain. Find the perimeter when $x = 2$ ft.

____

Determine whether each binomial is the difference of perfect squares. If so, factor it. If not, explain why.

6. $x^2 - 16$

____

7. $9b^4 - 200$

____

8. $1 - m^6$

____

9. $36s^2 - 4t^2$

____

10. $x^2y^2 + 190$

____

Problem Solving

Write the correct answer.

1. A rectangular fountain has an area of $(16x^2 + 8x + 1)$ ft^2. The dimensions of the rectangle have the form $ax + b$, where a and b are whole numbers. Write an expression for the perimeter of the fountain. Then find the perimeter when $x = 2$ feet.

____

____

2. A square tabletop has an area of $(9x^2 - 90x + 225)$ cm^2. The dimensions of the tabletop have the form $cx - d$, where c and d are whole numbers. Write an expression for the perimeter of the tabletop. Then find the perimeter when $x = 25$ centimeters.

____

____

3. The floor plan of a daycare center is shown.

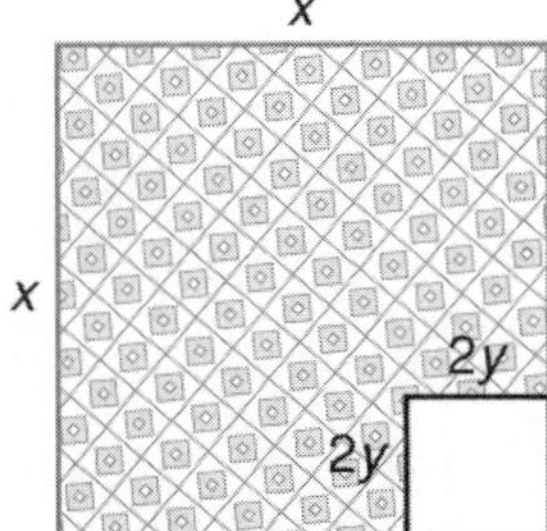

The arts and crafts area in the lower right corner is not carpeted. The rest of the center is carpeted. Write an expression, in factored form, for the area of the floor that is carpeted.

____

4. A plate with a decorative border is shown.

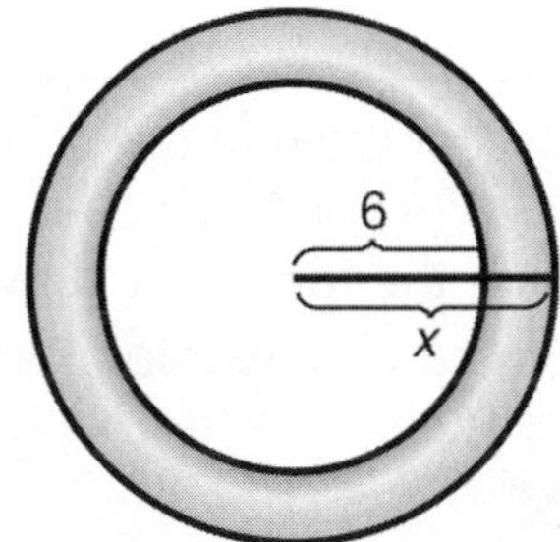

Write an expression, in factored form, for the area of the border. (*Hint:* First factor out the GCF.)

____

Nelson is making open top boxes by cutting out corners from a sheet of cardboard, folding the edges up, and then taping them together. Select the best answer.

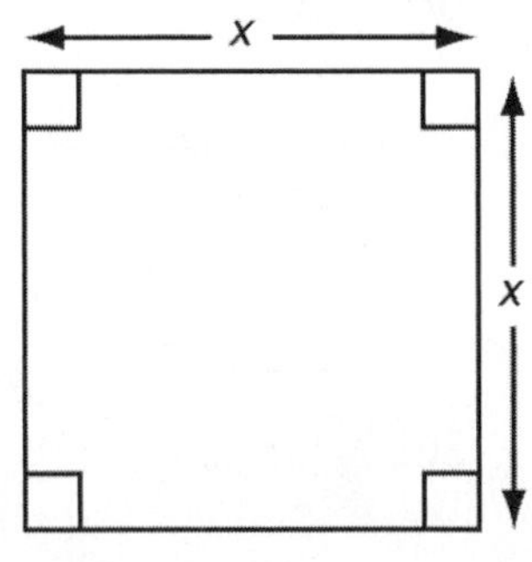

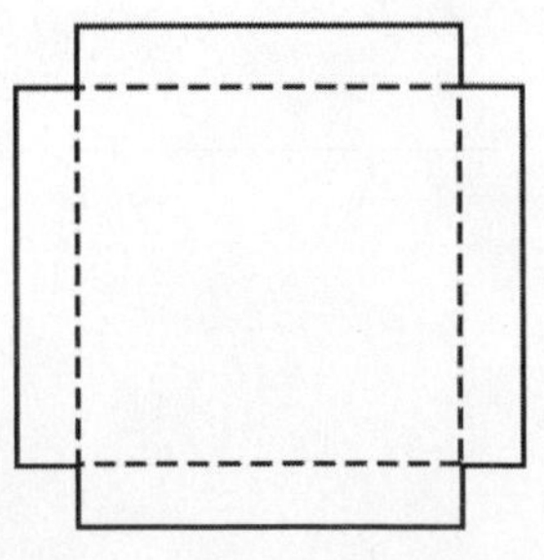

5. Nelson cut corners so that each corner was a square with side lengths of 4. What is the total area of the remaining piece of cardboard?

   A $x^2 - 8x + 16$ C $x^2 - 16x + 64$

   B $x^2 + 8x + 16$ D $x^2 + 16x + 64$

6. What are the dimensions of the square corners if the total remaining area is $x^2 - 4x + 4$?

   F 1 by 1 H 4 by 4

   G 2 by 2 J 8 by 8

Name ____________________ Class ____________ Date ________

7-6

Choosing a Factoring Method

Extension: Factoring Polynomials with More Than One Variable

Essential question: *How can you factor polynomials with more than one variable?*

Video Tutor

CC.9-12.A.SSE.2

1 EXPLORE Factoring Polynomials with Two Variables

Factor each polynomial completely. Explain each step.

$2x^2 - 162$

$2(x^2 - 81)$ Factor the GCF.

______________ Difference of squares

$3m^2 - 3n^2$

3______________ ______________

______________ ______________

REFLECT

1a. Compare the methods of factoring the two polynomials.

____

1b. How would the factoring change for the polynomial $3m^2 - 12n^2$?

____

____

To factor a perfect square trinomial with more than variable you can use the same patterns you used with perfect square trinomials in one variable.

$$a^2 + 2ab + b^2 = (a + b)(a + b)$$
$$a^2 - 2ab + b^2 = (a - b)(a - b)$$

CC.9-12.A.SSE.2

2 EXAMPLE Factoring a Perfect Square Trinomial

Factor the trinomial completely. Explain each step.

$3g^2 + 12gh + 12h^2$

3______________ ______________

______________ ______________

REFLECT

2a. Which pattern would you use to factor $16a^2 - 48ab + 36b^2$? Explain how you know and then factor the trinomial.

____

____

If there is no obvious pattern shown by the trinomial, you can find the factors of the coefficient of the third term and check their sums to find how to factor.

CC.9–12.A.SSE.2

3 EXAMPLE Factoring a Polynomial

Factor $3x^2 + 21xy + 36y^2$ completely. Explain your steps.

3______________________ ______________________

Find the factors of 12 that add to 7.

Factors of 12	Sum of factors
1 and 12	
and	
and	

______________________ Factor according to the sum.

REFLECT

3a. Would finding the factors and their sum be enough to factor the polynomial $2x^2 + 11xy + 12y^2$? Why or why not?

____

____

____

3b. What additional conditions must you consider to factor $2x^2 + 11xy + 12y^2$?

____

____

____

Sometimes grouping will allow you to factor a polynomial.

CC.9–12.A.SSE.1b

4 EXAMPLE Factoring a Polynomial Using Grouping

Factor $9x^3 - 9xy + 2y - 2x^2$ completely. Explain your steps.

There is no GCF for all the terms. Since the polynomial has four terms, factor by grouping.

$(9x^3 - \underline{\quad}) + (\underline{\quad} - \underline{\quad})$	Group terms that have a common factor. The common factor of $9x^3y$ and $-9xy$ is $\underline{\quad}$. The common factor of $2y$ and $-2x^2$ is $\underline{\quad}$.
$\underline{\quad}(\underline{\quad}) + (\underline{\quad})(\underline{\quad})$	Factor out the GCF of each group.
$\underline{\quad}(x^2 - y) + (\underline{\quad})(\underline{\quad})(\underline{\quad})$	The polynomial contains the binomial opposites $(x^2 - y)$ and $(\underline{\quad})$. Write $(y - x^2)$ as $(-1)(\underline{\quad})$.
$\underline{\quad}(x^2 - y) - (\underline{\quad})(\underline{\quad})$	Simplify.
$(\underline{\quad})(\underline{\quad})$	Factor out $(\underline{\quad})$, the common factor of the products.

REFLECT

4a. Describe the steps you would use in factoring $8x^2 - 2x + 24xy - 6y$.

PRACTICE

Choose a factoring method to factor each polynomial completely. Explain each step.

1. $x^2 + 6xy + 9x^2$

2. $4x^2 - 4xy - 8y^2$

3. $x^2 - 4y^2$

4. $g^2 + 3gh - 10h^2$

Factor each polynomial completely.

5. $2m^2 + 5mn - 3n^2$

6. $4x^2 - 9y^2$

7. $g^2 - 7gh + 10h^2$

8. $16b^2 - 49c^2$

9. $a^3 - 3a^2b - 4ab^2$

10. $6a^2 + 3ab - 18b^2$

11. $2t^3 + 12t^2w + 18tw^2$

12. $6c^3 - 27c^2d + 12cd^2$

13. $x^3y - 5x^2y + 4x - 20$

14. $x^4y^2 + 4x^2y^2 - 7x^2 - 28$

15. Factor $x^4 - y^4$ completely. (*Hint*: What special form does this polynomial appear to follow?)

16. Jaime and Sam both factored the polynomial $2x^2 + 10xy + 8y^2$. Which student is correct? Explain.

Jaime	**Sam**
$2x^2 + 10xy + 8y^2$	$2x^2 + 10xy + 8y^2$
$2(x^2 + 5xy + 4y^2)$	$(2x + 2y)(x + 4y)$
$2(x + y)(x + 4y)$	

Name________________ Class________________ Date________________

7-6

Additional Practice

Tell whether each polynomial is completely factored. If not, factor it.

1. $6(st^2 + 12)$ ________________

2. $5(m^2 + 9m)$ ________________

3. $2p(p^4 - 9)$ ________________

4. $(x - 8y)(2x + 3y)$ ________________

5. $3k^3(5jk^2 + 19j)$ ________________

6. $7(14g^4 - 4g + 10)$ ________________

Factor each polynomial completely.

7. $24xy^2 + 40y$ ________________

8. $5r^3 - 10rs$ ________________

9. $3x^3y + x^2y^2$ ________________

10. $-3a^2b + 12ab - 12b$ ________________

11. $5t^3 - 45ts^2 + 3t^2 - 27s^2$ ________________

12. $2y^2 - 6xy - 56x^2$ ________________

13. $6a^3 + 39a^2 + 45a$ ________________

14. $x^3y - 9xy^3$ ________________

15. $12n^3 - 48$ ________________

16. $3c^4 + 24c^3d + 48c^2d^2$ ________________

17. $3cd^3 + 4d - 2c$ ________________

18. $10w^6 - 160w^2v^4$ ________________

Problem Solving

Write the correct answer.

1. A rectangular stage set up in a theater has an area of $(15x^2 + 3xy - 12y^2)$ square feet. Factor the polynomial completely.

____

2. The area of a circular rug is $(16\pi k^2 - 16\pi k + 4\pi)$ m^2. Factor the expression completely. Then find the area of the rug if $k = 1$ meter.

____

____

3. An artist framed a picture. The dimensions of the picture and frame are shown below.

Completely factor the expression for the area of the frame.

____

4. The attendance for a team's basketball game can be approximated with the polynomial $-5x^2 + 80x + 285$, where x is the number of wins the team had in the previous month. Factor the polynomial completely. Then estimate the attendance when the team won 4 games in the previous month.

____

____

Select the best answer.

5. The volume of a box can be modeled by the expression $7x^4 - 28y^2$. Which shows this expression completely factored?

   A $7(x^4 - 4y^2)$

   B $7(x^2 - 2y)^2$

   C $(7x^2 + 4y)(x^2 - 7y)$

   D $7(x^2 + 2y)(x^2 - 2y)$

6. The area of a Japanese rock garden is $(30x^2 + 3xy - 6y^2)$ square feet. Factor the polynomial completely.

   F $3(10x^2 + xy - 2y^2)$

   G $3(2x + y)(5x - 2y)$

   H $(6x + 3y)(5x - 2y)$

   J $(15x - 6y)(2x + y)$

7. The money made from the sales of x mountain bikes is approximated by $20x^2 + 10x + 90$. Factor the expression completely.

   A $2(10x + 9)(x + 5)$

   B $5(4x^2 + 2x + 18)$

   C $10(2x^2 + x + 9)$

   D The expression cannot be factored.

8. Kyle stood on a bridge and threw a rock up and over the side. The height of the rock, in meters, can be approximated by $-5t^2 + 5t + 24$, where t is the time in seconds after Kyle threw it. Completely factor the expression.

   F $-5(t^2 + t + 24)$

   G $(-5t + 3)(t + 8)$

   H $-1(5t + 8)(t + 3)$

   J The expression cannot be factored.

Name_______________________ Class_______________ Date__________

Performance Tasks

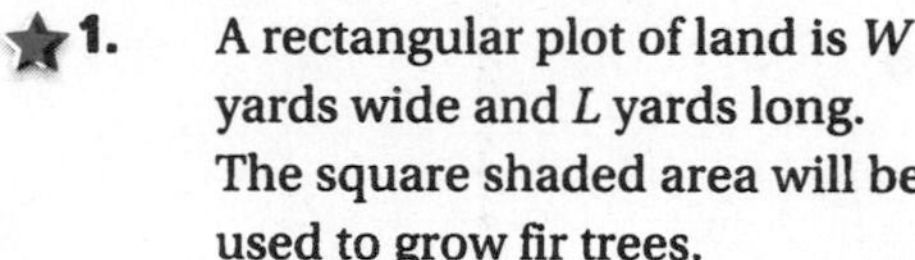

★1. A rectangular plot of land is W yards wide and L yards long. The square shaded area will be used to grow fir trees.

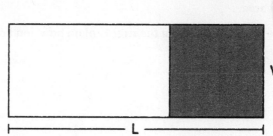

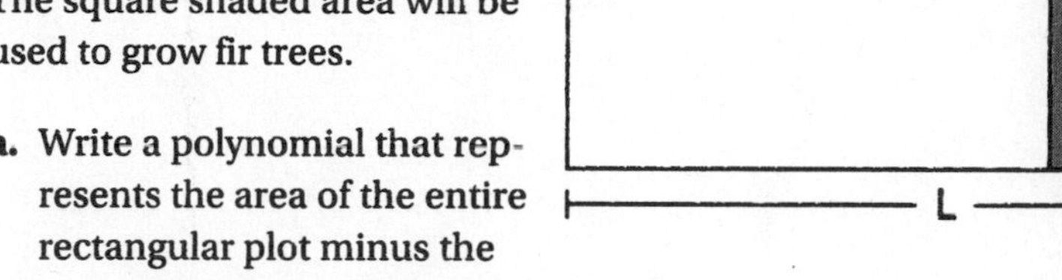

a. Write a polynomial that represents the area of the entire rectangular plot minus the area of the shaded square.

b. Rewrite your polynomial from part **a** in factored form. How does this relate to the dimensions of the area not used to grow fir trees?

★2. Baljit builds a square frame that is 1 inch wider than twice the width of a square frame from the store. He writes the area enclosed by his frame with the polynomial $4x^2 + 4x + 1$.

a. Factor the polynomial that Baljit wrote. Explain how the factorization yields an expression for the width of the frame Baljit builds.

b. What is a variable expression for the area enclosed by the frame from the store? Explain how you know.

3. The area of a rectangular rug is given by the polynomial $x^2 + 4x$. The variable x represents the width of the rug in feet.

a. Factor the polynomial. How does the length of the rug compare to the width of the rug?

b. The rug has an area of 21 square feet. Make a table to find the value of x that gives the required area.

c. What are the dimensions of the rug? Explain how you know.

4. There are two square workout mats at a gym.

a. Let x represent the length of the larger mat, and let y represent the length of the smaller mat. Write a binomial that represents how much more area the larger mat has than the smaller mat.

b. Factor the binomial for the difference in the mat areas. Interpret what the factors could mean in this context.

c. One mat has 4 times the area of the other mat. Use this to rewrite the binomial from part **a** using only the variable y.

CHAPTER 7 COMMON CORE ASSESSMENT READINESS

Name ______________________ Class ______________ Date __________

MULTIPLE CHOICE

1. One way to factor $6x^3 + 21x^2y + 15xy^2$ is to first find the greatest common factor, or GCF. What is the GCF?

   A. 3

   B. $3x$

   C. $3y$

   D. $3xy$

2. Jon has rewritten the expression $15x^3 - 10x^2 + 27x - 18$ in order to factor it. Which is a reasonable next step for Jon to perform?

   F. Use the Commutative Property to rewrite the terms in a different order.

   G. Factor 2 from the second and fourth terms.

   H. Group the first two terms and factor out the greatest common factor, $5x^2$.

   J. Factor x from each of the four terms.

3. What is the factored form of $n^2 - 5n + 6$?

   A. $(n - 6)(n + 1)$

   B. $(n + 6)(n - 1)$

   C. $(n + 2)(n + 3)$

   D. $(n - 2)(n - 3)$

4. What is the factored form of $3c^2 + c - 4$?

   F. $(3c - 2)(c + 2)$

   G. $(3c + 2)(c + 2)$

   H. $(3c + 4)(c - 1)$

   J. $(3c - 1)(c + 4)$

5. The amount of paint needed to cover a wall is proportional to its area. The wall is rectangular and has an area of $(6a^2 + 12a)$ square meters. Factor this polynomial to find possible expressions for the length and width of the wall. (Assume the factors are polynomials.)

   A. $6a(a + 2)$; possible dimensions: $6a$ meters by $(a + 2)$ meters

   B. $6a^2(a + 2)$; possible dimensions: $6a^2$ meters by $(a + 2)$ meters

   C. $6(a + 2a)$; possible dimensions: 6 meters by $(a + 2a)$ meters

   D. $6a(6a + 12)$; possible dimensions: $6a$ meters by $(6a + 12)$ meters

6. Which of the following polynomials have a common binomial factor?

   F. $(x^2 + 4)$ and $(x^2 + 4x + 4)$

   G. $(x^2 + 4)$ and $(x^2 - 4x + 4)$

   H. $(x^2 - 4)$ and $(x^2 + 4x - 4)$

   J. $(x^2 - 4)$ and $(x^2 + 4x + 4)$

7. Which expression is not equivalent to the polynomial $6x^3 + 15x^2 - 9x$?

   A. $3(2x^3 + 5x^2 - 3x)$

   B. $3x(2x^2 + 5x - 3)$

   C. $3x(x + 3)(x - 1)$

   D. $3x(2x - 1)(x + 3)$

CONSTRUCTED RESPONSE

8. Complete the diagram and the equation that represent the binomial multiplication shown by the algebra tiles.

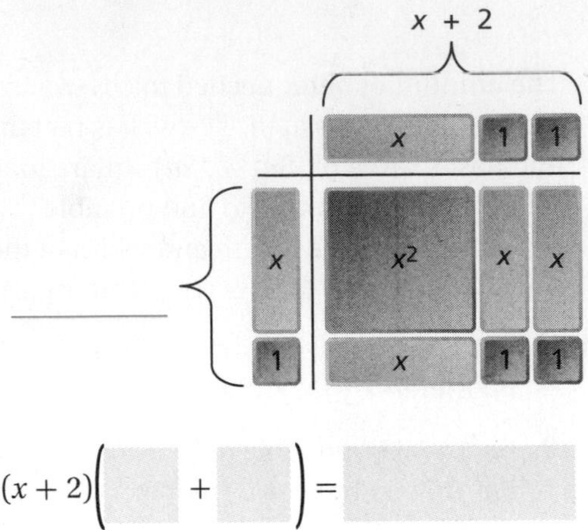

$(x + 2)(\quad + \quad) = $

9. Show how to factor the polynomial $10a^2b - 20ab - 12b + 6ab$ completely.

10. The area of a square room (in square feet) is given by the polynomial $16x^2 + 40x + 25$. The length of each wall can be written in the form $cx + d$, where c and d are whole numbers.

a. Show how to write an expression in terms of x for the perimeter of the room.

b. Find the perimeter when $x = 2$ feet.

11. A small square prism is positioned inside a larger square prism as shown, h is the height of the prisms, S is the base length of the larger prism, and s is the base length of the smaller prism. The volume of a prism is the product of the lengths of the edges.

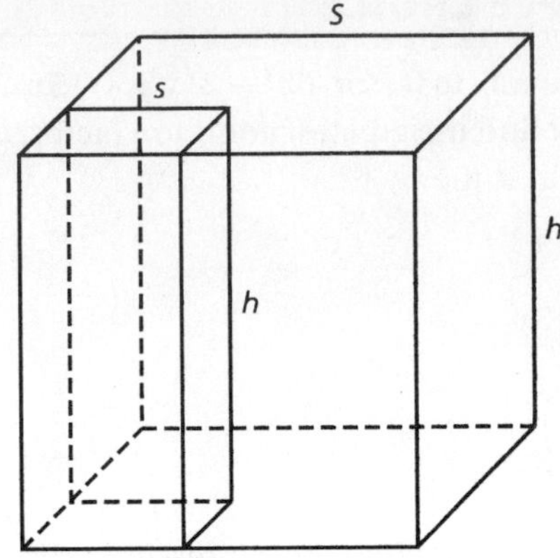

a. Write a subtraction expression for the difference in volumes between the two square prisms.

b. Write the expression in part (a) as a product in two different ways.

c. Find the difference in volumes when $h = 10$ cm, $S = 30$ cm, and $s = 20$ cm. Tell which form of the expression you used and why.

CHAPTER 8

Quadratic Functions and Equations

Chapter Focus

You will study quadratic functions and equations in this chapter. You will graph quadratic functions of the form $f(x) = ax^2 + bx + c$ and learn how to transform the graph of a quadratic function in the coordinate plane. You will also explore several ways to solve quadratic equations of the form $ax^2 + bx + c = 0$, and you will apply these techniques to solve systems of linear and quadratic equations.

Chapter at a Glance

COMMON CORE

Lesson		Standards for Mathematical Content
8-1	Identifying Quadratic Functions	CC.9-12.F.IF.4, CC.9-12.F.BF.1, CC.9-12.F.BF.3
8-2	Characteristics of Quadratic Functions	CC.9-12.F.BF.1, CC.9-12.F.BF.3
8-3	Graphing Quadratic Functions	CC.9-12.F.IF.7a
8-4	Transforming Quadratic Functions	CC.9-12.F.BF.1, CC.9-12.F.BF.3
8-5	Solving Quadratic Equations by Graphing	CC.9-12.A.CED.2, CC.9-12.A.REI.11
8-6	Solving Quadratic Equations by Factoring	CC.9-12.A.CED.1, CC.9-12.A.REI.4b
8-7	Solving Quadratic Equations by Using Square Roots	CC.9-12.A.CED.1, CC.9-12.A.REI.4b
8-8	Completing the Square	CC.9-12.A.REI.4b
8-9	The Quadratic Formula and the Discriminant	CC.9-12.A.REI.4a, CC.9-12.A.REI.4b
8-10	Nonlinear Systems	CC.9-12.A.REI.7
	Performance Tasks	
	Assessment Readiness	

CHAPTER 8

Unpacking the Standards

Understanding the standards and the vocabulary terms in the standards will help you know exactly what you are expected to learn in this chapter.

COMMON CORE **CC.9-12.F.IF.7a**

Graph … quadratic functions and show intercepts, maxima, and minima.

Key Vocabulary

quadratic function *(función cuadrática)* A function that can be written in the form $f(x) = ax^2 + bx + c$, where *a*, *b*, and *c* are real numbers and $a \neq 0$, or in the form $f(x) = a(x - h)^2 + k$, where *a*, *h*, and *k* are real numbers and $a \neq 0$.

x-intercept *(intersección con el eje x)* The *x*-coordinate(s) of the point(s) where a graph intersects the *x*-axis.

y-intercept *(intersección con el eje y)* The *y*-coordinate(s) of the point(s) where a graph intersects the *y*-axis.

maximum/minimum value of a function *(máximo/mínimo de una función)* The *y*-value of the highest/lowest point on the graph of the function.

What It Means For You Lessons 8-1, 8-2, 8-3, 8-4, 8-5, 8-9, 8-10

The graph of a quadratic function has key features that are helpful when interpreting a real-world quadratic model: the intercepts and the maximum or minimum value.

EXAMPLE **Graph of $y = x^2 + 2x - 3$**

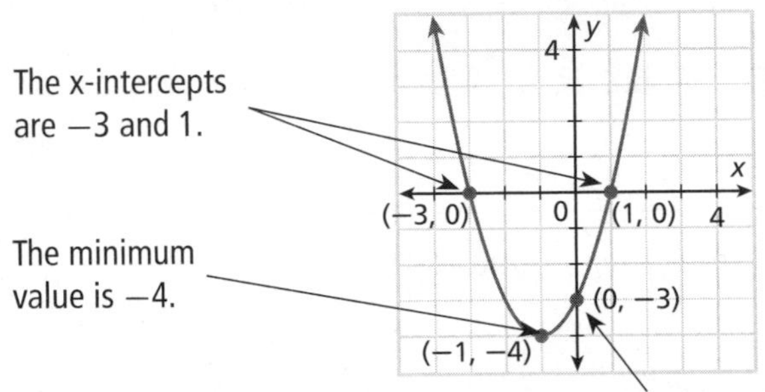

COMMON CORE **CC.9-12.F.BF.3**

Identify the effect on the graph of replacing $f(x)$ by $f(x) + k$, $k\,f(x)$, $f(kx)$, and $f(x + k)$ for specific values of k (both positive and negative); …

Key Vocabulary

function notation *(notación de función)* If *x* is the independent variable and *y* is the dependent variable, then the function notation for *y* is *f*(*x*), read "*f* of *x*," where *f* names the function.

What It Means For You Lessons 8-1, 8-4

You can change a function by adding or multiplying by a constant. The result will be a new function that is a transformation of the original function.

EXAMPLE **Compression and Stretch/Reflection of *f*(*x*)**

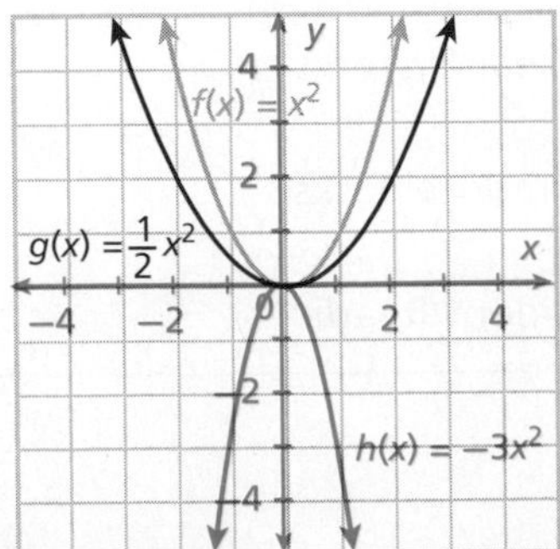

CHAPTER 8

COMMON CORE **CC.9-12.A.REI.4b**

Solve quadratic equations by inspection (e.g., for $x^2 = 49$), taking square roots, completing the square, the quadratic formula and factoring, as appropriate to the initial form of the equation. ...

Key Vocabulary

quadratic equation *(ecuación cuadrática)* An equation that can be written in the form $ax^2 + bx + c = 0$, where a, b, and c are real numbers and $a \neq 0$.

completing the square *(completar el cuadrado)* A process used to form a perfect-square trinomial. To complete the square of $x^2 + bx$, add $\left(\frac{b}{2}\right)^2$.

Quadratic Formula *(fórmula cuadrática)* The formula

$$x = \frac{-b \pm \sqrt{b^2 - 4ac}}{2a}$$

which gives solutions, or roots, of equations in the form $ax^2 + bx + c = 0$, where a, b, and c are real numbers and $a \neq 0$.

What It Means For You — Lessons 8-6, 8-7, 8-8, 8-9, 8-10

Knowing how to solve quadratic equations gives you tools to understand many situations, including the laws of motion. Recognizing the best solution method for a situation allows you to work efficiently.

EXAMPLE Solving a Quadratic Equation

The height h in feet of a baseball leaving a certain batter's bat is $h(t) = -16t^2 + 63t + 4$, where t is in seconds. When does the ball hit the ground?

$-16t^2 + 63t + 4 = 0$ *The ball hits the ground when $h = 0$.*

$-1(16t + 1)(t - 4) = 0$ *You can factor the equation.*

$t = -\frac{1}{16}$ or $t = 4$ *The factors give these solutions.*

The ball hits the ground in 4 seconds. (The negative value is not reasonable in the real-world context.)

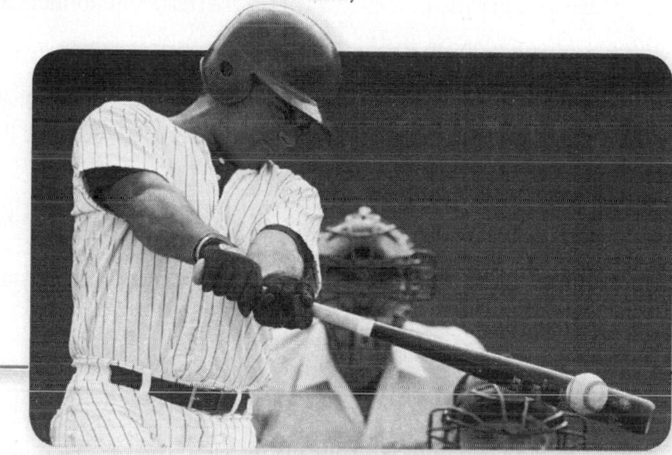

CHAPTER 8

CC.9-12.A.REI.7

Solve a simple system consisting of a linear equation and a quadratic equation in two variables algebraically and graphically.

Key Vocabulary

linear equation in two variables *(ecuación lineal en dos variables)* An equation that can be written in the form $Ax + By = C$ where A, B, and C are constants and A and B are not both 0.

What It Means For You — Lessons 8-10

Solving a system of equations in two variables involves finding the ordered pair or pairs of values that make both equations true. You can do this algebraically or graphically.

EXAMPLE Solving a System of Equations

$$\begin{cases} y = x^2 - 2x - 3 \\ y = -x - 1 \end{cases}$$

$$x^2 - 2x - 3 = -x - 1$$
$$x^2 - x - 2 = 0$$
$$(x - 2)(x + 1) = 0$$

Solutions: $(2, -3)$, $(-1, 0)$

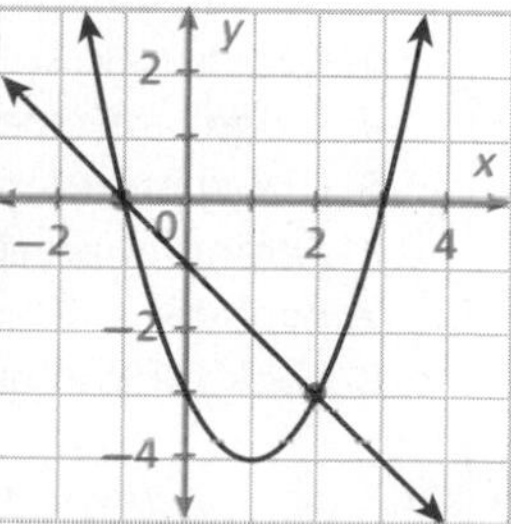

Key Vocabulary

completing the square *(completar el cuadrado)* A process used to form a perfect-square trinomial. To complete the square of $x^2 + bx$, add $\left(\frac{b}{2}\right)^2$.

discriminant *(discriminante)* The discriminant of the quadratic equation $ax^2 + bx + c = 0$ is $b^2 - 4ac$.

maximum/minimum value of a function *(máximo/mínimo de una función)* The y-value of the highest/lowest point on the graph of the function.

parabola *(parábola)* The shape of the graph of a quadratic function.

quadratic equation *(ecuación cuadrática)* An equation that can be written in the form $ax^2 + bx + c = 0$, where a, b, and c are real numbers and $a \neq 0$.

Quadratic Formula *(fórmula cuadrática)* The formula $x = \frac{-b \pm \sqrt{b^2 - 4ac}}{2a}$ which gives solutions, or roots, of equations in the form $ax^2 + bx + c = 0$, where a, b, and c are real numbers and $a \neq 0$.

quadratic function *(función cuadrática)* A function that can be written in the form $f(x) = ax^2 + bx + c$, where a, b, and c are real numbers and $a \neq 0$, or in the form $f(x) = a(x - h)^2 + k$, where a, h, and k are real numbers and $a \neq 0$.

vertex of a parabola *(vértice de una parábola)* The highest or lowest point on the parabola.

x-intercept *(intersección con el eje x)* The x-coordinate(s) of the point(s) where a graph intersects the x-axis.

y-intercept *(intersección con el eje y)* The y-coordinate(s) of the point(s) where a graph intersects the y-axis.

Zero Product Property *(Propiedad del producto cero)* For real numbers p and q, if $pq = 0$, then $p = 0$ or $q = 0$.

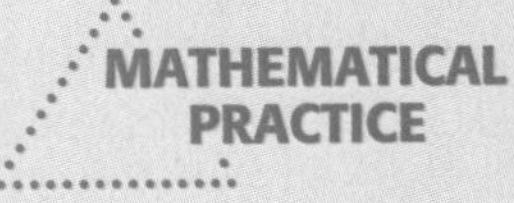

The Common Core Standards for Mathematical Practice describe varieties of expertise that mathematics educators at all levels should seek to develop in their students. Opportunities to develop these practices are integrated throughout this program.

1. **Make sense of problems and persevere in solving them.**
2. **Reason abstractly and quantitatively.**
3. **Construct viable arguments and critique the reasoning of others.**
4. **Model with mathematics.**
5. **Use appropriate tools strategically.**
6. **Attend to precision.**
7. **Look for and make use of structure.**
8. **Look for and express regularity in repeated reasoning**

Name ________________ Class ________ Date ________

8-1

Video Tutor

Identifying Quadratic Functions

Connection: Connecting $f(x) = x^2$ to $g(x) = ax^2$

Essential question: *What is the effect of the constant a on the graph of $g(x) = ax^2$?*

CC.9–12.F.IF.4

1 ENGAGE Understanding the Parent Quadratic Function

Any function that can be written as $f(x) = ax^2 + bx + c$ where a, b, and c are constants and $a \neq 0$ is a **quadratic function**. Notice that the highest exponent of the variable x is 2.

The most basic quadratic function is $f(x) = x^2$. It is called the *parent* quadratic function. To graph the parent function, make a table of values like the one below. Then plot the ordered pairs and draw the graph. The U-shaped curve is called a **parabola**. The turning point on the parabola is called its **vertex**.

x	$f(x) = x^2$
−3	9
−2	4
−1	1
0	0
1	1
2	4
3	9

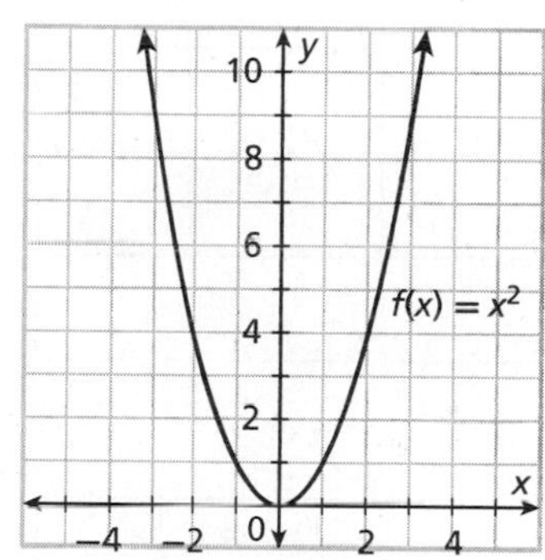

REFLECT

1a. What is the domain of $f(x) = x^2$? What is the range?

____

1b. What symmetry does the graph of $f(x) = x^2$ have? Why does it have this symmetry?

____

____

1c. For what values of x is $f(x) = x^2$ increasing? For what values is it decreasing?

____

____

To understand the effect of the constant a on the graph of $g(x) = ax^2$, you will graph the function using various values of a.

CC.9–12.F.BF.3

2 EXAMPLE Graphing $g(x) = ax^2$ when $a > 0$

Graph each quadratic function. (The graph of the parent function $f(x) = x^2$ is shown in gray.)

A $g(x) = 2x^2$

x	$g(x) = 2x^2$
−3	
−2	
−1	
0	
1	
2	
3	

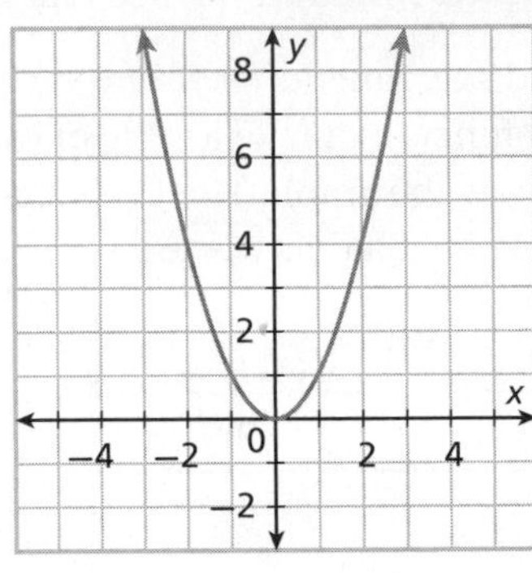

B $g(x) = \frac{1}{2}x^2$

x	$g(x) = \frac{1}{2}x^2$
−3	
−2	
−1	
0	
1	
2	
3	

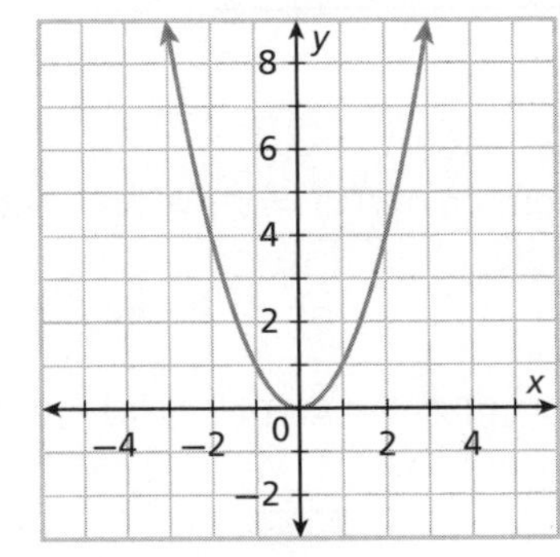

REFLECT

2a. The graph of the parent function $f(x) = x^2$ includes the point $(-1, 1)$ because $f(-1) = (-1)^2 = 1$. The corresponding point on the graph of $g(x) = 2x^2$ is $(-1, 2)$ because $g(-1) = 2(-1)^2 = 2$. In general, how does the y-coordinate of a point on the graph of $g(x) = 2x^2$ compare with the y-coordinate of a point on the graph of $f(x) = x^2$ when the points have the same x-coordinate?

____

____

2b. Describe how the graph of $g(x) = 2x^2$ compares with the graph of $f(x) = x^2$. Use either the word *stretch* or *shrink*, and include the direction of the movement.

____

2c. How does the y-coordinate of a point on the graph of $g(x) = \frac{1}{2}x^2$ compare with the y-coordinate of a point on the graph of $f(x) = x^2$ when the points have the same x-coordinate?

____

____

2d. Describe how the graph of $g(x) = \frac{1}{2}x^2$ compares with the graph of $f(x) = x^2$. Use either the word *stretch* or *shrink*, and include the direction of the movement.

____

CC.9–12.F.BF.3

3 EXAMPLE Graphing $g(x) = ax^2$ when $a < 0$

Graph each quadratic function. (The graph of the parent function $f(x) = x^2$ is shown in gray.)

A $g(x) = -2x^2$

x	$g(x) = -2x^2$
−3	
−2	
−1	
0	
1	
2	
3	

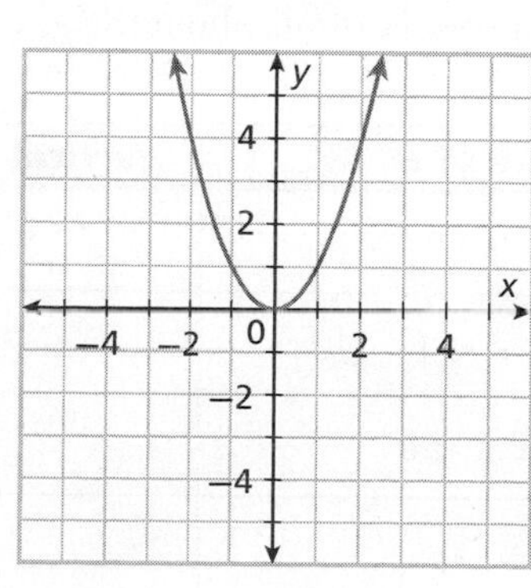

B $g(x) = -\frac{1}{2}x^2$

x	$g(x) = -\frac{1}{2}x^2$
−3	
−2	
−1	
0	
1	
2	
3	

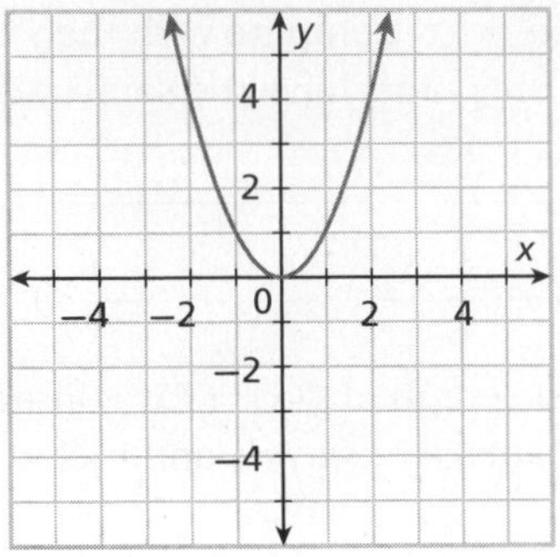

REFLECT

3a. In part A of the previous example, you drew the graph of $g(x) = ax^2$ where $a = 2$. In part A of this example, you drew the graph of $g(x) = ax^2$ where $a = -2$. How do the two graphs compare? How does the graph of $g(x) = -2x^2$ compare with the graph of $f(x) = x^2$?

3b. In part B of the previous example, you drew the graph of $g(x) = ax^2$ where $a = \frac{1}{2}$. In part B of this example, you drew the graph of $g(x) = ax^2$ where $a = -\frac{1}{2}$. How do the two graphs compare? How does the graph of $g(x) = -\frac{1}{2}x^2$ compare with the graph of $f(x) = x^2$?

3c. Summarize your observations about the graph of $g(x) = ax^2$.

Value of a	Vertical stretch or shrink?	Reflection across x-axis?
$a > 1$	Vertical stretch	No
$0 < a < 1$		
$-1 < a < 0$		
$a = -1$		
$a < -1$		

Writing Equations from Graphs A function whose graph is a parabola with vertex (0, 0) always has the form $f(x) = ax^2$. To write the rule for the function, you can substitute the x- and y-coordinates of a point on the graph into the equation $y = ax^2$ and solve for a.

CC.9–12.F.BF.1

4 EXAMPLE Writing the Equation for a Quadratic Function

Write the equation for the quadratic function whose graph is shown.

Use the point (2, −1) to find a.

$y = ax^2$

$\square = a\left(\square\right)^2$

$\square = a\left(\square\right)$

$\square = a$

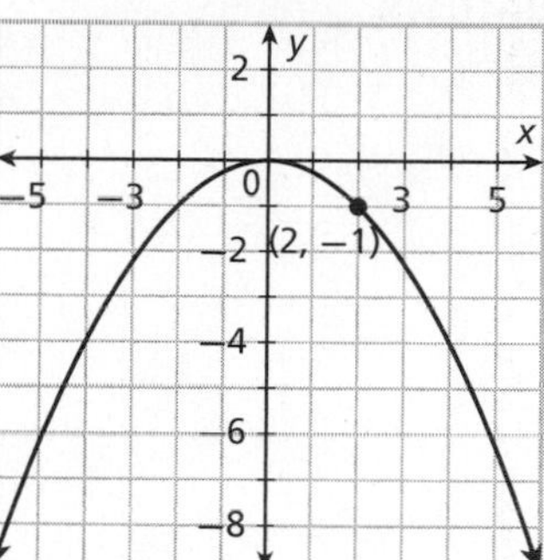

The equation for the function is ______________.

REFLECT

4a. Without actually graphing the function whose equation you found, how can check that your equation is reasonable?

4b. Error Analysis Knowing that the graph of $f(x) = ax^2$ is a parabola that has its vertex at (0, 0) and passes through the point (−2, 2), a student says that the value of a must be $-\frac{1}{2}$. Explain why this value of a is not reasonable.

4c. A quadratic function has a *minimum value* when the function's graph opens up, and it has a *maximum value* when the function's graph opens down. In each case, the minimum or maximum value is the y-coordinate of the vertex of the function's graph. Under what circumstances does the function $f(x) = ax^2$ have a minimum value? A maximum value? What is the minimum or maximum value in each case?

4d. A function is called *even* if $f(-x) = f(x)$ for all x in the domain of the function. Show that the function $f(x) = ax^2$ is even for any value of a.

PRACTICE

Graph each quadratic function.

1. $f(x) = 3x^2$

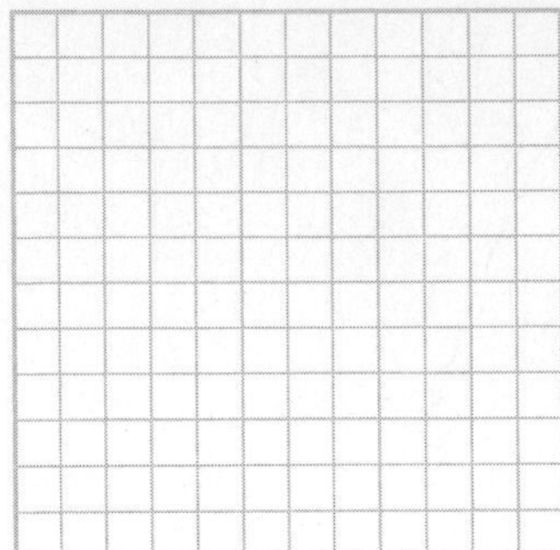

2. $f(x) = -\frac{3}{4}x^2$

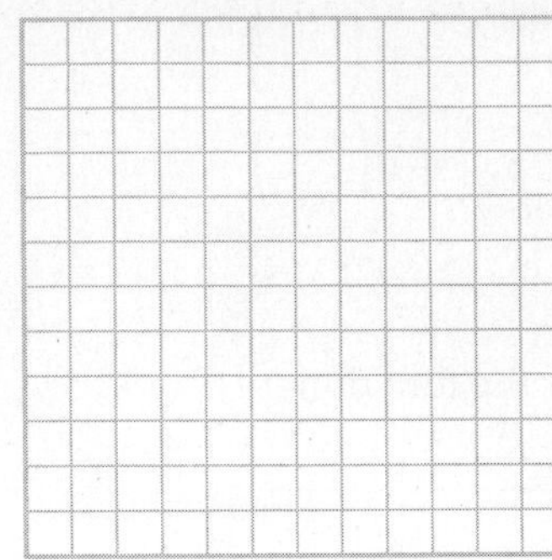

3. $f(x) = 0.6x^2$

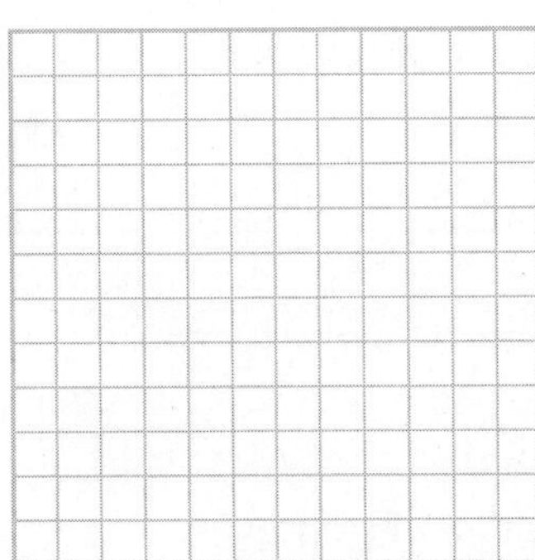

4. $f(x) = -1.5x^2$

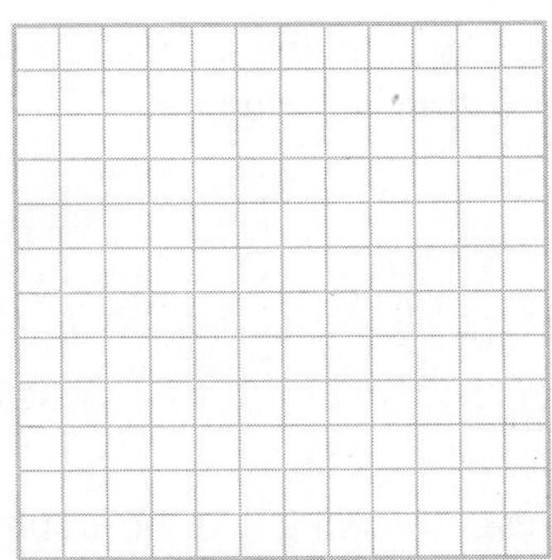

Write the equation for each quadratic function whose graph is shown.

5.

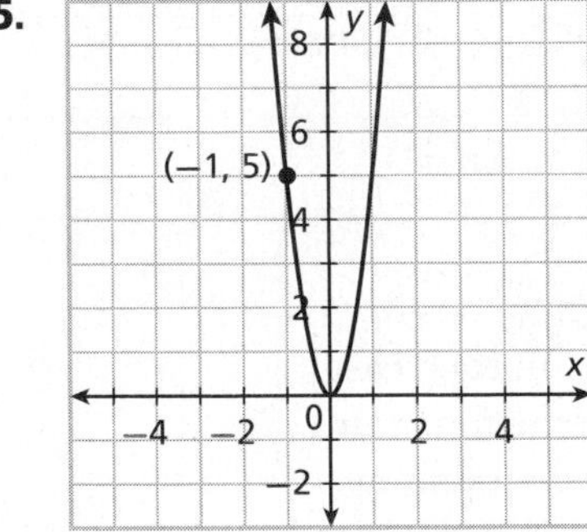

6.

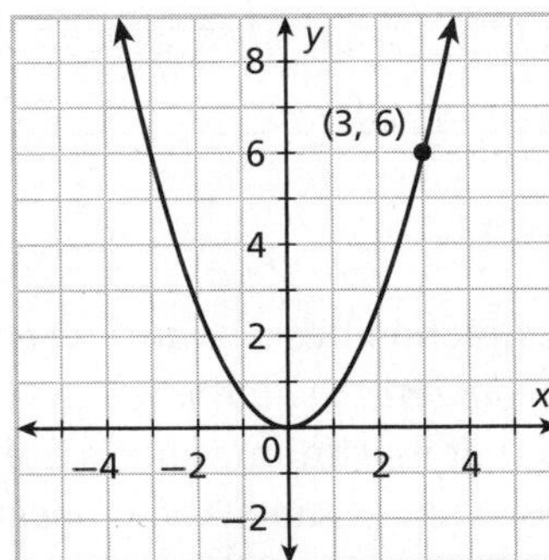

7.

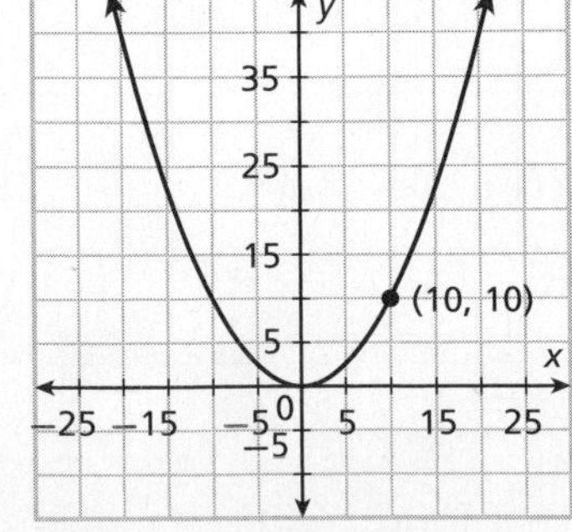

8.

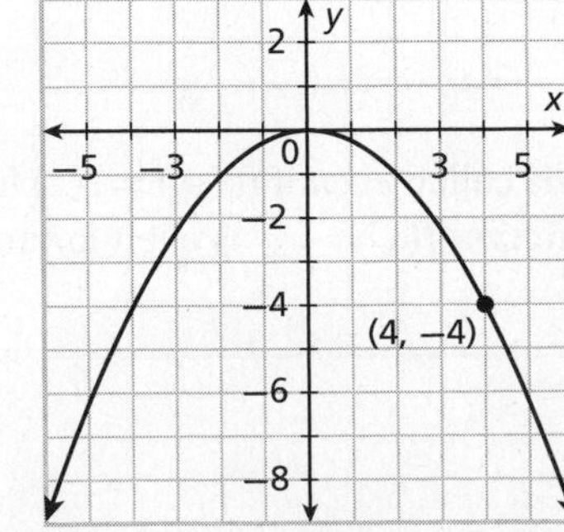

Name______________________ Class______________ Date__________ 8-1

Additional Practice

Use a table of values to graph each quadratic function. Then describe how each function is related to the parent function $y = x^2$.

1. $y = -\frac{1}{2}x^2$

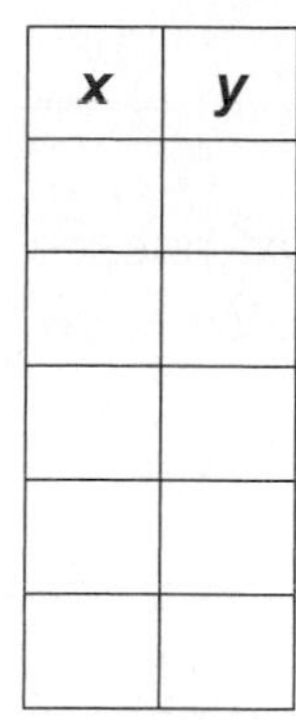

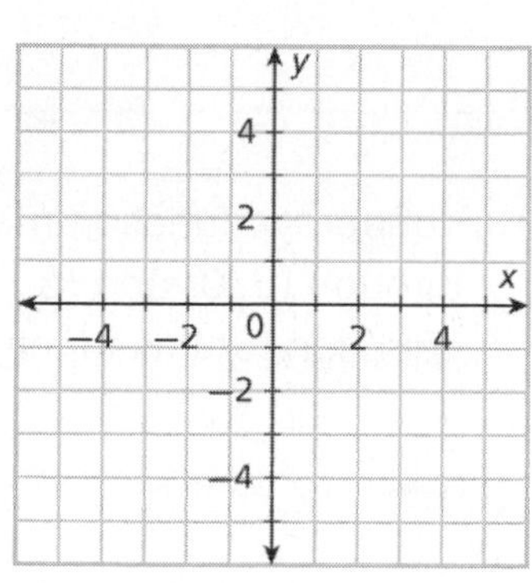

____

____

2. $y = 2x^2$

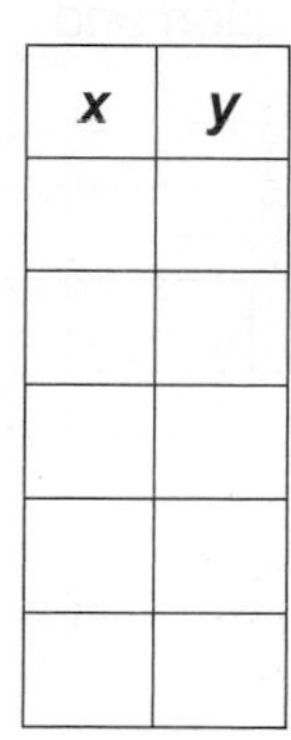

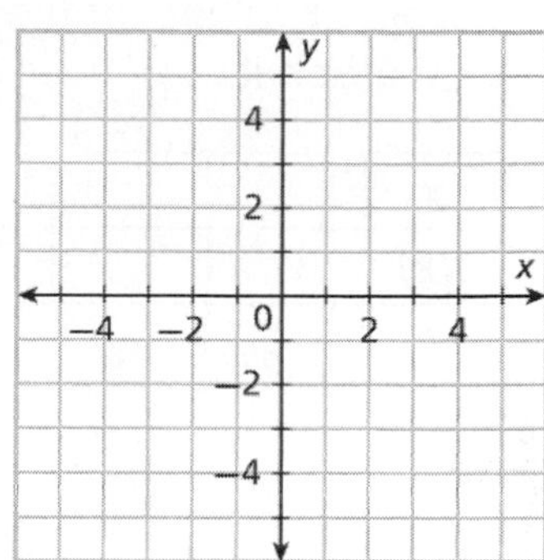

____

____

Tell whether the graph of each quadratic function opens upward or downward. Explain.

3. $y = -3x^2$

____

4. $y = 5x^2$

____

For each parabola, a) write the equation of the function; b) give the minimum or maximum value of the function; c) find the domain and range.

5. 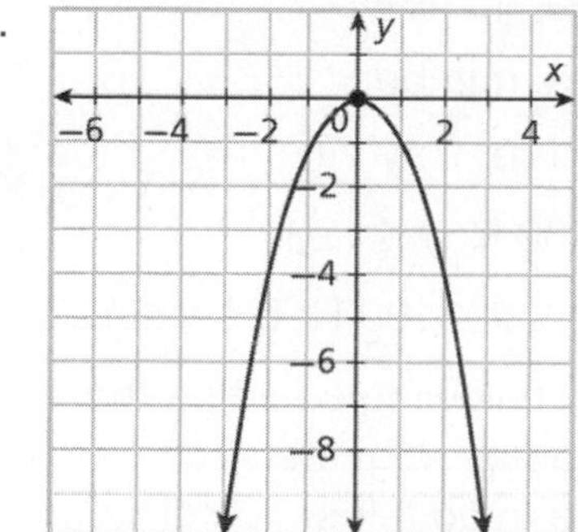

a. ______________________________

b. ______________________________

c. ______________________________

6. 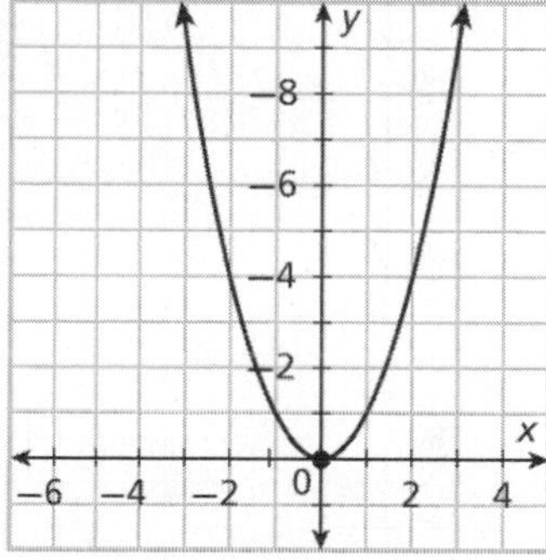

a. ______________________________

b. ______________________________

c. ______________________________

Problem Solving

Write the correct answer.

1. Kay is designing an arch for a bridge support. She uses the function $y = -0.25x^2$ to model the arch. Make a table of values for the function and then graph it.

x					
f(x)					

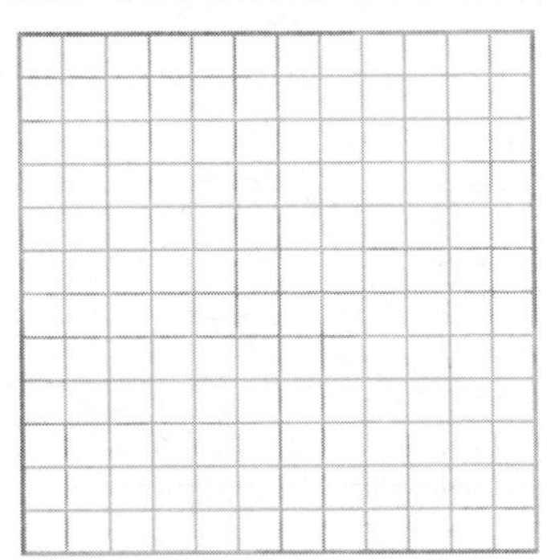

2. A quadratic function $f(x) = ax^2$ passes through (0, 0) and (5, 5). Write an equation for this function.

____

3. A quadratic function $f(x) = ax^2$ passes through (0, 0) and (3, –36). Write an equation for this function.

____

4. A quadratic function $f(x) = ax^2$ passes through (0, 0) and (–0.5, 6). Write an equation for this function.

____

Radio telescopes are built in the shape of a parabola. The graph below shows a radio telescope dish in cross-section. Select the best answer.

Receiving Dish

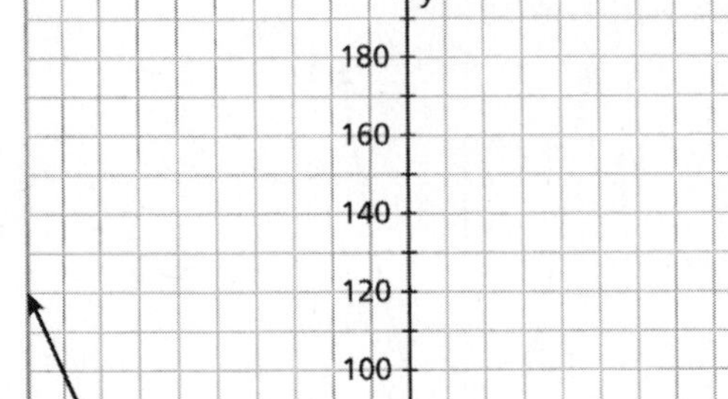

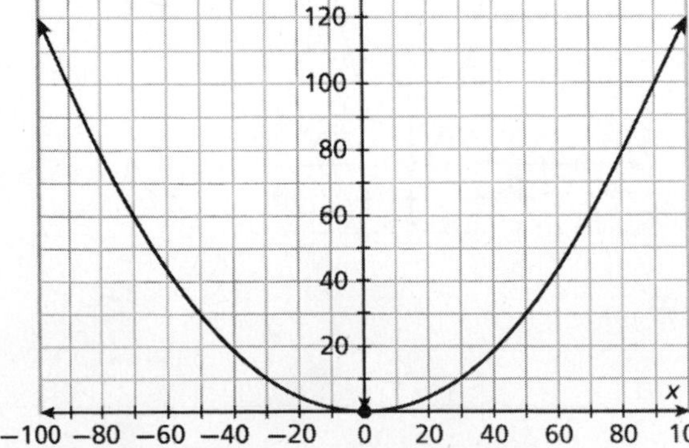

5. What is the vertex of this parabola?

A (0, 120) C (–100, 120)

B (0, 0) D (100, 120)

6. What are the domain and range of this function?

F D: all real numbers
R: all real numbers

G D: $x \geq -100$, R: $y \geq 0$

H D: $x \leq 100$ R: $y \leq 120$

J D: $-100 \leq x \leq 100$ R: $0 \leq y \leq 120$

7. Which of the following could be the equation used by engineers to construct the radio telescope dish?

A $y = 0.12x^2$

B $y = -0.12x^2$

C $y = 0.012x^2$

D $y = -0.012x^2$

Name ______________________ Class ______________ Date ________

8-2

Characteristics of Quadratic Functions

Connection: Connecting $f(x) = x^2$ to $g(x) = (x - h)^2 + k$

Essential question: *What is the effect of the constants h and k on the graph of* $g(x) = (x - h)^2 + k$*?*

Video Tutor

CC.9–12.F.BF.3

1 EXAMPLE Graphing Functions of the Form $g(x) = x^2 + k$

Graph each quadratic function. (The graph of the parent function $f(x) = x^2$ is shown in gray.)

A $g(x) = x^2 + 2$

x	$g(x) = x^2 + 2$
−3	
−2	
−1	
0	
1	
2	
3	

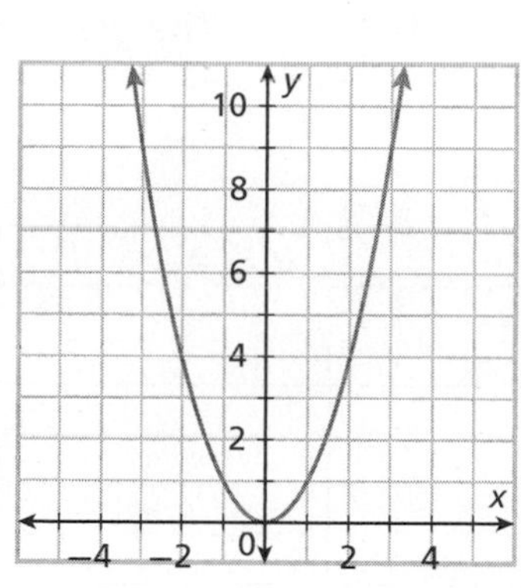

B $g(x) = x^2 - 2$

x	$g(x) = x^2 - 2$
−3	
−2	
−1	
0	
1	
2	
3	

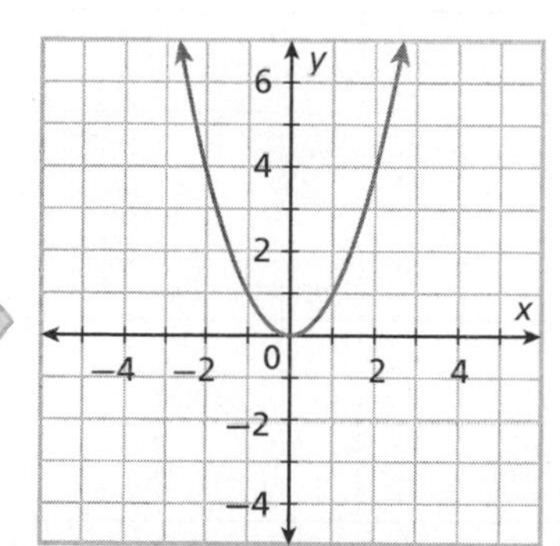

REFLECT

1a. How is the graph of $g(x) = x^2 + 2$ related to the graph of $f(x) = x^2$?

____

1b. How is the graph of $g(x) = x^2 - 2$ related to the graph of $f(x) = x^2$?

____

1c. In general, how is the graph of $g(x) = x^2 + k$ related to the graph of $f(x) = x^2$?

____

CC.9–12.F.BF.3

2 EXAMPLE Graphing Functions of the Form $g(x) = (x - h)^2$

Graph each quadratic function. (The graph of the parent function $f(x) = x^2$ is shown in gray.)

A $g(x) = (x - 1)^2$

x	$g(x) = (x - 1)^2$

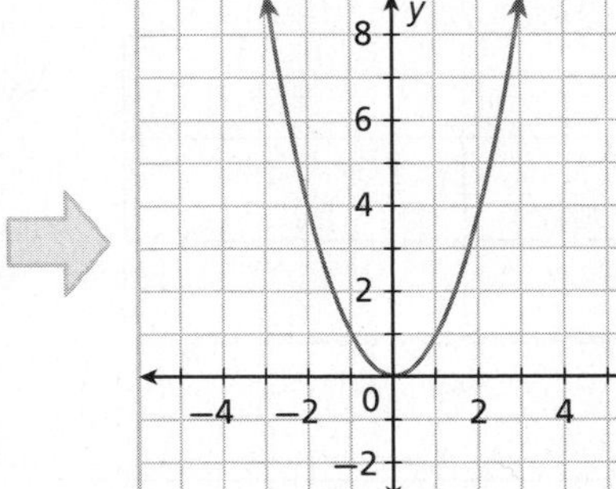

B $g(x) = (x + 1)^2$

x	$g(x) = (x + 1)^2$

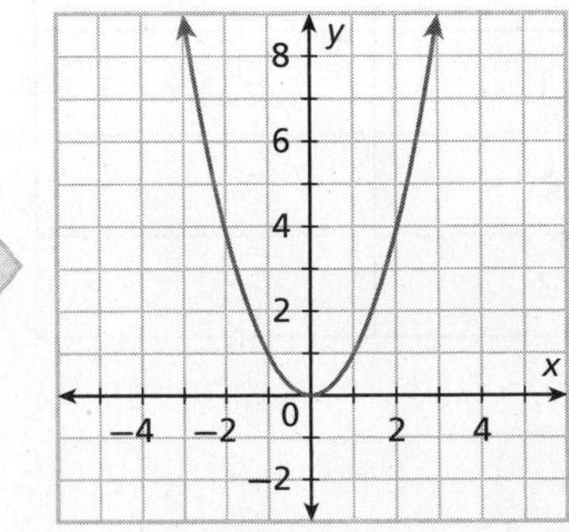

REFLECT

2a. How is the graph of $g(x) = (x - 1)^2$ related to the graph of $f(x) = x^2$?

____

2b. How is the graph of $g(x) = (x + 1)^2$ related to the graph of $f(x) = x^2$?

____

2c. In general, how is the graph of $g(x) = (x - h)^2$ related to the graph of $f(x) = x^2$?

____

CC.9–12.F.BF.1

3 EXAMPLE Writing Equations for Quadratic Functions

Write the equation for the quadratic function whose graph is shown.

A Compare the given graph to the graph of the parent function $f(x) = x^2$.

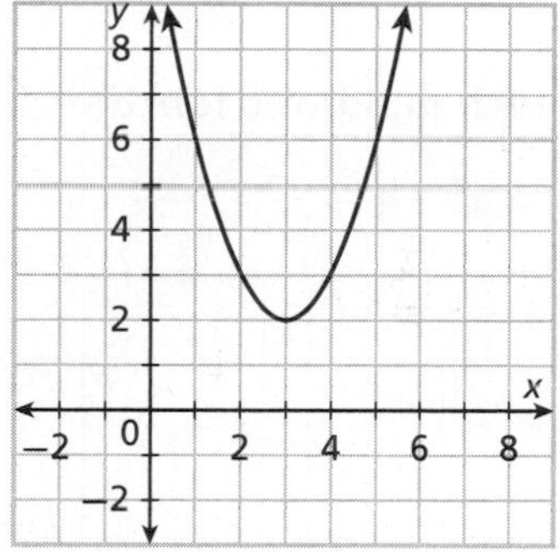

Complete the table below to describe how the parent function must be translated to get the graph shown here.

Type of Translation	Number of Units	Direction
Horizontal Translation		
Vertical Translation		

B Determine the values of h and k for the function $g(x) = (x - h)^2 + k$.

- h is the number of units that the parent function is translated horizontally. For a translation to the right, h is positive; for a translation to the left, h is negative.
- k is the number of units that the parent function is translated vertically. For a translation up, k is positive; for a translation down, k is negative.

So, $h =$ ________ and $k =$ ________. The equation is ______________________.

REFLECT

3a. What can you do to check that your equation is correct?

____

3b. **If the graph of a quadratic function is a translation of the graph of the parent function, explain how you can use the vertex of the translated graph to help you determine the equation for the function.**

3c. **Error Analysis** **A student says that the graph of $g(x) = (x + 2)^2 + 1$ is the graph of the parent function translated 2 units to the right and 1 unit up. Explain what is incorrect about this statement.**

PRACTICE

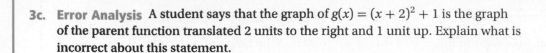

Graph each quadratic function.

1. $f(x) = x^2 + 4$

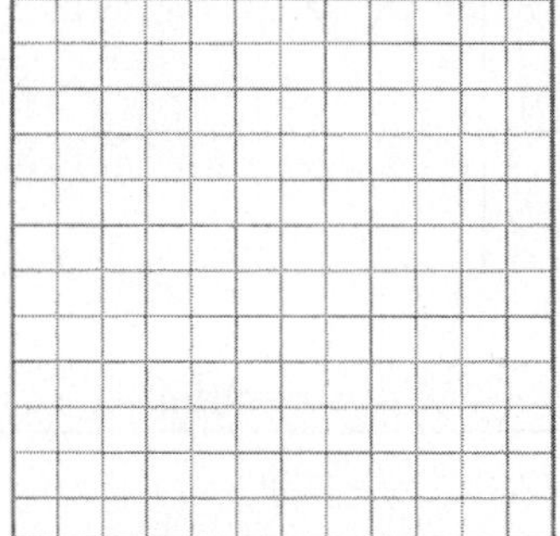

2. $f(x) = x^2 - 5$

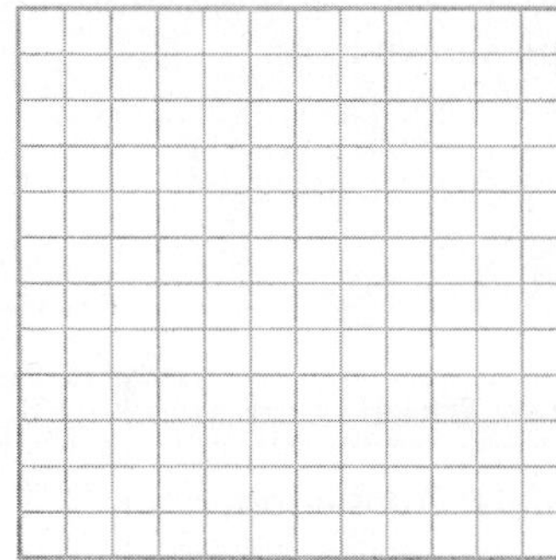

3. $f(x) = (x - 2)^2$

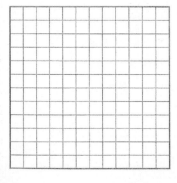

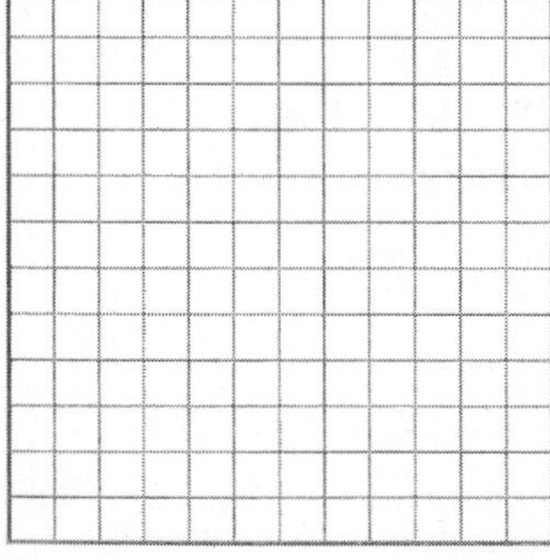

4. $f(x) = (x + 3)^2$

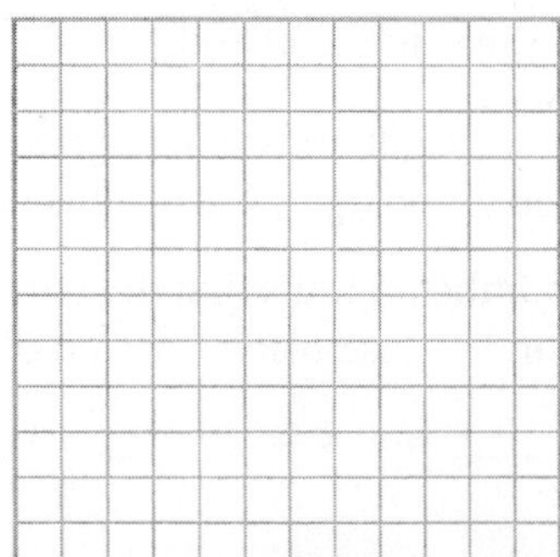

5. $f(x) = (x - 5)^2 - 2$

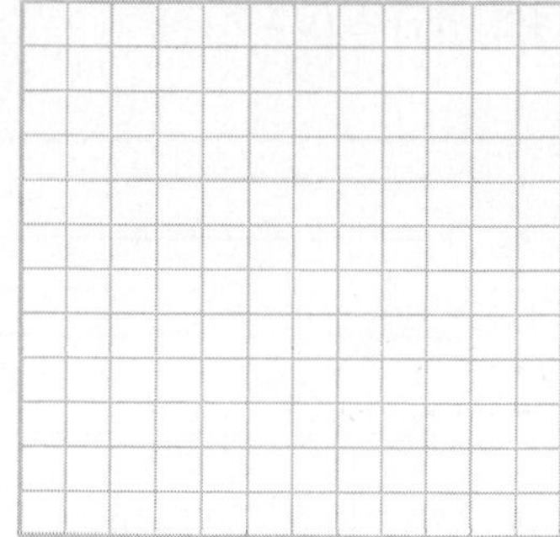

6. $f(x) = (x - 1)^2 + 1$

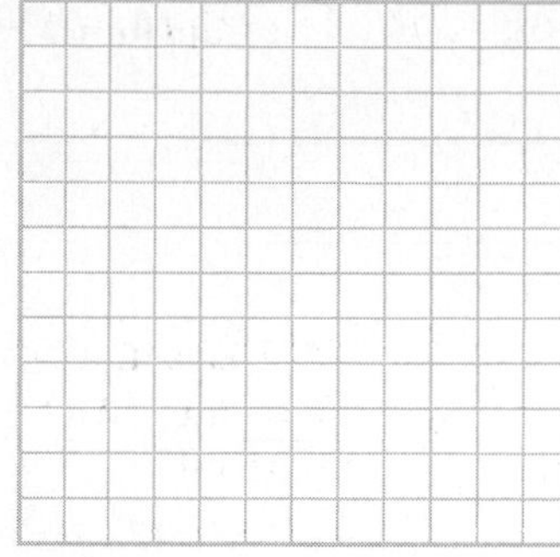

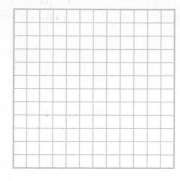

7. $f(x) = (x + 4)^2 + 3$

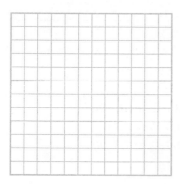

8. $f(x) = (x + 2)^2 - 4$

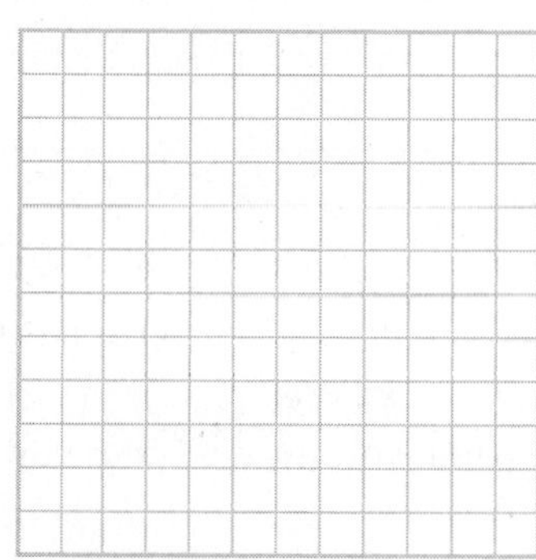

Write a rule for the quadratic function whose graph is shown.

9.

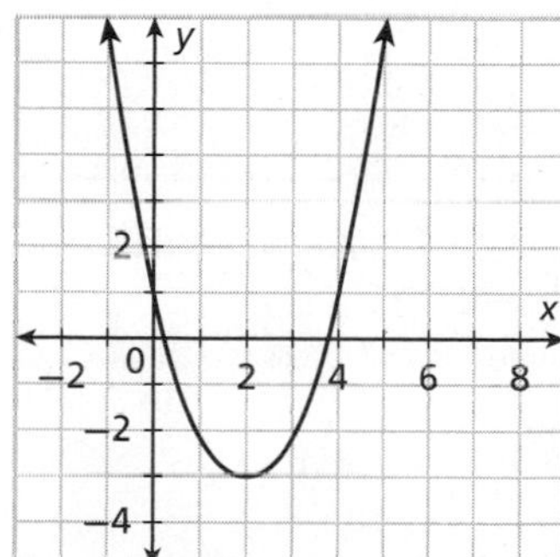

10.

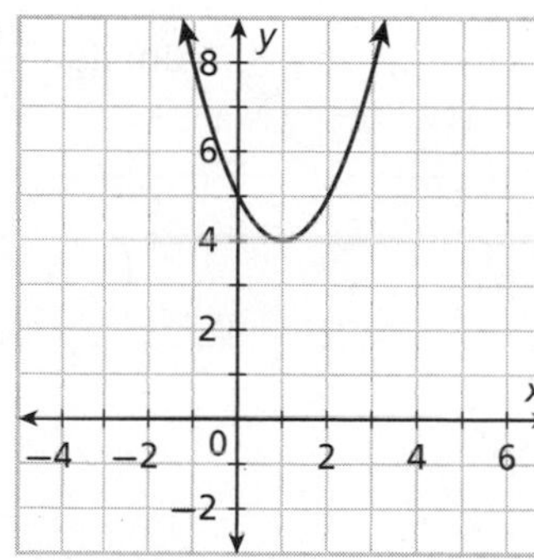

11.

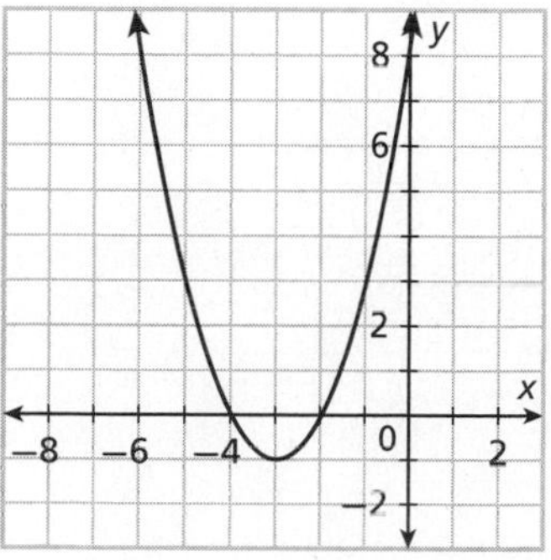

12.

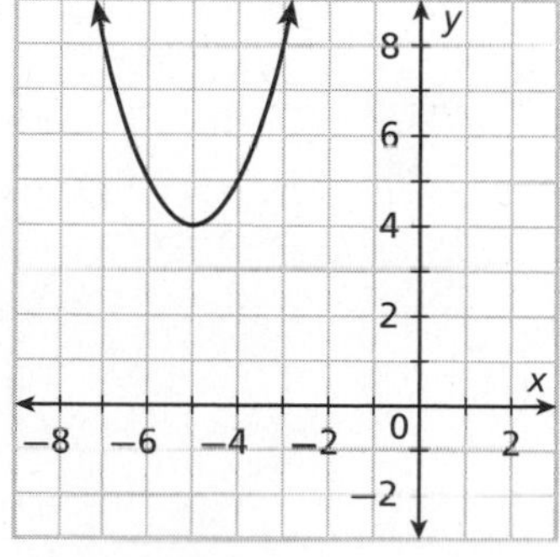

Determine the domain, range, vertex, and axis of symmetry of the function.

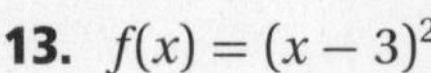

13. $f(x) = (x - 3)^2$

14. $f(x) = x^2 + 4$

15. $f(x) = (x + 5)^2$

16. $f(x) = x^2 - 7$

17. $f(x) = (x + 1)^2 - 6$

18. $f(x) = (x - 2)^2 + 8$

19. A function is called *even* if $f(-x) = f(x)$ for all x in the domain of the function. For instance, if $f(x) = x^2$, then $f(-x) = (-x)^2 = x^2 = f(x)$. In other words, you get the same value when you square $-x$ as you do when you square x. So, $f(x) = x^2$ is an even function.

a. Is $f(x) = x^2 - 1$ an even function? Explain.

b. Is $f(x) = (x - 1)^2$ an even function? Explain.

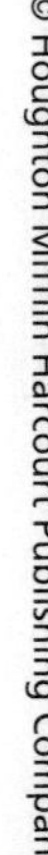

Name ____________ Class ________ Date ________

8-2

Additional Practice

Write a rule for the quadratic function whose graph is given.

1.

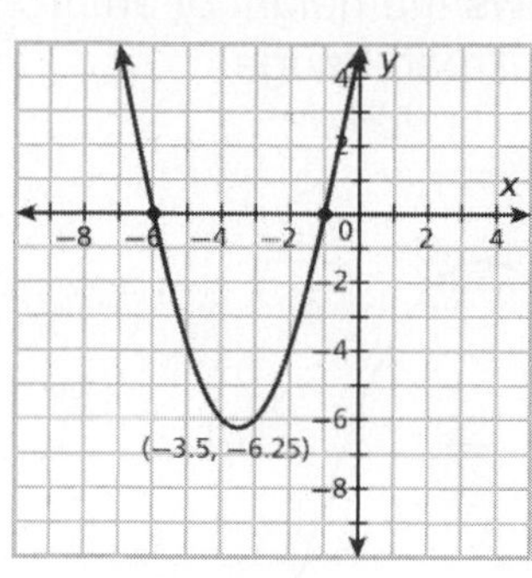

____

2.

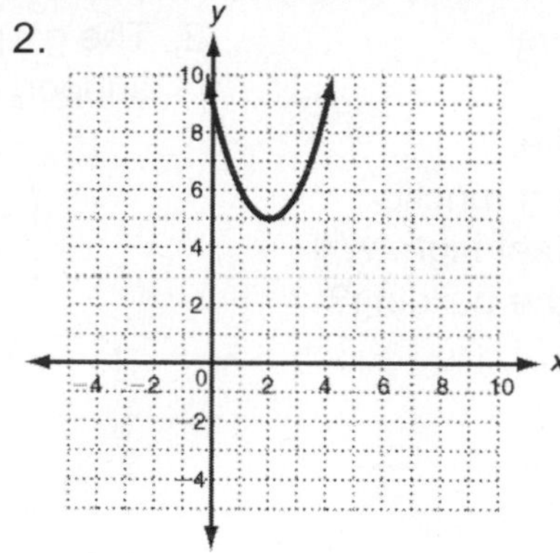

____

3.

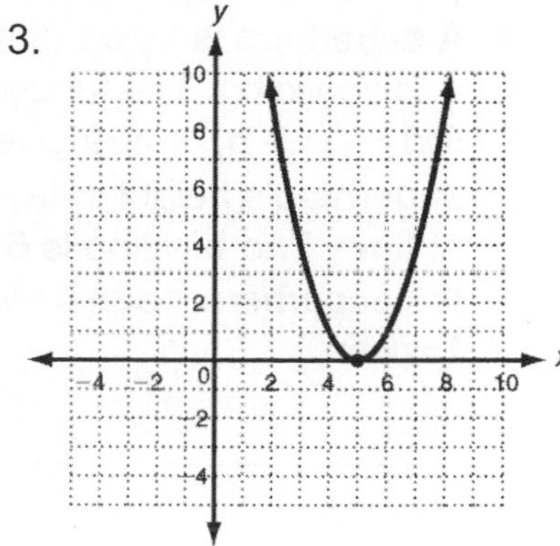

____

4.

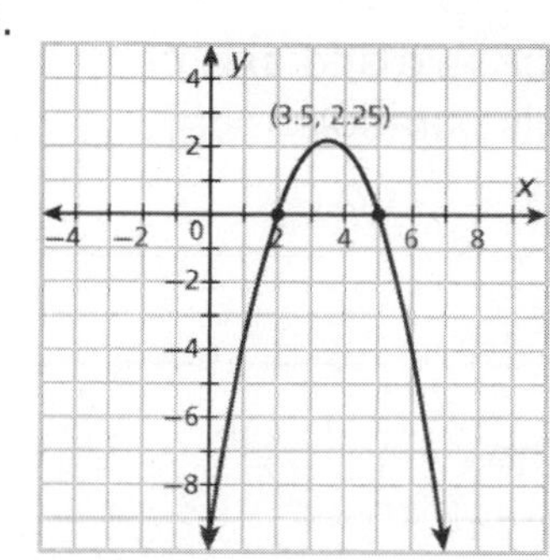

____

5.

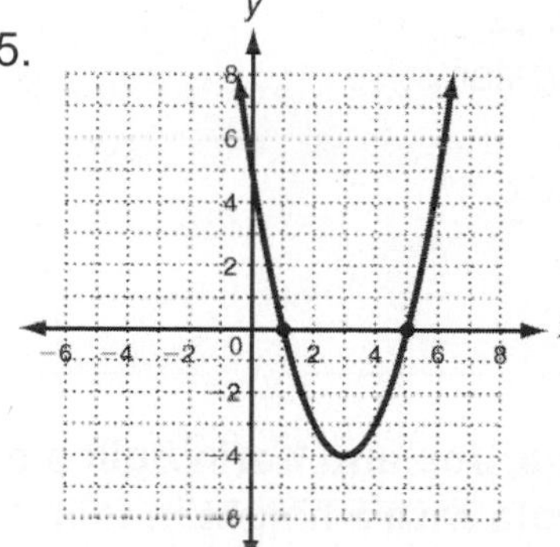

____

6.

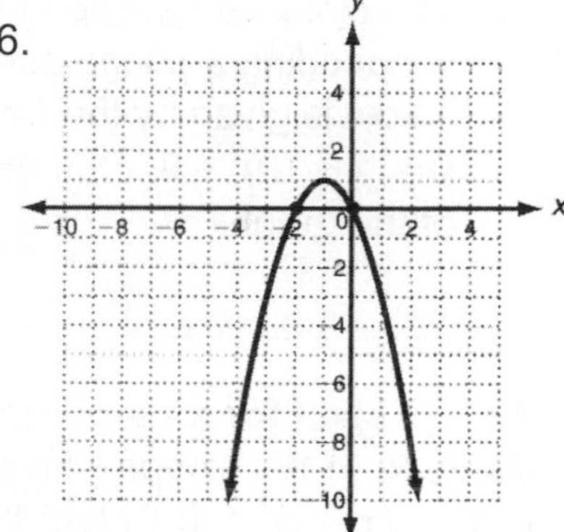

____

For each quadratic function, find the domain, range, vertex, and axis of symmetry.

7. $y = (x - 1)^2 + 1$

____

____

____

8. $y = -(x - 2)^2 + 4$

____

____

____

9. $y = (x + 5)^2 - 3$

____

____

____

10. $y = (x - 1)^2 - 5$

____

____

____

11. $y = -(x + 2)^2 - 22$

____

____

____

12. $y = (x + 1)^2 - 36$

____

____

____

Problem Solving

Write the correct answer.

1. A superhero is trying to fly over a tall building. The function $f(x) = -(x - 6)^2 + 620$ gives the superhero's height in feet as a function of time. The building is 612 feet high. Will the superhero make it over the building? Explain.

____

____

____

2. The graph shows the height of an arch support for a railroad bridge.

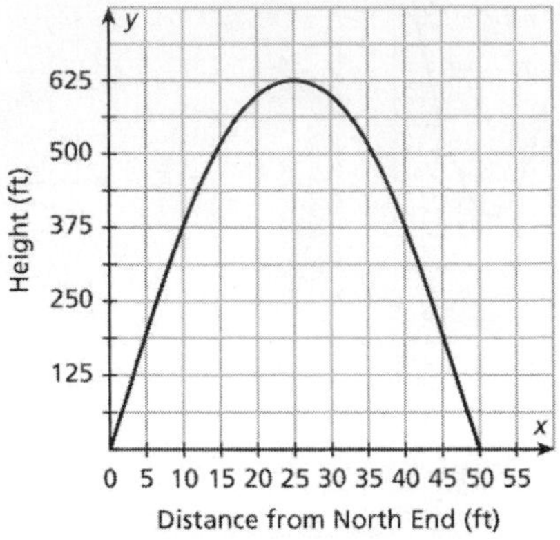

Find the function rule and axis of symmetry of this parabola.

____

____

3. The distance between the cables suspending a bridge and the water below is given by the function $y = (x - 10)^2 + 8$. Find the vertex of the graph.

____

As a project for a carpentry class, Joe and Karin built a dome. The dome is in the shape of a parabola with a height in feet given by $f(x) = -(x - 2)^2 + 4$. Select the best answer.

4. Joe wants to place a support in the middle of the dome, along the axis of symmetry. What is the axis of symmetry?

   A $x = 4$ C $y = 4$

   B $x = 2$ D $y = 2$

5. Neither Joe nor Karin can stand up inside the dome. How tall is the center of the dome? (*Hint:* The top of the dome is the vertex of the parabola.)

   F 1 ft H 4 ft

   G 2 ft J 6 ft

6. Karin graphs the parabola and finds the domain to see how wide the dome is. What is the domain of this parabola?

   A $0 \le f(x) \le 2$ C $0 \le x \le 2$

   B $0 \le f(x) \le 4$ D $0 \le x \le 4$

7. What is the vertex of the parabola that Karin graphed?

   F (4, 2) H (–2, 4)

   G (2, 4) J (2, –4)

Name________________________ Class________________ Date__________

8-3

Video Tutor

Graphing Quadratic Functions

Going Deeper

Essential question: *How can you describe key attributes of the graph of $f(x) = ax^2 + bx + c$ by analyzing its equation?*

To graph a function of the form $f(x) = ax^2 + bx + c$, called *standard form*, you can analyze the key features of the graph by factoring.

CC.9–12.F.IF.7a

1 EXAMPLE Graphing $f(x) = x^2 + bx + c$

Graph the function $f(x) = x^2 + 2x - 3$ by factoring.

A You can determine the x-intercepts of the graph by factoring to solve $f(x) = 0$:

$f(x) = x^2 + 2x - 3 = (x - \square)(x + \square)$, so $f(x) = 0$ when $x =$ __________ or $x =$ __________.

The graph of $f(x) = x^2 + 2x - 3$ intersects the x-axis at $(\square, \square)$ and $(\square, \square)$.

B The axis of symmetry of the graph is a vertical line that is halfway between the two x-intercepts and passes through the vertex. The axis of symmetry is $x = \square$. So, the vertex is $(\square, \square)$.

C Find another point on the graph and reflect it across the axis of symmetry. Use the point (2, 5). The x-value is $\square$ units from the axis of symmetry, so its reflection is $(\square, \square)$.

D Use the five points to graph the function.

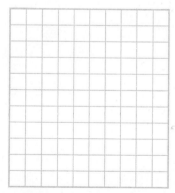

REFLECT

1a. A useful point to plot is where the y-intercept occurs. How can you find the y-intercept? What point is the reflection across the axis of symmetry of the point where the y-intercept occurs?

____

____

PRACTICE

Write the rule for the quadratic function in the form you would use to graph it. Then graph the function.

1. $f(x) = x^2 + 4x + 3$

____

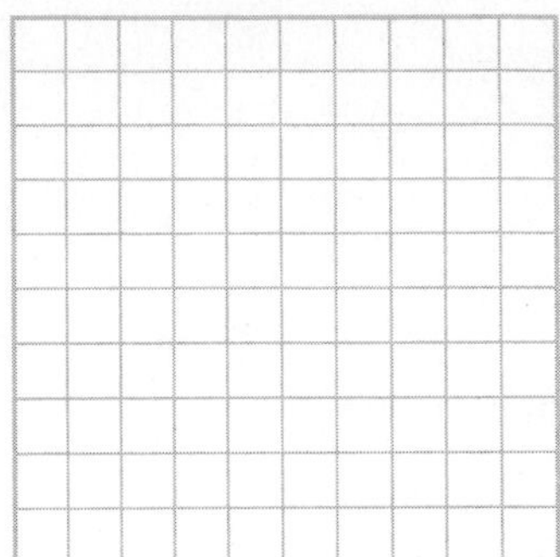

2. $f(x) = x^2 - 2x - 3$

____

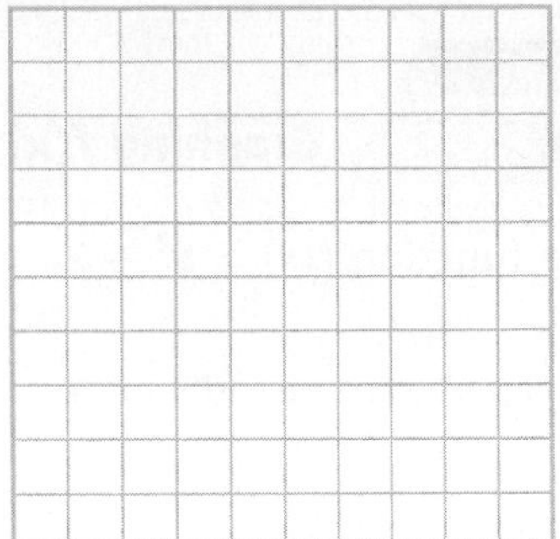

3. $f(x) = x^2 - 4$

____

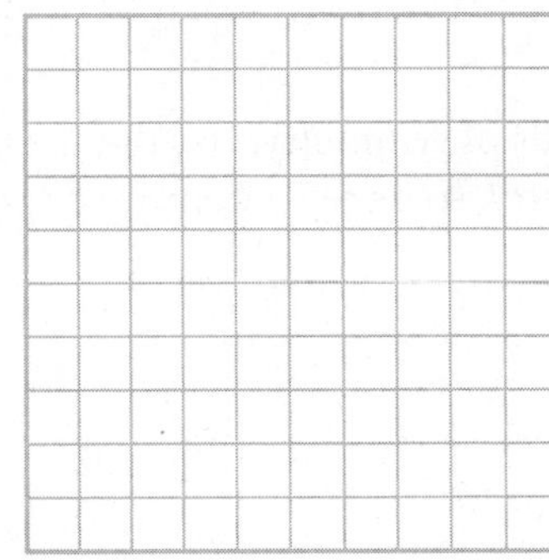

4. $f(x) = x^2 - 6x + 5$

____

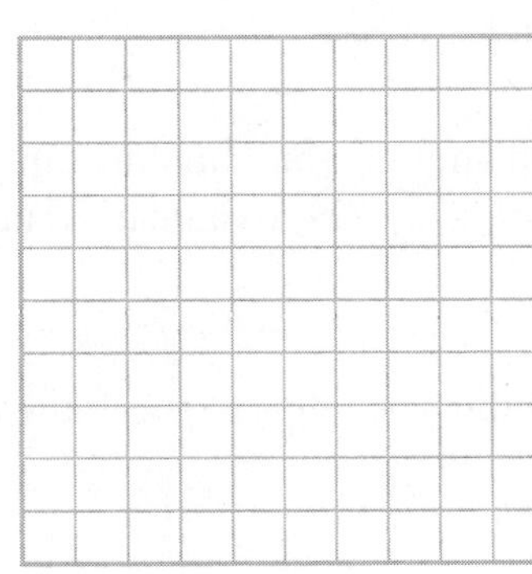

5. $f(x) = x^2 + 2x - 8$

____

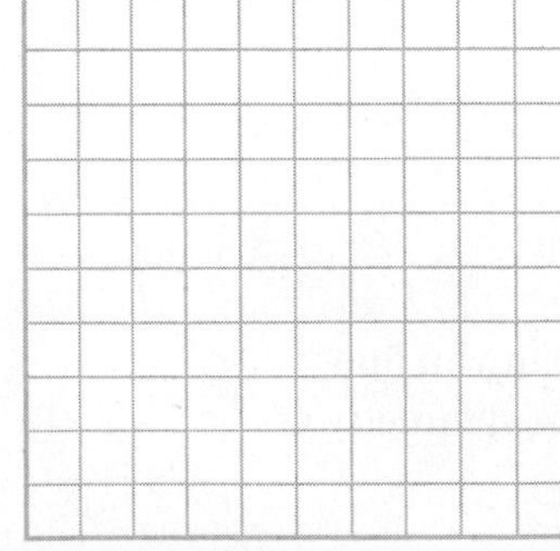

6. $f(x) = x^2 - 7x + 10$

____

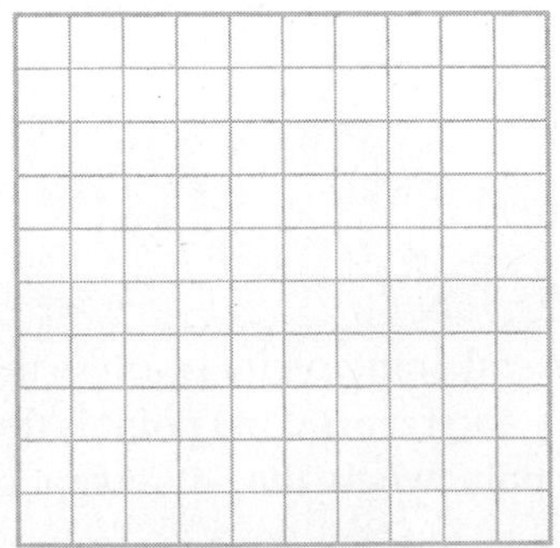

Additional Practice

Graph each quadratic function.

1. $y = x^2 + 4x - 4$

   axis of symmetry: ______________

   vertex: ______________

   y-intercept: ______________

   two other points: ______________

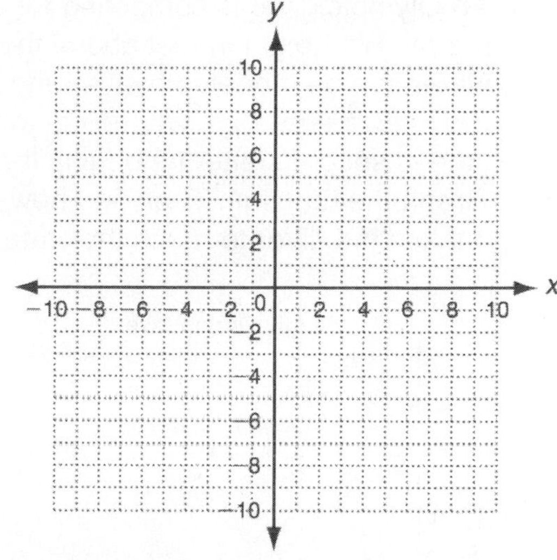

2. $y + 2x^2 - 4x - 6 = 0$

   axis of symmetry: ______________

   vertex: ______________

   y-intercept: ______________

   two other points: ______________

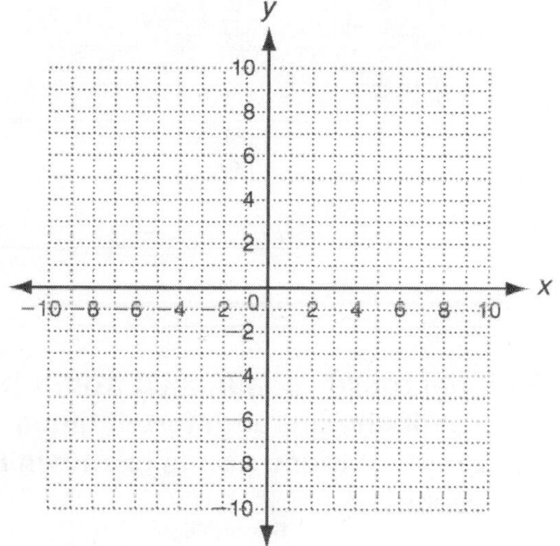

3. The height in feet of a soccer ball that is kicked can be modeled by the function $f(x) = -8x^2 + 24x$, where x is the time in seconds after it is kicked. Graph this function. Find the soccer ball's maximum height and the time it takes the ball to reach this height. Then find how long the soccer ball is in the air.

   maximum height: ______________

   time to reach maximum height: ______________

   time in the air: ______________

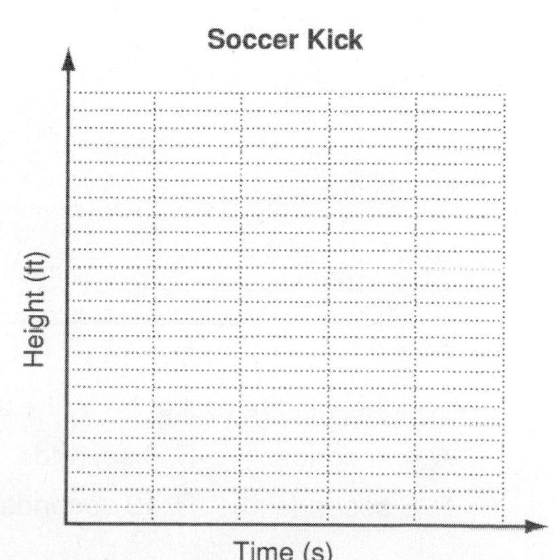

Problem Solving

Write the correct answer.

1. An Olympic diver is competing for a medal. His height in feet above the water can be modeled by the function $f(x) = -3x^2 + 6x + 24$, where x is the time in seconds after he begins the dive. Graph the function. Then find how long it takes the diver to reach the water.

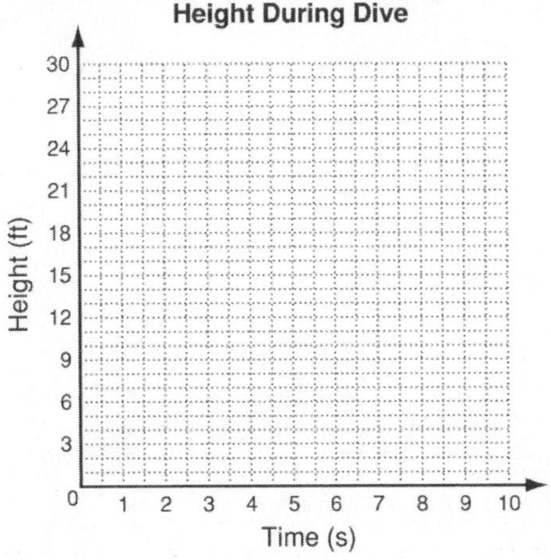

____

____

2. Tanisha kicks a soccer ball during a game. The height of the ball, in feet, can be modeled by the function $f(x) = -16x^2 + 48x$, where x is the time in seconds after she kicks the ball. Graph the function. Find the maximum height of the ball and how long it takes the ball to reach that height.

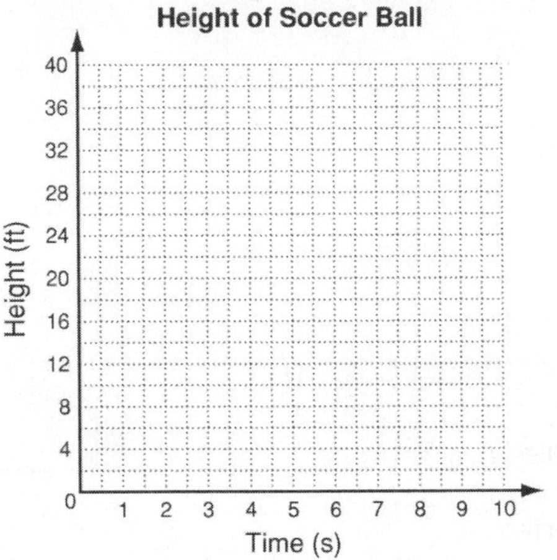

____

____

A model rocket is launched from a platform into the air. Keona records its height at different times until it reaches its peak at 259 ft. Her graph of these points is shown below. Use this graph to answer questions 3-5.

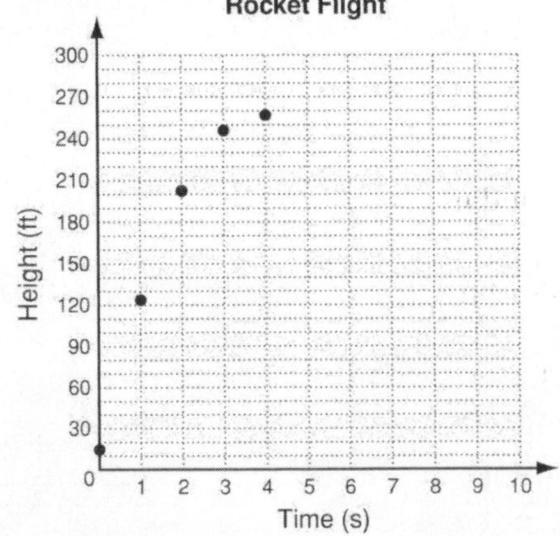

3. Keona wants to complete her graph by plotting the heights of the rocket as it descended. Which of the following points will she graph?

   F (4, 180) H (6, 200)

   G (5, 150) J (10, 0)

4. How long will the rocket be in the air?

   A 4 seconds C 8 seconds

   B 6 seconds D 10 seconds

5. Which of the following equations models the flight of the ball where x is the time in seconds and y is the height in feet?

   A $16x^2 + 15x + 125$

   B $16x^2 + 125x + 15$

   C $-16x^2 + 125x + 15$

   D $-16x^2 + 15x + 125$

Name ________________ Class ________________ Date ________________

8-4

Video Tutor

Transforming Quadratic Functions
Going Deeper

Essential question: *How can you obtain the graph of* $g(x) = a(x-h)^2 + k$ *from the graph of* $f(x) = x^2$*?*

CC.9-12.F.BF.3

1 ENGAGE Understanding How to Graph $g(x) = a(x - h)^2 + k$

The sequence of graphs below shows how you can obtain the graph of $g(x) = 2(x - 3)^2 + 1$ from the graph of the parent quadratic function $f(x) = x^2$ using transformations.

1. Start with the graph of $y = x^2$.

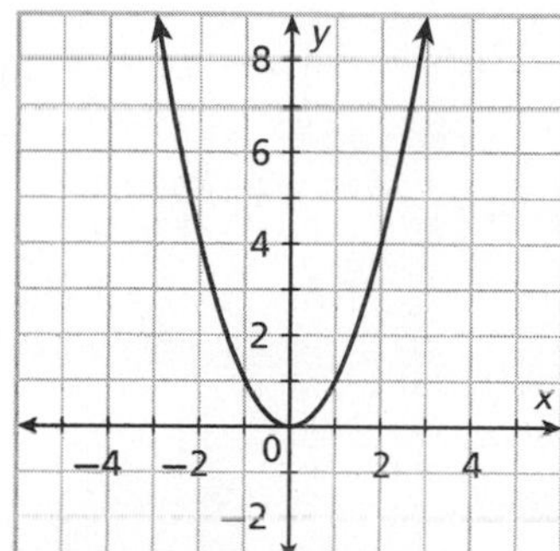

2. Stretch the graph vertically by a factor of 2 to obtain the graph of $y = 2x^2$.

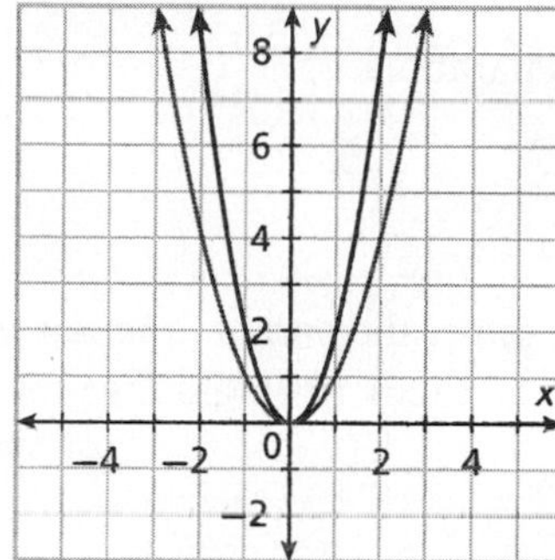

3. **Translate the graph of $y = 2x^2$ right 3 units and up 1 unit to obtain the graph of $y = 2(x - 3)^2 + 1$.**

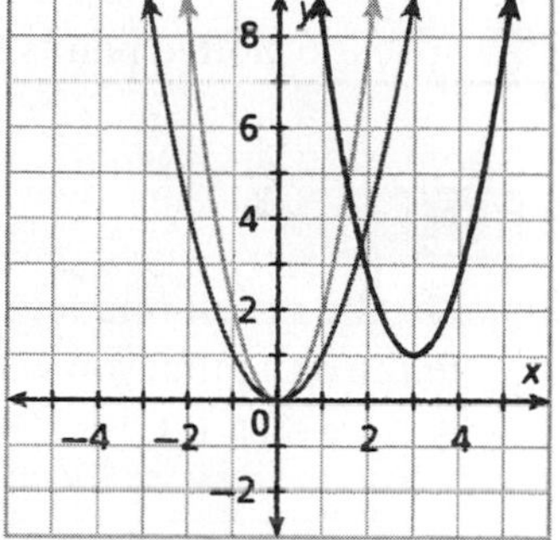

REFLECT

1a. The vertex of the graph of $f(x) = x^2$ is ____________, while the vertex of the graph of $g(x) = 2(x - 3)^2 + 1$ is ____________.

1b. If you start at the vertex of the graph of $f(x) = x^2$ and move 1 unit to the right or left, how must you move vertically to get back to the graph? ____________

1c. If you start at the vertex of the graph of $g(x) = 2(x - 3)^2 + 1$ and move 1 unit to the right or left, how must you move vertically to get back to the graph? ____________

1d. Based on your answers to Questions 1a–c, describe how you could graph $g(x) = a(x - h)^2 + k$ directly, without using transformed graphs.

____

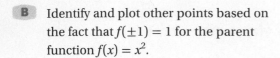

CC.9-12.F.BF.3

2 EXAMPLE Graphing $g(x) = a(x - h)^2 + k$

Graph $g(x) = -3(x + 1)^2 - 2$.

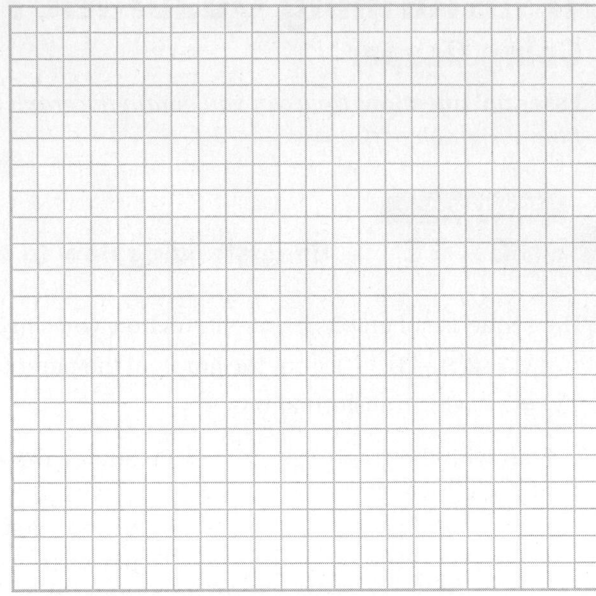

A Identify and plot the vertex.

Vertex: ___________

B Identify and plot other points based on the fact that $f(\pm 1) = 1$ for the parent function $f(x) = x^2$.

If you move 1 unit right or left from the vertex in part A, how must you move vertically to be on the graph of $g(x)$? What points are you at?

____

C Use the plotted points to draw a parabola.

REFLECT

2a. List the transformations of the graph of the parent function $f(x) = x^2$, in the order that you would perform them, to obtain the graph of $g(x) = -3(x + 1)^2 - 2$.

____

____

____

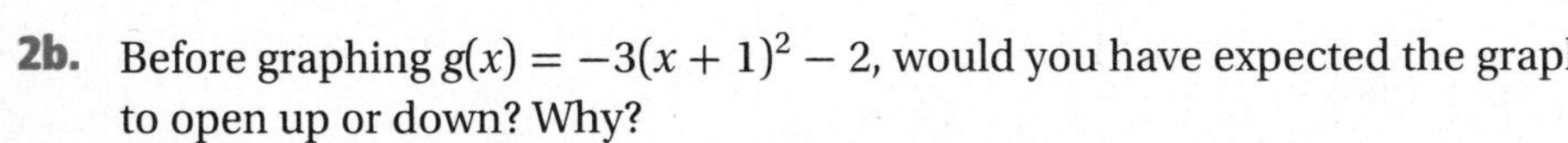

2b. Before graphing $g(x) = -3(x + 1)^2 - 2$, would you have expected the graph to open up or down? Why?

____

____

____

2c. Suppose you changed the -3 in $g(x) = -3(x + 1)^2 - 2$ to -4. Which of the points that you identified in parts A and B of the example would change? What coordinates would they now have?

____

____

____

CC.9–12.F.BF.1

3 EXAMPLE Writing a Quadratic Function from a Graph

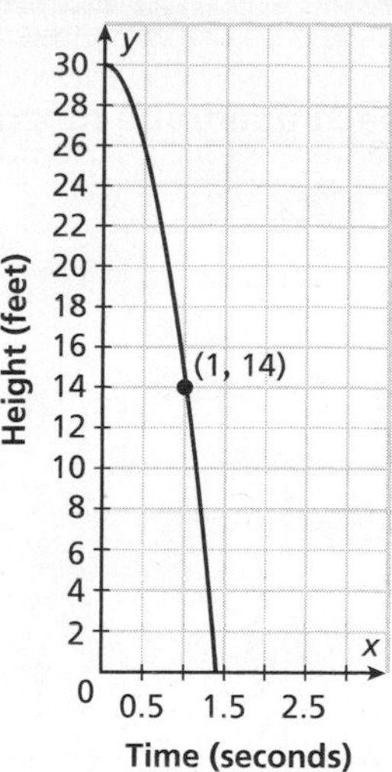

A house painter standing on a ladder drops a paintbrush, which falls to the ground. The paintbrush's height above the ground (in feet) is given by a function of the form $f(t) = a(t - h)^2 + k$ where t is the time (in seconds) since the paintbrush was dropped.

Because $f(t)$ is a quadratic function, its graph is a parabola. Only the portion of the parabola that lies in Quadrant I and on the axes is shown because only nonnegative values of t and $f(t)$ make sense in this situation. The vertex of the parabola lies on the vertical axis.

Use the graph to find an equation for $f(t)$.

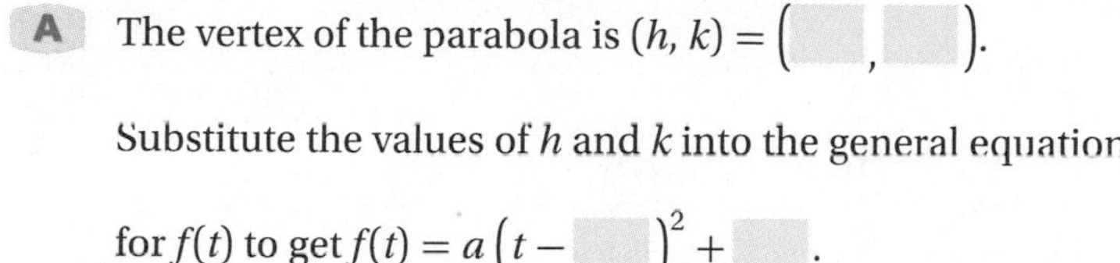

A The vertex of the parabola is $(h, k) = (\square, \square)$.

Substitute the values of h and k into the general equation for $f(t)$ to get $f(t) = a\left(t - \square\right)^2 + \square$.

B From the graph you can see that $f(1) =$ ________. Substitute 1 for t and ________ for $f(t)$ to determine the value of a for this function:

$$\square = a\left(1 - \square\right)^2 + \square$$

$$\_\_\_\_\_\_ = a$$

C Write the equation for the function: $f(t) =$ ________________

REFLECT

3a. Using the graph, estimate how much time elapses until the paintbrush hits the ground: $t \approx$ ________

3b. Using the value of t from Question 3a and the equation for the height function from part C of the example, find the value of $f(t)$. How does this help you check the reasonableness of the equation?

____

____

PRACTICE

Graph each quadratic function.

1. $f(x) = 2(x - 2)^2 + 3$

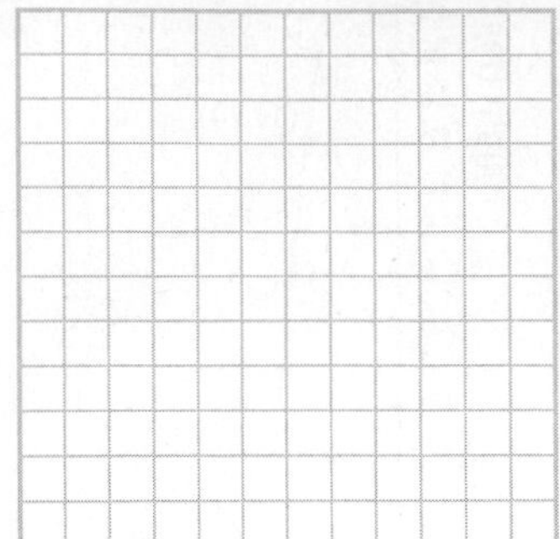

2. $f(x) = -(x - 1)^2 + 2$

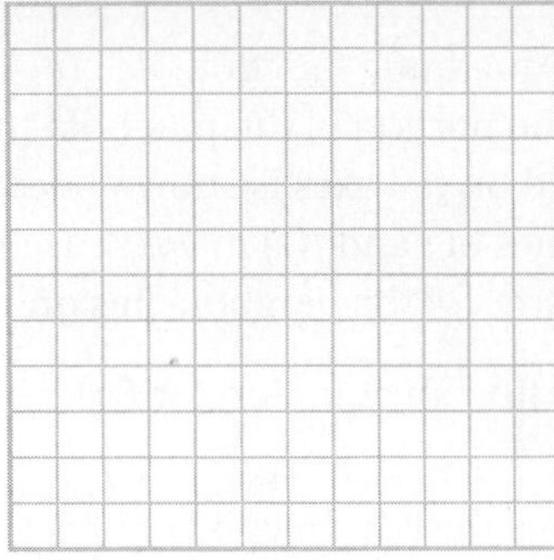

3. $f(x) = \frac{1}{2}(x - 2)^2$

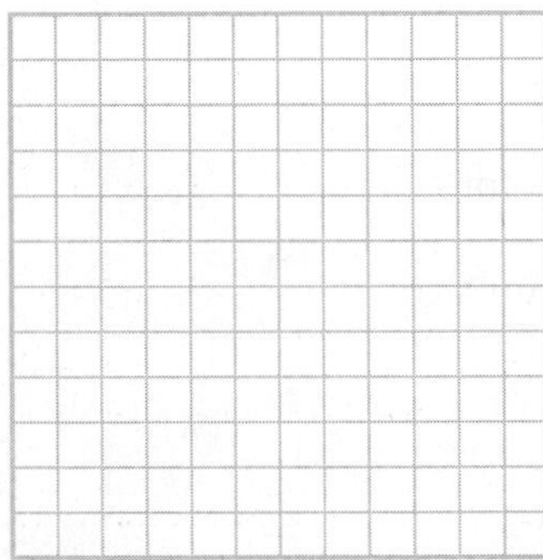

4. $f(x) = -\frac{1}{3}x^2 - 3$

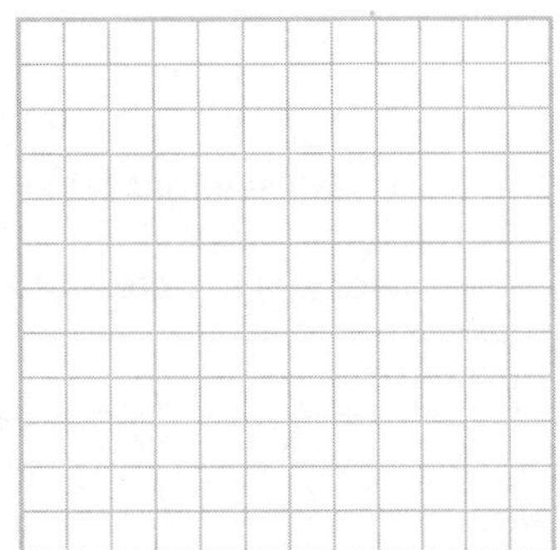

5. A roofer working on a roof accidentally drops a hammer, which falls to the ground. The hammer's height above the ground (in feet) is given by a function of the form $f(t) = a(t - h)^2 + k$ where t is the time (in seconds) since the hammer was dropped.

Because $f(t)$ is a quadratic function, its graph is a parabola. Only the portion of the parabola that lies in Quadrant I and on the axes is shown because only nonnegative values of t and $f(t)$ make sense in this situation. The vertex of the parabola lies on the vertical axis.

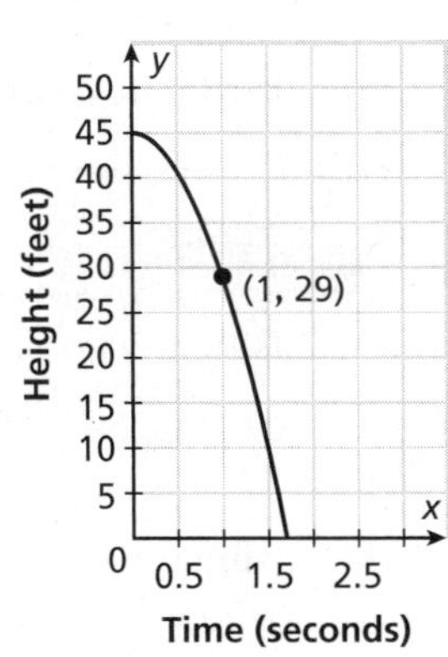

a. Use the graph to find an equation for $f(t)$.

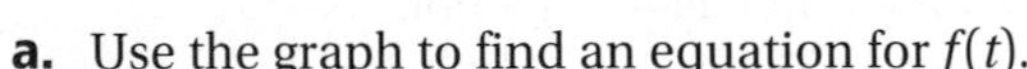

b. Explain how you can use the graph's t-intercept to check the reasonableness of your equation.

Name________________ Class__________ Date__________

8-4

Additional Practice

Order the functions from narrowest graph to widest.

1. $f(x) = 3x^2$; $g(x) = -2x^2$

____

2. $f(x) = \frac{1}{2}x^2$; $g(x) = 5x^2$; $h(x) = x^2$

____

3. $f(x) = 4x^2$; $g(x) = -3x^2$; $h(x) = \frac{1}{4}x^2$

____

4. $f(x) = 0.5x^2$; $g(x) = \frac{1}{4}x^2$; $h(x) = \frac{1}{3}x^2$

____

Compare the graph of each function with the graph of $f(x) = x^2$.

5. $g(x) = 5x^2 + 10$ _______________

____

6. $g(x) = \frac{1}{8}x^2 - 3$ _______________

____

7. $g(x) = -3x^2 + 8$ _______________

____

8. $g(x) = -\frac{3}{4}x^2 + \frac{1}{4}$ _______________

____

9. Two sandbags are dropped from a hot air balloon, one from a height of 400 feet and the other from a height of 1600 feet.

   a. Write the two height functions.

   $h_1(t) =$ __________ $h_2(t) =$ __________

   b. Sketch and compare their graphs.

   ____

   ____

   c. Tell when each sandbag reaches the ground.

   ____

   ____

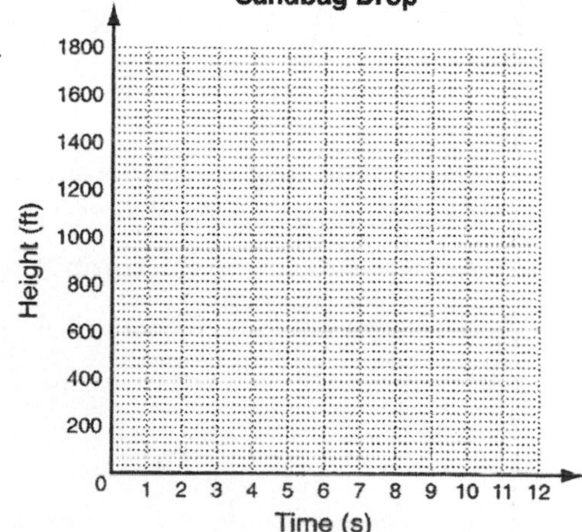

Problem Solving

Write the correct answer.

1. Two construction workers working at different heights on a skyscraper dropped their hammers at the same time. The first was working at a height of 400 ft, the second at a height of 160 ft. Write the two functions that describe the heights of the hammers.

____

____

2. Graph the two functions you found in problem 1 on the grid below.

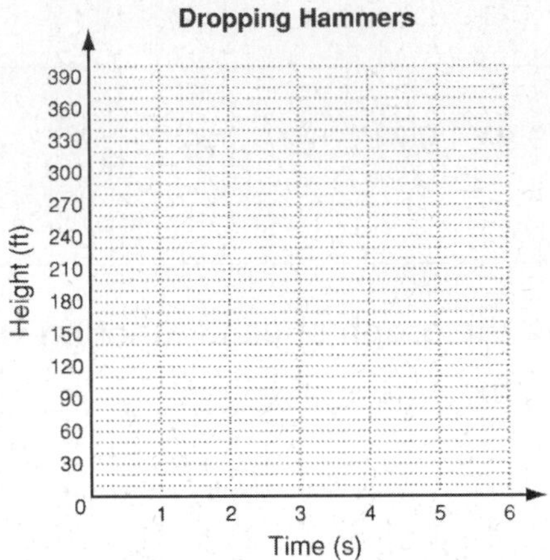

3. Based on the graphs you drew in problem 2, how long will it take each hammer to reach the ground?

____

____

The pull of gravity varies from planet to planet. The graph shows the height of objects dropped from 500 ft on the surface of four planets. Use this graph to answer questions 4–6. Select the best answer.

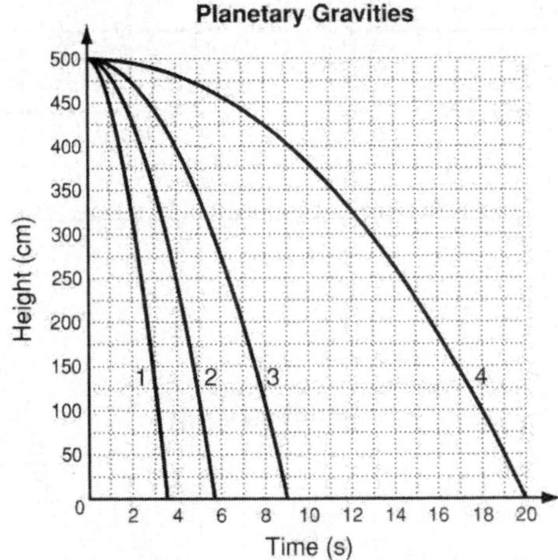

4. Of the four planets, Jupiter has the strongest gravity. Which of the four graphs represents the height of the object dropped on Jupiter?

   F Graph 1 H Graph 3

   G Graph 2 J Graph 4

5. Which of the graphs represents an object dropped on Earth?

   A Graph 1 C Graph 3

   B Graph 2 D Graph 4

6. Due to its small size, Pluto has a very weak pull of gravity. Which of the equations below represents the graph of the object dropped on Pluto?

   A $h(t) = -41x^2 + 500$

   B $h(t) = -16x^2 + 500$

   C $h(t) = -6x^2 + 500$

   D $h(t) = -1.25x^2 + 500$

Name ______________________ Class ______________ Date ____________

8-5

Solving Quadratic Equations by Graphing

Going Deeper

Essential question: *How can you solve a quadratic equation by graphing?*

Video Tutor

PREP FOR CC.9–12.A.REI.11

1 EXPLORE Finding Intersections of Lines and Parabolas

The graphs of three quadratic functions are shown.

Parabola A is the graph of $f(x) = x^2$.

Parabola B is the graph of $f(x) = x^2 + 4$.

Parabola C is the graph of $f(x) = x^2 + 8$.

A On the same coordinate grid, graph the function $g(x) = 4$. What type of function is this? Describe its graph.

____

B At how many points does the graph of $g(x)$ intersect each parabola?

Intersections with parabola A: __________

Intersections with parabola B: __________

Intersections with parabola C: __________

C Use the graph to find the x-coordinate of each point of intersection of the graph of $g(x)$ and parabola A. Show that each x-coordinate satisfies the equation $x^2 = 4$.

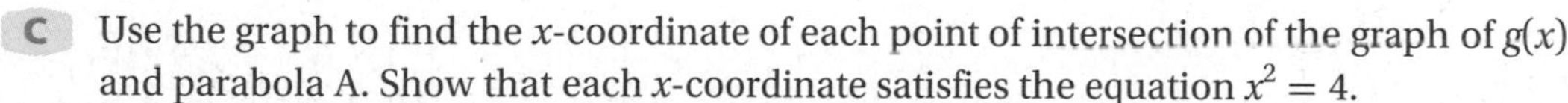

____

D Use the graph to find the x-coordinate of each point of intersection of the graph of $g(x)$ and parabola B. Show that each x-coordinate satisfies the equation $x^2 + 4 = 4$.

____

REFLECT

1a. Describe how you could solve an equation like $x^2 + 5 = 7$ graphically.

____

____

You can solve an equation of the form $a(x-h)^2+k=c$, which is called a *quadratic equation*, by graphing the functions $f(x)=a(x-h)^2+k$ and $g(x)=c$ and finding the x-coordinate of each point of intersection.

CC.9–12.A.REI.11

2 EXAMPLE Solving Quadratic Equations Graphically

Solve $2(x-4)^2+1=7$.

A Graph $f(x)=2(x-4)^2+1$.

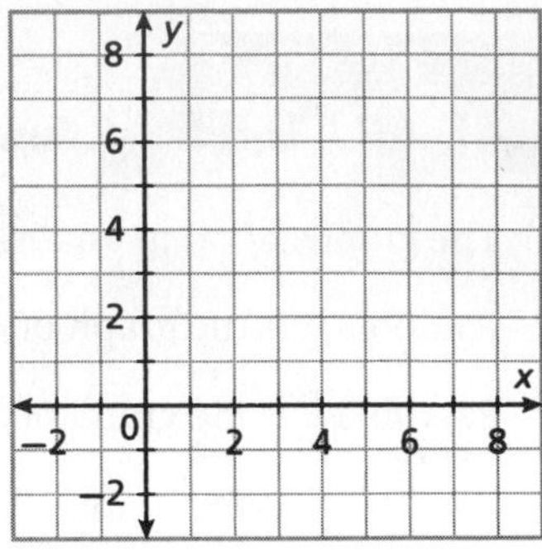

What is the vertex? ____________

If you move 1 unit right or left from the vertex, how must you move vertically to be on the graph of $f(x)$? What points are you at?

____

B Graph $g(x)=7$.

C At how many points do the graphs of $f(x)$ and $g(x)$ intersect? If possible, find the x-coordinate of each point of intersection exactly. Otherwise, give an approximation of the x-coordinate of each point of intersection.

____

D For each x-value from part C, find the value of $f(x)$. How does this show that you have found actual or approximate solutions of $2(x-4)^2+1=7$?

____

____

____

REFLECT

2a. If you solved the equation $4(x-3)^2+1=5$ graphically, would you be able to obtain exact or approximate solutions? Explain.

____

____

2b. For what value of c would the equation $4(x-3)^2+1=c$ have exactly one solution? How is that solution related to the graph of $f(x)$?

____

____

CC.9–12.A.CED.2

3 EXAMPLE Solving a Real-World Problem

While practicing a tightrope walk at a height of 20 feet, a circus performer slips and falls into a safety net 15 feet below. The function $h(t) = -16t^2 + 20$, where t represents time measured in seconds, gives the performer's height above the ground (in feet) as he falls. Write and solve an equation to find the elapsed time until the performer lands in the net.

A Write the equation that you need to solve. ______________________

B You will solve the equation using a graphing calculator. Because the calculator requires that you enter functions in terms of x and y, use x and y to write the equations for the two functions that you will graph. ______________________

C When setting a viewing window, you need to decide what portion of each axis to use for graphing. What interval on the x-axis and what interval on the y-axis are reasonable for this problem? Explain.

____

____

____

D Graph the two functions, and use the calculator's trace or intersect feature to find the elapsed time until the performer lands in the net. Is your answer exact or an approximation?

____

REFLECT

3a. Although the graphs also intersect to the left of the y-axis, why is that point irrelevant to the problem?

____

3b. The distance d (in feet) that a falling object travels as a function of time t (in seconds) is given by $d(t) = 16t^2$. Use this fact to explain the model given in the problem, $h(t) = -16t^2 + 20$. In particular, explain why the model includes the constant 20 and why $-16t^2$ includes a negative sign.

____

____

____

3c. At what height would the circus performer have to be for his fall to last exactly 1 second? Explain.

____

____

____

PRACTICE

Solve each quadratic equation by graphing. Indicate whether the solutions are exact or approximate.

1. $(x + 2)^2 - 1 = 3$

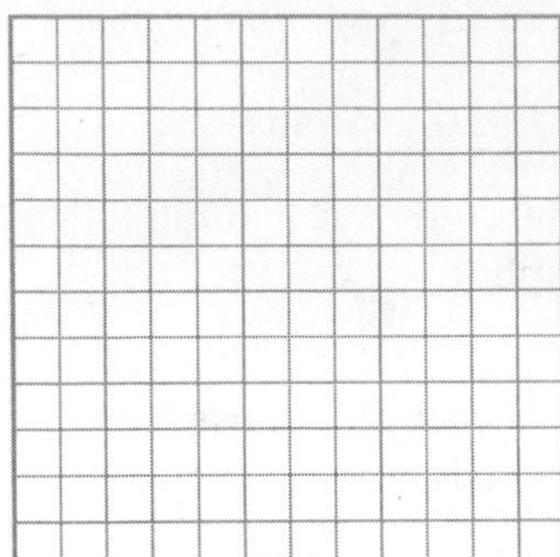

2. $2(x - 3)^2 + 1 = 5$

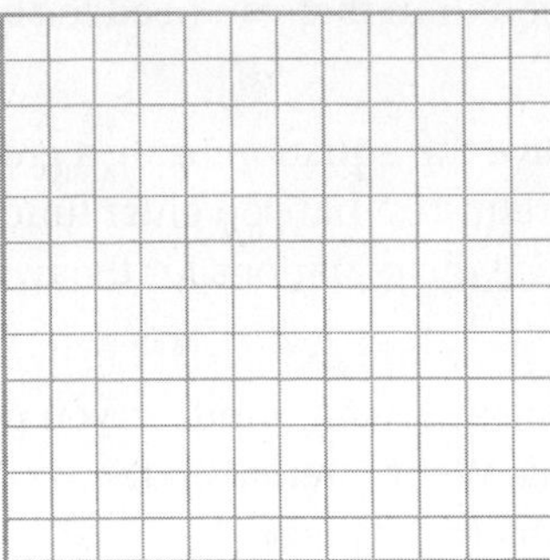

3. $-\frac{1}{2}x^2 + 2 = -4$

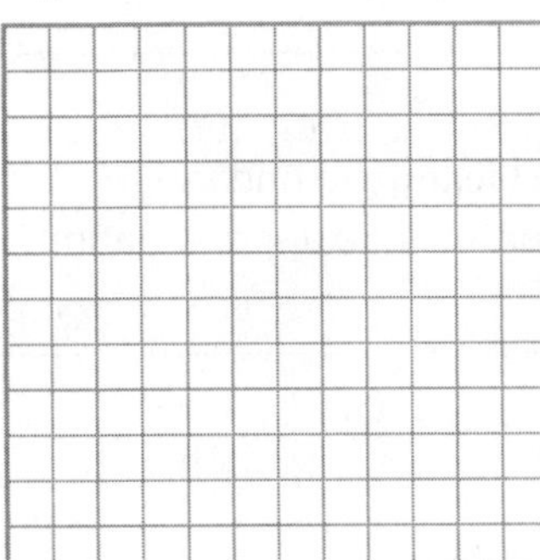

4. $-(x - 3)^2 - 2 = -6$

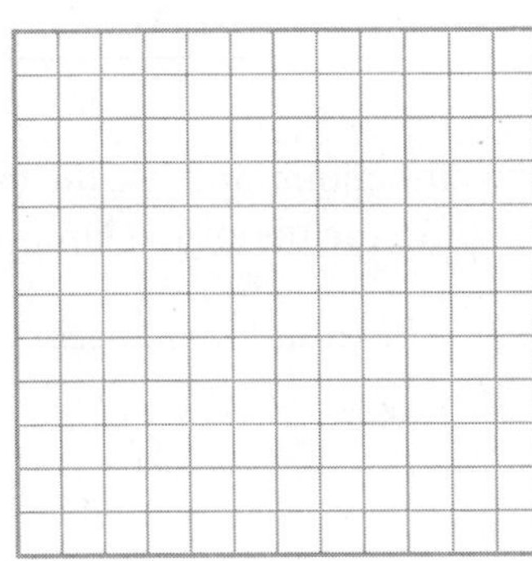

5. As part of an engineering contest, a student who has designed a protective crate for an egg drops the crate from a window 18 feet above the ground. The height (in feet) of the crate as it falls is given by $h(t) = -16t^2 + 18$ where t is the time (in seconds) since the crate was dropped.

a. Write and solve an equation to find the elapsed time until the crate passes a window 10 feet directly below the window from which it was dropped.

b. Write and solve an equation to find the elapsed time until the crate hits the ground.

c. Is the crate's rate of fall constant? Explain.

Name________________________ Class______________ Date____________

Additional Practice

Solve each equation by graphing the related function.

1. $x^2 - 6x + 9 = 0$

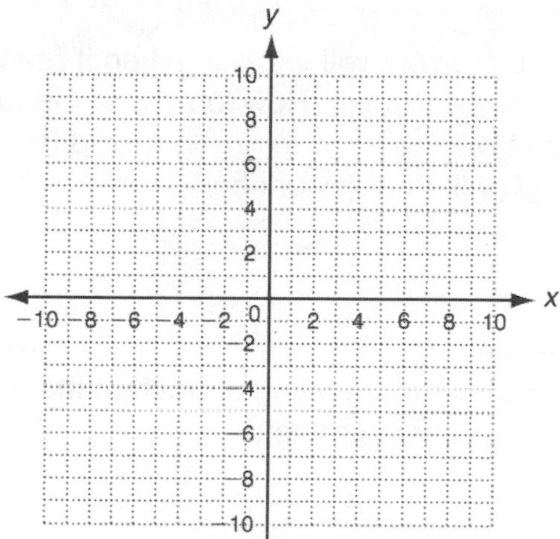

2. $x^2 = 4$

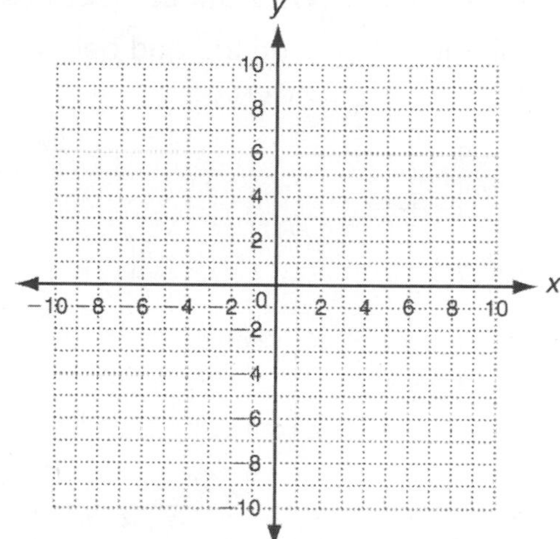

3. $2x^2 + 4x = 6$

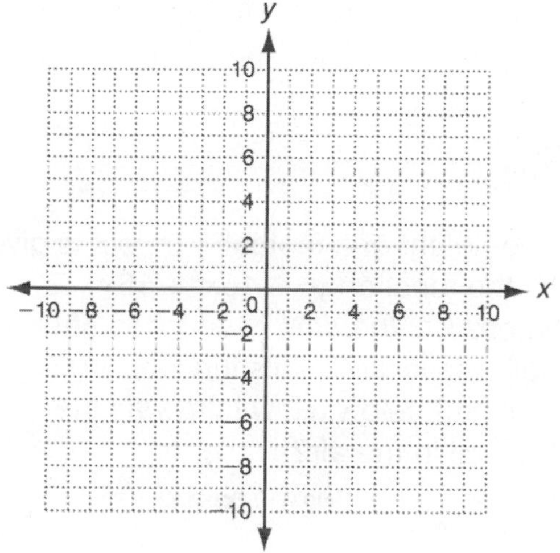

4. $x^2 = 5x - 10$

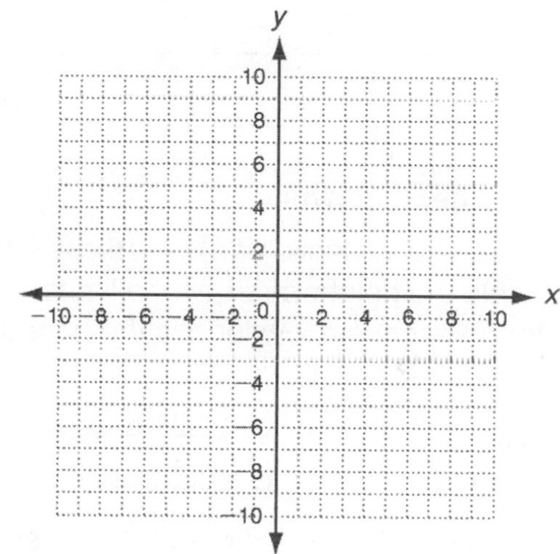

5. Water is shot straight up out of a water soaker toy. The quadratic function $y = -16x^2 + 32x$ models the height in feet of a water droplet after x seconds. How long is the water droplet in the air?

____

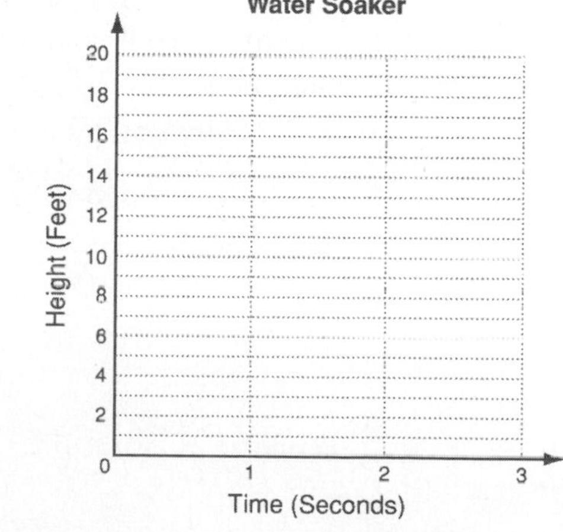

Problem Solving

The path of a certain firework in the air is modeled by the parabolic function $y = -16x^2 + 256x - 624$ where x is the number of seconds after the fuse is lit. Write the correct answer.

1. Graph the function on the grid below.

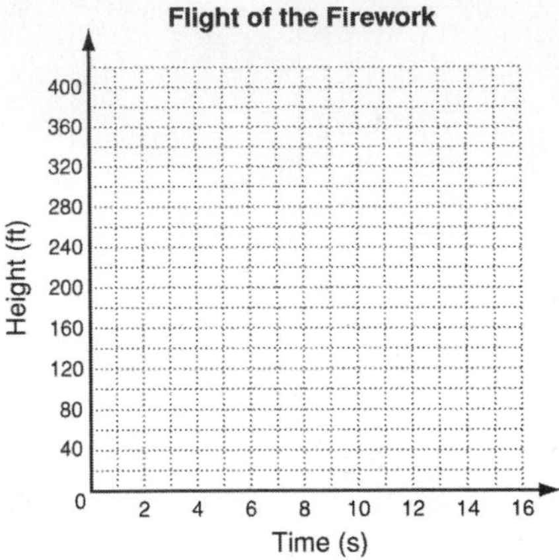

2. The firework will explode when it reaches its highest point. How long after the fuse is lit will the firework explode and how high will the firework be?

____

____

3. Based on the graph of the firework, what are the two zeros of this function?

____

____

4. What is the meaning of each of the zeros you found in problem 3?

____

____

____

Select the best answer.

5. The quadratic function $f(x) = -16x^2 + 90x$ models the height of a baseball in feet after x seconds. How long is the baseball in the air?

   A 2.8125 s　　C 11.25 s

   B 5.625 s　　D 126.5625 s

6. The height of a football y in feet is given by the function $y = -16x^2 + 56x + 2$ where x is the time in seconds after the ball was kicked. This function is graphed below. How long was the football in the air?

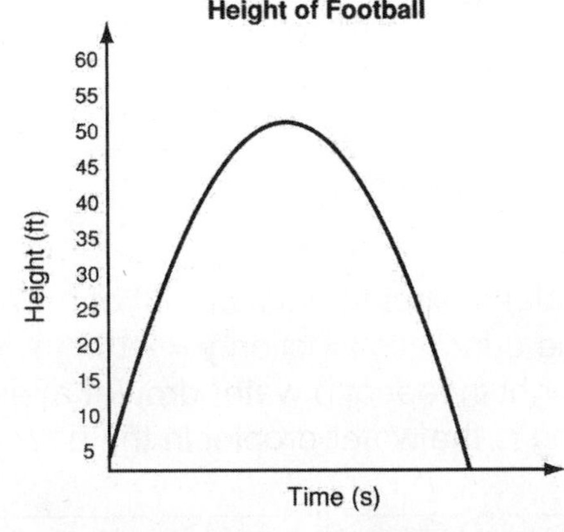

   A 0.5 seconds　　C 2 seconds

   B 1.75 seconds　　D 3.5 seconds

7. The function $y = -0.04x^2 + 2x$ models the height of an arch support for a bridge, where x is the distance in feet from where the arch supports enter the water. How many real solutions does this function have?

   F 0　　H 2

   G 1　　J 3

Name ____________________ Class ____________ Date ________

8-6

Video Tutor

Solving Quadratic Equations by Factoring

Going Deeper

Essential question: *How can you solve quadratic equations by factoring?*

CC.9–12.A.REI.4b

1 ENGAGE Understanding the Zero-Product Property and Recognizing Zeros of Quadratic Functions

You already know how to solve simple quadratic equations of the form $x^2 = a$, where a is a perfect square. For example, you can solve the equation $x^2 = 36$ by using the definition of ________________. The solutions of the equation are $x =$ ______ and $x =$ ______.

Another method for solving $x^2 = 36$ involves factoring. Start by subtracting 36 from both sides, resulting in $x^2 - 36 = 0$. This makes the left side of the equation a difference of two squares that can be factored as $(x + \square)(x - \square)$.

The **zero-product property** states that the product of any group of numbers is 0 if at least one of the numbers is 0 because 0 times any number is 0. Applying the zero-product property to $(x + 6)(x - 6) = 0$ gives the following:

$x + \square = 0$ or $x - \square = 0$

$x =$ ______ or $x =$ ______

The solutions of the equation $x^2 - 36 = 0$ are called the **zeros** of the related function $f(x) = x^2 - 36$ because they satisfy the equation $f(x) = 0$. To see this, you can substitute 6 and -6 for x in $f(x) = x^2 - 36$. The result is $f(6) = 0$ and $f(-6) = 0$.

REFLECT

1a. Describe how to use the zero-product property to solve the equation $(x + 4)(x - 12) = 0$. Then identify the solutions.

____

1b. How can you use your answer to Question 1a to identify the zeros of the function $f(x) = x^2 - 8x - 48$?

____

____

You can use the zero-product property to solve any quadratic equation written in standard form, $ax^2 + bx + c = 0$, provided the quadratic expression is factorable. You can also use the zero-product property to find the zeros of any quadratic function $f(x) = ax^2 + bx + c$ whose rule is factorable once you set $f(x)$ equal to 0.

CC.9–12.A.REI.4b

2 EXAMPLE Solving a Quadratic Equation

Find the solutions of $x^2 + 13x = -36$.

A Write the equation in standard form. $x^2 + 13x$ ___ $36 = 0$

B Factor the trinomial. The constant term is positive so its factors are either both positive or both negative. The coefficient of x is positive, so both factors of the constant term must be ________. The binomial factors will be of the form $(x$ ___ $p)(x$ ___ $q)$.

Factors of 36	Sum of Factors
1 and 36	

The factored trinomial is $(x +$ ___ $)(x +$ ___ $)$, so the equation becomes $(x +$ ___ $)(x +$ ___ $) = 0$.

C Use the zero-product property.

$x +$ ___ $= 0$ or $x +$ ___ $= 0$

$x =$ ______ or $x =$ ______

REFLECT

2a. Suppose the equation was $x^2 - 13x = -36$. Describe how solving the equation would be different than what is shown in the Example. Find the solutions of the equation.

2b. Can the zero-product property be used to solve any quadratic equation? If so, explain why. If not, give an example of an equation that cannot be solved.

CC.9–12.A.REI.4b

3 EXAMPLE Finding the Zeros of a Quadratic Function

Find the zeros of $f(x) = x^2 - 4x - 12$.

A Set the function equal to 0 and recognize the factoring pattern.

$x^2 - 4x - 12 =$ ____

$(x$ ____ $p)(x$ ____ $q) =$ ____

Explain your choice of factoring pattern.

____

____

B Find the factors of -12 that have a sum of -4. Then write the equation in factored form.

Factors of –12	Sum of Factors
1 and –12	

So, the factored form of the equation is $(x +$ ____ $)(x -$ ____ $) = 0$.

C Use the zero product property to solve the equation and identify the zeros.

$x +$ ____ $= 0$ or $x -$ ____ $= 0$

$x =$ ____ or $x =$ ____

So, the zeros of $f(x) = x^2 - 4x - 12$ are ____ and ____.

REFLECT

3a. Show that each zero satisfies $f(x) = 0$.

____

3b. If you were to graph the function $f(x) = x^2 - 4x - 12$, what points would be associated with the zeros of the function? What is special about these points and their x-coordinates?

____

____

To solve a quadratic equation by factoring, first rewrite the equation so one side equals 0, then factor. By the zero-product property, at least one of the factors must equal 0. Set each factor equal to 0 and solve each linear equation separately to find the solutions.

CC.9–12.A.REI.4b

4 EXAMPLE Solving $ax^2 + bx + c = 0$ by Factoring

Solve $7x^2 + 20x = x + 6$ by factoring.

A Use the addition and subtraction properties of equality as needed to rewrite the equation so that one side equals 0.

$$\underline{\qquad\qquad\qquad\qquad} = 0$$

B Factor the left side of the equation.

$$(\square x + \square)(\square x - \square) = 0$$

C Set each factor equal to 0, and solve.

$\square x + \square = 0$ or $\square x - \square = 0$

$x = \square$ or $x = \square$

REFLECT

4a. Why is it necessary to rewrite the equation so that one side equals 0 before factoring?

4b. How is solving the equation $7x^2 + 12x = x + 6$ like solving the equation in the Example and how is it different?

4c. How could you write a quadratic equation in standard form with solutions $x = \frac{1}{4}$ and $x = -\frac{3}{2}$?

Special Cases The following example includes some special cases to consider.

1. Always look for a common factor before you begin. If $c = 0$, then x is a common factor of $ax^2 + bx$.
2. Consider the perfect square trinomial and difference of squares patterns:

$$(a + b)^2 = a^2 + 2ab + b^2$$
$$(a - b)^2 = a^2 - 2ab + b^2$$
$$(a + b)(a - b) = a^2 - b^2$$

CC.9-12.A.REI.4b

5 EXAMPLE Solving $ax^2 + bx + c = 0$ by Factoring

Solve the equation by factoring.

A $12x^2 + 6x - 6 = 0$

Both a and c have many factor pairs, so there are a lot of possible factors. However, notice that 6 is a common factor for each term.

$6(\quad) = 0$ — First, factor out the 6.

$6(\quad)(\quad) = 0$ — Factor the remaining trinomial.

$\quad = 0$ or $\quad = 0$ — Set each factor equal to 0.

$x = \quad$ or $x = \quad$ — Solve.

B $4x^2 - 25 = 0$

The left side of the equation has the form $a^2 - b^2$, a difference of squares.

$a^2 = 4x^2$, so $a =$ ______, and $b^2 = 25$, so $b =$ ______.

$(\quad)(\quad) = 0$ — Factor the difference of squares.

$\quad = 0$ or $\quad = 0$ — Set each factor equal to 0.

$x = \quad$ or $x = \quad$ — Solve.

C $3x^2 + 9x = 0$

Because $c = 0$, x is a common factor. There is also a common factor of 3.

$\quad(\quad) = 0$ — Factor out the common factor.

$\quad = 0$ or $\quad = 0$ — Set each factor equal to 0.

$x = \quad$ or $x = \quad$ — Solve.

REFLECT

5a. Why can you ignore the common factor of 6 in Part A once it is factored out?

____

5b. Why can't you ignore the common factor of $3x$ in part C?

____

CC.9–12.A.CED.1

6 EXAMPLE Modeling the Height of a Diver

Physics students are measuring the heights and times of divers jumping off diving boards. The function that models a diver's height (in meters) above the water is

$$h(t) = -5t^2 + vt + h_0$$

where v is the diver's initial upward velocity in meters per second, h_0 is the diver's height above the water in meters, and t is the time in seconds. A diver who is 3 meters above the water jumps off a diving board with an initial upward velocity of 14 m/s. How many seconds will it take for the diver to hit the water? That is, when does $h(t) = 0$?

A Write the equation $h(t) = 0$, substituting in known values. $-5t^2 + \_\_\_\_ t + \_\_\_\_ = 0$

B Factor the left side of the equation. $(\_\_\_\_)(\_\_\_\_) = 0$

C Set each factor equal to zero and solve. $t =$ ______ or $t =$ ______

D Which value of t makes sense in the context of the problem? Why?

____

REFLECT

6a. Suppose a diver who is 10 meters above the water jumps off a diving board with an initial upward velocity of 5 m/s. How many seconds will it take for the diver to hit the water? Explain your reasoning.

____

____

____

6b. If an object is dropped, its initial velocity is 0. How would this affect the function that models the object's height?

____

PRACTICE

Solve.

1. $m^2 + 8m + 16 = 0$

2. $n^2 - 10n = 24$

3. $x^2 + 25x = 0$

4. $y^2 - 30 = 13y$

5. $z^2 - 9 = 0$

6. $p^2 = 54 - 3p$

7. $x^2 + 11x - 42 = 0$

8. $g^2 - 14g = 51$

9. $n^2 - 81 = 0$

10. $y^2 = 25y$

Find the zeros of the function.

11. $f(x) = x^2 + 11x + 30$

12. $f(x) = x^2 - x - 20$

13. $f(x) = x^2 + 6x - 7$

14. $f(x) = x^2 + 2x + 1$

Solve by factoring.

15. $2x^2 + 15x + 7 = 0$

16. $7z^2 - 30z + 27 = 0$

17. $8x^2 - 10x - 3 = 0$

18. $30d^2 + 7d - 15 = 0$

19. $10g^2 + 23g + 12 = 0$

20. $5y^2 - 2y - 7 = 0$

21. $2n^2 + 15 = 11n$

22. $6a^2 + 10a = 3a + 10$

Solve by factoring.

23. $12x^2 - x = 20$

____

24. $9z^2 - 25 = 0$

____

25. $36h^2 - 12h + 1 = 0$

____

26. $12n^2 + 48 = 80n$

____

27. $18x^2 + 24x = -8$

____

28. $12y^2 + 3y = 54$

____

29. A cat jumps off a three foot high kitchen counter at an initial upward velocity of 2 feet per second. The function $h(t) = -16t^2 + vt + s$ models the cat's height (in feet) above the kitchen floor, where v is the initial upward velocity of the cat in feet per second.

a. Write an equation to find the time when $h(t) = 0$.

$$-16t^2 + \underline{\quad} t + \underline{\quad} = 0$$

b. Solve the equation to find the two values for t.

$t =$ _______ or $t =$ _______

c. Explain the two values for t in the context of the situation.

____

____

____

Name________________________ Class______________ Date__________ **8-6**

Additional Practice

Use the Zero Product Property to solve each equation. Check your answers.

1. $(x-1)(x-5)=0$

   $x-1=0$ or $x-5=0$

   $x=$ ____ or $x=$ ____

2. $(x-2)(x-9)=0$

   $x-2=0$ or $x-9=0$

   $x=$ ____ or $x=$ ____

3. $(x-2)(x+4)=0$

   ____

4. $(2x+1)(x-6)=0$

   ____

Solve each quadratic equation by factoring.

5. $x^2-3x=0$ ____________
6. $x^2+4x+3=0$ ____________
7. $x^2+5x-6=0$ ____________
8. $x^2+11x+24=0$ ____________
9. $x^2-12x+11=0$ ____________
10. $x^2+18x+65=0$ ____________
11. $x^2-4x-12=0$ ____________
12. $x^2+11x+10=0$ ____________
13. $x^2+12x+35=0$ ____________
14. $2x^2-3x-5=0$ ____________
15. $3x^2-5x-2=0$ ____________
16. $x^2=3x+40$ ____________
17. $x^2-14=5x$ ____________
18. $2x-1=-8x^2$ ____________
19. $x=10x^2-2$ ____________
20. $2x^2=13x+7$ ____________
21. $6x^2+x=5$ ____________
22. $x^2=5x$ ____________
23. The height of a flare fired from the deck of a ship in distress can be modeled by $h=-16t^2+104t+56$, where h is the height of the flare above water and t is the time in seconds. Find the time it takes the flare to hit the water. ____________________

Problem Solving

Write the correct answer.

1. The height of an acorn falling out of a tree is $h = -16t^2 + 25$ where h is height in feet and t is time in seconds. Determine how long it takes the acorn to reach the ground. Check your answer by graphing the function.

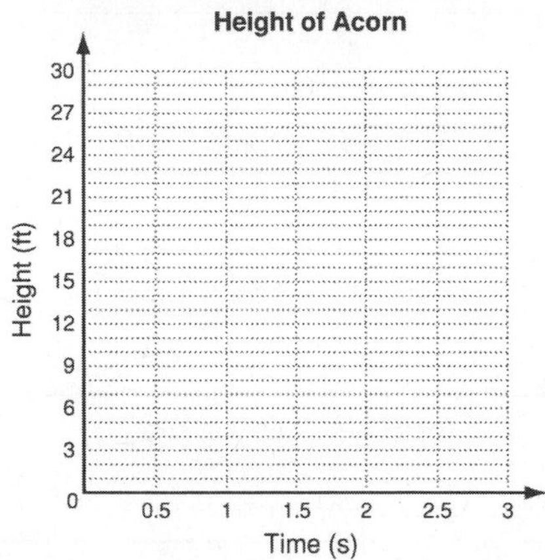

2. An architect is designing a building with a right triangular footprint.

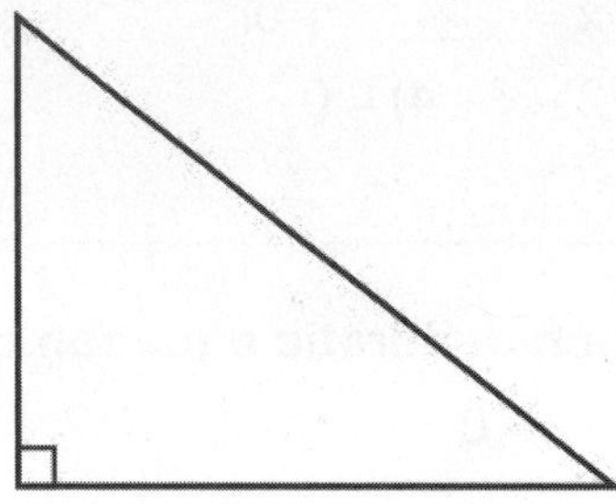

The hypotenuse of the triangle is 80 feet longer than one leg of the triangle and 40 feet longer than the other leg. Use the Pythagorean Theorem to find the dimensions of the footprint of the building.

3. Robert threw a rock off a bridge into the river. The distance from the rock to the river is modeled by the equation $h = -16t^2 - 16t + 60$, where h is the height in feet and t is the time in seconds. Find how long it took the rock to enter the water.

4. During a game of golf, Kayley hits her ball out of a sand trap. The equation $h = -16t^2 + 20t - 4$ models the height of the golf ball in feet in relation to the number of t seconds since it was hit. Find how long it takes Kayley's golf ball to reach the green.

A new store is being built in the shape of a rectangle with a parking lot in the shape of an isosceles trapezoid. The parking lot and the store will share a side as shown. Select the best answer.

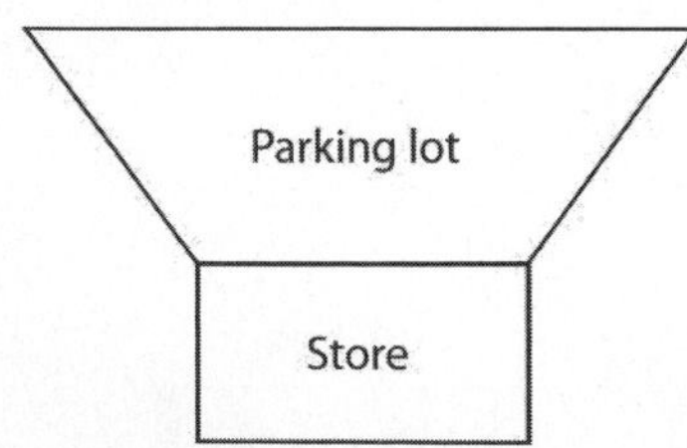

5. The parking lot will have an area of 160 square meters. The shorter base is 4 m longer than the height of the trapezoid, and the longer base is 8 m longer than the height. What is the length of the shorter base?

   F 10 meters H 18 meters

   G 14 meters J 20 meters

6. The area of the store is to be 154 square meters. If the depth is given as $\frac{1}{14}x^2 + \frac{15}{14}x$, what is the value of x?

   A 7 C 14

   B 11 D 28

7. What is the depth of the store in meters?

   F 7 H 14

   G 11 J 28

Name_______________________ Class_____________ Date_________

8-7

Video Tutor

Solving Quadratic Equations by Using Square Roots

Going Deeper

Essential question: *How can you solve a quadratic equation using square roots?*

PREP FOR CC.9–12.A.REI.4b

1 ENGAGE Understanding Square Roots

You know that $2^2 = 4$ and $(-2)^2 = 4$ and that the numbers 2 and -2 are called the *square roots* of 4.

In general, if $x^2 = a$, then x is a **square root** of a. Every positive number a has two square roots. This is illustrated in the diagram using the graph of $y = x^2$ and letting $y = a$. Notice that one square root of a is positive and is written $\sqrt{a}$, while the other is negative and is written $-\sqrt{a}$. The symbol $\sqrt{}$ is called a *radical sign,* and the number underneath the radical sign is called the *radicand.*

When the radicand is a perfect square, you can simplify a square root. For instance, because 4 is a perfect square, you can write the square roots of 4 as $\pm\sqrt{4} = \pm 2$.

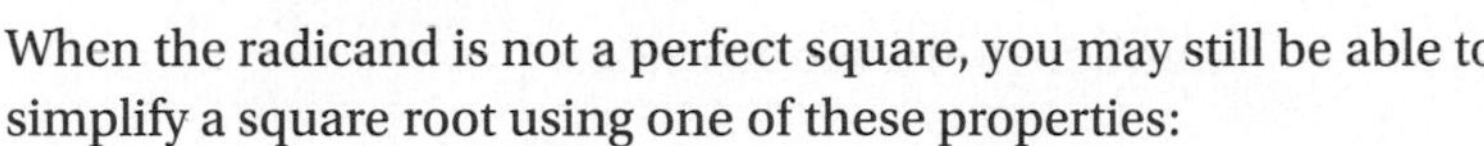

When the radicand is not a perfect square, you may still be able to simplify a square root using one of these properties:

Product Property of Radicals: For nonnegative a and b, $\sqrt{ab} = \sqrt{a} \cdot \sqrt{b}$.

Quotient Property of Radicals: For nonnegative a and positive b, $\sqrt{\frac{a}{b}} = \frac{\sqrt{a}}{\sqrt{b}}$.

For instance, because 12 has 4 as one of its factors, you can use the product property to write the square roots of 12 as $\pm\sqrt{12} = \pm\sqrt{4 \cdot 3} = \pm\sqrt{4} \cdot \sqrt{3} = \pm 2\sqrt{3}$.

REFLECT

1a. Does 0 have any square roots? Why or why not?

____

1b. Does a negative number have any square roots? Why or why not?

____

1c. Explain how you would simplify the square roots of $\frac{5}{4}$.

____

Solving a quadratic equation algebraically involves isolating the squared expression in the equation. Once you have the equation in the form $(x - h)^2 = c$, you can use the definition of a square root to write $x - h = \pm\sqrt{c}$ and finish solving for x.

CC.9–12.A.REI.4b

2 EXAMPLE Solving Quadratic Equations Algebraically

Solve each quadratic equation.

A $2x^2 - 7 = 9$ Equation to be solved

Add 7 to both sides.

$2x^2 =$ Simplify.

$\frac{2x^2}{} = \frac{}{}$ Divide both sides by 2.

$x^2 =$ Simplify.

$x =$ Definition of a square root

$x =$ Simplify the square roots.

B $-3(x - 6)^2 + 19 = 7$ Equation to be solved

Subtract 19 from both sides.

$-3(x - 6)^2 =$ Simplify.

$\frac{-3(x - 6)^2}{} = \frac{}{}$ Divide both sides by −3.

$(x - 6)^2 =$ Simplify.

$x - 6 =$ Definition of a square root

$x - 6 =$ or $x - 6 =$ Simplify the square roots.

$x =$ $x =$ Add 6 to both sides.

REFLECT

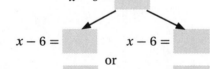

2a. How can you check the solutions of a quadratic equation?

3 EXAMPLE Solving a Real-World Problem

A person standing on a second-floor balcony drops keys to a friend standing below the balcony. The keys are dropped from a height of 10 feet. The height (in feet) of the keys as they fall is given by the function $h(t) = -16t^2 + 10$ where t is the time (in seconds) since the keys were dropped. The friend catches the keys at a height of 4 feet. Write and solve an equation to find the elapsed time before the keys are caught.

$-16t^2 + 10 = \square$	Write the equation to be solved.
$\underline{\square} \quad \underline{\square}$	Subtract 10 from both sides.
$-16t^2 = \square$	Simplify.
$\dfrac{-16t^2}{\square} = \dfrac{\square}{\square}$	Divide both sides by -16.
$t^2 = \square$	Simplify. Express the right side as a decimal.
$t = \square$	Definition of a square root
$t \approx \square$	Use a calculator to approximate the square roots.

The elapsed time before the keys are caught is about ______________.

REFLECT

3a. Although the equation that you solved has two solutions, one of them is rejected. Why?

____

3b. The exact positive solution of the equation is $t = \frac{\sqrt{6}}{4}$. Explain how to obtain this result, and show that it gives the same approximate solution.

____

____

3c. Suppose the friend decides not to catch the keys and lets them fall to the ground instead. What equation must you solve to find the elapsed time until the keys hit the ground? What is that elapsed time?

____

PRACTICE

1. Write the square roots of 64 in simplified form. ________

2. Write the square roots of 32 in simplified form. ________

3. Write the square roots of $\frac{8}{9}$ in simplified form. ________

4. Explain why the square roots of 37 cannot be simplified.

____

Solve each quadratic equation. Simplify solutions when possible.

5. $x^2 = 18$

____

6. $-4x^2 = -20$

____

7. $x^2 + 4 = 10$

____

8. $2x^2 = 200$

____

9. $(x - 5)^2 = 25$

____

10. $(x + 1)^2 = 16$

____

11. $2(x - 7)^2 = 98$

____

12. $-5(x + 3)^2 = -80$

____

13. $0.5(x + 2)^2 - 4 = 14$

____

14. $3(x - 1)^2 + 1 = 19$

____

15. To study how high a ball bounces, students drop the ball from various heights. The function $h(t) = -16t^2 + h_0$ gives the height (in feet) of the ball at time t measured in seconds since the ball was dropped from a height h_0.

    a. The ball is dropped from a height $h_0 = 8$ feet. Write and solve an equation to find the elapsed time until the ball hits the floor.

    ____

    b. Does doubling the drop height also double the elapsed time until the ball hits the floor? Explain why or why not.

    ____

    ____

    c. When dropped from a height $h_0 = 16$ feet, the ball rebounds to a height of 8 feet and then falls back to the floor. Find the total time for this to happen. (Assume the ball takes the same time to rebound 8 feet as it does to fall 8 feet.)

    ____

Additional Practice

Solve using square roots. Check your answer.

1. $x^2 = 81$

   $x = \pm\sqrt{81}$

   $x = \pm$

   The solutions are ______ and ______.

2. $x^2 = 100$

   $x = \pm\sqrt{\_\_\_\_}$

   $x = \pm$______

   The solutions are ______ and ______.

3. $x^2 = 225$

   $x = \pm\sqrt{\_\_\_\_}$

   $x =$ ______

4. $441 = x^2$

   $\pm\sqrt{\_\_\_\_} = x$

   ______ $= x$

5. $x^2 = -400$

   ____

6. $3x^2 = 108$

   ____

7. $100 = 4x^2$

   ____

8. $x^2 + 7 = 71$

   ____

9. $49x^2 - 64 = 0$

   ____

10. $-2x^2 = -162$

    ____

11. $9x^2 + 100 = 0$

    ____

12. $0 = 81x^2 - 121$

    ____

13. $100x^2 = 25$

    ____

14. $100x^2 = 121$

    ____

Solve. Round to the nearest hundredth.

15. $8x^2 = 56$

    ____

16. $5 - x^2 = 20$

    ____

17. $x^2 + 35 = 105$

    ____

18. The height of a skydiver jumping out of an airplane is given by $h = -16t^2 + 3200$. How long will it take the skydiver to reach the ground? Round to the nearest tenth of a second.

    ____

19. The height of a triangle is twice the length of its base. The area of the triangle is 50 m^2. Find the height and base to the nearest tenth of a meter.

    ____

20. The height of an acorn falling out of a tree is given by $h = -16t^2 + b$. If an acorn takes 1 second to fall to the ground. What is the value of b?

    ____

Problem Solving

A furniture maker has designed a bookcase with the proportions shown in the diagram below. Write the correct answer.

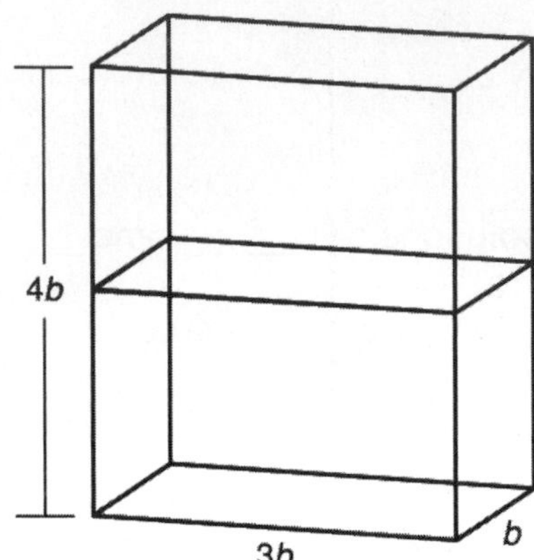

1. A customer has requested a bookcase with the two shelves having a total area of 864 square inches. What should b equal to meet the customer's specifications?

____

2. Barnard has a stain on his wall and would like to cover it up with a bookcase. What should b equal in order for the back of the bookcase to cover an area of 4800 square inches?

____

3. Bria would like to display her collection of soap carvings on top of her bookcase. The collection takes up an area of 400 square inches. What should b equal for the top of the bookcase to have the correct area? Round your answer to the nearest tenth of an inch.

____

4. Eliana would like to cover the side panels with silk. She has 1600 square inches of silk. What should b equal so that she can use all of her silk to completely cover the sides? Round your answer to the nearest tenth of an inch.

____

Select the best answer.

5. Carter plans to wallpaper the longest wall in his living room. The wall is twice as long as it is high and has an area of 162 square feet. What is the height of the wall?

   A 8 feet C 12 feet

   B 9 feet D 18 feet

6. An apple drops off the apple tree from a height of 8 feet. How long does it take the apple to reach the ground? Use the function $f(x) = -16x^2 + c$, where c is the initial height of a falling object, to find the answer.

   F 0.5 seconds H 1 second

   G 0.71 seconds J 2.23 seconds

7. Trinette cut a square tablecloth into 4 equal pieces that she used to make two pillow covers. The area of the tablecloth was 3600 square inches. What is the side length of each piece Trinette used to make the pillow covers?

   A 20 inches C 60 inches

   B 30 inches D 90 inches

8. Elton earns x dollars per hour at the bookstore. His mother, Evelyn, earns x^2 dollars per hour as a career counselor. Twice Evelyn's wage equals $84.50. What is Elton's hourly wage? Round your answer to the nearest cent.

   F $4.60 H $9.19

   G $6.50 J $13.00

Name________________________ Class______________ Date__________

8-8

Completing the Square
Going Deeper

Essential question: *How can you solve quadratic equations without factoring?*

PREP FOR CC.9–12.A.REI.4a

1 EXPLORE Completing the Square

The diagram below represents the expression $x^2 + 6x + c$ with the constant term missing.

A Complete the diagram by filling the bottom right corner with 1-tiles to form a square.

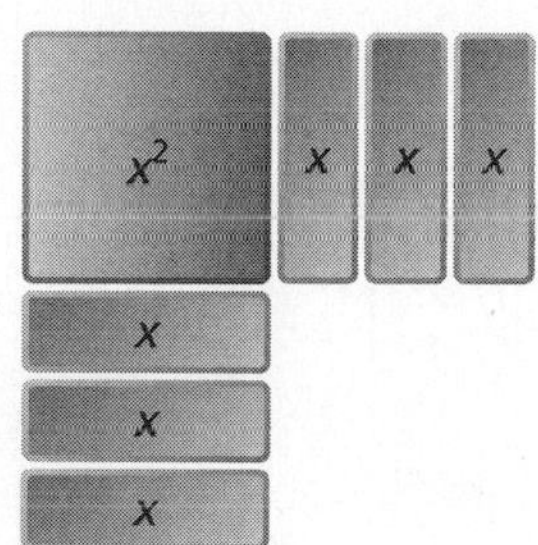

B How many 1-tiles did you add to the expression? ________

C Write the trinomial represented by the algebra tiles for the complete square.

$$\square x^2 + \square x + \square$$

D You should recognize this trinomial as an example of the special case $(a + b)^2 = a^2 + 2ab + b^2$. Recall that trinomials of this form are called perfect square trinomials. Since the trinomial is a perfect square, you can factor it into two binomials that are the same.

$$\square x^2 + \square x + \square = \left(\square x + \square\right)^2$$

REFLECT

1a. Look at the algebra tiles above. The x-tiles are divided equally, with 3 tiles on the right and bottom sides of the x^2-tile. How does the number 3 relate to the total number of x-tiles? How does the number 3 relate to the number of 1-tiles you added?

____

1b. How would algebra tiles be arranged to form a perfect square trinomial $x^2 + 8x + c$? How many 1-tiles must be added? How is this number related to the number of x-tiles?

____

____

Completing the Square Finding the value of c needed to make an expression such as $x^2 + 6x + c$ into a perfect square trinomial is called **completing the square**.

Using algebra tiles, half of the x-tiles are placed along the right and bottom sides of the x^2-tile. The number of 1-tiles added is the square of the number of x-tiles on either side of the x^2-tile.

To complete the square for the expression $x^2 + bx + c$, replace c with $\left(\frac{b}{2}\right)^2$. The perfect square trinomial is $x^2 + bx + \left(\frac{b}{2}\right)^2$ and factors as $\left(x + \frac{b}{2}\right)^2$.

PREP FOR CC.9–12.A.REI.4a

2 EXAMPLE Completing the Square

Complete the square to form a perfect square trinomial. Then factor the trinomial.

A $x^2 + 12x + c$

Identify b. $b =$ ______

Find c. $c = \left(\frac{b}{2}\right)^2 = \left(\frac{\square}{2}\right)^2 =$ ______

Write the trinomial. $x^2 + \square x + \square$

Factor the trinomial. $x^2 + \square x + \square = (\square)^2$

B $z^2 - 26z + c$

Identify b. $b =$ ______

Find c. $c = \left(\frac{b}{2}\right)^2 = \left(\frac{\square}{2}\right)^2 =$ ______

Write the trinomial. $z^2 + \square z + \square$

Factor the trinomial. $z^2 + \square z + \square = (\square)^2$

REFLECT

2a. In Part A, b is positive and in Part B, b is negative. Does this affect the sign of c? Why or why not?

____

____

2b. How can you confirm that you have factored each trinomial correctly?

____

____

CC.9-12.A.REI.4b

3 ENGAGE Solving Quadratic Equations by Completing the Square

You have solved quadratic equations by factoring and using the zero-product property. You can also solve quadratic equations by completing the square. This method is especially useful if the quadratic equation is difficult or impossible to factor. To solve a quadratic equation by completing the square, follow these steps:

1. Write the equation in the form $x^2 + bx = c$.
2. Complete the square by adding $\left(\frac{b}{2}\right)^2$ to both sides of the equation.
3. Factor the perfect square trinomial.
4. Apply the definition of a square root.
5. Write two equations, one using the positive square root and one using the negative square root.
6. Solve both equations.

REFLECT

3a. Which property explains why you need to add $\left(\frac{b}{2}\right)^2$ to both sides of the equation?

3b. What would be the first two steps in solving $x^2 + 10x - 11 = 0$ by completing the square?

3c. Could you use another method besides completing the square to solve the equation $x^2 + 10x - 11 = 0$? If so, describe how you would apply the alternate method.

3d. How would you apply the definition of a square root to eliminate the exponent in the equation $(x + 5)^2 = 36$?

3e. Look at step 4 above. Explain why there can be two, one, or zero real solutions of a quadratic equation.

CC.9-12.A.REI.4b

4 EXAMPLE Solving Quadratic Equations by Completing the Square

Solve the equation by completing the square.

A $x^2 - 2x - 1 = 0$

Write the equation in the form $x^2 + bx = c$. __________

Add $\left(\frac{b}{2}\right)^2$ to both sides of the equation. __________

Factor the perfect square trinomial. __________

Apply the definition of a square root. __________

Write two equations. __________

Solve the equations. __________

B $x^2 - 8x + 16 = 0$

Write the equation in the form $x^2 + bx = c$. __________

Add $\left(\frac{b}{2}\right)^2$ to both sides of the equation. __________

Factor the perfect square trinomial. __________

Apply the definition of a square root. __________

Write two equations. __________

Solve the equations. __________

REFLECT

4a. Can you solve either equation by factoring? If so, which method is easier?

4b. Use completing the square to explain why $x^2 - 2x + 3 = 0$ has no solution.

4c. What method would you use to solve the equation $x^2 + 3x - 4 = 0$? Explain why you would choose this method.

Completing the Square when *a* is a Perfect Square To find the value of c for which $ax^2 + bx + c$ is a perfect square when a is a perfect square, write $ax^2 + bx + c = (mx + n)^2$. Use FOIL to multiply $(mx + n)^2$, and compare the coefficients.

$$ax^2 + bx + c = (mx + n)^2$$
$$= m^2x^2 + 2mnx + n^2$$

Corresponding coefficients must be equal, so $a = m^2$, $b = 2mn$, and $c = n^2$. Thus, $m = \sqrt{a}$ and $n = \frac{b}{2m} = \frac{b}{2\sqrt{a}}$. The constant term, c, is $n^2 = \left(\frac{b}{2\sqrt{a}}\right)^2 = \frac{b^2}{4a}$. (Alternately, $m = -\sqrt{a}$ and $n = -\frac{b}{2\sqrt{a}}$. However, this does not change the overall result, so you need only consider the case of $m = \sqrt{a}$.)

CC.9–12.A.REI.4b

5 EXAMPLE Solving $ax^2 + bx = c$ when a is a Perfect Square

Solve $4x^2 + 8x = 21$ by completing the square.

A Add $\frac{b^2}{4a}$ to both sides of the equation. Since $a =$ ____ and $b =$ ____, $\frac{b^2}{4a} = \frac{\square^2}{4(\square)} = \square$.

$$4x^2 + 8x + \square = 21 + \square$$

B Factor the left side of the equation as a perfect square trinomial.

$$(\square x + \square)^2 = \square$$

C Apply the definition of a square root. Write two equations, and solve each equation to find the two solutions.

$$(\square x + \square) = \pm \square$$

$\square x + \square = \square$ or $\square x + \square = -\square$

$x =$ ______ or $x =$ ______

REFLECT

5a. Compare the steps for solving an equation of the form $ax^2 + bx = c$ when $a \neq 1$ and a is a perfect square with solving $x^2 + bx = c$.

____

____

____

5b. Why does a have to be a perfect square for this procedure to work?

____

____

Completing the Square when a is Not a Perfect Square To find the value of c for which $ax^2 + bx + c$ is a perfect square when a is not a perfect square, you can multiply each term by a number that makes the coefficient of x^2 be a perfect square. One possible value is a. Remember that when you are solving an equation by completing the square, you need to multiply both sides by a. Then solve in the same manner as before.

CC.9–12.A.REI.4b

6 EXAMPLE Solving $ax^2 + bx = c$ when a is Not a Perfect Square

Solve $2x^2 + 6x = 5$. Leave your answer in exact form.

A The coefficient of x^2 is not a perfect square. Multiply both sides by 2.

$$2(2x^2 + 6x) = 2(5)$$

$$\square x^2 + \square x = 10$$

B Add $\frac{b^2}{4a}$ to both sides of the equation. In this case, $\frac{b^2}{4a} = \frac{\square^2}{4(\square)} = \square$.

$$\square x^2 + \square x + \square = 10 + \square$$

C Factor the left side of the equation as a perfect square trinomial.

$$\left(\square x + \square\right)^2 = 19$$

D Apply the definition of a square root. Write two equations, and solve each equation to find the two solutions.

$$\left(\square x + \square\right) = \square$$

$\square x + \square = \square$ or $\square x + \square = \square$

$x =$ ________ or $x =$ ________

REFLECT

6a. Why is 2 the best value to multiply both sides of the equation by before completing the square? Are other values possible? Explain.

____

____

____

6b. You want to solve $12x^2 - 3x = 51$ by completing the square. What is the smallest whole number you could multiply 12 by? Explain.

____

Completing the square can be useful when graphing quadratic functions, especially if the function cannot be factored. If the function cannot be factored, complete the square to rewrite the function in *vertex form*: $f(x) = a(x - h)^2 + k$. Completing the square in this situation is similar to solving equations by completing the square, but instead of adding a term to both sides of the equation, you will both add and subtract it from the function's rule.

Projectile Motion The height of an object moving under the force of gravity, with no other forces acting on it, can be modeled by the following quadratic function.

$$h(t) = -16t^2 + vt + h_0$$

The variables in the function represent the following quantities:
t is the time in seconds,
$h(t)$ is the height of the object above the ground in feet,
v is the initial vertical velocity of the object in feet per second, and
h_0 is the initial height of the object in feet.

CC.9–12.F.IF.8a

7 EXAMPLE Graphing a Projectile Motion Model

A person standing at the edge of a 48-foot cliff tosses a ball up and just off the edge of the cliff with an initial upward velocity of 8 feet per second. Graph the function that models the motion of the ball.

A Identify the values of v and h_0 for the projectile motion function.

Initial vertical velocity, $v =$ ____________________

Initial height, $h_0 =$ ____________________

B Write the equation for the projectile motion function.

____

C Complete the square to find the vertex of the function's graph.

$h(t) = -16t^2 + \square t + \square$

$= -16(\square) + \square$ Factor out −16.

$= -16(\square + \square - \square) + \square$ Complete the square.

$= -16((t - \square)^2 - \square) + \square$ Factor the perfect square trinomial.

$= -16(t - \square)^2 + \square + \square$ Distribute the −16.

$= -16(t - \square)^2 + \square$ Combine the last two terms.

Write the coordinates of the vertex. $(\square, \square)$

D Graph the function by plotting a couple of points besides the vertex. Because only nonnegative values of t and $h(t)$ make sense for this situation, one point that you should plot is the point where the $h(t)$-intercept occurs. Since $h(0) = \underline{\qquad\qquad}$, the graph starts at the point $\left(0, \square\right)$. Determining when the ball hits the ground gives you another point that you can plot:

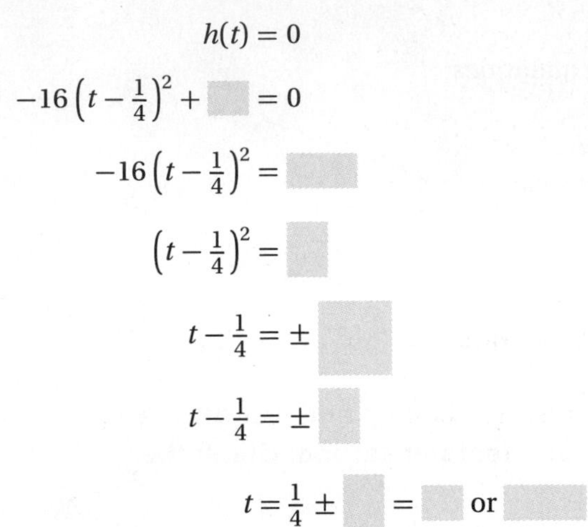

$$h(t) = 0$$

$$-16\left(t - \tfrac{1}{4}\right)^2 + \square = 0$$

$$-16\left(t - \tfrac{1}{4}\right)^2 = \square$$

$$\left(t - \tfrac{1}{4}\right)^2 = \square$$

$$t - \tfrac{1}{4} = \pm \square$$

$$t - \tfrac{1}{4} = \pm \square$$

$$t = \tfrac{1}{4} \pm \square = \square \text{ or } \square$$

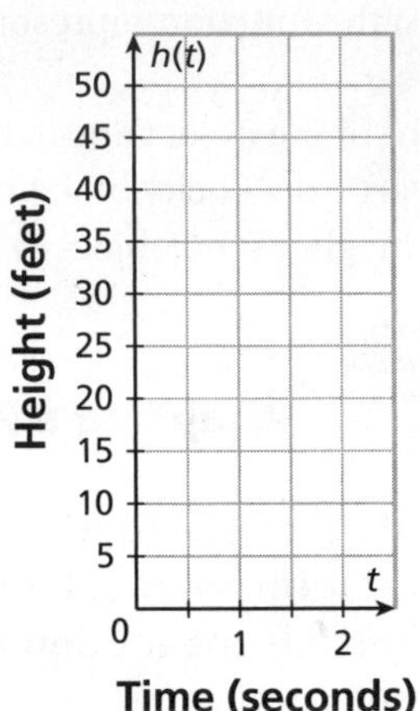

Reject the negative t-value. So, $\left(\square, 0\right)$ is another point on the graph.

REFLECT

7a. How long is the ball in the air? When is the ball at its highest? What is its height at that time?

____

7b. State the domain and range of the function in the context of the situation.

____

7c. The units of $h(t)$ and h_0 are in feet, the units of t are in seconds, and the units of v are in feet per second. What are the units of the coefficient -16? Explain.

____

____

____

PRACTICE

1. The diagram represents the expression $x^2 + 4x + c$ with the constant term missing. Complete the square by filling in the bottom right corner with 1-tiles, and write the expression as a trinomial and in factored form.

____

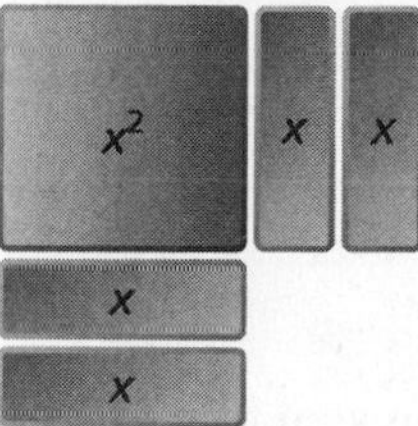

Complete the square to form a perfect square trinomial. Then factor the trinomial.

2. $m^2 + 10m +$ ☐

____

3. $g^2 - 20g +$ ☐

____

4. $y^2 + 2y +$ ☐

____

5. $w^2 - 11w +$ ☐

____

Solve the equation by completing the square.

6. $s^2 + 15s = -56$

____

7. $r^2 - 4r = 165$

____

8. $y^2 + 19y + 78 = 0$

____

9. $x^2 - 19x + 84 = 0$

____

10. $t^2 + 2t - 224 = 0$

____

11. $x^2 + 18x - 175 = 0$

____

12. $g^2 + 3g = -6$

____

13. $p^2 - 3p = 18$

____

14. $z^2 = 6z - 2$

____

15. $x^2 + 25 = 10x$

____

16. $9z^2 + 48z = 36$

____

17. $49x^2 + 28x = 60$

____

Solve the equation by completing the square.

18. $121r^2 - 44r = 5$

19. $4x^2 + 20x - 11 = 0$

20. $2x^2 + 9 = 9x$

21. $3x^2 + 4x = 20$

22. A carpenter is making the tabletop shown below. The surface area will be 24 square feet.

a. Write an equation to represent this situation.

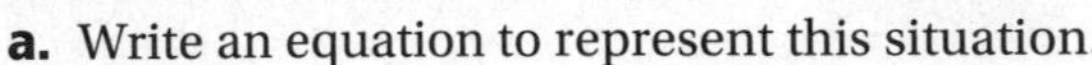

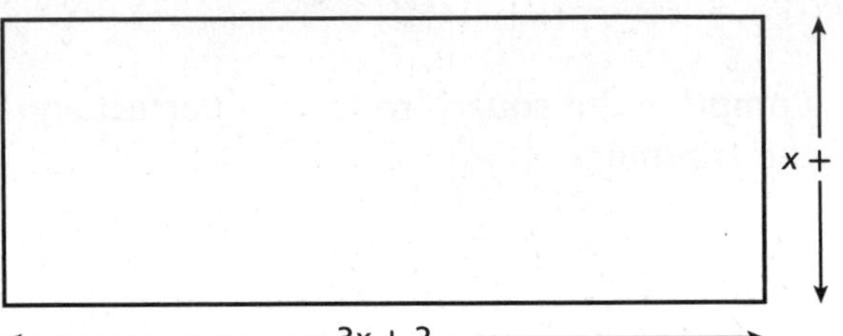

b. Solve the equation. Which solution(s) make sense in this situation? Explain.

c. What are the dimensions of the tabletop?

23. A model rocket is launched from a 12-foot platform with an initial upward velocity of 64 feet per second.

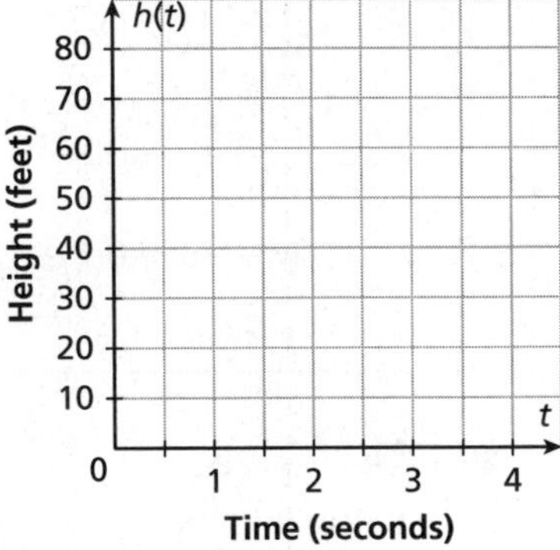

a. Write a quadratic function in standard form that models the height of the rocket.

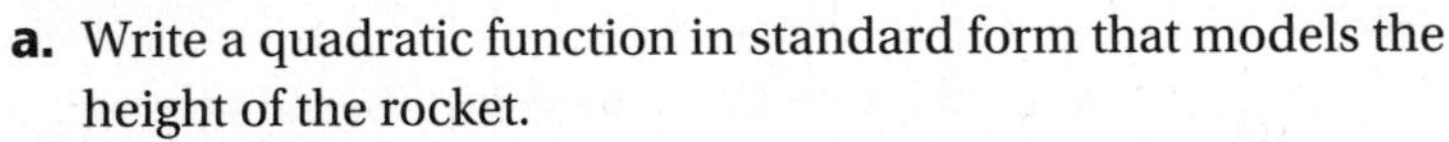

b. Write the quadratic function in vertex form that models the height of the rocket.

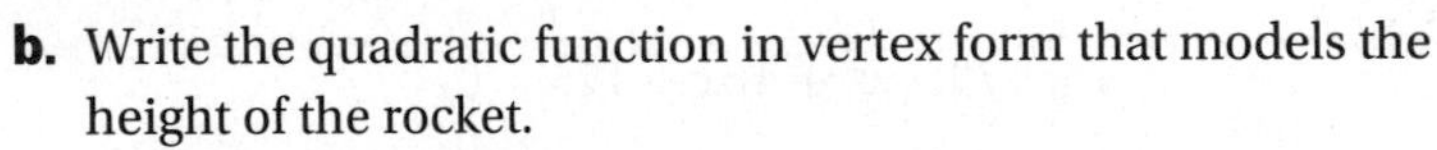

c. Graph the function.

d. State the domain and range of the function in the context of the situation.

Name________________________ Class________________ Date____________

8-8

Additional Practice

Complete the square to form a perfect square trinomial.

1. $x^2 + 4x +$ ☐
2. $x^2 - 16x +$ ☐
3. $x^2 + 7x +$ ☐

Solve each equation by completing the square.

4. $x^2 + 6x = -8$ ________
5. $x^2 + 4x = 12$ ________
6. $x^2 - 2x = 15$ ________
7. $x^2 - 8x + 13 = 0$ ________
8. $x^2 + 6x + 34 = 0$ ________
9. $x^2 - 2x - 35 = 0$ ________
10. $2x^2 + 16x + 42 = 0$ ________
11. $4x^2 - 7x - 2 = 0$ ________
12. $2x^2 + 9x + 4 = 0$ ________

13. A rectangular pool has an area of 880 ft^2. The length is 10 feet longer than the width. Find the dimensions of the pool. Solve by completing the square. Round answers to the nearest tenth of a foot.

____

14. A small painting has an area of 400 cm^2. The length is 4 more than 2 times the width. Find the dimensions of the painting. Solve by completing the square. Round answers to the nearest tenth of a centimeter.

____

Problem Solving

The Ward family is redecorating several rooms of their house. Write the correct answer.

1. The Wards decided to use carpet tiles in the family room. The room has an area of 176 square feet and is 5 feet longer than it is wide. Find the dimensions of the family room.

____

2. Angelique wants to have a rug that is 9 feet long and 7 feet wide in her bedroom. The rug will cover the whole floor except a border that is x feet wide. The area of her room is 167 square feet.

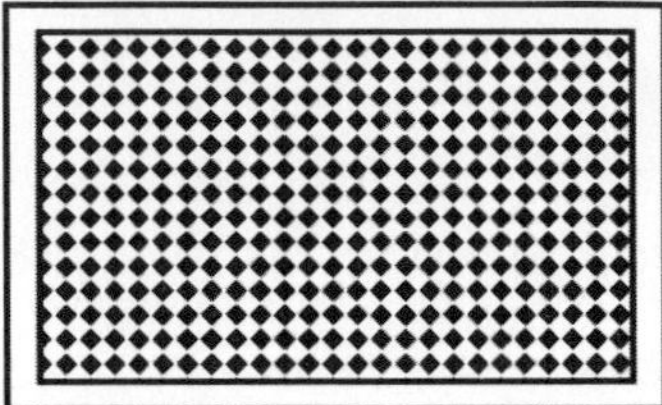

Find the width of the border, x. Round your answer to the nearest tenth of a foot.

____

____

3. Giselle is going to frame a portrait of the family and place it on the mantle in the family room. The portrait is 10 inches longer than it is tall and will take up a total area of 1344 square inches once it is inside the 2 inch thick frame. Find the dimensions and area of the unframed portrait.

____

____

Select the best answer.

4. The landing for the steps leading up to a county courthouse is shaped like a trapezoid. The area of the landing is 1500 square feet. The shorter base of the trapezoid is 15 feet longer than the height. The longer base is 5 feet longer than 3 times the height. What is the length of the longer base?

   A 25 feet C 80 feet

   B 40 feet D 95 feet

5. The height of a pumpkin launched from a cannon is given by the function $h = -16t^2 + 240t + 16$ where t is the time in seconds. How many seconds is the pumpkin in the air? Round your answer to the nearest tenth of a second.

   F 7.5 seconds H 16 seconds

   G 15.1 seconds J 32 seconds

6. Georgia works part-time at a daycare while she is going to college. She earned \$160 last week. Georgia worked 12 more hours than the amount she is paid per hour. What is Georgia's hourly pay rate?

   A \$6.00 C \$12.00

   B \$8.00 D \$20.00

7. Part of the set for a play is a triangular piece of plywood. The area of the triangle is 20 square feet. The base is 3 feet longer than the height. What is the height of the triangle? Round your answer to the nearest tenth of a foot.

   F 3 feet H 3.9 feet

   G 3.2 feet J 5 feet

Name ____________ Class ____________ Date ____________

8-9

Video Tutor

The Quadratic Formula and the Discriminant

Going Deeper

Essential question: *How can you derive the quadratic formula and use it to solve quadratic equations?*

You have learned how to solve quadratic equations by completing the square. You can complete the square on the general form of a quadratic equation to derive a formula that can be used to solve any quadratic equation.

CC.9-12.A.REI.4a

1 EXPLORE Deriving the Quadratic Formula

Solve the general form of the quadratic equation, $ax^2 + bx + c = 0$, by completing the square to find the values of x in terms of a, b, and c.

A Subtract c from both sides of the equation.

$$ax^2 + bx = \square$$

B Multiply both sides of the equation by $4a$ to make the coefficient of x^2 a perfect square.

$$4a^2x^2 + \square x = -4ac$$

C Add b^2 to both sides of the equation to complete the square. Then write the trinomial as the square of a binomial.

$$4a^2x^2 + 4abx + b^2 = -4ac + \square$$

$$\left(\square\right)^2 = b^2 - 4ac$$

D Apply the definition of a square root and solve for x.

$$\square = \pm\sqrt{\square}$$

$$2ax = -\square \pm \sqrt{\square}$$

$x =$ ____________

The formula $x = \dfrac{-b \pm \sqrt{b^2 - 4ac}}{2a}$ is called the **quadratic formula**.
For any quadratic equation written in standard form, $ax^2 + bx + c = 0$, the quadratic formula gives the solutions of the equation.

REFLECT

1a. In Part B, why did you multiply both sides of the equation by $4a$?

1b. In Part C, explain why you added b^2 to each side to complete the square.

1c. Provided the expression under the radical sign, $b^2 - 4ac$, is positive, how many solutions will the quadratic formula give for a quadratic equation? Explain.

1d. If the expression under the radical sign, $b^2 - 4ac$, is 0, how many solutions will the quadratic formula give for a quadratic equation? What if the expression is negative?

1e. Another method of deriving the quadratic formula is to first divide each term by a, and then complete the square. Complete the derivation below. (In this derivation, you will use the quotient property of square roots, which says that $\sqrt{\frac{a}{b}} = \frac{\sqrt{a}}{\sqrt{b}}$. For a square root of a fraction, this property allows you to simplify the numerator and denominator separately. For instance, $\sqrt{\frac{5}{9}} = \frac{\sqrt{5}}{\sqrt{9}} = \frac{\sqrt{5}}{3}$.)

$ax^2 + bx + c = 0$

$ax^2 + bx = -c$ — Subtract c from both sides.

$x^2 + \frac{\quad}{\quad}x = -\frac{c}{a}$ — Divide each term by a.

$x^2 + \frac{b}{a}x + \left(\frac{b}{2a}\right)^2 = \left(\frac{b}{2a}\right)^2 - \frac{c}{a}$ —

$\left(\quad\right)^2 = \frac{b^2 - 4ac}{4a^2}$ — Factor the left side, and write the right side as a single fraction.

$x + \frac{b}{2a} = \pm\sqrt{\frac{b^2 - 4ac}{4a^2}}$ —

$x + \frac{b}{2a} = \pm\frac{\sqrt{b^2 - 4ac}}{\sqrt{4a^2}}$ — Apply the quotient property of radicals.

$x + \frac{b}{2a} = \pm\frac{\sqrt{b^2 - 4ac}}{\quad}$ — Simplify the radical in the denominator.

$x = \frac{-b \pm \sqrt{b^2 - 4ac}}{2a}$ — Solve for x.

CC.9-12.A.REI.4b

2 ENGAGE Using the Quadratic Formula

You have learned to solve quadratic equations by factoring and by completing the square. You can use the quadratic formula you derived in the Explore to solve quadratic equations as well.

The standard form of a quadratic equation is $ax^2 + bx + c = 0$. As you saw from the Explore, if you complete the square on the standard form of the equation and solve for x, you will generate the quadratic formula:

$$x = \frac{-b \pm \sqrt{b^2 - 4ac}}{2a}$$

To solve a quadratic equation by using the quadratic formula, write the equation in standard form, $ax^2 + bx + c = 0$. Then substitute the values of a, b, and c into the quadratic formula, and simplify.

REFLECT

2a. The expression under the radical in the quadratic formula, $b^2 - 4ac$, is called the **discriminant**. If $d = b^2 - 4ac$, how many solutions does a quadratic equation have if $d > 0$? if $d = 0$? if $d < 0$? Justify your answers.

2b. Describe the solutions of a quadratic equation when $b = 0$.

2c. Describe the solutions of a quadratic equation when $c = 0$.

3 EXAMPLE Solving Quadratic Equations Using the Quadratic Formula

Use the quadratic formula to solve the quadratic equation.

A $6x^2 + 5x - 4 = 0$

Identify the following. Include negative signs as needed.

$a =$ ________; $b =$ ________; $c =$ ________

Use the quadratic formula $x = \frac{-b \pm \sqrt{b^2 - 4ac}}{2a}$.

$x = \frac{-\square \pm \sqrt{\square^2 - 4 \cdot \square \cdot \square}}{2 \cdot \square}$ Substitute the values into the quadratic formula.

$= \frac{-\square \pm \sqrt{\square}}{\square}$ Simplify the expression under the radical sign. Simplify the denominator.

$= \frac{-\square \pm \square}{\square}$ Evaluate the square root.

Separate the two solutions indicated by the $\pm$ sign, and simplify.

$x = \frac{-\square + \square}{\square}$ or $x = \frac{-\square - \square}{\square}$

$= \square$ $= \square$

B $x^2 + 7 = 4x$

Write the equation in standard form. ________________

Identify the following.

$a =$ ________; $b =$ ________; $c =$ ________

Use the quadratic formula $x = \frac{-b \pm \sqrt{b^2 - 4ac}}{2a}$.

$x = \frac{-\square \pm \sqrt{\square^2 - 4 \cdot \square \cdot \square}}{2 \cdot \square}$ Substitute the values into the quadratic formula.

$= \frac{\square \pm \sqrt{\square}}{\square}$ Simplify the expression under the radical sign. Simplify the denominator.

The discriminant is ________, so there is ________ solution.

C $5x^2 + 9.8 = -14x$

Write the equation in standard form. ______________________

Identify the following.

$a =$ __________; $b =$ __________; $c =$ __________

Use the quadratic formula $x = \dfrac{-b \pm \sqrt{b^2 - 4ac}}{2a}$.

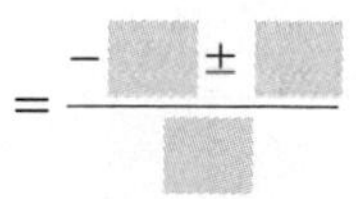

$x = \dfrac{-\square \pm \sqrt{\square^2 - 4 \cdot \square \cdot \square}}{2 \cdot \square}$ Substitute the values into the quadratic formula.

$= \dfrac{-\square \pm \sqrt{\square}}{\square}$ Simplify the expression under the radical sign. Simplify the denominator.

$= \dfrac{-\square \pm \square}{\square}$ Take the square root.

The discriminant is __________, so there is __________ solution.

$x = -\dfrac{\square}{\square}$

REFLECT

3a. Is it possible to solve the equation from Part A by factoring? Explain.

____

____

3b. Is it possible to solve the equation from Part B by factoring? Explain.

____

____

3c. Is it possible to solve the equation from Part C by factoring? Explain.

____

____

____

PRACTICE

State how many real solutions the equation has. Do not solve the equation.

1. $3x^2 + 8x + 6 = 0$ ______________

2. $z^2 = 9$ ______________

3. $9d^2 + 16 = 24d$ ______________

4. $-2x^2 = 25 - 10x$ ______________

Solve the equation using the quadratic formula. Round to the nearest hundredth, if necessary.

5. $16 + r^2 - 8r = 0$

____

6. $3x^2 = 10 - 4x$

____

7. $2s^2 = 98$

____

8. $z^2 = 2.5z$

____

9. $3x^2 + 16x - 84 = 0$

____

10. $34z^2 + 19z = 15$

____

11. $6q^2 + 25q + 24 = 0$

____

12. $7x^2 + 100x = 4$

____

State what method you would use to solve the equation. Justify your answer. You do not need to solve the equation.

13. $4x^2 + 25 = 20x$

____

14. $2z^2 = 20$

____

15. $4x^2 + 25 = 18x$

____

16. $g^2 - 3g - 4 = 0$

____

17. A football player kicks a ball with an initial upward velocity of 47 feet per second. The initial height of the ball is 3 feet. The function $h(t) = -16t^2 + vt + h_0$ models the height (in feet) of the ball, where v is the initial upward velocity and h_0 is the initial height. If no one catches the ball, how long will it be in the air?

____

Name ______________________ Class ______________ Date ____________

8-9

Additional Practice

Solve using the quadratic formula.

1. $x^2 + x = 12$

____

2. $4x^2 - 17x - 15 = 0$

____

3. $2x^2 - 5x = 3$

____

4. $3x^2 + 14x - 5 = 0$

____

Find the number of real solutions of each equation using the discriminant.

5. $x^2 + 25 = 0$

____

6. $x^2 - 11x + 28 = 0$

____

7. $x^2 + 8x + 16 = 0$

____

Solve using any method.

8. $x^2 + 8x + 15 = 0$

____

9. $x^2 - 49 = 0$

____

10. $6x^2 + x - 1 = 0$

____

11. $x^2 + 8x - 20 = 0$

____

12. In the past, professional baseball was played at the Astrodome in Houston, Texas. The Astrodome has a maximum height of 63.4 m. The height of a baseball t seconds after it is hit straight up in the air with a velocity of 45 ft/s is given by $h = -9.8t^2 + 45t + 1$. Will a baseball hit straight up with this velocity hit the roof of the Astrodome? Use the discriminant to explain your answer.

____

____

Problem Solving

Write the correct answer.

1. Theo's flying disc got stuck in a tree 14 feet from the ground. Theo threw his shoe up at the disc to dislodge it. The height in feet h of the shoe is given by the equation $h = -16t^2 + 25t + 6$, where t is the time in seconds. Determine whether the shoe hit the disc. Use the discriminant to explain your answer.

____

____

2. A picture frame holds a 4-in. by 6-in. photograph. The frame adds a border x inches wide around three sides of the photo. On the fourth side the frame forms a border that is $3x - 0.5$ in. wide.

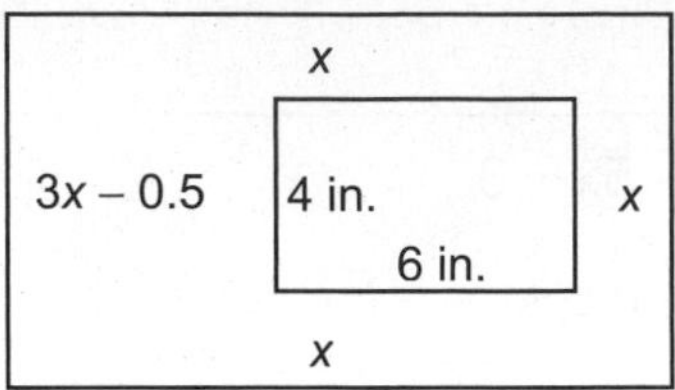

The combined area of the photograph and the frame is 80.5 in^2. Write a quadratic equation for the combined area. Then use the quadratic formula to find x.

____

____

3. The manager of a park enclosed an area for small dogs to play. He made the length 15 feet longer than the width and enclosed an area covering 1350 square feet. What are the dimensions of the dogs' play area?

____

The equation $-5x^2 + 72x + 378$ models the number of students enrolled in a school where x is the number of years since the school first opened in 1990. Select the best answer.

4. How many students did the school have when it opened?

   A 68

   B 72

   C 378

   D 445

5. Which equation can be used to find the year in which 502 students were enrolled?

   F $-5x^2 + 72x + 502 = 0$

   G $-5x^2 + 72x - 124 = 0$

   H $-5x^2 + 72x - 502 = 0$

   J $-5x^2 + 72x + 124 = 0$

6. In which year were 502 students enrolled?

   A 1992   C 1998

   B 1996   D 2002

7. In which year were 598 students enrolled?

   F 1995   H 2000

   G 1998   J 2010

8. Which statement is true?

   A Enrollment exceeded 650 students at one point.

   B Enrollment never exceeded 650 students.

   C The highest enrollment of any year was exactly 650 students.

   D There were two years where 650 students were enrolled.

Name________________________ Class______________ Date__________

8-10

Video Tutor

Nonlinear Systems
Going Deeper

Essential question: *How can you solve a system of equations when one equation is linear and the other is quadratic?*

To estimate the solution to a system of equations, you can graph both equations on the same coordinate plane and find the intersection points. Or you can solve the equations algebraically using substitution or elimination.

CC.9–12.A.REI.7

1 EXAMPLE Solving by Graphing and Algebraically

Solve the system of equations.

$$f(x) = -8x + 48$$
$$g(x) = -2(x - 2)^2 + 32$$

A Solve the system of equations by graphing.

Start by graphing the quadratic function. The vertex is (___ , ___). Describe the transformation of the parent quadratic function that produces the graph of $g(x)$.

____

____

To make the graph more accurate, plot the points where the x-intercepts occur. The x-intercepts are the solutions of the equation $g(x) = 0$:

$-2(x - 2)^2 + 32 = 0$

$-2(x - 2)^2 =$ ___

$(x - 2)^2 =$ ___

$x - 2 = \pm$ ___

$x =$ ___ $\pm$ ___ $=$ ___ or ___

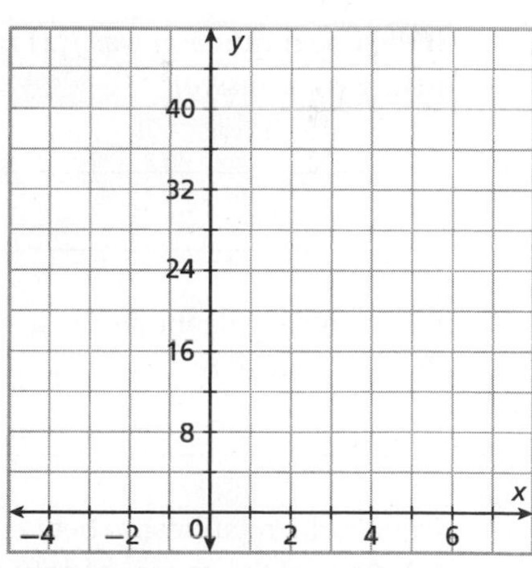

So, the points (___ , 0) and (___ , 0) are on the graph.
Use these points and the vertex to draw the graph.

Now graph the linear function. The y-intercept is _____,
and the slope is _____.

The line and the parabola intersect at two points. Identify the coordinates of those points.

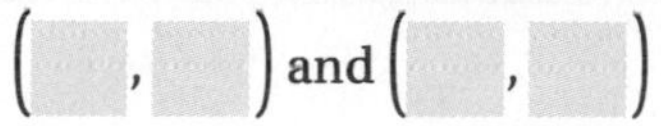

(___ , ___) and (___ , ___)

B Solve the system of equations algebraically.

Write the functions in terms of y.

$$y = -8x + 48$$
$$y = -2(x - 2)^2 + 32$$

Both equations are solved for y, so set the right sides equal to each other and solve for x.

$-8x + 48 = -2(x - 2)^2 + 32$

$-8x + 48 =$ ______ Simplify the right side.

$8x - 48 =$ ______ $8x - 48$ Add $8x - 48$ to both sides.

$0 =$ ______ Simplify both sides.

$0 = -2($ ______ $)($ ______ $)$ Factor the right side.

$x =$ ______ or $x =$ ______ Use the zero-product property to solve for x.

Substitute these values of x into the equation of the line to find the corresponding y-values.

$y = -8(2) + 48 =$ ______

$y = -8(6) + 48 =$ ______

The solutions are (______ , ______) and (______ , ______).

REFLECT

1a. If the linear function was $f(x) = 8x + 48$, how many solutions would there be? Justify your answer.

1b. When solving algebraically, why do you substitute the x-values into the equation of the line instead of the equation of the parabola?

1c. Explain the relationship between the intersection points of the graphs and the solutions of the system of equations.

1d. Describe how to check that the solutions are correct.

CC.9–12.A.REI.7

2 EXPLORE Determining the Possible Number of Solutions

In the previous example, the system of equations had two solutions. You can use a graph to understand other possible numbers of solutions of a system of equations involving a linear equation and a quadratic equation.

The graph of the quadratic function $f(x) = -x^2 + 10x - 27$ is shown below.

Graph each linear function below on the same coordinate plane as the parabola.

Line 1: $g(x) = 2x - 11$

Line 2: $h(x) = -2x + 14$

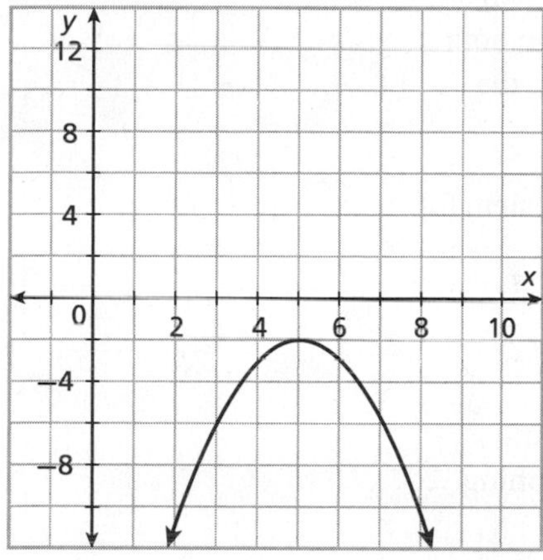

REFLECT

2a. At how many points do the parabola and Line 1 intersect? ___________

How many solutions are there for the system consisting of the quadratic function and the first linear function? ___________

2b. At how many points do the parabola and Line 2 intersect? ___________

How many solutions are there for the system consisting of the quadratic function and the second linear function? ___________

2c. A system of equations consisting of one quadratic equation and one linear equation can have ___________, ___________, or 2 real solutions.

2d. How many solutions does the following system of equations have? Explain your reasoning.

$$f(x) = -x^2 + 10x - 27$$
$$k(x) = -x + 1$$

____

____

2e. How many solutions does the following system of equations have? Explain your reasoning.

$$f(x) = -x^2 + 10x - 27$$
$$p(x) = -2$$

____

____

You can use the Intersect feature on a graphing calculator to solve systems of equations.

CC.9–12.A.REI.7

3 EXAMPLE Solving Systems Using Technology

Use a graphing calculator to solve the system of equations.

$$f(x) = -4.9x^2 + 50x + 25$$
$$g(x) = 30x$$

A Enter the functions as Y_1 and Y_2 on a graphing calculator. Then graph both functions. Sketch the graphs on the coordinate plane at the right.

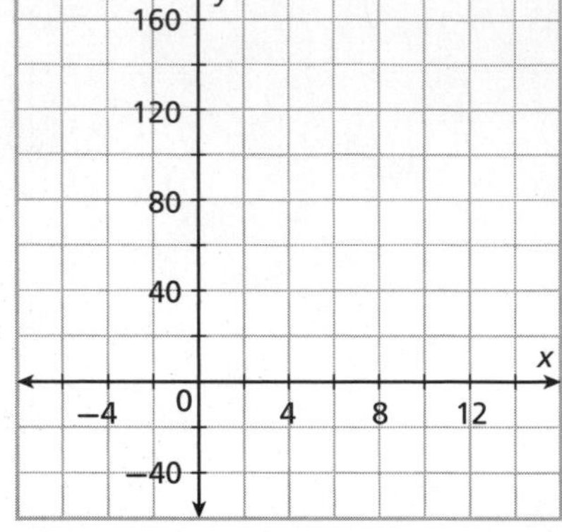

Estimate the solutions of the system from the graph.

____

B Solve the system directly by using the Intersect feature of the graphing calculator.

Press 2nd and CALC, then select Intersect. Press Enter for the first curve and again for the second curve. For Guess?, press the left or right arrows to move the cursor close to one of the intersections, then press Enter again. Repeat, moving the cursor close to the other intersection to find the second solution. Round your solutions to the nearest tenth.

____

REFLECT

3a. Are the solutions you get using the Intersect feature of a graphing calculator always exact? Explain.

____

3b. How can you check the accuracy of your estimated solutions?

____

3c. Use a graphing calculator to solve the system of equations $f(x)$ and $h(x)$ where $h(x) = 30x + 50$. What is the result? Explain.

____

____

PRACTICE

Solve the system of equations algebraically. Round to the nearest tenth, if necessary.

1. $f(x) = x^2 - 2$
$g(x) = -2$

____

2. $y = (x - 3)^2$
$y = x$

____

3. $y = -2x^2 - 4x + 1$
$y = -\frac{1}{2}x + 3$

____

4. $f(x) = x^2$
$g(x) = 1$

____

5. $y = x^2 + 4x - 5$
$y = 3x - 2$

____

6. $f(x) = -16x^2 + 15x + 10$
$g(x) = 14 - x$

____

The graph of a system of equations is shown. State how many solutions the system has. Then estimate the solution(s).

7. ____________________

____

8. 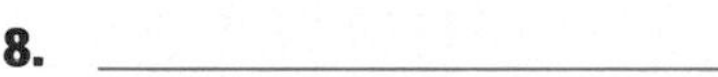

____

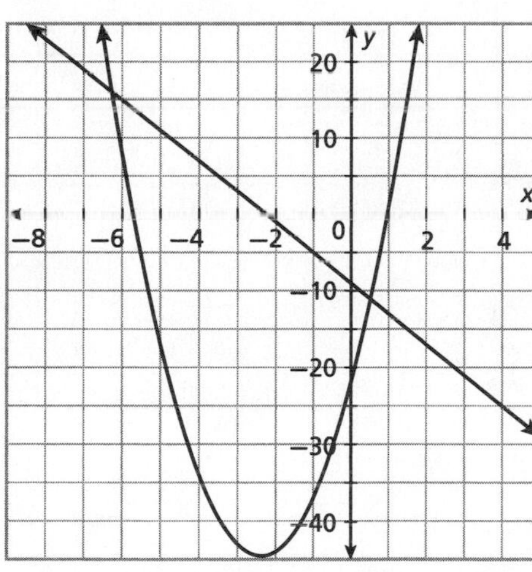

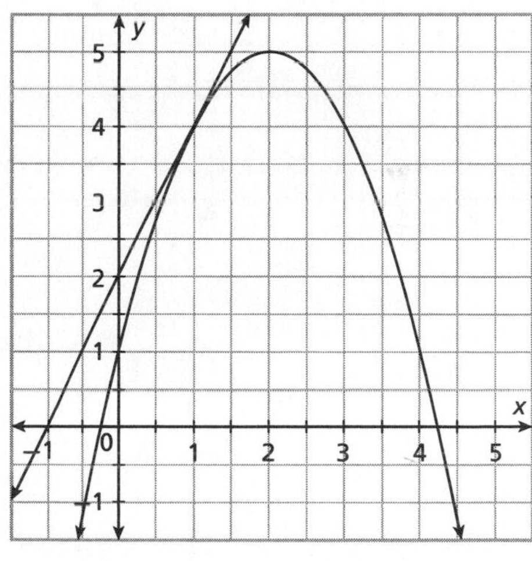

Estimate the solutions to the system of equations graphically. Confirm the solutions by substituting the values into the equations.

9. $f(x) = x^2$
$g(x) = 1$

10. $y = x^2 - 1$
$y = 0.5x - 3$

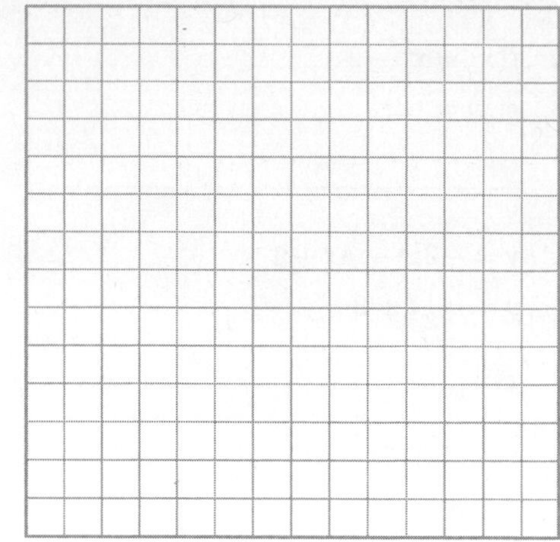

11. $f(x) = -16x^2 + 15x + 10$
$g(x) = 14 - x$

12. $f(x) = 3(x - 1)^2 + 4$
$g(x) = -4x + 9$

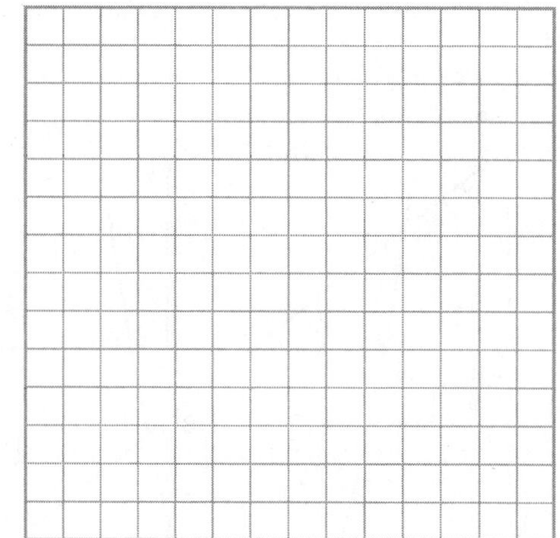

Solve the system of equations using the Intersect feature of a graphing calculator. Round your answers to the nearest tenth.

13. $y = -x^2 + 6x + 7$
$y = 2x + 6$

14. $f(x) = -x^2 + x - 2$
$g(x) = 2x - 3$

Additional Practice

Solve each system by graphing. Check your answers.

1. $\begin{cases} y = x^2 - x - 2 \\ y = -x + 2 \end{cases}$

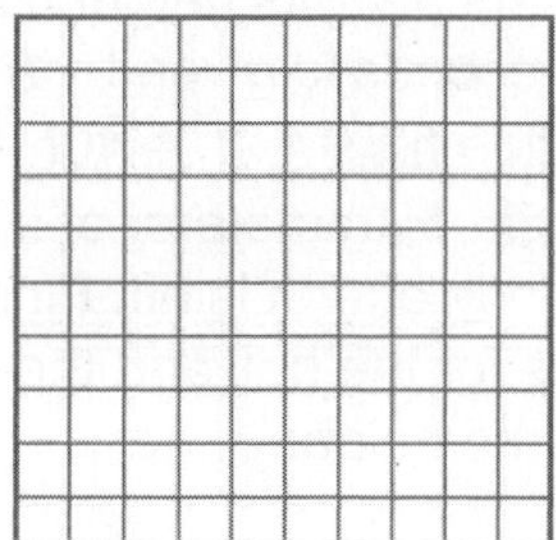

____

2. $\begin{cases} y = x^2 + x - 6 \\ y = -x - 3 \end{cases}$

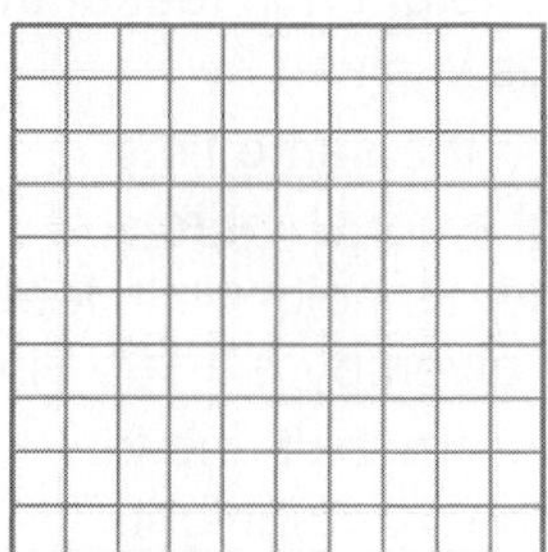

____

Solve each system by substitution. Check your answers.

3. $\begin{cases} y = -2x^2 + x + 4 \\ y = -5x + 8 \end{cases}$

____

4. $\begin{cases} y = -2x^2 - 3x + 2 \\ y = -x + 6 \end{cases}$

____

5. $\begin{cases} y = 3x^2 + 2x - 1 \\ x + y = 5 \end{cases}$

____

6. $\begin{cases} y = x^2 - 16 \\ y = x + 4 \end{cases}$

____

7. $\begin{cases} y = x^2 - 1 \\ x + 2y = 8 \end{cases}$

____

8. $\begin{cases} y = x^2 + 3x + 2 \\ 2x + y = -4 \end{cases}$

____

9. $\begin{cases} y = 2x^2 + 3x - 1 \\ 2x + y = -4 \end{cases}$

____

10. $\begin{cases} y = -x^2 + 2x - 4 \\ 3x + y = -4 \end{cases}$

____

Problem Solving

Write the correct answer.

1. A ball is thrown upward with an initial velocity of 40 feet per second from ground level. The height h in feet of the ball after t seconds is given by $h = -16t^2 + 40t$. At the same time, a balloon is rising at a constant rate of 10 feet per second. Its height h in feet after t seconds is given by $h = 10t$. Find the time it takes for the ball and the balloon to reach the same height.

____

2. A bird starts flying up from the grass in a park and climbs at a steady rate of 0.5 meters per second. Its height h in meters after t seconds is given by $h = 0.5t$. The equation $h = -4.9t^2 + 40t + 3$ models the height h, in meters, of a baseball t seconds after it is hit. Find the time it takes for the ball and the bird to reach the same height.

____

3. A skateboard company's monthly sales income can be modeled by the equation $C(s) = 0.5s^2 + 25s + 500$, where s represents the number of skateboards sold. The monthly cost of running the business is $C(s) = 25s + 812.5$. How many skateboards must the company sell in a month before the sales income equals or exceeds the cost of running the business?

____

4. The deer population in a park can be modeled by the equation $P(y) = 4y^2 - 10y + 60$, where y is the number of years after 2010. The deer population in another park can be modeled by $P(y) = 10y + 80$, where y is the number of years after 2010. In which year will the two parks have approximately the same number of deer?

____

Select the best answer.

5. A seagull is flying upwards such that its height h in feet above the sea after t seconds is given by $h = 3t$. At the same time, the height h in feet of a rock falling off a cliff above the sea after t seconds is given by $h = -16t^2 + 50$. Find the approximate time it takes for the rock and the bird to be at the same height.

   A 1.68 seconds   C 3.36 seconds

   B 3.13 seconds   D 16.67 seconds

6. A juggler at a fun park throws a ball upwards such that the ball's height h in feet above the ground after t seconds is given by $h = -16t^2 + 20t + 5$. At the same time, a scenic elevator begins climbing a tower at a constant rate of 20 feet per second. Its height h in feet after t seconds is given by $h = 20t$. Find the approximate time it takes for the ball and the elevator to reach the same height.

   F 0.56 seconds   H 4 seconds

   G 1.12 seconds   J 11.18 seconds

Name________________________ Class________________ Date__________

Performance Tasks

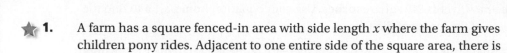

COMMON CORE

CC.9-12.A.CED.1
CC.9-12.A.CED.2
CC.9-12.A.REI.4
CC.9-12.F.BF.1

★ **1.** A farm has a square fenced-in area with side length x where the farm gives children pony rides. Adjacent to one entire side of the square area, there is a roped-off rectangular area where the children line up. This rectangle is 4 yards wide and x yards long.

a. The total area of the square and rectangular areas together is 2,700 square yards. Write an equation that represents this situation.

b. Use your equation from part **a** to find the dimensions of the roped-off rectangular area.

★ **2.** Jo is testing a computer game. A character runs across the screen at a rate r given by the equation $r = 30t$, where t is the number of seconds after the game begins. The rate r is in pixels per second.

a. Write an equation to represent the distance d the character travels, in pixels, after t seconds.

b. A computer monitor measures 12 inches across, and has a resolution of 85 pixels per inch. About how long does it take the character to run across the screen? Round to the nearest tenth of a second.

3. Marge has a flyer that is 10 inches wide and 12 inches long. To increase the size of the flyer, she will increase the length and width of the flyer by the same percent.

a. Write an equation that gives the new area A of the flyer in terms of x, where x is the percent increase in the length of the original flyer written as a decimal.

b. The area of the new flyer is 270 square inches. Use your equation from part **a** to find the percent increase of the length of the flyer.

c. Explain an alternate way of finding the percent increase of the length of the flyer, without using the equation from part **a**.

4. A restaurant decides to add homemade desserts to their menu. When they sell the desserts for \$7 each, they sell 80 desserts in a week. When they raise the price to \$9 each, they sell 40 deserts in a week.

a. Write a linear function $f(x)$ that relates x desserts sold to the price $f(x)$ of the desserts.

b. The desserts cost the restaurant \$2 each to make. Write a profit function $P(x)$ that gives the total profit for selling x desserts. (*Hint:* total profit = profit per item times number of items sold.)

c. Use your profit function to find the number of desserts that maximizes profit, and then find the price that maximizes profit.

CHAPTER 8 COMMON CORE ASSESSMENT READINESS

Name ______________________ Class ____________ Date ________

MULTIPLE CHOICE

1. The graph of $f(x) = 9x^2 + 3$ has what vertex?

A. (9, 3) **C.** (0, 3)

B. (3, 0) **D.** (9, −3)

2. The graph of which function is stretched vertically and reflected in the x-axis as compared to the parent quadratic function?

F. $g(x) = 2x^2$ **H.** $g(x) = 0.4x^2$

G. $g(x) = -2x^2$ **J.** $g(x) = -0.4x^2$

3. The graph of $g(x) = (x - 2)^2 + 3$ can be obtained from the graph of $f(x) = x^2$ using which transformation?

A. Translate −2 units horizontally and 3 units vertically.

B. Translate 3 units horizontally and −2 units vertically.

C. Translate 2 units horizontally and 3 units vertically.

D. Translate 2 units horizontally and −3 units vertically.

4. Which function has a maximum value?

F. $f(x) = -x^2$ **H.** $f(x) = x^2 - 5$

G. $f(x) = (x - 10)^2$ **J.** $f(x) = (x + 100)^2$

5. A parabola has its vertex at (10, 5). One point on the parabola is (12, 8). Which is another point on the parabola?

A. (8, 12) **C.** (12, −8)

B. (−12, 8) **D.** (8, 8)

6. How many real solutions does the equation $2(x - 1)^2 + 5 = 3$ have?

F. No solution **H.** Two solutions

G. One solution **J.** Three solutions

7. What are the solutions of the following system of equations?

$$f(x) = x^2 - 4x + 13$$
$$g(x) = x + 9$$

A. (0, 4); (0, 13) **C.** (1, 10); (4, 13)

B. (0, 10); (4, 13) **D.** (2, 9); (0, 9)

8. What values of a, b, and c should be substituted in the quadratic formula to solve $5x^2 - 3x + 2 = 0$?

F. $a = 5; b = -3; c = -2$

G. $a = 5; b = 3; c = -2$

H. $a = 5; b = 3; c = 2$

J. $a = 5; b = -3; c = 2$

9. What are the solutions of $y^2 - 8y + 7 = 0$?

A. −1, −7 **C.** −1, −8

B. 1, 7 **D.** 1, 8

10. What number should be added to both sides to complete the square on $r^2 - 5r = 12$?

F. 6.25 **H.** 36

G. 25 **J.** 144

11. The graph of which function is shown?

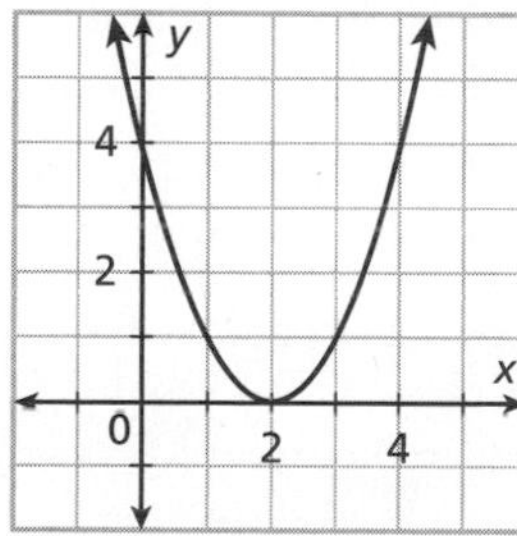

A. $f(x) = x^2 - 2$

B. $f(x) = x^2 + 2$

C. $f(x) = x^2 + 4x + 4$

D. $f(x) = x^2 - 4x + 4$

CONSTRUCTED RESPONSE

12. a. Graph $g(x) = -2x^2 + 3$.

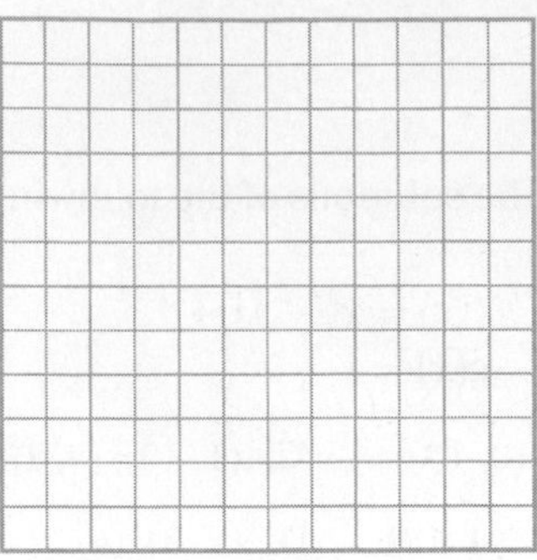

b. Describe the transformations that you would have to perform on the graph of $f(x) = x^2$ to obtain the graph of $g(x)$.

____

____

____

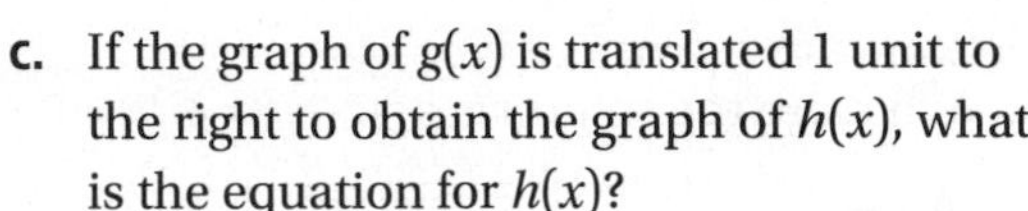

c. If the graph of $g(x)$ is translated 1 unit to the right to obtain the graph of $h(x)$, what is the equation for $h(x)$?

____

____

13. a. Find the approximate solutions of $(x + 1)^2 + 2 = 7$ by graphing $f(x) = (x + 1)^2 + 2$ and $g(x) = 7$.

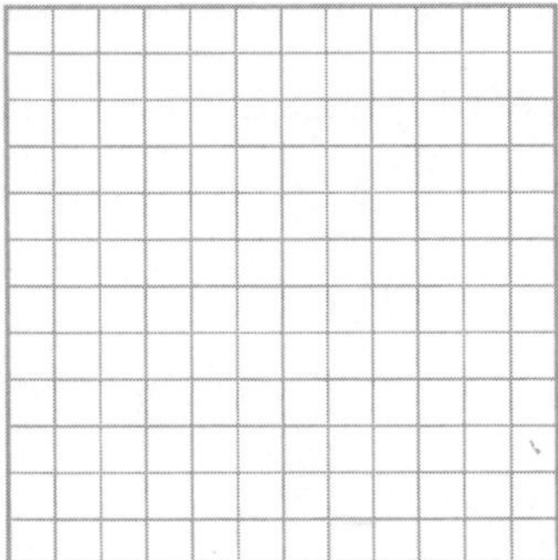

____

b. Find the exact solutions of $(x + 1)^2 + 2 = 7$ by using square roots.

____

14. Solve the quadratic equation by completing the square. Show all work. Round solutions to the nearest tenth, if necessary.

$$11 = 2x^2 + 5x$$

____

____

____

____

____

____

15. A diver leaves a 3-foot-high diving board with an initial upward velocity of 11 feet per second. Use the projectile motion model, $h(t) = -16t^2 + vt + h_0$, for the following. Note that the projectile motion model does not apply after the diver enters the water.

a. Write the function that represents the diver's height as a function of time.

____

b. Graph the function.

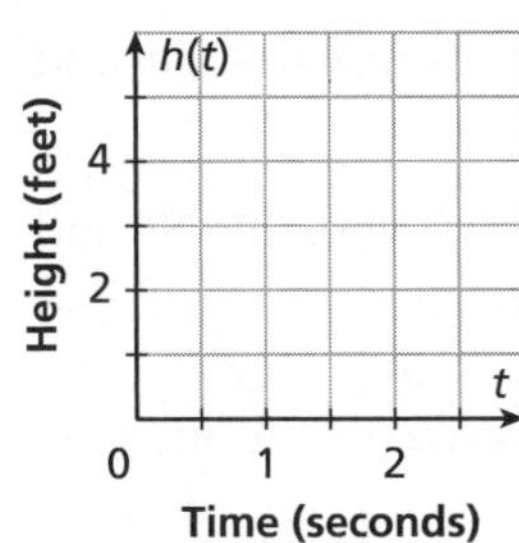

c. What is the diver's maximum height above the water?

____

d. How much time elapses before the diver enters the water? Round your answer to the nearest hundredth of a second.

____

e. What are the domain and range of the function in terms of the situation?

____

CHAPTER 9

Exponential Functions

Chapter Focus

In this chapter you will learn that a geometric sequence, such as 4, 8, 16, 32, is an ordered list of numbers in which the ratio of consecutive terms is constant. You will write rules for geometric sequences and make the connection between geometric sequences and exponential functions. You will learn the characteristics of the basic growth and decay functions and then use your graphing calculator to explore transformations of these exponential functions. You will also use technology to find an exponential model for a set of data. Finally, you will compare the growth of linear and exponential functions.

Chapter at a Glance

Lesson		Standards for Mathematical Content
9-1	Geometric Sequences	CC.9-12.F.BF.1a, CC.9-12.F.LE.2
9-2	Exponential Functions	CC.9-12.F.BF.3, CC.9-12.F.LE.2
9-3	Exponential Growth and Decay	CC.9-12.F.IF.7e, CC.9-12.F.LE.1c, CC.9-12.F.LE.2
9-4	Linear, Quadratic, and Exponential Models	CC.9-12.A.REI.1, CC.9-12.A.REI.11, CC.9-12.S.ID.6a, CC.9-12.S.ID.6b
9-5	Comparing Functions	CC.9-12.F.LE.1, CC.9-12.F.LE.3
	Performance Tasks	
	Assessment Readiness	

CHAPTER 9

Unpacking the Standards

Understanding the standards and the vocabulary terms in the standards will help you know exactly what you are expected to learn in this chapter.

COMMON CORE **CC.9-12.F.BF.2**

Write arithmetic and geometric sequences both recursively and with an explicit formula, use them to model situations, and translate between the two forms.

Key Vocabulary

arithmetic sequence *(sucesión aritmética)* A sequence whose successive terms differ by the same nonzero number d, called the *common difference.*

geometric sequence *(sucesión geométrica)* A sequence in which the ratio of successive terms is a constant r, called the *common ratio,* where $r \neq 0$ and $r \neq 1$.

recursive formula *(fórmula recurrente)* A formula for a sequence in which one or more previous terms are used to generate the next term.

What It Means For You — Lesson 9-1

You can write rules for arithmetic and geometric sequences as a function of the term number or with respect to the previous term. You can use the form that is more useful for a particular situation.

EXAMPLE **Explicit and Recursive Formulas**

In the geometric sequence below, each term is twice the previous term. So, the common ratio is $r = 2$.

1	2	3	4	← Position, n
↓	↓	↓	↓	
3	6	12	24	← Term, a_n
a_1	a_2	a_3	a_4	

Explicit formula: $a_n = a_1r^{n-1}$, so $a_n = 3 \cdot 2^{n-1}$

Recursive formula: The recursive formula gives the first term and for finding successive terms:
$a_n = a_{n-1}r$, so $a_1 = 3$, $a_n = 2a_{n-1}$

COMMON CORE **CC.9-12.F.IF.7e**

Graph exponential … functions, showing intercepts and end behavior, …

Key Vocabulary

exponential function *(función exponencial)* A function of the form $f(x) = ab^x$, where a and b are real numbers with $a \neq 0$, $b > 0$, and $b \neq 1$.

What It Means For You — Lessons 9-2, 9-3

The graph of an exponential function $f(x) = ab^x$ has y-intercept a. If $a > 0$, the function may model growth or decay.

EXAMPLE

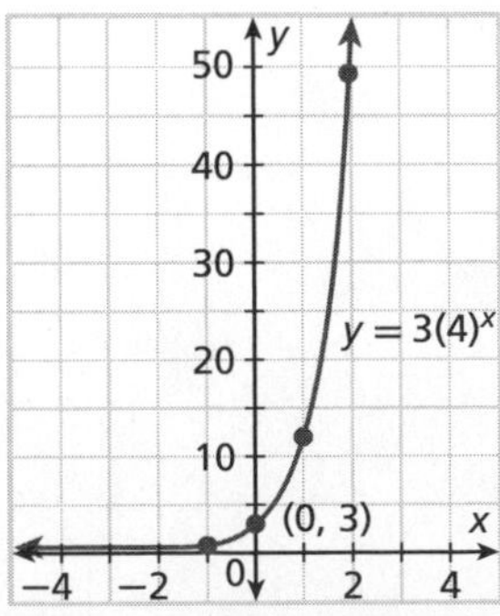

The graph nears the x-axis as x decreases and rises faster and faster as x increases.

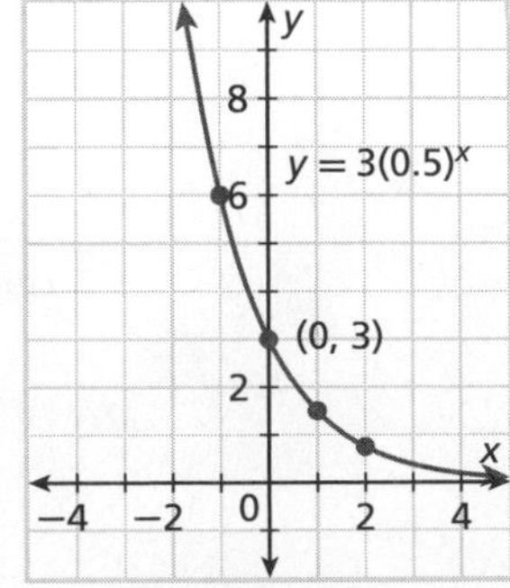

The graph nears the x-axis as x increases and rises faster and faster as x decreases.

CHAPTER 9

CC.9-12.F.LE.1

Distinguish between situations that can be modeled with linear functions and with exponential functions.

Key Vocabulary

linear function *(función lineal)* A function that can be written in the form $y = mx + b$, where x is the independent variable and m and b are real numbers. Its graph is a line.

What It Means For You — Lesson 9-5

A linear function models a *constant amount* of change for equal intervals. An exponential function models a *constant factor*, or *constant ratio* of change for equal intervals.

EXAMPLE **Exponential model**

Value of a car	
Car's Age (yr)	Value ($)
0	20,000
1	17,000
2	14,450
3	12,282.50

Age: +1, +1, +1. Value: × 0.85, × 0.85, × 0.85. Ratio is constant.

NON-EXAMPLE **Nonlinear, non-exponential model**

Height of Bridge Suspension Cables	
Cable's Distance from Tower (ft)	Cable's Height (ft)
0	400
100	256
200	144
300	64

Distance: + 100, + 100, + 100. Height: − 144, × 0.64; − 112, × 0.56; − 80, × 0.44.

Neither difference nor ratio is constant.

CHAPTER 9

CC.9-12.F.LE.2

Construct linear and exponential functions, including arithmetic and geometric sequences, given a graph, a description of a relationship, or two input-output pairs (include reading these from a table).

What It Means For You — Lessons 9-1, 9-2, 9-3

You can construct a model of a linear or exponential function from different descriptions or displays of the same situation.

EXAMPLE **Geometric Sequence**

A ball is dropped 81 inches onto a hard surface. The table shows the ball's height on successive bounces. Write a model for the height reached as a function of the number of bounces.

Bounce	1	2	3	4
Height (in.)	54	36	24	16

Consecutive terms have a common ratio of $\frac{2}{3}$. You can write a model as an exponential function or as a geometric sequence:

Exponential function: $f(x) = 81\left(\frac{2}{3}\right)^x$, where x is the bounce number

Geometric sequence: $a_1 = 54$, $a_n = \frac{2}{3}a_{n-1}$, where n is the bounce number

Key Vocabulary

common ratio *(razón común)* In a geometric sequence, the constant ratio of any term and the previous term.

exponential decay *(decremento exponencial)* An exponential function of the form $f(x) = ab^x$ in which $0 < b < 1$. If r is the rate of decay, then the function can be written $y = a(1 - r)^t$, where a is the initial amount and t is the time.

exponential function *(función exponencial)* A function of the form $f(x) = ab^x$, where a and b are real numbers with $a \neq 0$, $b > 0$, and $b \neq 1$.

exponential growth *(crecimiento exponencial)* An exponential function of the form $f(x) = ab^x$ in which $b > 1$. If r is the rate of growth, then the function can be written $y = a(1 + r)^t$, where a is the initial amount and t is the time.

geometric sequence *(sucesión geométrica)* A sequence in which the ratio of successive terms is a constant r, called the *common ratio*, where $r \neq 0$ and $r \neq 1$.

linear function *(función lineal)* A function that can be written in the form $y = mx + b$, where x is the independent variable and m and b are real numbers. Its graph is a line.

recursive formula *(fórmula recurrente)* A formula for a sequence in which one or more previous terms are used to generate the next term.

CHAPTER 9

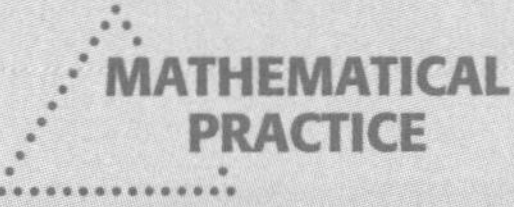

The Common Core Standards for Mathematical Practice describe varieties of expertise that mathematics educators at all levels should seek to develop in their students. Opportunities to develop these practices are integrated throughout this program.

1. **Make sense of problems and persevere in solving them.**
2. **Reason abstractly and quantitatively.**
3. **Construct viable arguments and critique the reasoning of others.**
4. **Model with mathematics.**
5. **Use appropriate tools strategically.**
6. **Attend to precision.**
7. **Look for and make use of structure.**
8. **Look for and express regularity in repeated reasoning**

Name________________ Class__________ Date__________

9-1

Video Tutor

Geometric Sequences

Essential question: *How can you write a rule for a geometric sequence?*

In a **geometric sequence**, the ratio of consecutive terms is constant. The constant ratio is called the **common ratio**, often written as *r*.

CC.9–12.F.BF.1a

1 EXAMPLE Writing Rules for a Geometric Sequence

Makers of Japanese swords in the 1400s repeatedly folded and hammered the metal to form layers. The folding process increased the strength of the sword.

The table shows how the number of layers depends on the number of folds. Write a recursive rule and an explicit rule for the geometric sequence described by the table.

Number of Folds	*n*	1	2	3	4	5
Number of Layers	*f(n)*	2	4	8	16	32

A Find the common ratio by calculating the ratios of consecutive terms.

$\frac{4}{2} =$ ______ $\frac{8}{4} =$ ______

$\frac{16}{8} =$ ______ $\frac{32}{16} =$ ______

The common ratio, *r*, is ________.

B Write a recursive rule for the sequence.

$f(1) =$ ______ and

The first term is ________.

$f(n) =$ ______ $\cdot$ ______ for $n \geq 2$

Every other term is the ________ of the previous term and the common ratio.

C Write an explicit rule for the sequence by writing each term as the product of the first term and a power of the common ratio.

n	*f(n)*
1	$2(2)^0 = 2$
2	$2(2)^1 = 4$
3	$2(2)^{\square} = 8$
4	$2(2)^{\square} = 16$
5	$2(2)^{\square} = 32$

Generalize the results from the table: $f(n) =$ ______ $\cdot\, 2^{n\,-\,\square}$

REFLECT

1a. Explain how you know that the sequence 4, 12, 36, 108, 324, ... is a geometric sequence.

1b. A geometric sequence has a common ratio of 5. If you know that the 6th term of the sequence is 30, how could you find the 7th term?

CC.9–12.F.BF.1a

2 EXPLORE Writing General Rules for Geometric Sequences

Use the geometric sequence 6, 24, 96, 384, 1536, ... to help you write a recursive rule and an explicit rule for any geometric sequence. For the general rules, the values of *n* are consecutive integers starting with 1.

A Find the common ratio.

Numbers	**Algebra**
6, 24, 96, 384, 1536, ...	$f(1), f(2), f(3),$ ____ , ____ , ...
Common ratio = ____	Common ratio = r

B Write a recursive rule.

Numbers	**Algebra**
$f(1) =$ ____ and	Given $f(1)$,
$f(n) = f(n-1) \cdot$ ____ for $n \geq 2$	$f(n) = f(n-1) \cdot$ ____ for $n \geq 2$

C Write an explicit rule.

Numbers	**Algebra**
$f(n) =$ ____ $\cdot$ ____$^{n-1}$	$f(n) =$ ____ $\cdot$ ____$^{n-1}$

REFLECT

2a. The first term of a geometric sequence is 81 and the common ratio is $\frac{1}{3}$. Explain how you could find the 4th term of the sequence.

2b. What information do you need to know in order to find the 5th term of a geometric sequence by using its explicit rule?

2c. What is the recursive rule for the sequence $f(n) = 5(4)^{n-1}$?

Relating Geometric Sequences and Exponential Functions

The graph shows the heights to which a ball bounces after it is dropped. Write an explicit rule for the sequence of bounce heights.

A Represent the sequence in a table.

n	1	2	3	4
$f(n)$				

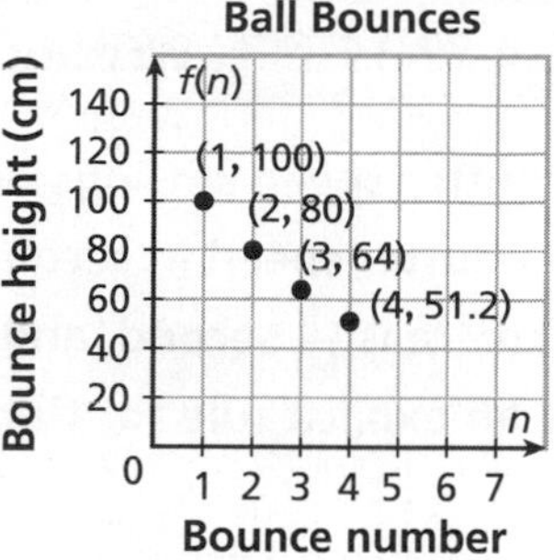

B Examine the sequence.

Is the sequence geometric? Explain.

____

What is the common ratio? ________

C Write an explicit rule for the sequence.

$f(n) = f(1) \cdot r^{n-1}$ Write the general rule.

$f(n) = \square \cdot \square^{n-1}$ Substitute ________ for $f(1)$ and ________ for r.

So, the sequence has the rule ________________ where n is the bounce number and $f(n)$ is the ________________.

REFLECT

3a. A geometric sequence is equivalent to an exponential function with a restricted domain. On the graph above, draw an exponential curve that passes through the given points. Then write an exponential function of the form $f(n) = ab^n$, where a is the initial amount (or y-intercept) and b is the common ratio, for the curve that you drew and give the function's domain.

____

3b. Show that the explicit rule for the sequence is equivalent to the exponential function. Justify the steps you take.

____

____

____

The explicit and recursive rules for a geometric sequence can also be written in subscript notation.

Explicit: $a^n = a_1 \cdot r^{n-1}$

Recursive: a_1 is given and $a_n = a_{n-1} \cdot r$ for $n \geq 2$

CC.9–12.F.LE.2

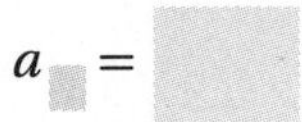

4 EXAMPLE Writing a Geometric Sequence Given Two Terms

The shutter speed settings on a camera form a geometric sequence where a_n is the shutter speed in seconds and n is the setting number. The fifth setting on the camera is $\frac{1}{60}$ second, and the seventh setting on the camera is $\frac{1}{15}$ second. Write an explicit rule for the sequence using subscript notation.

A Identify the given terms in the sequence.

$a_5 = \square$	The fifth setting is $\frac{1}{60}$ second, so the 5th term of the sequence is $\frac{1}{60}$.
$a_{\square} = \square$	The seventh setting is $\frac{1}{15}$ second, so the ________ term of the sequence is ________.

B Find the common ratio.

$a_7 = a_6 \cdot r$	Write the recursive rule for a_7.
$a_6 = \square \cdot r$	Write the recursive rule for a_6.
$a_7 = \square \cdot \square \cdot r$	Substitute the expression for a_6 into the rule for a_7.
$\square = \square \cdot r^2$	Substitute $\frac{1}{15}$ for a_7 and ________ for a_5.
$\square = r^2$	Multiply both sides by 60.
$\square = r$	Definition of positive square root

C Find the first term of the sequence.

$a_n = a_1 \cdot r^{n-1}$	Write the explicit rule.
$\square = a_1 \cdot \square^{\square - 1}$	Substitute $\frac{1}{60}$ for a_n, ________ for r, and 5 for n.
$\frac{1}{60} = a_1 \cdot \square$	Simplify.
$\square = a_1$	Divide both sides by 16.

D Write the explicit rule.

$a_n = a_1 \cdot r^{n-1}$	Write the general rule.
$a_n = \square \cdot \square^{n-1}$	Substitute ________ for a_1 and ________ for r.

REFLECT

4a. When finding the common ratio, why can you ignore the negative square root of 4 when solving the equation $4 = r^2$?

4b. If you graphed the explicit rule for the sequence, what would the graph look like?

PRACTICE

Write a recursive rule and an explicit rule for each geometric sequence.

1. 9, 27, 81, 243, ...

2. 5, −5, 5, −5, ...

3. 12, 3, $\frac{3}{4}$, $\frac{3}{16}$, ...

4. The table shows the beginning-of-month balances, rounded to the nearest cent, in Marla's savings account for the first few months after she made an initial deposit in the account.

Month	n	1	2	3	4
Account Balance ($)	$f(n)$	2010.00	2020.05	2030.15	2040.30

a. Explain how you know that the sequence of account balances is geometric.

b. Write recursive and explicit rules for the sequence of account balances.

c. What amount did Marla deposit initially? Explain.

5. The graph shows the number of players in the first four rounds of the U.S. Open women's singles tennis tournament.

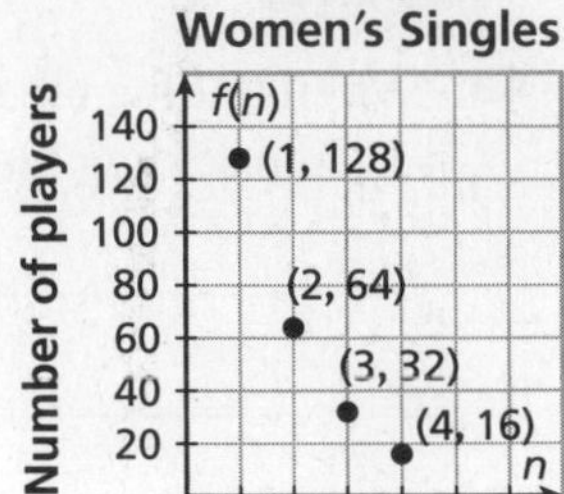

a. Write an explicit rule for the sequence of players in each round.

____

b. How many rounds are there in the tournament? (*Hint:* In the last round, only 2 players are left.)

____

6. The numbers of points that a player must accumulate to reach the next level of a video game form a geometric sequence, where a_n is the number of points needed to complete level n.

a. A player needs 1000 points to complete level 2 and 8,000,000 points to complete level 5. Write an explicit rule for the sequence using subscript notation.

____

b. How many points are needed for level 7? _______________

Write an explicit rule for each geometric sequence based on the given terms from the sequence. Assume that the common ratio *r* is positive.

7. $a_2 = 12$ and $a_4 = 192$

____

8. $a_5 = 0.32$ and $a_7 = 0.0128$

____

Each rule represents a geometric sequence. If the given rule is recursive, write it as an explicit rule. If the given rule is explicit, write it as a recursive rule. Assume that $f(1)$ is the first term of the sequence.

9. $f(n) = 6(3)^{n-1}$

____

10. $f(1) = 10; f(n) = f(n-1) \cdot 8$ for $n \geq 2$

____

11. An economist predicts that the cost of food will increase by 4% per year for the next several years.

a. Use the economist's prediction to write an explicit rule for a geometric sequence that gives the cost in dollars of a box of cereal in year n given that it costs \$3.20 in year 1.

____

b. What is the fourth term of the sequence, and what does it represent in this situation?

____

Name________________________ Class________________ Date____________

9-1

Additional Practice

Find the next three terms in each geometric sequence.

1. –5, –10, –20, –40, …

2. 7, 56, 448, 3584…

3. –10, 40, –160, 640, …

4. 40, 10, $\frac{5}{2}$, $\frac{5}{8}$, …

5. The first term of a geometric sequence is 6 and the common ratio is –8. Find the 7th term.

6. The first term of a geometric sequence is –3 and the common ratio is $\frac{1}{2}$. Find the 6th term.

7. The first term of a geometric sequence is –0.25 and the common ratio is –3. Find the 10th term.

8. What is the 12th term of the geometric sequence 4, 12, 36, …?

9. What is the 10th term of the geometric sequence 2, –6, 18, …?

10. What is the 6th term of the geometric sequence 50, 10, 2, …?

11. A shoe store is discounting shoes each month. A pair of shoes cost $80. The table shows the discount prices for several months. Find the cost of the shoes after 8 months. Round your answer to the nearest cent.

Month	Price
1	$80.00
2	$72.00
3	$64.80

Problem Solving

Write the correct answer.

1. A ball is dropped from 400 feet. The table shows the height of each bounce.

Bounce	Height (ft)
1	280
2	196
3	137.2

Find the height of the ball on the 6th bounce. Round your answer to the nearest tenth of a foot.

____

2. A plant starts with 1 branch. Every year, each branch becomes 3 branches. A sketch of the plant for the first 3 years is shown. How many branches will the plant have in year 10?

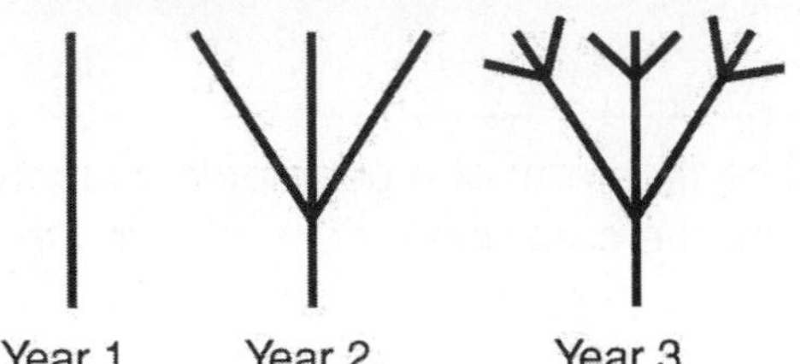

____

How many branches would the plant have in year 10 if the plant had 5 branches the first year? (Each branch still becomes 3 branches every year.)

____

3. Jeanette started selling bagels to offices in her area. Her sales for the first 3 months are shown in the table.

Month	Sales ($)
1	$200.00
2	$230.00
3	$264.50

If this trend continues, find the amount of Jeanette's sales in Month 8.

____

The table shows the number of houses in a new subdivision. Use the table to answer questions 4–7. Select the best answer.

Month	Houses
1	3
2	6
3	12
4	24

4. The number of houses forms a geometric sequence. What is r?

A 0.5 C 3

B 2 D 6

5. Assuming that the trend continues, how many houses would be in the subdivision in Month 6?

F 36 H 60

G 48 J 96

6. Management decides the subdivision is complete when the number of houses reaches 48. When will this happen?

A Month 5 C Month 7

B Month 6 D Month 8

7. Suppose the number of houses tripled every month. How many more houses would be in the subdivision in Month 4? (The number of houses in Month 1 is still 3.)

F 48 H 72

G 57 J 81

Name ______________________ Class ______________ Date ________

9-2

Exponential Functions

Going Deeper

Essential question: *How does changing the values of a, h, and k affect the graph of an exponential function?*

A general exponential growth function has the form $f(x) = ab^{x-h} + k$ where $b > 0$ and a, h, and k are real numbers with $a > 0$. Every value of b represents a different family of functions that can be transformed by changing the values of a, h, and k. The general exponential decay function has the same form, but $0 < b < 1$.

CC.9–12.F.BF.3

1 EXPLORE Changing *h* and *k*

Use your graphing calculator to help you with this activity.

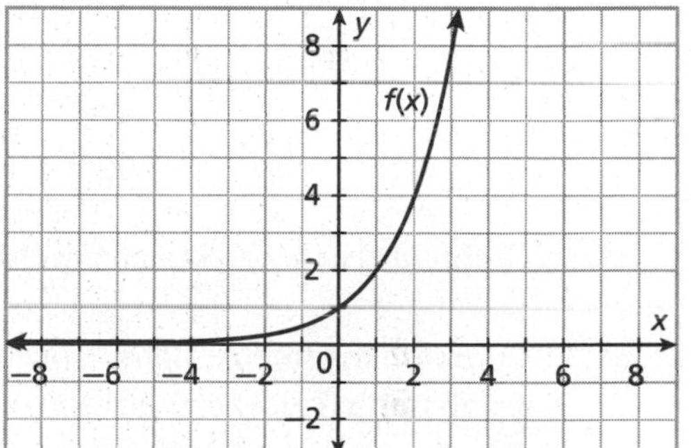

A Graph $f(x) = 2^x$. Confirm that it matches the graph shown at right.

B Graph $g(x) = 2^{x-4}$. Sketch and label $g(x)$ at right.

C Graph $h(x) = 2^{x+6}$. Sketch and label $h(x)$ at right.

D Compare the three graphs. How is the graph of $g(x)$ related to the graph of $f(x)$? How is the graph of $h(x)$ related to the graph of $f(x)$?

____

____

____

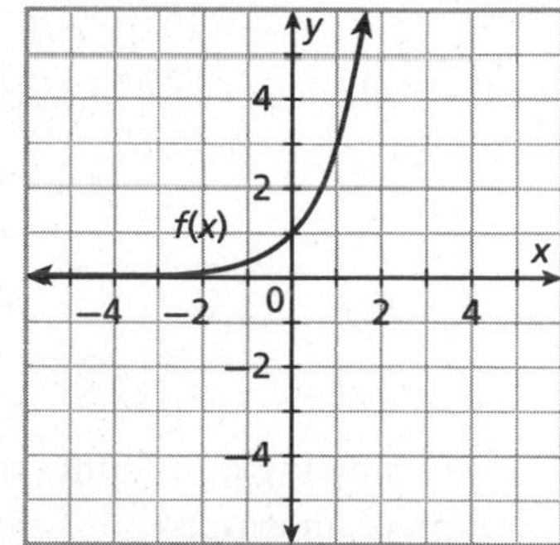

E Delete all equations from the equation editor. Then graph $f(x) = 3^x$. Confirm that it matches the graph shown at right.

F Graph $g(x) = 3^x + 3$. Sketch and label $g(x)$ at right.

G Graph $h(x) = 3^x - 5$. Sketch and label $h(x)$ at right.

H Compare the three graphs. How is the graph of $g(x)$ related to the graph of $f(x)$? How is the graph of $h(x)$ related to the graph of $f(x)$?

____

____

____

REFLECT

1a. How do you think the value of h affects the graph of $g(x) = b^{x-h}$?

1b. How do you think the value of k affects the graph of $g(x) = b^x + k$?

CC.9–12.F.BF.3

2 EXPLORE Changing *a*

Use your graphing calculator to help you with this activity.

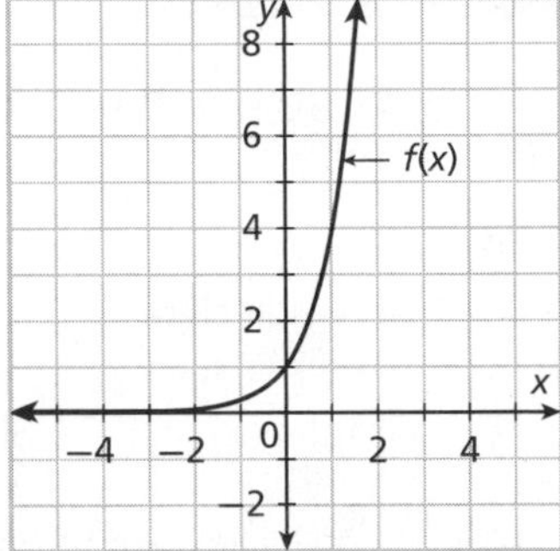

A Graph $f(x) = 4^x$. Confirm that it matches the graph shown.

B Graph $g(x) = 3(4)^x$. Sketch and label $g(x)$ at right.

C Graph $h(x) = \frac{1}{2}(4)^x$. Sketch and label $h(x)$ at right.

D Compare the three graphs. How is the graph of $g(x)$ related to the graph of $f(x)$? How is the graph of $h(x)$ related to the graph of $f(x)$?

REFLECT

2a. For $a > 0$, how do you think the value of a affects the graph of $g(x) = ab^x$?

2b. Without graphing, explain how the graph of $g(x) = 4(2)^{x+1} - 7$ compares to the graph of $f(x) = 2^x$.

The following table summarizes how the values of the parameters a, h, and k affect the graph of an exponential growth function or an exponential decay function.

$f(x) = ab^{x-h} + k$	
Parameter	**Effect**
h	If $h > 0$, the graph of the parent function is translated $\|h\|$ units to the right. If $h < 0$, the graph of the parent function is translated $\|h\|$ units to the left.
k	If $k > 0$, the graph of the parent function is translated $\|k\|$ units up. If $k < 0$, the graph of the parent function is translated $\|k\|$ units down.
a	If $a > 1$, the graph of the parent function is stretched vertically by a factor of a. If $0 < a < 1$, the graph of the parent function is shrunk vertically by a factor of a.

CC.9–12.F.BF.3

3 EXAMPLE Graphing $f(x) = b^{x-h} + k$

Graph each exponential decay function.

A $g(x) = \left(\frac{1}{2}\right)^x - 5$

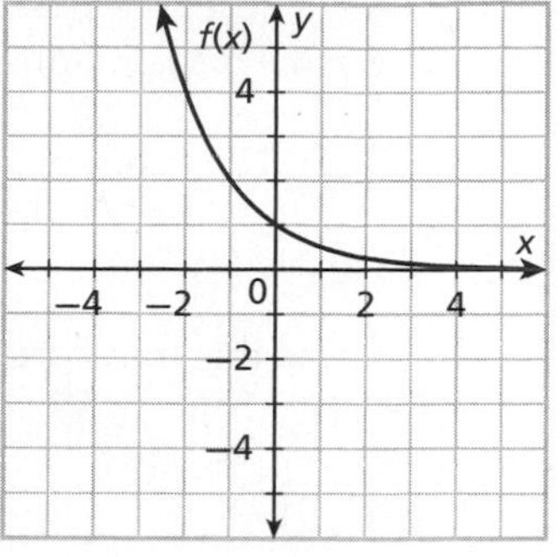

- First graph the parent function, $f(x) = \left(\frac{1}{2}\right)^x$. The graph of $f(x)$ is shown at right.
- The graph of $g(x)$ is a translation of the graph of $f(x)$ by how many units and in which direction?

  ____

- Use this transformation to sketch the graph of $g(x)$ at right.

B $g(x) = \left(\frac{1}{3}\right)^{x+2} + 1$

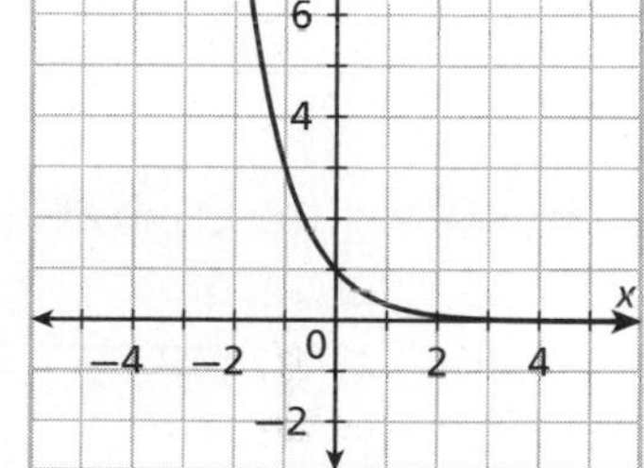

- The parent function $f(x)$ is ______________. The graph of $f(x)$ is shown at right.
- The graph of $g(x)$ is a translation of the graph of $f(x)$ by how many units and in which direction or directions?

  ____

- Use this transformation to sketch the graph of $g(x)$ at right.

REFLECT

3a. How is the graph of $g(x) = 0.25^{x-3}$ related to the graph of $f(x) = 0.25^x$?

____

3b. How is the graph of $h(x) = 0.25^{x+3}$ related to the graph of $f(x) = 0.25^x$?

____

3c. How is the graph of $g(x) = 0.25^{x-3}$ related to the graph of $h(x) = 0.25^{x+3}$?

____

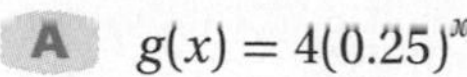

CC.9–12.F.BF.3

4 EXAMPLE Graphing $f(x) = ab^x$

Graph each exponential decay function.

A $g(x) = 4(0.25)^x$

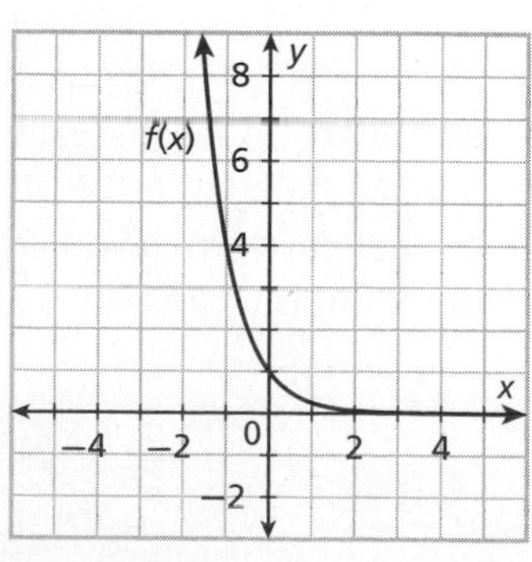

- First graph the parent function, $f(x) = 0.25^x$. The graph of $f(x)$ is shown at right.
- The graph of $g(x)$ is a vertical stretch of the graph of $f(x)$ by

  a factor of ________.

- Use this transformation to sketch the graph of $g(x)$ at right.

B $g(x) = \frac{1}{2}\left(\frac{1}{2}\right)^x$

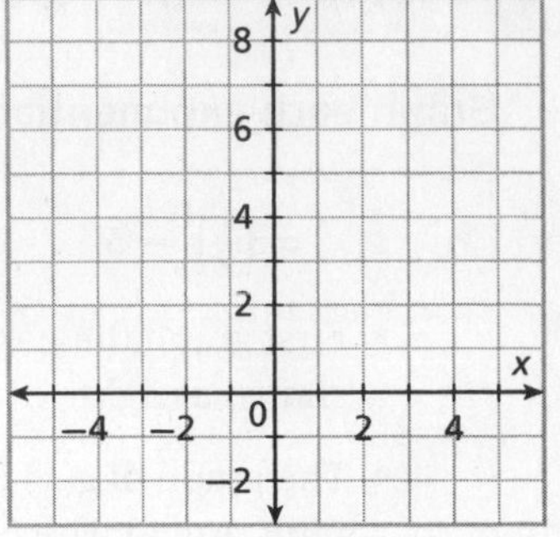

- The parent function $f(x)$ is ______________. Graph $f(x)$ on the coordinate plane at right.
- How is the graph of $g(x)$ related to the graph of $f(x)$?

____

____

- Use this transformation to sketch the graph of $g(x)$ at right.

REFLECT

4a. How is the graph of $g(x) = 9\left(\frac{2}{3}\right)^x$ related to the graph of $f(x) = \left(\frac{2}{3}\right)^x$?

____

____

4b. How is the graph of $h(x) = \frac{1}{3}\left(\frac{2}{3}\right)^x$ related to the graph of $f(x) = \left(\frac{2}{3}\right)^x$?

____

____

4c. How is the graph of $h(x) = \frac{1}{3}\left(\frac{2}{3}\right)^x$ related to the graph of $g(x) = 9\left(\frac{2}{3}\right)^x$?

____

____

4d. Use properties of exponents to explain why the graph of $g(x) = \left(\frac{1}{2}\right)^{x-3}$ may be considered a vertical stretch of the graph of $f(x) = \left(\frac{1}{2}\right)^x$. What is the factor of the vertical stretch?

____

____

Using the properties of exponents, you can rewrite the expression $ab^{x-h} + k$ as follows:

$$ab^{x-h} + k = ab^x \cdot b^{-h} + k = \left(ab^{-h}\right) b^x + k$$

where ab^{-h} is a constant because a, b, and h are constants. This means that the parameter h in the function $f(x) = ab^{x-h} + k$ can be eliminated by combining it with the parameter a. Therefore, when you are asked to find the equation of an exponential growth or decay function, you can assume that it has the form $f(x) = ab^x + k$.

CC.9–12.F.LE.2

5 EXAMPLE Writing an Equation from a Graph

Write an equation of the exponential growth function $g(x)$ whose graph is shown.

A Let $g(x) = ab^x + k$. First find the value of k.

Since the graph has the line $y = 1$ as a horizontal asymptote, there is a vertical translation of the parent function.

So, $k =$ ____________.

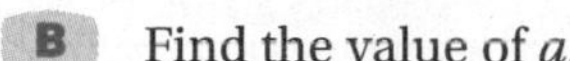

B Find the value of a.

The y-intercept of the graph of $g(x)$ is ____________.

If the graph of $g(x)$ is translated so that the x-axis is the asymptote, then the y-intercept of the graph will be ____________.

The y-intercept of the parent exponential growth function $f(x) = b^x$ is ____________.

This means the graph of the parent function is stretched vertically by a factor of ____________.

So, $a =$ ____________.

C Find the value of b.

The graph of $g(x)$ passes through $(1, 7)$.

If the graph is translated as in part A, then it passes through $(1,$ ______$)$.

Shrinking produces the graph of the parent function passing through $(1,$ ______$)$.

The graph of the parent function passes through $(1, b)$, so $b =$ ____________.

D Write the equation.

Using the values of the parameters from above, $g(x) =$ ____________.

REFLECT

5a. How did you use the fact that $g(x)$ passes through $(1, 7)$ to find a point through which the parent function passes?

____

____

5b. How can you check that you wrote a correct equation?

____

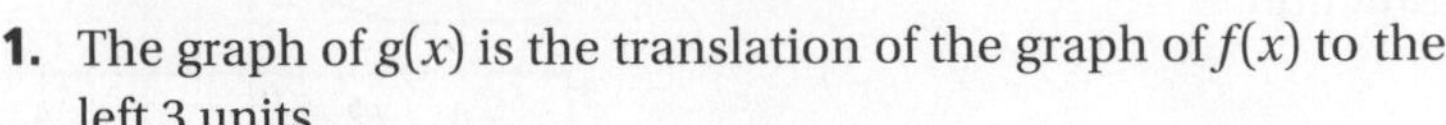

The graph of $f(x) = 2.5^x$ is shown. Write the function rules for $g(x)$ and $h(x)$ based on the descriptions given. Then sketch and label the graphs of $g(x)$ and $h(x)$ on the same coordinate plane.

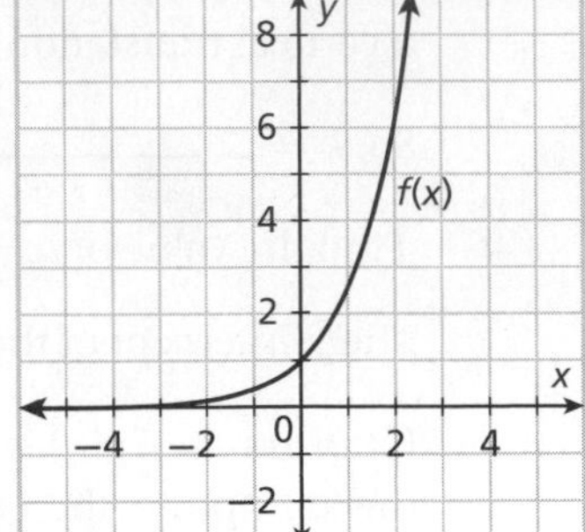

1. The graph of $g(x)$ is the translation of the graph of $f(x)$ to the left 3 units.

____

2. The graph of $h(x)$ is the translation of the graph of $f(x)$ up 2 units.

____

The graph of $f(x) = 3^x$ is shown. Write the function rules for $g(x)$ and $h(x)$ based on the descriptions given. Then sketch and label the graphs of $g(x)$ and $h(x)$ on the same coordinate plane.

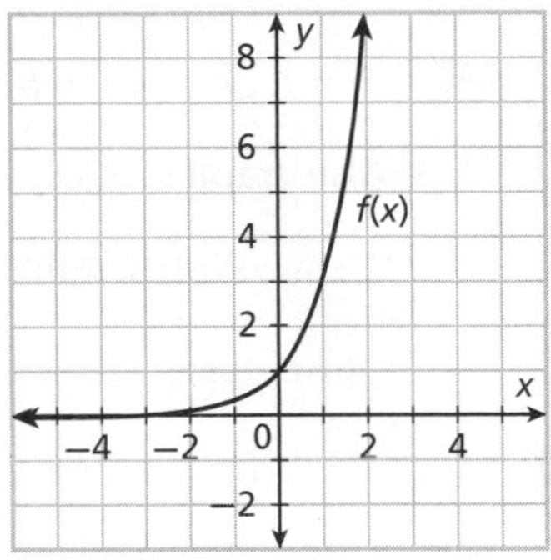

3. The graph of $g(x)$ is the translation of the graph of $f(x)$ to the right 2 units and down 1 unit.

____

4. The graph of $h(x)$ is a vertical stretch of the graph of $f(x)$ by a factor of 2.5.

____

Given $f(x) = 2^x$, write the function rules for $g(x)$, $h(x)$, $j(x)$, and $k(x)$ based on the descriptions given. Then give the range of each function.

5. The graph of $g(x)$ is a vertical shrink of the graph of $f(x)$ by a factor of $\frac{1}{3}$ and a vertical translation 6 units up.

____

6. The graph of $h(x)$ is a vertical stretch of the graph of $f(x)$ by a factor of 5 and a horizontal translation 4 units left.

____

7. The graph of $j(x)$ is a vertical stretch of the graph of $f(x)$ by a factor of 1.2, a horizontal translation 2 units right, and a vertical translation 4 units down.

____

8. The graph of $k(x)$ is a vertical shrink of the graph of $f(x)$ by a factor of 0.1, a horizontal translation 1 unit left, and a vertical translation 3 units up.

____

9. Error Analysis A student is told that the graph shown at right is a vertical translation of $f(x) = 1.5^x$ and determines that the equation of the function must be $f(x) = 1.5^x - 3$ because the y-intercept is -3. Explain and correct the error in the student's reasoning.

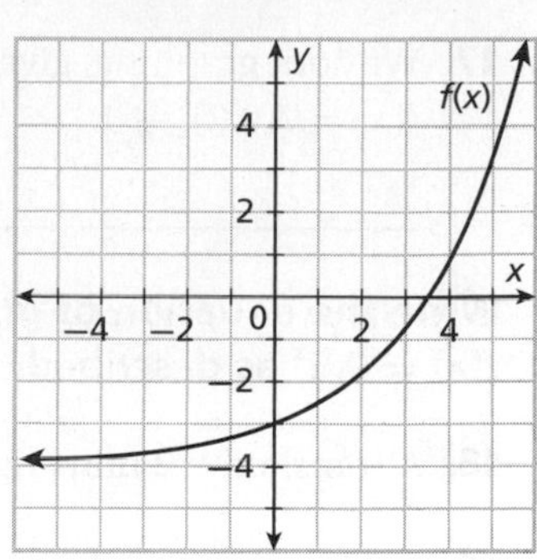

____

____

____

Write an equation of the exponential function $g(x)$ whose graph is shown.

10.

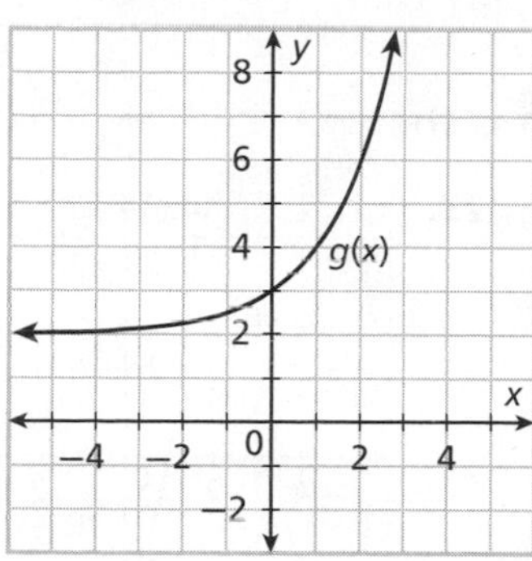

____

11.

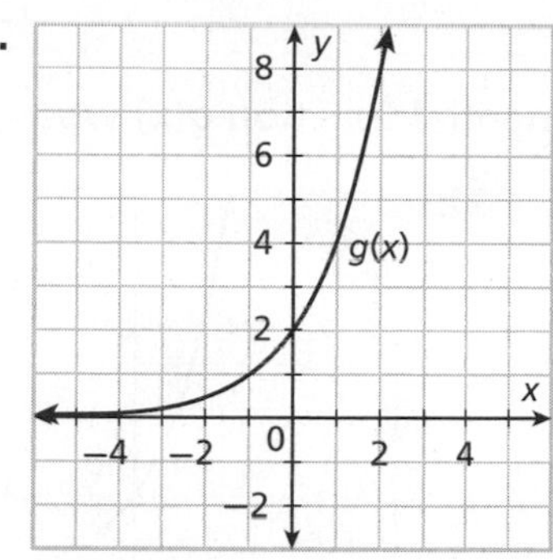

____

12.

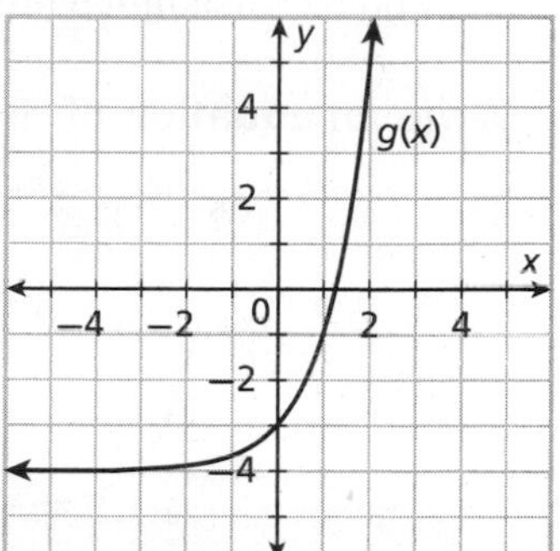

____

Graph each exponential decay function.

13. $f(x) = \left(\frac{1}{4}\right)^x + 1$

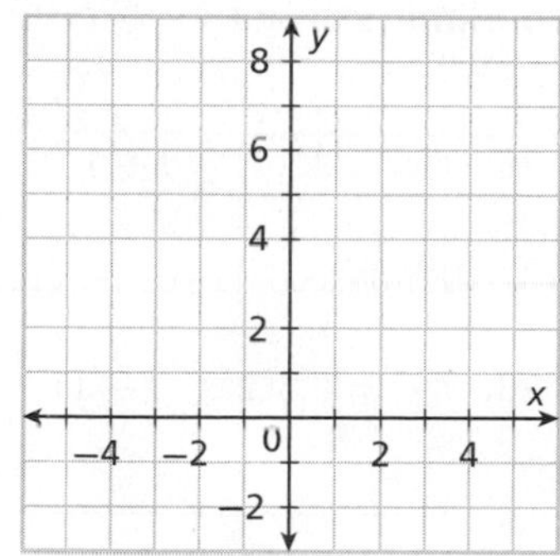

14. $f(x) = 0.5^{x-2} - 1$

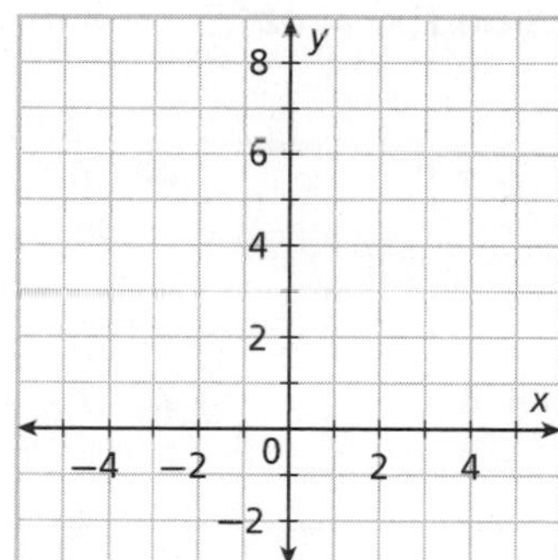

15. $f(x) = 3\left(\frac{1}{3}\right)^x$

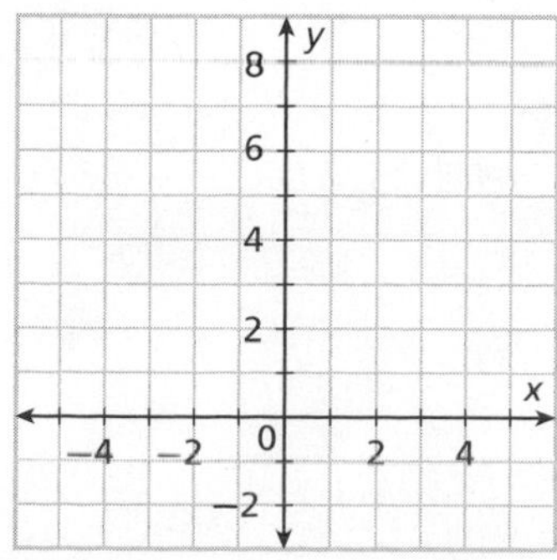

16. $f(x) = 2(0.5)^{x+1}$

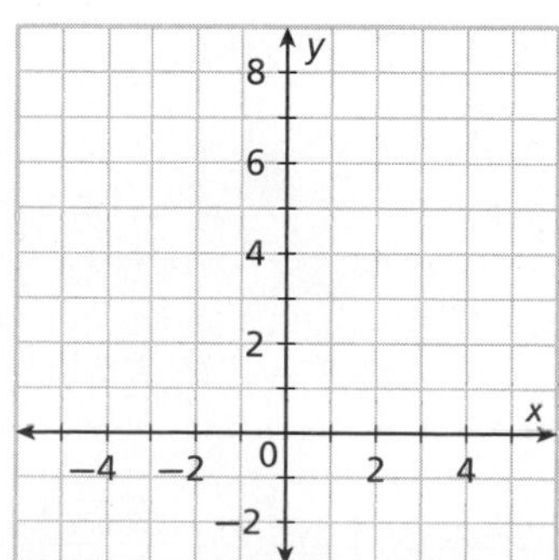

17. Without graphing, give the y-intercept and the horizontal asymptote of the graph of $f(x) = 7(0.2)^x - 4$.

____

Write the equation of $g(x)$ given that $g(x)$ is a transformation of the graph of $f(x) = 0.6^x$ as described.

18. A translation 2 units right and 1 unit up _______________

19. A vertical stretch by a factor of 3.5 _______________

20. A vertical shrink by a factor of 0.1 and a translation 5 units left _______________

Write an equation of the exponential function $g(x)$ whose graph is shown.

21.

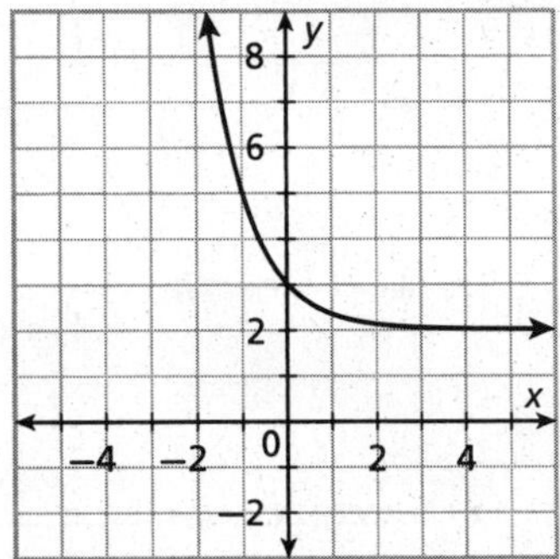

22.

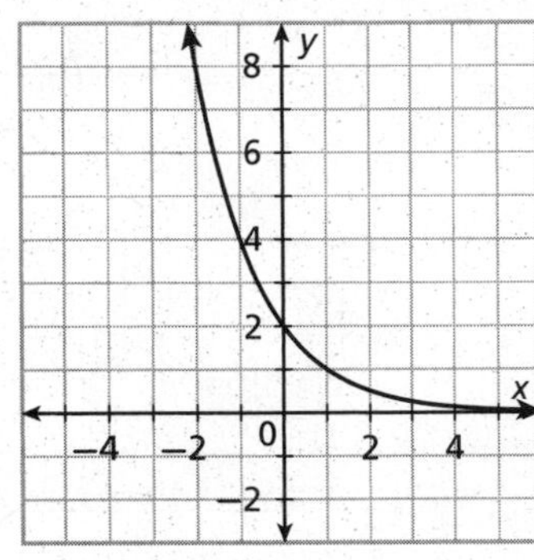

23.

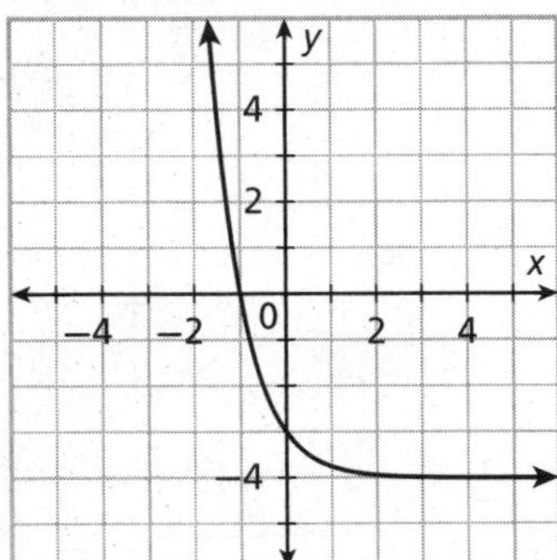

_______________ _______________ _______________

Rewrite the function $f(x) = ab^{x-h} + k$ in the form $f(x) = ab^x + k$ to eliminate the parameter h.

24. $f(x) = 100(5^{x-2}) + 8$

____

25. $f(x) = 216(3^{x-3}) - 4$

____

26. $f(x) = 32(2^{x-5}) + 1$

____

27. $f(x) = 3(4^{x+3}) + 6$

____

28. $f(x) = 0.4(5^{x+3}) + 9$

____

29. $f(x) = 0.5(2^{x+5}) - 11$

____

Name ______________________ Class ____________ Date ____________

Additional Practice

Given $f(x) = 3^x$, write function rules for $g(x)$, $h(x)$, $j(x)$, $k(x)$, and $m(x)$ based on the descriptions given.

1. The graph of $g(x)$ is a translation of the graph of $f(x)$ to the right 5 units.

   ____

2. The graph of $h(x)$ is a translation of the graph of $f(x)$ down 7 units.

   ____

3. The graph of $j(x)$ is a translation of the graph of $f(x)$ to the right 2 units and up 4 units.

   ____

4. The graph of $k(x)$ is a vertical stretch of the graph of $f(x)$ by a factor of 4.5.

   ____

5. The graph of $m(x)$ is a vertical shrink of the graph of $f(x)$ by a factor of 0.5 and a translation 6 units to the left.

   ____

Graph each exponential function.

6. $y = 5(2)^x$

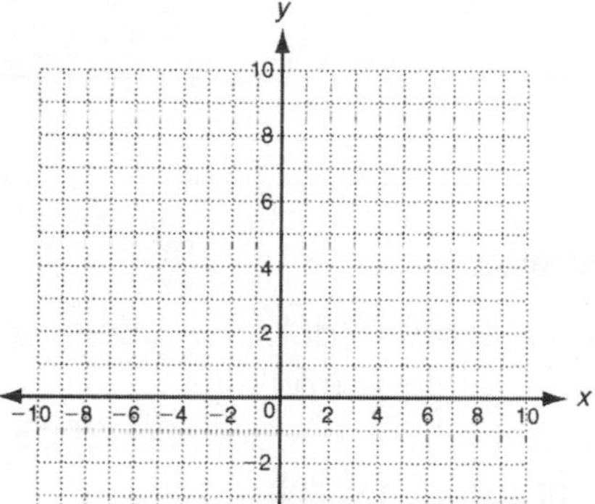

7. $y = -2(3)^x$

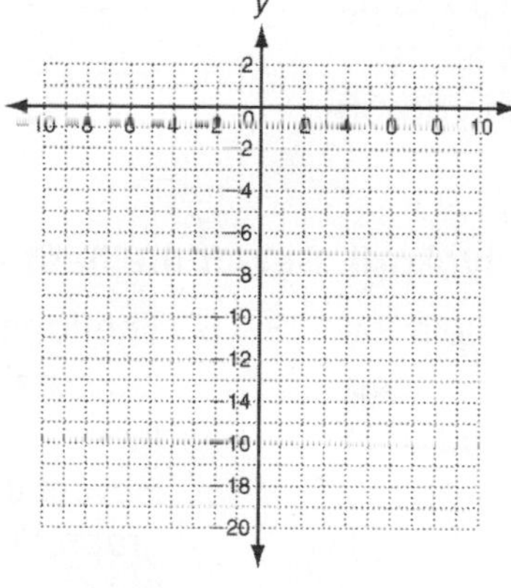

8. $y = 3\left(\frac{1}{2}\right)^x$

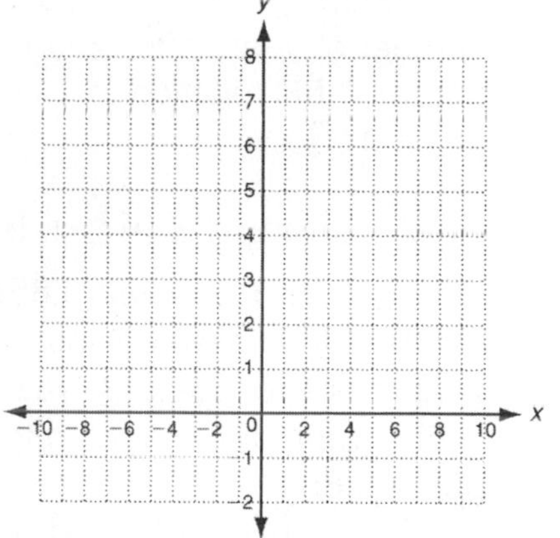

In the year 2000, the population of Virginia was about 7,400,000. Between the years 2000 and 2004, the population in Virginia grew at a rate of 5.4%. At this growth rate, the function $f(x) = 7{,}400{,}000(1.054)^x$ gives the population x years after 2000.

9. In what year will the population reach 15,000,000? ____________

10. In what year will the population reach 20,000,000? ____________

Problem Solving

Write the correct answer.

1. The function $f(x) = 6(1.5)^x$ models the length of a photograph in inches after the photo has been enlarged by 50% x times. Graph the function.

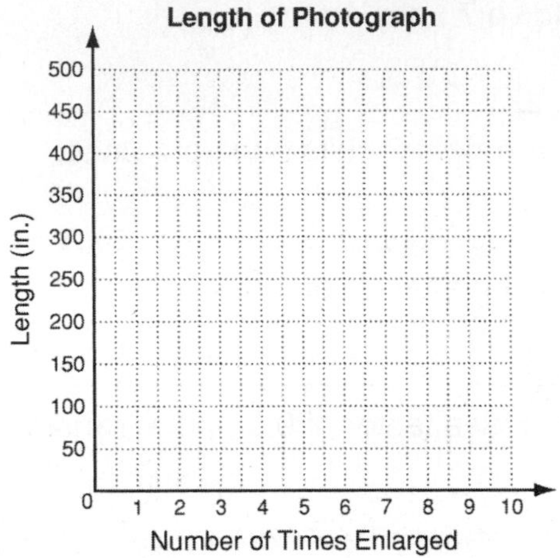

2. A population of 550 rabbits is increasing by 2.5% each year. The function $y = 5.5(1.025)^x$ gives the population of rabbits, in hundreds, x years from now. How is the graph of this function related to the graph of $y = 1.025^x$?

____

____

3. The function $y = 0.2(1.0004)^x$ models the balance, in thousands of dollars on a customer's line of credit x days after the end of the grace period (the time when no interest accumulates). How is the graph of this function related to the graph of $y = 1.0004^x$?

____

____

4. The function $f(x) = 2300(0.995)^x$ models enrollment in a high school, where x is the number of years after 2005. How is the graph of this function related to the graph of $y = 0.995^x$?

____

____

A lake was stocked with fish in early April. Select the best answer.

5. The function $f(x) = 300(0.85)^x$ models the number of landlocked salmon in the lake x months after the lake was stocked. How is the graph of $f(x)$ related to the graph of $g(x) = 0.85^x$?

   A Vertical shrink by a factor of 0.85

   B Vertical stretch by a factor of 300

   C Translation to the right by 0.85 units

   D Translation to the right by 300 units

6. The function $f(x) = 0.075(1.2)^x$ models the number of rainbow trout, in thousands, in the lake x years after 2005. How is the graph of $f(x)$ related to the graph of $g(x) = 1.2^x$?

   F Translation to the left by 0.075 units

   G Translation to the left by 1.2 units

   H Vertical shrink by a factor of 0.075

   J Vertical stretch by a factor of 1.2

Name _______________ Class _______________ Date _______________

9-3

Video Tutor

Exponential Growth and Decay

Going Deeper

Essential question: *How do you write, graph, and interpret exponential growth and decay functions?*

When you graph a function $f(x)$ in a coordinate plane, the x-axis represents the independent variable and the y-axis represents the dependent variable. Therefore, the graph of $f(x)$ is the same as the graph of the equation $y = f(x)$. You will use this form when you use a calculator to graph functions.

CC.9-12.F.IF.7e

1 EXPLORE Describing End Behavior of a Growth Function

A Use a graphing calculator to graph the exponential growth function $f(x) = 200(1.10)^x$ using Y_1 for $f(x)$. Use a viewing window from −20 to 20 for x, with a scale of 2, and from −100 to 1000 for y, with a scale of 50. Make a copy of the curve below.

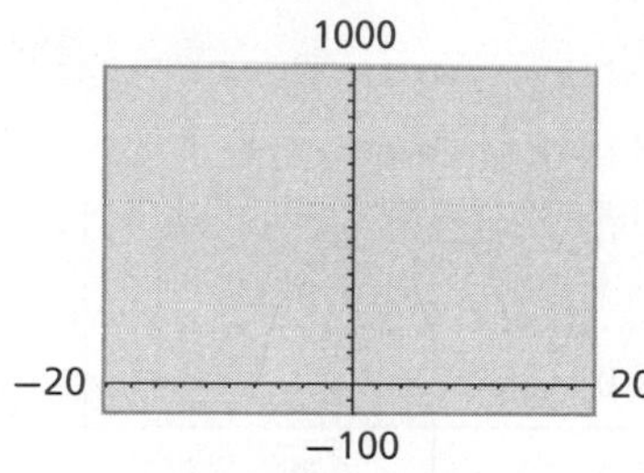

B To describe the *end behavior* of a function, you describe the function values as x increases or decreases without bound. Using the TRACE feature, move the cursor to the right along the curve. Describe the end behavior as x increases without bound.

____

C Using the TRACE feature, move the cursor to the left along the curve. Describe the end behavior as x decreases without bound.

____

REFLECT

1a. Describe the domain and the range of the function.

____

1b. Identify the y-intercept of the graph of the function. _______________

1c. An *asymptote* of a graph is a line the graph approaches more and more closely. Identify an asymptote of this graph _______________

1d. Why is the value of the function always greater than 0?

____

Recall that a function of the form $y = ab^x$ represents exponential growth when $a > 0$ and $b > 1$. If b is replaced by $1 + r$ and x is replaced by t, then the function is the **exponential growth model** $y = a(1 + r)^t$, where a is the *initial amount*, the base $(1 + r)$ is the *growth factor*, r is the *growth rate*, and t is the *time interval*. The value of the model increases with time.

CC.9–12.F.LE.2

2 EXAMPLE Modeling Exponential Growth

Alex buys a rare trading card for $4. The value of the card increases 40% per year for four years.

A Identify the initial amount and the growth rate.

$a =$ ____________________

$r =$ ____________________

B Write an exponential growth equation for this situation:

$y = \square\left(1 + \square\right)^t$

C Copy and complete the table. Round to the nearest cent.

Time (years) t	Value ($) y
0	
1	
2	
3	
4	

D Graph the points from the table using appropriate scales. Draw a smooth curve connecting the points. Label the axes.

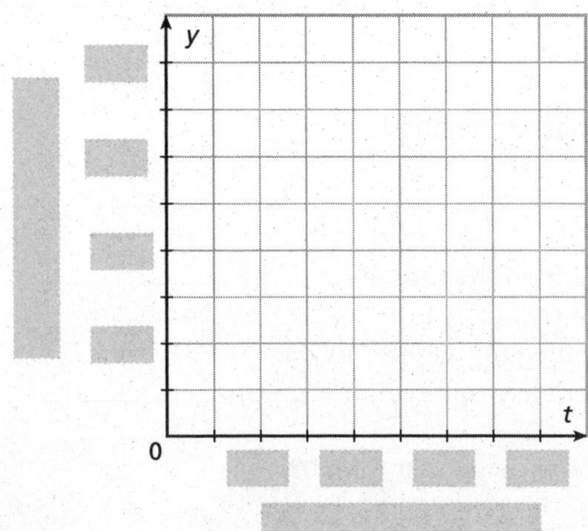

REFLECT

2a. Identify the *y*-intercept of the graph. What does it represent?

2b. What is the growth factor $(1 + r)$ written as a percent?

2c. Use the graph to estimate the value of the card in 3.5 years. Then explain why it makes sense to connect the points from the table with a smooth curve when graphing this function.

2d. Describe the domain and range of the function $y = 4(1.4)^t$ outside of the context of this problem. Do all of these values make sense in the context of this situation? Why or why not?

CC.9–12.F.IF.7e

3 EXPLORE Describing End Behavior of a Decay Function

A Use a graphing calculator to graph the exponential decay function $f(x) = 500(0.8)^x$ using Y_1 for $f(x)$. Use a viewing window from -10 to 10 for x, with a scale of 1, and from -500 to 5,000 for y, with a scale of 500. Make a copy of the curve below.

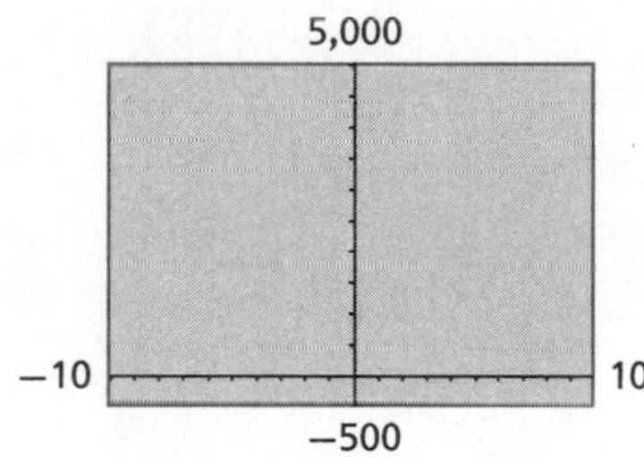

B Using the TRACE feature, move the cursor to the right along the curve. Describe the end behavior as x increases without bound.

C Using the TRACE feature, move the cursor to the left along the curve. Describe the end behavior as x decreases without bound.

REFLECT

3a. Describe the domain and the range of the function.

3b. Identify the y-intercept of the graph of the function. ______

3c. Identify an asymptote of this graph. Why is this line an asymptote?

Recall that a function of the form $f(x) = ab^x$ represents exponential decay when $a > 0$ and $0 < b < 1$. If b is replaced by $1 - r$ and x is replaced by t, then the function is the **exponential decay model** $y = a(1 - r)^t$, where a is the *initial amount*, the base $(1 - r)$ is the *decay factor*, r is the *decay rate*, and t is the *time interval.*

CC.9–12.F.LE.2

4 EXAMPLE Modeling Exponential Decay

You pay $12,000 for a car. The value then depreciates at a rate of 15% per year. That is, the car loses 15% of its value each year.

A Write an exponential decay equation for this situation.

$$y = \square(1 - \square)^t$$

B Complete the table. Round to the nearest dollar.

Time (years) t	Value ($) y
0	
1	
2	
3	
4	
5	
6	

C Graph the points and connect them with a smooth curve. Label the axes.

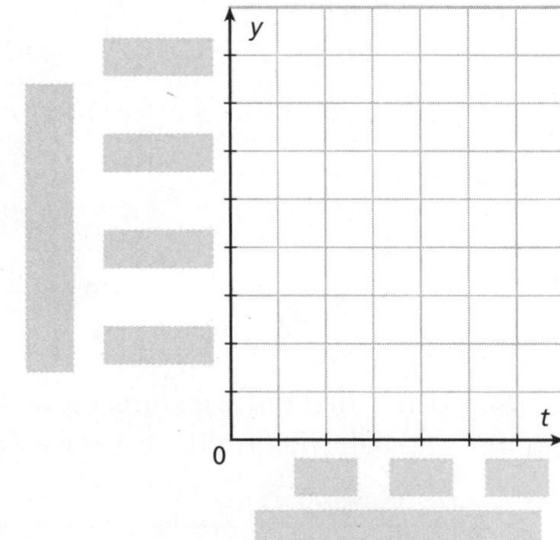

REFLECT

4a. Identify the y-intercept of the graph. What does it represent?

4b. What is the decay factor $(1 - r)$ written as a percent?

4c. What values make sense for the domain and range of this function?

____

____

4d. Predict the value of the car after 10 years.

____

4e. In how many years was the value of the car $8000?

____

4f. Explain why exponential functions of this type are referred to as exponential *decay* functions.

____

CC.9–12.F.LE.1c

5 EXAMPLE Comparing Exponential Growth and Exponential Decay

The graph shows the value of two different shares of stock over the period of four years since they were purchased. The values have been changing exponentially. Describe and compare the behaviors of the two stocks.

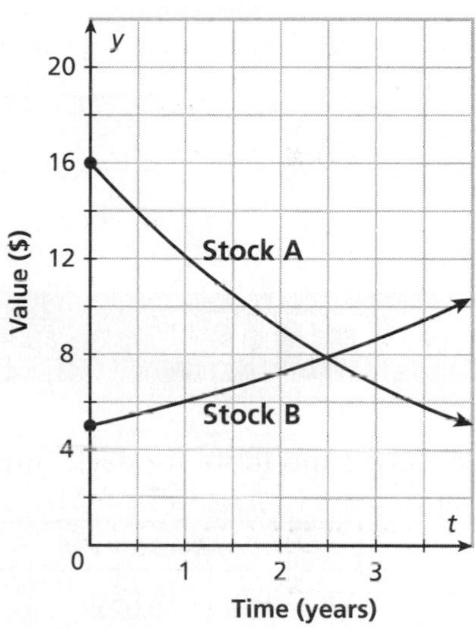

A The model for the graph representing Stock A is an exponential __________ model.

The initial value is __________ and the decay factor is ☐ ÷ ☐ = ☐.

B The model for the graph representing Stock B is an exponential __________ model. The initial value is __________ and the growth factor is ☐ ÷ ☐ = ☐.

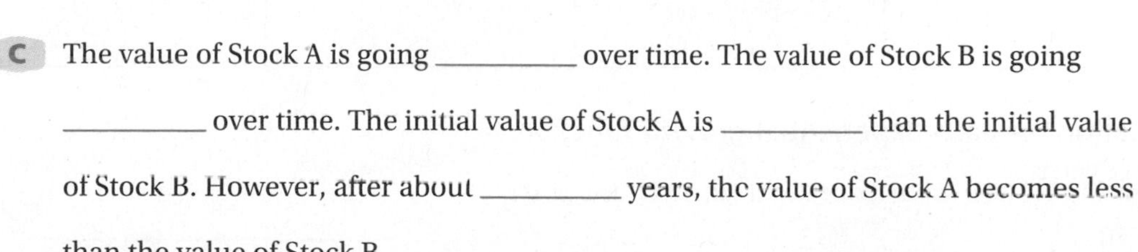

C The value of Stock A is going __________ over time. The value of Stock B is going __________ over time. The initial value of Stock A is __________ than the initial value of Stock B. However, after about __________ years, the value of Stock A becomes less than the value of Stock B.

REFLECT

5a. What is the growth rate for the increasing function above? Explain your reasoning.

5b. What is the decay rate for the decreasing function above? Explain your reasoning.

5c. How did the values of the stocks compare initially? after four years?

5d. In how many years was the value of Stock A about equal to the value of Stock B? Explain your reasoning.

5e. In how many years was the value of Stock A about twice the value of Stock B? Explain your reasoning.

PRACTICE

Complete the table for each function.

	Function	Initial Amount	Growth Rate	Growth Factor
1.	$y = 1250(1 + 0.02)^t$			
2.	$y = 40(1 + 0.5)^t$			
3.	$y = 50(1.06)^t$			

Write an equation for each exponential growth function.

4. Eva deposits $1500 in an account that earns 4% interest each year.

5. Lamont buys a house for $255,000. The value of the house increases 6% each year.

6. Brian invests $2000. His investment grows at a rate of 16% per year.

7. Sue is a coin collector. At the end of 2005 she bought a coin for \$2.50 whose value had been growing 20% per year for 3 years. The value continued to grow at this rate until she sold the coin 4 years later.

a. Write an exponential growth equation for this situation, using the amount Sue paid as the value at time 0. ____________________

b. Complete the table.

Time (years) t	Value (\$) y
−3	
−2	
−1	
0	
1	
2	
3	
4	

c. Graph and connect the points.

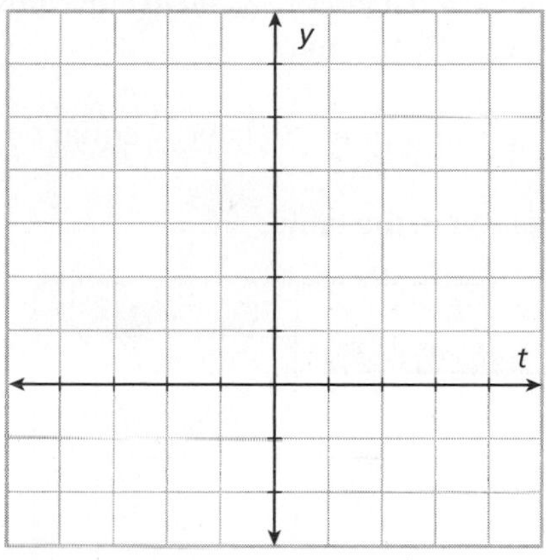

d. Describe the domain and range for this situation.

____

____

e. Identify the y-intercept. What does it represent?

____

f. What was the value of the coin at the end of 2003? at the time Sue sold the coin? Explain your reasoning.

____

____

____

8. Suppose you invest \$1600 on your 16th birthday and your investment earns 8% interest each year. What will be the value of the investment on your 30th birthday? Explain your reasoning.

____

9. Identify the initial amount, the decay factor, and the decay rate for the function $y = 2.50(0.4)^t$. Explain how you found the decay rate.

____

10. Mr. Nevin buys a car for $18,500. The value depreciates 9% per year. Write an equation for this function ______________

11. You are given a gift of $2,500 in stock on your 16th birthday. The value of the stock declines 10% per year.

a. Write an exponential decay equation for this situation. ______________

b. Complete the table.

Time (years), *t*	Value ($), *y*
0	
1	
2	
3	
4	
5	

c. Graph and connect the points. Label the axes.

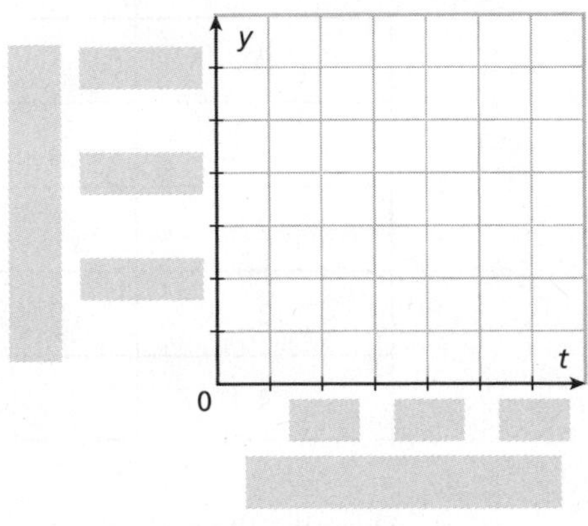

d. Predict the value of the stock on your 22nd birthday. ______________

12. The value of two parcels of land has been changing exponentially in the years since they were purchased, as shown in the graph. Describe and compare the values of the two parcels of land.

____

____

____

____

____

____

____

____

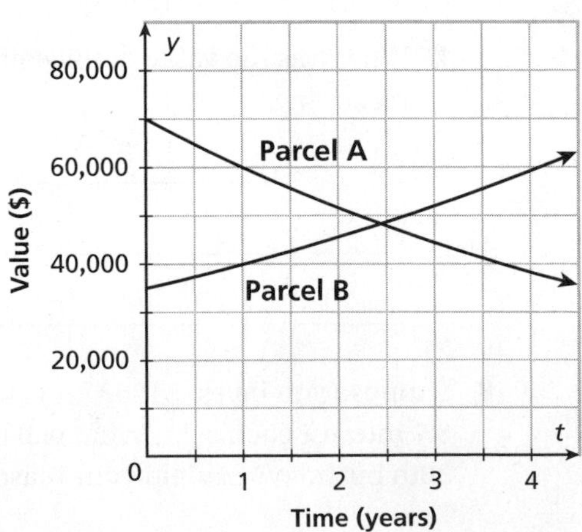

Name________________________ Class______________ Date______________

Additional Practice

Write an exponential growth function to model each situation. Then find the value of the function after the given amount of time.

1. Annual sales for a fast food restaurant are $650,000 and are increasing at a rate of 4% per year; 5 years ____________________

   ____

2. The population of a school is 800 students and is increasing at a rate of 2% per year; 6 years ____________________

   ____

3. During a certain period of time, about 70 northern sea otters had an annual growth rate of 18%; 4 years ____________________

   ____

Write a compound interest function to model each situation. Then find the balance after the given number of years.

4. $50,000 invested at a rate of 3% compounded monthly; 6 years ____________________

   ____

5. $43,000 invested at a rate of 5% compounded annually; 3 years ____________________

   ____

6. $65,000 invested at a rate of 6% compounded quarterly; 12 years ____________________

   ____

Write an exponential decay function to model each situation. Then find the value of the function after the given amount of time.

7. The population of a town is 2500 and is decreasing at a rate of 3% per year; 5 years ____________________

   ____

8. The value of a company's equipment is $25,000 and decreases at a rate of 15% per year; 8 years ____________________

   ____

9. The half-life of Iodine-131 is approximately 8 days. Find the amount of Iodine-131 left from a 35 gram sample after 32 days. ____________________

Problem Solving

Write the correct answer.

1. A condo in Austin, Texas, was worth \$80,000 in 1990. The value of the condo increased by an average of 3% each year. Write an exponential growth function to model this situation. Then find the value of the condominium in 2005.

____

____

2. Markiya deposited \$500 in a savings account. The annual interest rate is 2%, and the interest is compounded monthly. Write a compound interest function to model this situation. Then find the balance in Markiya's account after 4 years.

____

____

3. The population of a small Midwestern town is 4500. The population is decreasing at a rate of 1.5% per year. Write an exponential decay function to model this situation. Then find the number of people in the town after 25 years.

____

____

4. Twelve students at a particular high school passed an advanced placement test in 2000. The number of students who passed the test increased by 16.4% each year thereafter. Find the number of students who passed the test in 2004.

____

____

Half-lives range from less than a second to billions of years. The table below shows the half-lives of several substances. Select the best answer.

Half-Lives	
Nitrogen-16	7 s
Technetium-99	6 h
Sulfur-35	87 days
Tritium	12.3 yr
Uranium-238	4.5 billion yrs

5. About how many grams of a 500 g sample of Technetium-99 is left after 2 days?

   A 1.95 g C 31.25 g

   B 7.81 g D 62.5 g

6. Which equation can be used to find how much of a 50 g sample of Nitrogen-16 is left after 7 minutes?

   F $A = 50(0.5)^1$ H $A = 50(0.5)^{42}$

   G $A = 50(0.5)^7$ J $A = 50(0.5)^{60}$

7. How many billions of years will it take 1000 grams of Uranium-238 to decay to just 125 grams?

   A 0.125 C 9

   B 3 D 13.5

8. A researcher had 37.5 g left from a 600 g sample of Sulfer-35. How many half-lives passed during that time?

   F 4 H 7

   G 5 J 16

9. Look at problem 8. How many days passed during that time?

   A 7 C 348

   B 16 D 435

Name ____________________ Class ____________ Date ________

9-4

Video Tutor

Linear, Quadratic, and Exponential Models

Extension: Exponential models and regression

Essential question: *How can you model and solve problems involving exponential data?*

You can apply the properties of equations you already know to solve equations involving exponents. You will also need the following property.

Equating Exponents when Solving Equations		
Words	**Algebra**	**Example**
Two powers with the same positive base other than 1 are equal if and only if the exponents are equal.	If $b > 0$ and $b \neq 1$, then $b^x = b^y$ if and only if $x = y$.	If $2^x = 2^9$, then $x = 9$. If $x = 9$, then $2^x = 2^9$.

CC.9–12.A.REI.1

1 EXAMPLE Solving Equations by Equating Exponents

Solve each equation.

A $\frac{5}{2}(2)^x = 80$

$\square \cdot \frac{5}{2}(2)^x = \square \cdot 80$ — Multiply to isolate the power $(2)^x$.

$(2)^x = 32$ — Simplify.

$(2)^{\square} = 2^{\square}$ — Write 32 as a power of 2.

$x = \square$ — $b^x = b^y$ if and only if $x = y$.

B $4\left(\frac{5}{3}\right)^x = \frac{500}{27}$

$\square \cdot 4\left(\frac{5}{3}\right)^x = \square \cdot \frac{500}{27}$ — Multiply to isolate the power.

$\left(\frac{5}{3}\right)^x = \frac{125}{27}$ — Simplify.

$\left(\frac{5}{3}\right)^x = \left(\frac{5}{3}\right)^{\square}$ — Write the fraction as a power of $\frac{5}{3}$.

$x = \square$ — $b^x = b^y$ if and only if $x = y$.

REFLECT

1a. How can you check a solution?

1b. How can you work backward to write $\frac{125}{27}$ as a power of $\frac{5}{3}$?

1c. Is it possible to solve the equation $2^x = 96$ using the method in the Example? Why or why not?

Some equations can't be solved using the method in the Example because it isn't possible to write both sides of the equation as a whole number power of the same base. Instead, you can consider the expressions on either side of the equation as the rules for two different functions. You can then solve the original equation in one variable by graphing the two functions. The solution is the input value for the point where the two graphs intersect.

CC.9–12.A.REI.11

2 EXAMPLE Writing an Equation and Solving by Graphing

A town has 78,918 residents. The population is increasing at a rate of 6% per year. The town council is offering a prize for the best prediction of how long it will take for the population to reach 100,000. Make a prediction.

A Write an exponential model to represent the situation. Let *y* represent the population and *x* represent time (in years).

$$y = 78{,}918\left(1 + \boxed{}\right)^x$$

B Write an equation in one variable to represent the time, *x*, when the population reaches 100,000.

$$\boxed{} = 78{,}918\left(1 + \boxed{}\right)^x$$

C Write functions for the expressions on either side of the equation.

$$f(x) = \boxed{}$$

$$g(x) = 78{,}918\left(1 + \boxed{}\right)^x$$

D What type of function is $f(x)$? What type of function is $g(x)$?

E Graph the functions on a graphing calculator. Let $Y_1 = f(x)$ and $Y_2 = g(x)$. Sketch the graph of Y_2 below. (Y_1 is already graphed for you.) Include the missing window values.

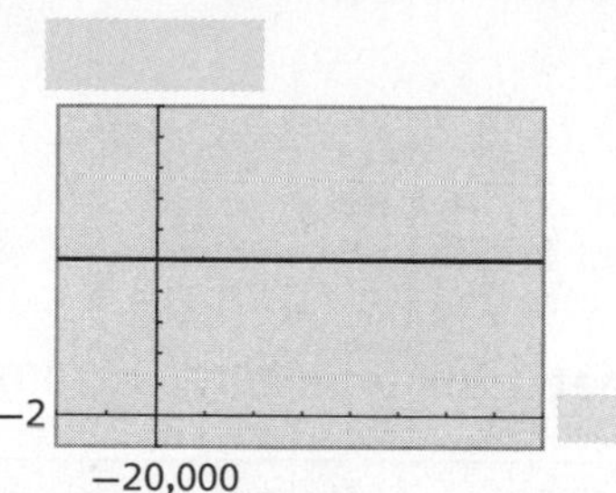

F Use the intersect feature on the CALC menu to find the input value where the graphs intersect. (Do not round.)

____

G Make a prediction as to the number of years until the population reaches 100,000.

____

REFLECT

2a. Suppose the contest is announced on January 1, and the town has 78,918 residents on that date. Explain how to predict *the date* on which the population will be 100,000.

____

2b. Explain why the x-coordinate of the point where the graphs of $Y_1 = f(x)$ and $Y_2 = g(x)$ intersect is the solution of the equation in Part B.

____

In the previous Example you knew the growth rate and were able to write an exponential model for the situation. However, in many real-world situations you only may have data points with which to create a model. For situations that can be modeled exponentially, you can use the exponential regression feature on a graphing calculator to create a model for the data.

CC.9–12.S.ID.6a

3 EXAMPLE Fitting a Function to Data

The table shows the number of internet hosts from 2001 to 2007.

Number of Internet Hosts							
Years since 2001	0	1	2	3	4	5	6
Number (millions)	110	147	172	233	318	395	490

A Enter the data from the table on a graphing calculator, with years since 2001 in List 1 and number of internet hosts in List 2. Then set up a scatter plot of the data, as shown, and graph it. Copy the points below.

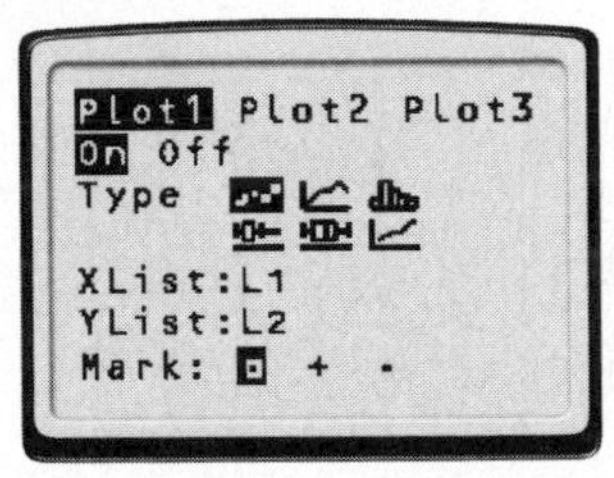

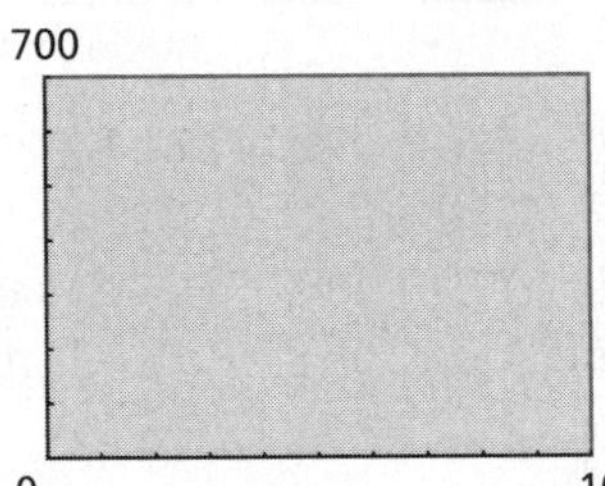

B The data fall along a curve, so an exponential function might fit the data. Use your calculator's statistical calculation features to find the exponential regression model. Record the results rounded to three significant digits.

Function $y =$ ____________ Correlation coefficient $r =$ ____________

REFLECT

3a. What does the correlation coefficient suggest about the model?

____

3b. Use your rounded function model to predict the number of internet hosts in 2010 and in 2020. Round to three significant digits.

2010: ____________ 2020: ____________

3c. Are these predictions likely to be accurate? Explain.

____

____

Residuals You have used residuals to assess how well a linear model fits a data set. You can also use residuals for exponential and other models. Remember that if (x, y_d) is a data point and the corresponding point on the model is (x, y_m), then the corresponding *residual* is the difference $y_d - y_m$.

Recall that a model is a good fit for the data when the following are true:

- The numbers of positive and negative residuals are roughly equal.
- The residuals are randomly distributed about the x-axis, with no pattern.
- The absolute values of the residuals are small relative to the data.

CC.9–12.S.ID.6b

4 EXAMPLE Plotting and Analyzing Residuals

Continue working with the data from the first Example to plot and analyze the residuals.

A Enter the regression equation from your calculator as the rule for equation Y_1. (It can be found with the statistical variables on the variables menu.) Then view the table to find the function values y_m for the model. Record the results in the table at the right. Round to three significant digits.

B Use the results of Part A to complete the residuals column of the table.

Number of Internet Hosts (millions)			
x	y_d	y_m	Residual $y_d - y_m$
0	110	110	0
1	147	142	5
2	172		
3	233		
4	318		
5	395		
6	490		

C Set up a residual scatter plot of the data, as shown, and graph it. Adjust the viewing window as needed. Copy the points below.

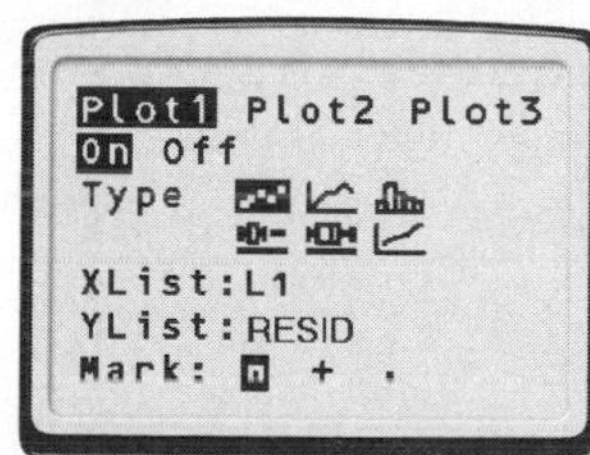

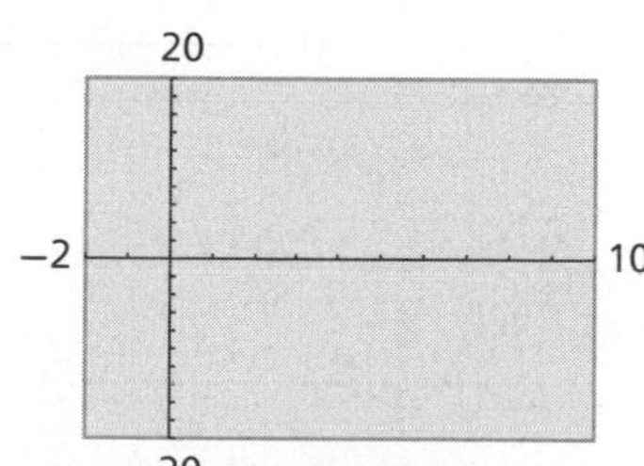

D At first glance, does the model fit the data well? Explain.

____

____

REFLECT

4a. Use the model $y = 110(1.29)^x$ from Part B of the first Example to find the function value for $x = 4$. Round to three significant digits. Compare the result with the value in the table above and with the actual value.

4b. Are the residuals in the calculator plotted on the residual plot exactly the same as the residuals in the table? Why or why not?

4c. One reason the model is a good fit for the data is that the absolute values of the residuals are small relative to the data. What does this claim mean? Give examples from the table to support this claim.

4d. Another reason the model fits the data well is that the residuals are randomly distributed about the x-axis with no pattern. Use a graphing calculator to find a *linear* regression model for these data. Describe the residual plot. What does it tell you about the model?

4e. Describe what the parameters a and b in the model represent. Is the number of internet hosts growing or decaying? Explain your reasoning. What is the growth or decay rate?

PRACTICE

Solve each equation without graphing.

1. $5(3)^x = 405$

$x =$ ____________

2. $\frac{1}{5}(5)^x = 5$

$x =$ ____________

3. $10(4)^x = 640$

$x =$ ____________

4. $7\left(\frac{1}{2}\right)^x = \frac{7}{8}$

$x =$ ____________

5. $\frac{3}{4}\left(\frac{2}{3}\right)^x = \frac{4}{27}$

$x =$ ____________

6. $3\left(\frac{3}{10}\right)^x = \frac{27}{100}$

$x =$ ____________

Solve each equation by graphing. Round to the nearest hundredth.

7. $6^x = 150$

$x \approx$ ____________

8. $5^x = 20$

$x \approx$ ____________

9. $(2.5)^x = 40$

$x \approx$ ____________

10. Last year a debate club sold 972 fundraiser tickets on their most successful day. This year the 4 club officers plan to match that number on a single day as follows:

To start off, on Day 0, each of the 4 officers of the club will sell 3 tickets and ask each buyer to sell 3 more tickets the next day. Every time a ticket is sold, the buyer of the ticket will be asked to sell 3 more tickets the next day.

If the plan works, on what day will the number of tickets sold be 972?

a. Write an equation in one variable to model the situation. ____________

b. If the plan works, on what day will the number sold be 972? ____________

11. There are 175 deer in a state park. The population is increasing at the rate of 12% per year. At this rate, when will the population reach 300?

a. Write an equation in one variable to model the situation. ____________

b. How long will it take for the population to reach 300?

____

c. Suppose there are 200 deer in another state park and that the deer population is increasing at a rate of 10% per year. Which park's deer population will reach 300 sooner? Explain.

____

____

12. A city has 642,000 residents on July 1, 2011. The population is decreasing at the rate of 2% per year. At that rate, in what month and year will the population reach 500,000? Explain how you found your answer.

____

____

The first two columns of the table show the population of Arizona (in thousands) in census years from 1900 to 2000.

13. Find an exponential function model for the data. Round to four significant digits.

____

14. Identify the parameters in the model, including the growth or decay rate, and explain what they represent.

____

____

____

15. Use the more precise model stored on your calculator to complete the third column of the table with population values based on the model. Round to three significant digits.

16. Use the results of Exercise 15 to complete the residuals column of the table.

17. Use your model from Exercise 13 to predict the population of Arizona in 1975 and in 2030, to the nearest thousand. Discuss the accuracy of the results. Which result is likely to be more accurate? Why?

Arizona Population y (in thousands) in Years x Since 1900			
x	y_d	y_m	$y_d - y_m$
0	123		
10	204		
20	334		
30	436		
40	499		
50	750		
60	1,302		
70	1,771		
80	2,718		
90	3,665		
100	5,131		

____

____

____

18. Make a residual plot. Does the model fit the data well? Explain.

____

____

____

____

____

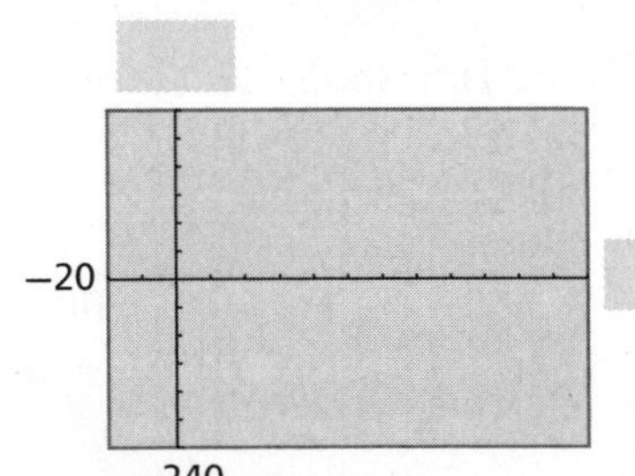

Name ______________________ Class ______________ Date ____________

9-4

Additional Practice

Solve each equation without graphing.

1. $3(2)^x = 384$

2. $6(5)^x = 750$

3. $0.25(6)^x = 324$

4. $4\left(\frac{1}{5}\right)^x = \frac{4}{125}$

5. $\frac{2}{5}\left(\frac{2}{3}\right)^x = \frac{32}{405}$

6. $\frac{1}{2}\left(\frac{5}{8}\right)^x = \frac{3125}{65{,}536}$

Solve each equation by graphing. Round to the nearest hundredth.

7. $6^x = 100$

8. $7^x = 420$

9. $5^x = 280$

10. $(2.5)^x = 130$

11. $(5.5)^x = 1525$

12. $(1.5)^x = 50$

There are 225 trout in a lake. The population is increasing at the rate of 15% per year. At this rate, when will the population reach 500 trout?

13. Write an equation in one variable to represent this situation.

14. How long will it take for the trout population to reach 500? Round the answer to the nearest tenth of a year.

15. Suppose there are 150 trout in another lake. The population of trout in that lake is increasing at a rate of 20% per year. Which lake's trout population will reach 500 sooner? Explain.

Problem Solving

Write the correct answer.

1. There are 250 wolves in a national park. The wolf population is increasing at a rate of 16% per year. Write an exponential model to represent the situation.

____

2. Use the model from Problem 1 to determine how long it will take the wolf population in the national park to reach 1000. Round the answer to the nearest hundredth.

____

3. A city has a population of 350,000 residents. The population is decreasing at the rate of 5% per year. Write an exponential model to represent the situation.

____

4. Use the model from Problem 3 to determine how long it will take the population of the city to reach 275,000 residents. Round the answer to the nearest hundredth.

____

A city has a population of 175,000 residents. The population of the city is increasing at the rate of 4% per year.

5. Write an exponential model to represent the situation.

   A $y = 175{,}000(1.04)x$

   B $y = 175{,}000(0.96)^x$

   C $y = 175{,}000(1.04)^x$

   D $y = 1.04(175{,}000)^x$

6. Use the model from Problem 5 to determine how long it will take the population of the city to reach 250,000 residents. Round the answer to the nearest tenth.

   F 9.1 years   H 0.1 year

   G 3.4 years   J 1.0 year

7. Another city has a population of 300,000 residents. The population of that city is decreasing at a rate of 2% per year. Write an exponential model to represent the situation.

   A $y = 300{,}000(1.02)^x$

   B $y = 300{,}000(0.98)x$

   C $y = 300{,}000(0.98)^x$

   D $y = 0.98(300{,}000)^x$

8. Use the model from Problem 7 to determine how long it will take the population of the second city to reach 250,000 residents. Round the answer to the nearest tenth.

   F 0.9 year   H 3.4 years

   G 1.0 year   J 9.0 years

Name _______________ Class _______________ Date _______________

9-5

Video Tutor

Comparing Functions

Going Deeper

Essential question: *How can you recognize, describe, and compare linear and exponential functions?*

CC.9-12.F.LE.1

1 ENGAGE Comparing Constant Change and Constant Percent Change

Suppose you are offered a job that pays $1000 the first month with a raise every month after that. You can choose a $100 raise or a 10% raise. Which option would you choose? What if the raise were 8%, 6%, or 4%?

A Work in groups and use multiple calculators to find the monthly salaries by following the steps described below. For the first three months, record the results in the table below, rounded to the nearest dollar.

- For the $100 raise, enter 1000, press ENTER, enter +100, press ENTER, and then press ENTER repeatedly.
- For the 10% raise, enter 1000, press ENTER, enter ×1.10, press ENTER, and then press ENTER repeatedly.
- For the other raises, replace 1.10 with these factors: 1.08, 1.06, and 1.04.

	Monthly Salary After Indicated Monthly Raise				
Month	**$100**	**10%**	**8%**	**6%**	**4%**
0	$1000	$1000	$1000	$1000	$1000
1	$1100	$1100	$1080	$1060	$1040
2					
3					

B Continue until you find the number of months it takes for each salary with a percent raise to exceed that month's salary with the $100 raise. Record the number of months in the table below.

	Number of Months Until Salary with Percent Raise Exceeds Salary with $100 Raise			
$100	**10%**	**8%**	**6%**	**4%**
---------	2			

REFLECT

1a. What is the change per unit interval in monthly salary for each option? Which of these is a constant rate of change in dollars per month? Explain your reasoning.

1b. Why are the differences from row to row in each percent column not constant? What *is* constant about the changes from row to row?

CC.9–12.F.LE.3

2 EXAMPLE Comparing Linear and Exponential Functions

Compare these two salary plans:

- Job A: \$1000 for the first month with a \$100 raise every month thereafter
- Job B: \$1000 for the first month with a 1% raise every month thereafter

Will Job B ever have a higher monthly salary than Job A?

A Write functions that represent the monthly salaries. Let *t* represent the number of elapsed months. Then tell whether the function is *linear* or *exponential*.

Job A: $S_A(t) = \_\_\_ + \_\_\_ t$ S_A is a/an ________ function.

Job B: $S_B(t) = \_\_\_ \cdot \_\_\_^t$ S_B is a/an ________ function.

B Graph the functions on a calculator and sketch them below. Label the functions and include the scale.

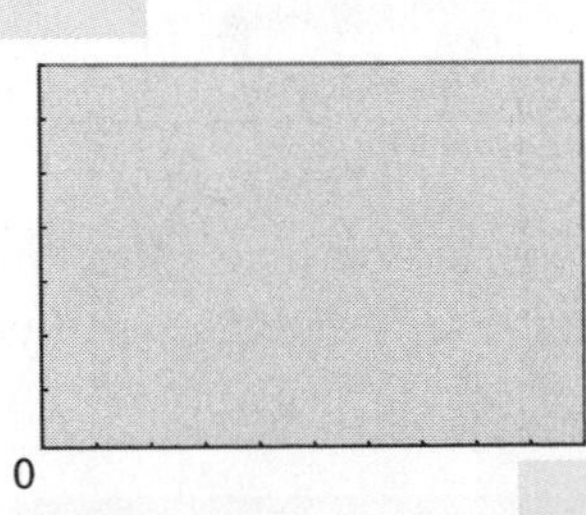

C Will Job B ever have a higher monthly salary than Job A? If so, after how many months will this happen? Explain your reasoning.

REFLECT

2a. Revise $S_B(t)$ and use the Table feature on your graphing calculator to find the interval in which the monthly salary for Job B finally exceeds that for Job A if the growth rate is 0.1%. Use intervals of 1,000. Repeat for a growth rate of 0.01%, using intervals of 10,000.

2b. Why does a quantity increasing exponentially eventually exceed a quantity increasing linearly?

2c. The table shows values for the monthly salary functions in four-month intervals rather than one-month intervals.

t	$S_A(t)$	$S_B(t)$
0	1000	1000.00
4	1400	1040.60
8	1800	1082.86
12	2200	1126.83
16	2600	1172.58
20	3000	1220.19

- Does $S_A(t)$ grow by equal differences over each four-month interval? Explain your reasoning.

- Does $S_A(t)$ grow by the same difference over the first eight-month interval as it does over the first four-month interval? Explain your reasoning.

- Does $S_B(t)$ grow by equal factors over each four-month interval? Explain your reasoning.

- Does $S_B(t)$ grow by the same factor over the first eight-month interval as it does over the first four month interval? Explain your reasoning.

Later you will prove that linear functions grow by the same difference over equal intervals and that exponential functions grow by equal factors over equal intervals.

PRACTICE

Tell whether each quantity is changing at a *constant rate* per unit of time, at a *constant percent rate* per unit of time, or *neither*.

1. Amy's salary is $40,000 in her first year on a job with a $2,000 raise every year thereafter. ______________

2. Carla's salary is $50,000 in her first year on a job plus a 1% commission on all sales. ______________

3. Enrollment at a school is 976 students initially and then it declines 2.5% each year thereafter. ______________

4. Companies X and Y each have 50 employees. If Company X increases its workforce by 2 employees per month, and Company Y increases its workforce by 2% per month, will Company Y ever have more employees than Company X? If so, when?

____

5. Centerville and Easton each have 2500 residents. Centerville's population decreases by 80 people per year, and Easton's population decreases by 3% per year. Will Centerville ever have a greater population than Easton? If so, when? Explain your reasoning.

____

____

____

Complete each statement with the correct function from the table at the right.

x	*f*(*x*)	*g*(*x*)
0	50	100
1	54	104
2	58	108
3	63	112
4	68	116
5	73	120

6. __________ grows at a constant rate per unit interval.

7. __________ grows at a constant percent rate per unit interval.

8. An equation for the linear function is as follows:

____

9. An equation for the exponential function is as follows:

____

10. In 1970, the populations of both Marston and Denton were 5000. The population of Marston increased by 5000 each decade from 1970 until 2010, while the population of Denton doubled each decade during the same period. Consider the ordered pairs (n, p) for each city where n is the number of decades since 1970 and p is the population of the city.

a. Tell whether the data for each city can be represented by a linear function or an exponential function. Explain your reasoning.

____

____

b. Complete the table for each city. Use the tables to justify your answers in part a.

Decades since 1970	Marston's population
0	5000
1	
2	
3	
4	

Decades since 1970	Denton's population
0	5000
1	
2	
3	
4	

____

____

c. Write a function that models the population for each town. Then use the model to predict each town's population in 2030.

____

____

11. Complete the proof that linear functions grow by equal differences over equal intervals.

Given: $x_2 - x_1 = x_4 - x_3$,
f is a linear function of the form $f(x) = mx + b$.

Prove: $f(x_2) - f(x_1) = f(x_4) - f(x_3)$

Proof:

$x_2 - x_1 = x_4 - x_3$	Given
$m(x_2 - x_1) = \underline{\quad}(x_4 - x_3)$	Mult. Prop. of Equality
$mx_2 - \underline{\quad} = mx_4 - \underline{\quad}$	Distributive Property
$mx_2 + b - mx_1 - b = mx_4 + \underline{\quad} - mx_3 - \underline{\quad}$	Add. and Subt. Prop. of Equality
$(mx_2 + b) - (mx_1 + b) = \underline{\qquad\qquad}$	Distributive Property
$f(x_2) - f(x_1) = \underline{\qquad\qquad}$	Definition of $f(x)$

12. Complete the proof that exponential functions grow by equal factors over equal intervals.

Given: $x_2 - x_1 = x_4 - x_3$
f is an exponential function of the form $f(x) = ab^x$.

Prove: $\dfrac{f(x_2)}{f(x_1)} = \dfrac{f(x_4)}{f(x_3)}$

Proof:

$x_2 - x_1 = x_4 - x_3$	Given
$b^{x_2 - x_1} = b^{x_4 - x_3}$	If $x = y$, then $b^x = b^y$.
$\dfrac{b^{x_2}}{b^{x_1}} = \dfrac{b^{x_4}}{\underline{\quad}}$	Quotient of Powers Prop.
$\dfrac{ab^{x_2}}{ab^{x_1}} = \dfrac{ab^{x_4}}{\underline{\quad}}$	Mult. Prop. of Equality
$\dfrac{f(x_2)}{f(x_1)} = \dfrac{\underline{\quad}}{\underline{\quad}}$	Definition of $f(x)$

Name________________________ Class______________ Date______________

9-5

Additional Practice

1. Two functions are given below. Complete the tables and find the rate of change over [0, 3] for each function. Then graph both functions on the same coordinate plane.

$y = 4x + 10$	
x	y
0	
1	
2	
3	
4	

$y = 1 + 4^x$	
x	y
0	
1	
2	
3	
4	

Rate of change ______________ ______________

a. Compare the rates of change.____

____

b. How do the y-values at $x = 0$ and $x = 3$ relate to the rates of change over [0, 3]? ______

____

2. An engineer designs reflector surfaces. Equations for the shapes of two of his designs are shown below. Complete the tables for each function. Compare the designs by finding and comparing average rates of change, minimums, and maximums over the interval [0, 3]. Then graph the functions on the same coordinate plane.

Design A: $y = 5 + 5x$	
x	y
0	
1	
2	
3	
4	

Design B: $y = 5 + 5^x$	
x	y
0	
1	
2	
3	
4	

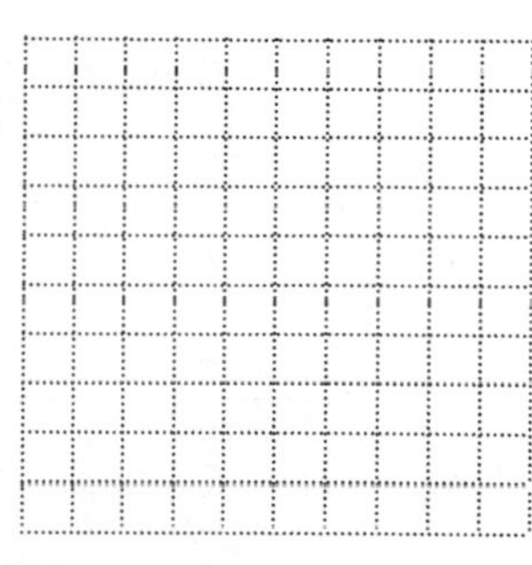

Rate of change ______________ ______________

Minimum value on [0, 3] ______________ ______________

Maximum value on [0, 3] ______________ ______________

Problem Solving

1. George and Julie each deposit money into their savings accounts monthly. Compare the accounts by finding slopes and *y*-intercepts.

George's Account

Month	0	1	2	3
Balance ($)	125	175	225	275

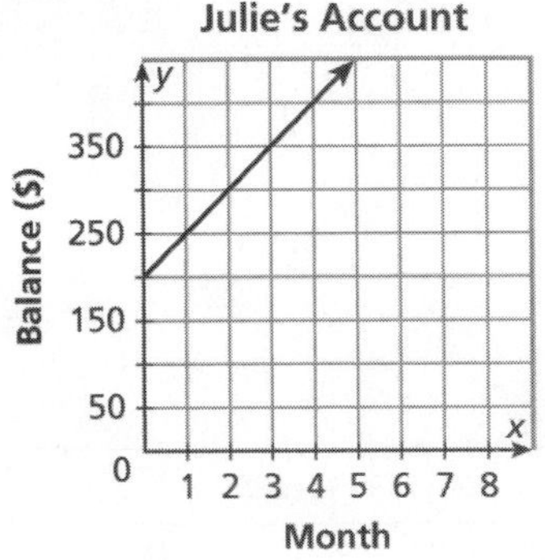

____

____

2. Miguel tracked the weekly spread of two strains of flu virus. His data are shown below. Compare the number of cases of flu by finding and interpreting average rates of change from week 0 to week 4.

Strain 1

Week	0	1	2	3	4	5
Cases	15	25	40	60	85	115

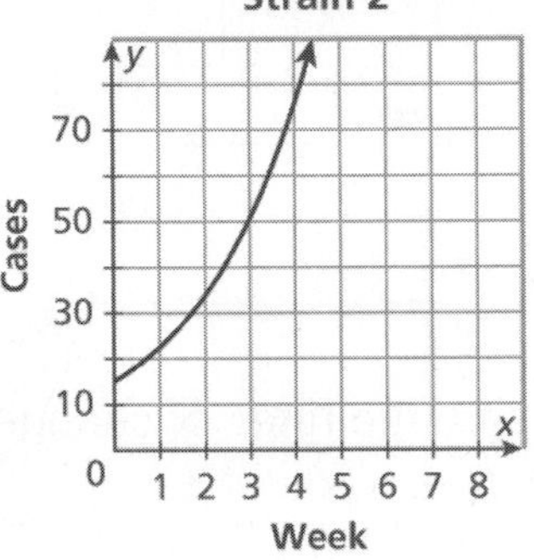

____

____

The table and graph below show functions used to model the changing population of the United States. Use the table or graph to select the best answers for 3 and 4.

Year (2000 = 0)	Population (millions)
0	282
2	288
4	293
6	298
8	304

www.census.gov/popest/geographic/NST-EST2008-01

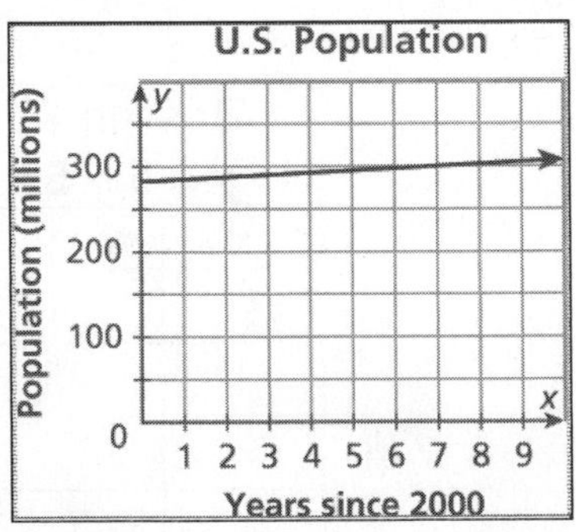

3. What is the rate of change in the table from the year 2000 to the year 2008?

A 1.75

B 2.75

C 22

D 73.25

4. What is the rate of change in the graph from the year 2000 to the year 2008?

F about 7.5 million people/year

G about 3.5 million people/year

H about 3 million people/year

J about 2.5 million people/year

Name________________________ Class________________ Date__________

CHAPTER 9

Performance Tasks

COMMON CORE

CC.9-12.F.IF.2
CC.9-12.F.BF.1
CC.9-12.F.LE.1
CC.9-12.F.LE.2
CC.9-12.F.LE.5

★ **1.** A scientist has a 400-gram sample of a radioactive substance. After one week, 348 grams of the substance remain. After two weeks, 302.76 grams remain.

a. What is the substance's weekly rate of decay as a percent?

b. What is the substance's approximate half-life? Round to the nearest whole week.

★ **2.** Seymour invests in a 5-year CD. Over the 5-year period, the CD earns a fixed annual interest rate, compounded once per year.

a. The equation $V(t) = 3000(1.049)^t$ gives the value $V(t)$, in dollars, of the CD after t years. What do the parameters 3000 and 1.049 represent?

b. What is the value of the CD after 5 years?

3. Arnold is eligible for a raise at his job, and he can choose one of two options, as described below. Once he chooses an option, he must stay with that option for the rest of the time he is at his job. He is currently making $40,000 per year.

Option 1: a pay increase of $2,500 per year

Option 2: a 6% pay increase per year

a. Write an equation to represent Arnold's pay each year under option 1

b. Write an equation to represent Arnold's pay each year under option 2.

c. If Arnold plans to be at his job for 4 more years, which option is a better choice? Explain your reasoning.

4. Nancy buys a new SUV for $39,000. Each year, the SUV will depreciate in value by about 7%. After 4 years, Nancy wants to sell or trade the SUV. She is told that if she had initially purchased options costing $5000, the SUV would have depreciated at $\frac{3}{4}$ the rate that it did. What is the value of the SUV after 4 years, with and without the options? How much money could Nancy have saved overall if she chose the options when she bought the SUV? Show your work.

Name _______________ Class _______________ Date _______________

MULTIPLE CHOICE

1. The table shows the number of people who have participated in an annual conference since it began in 2007.

Years since 2007, *n*	1	2	3
Participants, *p(n)*	12	36	108

Which function represents this situation?

A. $p(n) = \frac{1}{3}(4)^n$

B. $p(n) = 4(3)^n$

C. $p(n) = 4\left(\frac{1}{3}\right)^n$

D. $p(n) = 3(4)^n$

2. Amber buys a car for $17,500. The car depreciates (loses value) 8% each year. Which function shows *y*, the value of the car (in dollars) in *t* years?

F. $y = 17{,}500(0.08)^t$

G. $y = 17{,}500(0.8)^t$

H. $y = 17{,}500(0.92)^t$

J. $y = 17{,}500(1.08)^t$

3. Which statement is **NOT** true about the functions $f(x) = 1.2(1.05)^x$ and $g(x) = 1.2(1.07)^x$?

A. As *x* increases without bound, $f(x)$ and $g(x)$ both increase without bound.

B. As *x* increases to the right of 0, the value of $g(x)$ is greater than the value of $f(x)$ for every value of *x*.

C. The *y*-intercept of $g(x)$ is greater than the *y*-intercept of $f(x)$.

D. The *y*-intercept of $g(x)$ is equal to the *y*-intercept of $f(x)$.

4. Solve the equation $2\left(\frac{2}{3}\right)^x = \frac{8}{9}$.

F. $x = 1$

G. $x = 2$

H. $x = 3$

J. $x = 4$

5. An online music sharing club has 5,060 members. The membership is increasing at a rate of 2% per month. In approximately how many months will the membership reach 10,000?

A. 3.7 months

B. 34.4 months

C. 48.8 months

D. 98.8 months

6. The table shows attendance at games for a sports team from 2005 to 2009.

Years since 2005, *x*	**Attendance, *y***
0	320,143
1	300,656
2	283,752
3	265,700
4	250,978

Kion performs an exponential regression to find a model for the data set. Then he makes a scatter plot of the residuals. What is the approximate residual for 2008?

F. −720

G. −357

H. 184

J. 334

7. Which of the following can be represented by an exponential function?

   A. Ben deposits $20 in a savings account. Then he deposits $2 each month for the next 6 months.

   B. Leslie deposits $20 in a savings account. Then she makes a deposit each month for the next 6 months, putting in $2 more with each deposit.

   C. Dan runs a mile in 9 minutes. Then he runs a mile each day for the next 4 days, reducing his time by 6 seconds each day.

   D. Rick runs a mile in 8 minutes. Then he runs a mile each day for the next 4 days, reducing his time by 1.5% each day.

8. Keenville and Westbrook each have 1500 residents. The population of Keenville increases by 3% every year. The population of Westbrook increases by 80 residents every year. How long will it take for the population of Keenville to exceed the population of Westbrook?

   F. 1.1 years

   G. 1.8 years

   H. 36.7 years

   J. 45 years

9. Mr. Turner bought stock for $15,000. If the value of the stock decreases 4% each year, when will it be worth 80% of the original purchase price?

   A. in 5.5 years

   B. in 7.5 years

   C. in 20 years

   D. in 39 years

CONSTRUCTED RESPONSE

10. The table shows the number of phone calls made per day (in millions) in years since 1940.

Years, x	0	10	20	30	40
calls, y	98.8	171	288	494	853

   a. Fit a function to the data using four significant digits. Tell whether it is exponential or linear.

   ____

   b. Graph the function below. Label the axes.

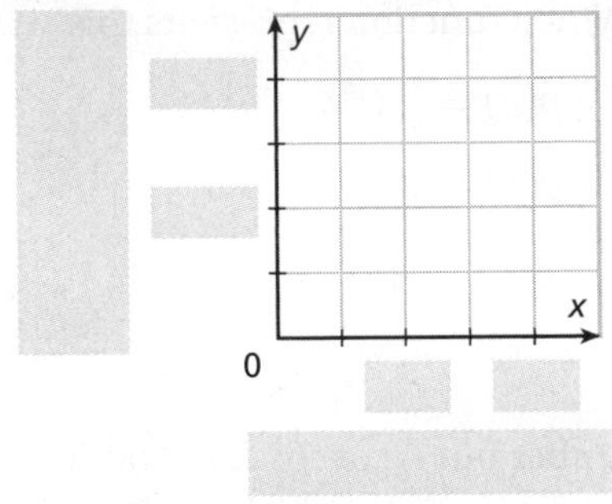

   c. Identify what the y-intercept represents.

   ____

   d. Use a graphing calculator to make a residual plot. Does the model fit the data well? Explain.

   ____

   ____

   ____

   ____

   e. Predict the calls per day in 1975 and in 1995. Which is more likely to be accurate? Explain.

   ____

   ____

   ____

   ____

CHAPTER 10

Data Analysis and Probability

Chapter Focus

In this chapter you will learn how to organize and analyze categorical data by using relative frequencies. You will analyze numerical data by calculating statistics that locate the center and measure the spread of the data. Then you will see how displaying numerical data in various ways helps you make sense of it, especially when the amount of data is substantial. You will also learn about probability of events, and distinguish between dependent and independent events in order to calculate their probabilities.

Chapter at a Glance

COMMON CORE

Lesson		Standards for Mathematical Content
10-1	Organizing and Displaying Data	CC.9-12.S.ID.5
10-2	Frequency and Histograms	CC.9-12.S.ID.1, CC.9-12.S.ID.2
10-3	Data Distributions	CC.9-12.S.ID.1, CC.9-12.S.ID.2
10-4	Misleading Graphs and Statistics	CC.9-12.S.ID.1, CC.9-12.S.ID.2, CC.9-12.S.ID.3
10-5	Experimental Probability	CC.9-12.S.CP.1
10-6	Theoretical Probability	CC.9-12.S.CP.1
10-7	Independent and Dependent Events	CC.9-12.S.CP.2, CC.9-12.S.CP.3, CC.9-12.S.CP.8(+)
	Performance Tasks	
	Assessment Readiness	

CHAPTER 10

Unpacking the Standards

Understanding the standards and the vocabulary terms in the standards will help you know exactly what you are expected to learn in this chapter.

COMMON CORE **CC.9-12.S.ID.1**

Represent data with plots on the real number line (dot plots, histograms, and box plots).

Key Vocabulary

histogram *(histograma)* A bar graph used to display data grouped in intervals.

box-and-whisker plot *(gráfica de mediana y rango)* A method of showing how data are distributed by using the median, quartiles, and minimum and maximum values; also called a box plot.

CHAPTER 10

What It Means For You — Lessons 10-2, 10-3, 10-4

Displaying numerical data on the real number line gives you an instant visual image of how the data are distributed, and helps you draw conclusions about the center and spread of the data.

EXAMPLE **Histogram**

A histogram gives you an overall picture of how data are distributed, but does not indicate any particular values or statistics.

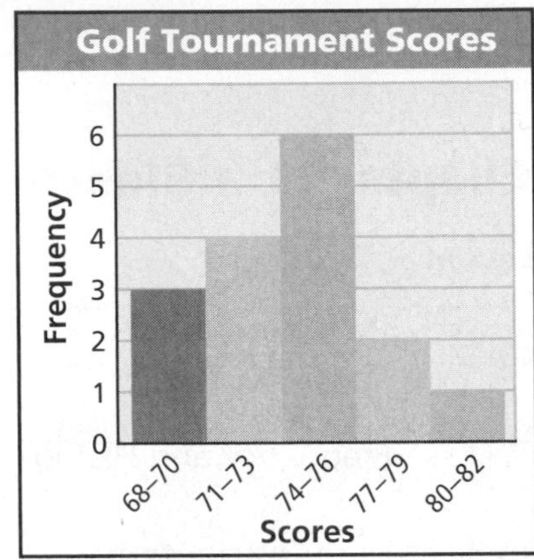

EXAMPLE **Box-and-whisker plot**

A box-and-whisker plot includes five statistical values.

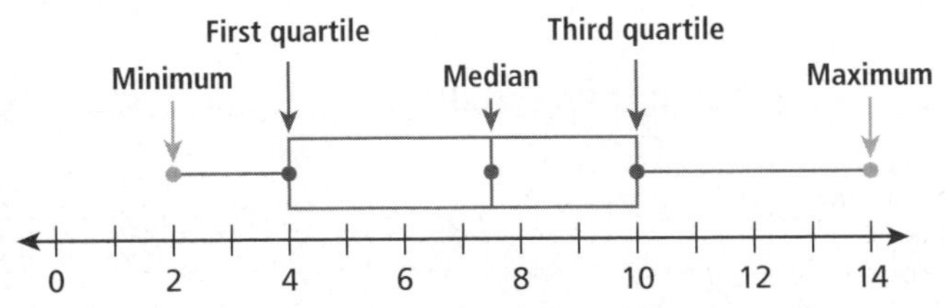

COMMON CORE **CC.9-12.S.ID.3**

Interpret differences in shape, center, and spread in the context of the data sets, accounting for possible effects of extreme data points (outliers).

Key Vocabulary

outlier *(valor extremo)* A data value that is far removed from the rest of the data.

What It Means For You — Lesson 10-4

Always examine the displays and statistics for a data set in its own particular context so that you can draw valid conclusions.

EXAMPLE **Outliers**

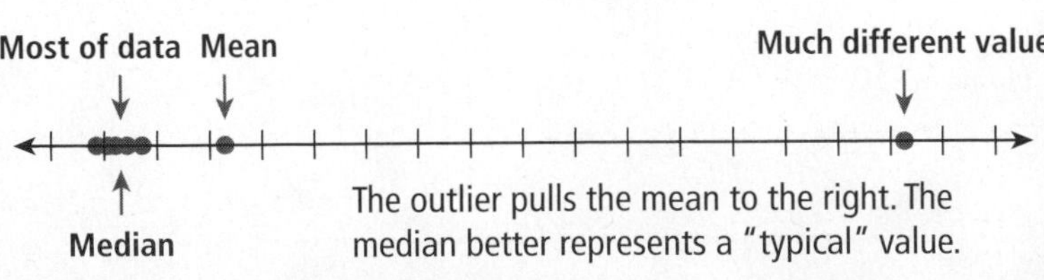

COMMON CORE **CC.9-12.S.ID.5**

Summarize categorical data for two categories in two-way frequency tables. Interpret relative frequencies in the context of the data (including joint, marginal, and conditional relative frequencies). Recognize possible associations and trends in the data.

Key Vocabulary

frequency table *(tabla de frequencia)* A table that lists the number of times, or frequency, that each data value occurs.

joint relative frequency *(frecuencia relativa conjunta)* The ratio of the frequency in a particular category divided by the total number of data values.

marginal relative frequency *(frecuencia relativa marginal)* The sum of the joint relative frequencies in a row or column of a two-way table.

conditional relative frequency *(frecuencia relativa condicional)* The ratio of a joint relative frequency to a related marginal relative frequency in a two-way table.

What It Means For You — Lesson 10-1

Two-way frequency tables give you a visual way to organize data categorized by two different variables so that you can more easily identify relationships.

EXAMPLE **A two-way relative frequency table**

The table shows the portions of households in a study that own a dog, a cat, both, or neither.

Joint relative frequencies

Owns a dog \ Owns a cat	Yes	No	Total
Yes	0.15	0.24	0.39
No	0.18	0.43	0.61
Total	0.33	0.67	1

Marginal relative frequencies

Here are a few conclusions you can draw from the table:

- 39% own a dog, and 33% own a cat.
- 15% own a dog and a cat, and 43% own neither.
- Of dog owners, $\frac{15}{39}\% \approx 38\%$ also own a cat.
- Of cat owners, $\frac{15}{33}\% \approx 45\%$ also own a dog.

CHAPTER 10

COMMON CORE **CC.9-12.S.CP.2**

Understand that two events *A* and *B* are independent if the probability of *A* and *B* occurring together is the product of their probabilities, and use this characterization to determine if they are independent.

Key Vocabulary

independent events *(sucesos independientes))* Events for which the occurrence or non-occurrence of one event does not affect the probability of the other event.

probability *(probabilidad)* A number from 0 to 1 (or 0% to 100%) that is the measure of how likely an event is to occur.

What It Means For You — Lessons 10-6, 10-7

Two events are independent if the occurrence of one event does not affect the occurrence of the other. When two events *A* and *B* are independent, the probability of both events occurring together is $P(A \text{ and } B) = P(A) \cdot P(B)$.

EXAMPLE **Independent Events**

You choose a marble without looking and put it back. Then you choose a second marble..

$P(\text{blue and then black}) = \frac{1}{2} \cdot \frac{1}{2} = \frac{1}{4}$

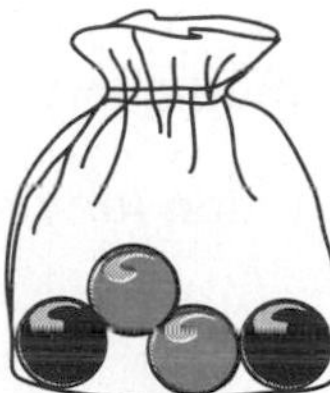

NON-EXAMPLE **Dependent Events**

You choose a marble without looking and don't put it back. Then you choose a second marble.

$P(\text{blue and then black}) = \frac{1}{2} \cdot \frac{2}{3} = \frac{1}{3}$

Key Vocabulary

box-and-whisker plot *(gráfica de mediana y rango)* A method of showing how data are distributed by using the median, quartiles, and minimum and maximum values; also called a box plot.

complement of an event *(complemento de un suceso)* All outcomes in the sample space that are not in an event E, denoted $\overline{E}$.

conditional probability *(probabilidad condicional)* The probability of event B, given that event A has already occurred or is certain to occur, denoted $P(B \mid A)$; used to find probability of dependent events.

dependent events *(sucesos dependientes)* Events for which the occurrence or nonoccurrence of one event affects the probability of the other event.

first quartile *(primer cuartil)* The median of the lower half of a data set, denoted Q_1. Also called *lower quartile.*

histogram *(histograma)* A bar graph used to display data grouped in intervals

independent events *(sucesos independientes)* Events for which the occurrence or non-occurrence of one event does not affect the probability of the other event.

interquartile range (IQR) *(rango entre cuartiles)* The difference of the third (upper) and first (lower) quartiles in a data set, representing the middle half of the data.

intersection *(intersección de conjuntos)* The intersection of two sets is the set of all elements that are common to both sets, denoted by $\cap$.

mean *(media)* The sum of all the values in a data set divided by the number of data values. Also called the *average.*

median *(mediana)* For an ordered data set with an odd number of values, the median is the middle value. For an ordered data set with an even number of values, the median is the average of the two middle values.

outlier *(valor extremo)* A data value that is far removed from the rest of the data.

probability *(probabilidad)* A number from 0 to 1 (or 0% to 100%) that is the measure of how likely an event is to occur.

range of a data set *(rango de un conjunto de datos)* The difference of the greatest and least values in the data set.

standard deviation *(desviación estándar)* A measure of dispersion of a data set. The standard deviation σ is the square root of the variance.

third quartile *(tercer cuartil)* The median of the upper half of a data set. Also called *upper quartile.*

union *(unión)* The union of two sets is the set of all elements that are in either set, denoted by $\cup$.

CHAPTER 10

Name ________________ Class ________ Date ______

10-1

Video Tutor

Organizing and Displaying Data
Extension: Two-Way Frequency Tables

Essential question: *How can categorical data be organized and analyzed?*

In previous lessons, you worked with numerical data involving variables such as age and height. In this lesson, you will analyze *categorical* data that involve variables such as pet preference and gender. The **frequency** of a data value is the number of times it occurs. A **frequency table** shows the frequency of each data value.

CC.9–12.S.ID.5

1 EXAMPLE Creating a Relative Frequency Table

The frequency table below shows the results of a survey that Jenna took at her school. She asked 40 randomly selected students whether they preferred dogs, cats, or other pets. Convert this table to a *relative frequency* table that uses decimals as well as one that uses percents.

Preferred Pet	Dog	Cat	Other	Total
Frequency	18	12	10	40

A Divide the numbers in the frequency table by the total to obtain relative frequencies as decimals. Record the results in the table below.

Preferred Pet	Dog	Cat	Other	Total
Relative Frequency	$\frac{18}{40} = 0.45$			

B Write the decimals as percents in the table below.

Preferred Pet	Dog	Cat	Other	Total
Relative Frequency	45%			

REFLECT

1a. How can you check that you have correctly converted frequencies to relative frequencies?

____

____

1b. Explain why the number in the Total column of a relative frequency table is always 1 or 100%.

____

____

In the previous example, the categorical variable was pet preference, and the variable had three possible data values: dog, cat, and other. The frequency table listed the frequency for each value of that single variable. If you have two categorical variables whose values have been paired, you list the frequencies of the paired values in a **two-way frequency table**.

CC.9–12.S.ID.5

2 EXAMPLE Creating a Two-Way Frequency Table

For her survey, Jenna also recorded the gender of each student. The results are shown in the two-way frequency table below. Each entry is the frequency of students who prefer a certain pet *and* are a certain gender. For instance, 8 girls prefer dogs as pets. Complete the table.

Gender \ Preferred Pet	Dog	Cat	Other	Total
Girl	8	7	1	
Boy	10	5	9	
Total				

A Find the total for each gender by adding the frequencies in each row. Write the row totals in the Total column.

B Find the total for each preferred pet by adding the frequencies in each column. Write the column totals in the Total row.

C Find the grand total, which is the sum of the row totals as well as the sum of the column totals. Write the grand total in the lower-right corner of the table (the intersection of the Total column and the Total row).

REFLECT

2a. Where have you seen the numbers in the Total row before?

____

2b. In terms of Jenna's survey, what does the grand total represent?

____

You can obtain the following *relative* frequencies from a two-way frequency table:

- A **joint relative frequency** is found by dividing a frequency that is not in the Total row or the Total column by the grand total.
- A **marginal relative frequency** is found by dividing a row total or a column total by the grand total.

A **two-way relative frequency table** displays both joint relative frequencies and marginal relative frequencies.

CC.9–12.S.ID.5

3 EXAMPLE Creating a Two-Way Relative Frequency Table

Create a two-way relative frequency table for Jenna's data.

A Divide each number in the two-way frequency table from the previous example by the grand total. Write the quotients as decimals.

Preferred Pet / Gender	Dog	Cat	Other	Total
Girl	$\frac{8}{40} = 0.2$			
Boy				
Total	$\frac{18}{40} = 0.45$			$\frac{40}{40} = 1$

B Check by adding the joint relative frequencies in a row or column to see if the sum equals the row or column's marginal relative frequency.

Girl row: $0.2 + \_\_\_ + \_\_\_ = \_\_\_$

Boy row: $\_\_\_ + \_\_\_ + \_\_\_ = \_\_\_$

Dog column: $0.2 + \_\_\_ = 0.45$

Cat column: $\_\_\_ + \_\_\_ = \_\_\_$

Other column: $\_\_\_ + \_\_\_ = \_\_\_$

REFLECT

3a. A joint relative frequency in a two-way relative frequency table tells you what portion of the entire data set falls into the intersection of a particular value of one variable and a particular value of the other variable. For instance, the joint relative frequency of students surveyed who are girls *and* prefer dogs as pets is 0.2, or 20%. What is the joint relative frequency of students surveyed who are boys and prefer cats as pets?

____

3b. A marginal relative frequency in a two-way relative frequency table tells you what portion of the entire data set represents a particular value of just one of the variables. For instance, the marginal relative frequency of students surveyed who prefer dogs as pets is 0.45, or 45%. What is the marginal relative frequency of students surveyed who are girls?

____

One other type of relative frequency that you can obtain from a two-way frequency table is a *conditional relative frequency*. A **conditional relative frequency** is found by dividing a frequency that is not in the Total row or the Total column by the frequency's row total or column total.

CC.9–12.S.ID.5

4 EXAMPLE Calculating Conditional Relative Frequencies

From Jenna's two-way frequency table you know that 16 students surveyed are girls and 12 students surveyed prefer cats as pets. You also know that 7 students surveyed are girls who prefer cats as pets. Use this information to find each conditional relative frequency.

A Find the conditional relative frequency that a student surveyed prefers cats as pets, given that the student is a girl.

Divide the number of girls who prefer cats as pets by the number of girls. Express your answer as a decimal and as a percent.

____

B Find the conditional relative frequency that a student surveyed is a girl, given that the student prefers cats as pets.

Divide the number of girls who prefer cats as pets by the number of students who prefer cats as pets. Express your answer as a decimal and as a percent.

____

REFLECT

4a. When calculating a conditional relative frequency, why do you divide by a row total or a column total and not by the grand total?

____

____

____

____

4b. You can obtain conditional relative frequencies from a two-way *relative* frequency table. For instance, in Jenna's survey, the relative frequency of girls who prefer cats as pets is 0.175, and the relative frequency of girls is 0.4. Find the conditional relative frequency that a student surveyed prefers cats as pets, given that the student is a girl.

____

CC.9–12.S.ID.5

5 EXAMPLE Finding Possible Associations Between Variables

Jenna conducted her survey because she was interested in the question, "Does gender influence what type of pet people prefer?" If there is no influence, then the distribution of gender within each subgroup of pet preference should roughly equal the distribution of gender within the whole group. Use the results of Jenna's survey to investigate possible influences of gender on pet preference.

A Identify the percent of all students surveyed who are girls: __________

B Determine each conditional relative frequency.

Of the 18 students who prefer dogs as pets, 8 are girls.
Percent who are girls, given a preference for dogs as pets: __________

Of the 12 students who prefer cats as pets, 7 are girls.
Percent who are girls, given a preference for cats as pets: __________

Of the 10 students who prefer other pets, 1 is a girl.
Percent who are girls, given a preference for other pets: __________

C Interpret the results by comparing each conditional relative frequency to the percent of all students surveyed who are girls.

The percent of girls among students who prefer dogs is fairly close to 40%, so gender does not appear to influence preference for dogs.

The percent of girls among students who prefer cats is much greater than 40%. What conclusion might you draw in this case?

____

The percent of girls among students who prefer other pets is much less than 40%. What conclusion might you draw in this case?

____

REFLECT

5a. Suppose you analyzed the data by focusing on boys rather than girls. How would the percent in Part A change? How would the percents in Part B change? How would the conclusions in Part C change?

____

____

5b. For pet preference to be completely uninfluenced by gender, about how many girls would have to prefer each type of pet? Explain.

____

____

PRACTICE

Antonio surveyed 60 of his classmates about their participation in school activities as well as whether they have a part-time job. The results are shown in the two-way frequency table below. Use the table to complete the exercises.

1. Complete the table by finding the row totals, column totals, and grand total.

Job \ Activity	Clubs Only	Sports Only	Both	Neither	Total
Yes	12	13	16	4	
No	3	5	5	2	
Total					

2. Create a two-way relative frequency table using decimals.

Job \ Activity	Clubs Only	Sports Only	Both	Neither	Total
Yes					
No					
Total					

3. Give each relative frequency as a percent.

a. The joint relative frequency of students surveyed who participate in school clubs only and have part-time jobs: ___________

b. The marginal relative frequency of students surveyed who do not have a part-time job: ___________

c. The conditional relative frequency that a student surveyed participates in both school clubs and sports, given that the student has a part-time job: _______________

4. Discuss possible influences of having a part-time job on participation in school activities. Support your response with an analysis of the data.

____

____

____

Name ____________________ Class ______________ Date __________

10-1

Additional Practice

The owner of an ice cream shop conducted a survey regarding customers' favorite flavors. The owner asked 80 randomly selected customers whether they preferred vanilla, chocolate, or strawberry. The results are shown in the frequency table below.

Flavor	Vanilla	Chocolate	Strawberry	Total
Frequency	22	34	24	80

1. Convert this table to a relative frequency table that uses decimals.

Flavor	Vanilla	Chocolate	Strawberry	Total
Relative Frequency				

2. Convert this table to a relative frequency table that uses percents.

Flavor	Vanillla	Chocolate	Strawberry	Total
Relative Frequency				

3. The owner also recorded the gender of each customer. The results are shown in the two-way frequency table below. Complete the table.

Gender/ Flavor	Vanilla	Chocolate	Strawberry	Total
Male	10	20	16	
Female	12	14	8	
Total				

4. Create a two-way relative frequency table for the data in Exercise 3.

Gender/ Flavor	Vanilla	Chocolate	Strawberry	Total
Male				
Female				
Total				

Problem Solving

A mobile phone company conducted a survey regarding how people communicate with their friends. The company asked 200 randomly selected customers whether they preferred texting, talking, or emailing. The results are shown in the frequency table below.

Communication	**Text**	**Talk**	**Email**	**Total**
Frequency	116	54	30	200

1. Convert this table to a relative frequency table that uses decimals.

Communication	**Text**	**Talk**	**Email**	**Total**
Relative Frequency				

2. The company also recorded the gender of each customer. The results are shown in the two-way frequency table below. Complete the table.

Gender/ Communication	**Text**	**Talk**	**Email**	**Total**
Male	75	36	14	
Female	41	18	16	
Total				

3. Create a two-way relative frequency table for the data in Problem 2.

Gender/ Communication	**Text**	**Talk**	**Email**	**Total**
Male				
Female				
Total				

Select the best answer.

4. Find the conditional relative frequency that a person surveyed prefers talking, given that the person is male.

A 0.6

B 0.112

C 0.288

D 0.24

5. Find the conditional relative frequency that a person surveyed is female, given that the person prefers texting.

F $\frac{1}{3}$

G $\frac{8}{15}$

H $\frac{75}{116}$

J $\frac{41}{116}$

Name ________________________ Class ______________ Date ________

10-2

Video Tutor

Frequency and Histograms
Going Deeper

Essential question: *How can you estimate statistics from data displayed in a histogram?*

Like a line plot, a histogram uses a number line to display data. Rather than display the data values individually as a line plot does, a histogram groups the data values into adjoining intervals of equal width and uses the heights of bars to indicate the number of data values that occur in each interval.

The number of data values in an interval is called the *frequency* of the interval. A histogram has a vertical frequency axis so that you can read the frequency for each interval. In the histogram at the right, you can see that 3 students had test scores in the interval 60–69, 9 students had test scores in the interval 70–79, and so on.

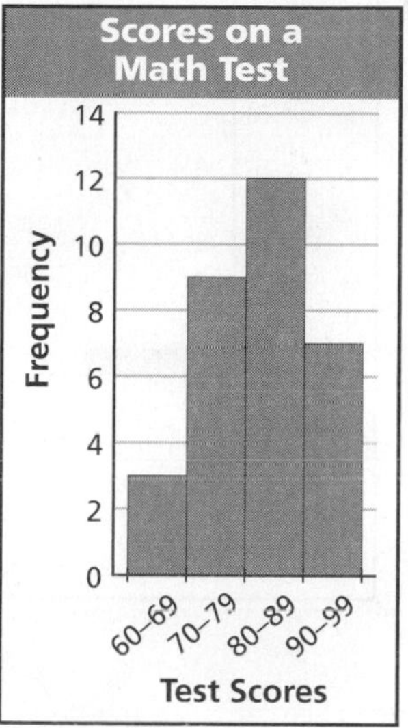

CC.9–12.S.ID.1

1 EXAMPLE Creating a Histogram

Listed below are the ages of the 100 U.S. senators at the time that the 112th Congress began on January 3, 2011. Create a histogram for this data set.

39, 39, 42, 44, 46, 47, 47, 47, 48, 49, 49, 49, 50, 50, 51, 51, 52, 52, 53, 53, 54, 54, 55, 55, 55, 55, 55, 55, 56, 56, 57, 57, 57, 58, 58, 58, 58, 58, 59, 59, 59, 59, 60, 60, 60, 60, 60, 60, 60, 61, 61, 62, 62, 62, 63, 63, 63, 63, 64, 64, 64, 64, 66, 66, 66, 67, 67, 67, 67, 67, 67, 67, 68, 68, 68, 68, 69, 69, 69, 70, 70, 70, 71, 71, 73, 73, 74, 74, 74, 75, 76, 76, 76, 76, 77, 77, 78, 86, 86, 86

A Create a frequency table. To do so, you must decide what the interval width will be and where to start the first interval. Since the data are ages that run from 39 to 86, you might decide to use an interval width of 10 and start the first interval at 30. So, the first interval includes any Senator who is in his or her 30s.

Use the data to complete the table at the right. When done, be sure to check that the sum of the frequencies is 100.

Age Interval	Frequency
30–39	2

B Use the frequency table to complete the histogram.

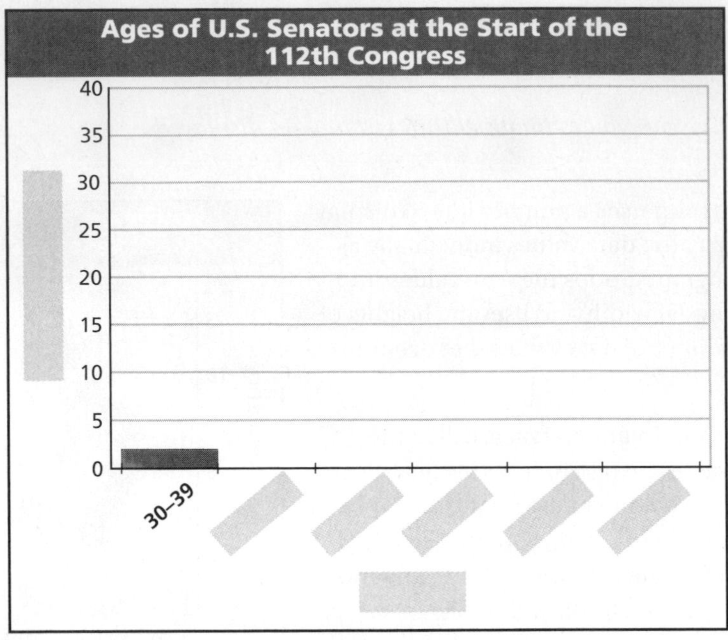

REFLECT

1a. Describe the shape of the distribution. Is it approximately symmetric, or does it have more data points to the right or to the left of its center? Explain.

1b. Estimate the center of the distribution. Explain your reasoning.

1c. Using the histogram alone, and not the data values on the first page of this lesson, estimate the maximum possible range and the minimum possible range. Explain your reasoning.

CC.9–12.S.ID.2

2 EXAMPLE Estimating Statistics from a Histogram

Although the first page of this lesson listed the ages all 100 senators, suppose you have only the histogram on the second page as a reference. Show how to estimate the mean and the median ages from the histogram.

A Estimate the mean. You know the frequency of each interval, but you don't know the individual data values. Use the midpoint of the interval as a substitute for each of those values. So, for the interval 30–39, you can estimate the sum of the data values by multiplying the midpoint, 35, by the frequency, 2. Complete the calculation below, rounding the final result to the nearest whole number.

$$\text{Mean} \approx \frac{35 \cdot 2 + \_\_ \cdot \_\_ + \_\_ \cdot \_\_ + \_\_ \cdot \_\_ + \_\_ \cdot \_\_ + \_\_ \cdot \_\_}{\_\_}$$

$$= \frac{\_\_}{\_\_} \approx \_\_$$

B Estimate the median. The median is the average of the 50th and 51st data values. In what interval do these values fall? Explain.

____

____

The median is the average of the 8th and 9th values in an interval with 37 values, so you can estimate that the median is the sum of the interval's least value and $\frac{8.5}{37} \approx 20\%$ of the interval width, 10. So, what is the estimate?

____

REFLECT

2a. How do the estimates of the mean and median support the observation that the distribution is approximately symmetric?

____

____

____

2b. Is it possible to estimate the mode from the histogram? If so, give the mode. If not, explain why not.

____

____

____

____

____

PRACTICE

The ages of the first 44 U.S. presidents on the date of their first inauguration are listed below.

42, 43, 46, 46, 47, 47, 48, 49, 49, 50, 51, 51, 51, 51, 51, 52, 52, 54, 54, 54, 54, 54, 55, 55, 55, 55, 56, 56, 56, 57, 57, 57, 57, 58, 60, 61, 61, 61, 62, 64, 64, 65, 68, 69

1. Complete the frequency table by organizing the data into six equal intervals.

Age Interval	Frequency
41–45	2

2. Use the frequency table to complete the histogram.

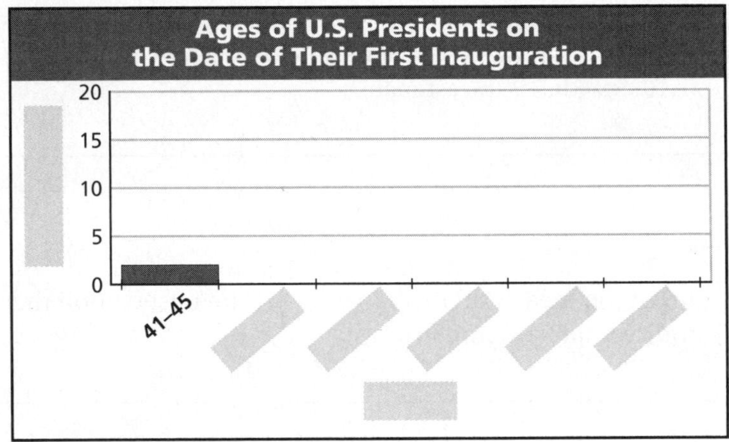

3. Describe the shape of the distribution. What measures of center would you use to characterize the data? Why?

____

____

4. Use the histogram to estimate the median.

____

Name ______________________ Class ______________ Date ____________

10-2

Additional Practice

1. The heights, in centimeters, of various plants two weeks after planting are given below. Use the data to make a frequency table with intervals.

Plant Height (cm)						
12	24	23	33	38	41	33
35	37	35	39	48	41	50

Plant Height	
Height in cm	Frequency

2. Use the frequency table in Exercise 1 to make a histogram.

Plant Height

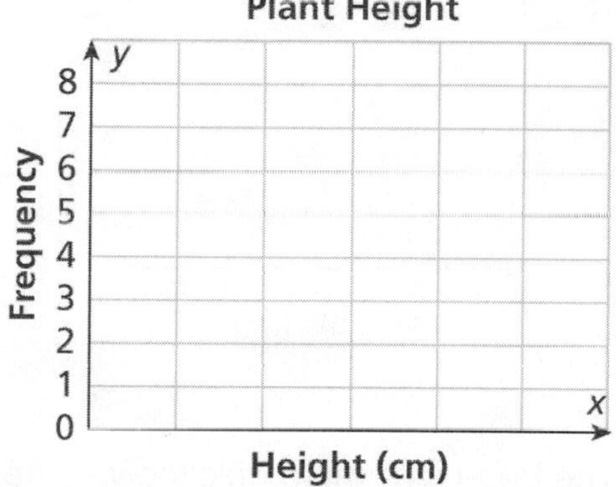

3. The number of calls per day received by a traveling Vet Van service for three weeks is given below. Use the data to make a frequency table with intervals.

Number of Calls						
18	22	13	15	16	21	22
26	17	14	12	13	18	14
16	22	23	20	21	18	22

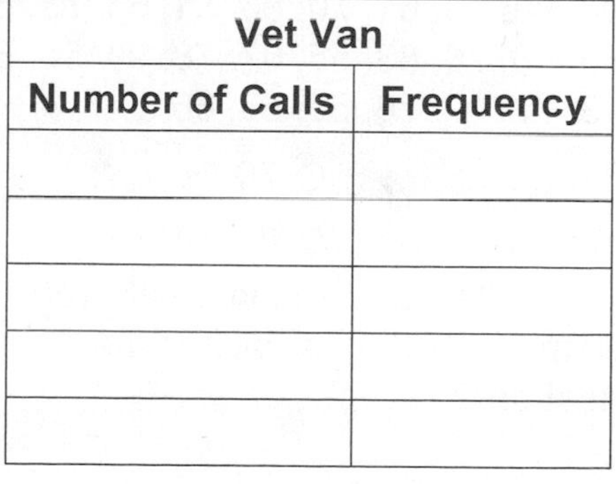

Vet Van	
Number of Calls	Frequency

4. Use the frequency table in Exercise 3 to make a histogram.

Vet Van

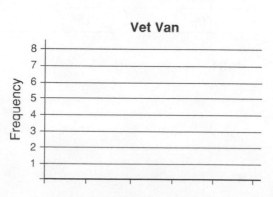

Frequency: 8, 7, 6, 5, 4, 3, 2, 1

Number of Calls

Problem Solving

The heights in inches of the 2005 NBA All-Star Game players are given below.

Players' Heights (in.)											
75	78	80	87	72	80	81	83	85	78	76	81
77	78	83	83	78	82	79	80	75	84	82	90

1. Use the data to make a frequency table with intervals. Use an interval of 5.

Players' Heights	
Heights (in.)	**Frequency**

2. Use your frequency table to make a histogram for the data.

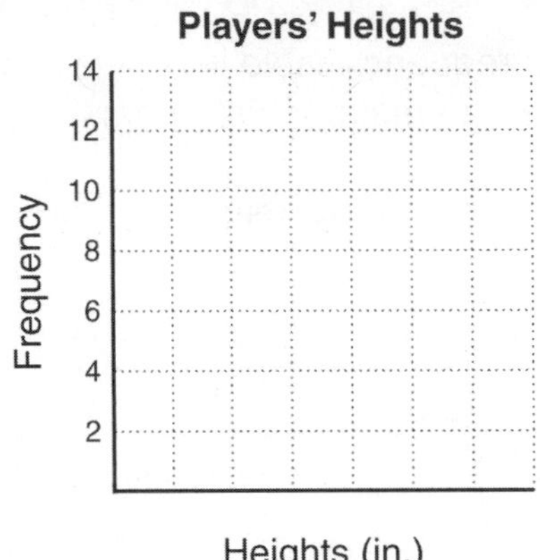

Select the best answer.

3. The file sizes, in megabytes, of 30 songs on an MP3 player are given below. If you create a histogram using intervals of 50-59, 60-69, 70-79, 80-89, and 90-99, which interval has the greatest bar?

   50, 99, 98, 58, 61, 70, 86, 51, 65, 73, 81, 97, 50, 66, 76, 83, 55, 67, 78, 90, 54, 52, 63, 73, 77, 92, 76, 55, 60, 66

   A 50-59   C 70-79
   B 60-69   D 80-89

4. Using the file sizes and intervals from Problem 3, which interval has the shortest bar?

   F 50-59   H 70-79
   G 60-69   J 80-89

5. The frequency table below gives the scores of 100 students on a standardized mathematics test. How many students scored below 600?

Standardized Test Scores	
Scores	**Cumulative Frequency**
200–299	1
300–399	2
400–499	16
500–599	31
600–699	35
700–799	15

   A 31   C 35
   B 50   D 599

Name ____________ Class ________ Date ________

10-3

Data Distributions

Going Deeper

Video Tutor

Essential question: *How can you characterize and compare the center and spread of data sets?*

Two commonly used measures of the center of a set of numerical data are the *mean* and *median*. Let n be the number of data values. The **mean** is the sum of the data values divided by n. When the data values are ordered from least to greatest, the **median** is either the middle value if n is odd or the average of the two middle values if n is even. The median divides the data set into two halves. The **first quartile** (Q_1) of a data set is the median of the lower half of the data. The **third quartile** (Q_3) is the median of the upper half.

Two commonly used measures of the spread of a set of numerical data are the *range* and *interquartile range*. The **range** is the difference between the greatest data value and the least data value. The **interquartile range** (IQR) is the difference between the third quartile and first quartile: $IQR = Q_3 - Q_1$.

CC.9–12.S.ID.2

1 EXAMPLE Finding Mean, Median, Range, and Interquartile Range

The April high temperatures (in degrees Fahrenheit) for five consecutive years in Boston are listed below. Find the mean, median, range, and interquartile range for this data set.

77 86 84 93 90

A Find the mean.

$$\text{Mean} = \frac{77 + 86 + 84 + 93 + 90}{\square} = \frac{\square}{\square} = \square$$

B Find the median.

Write the data values from least to greatest: ____________

Identify the middle value: ________

C Find the range.

$$\text{Range} = 93 - \square = \square$$

D Find the interquartile range.

Find the first and third quartiles. Do not include the median as part of either the lower half or the upper half of the data.

$$Q_1 = \frac{\square + \square}{2} = \square \text{ and } Q_3 = \frac{\square + \square}{2} = \square$$

Find the difference between Q_3 and Q_1: $IQR = \square - \square = \square$

REFLECT

1a. If 90°F is replaced with 92°F, will the median or mean change? Explain.

1b. Why is the IQR less than the range?

Standard Deviation Another measure of spread is **standard deviation**. It is found by squaring the deviations of the data values from the mean of the data values, then finding the mean of those squared deviations, and finally taking the square root of the mean of the squared deviations. The steps for calculating standard deviation are listed below.

1. Calculate the mean, $\bar{x}$.
2. Calculate each data value's deviation from the mean by finding $x - \bar{x}$ for each data value x.
3. Find $(x - \bar{x})^2$, the square of each deviation.
4. Find the mean of the squared deviations.
5. Take the square root of the mean of the squared deviations.

CC.9–12.S.ID.2

2 EXAMPLE Calculating the Standard Deviation

Calculate the standard deviation for the data from the previous example.

A Complete the table using the fact that the mean of the data is $\bar{x} = 86$.

Data value, x	Deviation from mean, $x - \bar{x}$	Squared deviation, $(x - \bar{x})^2$
77	$77 - 86 = -9$	$(-9)^2 = 81$
86		
84		
93		
90		

B Find the mean of the squared deviations.

$$\text{Mean} = \frac{81 + \square + \square + \square + \square}{\square} = \frac{\square}{\square} = \square$$

C Take the square root of the mean of the squared deviations. Use a calculator, and round to the nearest tenth.

Square root of mean $= \sqrt{\square} \approx \square$

REFLECT

2a. What is the mean of the deviations *before* squaring? Use your answer to explain why squaring the deviations is reasonable.

2b. In terms of the data values used, what makes calculating the standard deviation different from calculating the range?

2c. What must be true about a data set if the standard deviation is 0? Explain.

Numbers that characterize a data set, such as measures of center and spread, are called **statistics**. They are useful when comparing large sets of data.

CC.9–12.S.ID.2

3 EXAMPLE Comparing Statistics for Related Data Sets

The tables below list the average ages of players on 15 teams randomly selected from the 2010 teams in the National Football League (NFL) and Major League Baseball (MLB). Compare the average ages of NFL players to the average ages of MLB players.

NFL Players' Average Ages	
Team	**Average Age**
Bears	25.8
Bengals	26.0
Broncos	26.3
Chiefs	25.7
Colts	25.1
Eagles	25.2
Jets	26.1
Lions	26.4
Packers	25.9
Patriots	26.6
Saints	26.3
Seahawks	26.2
Steelers	26.8
Texans	25.6
Titans	25.7

MLB Players' Average Ages	
Team	**Average Age**
Astros	28.5
Cardinals	29.0
Cubs	28.0
Diamondbacks	27.8
Dodgers	29.5
Giants	29.1
Marlins	26.9
Mets	28.9
Nationals	28.6
Padres	28.7
Pirates	26.9
Phillies	30.5
Reds	28.7
Rockies	28.9
Yankees	29.3

A On a graphing calculator, enter the two sets of data into two lists, L_1 and L_2. Examine the data as you enter the values, and record your general impressions about how the data sets compare before calculating any statistics.

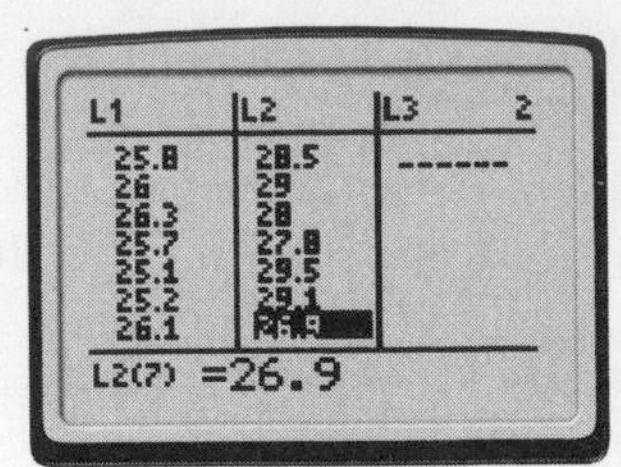

____

____

____

B Calculate the statistics for the NFL data in list L_1. Then do the same for the MLB data in L_2. Record the results in the table below. Your calculator may use the following notations and abbreviations for the statistics you're interested in.

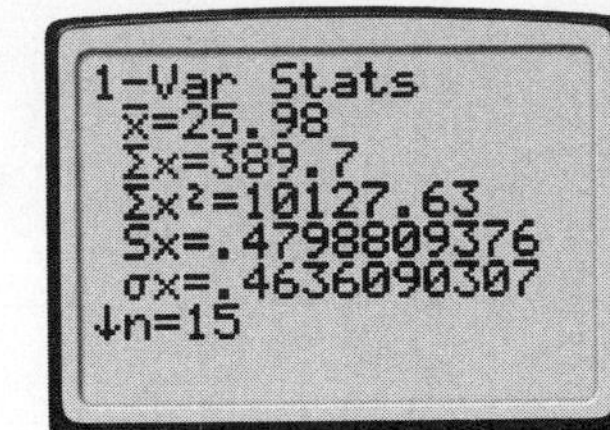

Mean: $\bar{x}$

Median: Med

IQR: May not be reported directly, but can be obtained by subtracting Q_1 from Q_3

Standard deviation: σx

	Center		Spread	
	Mean	**Median**	**IQR ($Q_3 - Q_1$)**	**Standard Deviation**
NFL				
MLB				

C Compare the corresponding statistics for the NFL data and the MLB data. Are your comparisons consistent for the two measures of center and the two measures of spread? Do your comparisons agree with your general impressions from Part A?

____

____

____

____

____

____

____

REFLECT

3a. Based on a comparison of the measures of center, what conclusion can you draw about the typical age of an NFL player and of an MLB player?

3b. Based on a comparison of the measures of spread, what conclusion can you draw about variation in the ages of NFL players and of MLB players?

3c. What do you notice about the mean and median for the NFL? For the MLB?

3d. What do you notice about the IQR and standard deviation for the NFL? For the MLB?

Sets of data can be graphed on a box plot. A box plot allows you to see the range, the minimum and maximum values, the median, and the first and third quartiles easily on a number line plot. A box plot also allows you to visually compare two sets of data, including *outliers*. An **outlier** is a value in a data set that is much greater or much less than the other values. A data value x is an outlier if $x < Q_1 - 1.5(\text{IQR})$ or $x > Q_3 + 1.5(\text{IQR})$.

CC.9–12.S.ID.1

4 EXAMPLE Interpreting a Box Plot

The table lists the total number of home runs hit at home games by each team in Major League Baseball (MLB) during the 2010 season. The data are displayed in the box plot below the table. Identify the statistics that are represented in the box plot, and describe the distribution of the data.

Home Runs in 2010 MLB Games Played at Home					
Team	**Home Runs**	**Team**	**Home Runs**	**Team**	**Home Runs**
Toronto	146	Tampa Bay	78	Cleveland	64
NY Yankees	115	San Francisco	75	Pittsburgh	64
Chicago Sox	111	Atlanta	74	Houston	63
Colorado	108	Chicago Cubs	74	NY Mets	63
Cincinnati	102	Washington	74	LA Dodgers	61
Milwaukee	100	Baltimore	72	Kansas City	60
Boston	98	Detroit	70	San Diego	59
Arizona	98	LA Angels	69	Minnesota	52
Philadelphia	94	Florida	69	Oakland	46
Texas	93	St. Louis	67	Seattle	35

Home Runs in 2010 MLB Games Played at Home

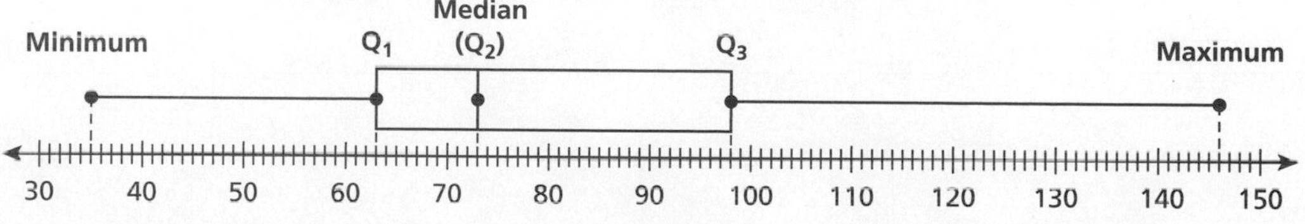

A A box plot displays a five-number summary of a data set. The five numbers are the statistics listed below. Use the box plot to determine each statistic.

Minimum	First Quartile	Median	Third Quartile	Maximum

B A box plot also shows the distribution of the data. Find the range of the lower half and the upper half of the data.

Range of lower half: ______ Range of upper half: ______

The data are more spread out in the upper half of the distribution than in the lower half.

REFLECT

4a. The lines that extend from the box in a box plot are sometimes called "whiskers." What *part* (lower, middle, or upper) and about what *percent* of the data does the box represent? What part and about what percent does each whisker represent?

4b. Which measures of spread can be determined from the box plot, and how are they found? Calculate each measure.

4c. In the table, the data value 146 appears to be much greater than the other data values. Determine whether 146 is an outlier.

4d. The mean of the data is about 78.5. Use the shape of the distribution to explain why the mean is greater than the median.

Comparing Data Using Box Plots

The table lists the total number of home runs hit at away games by each team in Major League Baseball (MLB) during the 2010 season. Display the data in a box plot.

Home Runs in 2010 MLB Games Played Away					
Team	**Home Runs**	**Team**	**Home Runs**	**Team**	**Home Runs**
Boston	**113**	Milwaukee	**82**	Atlanta	**65**
Toronto	**111**	Arizona	**82**	NY Mets	**65**
Minnesota	**90**	Tampa Bay	**82**	Colorado	**65**
San Francisco	**87**	Chicago Cubs	**75**	Cleveland	**64**
LA Angels	**86**	Washington	**75**	Oakland	**63**
NY Yankees	**86**	San Diego	**73**	Pittsburgh	**62**
Cincinnati	**86**	Philadelphia	**72**	Baltimore	**61**
St. Louis	**83**	Texas	**69**	Kansas City	**61**
Florida	**83**	Chicago Sox	**66**	LA Dodgers	**59**
Detroit	**82**	Seattle	**66**	Houston	**45**

A Find the values for the five-number summary.

Minimum	First Quartile	Median	Third Quartile	Maximum

B Determine whether the data set includes any outliers. Begin by finding the value of each expression below using the fact that the IQR $= Q_3 - Q_1 = 83 - 65 = 18$.

$Q_1 - 1.5(\text{IQR}) =$ ________ $\qquad Q_3 + 1.5(\text{IQR}) =$ ________

These values are sometimes called *fences* because they form the boundaries outside of which a data value is considered to be an outlier. Which data values, if any, are outliers for the away-game data? Why?

C The box plot shown below displays the number of home runs hit at home games during the 2010 MLB season. Draw a second box plot that displays the data for away games. The whiskers should extend only to the least and greatest data values that lie within the fences established in Part B. Show any outliers as individual dots.

Home Runs in 2010 MLB Games

Home games

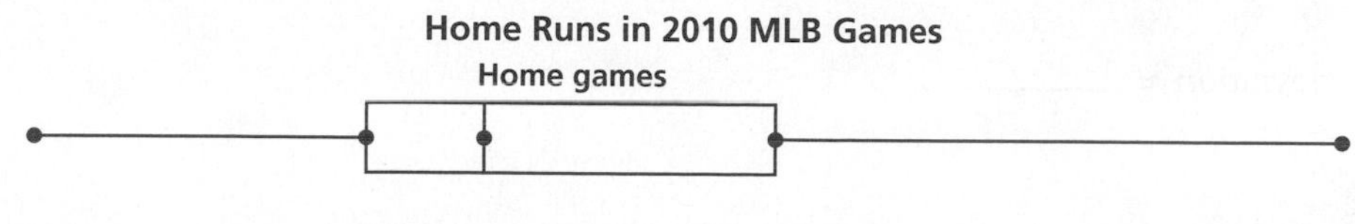

REFLECT

5a. Use the box plots to compare the center, spread, and shape of the two data distributions. Ignore any outliers.

____

____

____

____

PRACTICE

The numbers of students in each of a school's six Algebra 1 classes are listed below. Find each statistic for this data set.

28 30 29 26 31 30

1. Mean = ________

2. Median = ________

3. Range = ________

4. IQR = ________

5. Find the standard deviation of the Algebra 1 class data by completing the table and doing the calculations below it.

Data value, x	Deviation from mean, $x - \overline{x}$	Squared deviation, $(x - \overline{x})^2$
28		
30		
29		
26		
31		
30		

Mean of squared deviations = ________

Standard deviation ≈ ________

6. **Error Analysis** Suppose a student in the Algebra 1 class with 31 students transfers to the class with 26 students. The student claims that the measures of center and the measures of spread will all change. Correct the student's error.

7. The table lists the heights (in centimeters) of 8 males and 8 females on the U.S. Olympic swim team, all randomly selected from swimmers on the team who participated in the 2008 Olympic Games held in Beijing, China.

Heights of Olympic male swimmers	196	188	196	185	203	183	183	196
Heights of Olympic female swimmers	173	170	178	175	173	180	180	175

a. Use a graphing calculator to complete the table below.

	Center		**Spread**	
	Mean	**Median**	**IQR ($Q_3 - Q_1$)**	**Standard deviation**
Olympic male swimmers				
Olympic female swimmers				

b. Discuss the consistency of the measures of center for male swimmers and the measures of center for female swimmers, and then compare the measures of center for male and female swimmers.

c. What do the measures of spread tell you about the variation in the heights of the male and female swimmers?

8. The table shows the 2010 average salary for an MLB player by team for both the American League (AL) and the National League (NL).

MLB Players' Average 2010 Salaries (in Millions of Dollars)			
American League		**National League**	
Team	**Salary**	**Team**	**Salary**
New York	8.3	Chicago	5.4
Boston	5.6	Philadelphia	5.1
Detroit	4.6	New York	5.1
Chicago	4.2	St. Louis	3.7
Los Angeles	3.6	Los Angeles	3.7
Seattle	3.5	San Francisco	3.5
Minnesota	3.5	Houston	3.3
Baltimore	3.1	Atlanta	3.1
Tampa Bay	2.7	Colorado	2.9
Kansas City	2.5	Milwaukee	2.8
Cleveland	2.1	Cincinnati	2.8
Toronto	2.1	Arizona	2.3
Texas	1.9	Florida	2.1
Oakland	1.7	Washington	2.0
		San Diego	1.5
		Pittsburgh	1.3

a. Find the values for the five-number summary for each league.

	AL	NL
Min.		
Q_1		
Median		
Q_3		
Max.		

b. Complete the scale on the number line below. Then use the number line to create two box plots, one for each league. Show any outliers as individual dots.

MLB Player's Average 2010 Salaries (in Millions of Dollars)

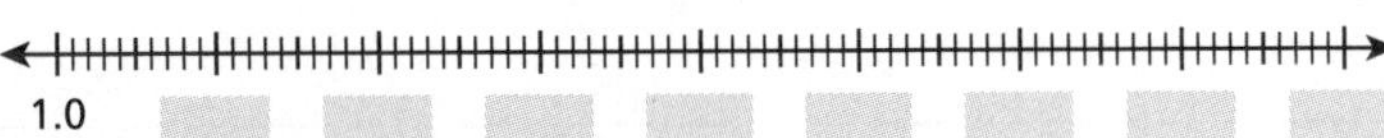

c. Compare the center, spread, and shape of the two data distributions. Ignore any outliers.

Name________________________ Class______________ Date______________ **10-3**

Additional Practice

Find the mean, median, mode, and range of each data set.

1. 22, 45, 30, 18, 22

2. 8, 10, 8, 14, 8, 15

3. 1.25, 0.5, 3.25, 0.75, 1.75

4. 95, 92, 96, 93, 94, 95, 93

Identify the outlier in each data set, and determine how the outlier affects the mean, median, mode, and range of the data.

5. 31, 35, 41, 40, 40, 98

6. 82, 24, 100, 96, 79, 93, 86

7. The amounts of Cathy's last six clothing purchases were $109, $72, $99, $15, $99, and $89. For each question, choose the mean, median, or mode, and give its value.
   a. Which value describes the average of Cathy's purchases? ______________
   b. Which value would Cathy tell her parents to convince them that she is not spending too much money on clothes? Explain.
   c. Which value would Cathy tell her parents to convince them that she needs an increase in her allowance? Explain.

Use the data to make a box-and-whisker plot.

8. 71, 79, 56, 24, 35, 37, 81, 63, 75

9. 210, 195, 350, 250, 260, 300

The finishing times of two runners for several one-mile races, in minutes, are shown in the box-and-whisker plots.

10. Who has the faster median time? ______________

11. Who has the slowest time? ______________

12. Overall, who is the faster runner? Explain.

Jamal

Tim

5 6 7

Problem Solving

Write the correct answer.

1. While window shopping, Sandra recorded the prices of shoes she would like to try on. The prices were $48, $63, $52, $99, and $58. Find the mean, median, and mode of the prices. Which best represents the typical shoe she looked at? Why?

____

____

2. The number of cans Xavier recycled each week for eight weeks is 24, 33, 76, 42, 35, 33, 45, and 33. Find the mean, median, and mode of the numbers of cans. How do the mean and median change when the outlier is removed?

____

____

3. The amounts due on the Harvey's electric bill, rounded to the nearest dollar, for the past six months were $64, $83, $76, $134, $76, and $71. Find the mean, median, and mode of the amounts. Which value should Mr. Harvey tell his family to convince them to cut down on electric use?

____

4. A manager at a bowling alley surveys adult patrons about their shoes sizes. He records sizes 11, 12, 8, 4, 8, 5, 8, 7, 9, 10, 8, 9, 8, and 10. Find the mean, median, and mode of the sizes. Which is most important to the manager when ordering new rental shoes?

____

The number of traffic citations given daily by two police departments over a two-week period is shown in the box-and-whisker plots. Choose the letter of the best answer.

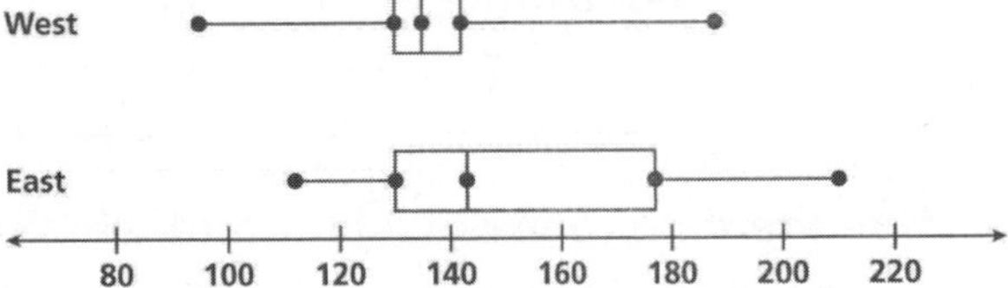

5. What is the best estimate of the difference in the greatest number of citations given by each department in one day?

   A 10 B 20

   C 30 D 35

6. What is the difference in the median number of citations between the two departments?

   F about 8

   G about 15

   H about 22

   J about 40

7. Which statement is NOT true?

   A The East department gave the greatest number of citations in one day.

   B The East department gave the least number of citations in one day.

   C The East department has a greater IQR than the West department.

   D The East department has the greater median number of citations in one day.

Name______________________ Class______________ Date__________

10-4

Misleading Graphs and Statistics

Connection: Outliers and Misleading Statistics

Essential question: *Which statistics are most affected by outliers, and what shapes can data distributions have?*

Video Tutor

CC.9–12.S.ID.1

1 EXAMPLE Using Line Plots to Display Data

Twelve employees at a small company make the following annual salaries (in thousands of dollars): 25, 30, 35, 35, 35, 40, 40, 40, 45, 45, 50, 60.

A Create a line plot of the data by putting an X above the number line to represent each data valuc. Stack the Xs for repeated data values.

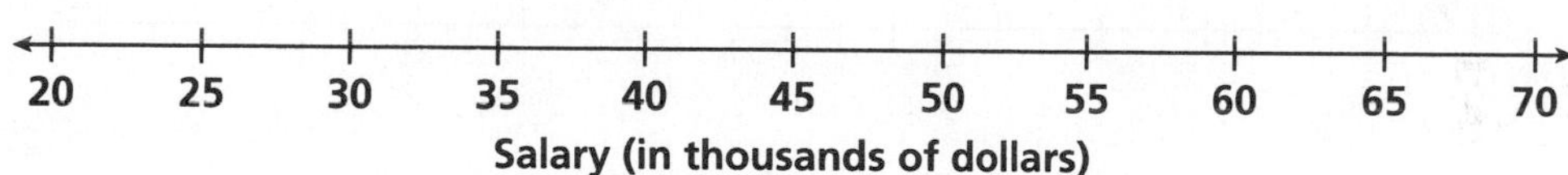

B Complete the table. Round to the nearest hundredth, if necessary.

Mean	Median	Range	IQR	Standard deviation

REFLECT

1a. *Quantitative data* are numbers, such as counts or measurements. *Qualitative data* are categories, such as attributes or preferences. For example, employees' salaries are quantitative data while employees' positions within a company are qualitative data. Is it appropriate to use a line plot for displaying quantitative data, qualitative data, or both? Explain.

____

____

1b. The line plot allows you to see how the data are distributed. Describe the overall shape of the distribution of employees' salaries.

____

1c. When you examine the line plot, do any data values appear to be different than the others? Explain.

____

Recall that an outlier is a value in a data set that is relatively much greater or much less than most of the other values in the data set and that you can determine whether a data value is an outlier by using the following rule.

Determining Whether a Data Value Is an Outlier
A data value x is an outlier if $x < Q_1 - 1.5(\text{IQR})$ or if $x > Q_3 + 1.5(\text{IQR})$.

CC.9–12.S.ID.3

2 EXPLORE Investigating the Effect of an Outlier in a Data Set

Suppose the list of salaries in the previous example is expanded to include the owner's salary, which is $150,000. Now the list of salaries is: 25, 30, 35, 35, 35, 40, 40, 40, 45, 45, 50, 60, 150.

A Create a line plot for the revised data set. Choose an appropriate scale for the number line.

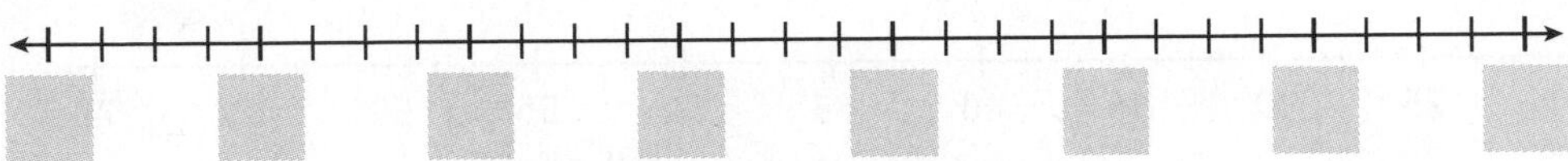

Salary (in thousands of dollars)

B Complete the table. Use a calculator and round to the nearest hundredth, if necessary.

Mean	Median	Range	IQR	Standard deviation

C Complete each sentence by stating whether the statistic increased, decreased, or stayed the same when the data value 150 was added to the original data set. If the statistic increased or decreased, say by what amount.

The mean ______________________________.

The median ______________________________.

The range ______________________________.

The IQR ______________________________.

The standard deviation ______________________________.

REFLECT

2a. Show that the data value 150 is an outlier, but the data value 60 is not. Use the inequalities given at the top of the previous page to support your answer.

2b. What effect does the outlier have on the overall shape of the distribution?

2c. For the original data set, you can conclude that the salary of a typical employee is $40,000 regardless of whether you used the mean or the median. For the revised data set, you could say that the salary of a typical employee is either $48,500 or $40,000 depending on whether you used the mean or the median. Which average salary is more reasonable for the revised data set? Explain your reasoning.

2d. Based on how the IQR and standard deviation are calculated, explain why the IQR was only slightly affected by the addition of the outlier while the standard deviation was dramatically changed.

2e. Because the median and the IQR are based on quartiles while the standard deviation is based on the mean, the center and spread of a data set are usually reported either as the median and IQR or as the mean and standard deviation. Which pair of statistics would you use for a data set that includes one or more outliers? Explain.

Shapes of Distributions A data distribution can be described as **symmetric**, **skewed to the left**, or **skewed to the right** depending on the general shape of the distribution in a line plot or other data display.

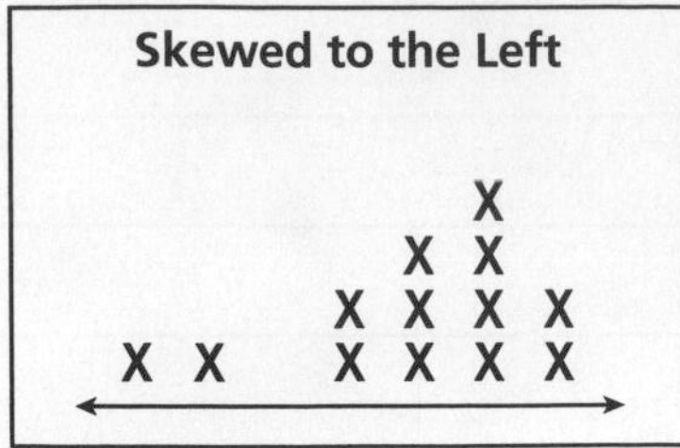

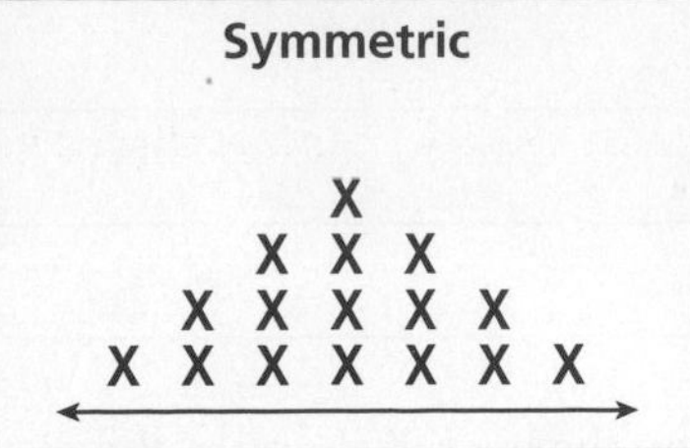

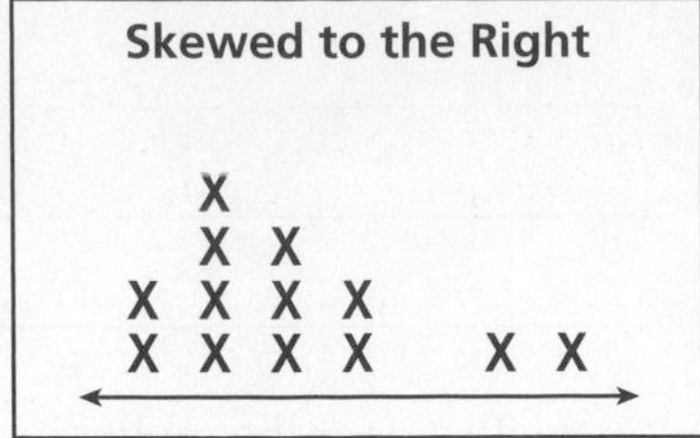

CC.9–12.S.ID.2

3 EXAMPLE Comparing Data Distributions

The tables list Sierra's and Jacey's scores on math tests in each quarter of the school year. Create a line plot for each student's scores and identify the distribution as symmetric, skewed to the left, or skewed to the right.

Sierra's Scores			
I	II	III	IV
88	86	92	88
94	90	87	91
91	95	94	91
92	91	88	93
90	94	96	89

Jacey's Scores			
I	II	III	IV
89	76	87	82
83	86	86	85
86	87	72	86
83	88	73	88
87	90	84	89

A Create and examine a line plot for Sierra's scores.

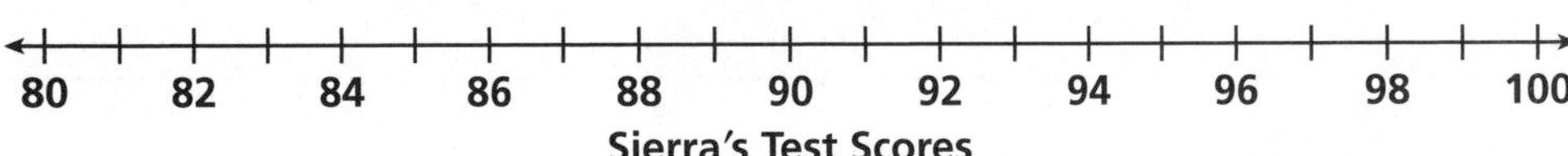

The distribution is centered on one value (91) with the data values to the left of the center balanced with the data values to the right, so the distribution is symmetric.

B Create and examine a line plot for Jacey's scores.

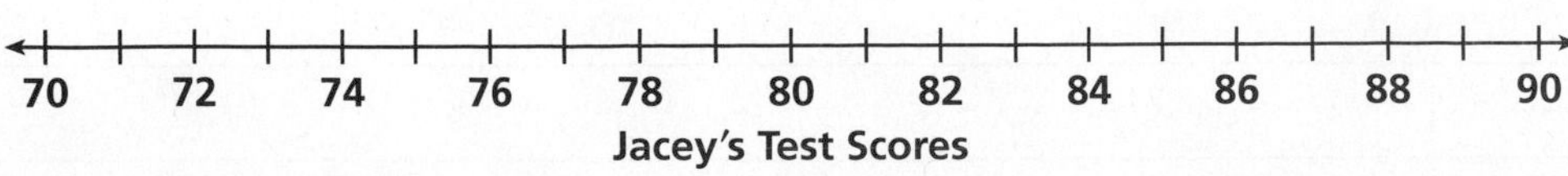

The data values cluster on the right with a few data values spread out to the left of the cluster, so the distribution is skewed to the left.

REFLECT

3a. Find the mean and median for Sierra's test scores. How do they compare?

3b. Will the mean and median in a symmetric distribution always be equal or approximately equal? Explain.

3c. Find the mean and median for Jacey's test scores. How do they compare?

3d. Will the mean and median in a skewed distribution always be different? Explain.

PRACTICE

1. a. Rounded to the nearest $50,000, the values (in thousands of dollars) of homes sold by a realtor are listed below. Use the number line to create a line plot for the data set.

300 250 200 250 350

400 300 250 400 300

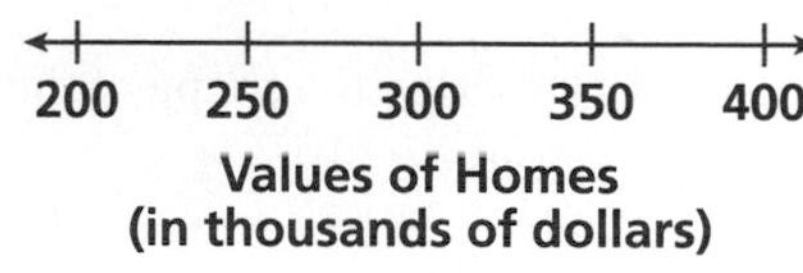

b. Suppose the realtor sells a home with a value of $650,000. Which statistics are affected when 650 is included in the data set?

c. Would 650 be considered an outlier? Explain.

2. In Exercise 1, find the mean and median for the data set with and without the data value 650. Why might the realtor want to use the mean instead of the median when advertising the typical value of homes sold?

3. The table shows Chloe's scores on math tests in each quarter of the school year.

Chloe's Scores			
I	II	III	IV
74	77	79	74
78	75	76	77
82	80	74	76
76	75	77	78
85	77	87	85

a. Use the number line below to create a line plot for Chloe's scores.

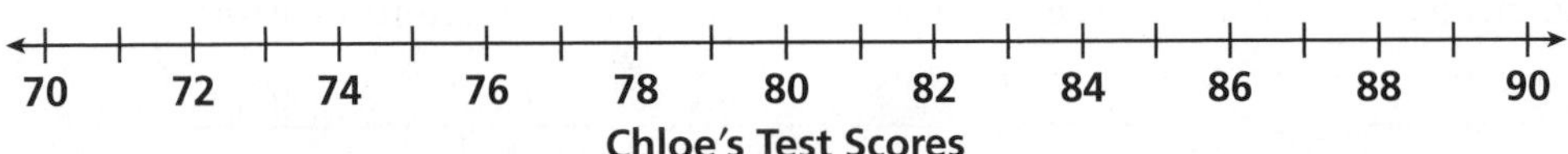

b. Complete the table below for the data set.

Mean	Median	Range	IQR	Standard deviation

c. Identify any outliers in the data set. Which of the statistics from the table above would change if the outliers were removed?

d. Describe the shape of the distribution.

e. Which measure of center and which measure of spread should be used to characterize the data? Explain.

4. Give an example of a data set with a symmetric distribution that also includes one or more outliers.

5. Suppose that a data set has an approximately symmetric distribution, with one outlier. What could you do if you wanted to use the mean and standard deviation to characterize the data?

Additional Practice

Rounded to the nearest $1000, the data below represent the prices of recently sold cars at two dealerships. For each data set, draw a line plot. Then find the mean, median, range, IQR, and standard deviation.

1. 22, 25, 30, 28, 23, 25, 20, 20, 21, 26

2. 38, 40, 38, 34, 38, 35, 33, 31, 33, 36

Identify the outlier in each data set, and determine how the outlier affects the mean, median, range, IQR, and standard deviation of the data.

3. 31, 35, 42, 40, 40, 97

4. 82, 26, 100, 95, 79, 92, 86

5. The amounts of Cathy's last six clothing purchases were $109, $72, $99, $15, $99, and $89.
   a. Is any value an outlier? If so, which value? ________________
   b. Is the other extreme data value an outlier? Explain how you know.
   c. What effect does the outlier have on the overall shape of the distribution?

Use the data to make a line plot. Then tell whether the plot is *symmetric*, *skewed to the left*, or *skewed to the right*.

6. 80, 80, 70, 20, 30, 70, 80, 70, 70

7. 230, 240, 250, 250, 260, 300, 240, 260

Problem Solving

Write the correct answer.

1. Sandra recorded the prices of shoes she would like to try on. The prices were \$48, \$64, \$52, \$79, \$67, \$73, and \$58. Find the mean, median, range, IQR, and standard deviation of the prices. Is any value an outlier? If so, which value?

2. The number of cans Xavier recycled each week for eight weeks is 24, 33, 76, 42, 35, 33, 44, and 33. Find the mean, median, range, IQR, and standard deviation of the data. Is any value an outlier? If so, which value?

3. Draw a line plot for the data 1, 2, 1, 3, 4, 5, 2, 2. Is the plot *symmetric*, *skewed to the left*, or *skewed to the right*?

4. Draw a line plot for the data 20, 30, 60, 40, 40, 50, 40, 30, 50. Is the plot *symmetric*, *skewed to the left*, or *skewed to the right*?

The numbers of traffic citations given daily by a police department over a ten-day period are 24, 18, 26, 20, 24, 20, 50, 24, 30, and 24. Choose the letter of the best answer.

5. Is any value an outlier? If so, which value?
   - A no outlier
   - B 24
   - C 18
   - D 50

6. Give the mean, median, range, IQR, and standard deviation for the number of citations. List the statistics in the given order.
   - F 24; 6; 26; 32; about 8.63
   - G 26; 24; 32; 6; about 8.63
   - J 32; 26; 24; 6; about 8.63
   - H 6; 24; 26; 32; about 8.63

7. Which statement is true?
   - A The distribution is skewed to the right.
   - B The distribution is skewed to the left.
   - C The distribution is symmetric.
   - D The distribution is not skewed in either direction.

Name________________________ Class______________ Date__________

10-5

Experimental Probability

Going Deeper

Essential question: *How do you find the experimental probability of an event?*

Video Tutor

CC.9-12.S.CP.1

1 EXPLORE Finding Experimental Probability

You can toss a paper cup to demonstrate *experimental probability*.

Consider tossing a paper cup. What are the three different ways the cup could land?

____

Toss a paper cup thirty times. Record your observations in the table.

Outcome	Number of Times
Open-end up	
Open-end down	
On its side	

REFLECT

1a. Which outcome do you think is most likely?

____

1b. Describe the three outcomes using the words *likely* and *unlikely*.

____

____

1c. Use the number of times each event occurred to calculate the probability of each event.

1d. What do you think would happen if you performed more trials?

____

____

____

Outcome	Experimental Probability
Open-end up	$\frac{\text{open} - \text{end up}}{30} = \frac{\square}{30}$
Open-end down	$\frac{\text{open} - \text{end down}}{30} = \frac{\square}{30}$
On its side	$\frac{\text{on its side}}{30} = \frac{\square}{30}$

1e. What is the sum of the three probabilities in question 1c?

____

You can use experimental probability to estimate the probability of an event. The **experimental probability** of the event is found by comparing the number of times an event occurs to the total number of trials.

Experimental Probability

$$\text{probability} \approx \frac{\text{number of times the event occurs}}{\text{total number of trials}}$$

CC.9–12.S.CP.1

2 EXAMPLE Calculating Experimental Probability

Martin has a bag of marbles. He removed one marble, recorded the color and then placed it back in the bag. He repeated this process several times and recorded his results in the table.

Color	Frequency
Red	12
Blue	10
Green	15
Yellow	13

A Number of trials = _______

B Complete the table of experimental probabilities. Write each answer in simplest form.

Color	Experimental Probability
Red	$\frac{\text{frequency of the event}}{\text{total number of trails}} = \frac{\square}{\square} = \frac{\square}{\square}$
Blue	$\frac{\text{frequency of the event}}{\text{total number of trails}} = \frac{\square}{\square} = \frac{\square}{\square}$
Green	$\frac{\text{frequency of the event}}{\text{total number of trails}} = \frac{\square}{\square} = \frac{\square}{\square}$
Yellow	$\frac{\text{frequency of the event}}{\text{total number of trails}} = \frac{\square}{\square}$

REFLECT

2a. What are two different ways you could find the experimental probability of the event that you do not draw a red marble?

____

____

____

Sometimes it is impossible or inconvenient to perform all the trials to find the experimental probability of an event. In cases where each outcome has the same chance of occurring, such as rolling a number cube or flipping a coin, you can calculate the *theoretical probability* of the event. This is the ratio of the number of ways the event can occur to the total number of equally likely outcomes.

CC.9–12.S.CP.1

3 EXPLORE

A You roll a number cube once. There are six equally likely outcomes. Complete the table of theoretical probabilities for the different outcomes.

Outcome (Number)	1	2	3	4	5	6
Theoretical Probability						

B Using theoretical probability, predict the number of times each number will be rolled out of 30 total rolls.

1: ________ times 3: ________ times 5: ________ times

2: ________ times 4: ________ times 6: ________ times

C Roll a number cube 30 times. Complete the table for the frequency of each number and then find its experimental probability.

Number						
Frequency						
Experimental Probability						

D Look at the tables you completed. How do the experimental probabilities compare with the theoretical probabilities?

____

____

E **Conjecture** By performing more trials, you tend to get experimental results that are closer to the theoretical probabilities. Combine your table from part C with those of your classmates to make one table for the class. How do the class experimental probabilities compare with the theoretical probabilities?

____

____

REFLECT

3a. Could the experimental probabilities ever be exactly equal to the theoretical probability? Why or why not?

____

____

____

PRACTICE

1. Toss a coin at least 30 times. Record the outcomes in the table.

Outcome	Number of Times	Experimental Probability
Heads		
Tails		

2. What do you think would happen if you performed many more trials?

____

____

3. Sonja has a bag of table tennis balls. She removed one ball, recorded the color and then placed it back in the bag. She repeated this process several times and recorded her results in the table. Find the experimental probability of each color. Write your answers in simplest form.

Color	Frequency
White	12
Blue	8
Red	5
Yellow	9
Green	6

White:________ Red:________ Green:________

Blue:________ Yellow:________

Use a spinner with eight equal sections numbered 1 through 8 for Exercises 4–6.

4. What is the theoretical probability of landing on a specific section of your spinner?

____

5. Spin the spinner 40 times. Complete the table.

Number	1	2	3	4	5	6	7	8
Frequency								
Experimental Probability								

6. Look at the table you completed. How do the experimental probabilities compare with the theoretical probabilities?

____

____

7. **Critical Thinking** Patricia finds that the experimental probability of her dog wanting to go outside between 4 P.M. and 5 P.M. is $\frac{7}{12}$. About what percent of the time does her dog not want to go outside between 4 P.M. and 5 P.M.?

____

Name_______________ Class__________ Date__________

10-5

Additional Practice

Identify the sample space and the outcome shown for each experiment.

1. spinning a spinner

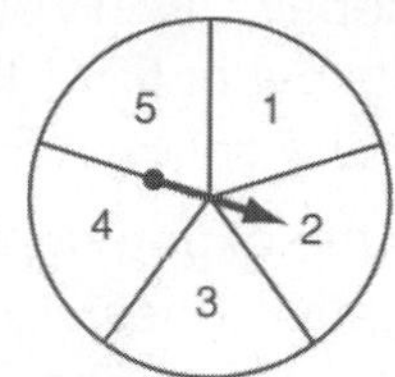

____

____

2. tossing two coins

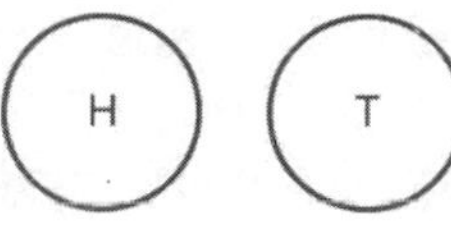

____

____

Write *impossible, unlikely, as likely as not, likely,* or *certain* to describe each event.

3. The mail was delivered before noon on 4 of the last 5 days. The mail will be delivered before noon today. _______________

4. Sean rolls a number cube and gets an even number. _______________

5. The pages of a book are numbered 1 – 350. Amelia begins reading on page 400. _______________

An experiment consists of rolling a standard number cube. Use the results in the table to find the experimental probability of each event.

Outcome	Frequency
1	6
2	7
3	4
4	10
5	8
6	5

6. rolling a 1 _______________

7. rolling a 5 _______________

8. not rolling a 3 _______________

9. not rolling a number less than 5 _______________

10. A tire manufacturer checks 80 tires and finds 6 of them to be defective.

    a. What is the experimental probability that a tire chosen at random will be defective? _______________

    b. The factory makes 200 tires. Predict the number of tires that are likely to be defective. _______________

11. A safety commission tested 1500 electric scooters and found that 15 of them had defective handles.

    a. What is the experimental probability that a scooter will have a defective handle? _______________

    b. The factory makes 40,000 scooters. Predict the number of scooters that are likely to have defective handles. _______________

Problem Solving

Write the correct answer.

1. A manufacturer of bottled juices has a contest where prizes are printed on the inside of the bottle caps. 2 million caps are printed with "Sorry"; 1.5 million say "Free Bottle"; 0.4 million say "T-Shirt"; and 0.1 million say "CD."
   a. Identify the sample space.

      ____

   b. If Tammy buys one bottle, is it impossible, unlikely, as likely as not, likely, or certain that she will get a cap that says "Sorry"?

      ____

   c. If Eagle buys one bottle, is it impossible, unlikely, as likely as not, likely, or certain that he will get a cap that says "CD"?

      ____

2. At the end of the 2005 season, Major League Baseball player Andruw Jones had 1408 hits out of 5271 times at bat during his entire career.
   a. What is the experimental probability that Andruw Jones will have a hit during any time at bat? (This statistic is called his *batting average* and is usually stated as a decimal rounded to the thousandths.)

      ____

   b. If Andruw has 570 at-bats during a season, predict the number of hits he will have during the season.

      ____

A pharmaceutical company tests the effectiveness of a diabetes screening test by administering it to several volunteers who actually know whether or not they have diabetes. The results are summarized in the table below. Select the best answer.

3. What is the experimental probability that this screening test will *not* identify someone who actually does have diabetes? (This type of result is called a false negative.)

   A 2.9 % C 20%

   B 16.6% D 28.6%

4. If this test is used on 1000 patients who do not know whether or not they have diabetes, about how many patients would the test predict *do* have diabetes?

   F 66 H 92

   G 79 J 101

		Volunteer _______ have diabetes.	
		does	does not
Test predicts that the person _______ have diabetes.	does	10	4
	does not	2	136

Name ____________ Class ____________ Date ____________

10-6

Video Tutor

Theoretical Probability

Connection: Probability and Set Theory

Essential question: *How can you use set theory to help you calculate theoretical probabilities?*

PREP FOR CC.9–12.S.CP.1

1 ENGAGE Introducing the Vocabulary of Sets

You will see that set theory is useful in calculating probabilities. A **set** is a well-defined collection of distinct objects. Each object in a set is called an **element** of the set. A set may be specified by writing its elements in braces. For example, the set S of prime numbers less than 10 may be written as $S = \{2, 3, 5, 7\}$.

The number of elements in a set S may be written as $n(S)$. For the set S of prime numbers less than 10, $n(S) = 4$.

The set with no elements is the **empty set** and is denoted by $\varnothing$ or $\{\ \}$. The set of all elements under consideration is the **universal set** and is denoted by U. The following terms describe how sets are related to each other.

Term	Notation	Venn Diagram
Set A is a **subset** of set B if every element of A is also an element of B.	$A \subset B$	U, B, A
The **intersection** of sets A and B is the set of all elements that are in both A and B.	$A \cap B$	U, A, B
The **union** of sets A and B is the set of all elements that are in A or B.	$A \cup B$	U, A, B
The **complement** of set A is the set of all elements in the universal set U that are not in A.	A^c	U, A

REFLECT

1a. For any set A, what is $A \cap \varnothing$? Explain.

____

____

Recall that a *probability experiment* is an activity involving chance. Each repetition of the experiment is a *trial* and each possible result is an *outcome*. The *sample space* of an experiment is the set of all possible outcomes. An *event* is a set of outcomes.

As you saw in the previous lesson, when all outcomes of an experiment are equally likely, the **theoretical probability** that an event A will occur is given by $P(A) = \frac{n(A)}{n(S)}$, where S is the sample space.

CC.9–12.S.CP.1

2 EXAMPLE Calculating Theoretical Probabilities

You roll a number cube. Event *A* is rolling an even number. Event *B* is rolling a prime number. Calculate each of the following probabilities.

A $P(A)$ **B** $P(A \cup B)$ **C** $P(A \cap B)$ **D** $P(A^c)$

A $P(A)$ is the probability of rolling an even number. To calculate $P(A)$, first identify the sample space S.

$S =$ ______________________, so $n(S) =$ ____________.

$A =$ ______________________, so $n(A) =$ ____________.

So, $P(A) = \frac{n(A)}{n(S)} = \frac{\square}{\square} = \frac{\square}{\square}$.

B $P(A \cup B)$ is the probability of rolling an even number *or* a prime number.

$A \cup B =$ ______________________, so $n(A \cup B) =$ ____________.

So, $P(A \cup B) = \frac{n(A \cup B)}{n(S)} = \frac{\square}{\square}$.

C $P(A \cap B)$ is the probability of rolling an even number *and* a prime number.

$A \cap B =$ ______________________, so $n(A \cap B) =$ ____________.

So, $P(A \cap B) = \frac{n(A \cap B)}{n(S)} = \frac{\square}{\square}$.

D $P(A^c)$ is the probability of rolling a number that is *not* even.

$A^c =$ ______________________, so $n(A^c) =$ ____________.

So, $P(A^c) = \frac{n(A^c)}{n(S)} = \frac{\square}{\square} = \frac{\square}{\square}$.

REFLECT

2a. Explain what $P(S)$ represents and then calculate this probability. Do you think this result is true in general? Explain.

____

____

You may have noticed in the example that $P(A) + P(A^c) = 1$. To see why this is true in general, note that an event and its complement represent all outcomes in the sample space, so $n(A) + n(A^c) = n(S)$.

$$P(A) + P(A^c) = \frac{n(A)}{n(S)} + \frac{n(A^c)}{n(S)}$$ Definition of theoretical probability

$$= \frac{n(A) + n(A^c)}{n(S)}$$ Add.

$$= \frac{n(S)}{n(S)} = 1$$ $n(A) + n(A^c) = n(S)$

You can write this relationship as $P(A) = 1 - P(A^c)$ and use it to help you find probabilities when it is more convenient to calculate the probability of the complement of an event.

Probabilities of an Event and Its Complement

The probability of an event and the probability of its complement have a sum of 1. So, the probability of an event is one minus the probability of its complement. Also, the probability of the complement of an event is one minus the probability of the event.

$$P(A) + P(A^c) = 1$$

$$P(A) = 1 - P(A^c)$$

$$P(A^c) = 1 - P(A)$$

CC.9–12.S.CP.1

3 EXAMPLE Using the Complement of an Event

You roll a blue number cube and white number cube at the same time. What is the probability that you do not roll doubles?

A Let A be the event that you do not roll doubles. Then A^c is the event that you do roll doubles.

Complete the table at right to show all outcomes in the sample space.

Circle the outcomes in A^c (rolling doubles).

White Number Cube

Blue Number Cube	1	2	3	4	5	6
1	1-1	1-2	1-3	1-4	1-5	1-6
2	2-1					
3	3-1					
4	4-1					
5	5-1					
6	6-1					

B Find the probability of rolling doubles.

$$P(A^c) = \frac{n(A^c)}{n(S)} = \frac{\quad}{\quad} = \frac{\quad}{\quad}$$

C Find the probability that you do not roll doubles.

$$P(A) = 1 - P(A^c) = 1 - \frac{\quad}{\quad} = \frac{\quad}{\quad}$$

REFLECT

3a. Describe a different way you could have calculated the probability that you do not roll doubles.

PRACTICE

You have a set of 10 cards numbered 1 to 10. You choose a card at random. Event *A* is choosing a number less than 7. Event *B* is choosing an odd number. Calculate each of the following probabilities.

1. $P(A)$

2. $P(B)$

3. $P(A \cup B)$

4. $P(A \cap B)$

5. $P(A^c)$

6. $P(B^c)$

7. A bag contains 5 red marbles and 10 blue marbles. You choose a marble without looking. Event *A* is choosing a red marble. Event *B* is choosing a blue marble. What is $P(A \cap B)$? Explain.

8. A standard deck of cards has 13 cards (2, 3, 4, 5, 6, 7, 8, 9, 10, jack, queen, king, ace) in each of 4 suits (hearts, clubs, diamonds, spades). You choose a card from a deck at random. What is the probability that you do not choose an ace? Explain.

9. You choose a card from a standard deck of cards at random. What is the probability that you do not choose a club? Explain.

10. **Error Analysis** A bag contains white tiles, black tiles, and gray tiles. $P(W)$, the probability of choosing a tile at random and choosing a white tile, is $\frac{1}{4}$. A student claims that the probability of choosing a black tile, $P(B)$, is $\frac{3}{4}$ since $P(B) = 1 - P(W) = 1 - \frac{1}{4} = \frac{3}{4}$. Do you agree? Explain.

Name ____________ Class ________ Date ________

10-6

Additional Practice

Find the theoretical probability of each outcome.

1. rolling a number less than 4 on a standard number cube ________
2. randomly choosing a day of the week and it is a weekend ________
3. spinning red on a spinner with equal sections of red, blue, and green ________
4. randomly choosing the letter N from the letters in NUMBER ________
5. The probability it will snow is 60%. What is the probability it will not snow? ________
6. The probability of tossing two coins and having them land heads up is $\frac{1}{4}$. What is the probability the coins will not land heads up? ________
7. A spinner has red, green, blue, and yellow. The probability of spinning a red is 0.4, the probability of spinning a blue is 0.05 and the probability of spinning a yellow is 0.25. What is the probability of spinning a green? ________
8. Miguel entered a contest offering prizes to the top 3 finishers. The probability of winning 1st is 12%, the probability of winning 2nd is 18% and probability of winning 3rd is 20%. What is the probability that Miguel will not win any prize? ________
9. The odds of winning a contest are 1:50. What is the probability of winning the contest? ________
10. The odds against a spinner landing on yellow are 3:1. What is the probability the spinner will not land on yellow? ________
11. The probability of a thunderstorm is 80%. What are the odds that there will be a thunderstorm? ________
12. The odds of selecting a red card from a box of cards are 2:5. What is the probability of not selecting a red card from a box? ________

The table shows how many of each letter are in a bag. Use the table for 13–16. Find the following.

13. *P*(A) ________

14. *P*(B) ________

15. odds in favor of C ________

16. odds against E ________

Letter	How Many in Bag
A	5
B	4
C	6
D	2
E	8

Problem Solving

Mahjong is a classic Chinese game frequently played with tiles. Each tile has numbers, pictures, or characters on them. Similar to a deck of playing cards, most of the tiles can be grouped into suits. From a certain set of mahjong tiles, the odds *in favor* of selecting a tile from the bamboo suit is 1:3.

1. What is the probability of selecting a tile from the bamboo suit?

____

2. What is the probability of selecting a tile that is *not* from the bamboo suit?

____

3. Any set of mahjong tiles has 36 tiles in the bamboo suit. How many tiles are in the entirety of this set? (*Hint:* Set up a proportion using your answer from question 1.)

____

4. This set of mahjong tiles also has 8 special tiles that represent flowers or seasons. What are the odds *against* selecting a tile that represents a flower or a season?

____

At a carnival game, you drop a ball into the top of the machine shown below. As the ball falls, it goes either left or right as it hits each peg. In total, the ball can follow 16 different paths. (See if you can find all 16 paths.) The ball eventually lands in one of the bins at the bottom and you win that amount of money. (One path to $0 is shown.) Select the best answer.

5. What is the probability of wining $2?

A $\frac{1}{16}$ C $\frac{1}{4}$

B $\frac{1}{8}$ D $\frac{1}{2}$

6. What is the probability of wining $1?

F $\frac{1}{8}$ H $\frac{1}{4}$

G $\frac{3}{16}$ J $\frac{3}{8}$

7. What are the odds in favor of winning nothing ($0)?

A 1:1 C 1:3

B 1:2 D 1:4

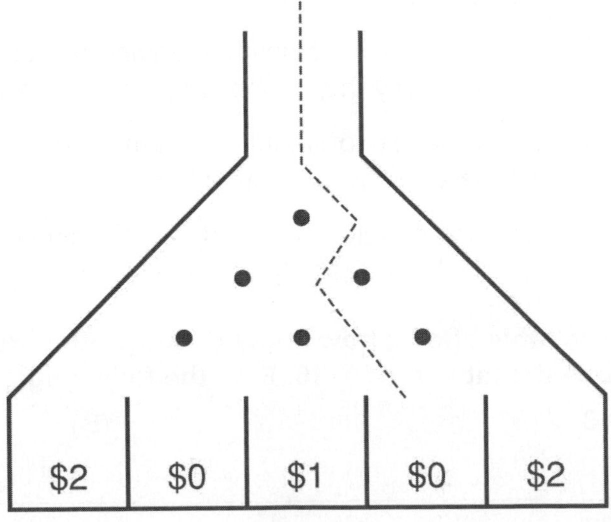

Name________________________ Class______________ Date__________

10-7

Video Tutor

Independent and Dependent Events

Going Deeper

Essential question: *How do you determine if two events are independent or dependent?*

Two events are **independent events** if the occurrence of one event does not affect the occurrence of the other event. For example, rolling a 1 on a number cube and choosing an ace at random from a deck of cards are independent events.

If two events *A* and *B* are independent events, then the fact that event *B* has occurred does not affect the probability of event *A*. In other words, for independent events *A* and *B*, $P(A) = P(A \mid B)$. You can use this as a criterion to determine whether two events are independent.

CC.9–12.S.CP.2

1 EXAMPLE Determining If Events are Independent

An airport employee collects data on 180 random flights that arrive at the airport. The data is shown in the two-way table. Is a late arrival independent of the flight being an international flight? Why or why not?

	Late Arrival	On Time	TOTAL
Domestic Flight	12	108	120
International Flight	6	54	60
TOTAL	18	162	180

A Let event *A* be the event that a flight arrives late. Let event *B* be the event that a flight is an international flight.

To find $P(A)$, first note that there is a total of ____________ flights.

Of these flights, there is a total of ____________ late flights.

So, $P(A) = \frac{\square}{\square} =$ ____________.

To find $P(A \mid B)$, first note that there is a total of ____________ international flights.

Of these flights, there is a total of ____________ late flights.

So, $P(A \mid B) = \frac{\square}{\square} =$ ____________.

B Compare $P(A)$ and $P(A \mid B)$.

So, a late arrival is independent of the flight being an international flight because

____

____

REFLECT

1a. In the example, you compared $P(A)$ and $P(A \mid B)$. Suppose you compare $P(B)$ and $P(B \mid A)$. What do you find? What does this tell you?

____

You can use a tree diagram to help you understand the formula for the probability of independent events. For example, consider tossing a coin two times. The outcome of one toss does not affect the outcome of the other toss, so the events are independent.

The tree diagram shows that the probability of the coin landing heads up on both tosses is $\frac{1}{4}$ because this is 1 of 4 equally-likely outcomes at the end of Toss 2. This probability is simply the product of the probabilities of the coin landing heads up on each individual toss: $\frac{1}{2} \cdot \frac{1}{2} = \frac{1}{4}$.

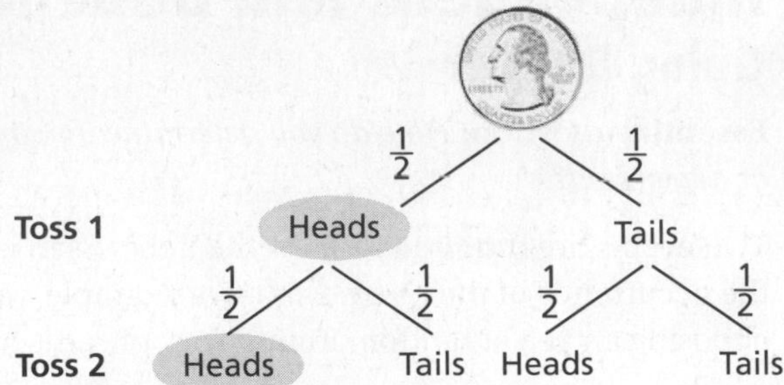

Probability of Independent Events

A and *B* are independent events if and only if $P(A \text{ and } B) = P(A) \cdot P(B)$.

CC.9–12.S.CP.2

2 EXAMPLE Using the Formula

You spin the spinner at right two times. What is the probability that you spin an even number on the first spin followed by an odd number on the second spin?

A Let event *A* be the event that you spin an even number on the first spin. Let event *B* be the event that you spin an odd number on the second spin.

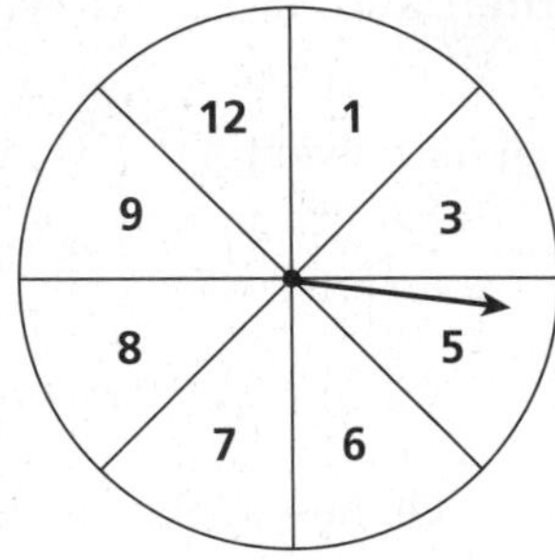

$P(A) = \frac{\square}{\square}$ $P(B) = \frac{\square}{\square}$

B The outcome of the first spin does not affect the outcome of the second spin, so the events are independent events.

$P(A \text{ and } B) = P(A) \cdot P(B)$ Use the formula for independent events.

$= (\_\_\_\_) \cdot (\_\_\_\_)$ Substitute.

$= \_\_\_\_\_\_$ Simplify.

So, the probability that you spin an even number on the first spin followed by an odd number on the second spin is ________.

REFLECT

2a. What is the probability that you spin an odd number on the first spin followed by an even number on the second spin? What do you notice?

____

____

____

The formula for the probability of independent events gives you another way to determine whether two events are independent. That is, two events A and B are independent events if $P(A \text{ and } B) = P(A) \cdot P(B)$.

CC.9–12.S.CP.2

3 EXAMPLE Showing that Events are Independent

The two-way table shows the data from the first example. Show that a flight arriving on time and a flight being a domestic flight are independent events.

	Late Arrival	On Time	TOTAL
Domestic Flight	12	108	120
International Flight	6	54	60
TOTAL	18	162	180

A Let event A be the event that a flight arrives on time. Let event B be the event that a flight is a domestic flight.

To find $P(A)$, $P(B)$, and $P(A \text{ and } B)$ note that there is a total of ________ flights.

There is a total of ________ on-time flights.

So, $P(A) = \frac{\square}{\square} = \frac{\square}{\square}$.

There is a total of ________ domestic flights.

So, $P(B) = \frac{\square}{\square} = \frac{\square}{\square}$.

There is a total of ________ on-time domestic flights.

So, $P(A \text{ and } B) = \frac{\square}{\square} = \frac{\square}{\square}$.

B Compare $P(A \text{ and } B)$ and $P(A) \cdot P(B)$.

$P(A) \cdot P(B) = (\_\_\_\_) \cdot (\_\_\_\_) = \_\_\_\_$

So, the events are independent events because

____

REFLECT

3a. Describe a different way you can show that a flight arriving on time and a flight being a domestic flight are independent events.

____

____

CC.9–12.S.CP.3

4 ENGAGE Introducing Dependent Events

Two events are **dependent events** if the occurrence of one event affects the occurrence of the other event.

Suppose you have a bag containing 2 blue marbles and 2 black marbles. You choose a marble without looking, put it aside, and then choose a second marble. Consider the following events.

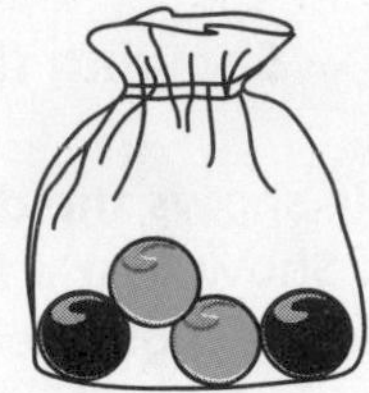

Event A: The first marble you choose is blue.

Event B: The second marble you choose is black.

Events A and B are dependent events, because the marble you choose for your first pick changes the sample space for your second pick. That is, the occurrence of event A affects the probability of event B.

The probability that event B occurs given that event A has already occurred is called the **conditional probability** of B given A and is written as $P(B \mid A)$. The formula used to determine conditional probability is given by

$$P(B \mid A) = \frac{P(A \text{ and } B)}{P(A)}.$$

Multiplying both sides by $P(A)$ results in $P(A) \cdot P(B \mid A) = P(A \text{ and } B)$. This is known as the Multiplication Rule.

Multiplication Rule

$P(A \text{ and } B) = P(A) \cdot P(B \mid A)$, where $P(B \mid A)$ is the conditional probability of event B, given that event A has occurred.

You can use the Multiplication Rule to find the probability of dependent or independent events. Note that when A and B are independent events, $P(B \mid A) = P(B)$ and the rule may be rewritten as $P(A \text{ and } B) = P(A) \cdot P(B)$, which is the rule for independent events.

REFLECT

4a. How can you write the Multiplication Rule in a different way by starting with the formula for the conditional probability $P(A \mid B)$ and multiplying both sides of that equation by $P(B)$?

CC.9–12.S.CP.8(+)

5 EXAMPLE Finding the Probability of Dependent Events

There are 5 tiles with the letters A, B, C, D, and E in a bag. You choose a tile without looking, put it aside, and then choose another tile. Find the probability that you choose a consonant followed by a vowel.

A Let event A be the event that the first tile is a consonant.
Let event B be the event that the second tile is a vowel.
Find $P(A)$ and $P(B \mid A)$.

$P(A) = \frac{\square}{\square}$ Of the 5 tiles, 3 are consonants.

$P(B \mid A) = \frac{\square}{\square} = \frac{\square}{\square}$ Of the 4 remaining tiles, 2 are vowels.

B Use the Multiplication Rule.

$P(A \text{ and } B) = P(A) \cdot P(B \mid A)$ Use the Multiplication Rule.

$= (\_\_\_\_) \cdot (\_\_\_\_)$ Substitute.

$= \_\_\_\_\_\_$ Multiply.

So, the probability that you choose a consonant followed by a vowel is ________.

REFLECT

5a. Complete the tree diagram below. Then explain how you can use it to check your answer.

1st tile A B C

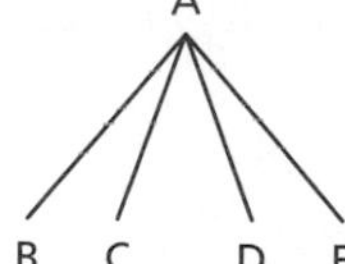

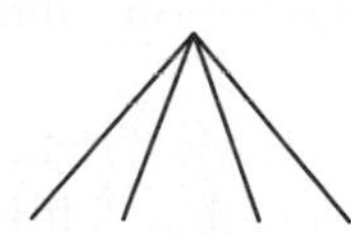

2nd tile B C D E A C D E

____

____

____

5b. What does your answer tell you about the likelihood of choosing a consonant followed by a vowel?

____

PRACTICE

1. A farmer wants to know if an insecticide is effective in preventing small insects called aphids from living on tomato plants. The farmer checks 80 plants. The data is shown in the two-way table. Is having aphids independent of being sprayed with the insecticide? Why or why not?

	Has Aphids	No Aphids	TOTAL
Was sprayed with insecticide	12	40	52
Was not sprayed with insecticide	14	14	28
TOTAL	26	54	80

____

____

____

You spin a spinner with 8 equal sections numbered 1 through 8 and you roll a number cube with sides numbered 1 through 6. Find the probability of each of the following. Write the probabilities as fractions.

2. The spinner lands on 1 and you roll a 5. ________

3. The spinner lands on an even number and you roll an even number. ________

4. The spinner lands on a prime number and you roll a number greater than 4. ________

5. The sum of the number on which the spinner lands and the number you roll is 14. ________

6. A student wants to know if right-handed people are more or less likely to play a musical instrument than left-handed people. The student collects data from 250 people, as shown in the two-way table. Show that being right handed and playing a musical instrument are independent events.

	Right Handed	Left Handed	TOTAL
Plays a musical instrument	44	6	50
Does not play a musical instrument	176	24	200
TOTAL	220	30	250

____

____

____

7. A basket contains 6 bottles of apple juice and 8 bottles of grape juice. You choose a bottle without looking, put it aside, and then choose another bottle. What is the probability that you choose a bottle of apple juice followed by a bottle of grape juice?

____

8. You have a set of ten cards that are numbered 1 through 10. You shuffle the cards and choose a card at random. You put the card aside and choose another card. What is the probability that you choose an even number followed by an odd number?

____

9. A bag contains 3 red marbles and 5 green marbles. You choose a marble without looking, put it aside, and then choose another marble.

a. What is the probability that you choose two red marbles? ________

b. Is the probability different if you replace the first marble before choosing the second marble? Explain.

____

____

10. There are 12 boys and 14 girls in Ms. Garcia's class. She chooses a student at random to solve a geometry problem at the board. Then she chooses another student at random to check the first student's work. Is she more likely to choose a boy followed by a girl, a girl followed by a boy, or are these both equally likely? Explain.

____

____

____

____

11. You roll a blue number cube and a red number cube at the same time. You are interested in the probability that you roll a 2 on the blue cube and that the sum of the numbers shown on the cubes is 7.

a. Are these dependent events or independent events? Explain.

____

____

____

____

b. What is the probability? ________

12. A bag contains 4 blue marbles and 4 red marbles. You choose a marble without looking, put it aside, and then choose another marble. Is there a greater than or less than 50% chance that you choose two marbles with different colors? Explain.

In Exercises 13-15, tell whether events *A* and *B* are dependent or independent. The find *P*(*A* and *B*).

13. You roll two number cubes.

Event *A*: You roll a 4 first.

Event *B*: You roll a 3 second.

14. You write each of the letters in COMMUTE on a separate slip of paper and put them in a hat. You randomly draw one letter, do not replace it in the hat, and then randomly draw a second letter.

Event *A*: The first letter is M.

Event *B*: The second letter is E.

15. You roll a number cube and flip a coin.

Event *A*: The number cube shows 3.

Event *B*: The coin shows tails.

Name________________________ Class______________ Date______________

10-7

Additional Practice

Tell whether each set of events is independent or dependent. Explain your answer.

1. You roll a die and flip a coin. ______________________________

____

2. You select one marble, do not replace it, then select another marble. ______________

____

3. A number cube is rolled three times. What is the probability of rolling a 2 each time? ______________

4. The numbers 1 – 40 are written on pieces of paper and put in a box. Two pieces of paper are randomly selected. What is the probability both numbers will be multiples of 4? ______________

5. A coin is tossed 4 times. What is the probability of getting 4 tails? ______________

6. **A bag contains 2 yellow, 12 red, and 6 green marbles.**
   a. What is the probability of selecting a red marble, replacing it, then selecting another red marble? ______________
   b. What is the probability of selecting a red marble, not replacing it, then selecting another red marble? ______________
   c. What is the probability of selecting 1 yellow marble, not replacing it, then selecting a green marble? ______________

7. **There are 7 girls and 3 boys in a class. Two students are to be randomly chosen for a special project.**
   a. What is the probability both students will be girls? ______________
   b. What is the probability both students will be boys? ______________
   c. What is the probability of selecting a boy and a girl? ______________

A music class consists of 9th and 10th graders as shown in the table. Two students will be selected at the same time.

Music Class		
	9th	**10th**
male	9	8
female	12	11

8. What is the probability both students are male? ______________

9. What is the probability both students are 9th graders? ______________

10. What is the probability one student is female and the second student is male? ______________

Problem Solving

Janeesa's backpack has 4 pens and 6 pencils in the front pocket. She reaches in, grabs one, and removes it. Then she reaches in again, grabs another, and removes it. Write the correct answer.

1. Are these two events independent or dependent? Explain.

2. What is the probability that Janeesa removes two pens?

3. What is the probability that Janeesa removes two pencils?

4. What is the probability that Janessa removes a pencil and then a pen?

5. What is the probability that she removes a pen and then a pencil?

6. Your answers to questions 4 and 5 should be numerically identical. Does that mean that the events are identical? Explain.

On a game show, a contestant tries to win a car by randomly picking tiles from a bag. Some of the tiles are printed with the digits in the price of the car and some are printed with strikes (red X's). Select the best answer.

7. When the prices of cars only had four digits, the game was played with 7 tiles—4 digits and 3 strikes. Whenever you picked a strike, it was removed from the bag. In this old version of the game, what was the probability of picking three strikes in a row?

   A $\frac{1}{343}$ C $\frac{6}{343}$

   B $\frac{1}{210}$ D $\frac{1}{35}$

8. When the prices of cars began to have five digits, the game was modified to use 6 tiles—5 digits and 1 strike. Whenever you picked a strike, it was put back in the bag. In this new version of the game, what is the probability of picking three strikes in a row?

   F $\frac{1}{216}$ H $\frac{1}{36}$

   G $\frac{1}{120}$ J $\frac{1}{20}$

Name________________ Class________________ Date________

CHAPTER 10

Performance Tasks

COMMON CORE

CC.9-12.S.ID.1
CC.9-12.S.ID.2
CC.9-12.S.CP.4
CC.9-12.S.CP.7

★ **1.** Jeremy had these scores on his weekly quizzes in History class.

93, 85, 88, 100, 84, 82, 95, 95, 91, 92, 98, 100, 68, 67, 80

Use the data to make a frequency table. Then draw a histogram based on your frequency table.

★ **2.** A computer game generates a random integer from 1 to 20. To guess the number, the user can click on different questions as shown:

AM I A MULTIPLE OF 5?

AM I LESS THAN 11?

AM I GREATER THAN 10?

Find the probability that the second question or third question is true.

★★ **3.** Gail counted the number of cars passing a certain store on Tuesday from 4 P.M. to 4:05 P.M. and on Saturday from 4 P.M. to 4:05 P.M. for 6 weeks. Her data sets are shown below.

Week	1	2	3	4	5	6
Cars on Tuesday	10	8	12	3	9	15
Cars on Saturday	24	8	31	36	29	32

continued

a. Choose the measure of center that best describes both data sets. Calculate that measure for both data sets, and use them to compare the data sets. Explain why the measure you chose is the best representation.

b. Draw two box-and-whisker plots on the same number line to represent the data.

c. The store owner is considering closing on Saturday afternoons. Do you think this would be a good idea? Explain why or why not.

4. A total of 82 ninth graders and 63 tenth graders were surveyed. They were asked if they currently ate lunch in the cafeteria, and if they did not, they were asked if they would eat lunch in the cafeteria if it had a salad bar. The results are shown in the table.

	Currently eat in cafeteria	Do not eat in cafeteria, but would with salad bar
9th graders	36	14
10th graders	25	10

a. What category of responses is not included in the two-way table? Add it to the table with the correct values.

b. Use the completed frequency table to make a new table showing the joint and marginal relative frequencies. Round to the nearest tenth of a percent.

c. The school board has decided that a salad bar should be added to the cafeteria if at least 30% of the students who currently do not eat in the cafeteria would start doing so. Should the salad bar be added?

CHAPTER 10  ASSESSMENT READINESS

Name ______________________ Class ______________ Date ________

MULTIPLE CHOICE

For Items 1–3, use the line plots below.

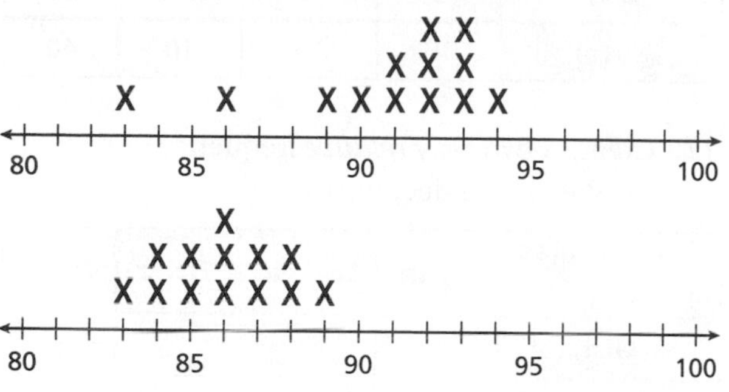

1. How do the medians of the two sets of test scores compare?

   A. The median for the first test is greater than the median for the second test.

   B. The median for the first test is less than the median for the second test.

   C. The medians for the first and second tests are equal.

   D. The relationship cannot be determined.

2. For which test is the median greater than the mean?

   F. First test only

   G. Second test only

   H. Both tests

   J. Neither test

3. Which measure of center is appropriate for comparing the two sets of test scores?

   A. The median only

   B. The mean only

   C. Either the median or the mean

   D. Neither the median nor the mean

For Items 4–6, use the histograms below.

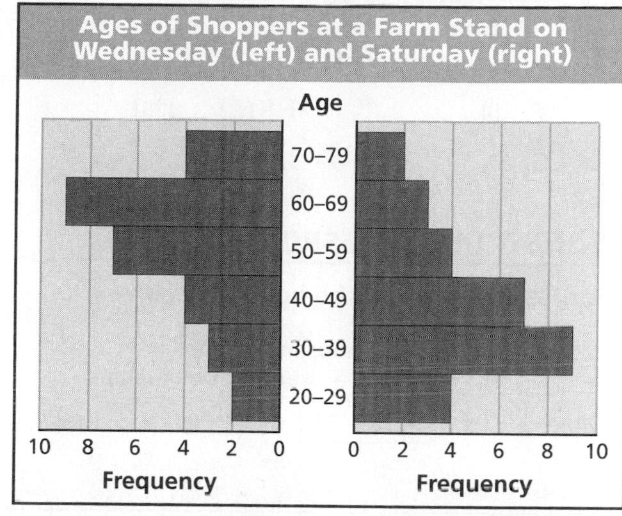

4. Which distribution is skewed toward older ages?

   F. Only the Wednesday distribution

   G. Only the Saturday distribution

   H. Both distributions

   J. Neither distribution

5. How do the spreads of the two distributions compare?

   A. The spread for the Wednesday data is much greater than the spread for the Saturday data.

   B. The spread for the Wednesday data is much less than the spread for the Saturday data.

   C. The spreads are roughly equal.

   D. The relationship cannot be determined.

6. Which measure of spread is appropriate for comparing the sets of ages?

   F. The interquartile range only

   G. The standard deviation only

   H. Either the interquartile range or the standard deviation

   J. Neither the interquartile range nor the standard deviation

7. If events A and B are independent, what must $P(A \text{ and } B)$ equal?

A. $P(A) \bullet P(B)$ **C.** $1 - (P(A) \bullet P(B))$

B. $P(A) + P(B)$ **D.** $1 - (P(A) + P(B))$

8. You roll a number cube. Event A is rolling an even number. Event B is rolling a multiple of 3. Event C is the union of A and B. What is the complement of event C?

F. {6} **H.** {1, 2, 3, 4, 5}

G. {1, 5} **J.** {2, 3, 4, 6}

CONSTRUCTED RESPONSE

For Items 9–11, use the box plot below.

Prices (in Thousands of Dollars) of Vehicles at a Used-Car Dealership

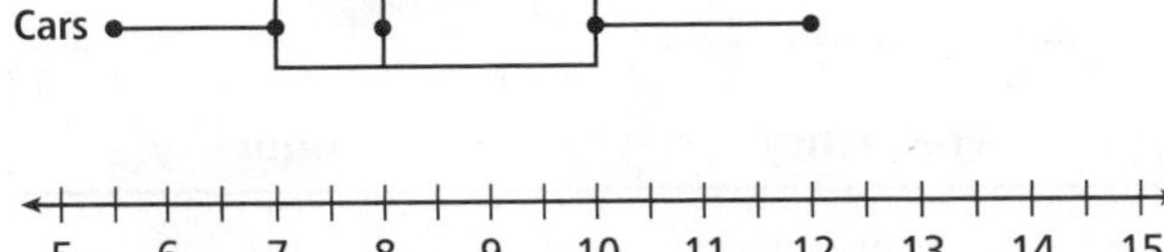

9. Suppose the dealership acquires a used luxury car that it intends to sell for $15,000. Would the price of the car be an outlier? Explain. (Assume that when the car's price is included in the data set, it has no effect on Q_3.)

____

____

10. The dealership also sells used SUVs. The prices (in thousands of dollars) of the SUVs are listed below. Add a box plot for the SUVs to the data display above.

6, 6, 7.5, 7.5, 8, 9, 11, 11, 11, 13, 14, 15

11. Compare the distribution of prices for the used SUVs with the distribution of prices for the used cars.

____

____

____

____

____

____

Derrick surveyed 40 of his classmates by asking each of them whether his or her favorite subject is math, English, or another subject. He also recorded the gender of each classmate surveyed. He recorded his results in the two-way frequency table below. Use the table to complete Items 11–15.

Gender \ Subject	Math	English	Other	Total
Girl	7	10	3	20
Boy	9	4	7	20
Total	16	14	10	40

12. Create a two-way *relative* frequency table for the data using decimals.

Gender \ Subject	Math	English	Other	Total
Girl				
Boy				
Total				

13. Find the joint relative frequency of surveyed students who are girls and prefer English.

____

14. Find the marginal relative frequency of surveyed students who prefer math.

____

15. Find the conditional relative frequency that a surveyed student prefers another subject, given that the student is a girl.

____

16. Discuss possible influences of gender on favorite subject.

____

____

____

____

____

Correlation of *Explorations in Core Math* to the Common Core State Standards

Standards	Algebra 1	Geometry	Algebra 2
Number and Quantity			
The Real Number System			
CC.9-12.N.RN.1 Explain how the definition of the meaning of rational exponents follows from extending the properties of integer exponents to those values, allowing for a notation for radicals in terms of rational exponents.	Lessons 6-1, 6-2		Lesson 5-6
CC.9-12.N.RN.2 Rewrite expressions involving radicals and rational exponents using the properties of exponents.	Lesson 6-2		Lesson 5-6
CC.9-12.N.RN.3 Explain why the sum or product of two rational numbers is rational; that the sum of a rational number and an irrational number is irrational; and that the product of a nonzero rational number and an irrational number is irrational.	Lesson 6-2		
Quantities			
CC.9-12.N.Q.1 Use units as a way to understand problems and to guide the solution of multi-step problems; choose and interpret units consistently in formulas; choose and interpret the scale and the origin in graphs and data displays.*	Lessons 1-8, 1-9, 3-2, 4-1, 4-9		Lessons 2-8, 10-1
CC.9-12.N.Q.2 Define appropriate quantities for the purpose of descriptive modeling.*	Lessons 4-9, 5-6		
CC.9-12.N.Q.3 Choose a level of accuracy appropriate to limitations on measurement when reporting quantities.*	Lesson 1-10		
The Complex Number System			
CC.9-12.N.CN.1 Know there is a complex number i such that $i^2 = -1$, and every complex number has the form $a + bi$ with a and b real.			Lesson 2-5
CC.9-12.N.CN.2 Use the relation $i^2 = -1$ and the commutative, associative, and distributive properties to add, subtract, and multiply complex numbers.			Lesson 2-9
CC.9-12.N.CN.3(+) Find the conjugate of a complex number; use conjugates to find moduli and quotients of complex numbers.			Lesson 2-9

(+) Advanced * = Also a Modeling Standard

Standards	Algebra 1	Geometry	Algebra 2
CC.9-12.N.CN.7 Solve quadratic equations with real coefficients that have complex solutions.			Lesson 2-6
CC.9-12.N.CN.9(+) Know the Fundamental Theorem of Algebra; show that it is true for quadratic polynomials.			Lesson 3-6
Algebra			
Seeing Structure in Expressions			
CC.9-12.A.SSE.1 Interpret expressions that represent a quantity in terms of its context.* **a.** Interpret parts of an expression, such as terms, factors, and coefficients. **b.** Interpret complicated expressions by viewing one or more of their parts as a single entity.	**Lessons 1-1, 1-8, 6-3, 7-1, 7-2, 7-6**		Lessons 2-8, 3-9, 9-5, 12-6
CC.9-12.A.SSE.2 Use the structure of an expression to identify ways to rewrite it.	**Lessons 6-5, 6-6, 7-2, 7-3, 7-4, 7-5, 7-6**		Lessons 3-6, 12-6
CC.9-12.A.SSE.3 Choose and produce an equivalent form of an expression to reveal and explain properties of the quantity represented by the expression. **a.** Factor a quadratic expression to reveal the zeros of the function it defines. **b.** Complete the square in a quadratic expression to reveal the maximum or minimum value of the function it defines. **c.** Use the properties of exponents to transform expressions for exponential functions.	**Lessons 8-3, 8-6, 8-8**		Lessons 4-5, 6-1, 6-7
CC.9-12.A.SSE.4 Derive the formula for the sum of a finite geometric series (when the common ratio is not 1), and use the formula to solve problems.			Lessons 9-4, 9-5
Arithmetic with Polynomials and Rational Expressions			
CC.9-12.A.APR.1 Understand that polynomials form a system analogous to the integers, namely, they are closed under the operations of addition, subtraction, and multiplication; add, subtract, and multiply polynomials.	**Lessons 6-4, 6-5**		Lessons 3-1, 3-2
CC.9-12.A.APR.2 Know and apply the Remainder Theorem: For a polynomial $p(x)$ and a number a, the remainder on division by $x - a$ is $p(a)$, so $p(a) = 0$ if and only if $(x - a)$ is a factor of $p(x)$.			Lessons 3-3, 3-4, 3-6
CC.9-12.A.APR.3 Identify zeros of polynomials when suitable factorizations are available, and use the zeros to construct a rough graph of the function defined by the polynomial.			Lesson 3-5
CC.9-12.A.APR.4 Prove polynomial identities and use them to describe numerical relationships.			Lesson 3-2

(+) Advanced * = Also a Modeling Standard

Standards	Algebra 1	Geometry	Algebra 2
CC.9-12.A.APR.5(+) Know and apply the Binomial Theorem for the expansion of $(x + y)^n$ in powers of x and y for a positive integer n, where x and y are any numbers, with coefficients determined for example by Pascal's Triangle. (The Binomial Theorem can be proved by mathematical induction or by a combinatorial argument.)			Lesson 3-2
CC.9-12.A.APR.6 Rewrite simple rational expressions in different forms; write $a(x)/b(x)$ in the form $q(x) + r(x)/b(x)$, where $a(x)$, $b(x)$, $q(x)$, and $r(x)$ are polynomials with the degree of $r(x)$ less than the degree of $b(x)$, using inspection, long division, or, for the more complicated examples, a computer algebra system.			Lesson 5-4
CC.9-12.A.APR.7(+) Understand that rational expressions form a system analogous to the rational numbers, closed under addition, subtraction, multiplication, and division by a nonzero rational expression; add, subtract, multiply, and divide rational expressions.			Lessons 5-2, 5-3
Creating Equations			
CC.9-12.A.CED.1 Create equations and inequalities in one variable and use them to solve problems.*	**Lessons 1-9, 2-1, 8-6, 8-7**	Lesson 1-4	Lessons 2-7, 3-9, 5-5
CC.9-12.A.CED.2 Create equations in two or more variables to represent relationships between quantities; graph equations on coordinate axes with labels and scales.*	**Lessons 1-7, 3-3, 3-4, 4-5, 4-6, 4-9, 4-10, 8-1, 8-2, 8-4, 8-5, 8-10, 9-2, 9-4**		Lessons 2-8, 3-9, 4-8, 6-1, 6-3, 6-6, 6-7, 11-6
CC.9-12.A.CED.3 Represent constraints by equations or inequalities, and by systems of equations and/or inequalities, and interpret solutions as viable or nonviable options in a modeling context.*	**Lessons 4-9, 5-6**		Lessons 2-8, 3-9, 9-5
CC.9-12.A.CED.4 Rearrange formulas to highlight a quantity of interest, using the same reasoning as in solving equations.*	**Lesson 1-6**	Lesson 1-5	Lessons 4-8, 10-1
Reasoning with Equations and Inequalities			
CC.9-12.A.REI.1. Explain each step in solving a simple equation as following from the equality of numbers asserted at the previous step, starting from the assumption that the original equation has a solution. Construct a viable argument to justify a solution method.	**Lessons 1-2, 1-3, 1-4, 1-5, 1-7, 9-4**		
CC.9-12.A.REI.2 Solve simple rational and radical equations in one variable, and give examples showing how extraneous solutions may arise.			Lessons 5-5, 5-8
CC.9-12.A.REI.3 Solve linear equations and inequalities in one variable, including equations with coefficients represented by letters.	**Lessons 1-2, 1-6, 2-2, 2-3, 2-4, 2-5, 2-6, 2-7**		

(+) Advanced   * = Also a Modeling Standard

Standards	Algebra 1	Geometry	Algebra 2
CC.9-12.A.REI.4 Solve quadratic equations in one variable. **a.** Use the method of completing the square to transform any quadratic equation in x into an equation of the form $(x - p)^2 = q$ that has the same solutions. Derive the quadratic formula from this form. **b.** Solve quadratic equations by inspection (e.g., for $x^2 = 49$), taking square roots, completing the square, the quadratic formula and factoring, as appropriate to the initial form of the equation. Recognize when the quadratic formula gives complex solutions and write them as $a \pm bi$ for real numbers a and b.	**Lessons 8-6, 8-7, 8-8, 8-9**		Lesson 2-6
CC.9-12.A.REI.5 Prove that, given a system of two equations in two variables, replacing one equation by the sum of that equation and a multiple of the other produces a system with the same solutions.	**Lesson 5-3**		
CC.9-12.A.REI.6 Solve systems of linear equations exactly and approximately (e.g., with graphs), focusing on pairs of linear equations in two variables.	**Lessons 5-1, 5-2, 5-3, 5-4, 5-6**		
CC.9-12.A.REI.7 Solve a simple system consisting of a linear equation and a quadratic equation in two variables algebraically and graphically.	**Lesson 8-10**	Lesson 12-7	Lesson 12-7
CC.9-12.A.REI.10 Understand that the graph of an equation in two variables is the set of all its solutions plotted in the coordinate plane, often forming a curve (which could be a line).	**Lesson 4-2**		
CC.9-12.A.REI.11 Explain why the x-coordinates of the points where the graphs of the equations $y = f(x)$ and $y = g(x)$ intersect are the solutions of the equation $f(x) = g(x)$; find the solutions approximately, e.g., using technology to graph the functions, make tables of values, or find successive approximations. Include cases where $f(x)$ and/or $g(x)$ are linear, polynomial, rational, absolute value, exponential, and logarithmic functions.*	**Lessons 1-7, 4-6, 8-5, 9-4**		Lesson 4-5
CC.9-12.A.REI.12 Graph the solutions to a linear inequality in two variables as a half-plane (excluding the boundary in the case of a strict inequality), and graph the solution set to a system of linear inequalities in two variables as the intersection of the corresponding half-planes.	**Lesson 5-5**		
Functions			
Interpreting Functions			
CC.9-12.F.IF.1 Understand that a function from one set (called the domain) to another set (called the range) assigns to each element of the domain exactly one element of the range. If f is a function and x is an element of its domain, then $f(x)$ denotes the output of f corresponding to the input x. The graph of f is the graph of the equation $y = f(x)$.	**Lessons 3-2, 4-1, 9-3**		Lesson 10-3

(+) Advanced   * = Also a Modeling Standard

Standards	Algebra 1	Geometry	Algebra 2
CC.9-12.F.IF.2 Use function notation, evaluate functions for inputs in their domains, and interpret statements that use function notation in terms of a context.	**Lessons 3-2, 3-3, 3-4, 3-6, 4-1, 4-5, 4-10, 8-1, 8-2, 8-4, 9-2**		Lessons 3-5, 4-4, 4-6, 4-8, 6-3, 6-6, 6-7, 9-1, 11-6
CC.9-12.F.IF.3 Recognize that sequences are functions, sometimes defined recursively, whose domain is a subset of the integers.	**Lessons 3-6, 4-1**		Lesson 9-1
CC.9-12.F.IF.4 For a function that models a relationship between two quantities, interpret key features of graphs and tables in terms of the quantities, and sketch graphs showing key features given a verbal description of the relationship.*	**Lessons 3-1, 3-4, 4-3, 4-5, 4-6, 4-10, 8-1, 8-4**		Lessons 2-8, 3-9, 4-8, 6-3, 6-7, 11-6
CC.9-12.F.IF.5 Relate the domain of a function to its graph and, where applicable, to the quantitative relationship it describes.*	**Lessons 3-2, 3-4, 4-1, 8-1, 8-2, 9-3**		Lessons 1-1, 6-3
CC.9-12.F.IF.6 Calculate and interpret the average rate of change of a function (presented symbolically or as a table) over a specified interval. Estimate the rate of change from a graph.*	**Lessons 4-3, 4-4**		Lesson 2-8
CC.9-12.F.IF.7 Graph functions expressed symbolically and show key features of the graph, by hand in simple cases and using technology for more complicated cases.* **a.** Graph linear and quadratic functions and show intercepts, maxima, and minima. **b.** Graph square root, cube root, and piecewise-defined functions, including step functions and absolute value functions. **c.** Graph polynomial functions, identifying zeros when suitable factorizations are available, and showing end behavior. **d.** (+) Graph rational functions, identifying zeros and asymptotes when suitable factorizations are available, and showing end behavior. **e.** Graph exponential and logarithmic functions, showing intercepts and end behavior, and trigonometric functions, showing period, midline, and amplitude.	**Lessons 3-4, 4-1, 4-5, 4-6, 4-10, 8-1, 8-2, 8-3, 8-4, 9-2, 9-3**		Lessons 2-1, 2-2, 2-8, 3-5, 3-7, 4-1, 4-2, 4-3, 4-6, 5-1, 5-4, 6-3, 6-7, 11-1, 11-2, 11-6
CC.9-12.F.IF.8 Write a function defined by an expression in different but equivalent forms to reveal and explain different properties of the function. **a.** Use the process of factoring and completing the square in a quadratic function to show zeros, extreme values, and symmetry of the graph, and interpret these in terms of a context. **b.** Use the properties of exponents to interpret expressions for exponential functions.	**Lessons 4-7, 8-3, 8-6**		Lessons 2-3, 2-4, 6-1, 6-7
CC.9-12.F.IF.9 Compare properties of two functions each represented in a different way (algebraically, graphically, numerically in tables, or by verbal descriptions).	**Lesson 4-1**		Lesson 6-2

(+) Advanced   * = Also a Modeling Standard

Standards	Algebra 1	Geometry	Algebra 2
Building Functions			
CC.9-12.F.BF.1 Write a function that describes a relationship between two quantities.* **a.** Determine an explicit expression, a recursive process, or steps for calculation from a context. **b.** Combine standard function types using arithmetic operations. **c.** (+) Compose functions.	Lessons 3-3, 3-4, 4-5, 4-10, 6-4, 8-1, 8-2, 8-4, 9-1		Lessons 3-1, 3-9, 4-8, 5-1, 5-2, 5-3, 5-4, 6-1, 6-3, 6-5, 6-7, 9-1, 9-2, 11-6
CC.9-12.F.BF.2 Write arithmetic and geometric sequences both recursively and with an explicit formula, use them to model situations, and translate between the two forms.*	Lesson 3-6		Lessons 9-3, 9-4
CC.9-12.F.BF.3 Identify the effect on the graph of replacing $f(x)$ by $f(x) + k$, $kf(x)$, $f(kx)$, and $f(x + k)$ for specific values of k (both positive and negative); find the value of k given the graphs. Experiment with cases and illustrate an explanation of the effects on the graph using technology.	Lessons 4-5, 4-10, 8-1, 8-2, 8-4, 9-2		Lessons 1-1, 1-2, 1-3, 2-1, 3-7, 3-8, 4-6, 4-7, 5-1, 5-7, 6-4, 11-2
CC.9-12.F.BF.4 Find inverse functions. **a.** Solve an equation of the form $f(x) = c$ for a simple function f that has an inverse and write an expression for the inverse. **b.** (+) Verify by composition that one function is the inverse of another. **c.** (+) Read values of an inverse function from a graph or a table, given that the function has an inverse. **d.** (+) Produce an invertible function from a non-invertible function by restricting the domain.	Lesson 3-3		Lessons 4-2, 6-6, 6-7
CC.9-12.F.BF.5(+) Understand the inverse relationship between exponents and logarithms and use this relationship to solve problems involving logarithms and exponents.			Lessons 4-3, 4-4, 4-5
Linear, Quadratic, and Exponential Models			
CC.9-12.F.LE.1 Distinguish between situations that can be modeled with linear functions and with exponential functions.* **a.** Prove that linear functions grow by equal differences over equal intervals, and that exponential functions grow by equal factors over equal intervals. **b.** Recognize situations in which one quantity changes at a constant rate per unit interval relative to another. **c.** Recognize situations in which a quantity grows or decays by a constant percent rate per unit interval relative to another.	Lessons 9-3, 9-5		
CC.9-12.F.LE.2 Construct linear and exponential functions, including arithmetic and geometric sequences, given a graph, a description of a relationship, or two input-output pairs (include reading these from a table).*	Lessons 3-3, 3-6, 4-6, 4-7, 9-1, 9-2, 9-3, 9-4		Lessons 9-3, 9-4

(+) Advanced   * = Also a Modeling Standard

Standards	Algebra 1	Geometry	Algebra 2
CC.9-12.F.LE.3 Observe using graphs and tables that a quantity increasing exponentially eventually exceeds a quantity increasing linearly, quadratically, or (more generally) as a polynomial function.*	**Lesson 9-5**		Lessons 4-1, 6-1
CC.9-12.F.LE.4 For exponential models, express as a logarithm the solution to $ab^{ct} = d$ where *a*, *c*, and *d* are numbers and the base *b* is 2, 10, or *e*; evaluate the logarithm using technology.*			Lesson 4-5
CC.9-12.F.LE.5 Interpret the parameters in a linear or exponential function in terms of a context.*	**Lessons 3-3, 4-8, 4-10, 9-3, 9-4**		Lesson 4-6
Trigonometric Functions			
CC.9-12.F.TF.1 Understand radian measure of an angle as the length of the arc on the unit circle subtended by the angle.			Lesson 10-2
CC.9-12.F.TF.2 Explain how the unit circle in the coordinate plane enables the extension of trigonometric functions to all real numbers, interpreted as radian measures of angles traversed counterclockwise around the unit circle.			Lesson 10-3
CC.9-12.F.TF.3(+) Use special triangles to determine geometrically the values of sine, cosine, tangent for $\pi/3$, $\pi/4$ and $\pi/6$, and use the unit circle to express the values of sine, cosines, and tangent for x, $\pi + x$, and $2\pi - x$ in terms of their values for x, where x is any real number.			Lesson 10-3
CC.9-12.F.TF.4(+) Use the unit circle to explain symmetry (odd and even) and periodicity of trigonometric functions.			Lesson 11-1
CC.9-12.F.TF.5 Choose trigonometric functions to model periodic phenomena with specified amplitude, frequency, and midline.*			Lesson 11-6
CC.9-12.F.TF.6(+) Understand that restricting a trigonometric function to a domain on which it is always increasing or always decreasing allows its inverse to be constructed.			Lesson 10-4
CC.9-12.F.TF.7(+) Use inverse functions to solve trigonometric equations that arise in modeling contexts; evaluate the solutions using technology, and interpret them in terms of the context.*			Lesson 10-4
CC.9-12.F.TF.8 Prove the Pythagorean identity $\sin^2(\theta) + \cos^2(\theta) = 1$ and use it to calculate trigonometric ratios.			Lesson 11-3
CC.9-12.F.TF.9(+) Prove the addition and subtraction formulas for sine, cosine, and tangent and use them to solve problems.			Lesson 11-4, 11-5

(+) Advanced   * = Also a Modeling Standard

Standards	Algebra 1	Geometry	Algebra 2
Geometry			
Congruence			
CC.9-12.G.CO.1 Know precise definitions of angle, circle, perpendicular line, parallel line, and line segment, based on the undefined notions of point, line, distance along a line, and distance around a circular arc.		Lessons 1-1, 1-4, 12-3	
CC.9-12.G.CO.2 Represent transformations in the plane using, e.g., transparencies and geometry software; describe transformations as functions that take points in the plane as inputs and give other points as outputs. Compare transformations that preserve distance and angle to those that do not (e.g., translation versus horizontal stretch).		Lessons 1-7, 7-2, 7-6, 9-1, 9-2, 9-3, 9-7, 10-5	
CC.9-12.G.CO.3 Given a rectangle, parallelogram, trapezoid, or regular polygon, describe the rotations and reflections that carry it onto itself.		Lesson 9-5	
CC.9-12.G.CO.4 Develop definitions of rotations, reflections, and translations in terms of angles, circles, perpendicular lines, parallel lines, and line segments.		Lessons 9-1, 9-2	
CC.9-12.G.CO.5 Given a geometric figure and a rotation, reflection, or translation, draw the transformed figure using, e.g., graph paper, tracing paper, or geometry software. Specify a sequence of transformations that will carry a given figure onto another.		Lessons 1-7, 4-1, 9-1, 9-2, 9-3, 9-4, 9-6	
CC.9-12.G.CO.6 Use geometric descriptions of rigid motions to transform figures and to predict the effect of a given rigid motion on a given figure; given two figures, use the definition of congruence in terms of rigid motions to decide if they are congruent.		Lessons 4-1, 9-1, 9-2, 9-3	
CC.9-12.G.CO.7 Use the definition of congruence in terms of rigid motions to show that two triangles are congruent if and only if corresponding pairs of sides and corresponding pairs of angles are congruent.		Lessons 4-4, 4-5	
CC.9-12.G.CO.8 Explain how the criteria for triangle congruence (ASA, SAS, and SSS) follow from the definition of congruence in terms of rigid motions.		Lessons 4-5, 4-6	
CC.9-12.G.CO.9 Prove geometric theorems about lines and angles.		Lessons 1-4, 2-6, 2-7, 3-2, 3-4, 4-5, 6-6, 12-5	
CC.9-12.G.CO.10 Prove theorems about triangles.		Lessons 4-3, 4-6, 4-9, 5-3, 5-4, 5-5, 5-6	
CC.9-12.G.CO.11 Prove theorems about parallelograms.		Lessons 6-2, 6-3, 6-4	
CC.9-12.G.CO.12 Make formal geometric constructions with a variety of tools and methods (compass and straightedge, string, reflective devices, paper folding, dynamic geometry software, etc.).		Lessons 1-2, 1-3, 3-3, 3-4	

(+) Advanced   * = Also a Modeling Standard

Standards	Algebra 1	Geometry	Algebra 2
CC.9-12.G.CO.13 Construct an equilateral triangle, a square, and a regular hexagon inscribed in a circle.		Lesson 6-1	
Similarity, Right Triangles, and Trigonometry			
CC.9-12.G.SRT.1 Verify experimentally the properties of dilations given by a center and a scale factor: **a.** A dilation takes a line not passing through the center of the dilation to a parallel line, and leaves a line passing through the center unchanged. **b.** The dilation of a line segment is longer or shorter in the ratio given by the scale factor.		Lesson 7-2	
CC.9-12.G.SRT.2 Given two figures, use the definition of similarity in terms of similarity transformations to decide if they are similar; explain using similarity transformations the meaning of similarity for triangles as the equality of all corresponding angles and the proportionality of all corresponding pairs of sides.		Lessons 7-2, 7-3	
CC.9-12.G.SRT.3 Use the properties of similarity transformations to establish the AA criterion for two triangles to be similar.		Lesson 7-3	
CC.9-12.G.SRT.4 Prove theorems about triangles.		Lessons 7-4, 8-1	
CC.9-12.G.SRT.5 Use congruence and similarity criteria for triangles to solve problems and prove relationships in geometric figures.		Lessons 4-5, 4-6, 6-2, 6-3, 6-4, 7-4, 7-5	
CC.9-12.G.SRT.6 Understand that by similarity, side ratios in right triangles are properties of the angles in the triangle, leading to definitions of trigonometric ratios for acute angles.		Lessons 5-8, 8-2	
CC.9-12.G.SRT.7 Explain and use the relationship between the sine and cosine of complementary angles.		Lesson 8-2	
CC.9-12.G.SRT.8 Use trigonometric ratios and the Pythagorean Theorem to solve right triangles in applied problems.		Lessons 5-7, 5-8, 8-2, 8-3, 8-4	
CC.9-12.G.SRT.9(+) Derive the formula $A = 1/2\ ab \sin(C)$ for the area of a triangle by drawing an auxiliary line from a vertex perpendicular to the opposite side.		Lesson 10-1	
CC.9-12.G.SRT.10(+) Prove the Laws of Sines and Cosines and use them to solve problems.		Lesson 8-5	Lessons 10-5, 10-6
CC.9-12.G.SRT.11(+) Understand and apply the Law of Sines and the Law of Cosines to find unknown measurements in right and non-right triangles (e.g., surveying problems, resultant forces).		Lessons 8-5, 8-6	Lessons 10-5, 10-6
Circles			
CC.9-12.G.C.1 Prove that all circles are similar.		Lesson 7-2	

(+) Advanced * = Also a Modeling Standard

Standards	Algebra 1	Geometry	Algebra 2
CC.9-12.G.C.2 Identify and describe relationships among inscribed angles, radii, and chords.		Lessons 12-1, 12-2, 12-4, 12-6	
CC.9-12.G.C.3 Construct the inscribed and circumscribed circles of a triangle, and prove properties of angles for a quadrilateral inscribed in a circle.		Lessons 5-2, 12-4	
CC.9-12.G.C.4(+) Construct a tangent line from a point outside a given circle to the circle.		Lesson 12-5	
CC.9-12.G.C.5 Derive using similarity the fact that the length of the arc intercepted by an angle is proportional to the radius, and define the radian measure of the angle as the constant of proportionality; derive the formula for the area of a sector.		Lesson 12-3	Lesson 10-1
Expressing Geometric Properties with Equations			
CC.9-12.G.GPE.1 Derive the equation of a circle of given center and radius using the Pythagorean Theorem; complete the square to find the center and radius of a circle given by an equation.		Lesson 12-7	Lesson 12-2
CC.9-12.G.GPE.2 Derive the equation of a parabola given a focus and directrix.		Lesson 5-1	Lesson 12-5
CC.9-12.G.GPE.3(+) Derive the equations of ellipses and hyperbolas given the foci, using the fact that the sum or difference of distances from the foci is constant.			Lessons 12-3, 12-4
CC.9-12.G.GPE.4 Use coordinates to prove simple geometric theorems algebraically.		Lessons 1-6, 4-2, 4-8, 5-3, 5-4, 6-5, 12-7	Lesson 12-1
CC.9-12.G.GPE.5 Prove the slope criteria for parallel and perpendicular lines and use them to solve geometric problems (e.g., find the equation of line parallel or perpendicular to a given line that passes through a given point).		Lessons 3-5, 3-6, 4-7	
CC.9-12.G.GPE.6 Find the point on a directed line segment between two given points that partitions the segment in a given ratio.		Lesson 1-6	
CC.9-12.G.GPE.7 Use coordinates to compute perimeters of polygons and areas of triangles and rectangles, e.g., using the distance formula.*		Lessons 4-2, 10-4	
Geometric Measurement and Dimension			
CC.9-12.G.GMD.1 Give an informal argument for the formulas for the circumference of a circle, area of a circle, volume of a cylinder, pyramid, and cone.		Lessons 10-2, 11-2, 11-3, 12-3	
CC.9-12.G.GMD.2(+) Give an informal argument using Cavalieri's principle for the formulas for the volume of a sphere and other solid figures.		Lessons 11-2, 11-4	
CC.9-12.G.GMD.3 Use volume formulas for cylinders, pyramids, cones, and spheres to solve problems.*		Lessons 11-2, 11-3, 11-4	

(+) Advanced * = Also a Modeling Standard

Standards	Algebra 1	Geometry	Algebra 2
CC.9-12.G.GMD.4 Identify the shapes of two-dimensional cross-sections of three-dimensional objects, and identify three-dimensional objects generated by rotations of two-dimensional objects.		Lesson 11-1	
Modeling with Geometry			
CC.9-12.G.MG.1 Use geometric shapes, their measures, and their properties to describe objects (e.g., modeling a tree trunk or a human torso as a cylinder).*		Lessons 10-2, 10-3, 12-6	
CC.9-12.G.MG.2 Apply concepts of density based on area and volume in modeling situations (e.g., persons per square mile, BTUs per cubic foot).*		Lessons 10-4, 11-2	
CC.9-12.G.MG.3 Apply geometric methods to solve design problems (e.g., designing an object or structure to satisfy physical constraints or minimize cost; working with typographic grid systems based on ratios).*		Lessons 7-5, 10-3, 11-2	
Statistics and Probability			
Interpreting Categorical and Quantitative Data			
CC.9-12.S.ID.1 Represent data with plots on the real number line (dot plots, histograms, and box plots).*	**Lessons 10-2, 10-3, 10-4**		Lesson 8-1
CC.9-12.S.ID.2 Use statistics appropriate to the shape of the data distribution to compare center (median, mean) and spread (interquartile range, standard deviation) of two or more different data sets.*	**Lessons 10-2, 10-3, 10-4**		
CC.9-12.S.ID.3 Interpret differences in shape, center, and spread in the context of the data sets, accounting for possible effects of extreme data points (outliers).*	**Lesson 10-4**		Lesson 8-1
CC.9-12.S.ID.4 Use the mean and standard deviation of a data set to fit it to a normal distribution and to estimate population percentages. Recognize that there are data sets for which such a procedure is not appropriate. Use calculators, spreadsheets, and tables to estimate areas under the normal curve.*			Lesson 8-8
CC.9-12.S.ID.5 Summarize categorical data for two categories in two-way frequency tables. Interpret relative frequencies in the context of the data (including joint, marginal, and conditional relative frequencies). Recognize possible associations and trends in the data.*	**Lesson 10-5**		

(+) Advanced * = Also a Modeling Standard

Standards	Algebra 1	Geometry	Algebra 2
CC.9-12.S.ID.6 Represent data on two quantitative variables on a scatter plot, and describe how the variables are related.* **a.** Fit a function to the data; use functions fitted to data to solve problems in the context of the data. **b.** Informally assess the fit of a function by plotting and analyzing residuals. **c.** Fit a linear function for a scatter plot that suggests a linear association.	**Lessons 3-5, 4-8, 9-4**		Lessons 1-4, 6-1, 6-7
CC.9-12.S.ID.7 Interpret the slope (rate of change) and the intercept (constant term) of a linear model in the context of the data.*	**Lessons 3-5, 4-8**		
CC.9-12.S.ID.8 Compute (using technology) and interpret the correlation coefficient of a linear fit.*	**Lesson 3-5**		
CC.9-12.S.ID.9 Distinguish between correlation and causation.*	**Lesson 3-5**		
Making Inferences and Justifying Conclusions			
CC.9-12.S.IC.1 Understand statistics as a process for making inferences about population parameters based on a random sample from that population.*			Lesson 8-2
CC.9-12.S.IC.2 Decide if a specified model is consistent with results from a given data-generating process, e.g., using simulation.*			Lesson 8-6
CC.9-12.S.IC.3 Recognize the purposes of and differences among sample surveys, experiments, and observational studies; explain how randomization relates to each.*			Lesson 8-3
CC.9-12.S.IC.4 Use data from a sample survey to estimate a population mean or proportion; develop a margin of error through the use of simulation models for random sampling.*			Lesson 8-5
CC.9-12.S.IC.5 Use data from a randomized experiment to compare two treatments; use simulations to decide if differences between parameters are significant.*			Lesson 8-4
CC.9-12.S.IC.6 Evaluate reports based on data.*			Lesson 8-3
Conditional Probability and the Rules of Probability			
CC.9-12.S.CP.1 Describe events as subsets of a sample space (the set of outcomes) using characteristics (or categories) of the outcomes, or as unions, intersections, or complements of other events ("or," "and," "not").*	**Lessons 10-5, 10-6**	Lesson 10-6	
CC.9-12.S.CP.2 Understand that two events *A* and *B* are independent if the probability of *A* and *B* occurring together is the product of their probabilities, and use this characterization to determine if they are independent.*	**Lesson 10-7**	Lesson 13-3	Lesson 7-3

(+) Advanced * = Also a Modeling Standard

Standards	Algebra 1	Geometry	Algebra 2
CC.9-12.S.CP.3 Understand the conditional probability of *A* given *B* as *P*(*A* and *B*)/*P*(*B*), and interpret independence of *A* and *B* as saying that the conditional probability of *A* given *B* is the same as the probability of *A*, and the conditional probability of *B* given *A* is the same as the probability of *B*.*	Lesson 10-7	Lessons 13-3, 13-4	Lessons 7-3, 7-4
CC.9-12.S.CP.4 Construct and interpret two-way frequency tables of data when two categories are associated with each object being classified. Use the two-way table as a sample space to decide if events are independent and to approximate conditional probabilities.*		Lesson 13-3	Lesson 7-3
CC.9-12.S.CP.5 Recognize and explain the concepts of conditional probability and independence in everyday language and everyday situations.*		Lessons 13-3, 13-4	Lessons 7-3, 7-4
CC.9-12.S.CP.6 Find the conditional probability of *A* given *B* as the fraction of *B*'s outcomes that also belong to *A*, and interpret the answer in terms of the model.*		Lesson 13-4	Lesson 7-4
CC.9-12.S.CP.7 Apply the Addition Rule, $P(A \text{ or } B) = P(A) + P(B) - P(A \text{ and } B)$, and interpret the answer in terms of the model.*		Lesson 13-5	Lesson 7-5
CC.9-12.S.CP.8(+) Apply the general Multiplication Rule in a uniform probability model, $P(A \text{ and } B) = P(A)P(B\|A) = P(B)P(A\|B)$, and interpret the answer in terms of the model.*	Lesson 10-7	Lesson 13-3	Lesson 7-3
CC.9-12.S.CP.9(+) Use permutations and combinations to compute probabilities of compound events and solve problems.*		Lesson 13-1	Lesson 7-1
Using Probability to Make Decisions			
CC.9-12.S.MD.3(+) Develop a probability distribution for a random variable defined for a sample space in which theoretical probabilities can be calculated; find the expected value.			Lesson 8-6
CC.9-12.S.MD.5(+) Develop a probability distribution for a random variable defined for a sample space in which probabilities are assigned empirically; find the expected value.			Lesson 8-6
CC.9-12.S.MD.6(+) Use probabilities to make fair decisions (e.g., drawing by lots, using a random number generator).*		Lesson 13-2	Lesson 7-2
CC.9-12.S.MD.7(+) Analyze decisions and strategies using probability concepts (e.g., product testing, medical testing, pulling a hockey goalie at the end of a game).*			Lesson 8-8

(+) Advanced   * = Also a Modeling Standard